PLAYFAIR
CRICKET ANNUAL 2013
66th edition
EDITED BY IAN MARSHALL
All statistics by the Editor unless otherwise stated

FOREWORD

With the snow blanketing the outfield at the Saffrons, my local cricket ground, it seems scarcely credible that we are less than four weeks away from the start of another season. It is a campaign that will run until Friday 27 September – one hopes before the autumn frosts have set in – which must surely be a record.

The year 2012 was one in which cricket sometimes struggled to draw attention to itself, given competition from the Olympics, Bradley Wiggins' Tour de France triumph, the Diamond Jubilee and much else besides. When the sport did hit the headlines, it was often for the wrong reasons: the disappointments against Pakistan when England seemed unable to cope with spin, losing the ICC top ranking to an exceptionally strong South Africa side – and of course the Kevin Pietersen saga.

This last 'crisis' was arguably an inevitable consequence of the lure of the riches associated with the IPL. So far, English cricket has been relatively well insulated against it: the franchises in India haven't been notably keen to sign up our players. But, more importantly, the ECB has been able to retain loyalty at the very top level through central contracts, which not only provide a good income for the players but also help to build the nucleus of a team, so that they are dedicated to the cause of England. Indeed, it is hard to imagine a period when England can ever have had such a professional and committed group of talented individuals to choose from. But the IPL is not going away, and nor does it seem likely that the burdens placed on our international cricketers will diminish, so we may find that this is only the first of many other similar dilemmas between the call to do one's national duty and the chance of earning huge sums from a format of the game that is physically much less demanding.

Fortunately, the last year ended on a high note with a first series win for England in India since 1984-85. Impressively led by new skipper Alastair Cook (who justifiably stars on our front cover), England will go into 2013 in much higher spirits than was the case for much of the previous twelve months With back-to-back Ashes series starting in July, England will start as strong favourites. While here we are waiting for the snow to melt, the Australians touring in India seem instead to have gone into meltdown, with four players suspended for disciplinary reasons.

Often Ashes series are personalised as battles between the captains, and at the start of this month the two men were very evenly matched: Cook had 7117 Test runs at 49.42 while Michael Clarke had 7150 runs at 52.96, and they were the two leading Test run-scorers in 2012. Yet, however even the comparisons between the skippers, it is with the ten men beside them that the balance shifts hugely in favour of England. Cook's team have greater batting depth and experience, a better seam attack and spin options that Australia can only dream about. If England can, for once, get off to a good start to the series, it is hard to see them losing a Test on home soil, or losing the series in Australia.

This year's *Playfair Cricket Annual* follows the tried and trusted formula of years gone by, though we will continue to provide weekly updates during the season on our website, playfaircricket.co.uk, where I will highlight as many personal best performances as possible, to complement the information contained within these pages. It is, in fact, a significant landmark for *Playfair*, too, and the article opposite pays tribute to the 50 years we have been published in this handy, pocket-sized format. But for those who want to try the book in a different way entirely, it is now also available as an ebook.

As ever, enjoy the season ahead.

Ian Marshall
Eastbourne, 12 March 2013.

FIFTY YEARS AGO

This year's edition marks 50 years since *Playfair* adopted its familiar pocket-sized format (137 x 98mm). Originally, the *News Chronicle Cricket Annual*, edited by Roy Webber, had been this size, while the *Playfair Cricket Annual*, edited by Peter West, was larger (178 x 119mm) and more expensive. During 1962, the last year in which both annuals were published, The Dickens Press (based in Upper Thames Street, London EC4) acquired *Playfair*, planning to continue publishing both books. In November, however, Webber died suddenly, and the decision was taken to merge the two annuals. The modern era of *Playfair* was born under the stewardship of Gordon Ross. The publishers' stated aim was to combine the best features of both annuals in one volume, though the action photographs that had been a feature of *Playfair* were dropped. In that first year of the new *Playfair*, the book was just 192 pages long, including nine pages of advertisements, and the price was 2/6 (12½p).

The change could not have come at a more significant time for English cricket, for as Ross said: 'No cricket season [has been] so important to the first-class game as that of 1963.' One reason for this was the introduction of limited-overs cricket to the schedule, with Gillette sponsoring (to the tune of £6500) a new limited-overs knockout tournament. In that first season, it was 65 overs a side, with a maximum of 15 overs per bowler. Commenting on how he believed the competition would work, Essex captain Trevor Bailey stated that those who expected the fixtures to be akin to a benefit match, with the ball regularly disappearing for six, might be disappointed. He also wondered if the short format would hinder the opportunities for spinners, but noted that in trial games during 1962 it had in fact been the spinners who had been the most successful. But the real reason for the introduction of the shorter format was the hope that it would bring fans back to the grounds. All of which sounds eerily familiar to the modern debate over twenty20 cricket.

There were other major developments taking place at that time, including the reinstatement of the follow-on, a proposal to revise the LBW law so that the ball would have to pitch in line with the stumps if an appeal were to be upheld (to compensate the bowlers, the stumps were to be widened), and a decision to keep wickets uncovered once a match had begun. But most significant of all was the ending of the distinction between amateurs and players. In 1962, 13 of the 17 county captains had been amateurs, almost all of them products of the public school system and Oxbridge. This preference was at its most striking in the case of Lancashire where 34-year-old Joseph Blackledge (Repton School) had been appointed captain despite never having previously played first-class cricket. For 1963, after he had averaged a little over 15, he was released to be replaced by veteran Australian Ken Grieves.

The 1963 Annual is also fascinating for some of the facts it throws up: by that stage only six men had scored more than 5000 Test runs, with Wally Hammond topping the list. The sheer volume of cricket played was staggering – some players appeared in 37 first-class matches during the 1962 season. Many bowlers delivered more than 1000 overs in the season, with Hampshire's Derek Shackleton (who enjoyed his 38th birthday during the campaign) leading the way with an astonishing 1717.1 overs. Despite all of this, the season was far shorter, with the first round of the County Championship starting on 1 May and the last game finishing on 6 September, with the Gillette Cup final at Lord's the day after; in 2013, the corresponding dates for the Championship are 5 April to 27 September.

So as The Beatles went to Number One in the charts for the first time, and the Profumo Scandal began to captivate a nation, it was also a new age for cricket – and for *Playfair*.

ACKNOWLEDGEMENTS AND THANKS

As ever, this book could not have been compiled without the help of many people giving freely of their time and expertise, so I must thank the following for all they have done to help ensure this edition of *Playfair Cricket Annual* could be written:

At the counties, I would like to thank the following for their help over the last year: Derbyshire – Tom Holdcroft and John Brown; Durham – Brian Hunt (get well soon); Essex – Ashley Neave, Rhys Ellingham and Tony Choat; Glamorgan – Andrew Hignell; Gloucestershire – Lizzie Allen and Adrian Bull; Hampshire – Tim Tremlett and Tony Weld; Kent – Alison Davies and Lorne Hart; Lancashire – Diana Lloyd and Alan West; Leicestershire – Elaine Pickering and Paul Rogers; Middlesex – Rebecca Hart and Don Shelley; Northamptonshire – Tony Kingston; Nottinghamshire – Helen Palmer and Roger Marshall; Somerset – Spencer Bishop and Gerald Stickley; Surrey – Steve Howes and Keith Booth; Sussex – Siobhan Edgar and Mike Charman; Warwickshire – Keith Cook, David Wainwright and Melvin Smith; Worcestershire – Joan Grundy and Dawn Pugh; Yorkshire – Ian Dews and John Potter.

Thanks to Chris Kelly for supplying the list of domestic umpires. To Alan Fordham, thank you for the Principal and Second XI Fixtures, and Philip August for the Minor Counties. Philip Bailey once again provided the first-class and List A career records, and he continues to be a vital help in compiling the book. He is keen that we should include twenty20 career records in the Annual – do say if you think this would be a useful addition.

At Headline, my thanks again go to Jonathan Taylor for his support and encouragement; Louise Rothwell was her usual firm self in reminding me that deadline day was looming, but as always did a wonderful job in getting the book printed in no time at all; Sam Habib continues to help running the *Playfair* website with infectious enthusiasm. John Skermer again played a vital role in checking the proofs. At Letterpart, the *Playfair* typesetter since 1994, Chris Leggett, Caroline Leggett and the whole team did a superb job on the setting. I know I always promise that it won't be such a late rush next year . . .

Finally, on a personal level, I must thank my young daughters, Kiri and Sophia, who have seen so very little of me in recent weeks; and of course my wife, Sugra, who has had to cope with an exhausted husband staggering out of the office after yet another marathon session in front of the computer – and has done so with wonderful grace and understanding.

GUIDE TO USING PLAYFAIR

As last year, *Playfair* is divided into five sections as follows: Test match cricket, county cricket, international limited-overs cricket (including Twenty20), other cricket (IPL, Champions League, women's limited-overs cricket, universities), and fixtures for the coming season. Each section, where appropriate, begins with a preview of forthcoming events, followed by a review of events during the previous season, then come the player records, and finally the records section.

ENGLAND v NEW ZEALAND

SERIES RECORDS
1929-30 to 2008

HIGHEST INNINGS TOTALS

England	in England	567-8d	Nottingham	1994
	in New Zealand	593-6d	Auckland	1974-75
New Zealand	in England	551-9d	Lord's	1973
	in New Zealand	537	Wellington	1983-84

LOWEST INNINGS TOTALS

England	in England	126	Birmingham	1999
	in New Zealand	64	Wellington	1977-78
New Zealand	in England	47	Lord's	1958
	in New Zealand	26	Auckland	1954-55

HIGHEST MATCH AGGREGATE 1445 for 33 wickets   Lord's   2004
LOWEST MATCH AGGREGATE 390 for 30 wickets   Lord's   1958

HIGHEST INDIVIDUAL INNINGS

England	in England	310*	J.H.Edrich	Leeds	1965
	in New Zealand	336*	W.R.Hammond	Auckland	1932-33
New Zealand	in England	206	M.P.Donnelly	Lord's	1949
	in New Zealand	222	N.J.Astle	Christchurch	2001-02

HIGHEST AGGREGATE OF RUNS IN A SERIES

England	in England	469	(av 78.16)	L.Hutton	1949
	in New Zealand	563	(av 563.00)	W.R.Hammond	1932-33
New Zealand	in England	462	(av 77.00)	M.P.Donnelly	1949
	in New Zealand	341	(av 85.25)	C.S.Dempster	1929-30

RECORD WICKET PARTNERSHIPS – ENGLAND

1st	223	G.Fowler (105)/C.J.Tavaré (109)	The Oval	1983
2nd	369	J.H.Edrich (310*)/K.F.Barrington (163)	Leeds	1965
3rd	245	J.Hardstaff jr (114)/W.R.Hammond (140)	Lord's	1937
4th	266	M.H.Denness (181)/K.W.R.Fletcher (216)	Auckland	1974-75
5th	242	W.R.Hammond (227)/L.E.G.Ames (103)	Christchurch	1932-33
6th	281	G.P.Thorpe (200*)/A.Flintoff (137)	Christchurch	2001-02
7th	149	A.P.E.Knott (104)/P.Lever (64)	Auckland	1970-71
8th	246	L.E.G.Ames (137)/G.O.B.Allen (122)	Lord's	1931
9th	163*	M.C.Cowdrey (128*)/A.C.Smith (69*)	Wellington	1962-63
10th	59	A.P.E.Knott (49)/N.Gifford (25*)	Nottingham	1973

RECORD WICKET PARTNERSHIPS – NEW ZEALAND

1st	276	C.S.Dempster (136)/J.E.Mills (117)	Wellington	1929-30
2nd	241	J.G.Wright (116)/A.H.Jones (143)	Wellington	1991-92
3rd	210	B.A.Edgar (83)/M.D.Crowe (106)	Lord's	1986
4th	155	M.D.Crowe (143)/M.J.Greatbatch (68)	Wellington	1987-88
5th	180	M.D.Crowe (142)/S.A.Thomson (69)	Lord's	1994
6th	141	M.D.Crowe (115)/A.C.Parore (71)	Manchester	1994
7th	148	L.R.P.L.Taylor (120)/D.L.Vettori (88)	Hamilton	2007-08
8th	104	D.A.R.Moloney (64)/A.W.Roberts (66*)	Lord's	1937
9th	118	J.V.Coney (174*)/B.L.Cairns (64)	Wellington	1983-84
10th	118	N.J.Astle (222)/C.L.Cairns (23*)	Christchurch	2001-02

BEST INNINGS BOWLING ANALYSIS

England	in England	7- 32	D.L.Underwood	Lord's	1969
	in New Zealand	7- 47	P.C.R.Tufnell	Christchurch	1991-92
		7- 47	R.J.Sidebottom	Napier	2007-08
New Zealand	in England	7- 74	B.L.Cairns	Leeds	1983
	in New Zealand	7-143	B.L.Cairns	Wellington	1983-84

BEST MATCH BOWLING ANALYSIS

England	in England	12-101	D.L.Underwood	The Oval	1969
	in New Zealand	12- 97	D.L.Underwood	Christchurch	1970-71
New Zealand	in England	11-169	D.J.Nash	Lord's	1994
	in New Zealand	10-100	R.J.Hadlee	Wellington	1977-78

HIGHEST AGGREGATE OF WICKETS IN A SERIES

England	in England	34	(av 7.47)	G.A.R.Lock	1958
	in New Zealand	24	(av 17.08)	R.J.Sidebottom	2007-08
New Zealand	in England	21	(av 26.61)	R.J.Hadlee	1983
	in New Zealand	15	(av 19.53)	R.O.Collinge	1977-78
		15	(av 24.73)	R.J.Hadlee	1977-78

RESULTS SUMMARY

ENGLAND v NEW ZEALAND – IN ENGLAND

	Tests	Series			Lord's			The Oval			Manchester			Leeds			Birmingham			Nottingham		
		E	NZ	D	E	NZ	D	E	NZ	D	E	NZ	D	E	NZ	D	E	NZ	D	E	NZ	D
1931	3	1	–	2	–	–	1	1	–	–	–	–	1									
1937	3	1	–	2	–	–	1	–	–	1	1	–	–									
1949	4	–	–	4	–	–	1	–	–	1	–	–	1	–	–	1						
1958	5	4	–	1	1	–	–	1	–	–	1	–	–	1	–	–	–	–	1			
1965	3	3	–	–	1	–	–							1	–	–	1	–	–			
1969	3	2	–	1	1	–	–	1	–	–										–	–	1
1973	3	2	–	1	–	–	1							1	–	–				1	–	–
1978	3	3	–	–	1	–	–	1	–	–										1	–	–
1983	4	3	1	–	1	–	–	1	–	–				–	1	–				1	–	–
1986	3	–	1	2	–	–	1	–	–	1										–	1	–
1990	3	1	–	2	–	–	1										1	–	–	–	–	1
1994	3	1	–	2	–	–	1				–	–	1							1	–	–
1999	4	1	2	1	–	1	–	–	1	–	–	–	1				1	–	–			
2004	3	3	–	–	1	–	–							1	–	–				1	–	–
2008	3	2	–	1	–	–	1				1	–	–							1	–	–
	50	27	4	19	6	1	8	5	1	3	3	–	4	4	1	1	3	–	1	6	1	2

ENGLAND v NEW ZEALAND – IN NEW ZEALAND

	Tests	Series			Christchurch			Wellington			Auckland			Dunedin			Hamilton			Napier		
		E	NZ	D	E	NZ	D	E	NZ	D	E	NZ	D	E	NZ	D	E	NZ	D	E	NZ	D
1929-30	4	1	–	3	1	–	–	–	–	1	–	–	2									
1932-33	2	–	–	2	–	–	1				–	–	1									
1946-47	1	–	–	1							–	–	1									
1950-51	2	1	–	1	–	–	1	1	–	–												
1954-55	2	2	–	–							1	–	–	1	–	–						
1958-59	2	1	–	1	1	–	–				–	–	1									
1962-63	3	3	–	–	1	–	–	1	–	–	1	–	–									
1965-66	3	–	–	3	–	–	1				–	–	1	–	–	1						
1970-71	2	1	–	1	1	–	–				–	–	1									
1974-75	2	1	–	1	–	–	1				1	–	–									
1977-78	3	1	1	1	1	–	–	–	1	–	–	–	1									
1983-84	3	–	1	2	–	1	–	–	–	1	–	–	1									
1987-88	3	–	–	3	–	–	1	–	–	1	–	–	1									
1991-92	3	2	–	1	1	–	–	–	–	1	1	–	–									
1996-97	3	2	–	1	1	–	–	1	–	–	–	–	1									
2001-02	3	1	1	1	1	–	–	–	–	1	–	1	–									
2007-08	3	2	1	–				1	–	–							–	1	–	1	–	–
	44	18	4	22	8	1	5	4	1	5	4	1	11	1	–	1	–	1	–	1	–	–

Totals	94	45	8	41																		

ENGLAND v AUSTRALIA

SERIES RECORDS

1876-77 to 2010-11

HIGHEST INNINGS TOTALS

England	in England	903-7d	The Oval	1938
	in Australia	636	Sydney	1928-29
Australia	in England	729-6d	Lord's	1930
	in Australia	659-8d	Sydney	1946-47

LOWEST INNINGS TOTALS

England	in England	52	The Oval	1948
	in Australia	45	Sydney	1886-87
Australia	in England	36	Birmingham	1902
	in Australia	42	Sydney	1887-88

HIGHEST MATCH AGGREGATE 1753 for 40 wickets Adelaide 1920-21
LOWEST MATCH AGGREGATE 291 for 40 wickets Lord's 1888

HIGHEST INDIVIDUAL INNINGS

England	in England	364	L.Hutton	The Oval	1938
	in Australia	287	R.E.Foster	Sydney	1903-04
Australia	in England	334	D.G.Bradman	Leeds	1930
	in Australia	307	R.M.Cowper	Melbourne	1965-66

HIGHEST AGGREGATE OF RUNS IN A SERIES

England	in England	732	(av 81.33)	D.I.Gower (6 Tests)	1985
	in Australia	905	(av 113.12)	W.R.Hammond	1928-29
Australia	in England	974	(av 139.14)	D.G.Bradman	1930
	in Australia	810	(av 90.00)	D.G.Bradman	1936-37

RECORD WICKET PARTNERSHIPS – ENGLAND

1st	323	J.B.Hobbs (178)/W.Rhodes (179)	Melbourne	1911-12
2nd	382	L.Hutton (364)/M.Leyland (187)	The Oval	1938
3rd	262	W.R.Hammond (177)/ D.R.Jardine (98)	Adelaide	1928-29
4th	310	P.D.Collingwood (206)/K.P.Pietersen (158)	Adelaide	2006-07
5th	206	E.Paynter (216*)/D.C.S.Compton (102)	Nottingham	1938
6th	215	L.Hutton (364)/J.Hardstaff jr (169*)	The Oval	1938
	215	G.Boycott (107)/A.P.E.Knott (135)	Nottingham	1977
7th	143	F.E.Woolley (133*)/J.Vine (36)	Sydney	1911-12
8th	124	E.H.Hendren (169)/H.Larwood (70)	Brisbane	1928-29
9th	151	W.H.Scotton (90)/W.W.Read (117)	The Oval	1884
10th	130	R.E.Foster (287)/W.Rhodes (40*)	Sydney	1903-04

RECORD WICKET PARTNERSHIPS – AUSTRALIA

1st	329	G.R.Marsh (138)/M.A.Taylor (219)	Nottingham	1989
2nd	451	W.H.Ponsford (266)/D.G.Bradman (244)	The Oval	1934
3rd	276	D.G.Bradman (187)/A.L.Hassett (128)	Brisbane	1946-47
4th	388	W.H.Ponsford (181)/D.G.Bradman (304)	Leeds	1934
5th	405	S.G.Barnes (234)/D.G.Bradman (234)	Sydney	1946-47
6th	346	J.H.W.Fingleton (136)/D.G.Bradman (270)	Melbourne	1936-37
7th	165	C.Hill (188)/H.Trumble (46)	Melbourne	1897-98
8th	243	R.J.Hartigan (116)/C.Hill (160)	Adelaide	1907-08
9th	154	S.E.Gregory (201)/J.M.Blackham (74)	Sydney	1894-95
10th	127	J.M.Taylor (108)/A.A.Mailey (46*)	Sydney	1924-25

BEST INNINGS BOWLING ANALYSIS

England	in England	10- 53	J.C.Laker	Manchester	1956
	in Australia	8- 35	G.A.Lohmann	Sydney	1886-87
Australia	in England	8- 31	F.Laver	Manchester	1909
	in Australia	9-121	A.A.Mailey	Melbourne	1920-21

BEST MATCH BOWLING ANALYSIS

England	in England	19- 90	J.C.Laker	Manchester	1956
	in Australia	15-124	W.Rhodes	Melbourne	1903-04
Australia	in England	16-137	R.A.L.Massie	Lord's	1972
	in Australia	13- 77	M.A.Noble	Melbourne	1901-02

HIGHEST AGGREGATE OF WICKETS IN A SERIES

England	in England	46	(av 9.60)	J.C.Laker	1956
	in Australia	38	(av 23.18)	M.W.Tate	1924-25
Australia	in England	42	(av 21.26)	T.M.Alderman (6 Tests)	1981
	in Australia	41	(av 12.85)	R.M.Hogg (6 Tests)	1978-79

RESULTS SUMMARY
ENGLAND v AUSTRALIA – IN ENGLAND

	Tests	Series			The Oval			Manchester			Lord's			Nottingham			Leeds			Birmingham			Sheffield			Cardiff		
		E	A	D	E	A	D	E	A	D	E	A	D	E	A	D	E	A	D	E	A	D	E	A	D	E	A	D
1880	1	1	–	–	1	–	–																						
1882	1	–	1	–	–	1	–																						
1884	3	1	–	2	–	–	1	–	–	1	1	–	–																
1886	3	3	–	–	1	–	–	1	–	–	1	–	–																
1888	3	2	1	–	1	–	–	1	–	–	–	1	–																
1890	2	2	–	–	1	–	–				1	–	–																
1893	3	1	–	2	1	–	–	–	–	1	–	–	1																
1896	3	2	1	–	1	–	–	–	1	–	1	–	–																
1899	5	–	1	4	–	–	1	–	–	1	–	1	–	–	–	1	–	–	1									
1902	5	1	2	2	1	–	–	–	1	–	–	–	1							–	–	1	–	1	–			
1905	5	2	–	3	–	–	1	1	–	–	–	–	1	1	–	–	–	–	1									
1909	5	1	2	2	–	–	1	–	–	1	–	1	–				–	1	–	1	–	–						
1912	3	1	–	2	1	–	–	–	–	1	–	–	1															
1921	5	–	3	2	–	–	1	–	–	1	–	1	–	–	1	–	–	1	–									
1926	5	1	–	4	1	–	–	–	–	1	–	–	1	–	–	1	–	–	1									
1930	5	1	2	2	–	1	–	–	–	1	–	1	–	1	–	–	–	–	1									
1934	5	1	2	2	–	1	–	–	–	1	1	–	–	–	1	–	–	–	1									
1938	4	1	1	2	1	–	–				–	–	1	–	–	1	–	1	–									
1948	5	–	4	1	–	1	–	–	–	1	–	1	–	–	1	–	–	1	–									
1953	5	1	–	4	1	–	–	–	–	1	–	–	1	–	–	1	–	–	1									
1956	5	2	1	2	–	–	1	1	–	–	–	1	–	–	–	1	1	–	–									
1961	5	1	2	2	–	–	1	–	1	–	–	1	–				1	–	–	–	–	1						
1964	5	–	1	4	–	–	1	–	–	1	–	–	1	–	–	1	–	1	–									
1968	5	1	1	3	1	–	–	–	1	–	–	–	1				–	–	1	–	–	1						
1972	5	2	2	1	–	1	–	1	–	–	–	1	–	–	–	1	1	–	–									
1975	4	–	1	3	–	–	1				–	–	1				–	–	1	–	1	–						
1977	5	3	–	2	–	–	1	1	–	–	–	–	1	1	–	–	1	–	–									
1980	1	–	–	1							–	–	1															
1981	6	3	1	2	–	–	1	1	–	–	–	–	1	–	1	–	1	–	–	1	–	–						
1985	6	3	1	2	1	–	–	–	–	1	–	1	–	–	–	1	1	–	–	1	–	–						
1989	6	–	4	2	–	–	1	–	1	–	–	1	–	–	1	–	–	1	–	–	–	1						
1993	6	1	4	1	1	–	–	–	1	–	–	1	–	–	–	1	–	1	–	–	1	–						
1997	6	2	3	1	1	–	–	–	1	–	–	–	1	–	1	–	–	1	–	1	–	–						
2001	5	1	4	–	–	1	–				–	1	–	–	1	–	1	–	–	–	1	–						
2005	5	2	1	2	–	–	1	–	–	1	–	1	–	1	–	–				1	–	–						
2009	5	2	1	2	1	–	–				1	–	–				–	1	–	–	–	1				–	–	1
156		**45**	**47**	**64**	**16**	**6**	**13**	**7**	**7**	**14**	**6**	**14**	**14**	**4**	**7**	**9**	**7**	**9**	**8**	**5**	**3**	**5**	–	**1**	–	–	–	**1**

	Tests	Series			Melbourne			Sydney			Adelaide			Brisbane			Perth		
		E	A	D	E	A	D	E	A	D	E	A	D	E	A	D	E	A	D
1876-77	2	1	1	–	1	1	–	–	–	–	–	–	–	–	–	–	–	–	–
1878-79	1	–	1	–	–	1	–	–	–	–	–	–	–	–	–	–	–	–	–
1881-82	4	–	2	2	–	–	2	–	2	–	–	–	–	–	–	–	–	–	–
1882-83	4	2	2	–	1	1	–	1	1	–	–	–	–	–	–	–	–	–	–
1884-85	5	3	2	–	2	–	–	–	2	–	1	–	–	–	–	–	–	–	–
1886-87	2	2	–	–	–	–	–	2	–	–	–	–	–	–	–	–	–	–	–
1887-88	1	1	–	–	–	–	–	1	–	–	–	–	–	–	–	–	–	–	–
1891-92	3	1	2	–	–	1	–	–	1	–	1	–	–	–	–	–	–	–	–
1894-95	5	3	2	–	2	–	–	1	1	–	–	1	–	–	–	–	–	–	–
1897-98	5	1	4	–	–	2	–	1	1	–	–	1	–	–	–	–	–	–	–
1901-02	5	1	4	–	–	2	–	1	1	–	–	1	–	–	–	–	–	–	–
1903-04	5	3	2	–	1	1	–	2	–	–	–	1	–	–	–	–	–	–	–
1907-08	5	1	4	–	1	1	–	–	2	–	–	1	–	–	–	–	–	–	–
1911-12	5	4	1	–	2	–	–	1	1	–	1	–	–	–	–	–	–	–	–
1920-21	5	–	5	–	–	2	–	–	2	–	–	1	–	–	–	–	–	–	–
1924-25	5	1	4	–	1	1	–	–	2	–	–	1	–	–	–	–	–	–	–
1928-29	5	4	1	–	1	1	–	1	–	–	1	–	–	1	–	–	–	–	–
1932-33	5	4	1	–	–	1	–	2	–	–	1	–	–	1	–	–	–	–	–
1936-37	5	2	3	–	–	2	–	1	–	–	–	1	–	1	–	–	–	–	–
1946-47	5	–	3	2	–	–	1	–	2	–	–	–	1	–	1	–	–	–	–
1950-51	5	1	4	–	1	1	–	–	1	–	–	1	–	–	1	–	–	–	–
1954-55	5	3	1	1	1	–	–	1	–	1	1	–	–	–	1	–	–	–	–
1958-59	5	–	4	1	–	2	–	–	–	1	–	1	–	–	1	–	–	–	–
1962-63	5	1	1	3	1	–	–	–	1	1	–	–	1	–	–	1	–	–	–
1965-66	5	1	1	3	–	–	2	1	–	–	–	1	–	–	–	1	–	–	–
1970-71	6	2	–	4	–	–	1	2	–	–	–	–	1	–	–	1	–	–	1
1974-75	6	1	4	1	1	–	1	–	1	–	–	1	–	–	1	–	–	1	–
1976-77	1	–	1	–	–	1	–	–	–	–	–	–	–	–	–	–	–	–	–
1978-79	6	5	1	–	–	1	–	2	–	–	1	–	–	1	–	–	1	–	–
1979-80	3	–	3	–	–	1	–	–	1	–	–	–	–	–	–	–	–	1	–
1982-83	5	1	2	2	1	–	–	–	–	1	–	1	–	–	1	–	–	–	1
1986-87	5	2	1	2	1	–	–	–	1	–	–	–	1	1	–	–	–	–	1
1987-88	1	–	–	1	–	–	–	–	–	1	–	–	–	–	–	–	–	–	–
1990-91	5	–	3	2	–	1	–	–	–	1	–	–	1	–	1	–	–	1	–
1994-95	5	1	3	1	–	1	–	–	–	1	1	–	–	–	1	–	–	1	–
1998-99	5	1	3	1	1	–	–	–	1	–	–	1	–	–	–	1	–	1	–
2002-03	5	1	4	–	–	1	–	1	–	–	–	1	–	–	1	–	–	1	–
2006-07	5	–	5	–	–	1	–	–	1	–	–	1	–	–	1	–	–	1	–
2010-11	5	3	1	1	1	–	–	1	–	–	1	–	–	–	–	1	–	1	–
	170	57	86	27	20	27	7	22	25	7	9	16	5	5	10	5	1	8	3
Totals	326	102	133	91															

Matches abandoned without a ball bowled (Manchester 1890 and 1938, Melbourne 1970-71) are excluded from these tables.

2000 RUNS

	Tests	I	NO	HS	Runs	Avge	100	50
D.G.Bradman (A)	37	63	7	334	5028	89.78	19	12
J.B.Hobbs (E)	41	71	4	187	3636	54.26	12	15
A.R.Border (A)	47	82	19	200*	3548	56.31	8	21
D.I.Gower (E)	42	77	4	215	3269	44.78	9	12
S.R.Waugh (A)	46	73	18	177*	3200	58.18	10	14
G.Boycott (E)	38	71	9	191	2945	47.50	7	14
W.R.Hammond (E)	33	58	3	251	2852	51.85	9	7
H.Sutcliffe (E)	27	46	5	194	2741	66.85	8	16
C.Hill (A)	41	76	1	188	2660	35.46	4	16
J.H.Edrich (E)	32	57	3	175	2644	48.96	7	13
G.A.Gooch (E)	42	79	0	196	2632	33.31	4	16
G.S.Chappell (A)	35	65	8	144	2619	45.94	9	12
M.A.Taylor (A)	33	61	2	219	2496	42.30	6	15
R.T.Ponting (A)	35	58	2	196	2476	44.21	8	9
M.C.Cowdrey (E)	43	75	4	113	2433	34.26	5	11
L.Hutton (E)	27	49	6	364	2428	56.46	5	14
R.N.Harvey (A)	37	68	5	167	2416	38.34	6	12
V.T.Trumper (A)	40	74	5	185*	2263	32.79	6	9
D.C.Boon (A)	31	57	8	184*	2237	45.65	7	8
W.M.Lawry (A)	29	51	5	166	2233	48.54	7	13
M.E.Waugh (A)	29	51	7	140	2204	50.09	6	11
S.E.Gregory (A)	52	92	7	201	2193	25.80	4	8
W.W.Armstrong (A)	42	71	9	158	2172	35.03	4	6
I.M.Chappell (A)	30	56	4	192	2138	41.11	4	16
K.F.Barrington (E)	23	39	6	256	2111	63.96	5	13
A.R.Morris (A)	24	43	2	206	2080	50.73	8	8

D.G.Bradman holds the unique record of scoring 2000 runs in both countries in this series (2674 runs in England and 2354 in Australia); J.B.Hobbs is the only other batsman to score 2000 runs in either country (2493 runs in Australia).

100 WICKETS

	Tests	Balls	Runs	Wkts	Avge	Best	5wI	10wM
S.K.Warne (A)	36	10757	4535	195	23.25	8- 71	11	4
D.K.Lillee (A)	29	8516	3507	167	21.00	7- 89	11	4
G.D.McGrath (A)	30	7280	3286	157	20.92	8- 38	10	–
I.T.Botham (E)	36	8479	4093	148	27.65	6- 78	9	2
H.Trumble (A)	31	7895	2945	141	20.88	8- 65	9	3
R.G.D.Willis (E)	35	7294	3346	128	26.14	8- 43	7	–
M.A.Noble (A)	39	6845	2860	115	24.86	7- 17	9	2
R.R.Lindwall (A)	29	6728	2559	114	22.44	7- 63	6	–
W.Rhodes (E)	41	5791	2616	109	24.00	8- 68	6	1
S.F.Barnes (E)	20	5749	2288	106	21.58	7- 60	12	1
C.V.Grimmett (A)	22	9224	3439	106	32.44	6- 37	11	2
D.L.Underwood (E)	29	8000	2770	105	26.38	7- 50	4	2
A.V.Bedser (E)	21	7065	2859	104	27.49	7- 44	7	2
G.Giffen (A)	31	6457	2791	103	27.09	7-117	7	1
W.J.O'Reilly (E)	19	7864	2587	102	25.36	7- 54	8	3
R.Peel (E)	20	5216	1715	101	16.98	7- 31	5	1
C.T.B.Turner (A)	17	5195	1670	101	16.53	7- 43	11	2
T.M.Alderman (A)	17	4717	2117	100	21.17	6- 47	11	1
J.R.Thomson (A)	21	4951	2418	100	24.18	6- 46	5	–

100 WICKET-KEEPING DISMISSALS

	Tests	Ct	St	Total
R.W.Marsh (A)	42	141	7	148
I.A.Healy (A)	33	123	12	135
A.P.E.Knott (E)	34	97	8	105

R.W.Marsh (141 catches) and W.A.S.Oldfield (A), (31 stumpings) hold the respective individual records in Anglo-Australian Tests.

TOURING TEAMS REGISTER 2013

Neither New Zealand nor Australia had selected their 2013 touring teams at the time of going to press. The following players who had represented those teams in Test matches since 1 November 2011 were still available for selection:

AUSTRALIA

Full Names	Birthdate	Birthplace	Team	Type	F-C Debut
BEER, Michael Anthony	09.06.84	Malvern	W Australia	RHB/SLA	2010-11
BIRD, Jackson Munro	11.12.86	Sydney	Tasmania	RHB/RFM	2011-12
CLARKE, Michael John	02.04.81	Liverpool	NSW	RHB/SLA	1999-00
COWAN, Edward James McKenzie	16.06.82	Paddington	Tasmania	LHB/LB	2003
CUMMINS, Patrick James	08.05.93	Sydney	NSW	RHB/RF	2010-11
HADDIN, Bradley James	23.10.77	Cowra	NSW	RHB/WK	1999-00
HARRIS, Ryan James	11.10.79	Sydney	Queensland	RHB/RF	2001-02
HASTINGS, John Wayne	04.11.85	Penrith	Victoria	RHB/RFM	2007-08
HENRIQUES, Moises Constantino	01.02.87	Funchal, Portugal	NSW	RHB/RFM	2006-07
HILFENHAUS, Benjamin William	15.03.83	Ulverstone	Tasmania	RHB/RFM	2005-06
HUGHES, Phillip Joel	30.11.88	Macksville	S Australia	LHB/OB	2007-08
JOHNSON, Mitchell Guy	02.11.81	Townsville	W Australia	LHB/LF	2001-02
KHAWAJA, Usman Tariq	18.12.86	Islamabad, Pak	NSW	LHB/RM	2007-08
LYON, Nathan Michael	20.11.87	Young	S Australia	RHB/OB	2010-11
MARSH, Shaun Edward	09.07.83	Narrogin	W Australia	LHB/SLA	2000-01
MAXWELL, Glenn James	14.10.88	Melbourne	Victoria	RHB/OB	2010-11
PATTINSON, James Lee	03.05.90	Melbourne	Victoria	LHB/RFM	2008-09
QUINEY, Robert John	20.08.82	Brighton	Victoria	LHB/RM	2006-07
SIDDLE, Peter Matthew	25.11.84	Traralgon	Victoria	RHB/RFM	2005-06
STARC, Mitchell Aaron	30.01.90	Sydney	NSW	LHB/LFM	2008-09
WADE, Matthew Scott	26.12.87	Hobart	Victoria	LHB/WK	2007-08
WARNER, David Andrew	27.10.86	Paddington	NSW	LHB/LB	2008-09
WATSON, Shane Robert	17.06.81	Ipswich	NSW	RHB/RMF	2000-01

NEW ZEALAND

Full Names	Birthdate	Birthplace	Team	Type	F-C Debut
ARNEL, Brent John	03.01.79	Te Awamutu	N Districts	RHB/RMF	2005-06
ASTLE, Todd Duncan	24.09.86	Palmerston N	Canterbury	RHB/LB	2008-09
BOULT, Trent Alexander	22.07.89	Rotorua	N Districts	RHB/LFM	2008-09
BRACEWELL, Douglas Alexander John	28.09.90	Tauranga	C Districts	RHB/RFM	2008-09
BROWNLIE, Dean Graham	30.07.84	Perth, Australia	Canterbury	RHB/RM	2009-10
FLYNN, Daniel Raymond	16.04.85	Rotorua	N Districts	LHB/SLA	2004-05
FRANKLIN, James Edward Charles	07.11.80	Wellington	Wellington	LHB/LFM	1998-99
GILLESPIE, Mark Raymond	17.10.79	Wanganui	Wellington	RHB/RFM	1999-00
GUPTILL, Martin James	30.09.86	Auckland	Auckland	RHB/OB	2005-06
McCULLUM, Brendon Barrie	27.09.81	Dunedin	Otago	RHB/WK	1999-00
MARTIN, Bruce Philip	25.04.80	Whangarei	Auckland	RHB/SLA	1999-00
MARTIN, Christopher Stewart	10.12.74	Christchurch	Auckland	RHB/RM	1997-98
MUNRO, Colin	11.03.87	Durban, SA	Auckland	LHB/RM	2006-07
NICOL, Robert James	28.05.83	Auckland	Canterbury	RHB/RM	2001-02
PATEL, Jeetan Singh	07.05.80	Wellington	Wellington	RHB/OB	1999-00
RUTHERFORD, Hamish Duncan	27.04.89	Dunedin	Otago	LHB	2008-09
RYDER, Jesse Daniel	06.08.84	Masterton	Wellington	LHB/RM	2002-03
SOUTHEE, Timothy Grant	11.12.88	Whangarei	N Districts	RHB/RMF	2006-07
TAYLOR, Luteru Ross Poutoa Lote	08.03.84	Lower Hutt	C Districts	RHB/OB	2002-03
VAN WYK, Cornelius Francoius Kruger	07.02.80	Wolmaransstad, SA	Canterbury	RHB/WK	2000-01
VETTORI, Daniel Luca	27.01.79	Auckland	N Districts	LHB/SLA	1996-97
WAGNER, Neil	13.03.86	Pretoria, SA	Otago	LHB/LMF	2005-06
WATLING, Bradley-John	09.07.85	Durban, SA	N Districts	RHB/WK	2004-05
WILLIAMSON, Kane Stuart	08.08.90	Tauranga	N Districts	RHB/OB	2007-08
YOUNG, Reece Alan	15.09.79	Auckland	Auckland	RHB/WK	1998-99

When the final squads are announced, a complete version of the touring parties and tour previews will be posted on www.playfaircricket.co.uk

STATISTICAL HIGHLIGHTS IN 2012 TESTS

Including Tests from No. 2025 (South Africa v Sri Lanka, 3rd Test) and No. 2027 (Australia v India, 2nd Test) to No. 2067 (Australia v Sri Lanka, 2nd Test).

TEAM HIGHLIGHTS

HIGHEST INNINGS TOTALS

659-4d	Australia v India	Sydney
648-9d	West Indies v Bangladesh	Khulna
637-2d	South Africa v England	The Oval
604-7d	Australia v India	Adelaide

LOWEST INNINGS TOTALS

51	Zimbabwe v New Zealand	Napier
72	England v Pakistan	Abu Dhabi
99	Pakistan v England	Dubai

HIGHEST MATCH AGGREGATE

1523-34	Bangladesh (556 & 167) v West Indies (527-4d & 273)	Mirpur

LARGE MARGINS OF VICTORY

Inns and 301 runs	New Zealand (495-7d) beat Zimbabwe (51 & 143)	Napier
Inns and 201 runs	Australia (460) beat Sri Lanka (156 & 103)	Melbourne
309 runs	South Africa (225 & 569) beat Australia (163 & 322)	Perth

ALL ELEVEN SCORING DOUBLE FIGURES

West Indies (449-9d, lowest 10) v Australia   Bridgetown

BATTING HIGHLIGHTS

TREBLE HUNDREDS

† = National record

H.M.Amla	311*†	South Africa v England	The Oval
M.J.Clarke	329*	Australia v India	Sydney

DOUBLE HUNDREDS

S.Chanderpaul	203*	West Indies v Bangladesh	Mirpur
M.J.Clarke (3)	210	Australia v India	Adelaide
	259*	Australia v South Africa	Brisbane
	230	Australia v South Africa	Adelaide

M.J.Clarke is the first batsman ever to score four double hundreds in a calendar year.

J.H.Kallis	224	South Africa v Sri Lanka	Cape Town
R.T.Ponting	221	Australia v India	Adelaide
C.A.Pujara	206*	India v England	Ahmedabad
M.N.Samuels	260	West Indies v Bangladesh	Khulna

HUNDRED IN EACH INNINGS OF A MATCH

K.O.A.Powell	117	110	West Indies v Bangladesh	Mirpur

FASTEST HUNDRED

D.A.Warner (180)	69 balls	Australia v India	Perth

This was the joint fourth fastest Test hundred of all time.

HUNDRED RUNS SCORED IN A SESSION

D.A.Warner (0-104*)   Australia v India   Perth

150 OR MORE RUNS FROM BOUNDARIES IN AN INNINGS

Runs	6s	4s			
166	1	40	M.J.Clarke (230)	Australia v South Africa	Adelaide
162	1	39	M.J.Clarke (329*)	Australia v India	Sydney

HUNDRED ON TEST DEBUT

Abul Hasan   113   Bangladesh v West Indies   Khulna

Only the second player, after R.A.Duff in 1901-02, to score a hundred on debut batting at No 10.

F.du Plessis   110*   South Africa v Australia   Adelaide

LONG INNINGS (Qualification: 600 mins and/or 400 balls)

Mins	Balls			
533	442	Azhar Ali (157)	Pakistan v England	Dubai
790	529	H.M.Amla (311)	South Africa v England	The Oval
609	468	M.J.Clarke (329*)	Australia v India	Sydney
516	404	R.T.Ponting (221)	Australia v India	Adelaide
618	455	M.N.Samuels (260)	West Indies v Bangladesh	Khulna

FIRST-WICKET PARTNERSHIP OF 100 IN EACH INNINGS

120/120   A.N.Petersen/G.C.Smith/J.A.Rudolph   South Africa v England   Headingley

NOTABLE PARTNERSHIPS

Qualifications: 1st-4th wkts: 250 runs; 5th-6th: 225; 7th: 200; 8th: 175; 9th: 150; 10th: 100. † = National record

First Wicket
254	C.H.Gayle/K.O.A.Powell	West Indies v New Zealand	North Sound

Second Wicket
287	Mohammad Hafeez/Azhar Ali	Pakistan v Sri Lanka	Colombo, SSC
259	G.C.Smith/H.M.Amla	South Africa v England	The Oval

Third Wicket
377*	H.M.Amla/J.H.Kallis	South Africa v England	The Oval
326	M.N.Samuels/S.Chanderpaul	West Indies v Bangladesh	Khulna
262	K.S.Williamson/L.R.P.L.Taylor	New Zealand v Sri Lanka	Colombo, PSS

Fourth Wicket
386	R.T.Ponting/M.J.Clarke	Australia v India	Adelaide
288	R.T.Ponting/M.J.Clarke	Australia v India	Sydney
259	E.J.M.Cowan/M.J.Clarke	Australia v South Africa	Brisbane

Fifth Wicket
334*	M.J.Clarke/M.E.K.Hussey	Australia v India	Sydney
296*	S.Chanderpaul/D.Ramdin	West Indies v Bangladesh	Mirpur
272	M.J.Clarke/M.E.K.Hussey	Australia v South Africa	Adelaide
228	M.J.Clarke/M.E.K.Hussey	Australia v South Africa	Brisbane

Seventh Wicket
204	M.N.Samuels/D.J.G.Sammy	West Indies v England	Nottingham

Ninth Wicket
184†	Mahmudullah/Abul Hasan	Bangladesh v West Indies	Khulna

Tenth Wicket
143†	D.Ramdin/T.L.Best	West Indies v England	Birmingham

T.L.Best's score of 95 was a record in Tests for a No 11 batsman.

BOWLING HIGHLIGHTS

SEVEN WICKETS IN AN INNINGS

Saeed Ajmal	7- 55	Pakistan v England	Dubai
S.C.J.Broad	7- 72	England v West Indies	Lord's
T.G.Southee	7- 64	New Zealand v India	Bangalore

TEN WICKETS IN A MATCH

R.Ashwin	12- 85	India v New Zealand	Hyderabad
S.C.J.Broad	11-165	England v West Indies	Lord's
H.M.R.K.B.Herath (2)	12-171	Sri Lanka v England	Galle
	11-108	Sri Lanka v New Zealand	Galle
M.S.Panesar	11-210	England v India	Mumbai
V.D.Philander	10-114	South Africa v New Zealand	Hamilton
K.A.J.Roach	10-146	West Indies v Australia	Port of Spain
Saeed Ajmal	10- 97	Pakistan v England	Dubai
S.Shillingford	10-219	West Indies v Australia	Roseau
G.P.Swann	10-181	England v Sri Lanka	Colombo, PSS

FIVE WICKETS IN AN INNINGS ON DEBUT

Sohag Gazi	6- 74	Bangladesh v West Indies	Mirpur

MOST OVERS IN AN INNINGS

Sohag Gazi	57.3-4-167-3	Bangladesh v West Indies	Khulna

MOST RUNS CONCEDED IN AN INNINGS

R.Ashwin	53-6-194-3	India v Australia	Adelaide

WICKET-KEEPING HIGHLIGHTS

SIX WICKET-KEEPING DISMISSALS IN AN INNINGS

M.J.Prior	5ct,1st	England v South Africa	Lord's

EIGHT WICKET-KEEPING DISMISSALS IN A MATCH

A.B.de Villiers	8ct	South Africa v England	The Oval
M.J.Prior	6ct,2st	England v South Africa	Lord's

NO BYES CONCEDED IN AN INNINGS OF 550

580-4d	L.D.Chandimal	Sri Lanka v South Africa	Cape Town
565-5d	A.B.de Villiers	South Africa v Australia	Brisbane
550	A.B.de Villiers	South Africa v Australia	Adelaide

FIELDING HIGHLIGHTS

FIVE CATCHES IN AN INNINGS IN THE FIELD

G.C.Smith	5ct	South Africa v Australia	Perth

SIX CATCHES IN A MATCH IN THE FIELD

J.H.Kallis	6ct	South Africa v Sri Lanka	Cape Town
G.C.Smith	6ct	South Africa v Australia	Perth

LEADING TEST AGGREGATES IN 2012

1000 RUNS IN 2012

	M	I	NO	HS	Runs	Avge	100	50
M.J.Clarke (A)	11	18	3	329*	1595	106.33	5	3
A.N.Cook (E)	15	29	3	190	1249	48.03	4	3
H.M.Amla (SA)	10	17	2	311*	1064	70.93	4	2
K.P.Pietersen (E)	14	25	1	186	1053	43.87	3	4
I.J.L.Trott (E)	15	28	2	143	1005	38.65	2	6

RECORD CALENDAR YEAR RUNS AGGREGATE

	M	I	NO	HS	Runs	Avge	100	50
M.Yousuf Youhana (P) (2006)	11	19	1	202	1788	99.33	9	3

RECORD CALENDAR YEAR RUNS AVERAGE

	M	I	NO	HS	Runs	Avge	100	50
G.St A.Sobers (WI) (1958)	7	12	3	365*	1193	132.55	5	3

1000 RUNS IN DEBUT CALENDAR YEAR

	M	I	NO	HS	Runs	Avge	100	50
M.A.Taylor (A) (1989)	11	20	1	219	1219	64.15	4	5
A.N.Cook (E) (2006)	13	24	2	127	1013	46.04	4	3

50 WICKETS IN 2012

	M	O	R	W	Avge	Best	5wI	10wM
H.M.R.K.B.Herath (SL)	10	537.2	1417	60	23.61	6-43	7	2
G.P.Swann (E)	14	634.2	1766	59	29.93	6-82	3	1

RECORD CALENDAR YEAR WICKETS AGGREGATE

	M	O	R	W	Avge	Best	5wI	10wM
M.Muralitharan (SL) (2006)	11	588.4	1521	90	16.90	8-70	9	5
S.K.Warne (A) (2005)	14	691.4	2043	90	22.70	6-46	6	2

MOST WICKET-KEEPING DISMISSALS IN 2012

	M	Dis	Ct	St
M.J.Prior (E)	15	36	29	7

RECORD CALENDAR YEAR DISMISSALS AGGREGATE

	M	Dis	Ct	St
I.A.Healy (A) (1993)	16	67	58	9
M.V.Boucher (SA) (1998)	13	67	65	2

20 CATCHES BY FIELDERS IN 2012

	M	Ct
G.C.Smith (SA)	10	23
D.J.G.Sammy (WI)	10	20

RECORD CALENDAR YEAR FIELDER'S AGGREGATE

	M	Ct
G.C.Smith (SA) (2008)	15	30

TEST MATCH SCORES
NEW ZEALAND v SOUTH AFRICA (1st Test)

At University Oval, Dunedin, on 7, 8, 9, 10, 11 (*no play*) March 2012.
Toss: New Zealand. Result: **MATCH DRAWN**.
Debuts: New Zealand – R.J.Nicol, C.F.K.van Wyk.

SOUTH AFRICA

*G.C.Smith	c Nicol b Martin	53	(2)	b Bracewell	115
A.N.Petersen	lbw b Boult	11	(1)	c Southee b Bracewell	25
H.M.Amla	c Taylor b Vettori	62		c Guptill b Bracewell	2
J.H.Kallis	c Taylor b Martin	0		c Nicol b Boult	113
A.B.de Villiers	lbw b Martin	0	(6)	c McCullum b Williamson	29
J.A.Rudolph	c Boult b Bracewell	52	(5)	not out	105
†M.V.Boucher	run out	4		not out	34
D.W.Steyn	c Taylor b Bracewell	9			
V.D.Philander	c Williamson b Martin	22			
M.Morkel	not out	13			
Imran Tahir	run out	10			
Extras	(LB 1, NB 1)	2		(B 2, LB 6, W 1, NB 3)	12
Total	(68.2 overs; 307 mins)	238		(5 wkts dec; 140 overs; 614 mins)	435

NEW ZEALAND

R.J.Nicol	c Smith b Philander	6	c Smith b Tahir	19
M.J.Guptill	b Morkel	16	c de Villiers b Philander	6
B.B.McCullum	c and b Tahir	48	not out	58
*L.R.P.L.Taylor	c Boucher b Morkel	44	not out	48
K.S.Williamson	c Boucher b Philander	11		
D.L.Vettori	c and b Kallis	46		
†C.F.K.van Wyk	c Smith b Philander	36		
D.A.J.Bracewell	b Steyn	25		
T.G.Southee	c Smith b Philander	0		
T.A.Boult	not out	33		
C.S.Martin	c Amla b Steyn	5		
Extras	(LB 3)	3	(LB 2, W 2, NB 2)	6
Total	(88.2 overs; 370 mins)	273	(2 wkts; 41 overs; 186 mins)	137

NEW ZEALAND	O	M	R	W		O	M	R	W
Martin	18	2	56	4		23	4	74	0
Southee	10	1	40	0	(4)	26	4	100	0
Boult	8	0	58	1	(2)	26	4	93	1
Bracewell	16.2	2	52	2	(3)	25	3	70	3
Vettori	15	4	31	1		32	5	65	0
Nicol	1	1	0	0		1	0	9	0
Williamson						7	4	16	1
SOUTH AFRICA									
Steyn	20.2	4	79	2		8	2	25	0
Philander	18	1	72	4		12	2	29	1
Morkel	18	5	52	2		9	2	33	0
Imran Tahir	24	6	55	1		8	2	33	1
Kallis	8	2	12	1		4	1	15	0

FALL OF WICKETS

	SA	NZ	SA	NZ
Wkt	1st	1st	2nd	2nd
1st	34	7	45	16
2nd	86	41	47	55
3rd	90	106	247	—
4th	90	116	283	—
5th	156	135	353	—
6th	161	188		
7th	179	229		
8th	214	229		
9th	222	239		
10th	238	273		

Umpires: Alim Dar (*Pakistan*) (71) and B.R.Doctrove (*West Indies*) (37).
Referee: R.S.Mahanama (*Sri Lanka*) (35). Test No. 2034/36 (NZ369/SA364)

NEW ZEALAND v SOUTH AFRICA (2nd Test)

At Seddon Park, Hamilton, on 15, 16, 17 March 2012.
Toss: South Africa. Result: **SOUTH AFRICA** won by nine wickets.
Debuts: None.

NEW ZEALAND

R.J.Nicol	c Boucher b Philander	2	b Philander		1
M.J.Guptill	b Steyn	22	c Amla b Steyn		1
B.B.McCullum	c Rudolph b Steyn	61	lbw b Philander		5
*L.R.P.L.Taylor	c Smith b Philander	44	lbw b Steyn		17
K.S.Williamson	c Smith b Steyn	0	c Boucher b Philander		77
D.L.Vettori	b Philander	0	c Boucher b Kallis		21
†C.F.K.van Wyk	lbw b Morkel	21	b Philander		20
D.A.J.Bracewell	c Boucher b Philander	0	b Morkel		0
M.R.Gillespie	c Petersen b Tahir	27	c Boucher b Philander		14
B.J.Arnel	lbw b Tahir	3	not out		8
C.S.Martin	not out	0	b Philander		0
Extras	(LB 3, NB 2)	5	(LB 4)		4
Total	**(61.2 overs; 286 mins)**	**185**	**(67.5 overs; 296 mins)**		**168**

SOUTH AFRICA

*G.C.Smith	c van Wyk b Martin	13	(2) not out		55
A.N.Petersen	lbw b Gillespie	29	(1) c van Wyk b Bracewell		1
D.W.Steyn	c van Wyk b Martin	4			
H.M.Amla	c Williamson b Gillespie	16	(3) not out		46
J.H.Kallis	c van Wyk b Gillespie	6			
A.B.de Villiers	b Vettori	83			
J.A.Rudolph	c van Wyk b Gillespie	1			
†M.V.Boucher	b Gillespie	24			
V.D.Philander	b Bracewell	14			
M.Morkel	not out	35			
Imran Tahir	c Gillespie b Williamson	16			
Extras	(B 1, LB 9, W 1, NB 1)	12	(NB 1)		1
Total	**(77.3 overs; 335 mins)**	**253**	**(1 wkt; 19.5 overs; 87 mins)**		**103**

SOUTH AFRICA	O	M	R	W		O	M	R	W
Steyn	18	5	49	3		16	5	31	2
Philander	15	3	70	4		15.5	3	44	6
Kallis	9	4	9	0	(5)	6	3	11	1
Morkel	14	2	42	1	(3)	13	5	26	1
Imran Tahir	5.2	1	12	2	(4)	17	2	52	0

NEW ZEALAND	O	M	R	W		O	M	R	W
Martin	16	6	38	2		3	1	18	0
Bracewell	18	7	50	1		5	0	14	1
Gillespie	15	2	59	5	(4)	4	0	24	0
Vettori	19	3	49	1	(3)	2	0	2	0
Arnel	9	2	46	0		3	0	18	0
Williamson	0.3	0	1	1		2	0	23	0
Nicol						0.5	0	4	0

FALL OF WICKETS

	NZ	SA	NZ	SA
Wkt	1st	1st	2nd	2nd
1st	11	14	1	5
2nd	44	18	7	—
3rd	133	63	7	—
4th	133	69	64	—
5th	133	84	99	—
6th	133	88	141	—
7th	133	151	142	—
8th	176	185	142	—
9th	184	219	160	—
10th	185	253	168	—

Umpires: B.R.Doctrove (*West Indies*) (38) and R.J.Kettleborough (*England*) (8).
Referee: R.S.Madugalle (*Sri Lanka*) (133). **Test No. 2035/37 (NZ370/SA365)**

NEW ZEALAND v SOUTH AFRICA (3rd Test)

At Basin Reserve, Wellington, on 23, 24, 25, 26, 27 March 2012.
Toss: New Zealand. Result: **MATCH DRAWN**.
Debuts: None.

SOUTH AFRICA

*G.C.Smith	c van Wyk b Bracewell	5	(2) c Bracewell b Vettori		41
A.N.Petersen	lbw b Martin	156	(1) run out		39
H.M.Amla	c van Wyk b Gillespie	63			
J.P.Duminy	c Taylor b Gillespie	103	not out		33
A.B.de Villiers	b Martin	38	(3) c Williamson b Bracewell		68
J.A.Rudolph	c van Wyk b Gillespie	11			
†M.V.Boucher	c Williamson b Gillespie	46			
D.W.Steyn	c Guptill b Gillespie	0			
V.D.Philander	c Flynn b Gillespie	29			
M.Morkel	not out	10			
M.de Lange					
Extras	(B 6, LB 1, W 3, NB 3)	13	(LB 3, W 3, NB 2)		8
Total	(9 wkts dec; 148.4 overs; 644 mins)	474	(3 wkts dec; 29.4 overs; 150 mins)		189

NEW ZEALAND

D.R.Flynn	c Boucher b Philander	45	(2) c Boucher b Morkel		0
M.J.Guptill	lbw b Philander	59	(1) c Rudolph b Morkel		18
B.B.McCullum	c Boucher b Steyn	31	lbw b Morkel		0
*L.R.P.L.Taylor	retired hurt	18			
K.S.Williamson	c Boucher b Steyn	39	(4) not out		102
D.G.Brownlie	c Steyn b Philander	29	(5) b Morkel		15
D.L.Vettori	c Rudolph b Philander	30	(6) b Morkel		0
†C.F.K.van Wyk	c sub (Imran Tahir) b de Lange	7	(7) c and b Morkel		39
D.A.J.Bracewell	b Philander	0	(8) not out		20
M.R.Gillespie	c de Villiers b Philander	10			
C.S.Martin	not out	2			
Extras	(LB 2, W 2, NB 1)	5	(LB 6)		6
Total	(96 overs; 438 mins)	275	(6 wkts; 80.4 overs; 346 mins)		200

NEW ZEALAND	O	M	R	W		O	M	R	W
Martin	28	5	95	2		10	0	44	0
Bracewell	30	3	106	1		6.4	0	47	1
Gillespie	33.4	7	113	6		6	0	55	0
Vettori	42	11	98	0		7	1	40	1
Brownlie	2	0	20	0					
Williamson	13	1	35	0					
SOUTH AFRICA									
Steyn	23	8	41	2	(4)	15	9	14	0
Philander	22	4	81	6		18.4	6	29	0
Morkel	20	6	54	0	(1)	16.4	7	23	6
De Lange	21	1	74	1	(3)	17.2	4	77	0
Duminy	10	0	23	0		13	2	51	0

FALL OF WICKETS

	SA	NZ	SA	NZ
Wkt	1st	1st	2nd	2nd
1st	13	86	77	1
2nd	106	136	106	1
3rd	306	145	189	32
4th	362	219	–	83
5th	381	242	–	83
6th	388	263	–	163
7th	404	263	–	–
8th	459	263	–	–
9th	474	275	–	–
10th	–	–	–	–

Umpires: Alim Dar (*Pakistan*) (72) and R.A.Kettleborough (*England*) (9).
Referee: R.S.Madugalle (*Sri Lanka*) (134). **Test No. 2036/38 (NZ371/SA366)**
L.R.P.L.Taylor retired hurt at 160-3.

SRI LANKA v ENGLAND (1st Test)

At Galle International Stadium, on 26, 27, 28, 29 March 2012.
Toss: Sri Lanka. Result: **SRI LANKA** won by 75 runs.
Debut: England – S.R.Patel.

SRI LANKA

H.D.R.L.Thirimanne	c Swann b Anderson	3	b Swann		6
T.M.Dilshan	c Strauss b Broad	11	b Broad		0
K.C.Sangakkara	c Prior b Anderson	0	c Bell b Swann		14
*D.P.M.D.Jayawardena	c Prior b Anderson	180	c Anderson b Swann		5
T.T.Samaraweera	run out	20	st Prior b Swann		36
L.D.Chandimal	c Bell b Patel	27	c Pietersen b Panesar		31
†H.A.P.W.Jayawardena	lbw b Anderson	23	(8) not out		61
H.K.S.R.Kaluhalamulla	run out	12	(7) lbw b Swann		18
H.M.R.K.B.Herath	lbw b Patel	5	b Swann		7
U.W.M.B.C.A.Welagedara	b Anderson	19	c Strauss b Panesar		13
R.A.S.Lakmal	not out	0	run out		13
Extras	(LB 14, NB 4)	18	(B 1, LB 4, W 1, NB 4)		10
Total	**(96.3 overs; 412 mins)**	**318**	**(84.3 overs; 339 mins)**		**214**

ENGLAND

*A.J.Strauss	lbw b Herath	26	c Dilshan b Herath		27
A.N.Cook	lbw b Lakmal	0	c H.A.P.W.Jayawardena b Herath		14
I.J.L.Trott	st H.A.P.W.Jayawardena b Herath	12	c Dilshan b Kaluhalamulla		112
K.P.Pietersen	b Welagedara	3	c D.P.M.D.Jayawardena b Kaluhalamulla		30
I.R.Bell	b Herath	52	lbw b Herath		13
†M.J.Prior	lbw b Herath	7	c Thirimanne b Herath		41
S.R.Patel	lbw b Herath	2	c Dilshan b Herath		9
S.C.J.Broad	lbw b Herath	28	not out		5
G.P.Swann	c Dilshan b Kaluhalamulla	24	lbw b Herath		1
J.M.Anderson	not out	23	c H.A.P.W.Jayawardena b Kaluhalamulla		5
M.S.Panesar	lbw b Kaluhalamulla	13	c Dilshan b Kaluhalamulla		0
Extras	(LB 2, W 1)	3	(LB 6, W 1)		7
Total	**(46.4 overs; 203 mins)**	**193**	**(99 overs; 387 mins)**		**264**

ENGLAND	O	M	R	W	O	M	R	W
Anderson	20.3	5	72	5	10.3	2	26	0
Broad	21	3	71	1	11	2	33	1
Panesar	23	11	42	0	(4) 24	6	59	2
Swann	23	3	92	0	(3) 30	5	82	6
Patel	9	1	27	2	9	4	9	0

SRI LANKA	O	M	R	W	O	M	R	W
Welagedara	11	2	46	4	13	2	40	0
Lakmal	9	2	45	1	10	5	22	0
Herath	9	5	74	6	38	9	97	6
Kaluhalamulla	7.4	0	26	2	(5) 26	2	74	4
Dilshan					(4) 12	1	25	0

FALL OF WICKETS

	SL	E	SL	E
Wkt	1st	1st	2nd	2nd
1st	11	0	4	31
2nd	11	40	8	48
3rd	15	43	14	118
4th	67	65	41	152
5th	128	72	72	233
6th	170	92	114	252
7th	191	122	115	256
8th	253	157	127	259
9th	307	157	167	264
10th	318	193	214	264

Umpires: Asad Rauf (*Pakistan*) (41) and R.J.Tucker (*Australia*) (19).
Referee: J.Srinath (*India*) (21).   Test No. 2037/25 (SL211/E919)

SRI LANKA v ENGLAND (2nd Test)

At P.Saravanamuttu Oval, Colombo, on 3, 4, 5, 6, 7 April 2012.
Toss: Sri Lanka. Result: **ENGLAND** won by eight wickets.
Debuts: None.

SRI LANKA

H.D.R.L.Thirimanne	lbw b Anderson	8	(2) c Strauss b Anderson		11
T.M.Dilshan	c Prior b Anderson	14	(3) c Anderson b Swann		35
K.C.Sangakkara	c Strauss b Anderson	0	(4) c Prior b Swann		21
*D.P.M.D.Jayawardena	lbw b Swann	105	(5) c Cook b Swann		64
T.T.Samaraweera	lbw b Bresnan	54	(6) b Swann		47
A.D.Mathews	c Strauss b Swann	57	(8) c Strauss b Finn		46
†H.A.P.W.Jayawardena	c Prior b Finn	7	(9) b Swann		2
H.K.S.R.Kaluhalamulla	c Pietersen b Swann	12	(7) b Swann		0
K.T.G.D.Prasad	not out	12	(1) c Bresnan b Finn		34
H.M.R.K.B.Herath	c Prior b Bresnan	2	c Anderson b Patel		2
R.A.S.Lakmal	b Swann	0	not out		4
Extras	(B 4)	4	(B 4, LB 6, W 2)		12
Total	(111.1 overs; 481 mins)	275	(118.5 overs; 498 mins)		278

ENGLAND

*A.J.Strauss	c H.A.P.W.Jayawardena b Dilshan	61	b Dilshan	0
A.N.Cook	c D.P.M.D.Jayawardena b Dilshan	94	not out	49
I.J.L.Trott	c D.P.M.D.Jayawardena b Herath	64	lbw b Herath	5
K.P.Pietersen	lbw b Herath	151	not out	42
I.R.Bell	c Kaluhalamulla b Prasad	18		
†M.J.Prior	c Prasad b Herath	11		
S.R.Patel	c Prasad b Kaluhalamulla	29		
T.T.Bresnan	b Herath	5		
G.P.Swann	c Dilshan b Herath	17		
J.M.Anderson	lbw b Herath	2		
S.T.Finn	not out	2		
Extras	(B 1, LB 2, W 1, NB 2)	6	(LB 1)	1
Total	(152.3 overs; 622 mins)	460	(2 wkts; 19.4 overs; 78 mins)	97

ENGLAND	O	M	R	W	O	M	R	W	FALL OF WICKETS				
										SL	E	SL	E
Anderson	22	5	62	3	20	6	36	1					
Finn	22	4	51	1	15.5	1	30	2	Wkt	1st	1st	2nd	2nd
Bresnan	21	3	47	2	(4) 14	5	24	0	1st	21	122	23	0
Patel	16	3	32	0	(5) 25	7	54	1	2nd	21	213	64	31
Swann	28.1	4	75	4	(3) 40	1	106	6	3rd	30	253	104	–
Pietersen					4	0	18	0	4th	154	347	125	–
SRI LANKA									5th	216	380	215	–
Lakmal	22	4	81	0					6th	227	411	215	–
Prasad	23	8	63	1					7th	258	419	238	–
Herath	53	9	133	6	(2) 9	0	37	1	8th	261	454	242	–
Dilshan	20	4	73	2	(1) 7.4	1	43	1	9th	270	458	251	–
Kaluhalamulla	34.3	4	107	1	(3) 3	0	16	0	10th	275	460	278	–

Umpires: Asad Rauf (*Pakistan*) (42) and B.N.J.Oxenford (*Australia*) (8).
Referee: J.Srinath (*India*) (22). **Test No. 2038/26 (SL212/E920)**

WEST INDIES v AUSTRALIA (1st Test)

At Kensington Oval, Bridgetown, Barbados, on 7, 8, 9, 10, 11 April 2012.
Toss: West Indies. Result: **AUSTRALIA** won by three wickets.
Debut: Australia – M.S.Wade.   ‡ K.O.A.Powell

WEST INDIES

Batsman	1st innings		2nd innings	
A.B.Barath	c Siddle b Harris	22	b Hilfenhaus	2
K.C.Brathwaite	c Wade b Siddle	57	c Wade b Hilfenhaus	0
K.A.Edwards	c and b Warner	61	lbw b Hilfenhaus	1
D.M.Bravo	c Hussey b Watson	51	c Wade b Siddle	32
S.Chanderpaul	not out	103	c Wade b Harris	12
N.Deonarine	c Wade b Harris	21	lbw b Harris	21
†C.S.Baugh	run out	22	c Harris b Hilfenhaus	23
*D.J.G.Sammy	c Cowan b Hilfenhaus	41	b Watson	14
K.A.J.Roach	c Clarke b Lyon	16	b Harris	25
F.H.Edwards	c Hussey b Warner	10	c Watson b Siddle	3
D.Bishoo	not out	18	not out	7
Extras	(B 12, LB 9, W 4, NB 2)	27	(B 4, LB 3, NB 1)	8
Total	(9 wkts dec; 153 overs)	449	(66.4 overs)	148

AUSTRALIA

Batsman	1st innings		2nd innings	
E.J.M.Cowan	c Baugh b Sammy	14	(2) c Chanderpaul b Deonarine	34
D.A.Warner	c Bravo b Sammy	42	(1) c Baugh b Sammy	22
S.R.Watson	c Baugh b Roach	39	c sub‡ b Deonarine	52
R.T.Ponting	run out	4	b Deonarine	14
*M.J.Clarke	c Deonarine b Bishoo	73	c and b Deonarine	6
M.E.K.Hussey	c Baugh b Roach	48	b Roach	32
†M.S.Wade	c Bravo b F.H.Edwards	28	c Bishoo b Roach	18
P.M.Siddle	c K.A.Edwards b F.H.Edwards	0		
R.J.Harris	not out	68	(8) not out	0
B.W.Hilfenhaus	b Roach	24	(9) not out	2
N.M.Lyon	not out	40		
Extras	(LB 16, W 5, NB 5)	26	(B 1, LB 3, W 2, NB 2)	8
Total	(9 wkts dec; 145 overs)	406	(7 wkts; 47 overs)	192

AUSTRALIA	O	M	R	W	O	M	R	W
Harris	29	8	83	2	(3) 8.4	2	31	3
Hilfenhaus	33	12	67	1	(1) 17	7	27	4
Siddle	31	10	83	1	(4) 17	2	32	2
Lyon	31	11	94	1	(5) 11	4	19	0
Clarke	2	0	4	0	(6) 1	0	2	0
Watson	15	5	46	1	(2) 12	1	30	1
Warner	10	0	45	2				
Hussey	2	0	6	0				

WEST INDIES	O	M	R	W	O	M	R	W
F.H.Edwards	31	4	92	2	(2) 6	0	19	0
Roach	29	8	72	3	(1) 12	0	45	2
Bishoo	45	10	125	1	(4) 8	0	44	0
Sammy	21	6	65	2	(3) 10	2	27	1
Deonarine	19	5	36	0	11	1	53	4

FALL OF WICKETS

	WI	A	WI	A
Wkt	1st	1st	2nd	2nd
1st	38	50	2	31
2nd	142	65	3	106
3rd	167	84	4	126
4th	240	133	17	131
5th	285	215	67	140
6th	316	249	75	177
7th	369	250	106	189
8th	402	285	116	–
9th	421	329	125	–
10th	–	–	148	–

Umpires: I.J.Gould (*England*) (26) and A.L.Hill (*New Zealand*) (29).
Referee: J.J.Crowe (*New Zealand*) (50).   Test No. 2039/109 (WI479/A741)

WEST INDIES v AUSTRALIA (2nd Test)

At Queen's Park Oval, Port of Spain, Trinidad, on 15, 16, 17, 18, 19 April 2012.
Toss: Australia. Result: **MATCH DRAWN**.
Debuts: None.

AUSTRALIA

D.A.Warner	c Sammy b Shillingford	29	(2) c Bravo b Roach		17
E.J.M.Cowan	lbw b Roach	28	(1) lbw b Roach		20
S.R.Watson	c Barath b Shillingford	56	b Roach		0
R.T.Ponting	c Sammy b Roach	7	c Powell b Edwards		41
*M.J.Clarke	c Shillingford b Deonarine	45	c and b Sammy		15
M.E.K.Hussey	c Brathwaite b Deonarine	73	b Roach		24
†M.S.Wade	c Bravo b Roach	11	not out		31
J.L.Pattinson	c Bravo b Shillingford	32			
B.W.Hilfenhaus	b Roach	5	(8) b Roach		0
N.M.Lyon	not out	7	(9) c Sammy b Shillingford		3
M.A.Beer	lbw b Roach	2			
Extras	(B 5, LB 5, W 1, NB 5)	16	(B 4, LB 1, W 1, NB 3)		9
Total	**(135 overs)**	**311**	**(8 wkts dec; 61.5 overs)**		**160**

WEST INDIES

A.B.Barath	lbw b Beer	7	c Clarke b Hilfenhaus	5
K.C.Brathwaite	lbw b Hilfenhaus	0		
K.O.A.Powell	lbw b Pattinson	19	(2) lbw b Hilfenhaus	4
D.M.Bravo	lbw b Hussey	38	not out	8
S.Chanderpaul	lbw b Lyon	94		
N.Deonarine	st Wade b Lyon	55		
†C.S.Baugh	lbw b Beer	21		
*D.J.G.Sammy	c Hussey b Lyon	1	(3) not out	30
S.Shillingford	c Cowan b Lyon	4		
K.A.J.Roach	c Wade b Lyon	0		
F.H.Edwards	not out	0		
Extras	(B 1, LB 8, W 1, NB 8)	18	(B 6)	6
Total	**(104.4 overs)**	**257**	**(2 wkts; 11 overs)**	**53**

WEST INDIES	O	M	R	W		O	M	R	W	FALL OF WICKETS				
Edwards	23	11	45	0		10	2	28	1		A	WI	A	WI
Roach	27	5	105	5	(3)	18	4	41	5	*Wkt*	*1st*	*1st*	*2nd*	*2nd*
Sammy	16	6	27	0	(4)	8	0	17	1	1st	53	0	26	6
Shillingford	49	17	92	3	(2)	23.5	4	55	1	2nd	65	26	26	13
Deonarine	20	6	32	2		2	0	14	0	3rd	83	38	57	–
										4th	167	100	93	–
AUSTRALIA										5th	178	230	95	–
Beer	25.4	9	56	2		4	1	10	0	6th	208	231	145	–
Hilfenhaus	16	4	39	1		4	0	22	2	7th	297	237	149	–
Lyon	29	9	68	5						8th	297	241	160	–
Pattinson	11	2	40	1						9th	309	249	–	–
Hussey	6	1	19	1						10th	311	257	–	–
Watson	12	5	14	0	(3)	3	1	15	0					
Warner	3	1	9	0										
Clarke	2	0	3	0										

Umpires: M.Erasmus (*South Africa*) (10) and I.J.Gould (*England*) (27).
Referee: J.J.Crowe (*New Zealand*) (51). **Test No. 2040/110 (WI480/A742)**

WEST INDIES v AUSTRALIA (3rd Test)

At Windsor Park, Roseau, Dominica, on 23, 24, 25, 26, 27 April 2012.
Toss: Australia. Result: **AUSTRALIA** won by 75 runs.
Debuts: None.

AUSTRALIA

Batsman	Dismissal 1	R		Dismissal 2	R
E.J.M.Cowan	lbw b Rampaul	1	(2)	c Sammy b Deonarine	55
D.A.Warner	c Powell b Shillingford	50	(1)	c Chanderpaul b Roach	11
S.R.Watson	c Deonarine b Sammy	41		c Sammy b Shillingford	5
R.T.Ponting	c Sammy b Shillingford	23		c Chanderpaul b Roach	57
*M.J.Clarke	c Barath b Shillingford	24		c Bravo b Shillingford	25
M.E.K.Hussey	c Sammy b Shillingford	10		c Sammy b Shillingford	32
†M.S.Wade	c Bravo b Shillingford	106		lbw b Deonarine	4
R.J.Harris	c Baugh b Roach	4		c Baugh b Deonarine	9
M.A.Starc	run out	35		b Roach	21
B.W.Hilfenhaus	b Shillingford	19		c Brathwaite b Shillingford	12
N.M.Lyon	not out	0		not out	12
Extras	(B 4, LB 6, W 3, NB 2)	15		(B 8, LB 9, W 1, NB 4)	22
Total	**(114.5 overs)**	**328**		**(85 overs)**	**259**

WEST INDIES

Batsman	Dismissal 1	R		Dismissal 2	R
A.B.Barath	c Cowan b Lyon	29		c Cowan b Hilfenhaus	0
K.C.Brathwaite	c Harris b Hilfenhaus	0		lbw b Clarke	14
K.O.A.Powell	b Lyon	40		b Clarke	24
D.M.Bravo	c Cowan b Warner	10		c Wade b Watson	45
S.Chanderpaul	lbw b Starc	68		lbw b Clarke	69
N.Deonarine	lbw b Harris	7		c and b Clarke	13
†C.S.Baugh	c Cowan b Lyon	5		c Ponting b Lyon	12
*D.J.G.Sammy	run out	10		c Hilfenhaus b Lyon	61
S.Shillingford	b Starc	0	(11)	not out	31
R.Rampaul	c Warner b Lyon	31		c Warner b Clarke	11
K.A.J.Roach	not out	9	(9)	c Clarke b Lyon	2
Extras	(B 1, LB 2, W 1, NB 5)	9		(B 3, LB 9)	12
Total	**(87.2 overs)**	**218**		**(96.3 overs)**	**294**

WEST INDIES	O	M	R	W		O	M	R	W
Roach	23	5	72	1	(2)	13	2	40	3
Rampaul	24	6	65	1	(1)	9	1	37	0
Sammy	21	7	48	1	(4)	10	4	20	0
Shillingford	42.5	9	119	6	(3)	39	7	100	4
Deonarine	4	0	14	0		14	1	45	3
AUSTRALIA									
Hilfenhaus	18	6	30	1		13	5	23	1
Starc	12.2	4	29	2		9	2	26	0
Harris	13	0	36	1	(4)	12	2	34	0
Watson	4	0	12	0	(6)	9	2	20	1
Lyon	33	7	69	4	(3)	29.3	6	87	3
Warner	5	0	21	1	(7)	1	0	6	0
Clarke	2	0	18	0	(5)	23	1	86	5

FALL OF WICKETS

	A	WI	A	WI
Wkt	1st	1st	2nd	2nd
1st	1	1	17	0
2nd	84	62	25	28
3rd	105	73	112	45
4th	142	85	168	155
5th	157	96	171	173
6th	164	103	196	180
7th	169	120	220	206
8th	226	120	230	234
9th	328	186	237	245
10th	328	218	259	294

Umpires: M.Erasmus (*South Africa*) (11) and A.L.Hill (*New Zealand*) (30).
Referee: J.J.Crowe (*New Zealand*) (52). **Test No. 2041/111 (WI481/A743)**

ENGLAND v WEST INDIES (1st Test)

At Lord's, London, on 17, 18, 19, 20, 21 May 2012.
Toss: England. Result: **ENGLAND** won by five wickets.
Debuts: England – J.M.Bairstow; West Indies – S.T.Gabriel.

WEST INDIES

A.B.Barath	c Anderson b Broad	42	c Prior b Bresnan		24
K.O.A.Powell	b Anderson	5	c Bell b Broad		8
K.A.Edwards	lbw b Anderson	1	run out		0
D.M.Bravo	run out	29	b Swann		21
S.Chanderpaul	not out	87	lbw b Swann		91
M.N.Samuels	c Bairstow b Broad	31	c Swann b Broad		86
†D.Ramdin	c Strauss b Broad	6	b Anderson		43
*D.J.G.Sammy	c Bresnan b Broad	17	c Prior b Broad		37
K.A.J.Roach	c and b Broad	6	c Bell b Broad		4
F.H.Edwards	c Prior b Broad	2	not out		10
S.T.Gabriel	c Swann b Broad	0	b Swann		13
Extras	(B 6, LB 8, NB 3)	17	(LB 7, NB 1)		8
Total	**(89.5 overs; 381 mins)**	**243**	**(130.5 overs; 575 mins)**		**345**

ENGLAND

*A.J.Strauss	c Ramdin b Roach	122	c Powell b Roach		1
A.N.Cook	b Roach	26	c K.A.Edwards b Sammy		79
I.J.L.Trott	c Ramdin b Sammy	58	(4) c Sammy b Roach		13
K.P.Pietersen	c Ramdin b Samuels	32	(5) c Ramdin b Gabriel		13
I.R.Bell	c Powell b Gabriel	61	(6) not out		63
J.M.Bairstow	lbw b Roach	16	(7) not out		0
†M.J.Prior	b Gabriel	19			
T.T.Bresnan	c Ramdin b Sammy	0			
S.C.J.Broad	b F.H.Edwards	10			
G.P.Swann	b Gabriel	30			
J.M.Anderson	not out	0	(3) c Ramdin b Roach		6
Extras	(B 9, LB 3, NB 12)	24	(B 4, LB 3, NB 11)		18
Total	**(113.3 overs; 533 mins)**	**398**	**(5 wkts; 46.1 overs; 202 mins)**		**193**

ENGLAND	O	M	R	W	O	M	R	W		FALL OF WICKETS			
Anderson	25	8	59	2	36	11	67	1			WI	E	WI	E
Broad	24.5	6	72	7	34	6	93	4		*Wkt*	*1st*	*1st*	*2nd*	*2nd*
Bresnan	20	7	39	0	36	11	105	1		1st	13	47	36	1
Swann	18	6	52	0	18.5	4	59	3		2nd	32	194	36	10
Trott	2	0	7	0	6	0	14	0		3rd	86	244	36	29
										4th	100	266	65	57
WEST INDIES										5th	181	292	222	189
F.H.Edwards	25	1	88	1	8	0	24	0		6th	187	320	261	–
Roach	25	3	108	3	13	2	60	3		7th	219	323	307	–
Gabriel	21.3	2	60	3	5	1	26	1		8th	231	342	313	–
Sammy	28	1	92	2	10	1	25	1		9th	243	397	325	–
Samuels	14	3	38	1	10.1	0	51	1		10th	243	398	345	–

Umpires: Alim Dar (*Pakistan*) (73) and M.Erasmus (*South Africa*) (12).
Referee: R.S.Mahanama (*Sri Lanka*) (36). **Test No. 2042/146 (E921/WI482)**

ENGLAND v WEST INDIES (2nd Test)

At Trent Bridge, Nottingham, on 25, 26, 27, 28 May 2012.
Toss: West Indies. Result: **ENGLAND** won by nine wickets.
Debuts: None.

WEST INDIES

A.B.Barath	c Anderson b Broad	0		lbw b Anderson		7
K.O.A.Powell	c Anderson b Broad	33		b Anderson		1
K.A.Edwards	b Anderson	7	(7)	lbw b Bresnan		0
D.M.Bravo	c Swann b Anderson	3	(3)	lbw b Bresnan		22
S.Chanderpaul	lbw b Swann	46	(4)	c Trott b Broad		11
M.N.Samuels	c Anderson b Bresnan	117	(5)	not out		76
†D.Ramdin	b Bresnan	1	(6)	lbw b Bresnan		6
*D.J.G.Sammy	c Pietersen b Bresnan	106		lbw b Bresnan		25
K.A.J.Roach	c Strauss b Bresnan	7		lbw b Anderson		14
S.Shillingford	st Prior b Swann	5		c Anderson b Swann		0
R.Rampaul	not out	6		c Bresnan b Anderson		0
Extras	(B 8, LB 18, W 1, NB 1)	28		(B 1, LB 2)		3
Total	**(109.2 overs; 463 mins)**	**370**		**(60.1 overs; 279 mins)**		**165**

ENGLAND

*A.J.Strauss	c Ramdin b Sammy	141		c Bravo b Samuels	45
A.N.Cook	c Ramdin b Rampaul	24		not out	43
I.J.L.Trott	lbw b Rampaul	35		not out	17
K.P.Pietersen	lbw b Rampaul	80			
I.R.Bell	lbw b Roach	22			
J.M.Bairstow	c Chanderpaul b Roach	4			
†M.J.Prior	b Sammy	16			
T.T.Bresnan	not out	39			
S.C.J.Broad	c Sammy b Shillingford	25			
G.P.Swann	c Sammy b Samuels	1			
J.M.Anderson	lbw b Samuels	0			
Extras	(B 9, LB 10, W 4, NB 18)	41		(B 5, NB 1)	6
Total	**(123.4 overs; 532 mins)**	**428**		**(1 wkt; 30.4 overs; 112 mins)**	**111**

ENGLAND	O	M	R	W	O	M	R	W
Anderson	30	12	73	2	20.1	6	43	4
Broad	27	4	81	2	17	5	58	1
Bresnan	27	4	104	4	(4) 17	5	37	4
Swann	20.2	4	62	2	(3) 6	1	24	1
Trott	5	0	24	0				

WEST INDIES	O	M	R	W	O	M	R	W
Roach	25	1	90	2	5	2	16	0
Rampaul	32	8	75	3	6	2	12	0
Sammy	34	3	120	2	6	0	32	0
Shillingford	26	4	110	1	(5) 8	1	28	0
Samuels	4.2	2	14	2	(4) 5.4	0	18	1

FALL OF WICKETS				
	WI	E	WI	E
Wkt	1st	1st	2nd	2nd
1st	9	43	5	89
2nd	26	123	14	–
3rd	42	267	31	–
4th	63	300	45	–
5th	125	308	61	–
6th	136	336	61	–
7th	340	363	110	–
8th	341	416	139	–
9th	360	426	148	–
10th	370	428	165	–

Umpires: Alim Dar (*Pakistan*) (74) and Asad Rauf (*Pakistan*) (43).
Referee: R.S.Mahanama (*Sri Lanka*) (37). **Test No. 2043/147 (E922/WI483)**

ENGLAND v WEST INDIES (3rd Test)

At Edgbaston, Birmingham, on 7 (*no play*), 8 (*no play*), 9, 10, 11 (*no play*) June 2012.
Toss: England. Result: **MATCH DRAWN**.
Debuts: West Indies – A.B.Fudadin, S.P.Narine.

WEST INDIES

A.B.Barath	lbw b Onions	41
K.O.A.Powell	c Swann b Bresnan	24
A.B.Fudadin	c Bell b Bresnan	28
D.M.Bravo	c and b Finn	6
M.N.Samuels	lbw b Bresnan	76
N.Deonarine	c Strauss b Onions	7
†D.Ramdin	not out	107
*D.J.G.Sammy	c Strauss b Finn	16
S.P.Narine	b Onions	11
R.Rampaul	c Prior b Finn	2
T.L.Best	c Strauss b Onions	95
Extras	(B 4, LB 8, W 1)	13
Total	**(129.3 overs; 550 mins)**	**426**

ENGLAND

*A.J.Strauss	c Bravo b Best	17
A.N.Cook	lbw b Rampaul	4
I.J.L.Trott	b Sammy	17
K.P.Pietersen	c Sammy b Samuels	78
I.R.Bell	not out	76
J.M.Bairstow	b Best	18
S.T.Finn	not out	0
†M.J.Prior		
T.T.Bresnan		
G.P.Swann		
G.Onions		
Extras	(B 1, LB 7, NB 3)	11
Total	**(5 wkts; 58 overs; 246 mins)**	**221**

ENGLAND	O	M	R	W
Onions	29.3	7	88	4
Bresnan	34	9	111	3
Finn	32	6	109	3
Swann	26	5	85	0
Trott	8	1	21	0

WEST INDIES	O	M	R	W
Best	12	2	37	2
Rampaul	14	1	55	1
Sammy	8	1	22	1
Narine	15	1	70	0
Samuels	9	0	29	1

FALL OF WICKETS

	WI	E
Wkt	*1st*	*1st*
1st	49	13
2nd	90	40
3rd	99	49
4th	128	186
5th	152	215
6th	208	–
7th	241	–
8th	267	–
9th	283	–
10th	426	–

Umpires: H.D.P.K.Dharmasena (*Sri Lanka*) (9) and A.L.Hill (*New Zealand*) (31).
Referee: R.S.Mahanama (*Sri Lanka*) (38).   **Test No. 2044/148 (E923/WI484)**

SRI LANKA v PAKISTAN (1st Test)

At Galle International Stadium, on 22, 23, 24, 25 June 2012.
Toss: Sri Lanka. Result: **SRI LANKA** won by 209 runs.
Debut: Pakistan – Mohammad Ayub. ‡B.M.A.J.Mendis

SRI LANKA

Batsman	1st innings		2nd innings	
N.T.Paranavitana	st Akmal b Ajmal	24	lbw b Ajmal	25
T.M.Dilshan	lbw b Ajmal	101	lbw b Junaid Khan	56
K.C.Sangakkara	not out	199	c Umar b Ajmal	1
*D.P.M.D.Jayawardena	b Ajmal	62	c Akmal b Junaid Khan	14
T.T.Samaraweera	st Akmal b Ajmal	6	c Younus Khan b Junaid Khan	15
A.D.Mathews	c and b Ajmal	0	not out	7
†H.A.P.W.Jayawardena	c Akmal b Hafeez	48	not out	9
H.K.S.R.Kaluhalamulla	c and b Rehman	8		
K.M.D.N.Kulasekara	c Ayub b Hafeez	0		
H.M.R.K.B.Herath	run out	0		
A.N.P.R.Fernando	b Hafeez	0		
Extras	(B 10, LB 7, W 5, NB 2)	24	(B 6, LB 2, NB 2)	10
Total	(153.2 overs; 640 mins)	472	(5 wkts dec; 41 overs; 194 mins)	137

PAKISTAN

Batsman	1st innings		2nd innings	
*Mohammad Hafeez	lbw b Kaluhalamulla	20	c D.P.M.D.Jayawardena b Kulasekara	4
Taufiq Umar	lbw b Kulasekara	9	b Kulasekara	10
Azhar Ali	c H.A.P.W.Jayawardena b Kulasekara	0	c Samaraweera b Herath	7
Younus Khan	lbw b Herath	29	c H.A.P.W.Jayawardena b Kulasekara	87
Saeed Ajmal	c Paranavitana b Kaluhalamulla	0	run out	12
Asad Shafiq	c H.A.P.W.Jayawardena b Herath	0	c D.P.M.D.Jayawardena b Herath	80
Mohammad Ayub	lbw b Herath	25	lbw b Fernando	22
†Adnan Akmal	run out	9	not out	40
Abdur Rehman	lbw b Kaluhalamulla	1	c Sangakkara b Kaluhalamulla	14
Umar Gul	c H.A.P.W.Jayawardena b Kaluhalamulla	2	c Samaraweera b Kaluhalamulla	4
Junaid Khan	not out	2	c sub‡ b Kaluhalamulla	8
Extras	(LB 2, W 1)	3	(B 9, LB 2, W 1)	12
Total	(54.3 overs; 220 mins)	100	(114 overs; 447 mins)	300

PAKISTAN	O	M	R	W		O	M	R	W
Umar Gul	27	8	76	0		4	0	11	0
Junaid Khan	18	5	52	0		13	2	44	3
Mohammad Hafeez	19.2	3	55	3					
Saeed Ajmal	46	9	146	5		17	3	47	2
Abdur Rehman	43	7	126	1	(3)	5	0	25	0
Younus Khan					(5)	2	0	2	0

SRI LANKA	O	M	R	W		O	M	R	W
Kulasekara	13	7	27	2		23	8	48	3
Fernando	9	2	28	0		15	4	56	1
Herath	21	6	30	3		42	9	91	2
Mathews	2	2	0	0		4	1	8	0
Kaluhalamulla	9.3	1	13	4		30	4	86	3

FALL OF WICKETS

	SL	P	SL	P
Wkt	1st	1st	2nd	2nd
1st	63	17	81	8
2nd	187	17	85	21
3rd	315	43	93	25
4th	335	43	114	38
5th	335	44	119	189
6th	415	65	–	212
7th	438	88	–	243
8th	439	94	–	266
9th	455	98	–	280
10th	472	100	–	300

Umpires: S.J.Davis (*Australia*) (37) and I.J.Gould (*England*) (28).
Referee: D.C.Boon (*Australia*) (8).   **Test No. 2045/41 (SL213/P368)**

SRI LANKA v PAKISTAN (2nd Test)

At Sinhalese Sports Club, Colombo, on 30 June, 1, 2, 3, 4 July 2012.
Toss: Sri Lanka. Result: **MATCH DRAWN**.
Debuts: None.

PAKISTAN

Mohammad Hafeez	b Herath	196	c Dilshan b Kaluhalamulla	21
Taufiq Umar	c H.A.P.W.Jayawardena b Mathews	65	not out	42
Azhar Ali	c Kulasekara b Kaluhalamulla	157		
Younus Khan	lbw b Herath	32		
*Misbah-ul-Haq	not out	66		
Asad Shafiq	run out	2		
†Adnan Akmal	c Dilshan b Herath	5	(4) not out	0
Abdur Rehman	not out	18	(3) b Kaluhalamulla	36
Saeed Ajmal				
Aizaz Cheema				
Junaid Khan				
Extras	(LB 5, W 1, NB 4)	10	(NB 1)	1
Total	**(6 wkts dec; 147 overs; 611 mins)**	**551**	**(2 wkts dec; 18 overs; 82 mins)**	**100**

SRI LANKA

N.T.Paranavitana	c Ali b Junaid Khan	0	lbw b Ajmal	32
T.M.Dilshan	lbw b Junaid Khan	121	lbw b Rehman	28
K.C.Sangakkara	c Umar b Rehman	192	not out	24
*D.P.M.D.Jayawardena	lbw b Junaid Khan	0	not out	1
T.T.Samaraweera	lbw b Ajmal	0		
H.K.S.R.Kaluhalamulla	lbw b Rehman	5		
A.D.Mathews	c Akmal b Junaid Khan	47		
†H.A.P.W.Jayawardena	c Akmal b Rehman	6		
K.M.D.N.Kulasekara	b Junaid Khan	0		
H.M.R.K.B.Herath	not out	10		
A.N.P.R.Fernando	c Ajmal b Rehman	1		
Extras	(B 4, LB 5)	9	(LB 1)	1
Total	**(124.4 overs; 552 mins)**	**391**	**(2 wkts; 22 overs; 89 mins)**	**86**

SRI LANKA	O	M	R	W		O	M	R	W
Kulasekara	27	6	84	0		5	0	23	0
Mathews	15	1	55	1					
Fernando	24	3	103	0	(2)	8	0	48	0
Kaluhalamulla	31	0	131	1	(3)	4	0	28	2
Herath	49	5	164	3	(4)	1	0	1	0
Dilshan	1	0	9	0					

PAKISTAN	O	M	R	W		O	M	R	W
Aizaz Cheema	24	5	86	0	(2)	2	0	11	0
Junaid Khan	28	6	73	5	(1)	4	0	21	0
Saeed Ajmal	34	0	106	0	(4)	7	0	34	1
Abdur Rehman	26.4	5	78	4	(3)	9	2	19	1
Mohammad Hafeez	8	0	29	0					
Azhar Ali	4	0	10	0					

FALL OF WICKETS

	P	SL	P	SL
Wkt	1st	1st	2nd	2nd
1st	78	11	51	48
2nd	365	236	99	78
3rd	435	250	–	–
4th	486	259	–	–
5th	491	278	–	–
6th	519	370	–	–
7th	–	378	–	–
8th	–	379	–	–
9th	–	385	–	–
10th	–	391	–	–

Umpires: I.J.Gould (*England*) (29) and S.J.A.Taufel (*Australia*) (72).
Referee: D.C.Boon (*Australia*) (9).

Test No. 2046/42 (SL214/P369)

SRI LANKA v PAKISTAN (3rd Test)

At Pallekele International Cricket Stadium, on 8, 9 (*no play*), 10, 11, 12 July 2012.
Toss: Sri Lanka. Result: **MATCH DRAWN**.
Debuts: None.

PAKISTAN

Mohammad Hafeez	b Perera	22	c Paranavitana b Fernando		52
Taufiq Umar	lbw b Perera	29	lbw b Kulasekara		4
Azhar Ali	c Samaraweera b Perera	0	c H.A.P.W.Jayawardena b Fernando		136
Younus Khan	c H.A.P.W.Jayawardena b Kulasekara	0	c Paranavitana b Herath		19
*Misbah-ul-Haq	c H.A.P.W.Jayawardena b Perera	40	c D.P.M.D.Jayawardena b Herath		5
Asad Shafiq	c H.A.P.W.Jayawardena b Herath	75	not out		100
†Adnan Akmal	b Herath	24	(10) not out		35
Mohammad Sami	c Perera b Mathews	9	(7) lbw b Fernando		3
Umar Gul	b Kulasekara	7	(8) lbw b Herath		0
Saeed Ajmal	lbw b Herath	6	(9) lbw b Herath		5
Junaid Khan	not out	3			
Extras	(LB 11)	11	(B 6, LB 8, W 7)		21
Total	**(72.5 overs; 310 mins)**	**226**	**(8 wkts dec; 128.4 overs; 538 mins)**		**380**

SRI LANKA

N.T.Paranavitana	b Ajmal	75	c Younus Khan b Junaid Khan		22
L.D.Chandimal	lbw b Junaid Khan	8	c Shafiq b Ajmal		65
K.C.Sangakkara	b Junaid Khan	0	not out		74
*D.P.M.D.Jayawardena	lbw b Sami	12	c Hafeez b Ajmal		11
T.T.Samaraweera	lbw b Herath	73	b Ajmal		10
A.D.Mathews	c Shafiq b Junaid Khan	9	not out		1
†H.A.P.W.Jayawardena	lbw b Gul	20			
N.L.T.C.Perera	b Junaid Khan	75			
K.M.D.N.Kulasekara	c Umar b Junaid Khan	33			
H.M.R.K.B.Herath	lbw b Ajmal	2			
C.R.D.Fernando	not out	0			
Extras	(B 16, LB 7, W 6, NB 1)	30	(B 2, LB 10)		12
Total	**(100.2 overs; 448 mins)**	**337**	**(4 wkts; 62 overs; 257 mins)**		**195**

SRI LANKA	O	M	R	W	O	M	R	W		FALL OF WICKETS				
Kulasekara	16	4	44	2	28	9	65	1			P	SL	P	SL
Perera	18	5	63	4	25	2	88	0		*Wkt*	*1st*	*1st*	*2nd*	*2nd*
Mathews	8	3	20	1	(5) 12	0	38	0		1st	35	14	16	44
Herath	18.5	6	40	3	(4) 39.4	4	99	4		2nd	41	14	110	132
Fernando	12	1	48	0	(4) 23	1	74	3		3rd	50	44	158	150
Samaraweera					1	0	2	0		4th	56	187	176	178
										5th	141	200	276	–
										6th	175	204	280	–
PAKISTAN										7th	198	236	281	–
Umar Gul	22	3	90	1	9	2	43	0		8th	217	320	299	–
Junaid Khan	28.2	3	70	5	10	0	45	1		9th	217	337		–
Mohammad Sami	17	1	69	1	(5) 8	0	23	0		10th	226	337		–
Saeed Ajmal	25	5	66	3	26	8	50	3						
Younus Khan	3	0	9	0										
Mohammad Hafeez	5	0	10	0	(3) 9	1	22	0						

Umpires: S.J.Davis (*Australia*) (38) and S.J.A.Taufel (*Australia*) (73).
Referee: D.C.Boon (*Australia*) (10).   Test No. 2047/43 (SL215/P370)
Adnan Akmal (10*) retired hurt at 162-5 and returned when the score was 175-6.

ENGLAND v SOUTH AFRICA (1st Test)

At The Oval, London, on 19, 20, 21, 22, 23 July 2012.
Toss: England. Result: **SOUTH AFRICA** won by an innings and 12 runs.
Debuts: None.

ENGLAND

*A.J.Strauss	lbw b Morkel	0	c Philander b Tahir		27
A.N.Cook	b Steyn	115	c de Villiers b Philander		0
I.J.L.Trott	c de Villiers b Morkel	71	c de Villiers b Steyn		10
K.P.Pietersen	c de Villiers b Kallis	42	b Morkel		16
I.R.Bell	b Kallis	13	c Kallis b Steyn		55
R.S.Bopara	c de Villiers b Steyn	0	b Steyn		22
†M.J.Prior	c de Villiers b Morkel	60	c Kallis b Tahir		40
T.T.Bresnan	b Tahir	8	not out		20
S.C.J.Broad	b Philander	16	c de Villiers b Steyn		0
G.P.Swann	not out	15	c Petersen b Steyn		7
J.M.Anderson	c de Villiers b Morkel	2	lbw b Tahir		4
Extras	(B 2, LB 24, W 3, NB 14)	43	(B 11, LB 15, W 1, NB 12)		39
Total	**(125.5 overs; 558 mins)**	**385**	**(97 overs; 429 mins)**		**240**

SOUTH AFRICA

*G.C.Smith	b Bresnan	131
A.N.Petersen	lbw b Anderson	0
H.M.Amla	not out	311
J.H.Kallis	not out	182
†A.B.de Villiers		
J.A.Rudolph		
J.P.Duminy		
V.D.Philander		
D.W.Steyn		
M.Morkel		
Imran Tahir		
Extras	(B 5, LB 4, W 2, NB 2)	13
Total	**(2 wkts dec; 189 overs; 803 mins)**	**637**

SOUTH AFRICA	O	M	R	W		O	M	R	W
Morkel	24.5	2	72	4		16	0	41	1
Philander	27	4	79	1		19	6	29	1
Steyn	30	7	99	2		21	6	56	5
Kallis	19	7	38	2	(5)	7	1	22	0
Imran Tahir	19	0	61	1	(4)	32	7	63	3
Duminy	6	1	10	0		2	1	3	0

ENGLAND	O	M	R	W
Anderson	41	7	116	1
Broad	34	6	118	0
Swann	52	10	151	0
Bresnan	37	2	140	1
Bopara	18	1	78	0
Pietersen	3	0	13	0
Trott	4	0	12	0

FALL OF WICKETS

	E	SA	E
Wkt	1st	1st	2nd
1st	0	1	2
2nd	170	260	32
3rd	251	–	57
4th	271	–	67
5th	272	–	117
6th	284	–	203
7th	313	–	210
8th	358	–	210
9th	383	–	218
10th	385	–	240

Umpires: Asad Rauf (*Pakistan*) (44) and S.J.Davis (*Australia*) (39).
Referee: J.J.Crowe (*New Zealand*) (53).   **Test No. 2048/139 (E924/SA367)**

ENGLAND v SOUTH AFRICA (2nd Test)

At Headingley, Leeds, on 2, 3, 4, 5, 6 August 2012.
Toss: England. Result: **MATCH DRAWN**.
Debut: England – J.W.A.Taylor.

SOUTH AFRICA

A.N.Petersen	c Prior b Broad	182	(8) not out		16
*G.C.Smith	c Bell b Bresnan	52		c Taylor b Pietersen	52
H.M.Amla	run out	9		c Cook b Pietersen	28
J.H.Kallis	c Cook b Anderson	19	(5)	c Prior b Broad	27
†A.B.de Villiers	b Broad	47	(4)	lbw b Broad	44
D.W.Steyn	b Finn	0	(9)	c and b Anderson	3
J.A.Rudolph	st Prior b Pietersen	19	(1)	lbw b Pietersen	69
J.P.Duminy	not out	48	(6)	lbw b Broad	0
V.D.Philander	c Bresnan b Finn	13	(7)	lbw b Broad	6
M.Morkel	c Cook b Broad	19		c Cook b Broad	10
Imran Tahir	c Cook b Anderson	0			
Extras	(B 5, LB 6)	11		(LB 2, W 1)	3
Total	**(139.2 overs; 619 mins)**	**419**		**(9 wkts dec; 67.4 overs; 305 mins)**	**258**

ENGLAND

*A.J.Strauss	c de Villiers b Steyn	37	(3)	c and b Duminy	22
A.N.Cook	lbw b Philander	24		b Rudolph b Steyn	46
I.J.L.Trott	c Smith b Steyn	35	(4)	not out	30
K.P.Pietersen	lbw b Morkel	149	(1)	c Tahir b Philander	12
I.R.Bell	c Smith b Kallis	11	(6)	not out	3
J.W.A.Taylor	b Morkel	34			
†M.J.Prior	c Steyn b Tahir	68	(5)	run out	7
T.T.Bresnan	c Smith b Philander	9			
S.C.J.Broad	c sub (F.du Plessis) b Tahir	1			
J.M.Anderson	b Tahir	8			
S.T.Finn	not out	0			
Extras	(B 7, LB 17, W 14, NB 11)	49		(LB 8, W 1, NB 1)	10
Total	**(126.4 overs; 570 mins)**	**425**		**(4 wkts; 33 overs; 154 mins)**	**130**

ENGLAND	O	M	R	W		O	M	R	W
Anderson	33.2	10	61	2		19	7	40	1
Broad	35	10	96	3		16.4	2	69	5
Finn	32	3	118	2		14	2	55	0
Bresnan	27	4	98	1		9	2	40	0
Trott	5	1	9	0					
Pietersen	7	0	26	1	(5)	9	1	52	3

SOUTH AFRICA	O	M	R	W		O	M	R	W
Morkel	32	9	96	2		10	4	33	0
Philander	30	10	72	2		6	1	26	1
Steyn	28	8	102	2		7	1	26	1
Kallis	12	3	34	1	(6)	4	2	7	0
Imran Tahir	23.4	0	92	3	(4)	4	0	20	0
Duminy	1	0	5	0	(5)	2	0	10	1

		FALL OF WICKETS			
		SA	E	SA	E
	Wkt	*1st*	*1st*	*2nd*	*2nd*
	1st	120	65	120	21
	2nd	132	85	129	75
	3rd	157	142	182	90
	4th	254	173	209	106
	5th	259	320	209	–
	6th	318	351	223	–
	7th	353	396	230	–
	8th	375	407	247	–
	9th	414	420	258	–
	10th	419	425	–	–

Umpires: S.J.Davis (*Australia*) (40) and R.J.Tucker (*Australia*) (20).
Referee: J.J.Crowe (*New Zealand*) (54). **Test No. 2049/140 (E925/SA368)**

ENGLAND v SOUTH AFRICA (3rd Test)

At Lord's, London, on 16, 17, 18, 19, 20 August 2012.
Toss: South Africa. Result: **SOUTH AFRICA** won by 51 runs.
Debuts: None.

SOUTH AFRICA

*G.C.Smith	c Prior b Anderson	14	(2) lbw b Swann		23
A.N.Petersen	c Prior b Finn	22	(1) lbw b Broad		24
H.M.Amla	b Finn	13	b Finn		121
J.H.Kallis	c Prior b Finn	3	lbw b Finn		31
†A.B.de Villiers	c Cook b Anderson	27	(6) c Strauss b Finn		43
J.A.Rudolph	b Swann	42	(7) c Prior b Finn		11
J.P.Duminy	c Prior b Anderson	61	(8) not out		26
V.D.Philander	st Prior b Swann	61	(4) c Bairstow b Anderson		35
D.W.Steyn	c Swann b Broad	26	(5) c Taylor b Broad		9
M.Morkel	c Prior b Finn	25	st Prior b Swann		9
Imran Tahir	not out	2	b Anderson		1
Extras	(B 7, LB 5, NB 1)	13	(B 6, LB 8, W 2, NB 2)		18
Total	**(101.2 overs; 437 mins)**	**309**	**(124.2 overs; 538 mins)**		**351**

ENGLAND

*A.J.Strauss	b Morkel	20	lbw b Philander		1
A.N.Cook	c Kallis b Steyn	7	lbw b Philander		3
I.J.L.Trott	lbw b Steyn	8	c Kallis b Steyn		63
I.R.Bell	c Petersen b Philander	58	c Smith b Philander		4
J.W.A.Taylor	c Smith b Morkel	10	run out		4
J.M.Bairstow	b Morkel	95	b Tahir		54
†M.J.Prior	c Kallis b Philander	27	c Smith b Philander		73
S.C.J.Broad	c Amla b Steyn	16	c Amla b Kallis		37
G.P.Swann	not out	37	run out		41
J.M.Anderson	c Rudolph b Steyn	12	not out		4
S.T.Finn	c Duminy b Morkel	10	c Kallis b Philander		0
Extras	(LB 10, W 1, NB 4)	15	(B 7, W 2, NB 1)		10
Total	**(107.3 overs; 468 mins)**	**315**	**(82.5 overs; 363 mins)**		**294**

ENGLAND	O	M	R	W		O	M	R	W
Anderson	29	5	76	3		25.2	4	73	2
Broad	24	4	69	1		21	2	85	2
Finn	18	2	75	4	(4)	27	5	74	4
Swann	24.2	6	63	2	(3)	47	14	94	2
Trott	6	1	14	0		4	0	11	0

SOUTH AFRICA	O	M	R	W	O	M	R	W
Morkel	28.3	6	80	4	17	3	58	0
Philander	24	9	48	2	14.5	4	30	5
Steyn	29	4	94	4	16	4	61	1
Kallis	12	3	29	0	11	2	50	1
Imran Tahir	14	3	54	0	24	3	88	1

	FALL OF WICKETS			
	SA	E	SA	E
Wkt	*1st*	*1st*	*2nd*	*2nd*
1st	22	29	46	5
2nd	49	38	50	6
3rd	50	39	131	34
4th	54	54	164	45
5th	105	178	259	134
6th	163	221	268	146
7th	235	252	282	208
8th	270	264	336	282
9th	307	283	348	294
10th	309	315	351	294

Umpires: H.D.P.K.Dharmasena (*Sri Lanka*) (10) and S.J.A.Taufel (*Australia*) (74).
Referee: J.J.Crowe (*New Zealand*) (55).   **Test No. 2050/141 (E926/SA369)**

WEST INDIES v NEW ZEALAND (1st Test)

At Sir Vivian Richards Stadium, North Sound, Antigua, on 25, 26, 27, 28, 29 July 2012.
Toss: New Zealand. Result: **WEST INDIES** won by nine wickets.
Debut: New Zealand – N.Wagner.

NEW ZEALAND

D.R.Flynn	c Powell b Narine	45	(2) lbw b Narine		20
M.J.Guptill	c Deonarine b Narine	97	(1) c Fudadin b Narine		67
B.B.McCullum	c Deonarine b Roach	25	b Roach		84
*L.R.P.L.Taylor	b Narine	45	lbw b Roach		21
N.Wagner	c Sammy b Narine	4	c Ramdin b Roach		13
K.S.Williamson	b Roach	19	b Roach		0
D.G.Brownlie	c Ramdin b Rampaul	23	c Gayle b Rampaul		5
†C.F.K.van Wyk	c Fudadin b Narine	11	b Roach		30
D.L.Vettori	c Deonarine b Sammy	17	c Ramdin b Rampaul		13
D.A.J.Bracewell	c Chanderpaul b Rampaul	39	lbw b Narine		0
C.S.Martin	not out	4	not out		0
Extras	(B 14, LB 1, W 1, NB 6)	22	(B 7, LB 8, NB 4)		19
Total	**(129.1 overs; 529 mins)**	**351**	**(105.2 overs; 425 mins)**		**272**

WEST INDIES

C.H.Gayle	c McCullum b Williamson	150	not out	64
K.O.A.Powell	c van Wyk b Wagner	134	c Brownlie b Bracewell	30
A.B.Fudadin	c McCullum b Williamson	55	not out	7
M.N.Samuels	b Martin	28		
S.Chanderpaul	c van Wyk b Martin	0		
N.Deonarine	b Martin	79		
†D.Ramdin	b Bracewell	3		
*D.J.G.Sammy	c and b Vettori	50		
S.P.Narine	run out	4		
K.A.J.Roach	not out	6		
R.Rampaul	lbw b Bracewell	1		
Extras	(LB 9, NB 3)	12	(W 1)	1
Total	**(163.3 overs; 679 mins)**	**522**	**(1 wkt; 19.3 overs; 86 mins)**	**102**

WEST INDIES	O	M	R	W	O	M	R	W		FALL OF WICKETS			
										NZ	WI	NZ	WI
Rampaul	23.1	9	44	2	17	3	52	2	*Wkt*	*1st*	*1st*	*2nd*	*2nd*
Roach	23	8	55	2	23.2	4	60	5	1st	97	254	47	77
Sammy	26	7	76	1	(4) 16	6	25	0	2nd	133	304	170	–
Narine	43	9	132	5	(3) 42	13	91	3	3rd	223	355	194	–
Samuels	6	2	14	0	3	1	22	0	4th	228	355	217	–
Fudadin	5	1	11	0					5th	233	410	217	–
Deonarine	3	1	4	0	(6) 4	2	7	0	6th	273	428	225	–
									7th	281	497	225	–
NEW ZEALAND									8th	308	502	251	–
Martin	30	9	134	3	(2) 4	0	12	0	9th	309	516	258	–
Bracewell	29.3	5	96	2	(1) 6	0	25	1	10th	351	522	272	–
Wagner	33	8	112	1	(4) 5	0	32	0					
Vettori	51	14	124	1	(5) 1.3	0	3	0					
Williamson	20	2	47	2	(3) 3	1	30	0					

Umpires: R.A.Kettleborough (*England*) (10) and P.R.Reiffel (*Australia*) (1).
Referee: R.S.Madugalle (*Sri Lanka*) (135).   **Test No. 2051/38 (WI485/NZ372)**

WEST INDIES v NEW ZEALAND (2nd Test)

At Sabina Park, Kingston, Jamaica, on 2, 3, 4, 5 August 2012.
Toss: West Indies. Result: **WEST INDIES** won by five wickets.
Debuts: None.

NEW ZEALAND

B.J.Watling	c Gayle b Roach	2	(2)	lbw b Deonarine	11
M.J.Guptill	run out	71	(1)	lbw b Deonarine	42
B.B.McCullum	c Ramdin b Best	0	(4)	c Fudadin b Deonarine	19
*L.R.P.L.Taylor	c Ramdin b Best	60	(5)	c Ramdin b Best	0
K.S.Williamson	c Sammy b Deonarine	22	(6)	c Sammy b Deonarine	8
D.G.Brownlie	c Ramdin b Roach	0	(7)	c Deonarine b Narine	35
†C.F.K.van Wyk	b Deonarine	16	(8)	c Chanderpaul b Narine	5
D.A.J.Bracewell	b Narine	14	(9)	c Fudadin b Narine	14
N.Wagner	c Best b Roach	23	(3)	c Ramdin b Best	6
T.G.Southee	c Sammy b Roach	18		c Narine b Roach	7
T.A.Boult	not out	14		not out	0
Extras	(B 6, LB 2, W 1, NB 11)	20		(LB 1, W 1, NB 5)	7
Total	**(82.5 overs; 350 mins)**	**260**		**(65.2 overs; 261 mins)**	**154**

WEST INDIES

C.H.Gayle	c Watling b Wagner	8		lbw b Boult	8
K.O.A.Powell	c Brownlie b Boult	10		lbw b Southee	6
A.B.Fudadin	lbw b Boult	5		b Wagner	27
M.N.Samuels	c Wagner b Bracewell	123		c Taylor b Bracewell	52
S.Chanderpaul	c Taylor b Southee	9		not out	43
N.Deonarine	c van Wyk b Boult	0	(7)	not out	15
†D.Ramdin	c Williamson b Wagner	15			
*D.J.G.Sammy	lbw b Southee	32			
S.P.Narine	c Guptill b Bracewell	1			
K.A.J.Roach	c Guptill b Bracewell	0	(6)	c Southee b Williamson	41
T.L.Best	not out	0			
Extras	(LB 4, W 2)	6		(B 4, LB 2, W 8)	14
Total	**(64.3 overs; 308 mins)**	**209**		**(5 wkts; 63.2 overs; 280 mins)**	**206**

WEST INDIES	O	M	R	W		O	M	R	W
Roach	17.5	2	70	4		12.2	3	34	1
Best	16	1	40	2		13	2	44	2
Sammy	10	1	31	0		6	2	19	0
Narine	26	7	66	1		12	1	19	3
Samuels	1	0	2	0					
Deonarine	12	3	43	2	(5)	22	7	37	4

NEW ZEALAND	O	M	R	W		O	M	R	W
Boult	17	2	58	3		12	1	46	1
Bracewell	15.3	3	46	3		13	0	38	1
Southee	19	5	70	2		14	4	30	1
Wagner	10	3	24	2		12	3	41	1
Williamson	3	0	7	0		7.2	1	18	1
Guptill						4	0	21	0
Brownlie						1	0	6	0

FALL OF WICKETS

	NZ	WI	NZ	WI
Wkt	1st	1st	2nd	2nd
1st	10	11	55	20
2nd	11	17	56	20
3rd	114	53	80	94
4th	161	82	80	113
5th	162	83	85	183
6th	170	113	98	–
7th	202	162	105	–
8th	202	177	142	–
9th	225	183	151	–
10th	260	209	154	–

Umpires: M.Erasmus (*South Africa*) (13) and P.R.Reiffel (*Australia*) (2).
Referee: R.S.Madugalle (*Sri Lanka*) (136). **Test No. 2052/39 (WI486/NZ373)**

INDIA v NEW ZEALAND (1st Test)

At Rajiv Gandhi International Stadium, Hyderabad, on 23, 24, 25, 26 August 2012.
Toss: India. Result: **INDIA** won by an innings and 115 runs.
Debuts: None.

INDIA

G.Gambhir	c van Wyk b Boult	22
V.Sehwag	c Guptill b Bracewell	47
C.A.Pujara	c Franklin b Patel	159
S.R.Tendulkar	b Boult	19
V.Kohli	c Guptill b Martin	58
S.K.Raina	c van Wyk b Patel	3
†*M.S.Dhoni	c Bracewell b Patel	73
R.Ashwin	st van Wyk b Patel	37
Z.Khan	c van Wyk b Boult	0
P.P.Ojha	not out	4
U.T.Yadav	run out	4
Extras	(B 6, LB 4, W 2)	12
Total	**(134.3 overs; 599 mins)**	**438**

NEW ZEALAND

B.B.McCullum	c Kohli b Ojha	22	(2)	lbw b Yadav	42
M.J.Guptill	c Kohli b Ashwin	2	(1)	lbw b Ojha	16
K.S.Williamson	c Sehwag b Ojha	32		c Sehwag b Ojha	52
*L.R.P.L.Taylor	c Kohli b Ashwin	2		b Ashwin	7
D.R.Flynn	lbw b Ashwin	16		lbw b Ashwin	11
J.E.C.Franklin	not out	43		c Sehwag b Ashwin	5
†C.F.K.van Wyk	lbw b Ojha	0		lbw b Ashwin	13
D.A.J.Bracewell	st Dhoni b Ojha	17		c Kohli b Ojha	1
J.S.Patel	c and b Ashwin	10		not out	6
T.A.Boult	c Gambhir b Ashwin	4		c Sehwag b Ashwin	0
C.S.Martin	b Ashwin	0		lbw b Ashwin	0
Extras	(B 4, LB 7)	11		(B 1, LB 10)	11
Total	**(61.3 overs; 244 mins)**	**159**		**(79.5 overs; 309 mins)**	**164**

NEW ZEALAND	O	M	R	W		O	M	R	W
Martin	27	4	76	1					
Boult	27	4	93	3					
Bracewell	19.1	1	88	1					
Franklin	13.2	0	40	0					
Patel	41	9	100	4					
Williamson	7	0	31	0					
INDIA									
Khan	11	4	33	0	(2)	13	5	17	0
Yadav	8	0	24	1	(3)	10	1	32	1
Ojha	21	6	44	3	(1)	28	9	48	3
Ashwin	16.3	5	31	6		26.5	9	54	6
Sehwag	2	0	4	0					
Raina	2	0	6	0	(5)	2	1	2	0
Tendulkar	1	0	6	0					

FALL OF WICKETS

	I	NZ	NZ
Wkt	1st	1st	2nd
1st	49	25	26
2nd	77	29	98
3rd	125	35	105
4th	250	55	138
5th	260	99	142
6th	387	111	145
7th	411	141	148
8th	414	153	160
9th	430	159	164
10th	438	159	164

Umpires: S.J.Davis (*Australia*) (41) and I.J.Gould (*England*) (30).
Referee: B.C.Broad (*England*) (52). **Test No. 2053/51 (I463/NZ374)**

INDIA v NEW ZEALAND (2nd Test)

At M.Chinnaswamy Stadium, Bangalore, on 31 August, 1, 2, 3 September 2012.
Toss: New Zealand. Result: **INDIA** won by five wickets.
Debuts: None.

NEW ZEALAND

M.J.Guptill	c Gambhir b Ojha	53	(2) b Yadav		7
B.B.McCullum	lbw b Khan	0	(1) c Dhoni b Yadav		23
K.S.Williamson	lbw b Ojha	17	c Sehwag b Ashwin		13
*L.R.P.L.Taylor	lbw b Ojha	113	lbw b Ojha		35
D.R.Flynn	lbw b Ashwin	33	c Sehwag b Ashwin		31
J.E.C.Franklin	c Raina b Ojha	8	st Dhoni b Ashwin		41
†C.F.K.van Wyk	c Raina b Khan	71	lbw b Ashwin		31
D.A.J.Bracewell	run out	43	lbw b Ojha		22
T.G.Southee	lbw b Ojha	14	b Ashwin		2
J.S.Patel	c Gambhir b Yadav	0	c Dhoni b Khan		22
T.A.Boult	not out	2	not out		4
Extras	(B 2, LB 9)	11	(B 4, LB 12, W 1)		17
Total	**(90.1 overs; 371 mins)**	**365**	**(73.2 overs; 305 mins)**		**248**

INDIA

G.Gambhir	b Southee	2	c Taylor b Boult	34
V.Sehwag	c Flynn b Bracewell	43	b Patel	38
C.A.Pujara	c Boult b Southee	9	c Flynn b Patel	48
S.R.Tendulkar	b Bracewell	17	b Southee	27
V.Kohli	lbw b Southee	103	not out	51
S.K.Raina	c van Wyk b Southee	55	b Patel	0
†*M.S.Dhoni	lbw b Southee	62	not out	48
R.Ashwin	not out	32		
Z.Khan	c van Wyk b Southee	7		
P.P.Ojha	c van Wyk b Southee	0		
U.T.Yadav	b Boult	4		
Extras	(B 11, LB 2, W 1, NB 5)	19	(B 4, LB 6, W 5, NB 1)	16
Total	**(96.5 overs; 457 mins)**	**353**	**(5 wkts; 63.2 overs; 291 mins)**	**262**

INDIA	O	M	R	W		O	M	R	W
Ojha	28.1	10	99	5	(3)	21	6	49	2
Khan	22	2	83	2	(1)	14.2	2	46	1
Yadav	16	1	90	1	(2)	15	0	68	2
Ashwin	24	5	82	1		22	1	69	5
Raina						1	1	0	0
NEW ZEALAND									
Boult	23.5	2	90	1		16	4	64	1
Southee	24	6	64	7		18	3	68	1
Bracewell	20	4	91	2		14	3	52	0
Franklin	10	4	17	0					
Patel	19	5	78	0	(4)	15.2	3	68	3

FALL OF WICKETS

	NZ	I	NZ	I
Wkt	1st	1st	2nd	2nd
1st	0	5	30	77
2nd	63	27	31	83
3rd	89	67	69	152
4th	196	80	111	158
5th	215	179	140	166
6th	246	301	195	–
7th	345	312	216	–
8th	353	320	222	–
9th	353	320	222	–
10th	365	353	248	–

Umpires: S.J.Davis (*Australia*) (42) and I.J.Gould (*England*) (31).
Referee: B.C.Broad (*England*) (53).   Test No. 2054/52 (I464/NZ375)

AUSTRALIA v SOUTH AFRICA (1st Test)

At Woolloongabba, Brisbane, on 9, 10 (*no play*), 11, 12, 13 November 2012.
Toss: South Africa. Result: **MATCH DRAWN**.
Debuts: Australia – R.J.Quiney; South Africa – R.K.Kleinveldt.

SOUTH AFRICA

*G.C.Smith	lbw b Pattinson	10	(2)	c Quiney b Pattinson	23
A.N.Petersen	c Hussey b Lyon	64	(1)	c Wade b Pattinson	5
H.M.Amla	lbw b Siddle	104		c Hussey b Siddle	38
J.H.Kallis	c Quiney b Pattinson	147		c Clarke b Lyon	49
†A.B.de Villiers	c Warner b Pattinson	40		not out	29
J.A.Rudolph	c Quiney b Lyon	31		lbw b Lyon	11
V.D.Philander	c Clarke b Siddle	11		not out	1
D.W.Steyn	c Wade b Hilfenhaus	15			
R.K.Kleinveldt	not out	17			
M.Morkel	c Siddle b Hilfenhaus	0			
J.P.Duminy	absent hurt	–			
Extras	(B 1, LB 1, W 3, NB 6)	11		(B 2, W 4, NB 4)	10
Total	**(151.4 overs; 636 mins)**	**450**		**(5 wkts; 68 overs; 294 mins)**	**166**

AUSTRALIA

E.J.M.Cowan	run out	136
D.A.Warner	c Kallis b Steyn	4
R.J.Quiney	c Steyn b Morkel	9
R.T.Ponting	c Kallis b Morkel	0
*M.J.Clarke	not out	259
M.E.K.Hussey	c sub (F.du Plessis) b Morkel	100
†M.S.Wade	not out	19
N.M.Lyon		
P.M.Siddle		
J.L.Pattinson		
B.W.Hilfenhaus		
Extras	(LB 14, W 1, NB 23)	38
Total	**(5 wkts dec; 138 overs; 627 mins)**	**565**

AUSTRALIA	O	M	R	W	O	M	R	W				
Hilfenhaus	32.4	9	73	2	15	3	26	0				
Pattinson	34	6	93	3	19	3	58	2				
Siddle	36	6	111	2	17	4	36	1				
Lyon	37	4	136	2	13	5	41	2				
Hussey	4	0	21	0								
Quiney	7	3	10	0	(5)	4	3	3	0			
Clarke	1	0	4	0								

SOUTH AFRICA	O	M	R	W
Steyn	30	3	129	1
Philander	30	3	103	0
Morkel	31	6	127	3
Kleinveldt	21	1	97	0
Kallis	12	3	30	0
Smith	9	0	36	0
Amla	2	0	9	0
Petersen	3	0	20	0

FALL OF WICKETS

	SA	A	SA
Wkt	1st	1st	2nd
1st	29	13	6
2nd	119	30	55
3rd	284	40	102
4th	374	299	129
5th	377	527	165
6th	403	–	–
7th	426	–	–
8th	446	–	–
9th	450	–	–
10th	–	–	–

Umpires: Asad Rauf (*Pakistan*) (45) and B.F.Bowden (*New Zealand*) (71).
Referee: R.S.Madugalle (*Sri Lanka*) (137). **Test No. 2055/86 (A744/SA370)**

AUSTRALIA v SOUTH AFRICA (2nd Test)

At Adelaide Oval, on 22, 23, 24, 25, 26 November 2012.
Toss: Australia. Result: **MATCH DRAWN**.
Debut: South Africa – F.du Plessis.

AUSTRALIA

D.A.Warner	c Smith b Morkel	119	(2)	c du Plessis b Kleinveldt	41
E.J.M.Cowan	c and b Kallis	10	(1)	b Kleinveldt	29
R.J.Quiney	c Smith b Morkel	0		c de Villiers b Kleinveldt	0
R.T.Ponting	b Kallis	4		b Steyn	16
*M.J.Clarke	b Morkel	230		lbw b Steyn	38
M.E.K.Hussey	b Steyn	103	(7)	c Steyn b Morkel	54
†M.S.Wade	c de Villiers b Morkel	6	(8)	c de Villiers b Morkel	18
P.M.Siddle	c Smith b Kleinveldt	6	(6)	c de Villiers b Morkel	1
J.L.Pattinson	c Smith b Steyn	42		not out	29
B.W.Hilfenhaus	c Kleinveldt b Morkel	0		not out	18
N.M.Lyon	not out	7			
Extras	(LB 11, W 1, NB 11)	23		(B 4, LB 10, NB 9)	23
Total	**(107.2 overs; 481 mins)**	**550**		**(8 wkts dec; 70 overs; 325 mins)**	**267**

SOUTH AFRICA

*G.C.Smith	c Wade b Siddle	122	(2)	c Ponting b Hilfenhaus	0
A.N.Petersen	run out	54	(1)	b Siddle	24
H.M.Amla	st Wade b Warner	11		c Clarke b Lyon	17
J.A.Rudolph	c Quiney b Lyon	29		c Cowan b Lyon	3
†A.B.de Villiers	lbw b Siddle	1		b Siddle	33
F.du Plessis	c Clarke b Hilfenhaus	78		not out	110
D.W.Steyn	c Ponting b Hilfenhaus	1	(8)	c Quiney b Siddle	0
R.K.Kleinveldt	b Hilfenhaus	0	(9)	b Siddle	3
J.H.Kallis	c Wade b Clarke	58	(7)	c Cowan b Lyon	46
M.Morkel	b Lyon	6		not out	8
Imran Tahir	not out	10			
Extras	(B 7, LB 2, W 3, NB 6)	18		(B 1, LB 1, W 1, NB 1)	4
Total	**(124.3 overs; 502 mins)**	**388**		**(8 wkts; 148 overs; 549 mins)**	**248**

SOUTH AFRICA	O	M	R	W		O	M	R	W		FALL OF WICKETS			
Steyn	23.4	4	79	2		17	5	50	2			A	SA	A	SA
Morkel	30	5	146	5		19	4	50	3		Wkt	1st	1st	2nd	2nd
Kallis	3.3	1	19	2							1st	43	138	77	3
Kleinveldt	20.1	4	81	1		19	2	65	3		2nd	44	169	77	36
Imran Tahir	23	0	180	0	(3)	14	1	80	0		3rd	55	233	91	45
Du Plessis	7	0	34	0	(5)	1	0	8	0		4th	210	233	98	45
											5th	482	240	103	134
AUSTRALIA											6th	494	246	173	233
Hilfenhaus	19.3	6	49	3		34	16	65	1		7th	501	250	206	234
Pattinson	9.1	0	41	0							8th	503	343	220	240
Lyon	44	7	91	2	(4)	50	31	49	3		9th	504	352	–	–
Siddle	30.5	6	130	2	(2)	33	15	65	4		10th	550	388	–	–
Clarke	7	1	22	1	(3)	18	5	34	0						
Hussey	1	0	7	0											
Warner	5	0	27	1	(5)	6	0	29	0						
Quiney	8	3	12	0	(6)	6	3	4	0						
Ponting					(7)	1	1	0	0						

Umpires: B.F.Bowden (*New Zealand*) (72) and R.A.Kettleborough (*England*) (11).
Referee: R.S.Madugalle (*Sri Lanka*) (138).   Test No. 2056/87 (A745/SA371)

AUSTRALIA v SOUTH AFRICA (3rd Test)

At W.A.C.A. Ground, Perth, on 30 November, 1, 2, 3 December 2012.
Toss: South Africa. Result: **SOUTH AFRICA** won by 309 runs.
Debuts: Australia – J.W.Hastings; South Africa – D.Elgar.

SOUTH AFRICA

*G.C.Smith	c Clarke b Watson	16	(2) c Lyon b Starc		84
A.N.Petersen	b Starc	30	(1) c and b Johnson		23
H.M.Amla	run out	11	c and b Johnson		196
J.H.Kallis	b Starc	2	c Johnson b Starc		37
†A.B.de Villiers	c Clarke b Hastings	4	c Wade b Starc		169
D.Elgar	c Wade b Johnson	0	lbw b Johnson		0
F.du Plessis	not out	78	c Clarke b Johnson		27
R.J.Peterson	c Wade b Lyon	31	c Johnson b Starc		0
V.D.Philander	c Hussey b Lyon	30	not out		14
D.W.Steyn	b Johnson	2	c Wade b Starc		8
M.Morkel	c Hastings b Lyon	17	b Starc		0
Extras	(LB 2, W 2)	4	(B 4, LB 4, W 3)		11
Total	**(74 overs; 330 mins)**	**225**	**(111.5 overs; 495 mins)**		**569**

AUSTRALIA

D.A.Warner	c de Villiers b Steyn	13	(2) c Smith b Philander		29
E.J.M.Cowan	c Kallis b Steyn	0	(1) c Elgar b Steyn		53
S.R.Watson	lbw b Philander	10	c Smith b Morkel		25
N.M.Lyon	c du Plessis b Steyn	7	(11) c Smith b Steyn		31
R.T.Ponting	lbw b Philander	4	c Kallis b Peterson		8
*M.J.Clarke	c de Villiers b Steyn	5	(5) st de Villiers b Peterson		44
M.E.K.Hussey	c Smith b Morkel	12	(6) c de Villiers b Steyn		26
†M.S.Wade	b Peterson	68	c Smith b Peterson		10
J.W.Hastings	c Petersen b Peterson	32	(8) c Smith b Morkel		20
M.G.Johnson	b Peterson	7	(9) c de Villiers b Philander		3
M.A.Starc	not out	0	(10) not out		68
Extras	(LB 5)	5	(LB 3, W 2)		5
Total	**(53.1 overs; 254 mins)**	**163**	**(82.5 overs; 377 mins)**		**322**

AUSTRALIA	O	M	R	W		O	M	R	W
Starc	16	3	55	2		28.5	3	154	6
Hastings	20	2	51	1	(4)	19	1	102	0
Watson	9	2	22	1	(2)	9	3	24	0
Johnson	17	3	54	2	(3)	25	1	110	4
Lyon	12	1	41	3		22	2	128	0
Hussey						4	0	26	0
Warner						3	0	14	0
Ponting						1	0	3	0

SOUTH AFRICA	O	M	R	W		O	M	R	W
Steyn	16	4	40	4		22.5	6	72	3
Philander	16	0	55	2		21	8	41	2
Morkel	13	6	19	1		16	2	57	2
Peterson	8.1	1	44	3		20	2	127	3
Elgar						1	0	4	0
Du Plessis						2	0	18	0

FALL OF WICKETS

	SA	A	SA	A
Wkt	1st	1st	2nd	2nd
1st	38	3	28	40
2nd	61	18	206	81
3rd	63	34	287	102
4th	67	35	436	130
5th	67	43	436	188
6th	75	45	538	198
7th	132	100	539	198
8th	196	140	557	204
9th	206	162	569	235
10th	225	163	569	322

Umpires: Asad Rauf (*Pakistan*) (46) and R.A.Kettleborough (*England*) (12).
Referee: R.S.Madugalle (*Sri Lanka*) (139). **Test No. 2057/88 (A746/SA372)**

BANGLADESH v WEST INDIES (1st Test)

At Shere Bangla National Stadium, Mirpur, on 13, 14, 15, 16, 17 November 2012.
Toss: West Indies. Result: **WEST INDIES** won by 77 runs.
Debuts: Bangladesh – Sohag Gazi; West Indies – V.Permaul.   ‡ N.Deonarine

WEST INDIES

C.H.Gayle	c Mahmudullah b Gazi	24	c Rahim b Rubel	19
K.O.A.Powell	b Gazi	117	c Rahim b Shakib	110
D.M.Bravo	c Rubel b Gazi	14	c Rahim b Rubel	76
M.N.Samuels	c Gazi b Shahadat	16	c Nafees b Gazi	1
S.Chanderpaul	not out	203	(11) lbw b Gazi	1
†D.Ramdin	not out	126	(5) lbw b Shakib	5
*D.J.G.Sammy			(6) lbw b Gazi	16
V.Permaul			(7) b Gazi	10
S.P.Narine			(8) not out	22
T.L.Best			b Gazi	0
R.Rampaul			(9) b Gazi	5
Extras	(B 4, LB 13, W 2, NB 8)	27	(B 1, LB 3, NB 4)	8
Total	**(4 wkts dec; 144 overs; 578 mins)**	**527**	**(74.2 overs)**	**273**

BANGLADESH

Tamim Iqbal	c Narine b Sammy	72	c Ramdin b Rampaul	5
Junaid Siddique	c Bravo b Rampaul	7	c Ramdin b Best	20
Shahriar Nafees	c Ramdin b Rampaul	31	c and b Best	23
Naeem Islam	c Ramdin b Sammy	108	lbw b Permaul	26
Shakib Al Hasan	c sub (A.B.Fudadin) b Rampaul	89	c Ramdin b Best	2
*†Mushfiqur Rahim	c and b Permaul	43	lbw b Best	16
Nasir Hossain	c Gayle b Best	96	b Permaul	21
Mahmudullah	c Powell b Narine	62	b Best	29
Sohag Gazi	b Narine	4	c sub‡ b Permaul	19
Shahadat Hossain	b Narine	13	c Powell b Rampaul	4
Rubel Hossain	not out	0	not out	0
Extras	(B 8, LB 12, W 3, NB 8)	31	(B 1, NB 1)	2
Total	**(148.3 overs; 635 mins)**	**556**	**(54.3 overs)**	**167**

BANGLADESH	O	M	R	W		O	M	R	W	FALL OF WICKETS				
											WI	B	WI	B
Sohag Gazi	47	7	145	3		23.2	2	74	6	Wkt	1st	1st	2nd	2nd
Shahadat Hossain	21	3	85	1	(4) 7	1	34	0	1st	32	25	20	10
Rubel Hossain	18	0	89	0	(2) 19	4	53	2	2nd	74	88	209	44
Mahmudullah	14	0	45	0	(3) 3	0	12	0	3rd	106	119	212	51
Shakib Al Hasan	34	4	104	0	11	2	56	2	4th	231	286	218	55
Naeem Islam	8	1	24	0	8	0	22	0	5th	–	362	225	85
Nasir Hossain	1	0	8	0	3	0	18	0	6th	–	368	244	106
Tamim Iqbal	1	0	10	0					7th	–	489	249	115
										8th	–	493	265	155
WEST INDIES										9th	–	554	265	159
Rampaul	32	2	118	3		11	1	32	2	10th	–	556	273	167
Best	23	3	77	1	(3) 12.3	2	24	5					
Sammy	23	3	83	2	(5) 3	0	13	0					
Narine	32.3	5	148	3	(2) 18	1	56	0					
Permaul	29	7	75	1	(4) 8	0	32	3					
Gayle	3	0	14	0									
Samuels	6	0	21	0	(6) 2	0	9	0					

Umpires: R.K.Illingworth (*England*) (1) and B.N.J.Oxenford (*Australia*) (9).
Referee: D.C.Boon (*Australia*) (11).   **Test No. 2058/9 (B74/WI487)**

BANGLADESH v WEST INDIES (2nd Test)

At Sheikh Abu Naser Stadium, Khulna, on 21, 22, 23, 24, 25 November 2012.
Toss: Bangladesh. Result: **WEST INDIES** won by ten wickets.
Debut: Bangladesh – Abul Hasan.

BANGLADESH

Batsman	Dismissal	R	Dismissal	R
Tamim Iqbal	b Sammy	32	b Best	28
Nazimuddin	c Powell b Edwards	4	lbw b Edwards	0
Shahriar Nafees	c Ramdin b Sammy	26	c Sammy b Best	21
Naeem Islam	b Edwards	16	b Best	2
Shakib Al Hasan	c Ramdin b Edwards	17	c Best b Permaul	97
*†Mushfiqur Rahim	c Ramdin b Edwards	38	b Permaul	10
Nasir Hossain	c Edwards b Permaul	52	b Best	94
Mahmudullah	c and b Sammy	76	c Ramdin b Permaul	2
Sohag Gazi	lbw b Edwards	0	b Best	7
Abul Hasan	c Sammy b Edwards	113	not out	7
Rubel Hossain	not out	5	c Bravo b Best	14
Extras	(B 4, LB 3, NB 1)	8	(LB 3, W 1, NB 1)	5
Total	**(91.1 overs)**	**387**	**(70.1 overs)**	**287**

WEST INDIES

Batsman	Dismissal	R	Dismissal	R
C.H.Gayle	c Rahim b Gazi	25	not out	20
K.O.A.Powell	c Shakib b Rubel	13	not out	9
D.M.Bravo	lbw b Gazi	127		
M.N.Samuels	c sub (Elias Sunny) b Rubel	260		
S.Chanderpaul	not out	150		
†D.Ramdin	c Rahim b Shakib	31		
*D.J.G.Sammy	c Mahmudullah b Shakib	0		
V.Permaul	c Gazi b Shakib	13		
S.P.Narine	c Nafees b Shakib	0		
F.H.Edwards	c Shakib b Gazi	2		
T.L.Best				
Extras	(B 10, LB 7, W 2, NB 8)	27	(W 1)	1
Total	**(9 wkts dec; 200.3 overs)**	**648**	**(0 wkts; 4.4 overs; 18 mins)**	**30**

WEST INDIES	O	M	R	W		O	M	R	W
Edwards	18.1	2	90	6		17	0	95	1
Best	10	3	31	0	(4)	12.1	1	40	6
Sammy	23	4	74	3	(6)	8	3	19	0
Narine	19	0	91	0	(2)	9	0	48	0
Permaul	19	2	79	1	(3)	20	2	67	3
Samuels	2	0	15	0					
Gayle					(5)	4	0	15	0

BANGLADESH	O	M	R	W		O	M	R	W
Sohag Gazi	57.3	4	167	3		1	0	8	0
Abul Hasan	24	0	113	0					
Rubel Hossain	31	8	86	2	(2)	2	0	14	0
Naeem Islam	14	1	43	0	(3)	1.4	1	8	0
Shakib Al Hasan	52	11	151	4					
Mahmudullah	10	0	42	0					
Nasir Hossain	12	1	29	0					

FALL OF WICKETS

	B	WI	B	WI
Wkt	1st	1st	2nd	2nd
1st	5	37	1	–
2nd	64	43	49	–
3rd	77	369	51	–
4th	93	546	62	–
5th	98	621	82	–
6th	185	621	226	–
7th	193	639	228	–
8th	193	639	254	–
9th	377	648	269	–
10th	387	–	287	–

Umpires: R.K.Illingworth (*England*) (2) and B.N.J.Oxenford (*Australia*) (10).
Referee: D.C.Boon (*Australia*) (12).

Test No. 2059/10 (B75/WI488)

INDIA v ENGLAND (1st Test)

At Sardar Patel Stadium, Motera, Ahmedabad, on 15, 16, 17, 18, 19 November 2012.
Toss: India. Result: **INDIA** won by nine wickets.
Debut: England – N.R.D.Compton.

INDIA

G.Gambhir	b Swann	45			
V.Sehwag	b Swann	117	(1) c Pietersen b Swann		25
C.A.Pujara	not out	206	(2) not out		41
S.R.Tendulkar	c Patel b Swann	13			
V.Kohli	b Swann	19	(3) not out		14
Yuvraj Singh	c Swann b Patel	74			
†*M.S.Dhoni	b Swann	5			
R.Ashwin	c Prior b Pietersen	23			
Z.Khan	c Trott b Anderson	7			
P.P.Ojha	not out	0			
U.T.Yadav					
Extras	(B 1, LB 10, NB 1)	12			–
Total	**(8 wkts dec; 160 overs; 640 mins)**	**521**	**(1 wkt; 15.3 overs; 51 mins)**		**80**

ENGLAND

*A.N.Cook	c Sehwag b Ashwin	41	b Ojha		176
N.R.D.Compton	b Ashwin	9	lbw b Khan		37
J.M.Anderson	c Gambhir b Ojha	2	(11) not out		0
I.J.L.Trott	c Pujara b Ashwin	0	(3) c Dhoni b Ojha		17
K.P.Pietersen	b Ojha	17	(4) b Ojha		2
I.R.Bell	c Tendulkar b Ojha	0	(5) lbw b Yadav		22
S.R.Patel	lbw b Yadav	10	(6) lbw b Yadav		0
†M.J.Prior	b Ojha	48	(7) c and b Ojha		91
T.T.Bresnan	c Kohli b Ojha	19	(8) c sub (A.M.Rahane) b Khan		20
S.C.J.Broad	lbw b Khan	25	(9) c and b Yadav		3
G.P.Swann	not out	3	(10) b Ashwin		17
Extras	(B 5, LB 12)	17	(B 14, LB 6, W 1)		21
Total	**(74.2 overs; 287 mins)**	**191**	**(154.3 overs; 614 mins)**		**406**

ENGLAND	O	M	R	W	O	M	R	W	FALL OF WICKETS				
Anderson	27	7	75	1	2	0	10	0		I	E	E	I
Broad	24	1	97	0					Wkt	1st	1st	2nd	2nd
Bresnan	19	2	73	0					1st	134	26	123	57
Swann	51	8	144	5	(2) 7.3	1	46	1	2nd	224	29	156	–
Patel	31	3	96	1	(3) 6	0	24	0	3rd	250	30	160	–
Pietersen	8	1	25	1					4th	283	69	199	–
									5th	413	69	199	–
INDIA									6th	444	80	356	–
Ashwin	27	9	80	3	(3) 43	9	111	1	7th	510	97	365	–
Khan	15	7	23	1	(5) 27.3	5	59	2	8th	519	144	378	–
Ojha	22.2	8	45	5	(2) 55	16	120	4	9th	–	187	406	–
Yuvraj Singh	3	0	12	0	(7) 4	0	17	0	10th	–	191	406	–
Yadav	7	2	14	1	(1) 23	2	70	3					
Sehwag					(4) 1	0	1	0					
Tendulkar					(6) 1	0	8	0					

Umpires: Alim Dar (*Pakistan*) (75) and A.L.Hill (*New Zealand*) (32).
Referee: R.S.Mahanama (*Sri Lanka*) (39).   **Test No. 2060/104 (I465/E927)**

INDIA v ENGLAND (2nd Test)

At Wankhede Stadium, Mumbai, on 23, 24, 25, 26 November 2012.
Toss: India. Result: **ENGLAND** won by ten wickets.
Debuts: None.

INDIA

G.Gambhir	lbw b Anderson	4	lbw b Swann		65
V.Sehwag	b Panesar	30	c Swann b Panesar		9
C.A.Pujara	st Prior b Swann	135	c Bairstow b Swann		6
S.R.Tendulkar	b Panesar	8	lbw b Panesar		8
V.Kohli	c Compton b Panesar	19	c sub (J.E.Root) b Swann		7
Yuvraj Singh	b Swann	0	c Bairstow b Panesar		8
†*M.S.Dhoni	c Swann b Panesar	29	c Trott b Panesar		6
R.Ashwin	lbw b Swann	68	c Patel b Panesar		11
Harbhajan Singh	lbw b Swann	21	c Trott b Swann		6
Z.Khan	c Bairstow b Swann	11	c Prior b Panesar		1
P.P.Ojha	not out	0	not out		6
Extras	(LB 1, NB 1)	2	(B 6, LB 3)		9
Total	**(115.1 overs; 462 mins)**	**327**	**(44.1 overs; 183 mins)**		**142**

ENGLAND

*A.N.Cook	c Dhoni b Ashwin	122	not out	18
N.R.D.Compton	c Sehwag b Ojha	29	not out	30
I.J.L.Trott	lbw b Ojha	0		
K.P.Pietersen	c Dhoni b Ojha	186		
J.M.Bairstow	c Gambhir b Ojha	9		
S.R.Patel	c Kohli b Ojha	26		
†M.J.Prior	run out	21		
S.C.J.Broad	c Pujara b Harbhajan	6		
G.P.Swann	not out	1		
J.M.Anderson	lbw b Harbhajan	2		
M.S.Panesar	c Khan b Ashwin	4		
Extras	(B 4, LB 2, W 1)	7	(B 8, LB 2)	10
Total	**(121.3 overs; 482 mins)**	**413**	**(0 wkts; 9.4 overs; 31 mins)**	**58**

ENGLAND	O	M	R	W		O	M	R	W
Anderson	18	3	61	1		4	1	9	0
Broad	12	1	60	0					
Panesar	47	12	129	5	(2)	22	3	81	6
Swann	34.1	7	70	4	(3)	18.1	6	43	4
Patel	4	1	6	0					

INDIA	O	M	R	W		O	M	R	W
Ashwin	42.3	6	145	2		3.4	0	22	0
Ojha	40	6	143	5		4	0	16	0
Khan	15	4	37	0					
Harbhajan Singh	21	1	74	2	(3)	2	0	10	0
Yuvraj Singh	3	0	8	0					

FALL OF WICKETS

	I	E	I	E
Wkt	1st	1st	2nd	2nd
1st	4	66	30	–
2nd	52	68	37	–
3rd	60	274	52	–
4th	118	298	65	–
5th	119	357	78	–
6th	169	382	92	–
7th	280	406	110	–
8th	315	406	128	–
9th	316	408	131	–
10th	327	413	142	–

Umpires: Alim Dar (*Pakistan*) (76) and A.L.Hill (*New Zealand*) (33).
Referee: R.S.Mahanama (*Sri Lanka*) (40). Test No. 2061/105 (I466/E928)

INDIA v ENGLAND (3rd Test)

At Eden Gardens, Kolkata, on 5, 6, 7, 8, 9 December 2012.
Toss: India. Result: **ENGLAND** won by seven wickets.
Debuts: None.

INDIA

G.Gambhir	c Trott b Panesar	60	c Prior b Finn		40
V.Sehwag	run out	23	b Swann		49
C.A.Pujara	b Panesar	16	run out		8
S.R.Tendulkar	c Prior b Anderson	76	c Trott b Swann		5
V.Kohli	c Swann b Anderson	6	c Prior b Finn		20
Yuvraj Singh	c Cook b Swann	32	b Anderson		11
†*M.S.Dhoni	c Swann b Finn	52	c Cook b Anderson		0
R.Ashwin	b Anderson	21	not out		91
Z.Khan	lbw b Panesar	6	lbw b Finn		0
I.Sharma	b Panesar	0	b Panesar		10
P.P.Ojha	not out	0	b Anderson		3
Extras	(B 5, LB 13, W 5, NB 1)	24	(B 8, LB 2)		10
Total	**(105 overs; 438 mins)**	**316**	**(84.4 overs; 346 mins)**		**247**

ENGLAND

*A.N.Cook	run out	190	st Dhoni b Ashwin		1
N.R.D.Compton	lbw b Ojha	57	not out		9
I.J.L.Trott	c Dhoni b Ojha	87	lbw b Ojha		3
K.P.Pietersen	lbw b Ashwin	54	c Dhoni b Ashwin		0
I.R.Bell	c Dhoni b Sharma	5	not out		28
S.R.Patel	c Sehwag b Ojha	33			
†M.J.Prior	c Dhoni b Khan	41			
G.P.Swann	c Sehwag b Ojha	21			
S.T.Finn	not out	4			
J.M.Anderson	c Sehwag b Ashwin	9			
M.S.Panesar	lbw b Ashwin	0			
Extras	(B 13, LB 4, NB 5)	22			
Total	**(167.3 overs; 679 mins)**	**523**	**(3 wkts; 12.1 overs; 40 mins)**		**41**

ENGLAND	O	M	R	W	O	M	R	W	FALL OF WICKETS				
Anderson	28	7	89	3	15.4	4	38	3		I	E	I	E
Finn	21	2	73	1	18	6	45	3	*Wkt*	*1st*	*1st*	*2nd*	*2nd*
Panesar	40	13	90	4	22	1	75	1	1st	47	165	86	4
Swann	16	3	46	1	28	9	70	2	2nd	88	338	98	7
Patel					1	0	9	0	3rd	117	359	103	8
									4th	136	395	107	–
INDIA									5th	215	420	122	–
Khan	31	6	94	1					6th	230	453	122	–
Sharma	29	8	78	1					7th	268	510	155	–
Ashwin	52.3	9	183	3	(1)	6.1	1	31	2	8th	292	510	159	–
Ojha	52	10	142	4	(2)	6	3	10	1	9th	296	523	197	–
Yuvraj Singh	3	1	9	0					10th	316	523	247	–

Umpires: H.D.P.K.Dharmasena (*Sri Lanka*) (11) and R.J.Tucker (*Australia*) (21).
Referee: J.J.Crowe (*New Zealand*) (56).   Test No. 2062/106 (I467/E929)

INDIA v ENGLAND (4th Test)

At Vidarbha C.A.Stadium, Nagpur, on 13, 14, 15, 16, 17 December 2012.
Toss: England. Result: **MATCH DRAWN**.
Debuts: India – R.A.Jadeja; England – J.E.Root.

ENGLAND

*A.N.Cook	lbw b Sharma	1	c Dhoni b Ashwin		13
N.R.D.Compton	c Dhoni b Sharma	3	lbw b Ojha		34
I.J.L.Trott	b Jadeja	44	c Kohli b Ashwin		143
K.P.Pietersen	c Ojha b Jadeja	73	b Jadeja		6
I.R.Bell	c Kohli b Chawla	1	not out		116
J.E.Root	c and b Chawla	73	not out		20
†M.J.Prior	b Ashwin	57			
T.T.Bresnan	lbw b Sharma	0			
G.P.Swann	lbw b Chawla	56			
J.M.Anderson	c Pujara b Chawla	4			
M.S.Panesar	not out	1			
Extras	(B 5, LB 12)	17	(B 8, LB 6, NB 6)		20
Total	**(145.5 overs; 543 mins)**	330	**(4 wkts dec; 154 overs; 578 mins)**		352

INDIA

G.Gambhir	c Prior b Anderson	37
V.Sehwag	b Anderson	0
C.A.Pujara	c Bell b Swann	26
S.R.Tendulkar	b Anderson	2
V.Kohli	lbw b Swann	103
†*M.S.Dhoni	run out	99
R.A.Jadeja	lbw b Anderson	12
R.Ashwin	not out	29
P.P.Chawla	b Swann	1
P.P.Ojha	b Panesar	3
I.Sharma	not out	2
Extras	(B 5, LB 7)	12
Total	**(9 wkts dec; 143 overs; 602 mins)**	326

INDIA	O	M	R	W		O	M	R	W
Sharma	28	9	49	3		15	3	42	0
Ojha	35	12	71	0		40	14	70	1
Jadeja	37	17	58	2	(5)	33	17	59	1
Chawla	21.5	1	69	4		26	6	64	0
Ashwin	24	3	66	1	(3)	38	11	99	2
Gambhir						2	0	4	0

ENGLAND	O	M	R	W
Anderson	32	5	81	4
Bresnan	26	5	69	0
Panesar	52	15	81	1
Swann	31	10	76	3
Trott	1	0	2	0
Root	1	0	5	0

FALL OF WICKETS

	E	I	E
Wkt	1st	1st	2nd
1st	3	1	48
2nd	16	59	81
3rd	102	64	94
4th	119	71	302
5th	139	269	–
6th	242	288	–
7th	242	295	–
8th	302	297	–
9th	325	317	–
10th	330	–	–

Umpires: H.D.P.K.Dharmasena (*Sri Lanka*) (12) and R.J.Tucker (*Australia*) (22).
Referee: J.J.Crowe (*New Zealand*) (57).   Test No. 2063/107 (I468/E930)

SRI LANKA v NEW ZEALAND (1st Test)

At Galle International Stadium, on 17, 18, 19 November 2012.
Toss: New Zealand. Result: **SRI LANKA** won by ten wickets.
Debut: Sri Lanka – F.D.M.Karunaratne.

NEW ZEALAND

M.J.Guptill	c Mathews b Eranga	11	b Kulasekara	13
B.B.McCullum	b Herath	68	c Kulasekara b Herath	13
K.S.Williamson	c Paranavitana b Eranga	0	c H.A.P.W.Jayawardena b Kulasekara	10
*L.R.P.L.Taylor	b Kulasekara	9	lbw b Herath	18
D.R.Flynn	c H.A.P.W.Jayawardena b Herath	53	b Herath	20
J.E.C.Franklin	lbw b Herath	3	st H.A.P.W.Jayawardena b Herath	2
†C.F.K.van Wyk	b Herath	28	not out	13
D.A.J.Bracewell	c D.P.M.D.Jayawardena b Herath	12	lbw b Herath	0
T.G.Southee	c Mathews b Eranga	16	st H.A.P.W.Jayawardena b Kaluhalamulla	16
J.S.Patel	not out	12	c Karunaratne b Herath	0
T.A.Boult	b Kulasekara	7	c D.P.M.D.Jayawardena b Kaluhalamulla	13
Extras	(LB 1, NB 1)	2		–
Total	**(82.5 overs; 329 mins)**	**221**	**(44.1 overs; 182 mins)**	**118**

SRI LANKA

N.T.Paranavitana	b Southee	0	not out	31
F.D.M.Karunaratne	lbw b Southee	0	not out	60
H.K.S.R.Kaluhalamulla	c Guptill b Southee	9		
K.C.Sangakkara	c McCullum b Boult	5		
*D.P.M.D.Jayawardena	c van Wyk b Patel	91		
T.T.Samaraweera	lbw b Southee	17		
A.D.Mathews	c van Wyk b Franklin	79		
†H.A.P.W.Jayawardena	c Bracewell b Patel	4		
K.M.D.N.Kulasekara	c and b Patel	8		
H.M.R.K.B.Herath	not out	11		
R.M.S.Eranga	c Bracewell b Boult	4		
Extras	(B 9, LB 8, NB 2)	19	(W 2)	2
Total	**(80.2 overs; 363 mins)**	**247**	**(0 wkts; 18.3 overs; 75 mins)**	**93**

SRI LANKA	O	M	R	W	O	M	R	W
Kulasekara	12.5	5	31	2	12	4	28	2
Eranga	16	5	51	3	4	2	10	0
Mathews	3	0	11	0				
Herath	30	5	65	5	(3) 18	3	43	6
Kaluhalamulla	21	1	62	0	(4) 10.1	0	37	2

NEW ZEALAND	O	M	R	W	O	M	R	W
Boult	16.2	3	46	2	4	1	15	0
Southee	18	4	46	4				
Bracewell	16	1	67	0	(2) 5.3	0	35	0
Franklin	7	2	16	1	3	0	15	0
Patel	23	7	55	3	(3) 5	1	22	0
Williamson					(5) 1	0	6	0

FALL OF WICKETS

	NZ	SL	NZ	SL
Wkt	1st	1st	2nd	2nd
1st	29	2	18	–
2nd	29	9	35	–
3rd	40	18	46	–
4th	130	20	60	–
5th	142	50	70	–
6th	155	206	79	–
7th	181	215	79	–
8th	196	229	96	–
9th	207	242	97	–
10th	221	247	118	–

Umpires: M.Erasmus (*South Africa*) (14) and N.J.Llong (*England*) (13).
Referee: J.Srinath (*India*) (23).   Test No. 2064/27 (SL216/NZ376)

SRI LANKA v NEW ZEALAND (2nd Test)

At P.Saravanamuttu Stadium, Colombo, on 25, 26, 27, 28, 29 November 2012.
Toss: New Zealand. Result: **NEW ZEALAND** won by 167 runs.
Debut: New Zealand – T.D.Astle.

NEW ZEALAND

M.J.Guptill	c Mathews b Kulasekara	4	c Dilshan b Eranga	11
B.B.McCullum	lbw b Eranga	4	st H.A.P.W.Jayawardena b Herath	35
K.S.Williamson	lbw b Herath	135	c Paranavitana b Kulasekara	18
*L.R.P.L.Taylor	lbw b Herath	142	run out	74
D.R.Flynn	lbw b Herath	53	lbw b Kulasekara	0
†C.F.K.van Wyk	b Dilshan	0	c Paranavitana b Herath	0
T.D.Astle	lbw b Herath	3	c Dilshan b Kaluhalamulla	35
D.A.J.Bracewell	c Herath b Kaluhalamulla	24	c Kulasekara b Herath	1
T.G.Southee	b Herath	15	not out	8
J.S.Patel	not out	25	st H.A.P.W.Jayawardena b Kaluhalamulla	6
T.A.Boult	b Herath	1	not out	6
Extras	(B 2, LB 2, NB 2)	6	(LB 4, NB 2)	6
Total	**(153 overs; 605 mins)**	**412**	**(9 wkts dec; 54 overs; 253 mins)**	**194**

SRI LANKA

N.T.Paranavitana	c van Wyk b Southee	40	lbw b Southee	0
T.M.Dilshan	b Southee	5	c van Wyk b Southee	14
K.C.Sangakkara	c Boult b Southee	0	b Bracewell	16
*D.P.M.D.Jayawardena	c Williamson b Boult	4	c van Wyk b Bracewell	5
A.D.Mathews	c Guptill b Southee	47	(6) c Guptill b Boult	84
T.T.Samaraweera	c Guptill b Boult	76	(5) run out	7
†H.A.P.W.Jayawardena	c Williamson b Patel	12	c van Wyk b Astle	29
H.K.S.R.Kaluhalamulla	lbw b Boult	39	c Guptill b Boult	0
K.M.D.N.Kulasekara	c Taylor b Southee	6	c Williamson b Southee	18
H.M.R.K.B.Herath	c Williamson b Boult	5	(11) not out	6
R.M.S.Eranga	not out	3	(10) c Williamson b Southee	0
Extras	(LB 3, W 1, NB 3)	7	(B 4, LB 11, W 1)	16
Total	**(94 overs; 442 mins)**	**244**	**(85.5 overs; 369 mins)**	**195**

SRI LANKA	O	M	R	W		O	M	R	W
Kulasekara	24	2	76	1		12	2	47	2
Eranga	22	0	91	1		10	1	39	1
Mathews	10	1	25	0					
Herath	49	10	103	6	(3)	21	3	67	3
Kaluhalamulla	39	3	94	1	(4)	11	1	37	2
Dilshan	9	2	19	1					

NEW ZEALAND	O	M	R	W		O	M	R	W
Southee	22	4	62	5		20	5	58	3
Boult	21	7	42	4		17.5	6	33	3
Patel	22	3	47	1	(4)	16	7	20	0
Astle	13	2	41	0	(5)	18	4	56	1
Bracewell	13	1	44	0	(3)	13	6	13	2
Williamson	3	1	5	0					
Flynn					(6)	1	1	0	0

FALL OF WICKETS				
	NZ	SL	NZ	SL
Wkt	1st	1st	2nd	2nd
1st	4	7	32	0
2nd	14	7	56	35
3rd	276	12	74	41
4th	290	102	74	46
5th	291	103	75	63
6th	300	128	172	119
7th	346	225	177	122
8th	374	232	180	168
9th	410	240	182	169
10th	412	244	—	195

Umpires: M.Erasmus (*South Africa*) (15) and N.J.Llong (*England*) (14).
Referee: J.Srinath (*India*) (24). **Test No. 2065/28 (SL217/NZ377)**

AUSTRALIA v SRI LANKA (1st Test)

At Bellerive Oval, Hobart, on 14, 15, 16, 17, 18 December 2012.
Toss: Australia. Result: **AUSTRALIA** won by 137 runs.
Debuts: None.

AUSTRALIA

D.A.Warner	run out	57	(2) c H.A.P.W.Jayawardena b Herath		68
E.J.M.Cowan	c Eranga b Welagedara	4	(1) b Welagedara		56
P.J.Hughes	b Welagedara	86	b Eranga		16
S.R.Watson	c D.P.M.D.Jayawardena b Welagedara	30	st H.A.P.W.Jayawardena b Herath		5
*M.J.Clarke	c Sangakkara b Eranga	74	(6) retired hurt		57
M.E.K.Hussey	not out	115	(7) not out		31
†M.S.Wade	not out	68	(5) c Kulasekara b Herath		11
P.M.Siddle			c H.A.P.W.Jayawardena b Welagedara		4
M.A.Starc			lbw b Welagedara		5
N.M.Lyon			b Herath		11
B.W.Hilfenhaus			lbw b Herath		0
Extras	(B 1, LB 3, W 1, NB 11)	16	(LB 10, NB 4)		14
Total	**(5 wkts dec; 131 overs; 547 mins)**	**450**	**(73.5 overs; 317 mins)**		**278**

SRI LANKA

F.D.M.Karunaratne	c Wade b Hilfenhaus	14	b Starc	30
T.M.Dilshan	b Starc	147	c Wade b Watson	11
K.C.Sangakkara	c Hussey b Siddle	4	lbw b Siddle	63
*D.P.M.D.Jayawardena	lbw b Watson	12	c Clarke b Siddle	19
T.T.Samaraweera	c Wade b Lyon	7	lbw b Siddle	49
A.D.Mathews	lbw b Siddle	75	c Wade b Siddle	19
†H.A.P.W.Jayawardena	lbw b Siddle	40	c Hussey b Starc	21
K.M.D.N.Kulasekara	c sub (J.C.Silk) b Lyon	23	c Wade b Starc	9
H.M.R.K.B.Herath	b Siddle	0	b Starc	8
R.M.S.Eranga	not out	5	c Wade b Starc	6
U.W.M.B.C.A.Welagedara	c Hussey b Siddle	0	not out	0
Extras	(B 2, LB 6, NB 1)	9	(B 10, LB 8, W 1, NB 1)	20
Total	**(109.3 overs; 469 mins)**	**336**	**(119.2 overs; 521 mins)**	**255**

SRI LANKA

	O	M	R	W		O	M	R	W
Kulasekara	32	2	80	0		12	3	24	0
Welagedara	26	1	130	3		22	3	89	3
Eranga	25	5	90	1	(4)	11	0	53	1
Mathews	15	3	41	0	(5)	5	2	5	0
Dilshan	7	0	30	0	(3)	2	0	2	0
Herath	26	4	75	0		21.5	2	95	5

AUSTRALIA

	O	M	R	W		O	M	R	W
Starc	24	3	104	1		28.2	7	63	5
Hilfenhaus	12.2	3	30	1					
Lyon	25	8	76	2	(4)	32	12	57	0
Siddle	25.3	11	54	5	(2)	26	11	50	4
Watson	20.4	5	55	1	(3)	27	6	54	1
Clarke	2	0	9	0					
Hussey					(5)	1	0	5	0
Warner					(6)	4	0	8	0
Wade					(7)	1	1	0	0

FALL OF WICKETS

	A	SL	A	SL
Wkt	1st	1st	2nd	2nd
1st	18	25	132	26
2nd	97	42	140	47
3rd	183	70	153	112
4th	198	87	165	151
5th	304	248	181	201
6th	–	289	250	218
7th	–	316	256	235
8th	–	320	271	247
9th	–	336	278	250
10th	–	336	–	255

Umpires: A.L.Hill (*New Zealand*) (34) and N.J.Llong (*England*) (15).
Referee: B.C.Broad (*England*) (54). **Test No. 2066/24 (A747/SL218)**
M.J.Clarke retired hurt at 238-5.

AUSTRALIA v SRI LANKA (2nd Test)

At Melbourne Cricket Ground, on 26, 27, 28 December 2012.
Toss: Sri Lanka. Result: **AUSTRALIA** won by an innings and 201 runs.
Debut: Australia – J.M.Bird.

SRI LANKA

F.D.M.Karunaratne	c Wade b Bird	5	run out		1
T.M.Dilshan	b Johnson	11	c Cowan b Johnson		0
K.C.Sangakkara	c Wade b Johnson	58	retired hurt		27
*D.P.M.D.Jayawardena	c Wade b Siddle	3	b Bird		0
T.T.Samaraweera	c Warner b Bird	10	lbw b Bird		1
A.D.Mathews	c Hussey b Siddle	15	b Johnson		35
†H.A.P.W.Jayawardena	c Hughes b Johnson	24	absent hurt		–
K.T.G.D.Prasad	c Wade b Johnson	0	(7) c Hughes b Lyon		17
H.M.R.K.B.Herath	c Cowan b Lyon	14	(8) not out		11
R.M.S.Eranga	not out	4	(9) c Cowan b Siddle		0
U.W.M.B.C.A.Welagedara	c Hussey b Lyon	0	absent hurt		–
Extras	(LB 5, NB 7)	12	(LB 10, NB 1)		11
Total	**(43.4 overs; 219 mins)**	**156**	**(24.2 overs; 130 mins)**		**103**

AUSTRALIA

E.J.M.Cowan	c D.P.M.D.Jayawardena b Prasad	36
D.A.Warner	c Prasad b Mathews	62
P.J.Hughes	run out	10
S.R.Watson	c Samaraweera b Prasad	83
*M.J.Clarke	c D.P.M.D.Jayawardena b Eranga	106
M.E.K.Hussey	c Herath b Dilshan	34
†M.S.Wade	c Eranga b Prasad	1
M.G.Johnson	not out	92
P.M.Siddle	c D.P.M.D.Jayawardena b Eranga	13
N.M.Lyon	c sub (L.D.Chandimal) b Mathews	1
J.M.Bird	b Eranga	0
Extras	(B 9, LB 5, W 6, NB 2)	22
Total	**(134.4 overs; 567 mins)**	**460**

AUSTRALIA	O	M	R	W		O	M	R	W
Johnson	14	2	63	4		8	0	16	2
Bird	13	5	32	2		9	1	29	2
Siddle	8	1	30	2		5.2	0	32	1
Watson	3	2	3	0					
Lyon	5.4	0	23	2	(4)	2	0	16	1

SRI LANKA	O	M	R	W
Welagedara	14.4	6	38	0
Eranga	27	2	109	3
Prasad	26	2	106	3
Mathews	16	3	60	2
Herath	39	7	95	0
Dilshan	12	1	38	1

FALL OF WICKETS

	SL	A	SL
Wkt	1st	1st	2nd
1st	13	95	1
2nd	19	117	1
3rd	37	117	3
4th	79	311	13
5th	99	313	74
6th	134	315	102
7th	134	376	103
8th	147	434	–
9th	156	451	–
10th	156	460	–

Umpires: Alim Dar (*Pakistan*) (77) and N.J.Llong (*England*) (16).
Referee: B.C.Broad (*England*) (55).
K.C.Sangakkara retired hurt at 62-4.

Test No. 2067/25 (A748/SL219)

AUSTRALIA v SRI LANKA (3rd Test)

At Sydney Cricket Ground, on 3, 4, 5, 6 January 2013.
Toss: Australia. Result: **AUSTRALIA** won by five wickets.
Debuts: None.

SRI LANKA

Batsman	1st innings	R	2nd innings	R
F.D.M.Karunaratne	c Hussey b Bird	5	c Wade b Bird	85
T.M.Dilshan	c Wade b Bird	34	c Hughes b Johnson	5
*D.P.M.D.Jayawardena	c Clarke b Starc	72	c Clarke b Siddle	60
H.D.R.L.Thirimanne	c Warner b Lyon	91	c Bird b Johnson	7
T.T.Samaraweera	lbw b Siddle	12	c Hussey b Lyon	0
A.D.Mathews	c Hussey b Starc	15	run out	16
†L.D.Chandimal	b Starc	24	not out	62
K.T.G.D.Prasad	c Starc b Siddle	2	c Wade b Starc	15
H.M.R.K.B.Herath	c Siddle b Bird	5	b Bird	10
R.A.S.Lakmal	c Hussey b Bird	5	b Johnson	0
A.N.P.R.Fernando	not out	17	c Wade b Bird	9
Extras	(LB 8, W 3, NB 1)	12	(B 1, LB 4, W 1, NB 3)	9
Total	(87.4 overs; 385 mins)	294	(81.2 overs; 380 mins)	278

AUSTRALIA

Batsman	1st innings	R	2nd innings	R
D.A.Warner	c Prasad b Dilshan	85	(2) c Jayawardena b Lakmal	0
E.J.M.Cowan	run out	4	(1) lbw b Herath	36
P.J.Hughes	c Chandimal b Herath	87	lbw b Herath	34
*M.J.Clarke	c Karunaratne b Herath	50	c Thirimanne b Dilshan	29
M.E.K.Hussey	run out	25	not out	27
†M.S.Wade	not out	102	b Herath	9
M.G.Johnson	c Chandimal b Fernando	13	not out	1
P.M.Siddle	c Chandimal b Fernando	38		
M.A.Starc	lbw b Herath	2		
N.M.Lyon	b Herath	4		
J.M.Bird	not out	6		
Extras	(LB 6, W 7, NB 3)	16	(LB 5)	5
Total	(9 wkts dec; 107 overs; 479 mins)	432	(5wkts; 42.5 overs; 160 mins)	141

AUSTRALIA	O	M	R	W	O	M	R	W
Starc	19	0	71	3	12	1	49	1
Bird	19.4	10	41	4	21.2	5	76	3
Siddle	15	3	46	2	(4) 17	4	42	1
Johnson	13	1	58	0	(3) 15	3	34	3
Lyon	19	2	69	1	15	1	66	1
Hussey	2	1	1	0	1	0	4	0

SRI LANKA	O	M	R	W	O	M	R	W
Lakmal	24	4	95	0	(2) 6	1	18	1
Fernando	20	1	114	2	(4) 2	0	14	0
Prasad	11	0	53	0				
Mathews	2	0	11	0				
Dilshan	19	2	58	1	(1) 18	2	57	1
Herath	31	3	95	4	(3) 16.5	0	47	3

FALL OF WICKETS

Wkt	SL 1st	A 1st	SL 2nd	A 2nd
1st	26	36	24	0
2nd	72	166	132	45
3rd	134	195	155	104
4th	167	251	158	108
5th	222	271	178	132
6th	250	307	178	–
7th	256	384	202	–
8th	271	387	235	–
9th	273	393	237	–
10th	294	–	278	–

Umpires: Alim Dar (*Pakistan*) (78) and A.L.Hill (*New Zealand*) (35).
Referee: B.C.Broad (*England*) (56).

Test No. 2068/26 (A749/SL220)

SOUTH AFRICA v NEW ZEALAND (1st Test)

At Newlands, Cape Town, on 2, 3, 4 January 2013.
Toss: New Zealand. Result: **SOUTH AFRICA** won by an innings and 27 runs.
Debuts: None.

NEW ZEALAND

M.J.Guptill	c de Villiers b Philander	1	c Amla b Steyn		0
*B.B.McCullum	b Philander	7	lbw b Peterson		51
K.S.Williamson	lbw b Philander	13	c Petersen b Kallis		15
D.G.Brownlie	c Smith b Philander	0	c Peterson b Morkel		109
D.R.Flynn	c and b Steyn	8	c de Villiers b Kallis		14
†B.J.Watling	c de Villiers b Philander	0	c Smith b Philander		42
J.E.C.Franklin	c Smith b Morkel	1	b Steyn		22
D.A.J.Bracewell	b Steyn	2	c Petersen b Philander		0
J.S.Patel	c Amla b Morkel	5	b Steyn		8
T.A.Boult	c de Villiers b Morkel	0	not out		2
C.S.Martin	not out	0	run out		0
Extras	(LB 6, NB 1)	7	(B 1, LB 8, W 3)		12
Total	**(19.2 overs, 100 mins)**	**45**	**(102.1 overs; 460 mins)**		**275**

SOUTH AFRICA

*G.C.Smith	lbw b Bracewell	1
A.N.Petersen	b Boult	106
H.M.Amla	lbw b Franklin	66
J.H.Kallis	c Watling b Boult	60
†A.B.de Villiers	b Martin	67
F.du Plessis	c Williamson b Martin	15
D.Elgar	c Watling b Boult	21
R.J.Peterson	b Martin	5
V.D.Philander	not out	0
D.W.Steyn		
M.Morkel		
Extras	(B 1, LB 2, W 2, NB 1)	6
Total	**(8 wkts dec; 95.2 overs; 416 mins)**	**347**

SOUTH AFRICA	O	M	R	W	O	M	R	W		FALL OF WICKETS		
Steyn	7.2	2	18	2	30	6	67	3		NZ	SA	NZ
Philander	6	3	7	5	24	8	76	2	Wkt	1st	1st	2nd
Morkel	6	2	14	3	21	6	50	1	1st	7	1	0
Kallis					11.1	3	31	2	2nd	14	108	29
Peterson					16	6	42	1	3rd	14	212	118
									4th	27	255	155
NEW ZEALAND									5th	27	281	229
Boult	21	2	78	3					6th	28	335	252
Bracewell	24	4	93	1					7th	31	342	252
Martin	19.2	4	63	3					8th	38	347	265
Franklin	14	1	50	1					9th	45	–	274
Patel	17	4	60	0					10th	45	–	275

Umpires: I.J.Gould (*England*) (32) and R.J.Tucker (*Australia*) (23).
Referee: D.C.Boon (*Australia*) (13).   Test No. 2069/39 (SA373/NZ378)

SOUTH AFRICA v NEW ZEALAND (2nd Test)

At St George's Park, Port Elizabeth, on 11, 12, 13, 14 January 2013.
Toss: South Africa. Result: **SOUTH AFRICA** won by an innings and 193 runs.
Debut: New Zealand – C.Munro.

SOUTH AFRICA

A.N.Petersen	c Patel b Bracewell	21
*G.C.Smith	c Watling b Wagner	54
H.M.Amla	c Watling b Boult	110
J.H.Kallis	c Watling b Bracewell	8
†A.B.de Villiers	c Williamson b Patel	51
F.du Plessis	c McCullum b Munro	137
D.Elgar	not out	103
R.J.Peterson	c Patel b Munro	8
D.W.Steyn	c Patel b Bracewell	5
R.K.Kleinveldt	not out	7
M.Morkel		
Extras	(B 6, LB 8, W 4, NB 3)	21
Total	**(8 wkts dec; 153.5 overs; 654 mins)**	**525**

NEW ZEALAND

M.J.Guptill	c Petersen b Steyn	1	b Kleinveldt		48
*B.B.McCullum	c Kallis b Peterson	13	lbw b Peterson		11
K.S.Williamson	c Smith b Steyn	4	b Peterson		11
D.G.Brownlie	c de Villiers b Kleinveldt	10	c de Villiers b Kallis		53
D.R.Flynn	lbw b Kleinveldt	0	c de Villiers b Kleinveldt		0
†B.J.Watling	c Smith b Morkel	63	b Steyn		63
C.Munro	c Elgar b Peterson	0	c Petersen b Morkel		15
D.A.J.Bracewell	c de Villiers b Steyn	7	c Petersen b Steyn		0
N.Wagner	lbw b Steyn	0	c de Villiers b Steyn		4
J.S.Patel	b Steyn	0	(11) not out		0
T.A.Boult	not out	17	(10) c Peterson b Morkel		3
Extras	(LB 5, W 1)	6	(LB 2, W 1)		3
Total	**(44.4 overs; 208 mins)**	**121**	**(86.4 overs; 358 mins)**		**211**

NEW ZEALAND	O	M	R	W	O	M	R	W
Boult	32	5	108	1				
Bracewell	34	6	94	3				
Wagner	33	4	135	1				
Patel	36.5	2	134	1				
Munro	18	4	40	2				

SOUTH AFRICA	O	M	R	W	O	M	R	W
Steyn	13	5	17	5	15.4	2	48	3
Morkel	12.4	6	26	1	16	6	36	2
Kleinveldt	11	3	53	2	15	8	44	2
Peterson	7	2	20	2	26	13	47	2
Kallis	1	1	0	0	9	3	18	1
Smith					1	0	10	0
Petersen					4	0	6	0

FALL OF WICKETS			
	SA	NZ	NZ
Wkt	1st	1st	2nd
1st	29	2	40
2nd	121	8	64
3rd	137	27	84
4th	223	27	84
5th	336	39	182
6th	467	39	203
7th	481	61	203
8th	508	62	204
9th	–	62	207
10th	–	121	211

Umpires: H.D.P.K.Dharmasena (*Sri Lanka*) (13) and I.J.Gould (*England*) (33).
Referee: D.C.Boon (*Australia*) (14).

Test No. 2070/40 (SA374/NZ379)

SOUTH AFRICA v PAKISTAN (1st Test)

At New Wanderers Stadium, Johannesburg, on 1, 2, 3, 4 February 2013.
Toss: South Africa. Result: **SOUTH AFRICA** won by 211 runs.
Debuts: Pakistan – Nasir Jamshed, Rahat Ali.

SOUTH AFRICA

*G.C.Smith	c Ahmed b Gul	24	(2) c Ahmed b Gul	52
A.N.Petersen	c Hafeez b Junaid Khan	20	(1) c Hafeez b Gul	27
H.M.Amla	c Azhar Ali b Younus Khan	37	not out	74
J.H.Kallis	c Shafiq b Gul	50	c Shafiq b Ajmal	7
†A.B.de Villiers	c Ahmed b Hafeez	31	not out	103
F.du Plessis	b Junaid Khan	41		
D.Elgar	c Ahmed b Hafeez	27		
R.J.Peterson	b Hafeez	0		
V.D.Philander	run out	1		
D.W.Steyn	not out	12		
M.Morkel	b Hafeez	0		
Extras	(B 4, LB 4, W 1, NB 1)	10	(LB 4, W 3, NB 5)	12
Total	**(85.2 overs; 370 mins)**	**253**	**(3 wkts dec; 62 overs; 281 mins)**	**275**

PAKISTAN

Mohammad Hafeez	c de Villiers b Steyn	6	c de Villiers b Philander	2
Nasir Jamshed	lbw b Steyn	2	c Peterson b Steyn	46
Azhar Ali	c de Villiers b Kallis	13	lbw b Kallis	18
Younus Khan	c Smith b Steyn	0	c de Villiers b Morkel	15
*Misbah-ul-Haq	c de Villiers b Kallis	12	c de Villiers b Steyn	64
Asad Shafiq	c de Villiers b Philander	1	c Kallis b Steyn	56
†Sarfraz Ahmed	c de Villiers b Steyn	2	b Philander	6
Umar Gul	c Smith b Philander	0	c de Villiers b Steyn	23
Saeed Ajmal	c de Villiers b Steyn	1	c de Villiers b Morkel	11
Junaid Khan	not out	8	lbw b Steyn	9
Rahat Ali	c du Plessis b Steyn	0	not out	3
Extras	(LB 3, W 1)	4	(B 4, LB 4, W 3, NB 4)	15
Total	**(29.1 overs; 148 mins)**	**49**	**(100.4 overs; 456 mins)**	**268**

PAKISTAN	O	M	R	W	O	M	R	W	FALL OF WICKETS
Umar Gul	19	2	56	2	14	2	58	2		SA	P	SA	P
Junaid Khan	18	8	33	2	13	1	63	0	Wkt	1st	1st	2nd	2nd
Rahat Ali	14	0	56	0	11	1	44	0	1st	46	9	82	7
Saeed Ajmal	23	4	68	4	(5) 18	1	74	1	2nd	46	12	87	64
Younus Khan	4	0	16	1	(6) 1	0	9	0	3rd	125	12	99	70
Mohammad Hafeez	7.2	1	16	4	(4) 5	0	32	0	4th	135	36	–	82
									5th	199	37	–	209
SOUTH AFRICA									6th	232	39	–	210
Philander	9	5	16	2	(2) 22	3	60	2	7th	239	39	–	218
Steyn	8.1	6	8	6	(1) 28.4	10	52	5	8th	240	40	–	240
Morkel	6	3	11	0	25	7	89	2	9th	243	41	–	261
Kallis	6	1	12	2	15	5	35	1	10th	253	49	–	268
Peterson					10	3	24	0					

Umpires: B.F.Bowden (*New Zealand*) (73) and B.N.J.Oxenford (*Australia*) (11).
Referee: J.J.Crowe (*New Zealand*) (58).   Test No. 2071/19 (SA375/P371)

SOUTH AFRICA v PAKISTAN (2nd Test)

At Newlands, Cape Town, on 14, 15, 16, 17 February 2013.
Toss: South Africa. Result: **SOUTH AFRICA** won by four wickets.
Debut: Pakistan – Mohammad Irfan.

PAKISTAN

Mohammad Hafeez	c Smith b Steyn	17	lbw b Steyn	0
Nasir Jamshed	c de Villiers b Philander	3	lbw b Philander	0
Azhar Ali	c de Villiers b Morkel	4	c de Villiers b Philander	65
Younus Khan	c de Villiers b Philander	111	b Steyn	14
*Misbah-ul-Haq	c Elgar b Morkel	0	c Smith b Peterson	44
Asad Shafiq	c Smith b Philander	111	b Philander	19
†Sarfraz Ahmed	c Petersen b Philander	13	b Peterson	5
Tanvir Ahmed	c Philander b Peterson	44	not out	10
Umar Gul	lbw b Philander	0	c Petersen b Philander	0
Saeed Ajmal	not out	21	b Peterson	4
Mohammad Irfan	b Peterson	6	c Petersen b Steyn	2
Extras	(LB 5, NB 3)	8	(LB 2, W 4)	6
Total	(116.2 overs; 505 mins)	338	(75.3 overs; 333 mins)	169

SOUTH AFRICA

*G.C.Smith	lbw b Ajmal	19	(2) lbw b Ajmal	29
A.N.Petersen	c Ali b Ajmal	17	(1) lbw b Gul	1
H.M.Amla	lbw b Ajmal	25	b Ajmal	58
F.du Plessis	c Khan b Ajmal	28	(6) lbw b Ajmal	15
J.H.Kallis	lbw b Ajmal	2	(4) lbw b Ajmal	21
†A.B.de Villiers	c Gul b Irfan	61	(5) c Sarfraz Ahmed b Tanvir Ahmed	36
D.Elgar	c Khan b Ajmal	23	not out	11
R.J.Peterson	c Gul b Hafeez	84	not out	1
V.D.Philander	c Jamshed b Irfan	22		
D.W.Steyn	c Sarfraz Ahmed b Irfan	10		
M.Morkel	not out	8		
Extras	(B 12, LB 8, NB 7)	27	(B 5, NB 5)	10
Total	(102.1 overs; 457 mins)	326	(6 wkts; 43.1 overs; 214 mins)	182

SOUTH AFRICA	O	M	R	W		O	M	R	W
Steyn	25	7	55	1		18.3	5	38	3
Philander	26	10	59	5		19	6	40	2
Morkel	20.3	6	59	2		3.1	0	8	0
Kallis	19.3	2	52	0	(5)	5.5	2	8	0
Peterson	23.2	0	94	2	(4)	29	8	73	3
Elgar	2	0	14	0					
PAKISTAN									
Umar Gul	20	5	74	0	(2)	8	0	46	1
Tanvir Ahmed	10	4	26	0	(5)	5	0	34	1
Mohammad Irfan	21	1	86	3	(1)	10	1	35	0
Saeed Ajmal	42	9	96	6	(3)	18.1	2	51	4
Mohammad Hafeez	9.1	1	24	1	(4)	1	1	11	0

FALL OF WICKETS

Wkt	P 1st	SA 1st	P 2nd	SA 2nd
1st	10	36	0	10
2nd	21	50	7	63
3rd	33	84	45	88
4th	33	102	114	150
5th	252	109	147	168
6th	259	164	152	180
7th	266	210	152	–
8th	268	277	152	–
9th	332	303	158	–
10th	338	326	169	–

Umpires: S.J.Davis (*Australia*) (43) and B.N.J.Oxenford (*Australia*) (12).
Referee: J.J.Crowe (*New Zealand*) (59).   **Test No. 2072/20 (SA376/P372)**

SOUTH AFRICA v PAKISTAN (3rd Test)

At SuperSport Park, Centurion, on 22, 23, 24 February 2013.
Toss: South Africa. Result: **SOUTH AFRICA** won by an innings and 18 runs.
Debuts: South Africa – K.J.Abbott; Pakistan – Ehsan Adil.

SOUTH AFRICA

*G.C.Smith	c Khan b Adil	5
A.N.Petersen	lbw b Rahat Ali	10
H.M.Amla	c Ahmed b Rahat Ali	92
F.du Plessis	c Ahmed b Adil	29
†A.B.de Villiers	c Shafiq b Rahat Ali	121
D.Elgar	lbw b Rahat Ali	7
R.J.Peterson	run out	28
V.D.Philander	c Hafeez b Khan	74
K.J.Abbott	b Rahat Ali	13
R.K.Kleinveldt	c Ajmal b Rahat Ali	0
D.W.Steyn	not out	5
Extras	(B 1, LB 6, W 6, NB 12)	25
Total	**(103.2 overs; 480 mins)**	**409**

PAKISTAN

Mohammad Hafeez	c Elgar b Abbott	18		b Steyn	0
Imran Farhat	lbw b Philander	30	(4)	c de Villiers b Abbott	43
Azhar Ali	b Philander	6	(2)	run out	27
Younus Khan	lbw b Abbott	33	(3)	c Smith b Steyn	11
*Misbah-ul-Haq	c Petersen b Abbott	10		c de Villiers b Kleinveldt	5
Asad Shafiq	lbw b Steyn	6		c Philander b Kleinveldt	6
†Sarfraz Ahmed	c Smith b Abbott	17		c Elgar b Steyn	40
Saeed Ajmal	c Smith b Abbott	0		lbw b Steyn	31
Ehsan Adil	c du Plessis b Abbott	9		c Kleinveldt b Abbott	12
Mohammad Irfan	c Elgar b Abbott	0	(11)	not out	6
Rahat Ali	not out	0	(10)	lbw b Peterson	22
Extras	(LB 17, W 8, NB 2)	27		(B 9, LB 10, W 11, NB 2)	32
Total	**(46.4 overs; 234 mins)**	**156**		**(78 overs; 367 mins)**	**235**

PAKISTAN	O	M	R	W		O	M	R	W
Mohammad Irfan	21.5	3	80	0					
Rahat Ali	27.2	1	127	6					
Ehsan Adil	12.1	2	54	2					
Saeed Ajmal	29	6	76	0					
Younus Khan	6	0	28	1					
Mohammad Hafeez	5	0	24	0					
Azhar Ali	2	0	13	0					

SOUTH AFRICA	O	M	R	W		O	M	R	W
Steyn	12	5	25	1		23	5	80	4
Philander	10	2	30	2		15	4	32	0
Kleinveldt	12	1	49	0	(4)	13	2	33	2
Abbott	11.4	6	29	7	(3)	17	7	39	2
Peterson	1	0	6	0		10	2	32	1

FALL OF WICKETS

		SA	P	P
Wkt	1st	1st	2nd	
1st	13	46	0	
2nd	38	56	39	
3rd	107	56	93	
4th	186	75	107	
5th	196	95	107	
6th	248	132	114	
7th	377	132	183	
8th	394	149	202	
9th	402	149	202	
10th	409	156	235	

Umpires: B.F.Bowden (*New Zealand*) (74) and S.J.Davis (*Australia*) (44).
Referee: J.J.Crowe (*New Zealand*) (60).   Test No. 2073/21 (SA377/P373)

ENGLAND TEST MATCH AVERAGES 2012

These averages cover the 12 Tests played by England included in this book, against Sri Lanka away, at home to West Indies and South Africa, and away to India.

BATTING AND FIELDING

	M	I	NO	HS	Runs	Avge	100	50	Ct/St
K.P.Pietersen	11	19	1	186	986	54.77	3	4	4
A.N.Cook	12	23	3	190	1090	54.50	4	2	9
I.R.Bell	11	19	5	116*	621	44.35	1	6	7
I.J.L.Trott	12	22	2	143	844	42.20	2	5	6
M.J.Prior	12	16	–	91	627	39.18	–	5	24/6
A.J.Strauss	8	15	–	141	547	36.46	2	1	12
N.R.D.Compton	4	8	2	57	208	34.66	–	1	1
J.M.Bairstow	5	7	1	95	196	32.66	–	2	5
G.P.Swann	11	14	4	56	271	27.10	–	1	11
T.T.Bresnan	8	9	2	39*	120	17.14	–	–	4
S.C.J.Broad	8	12	1	37	172	15.63	–	–	1
S.R.Patel	5	7	–	33	109	15.57	–	–	2
S.T.Finn	5	6	4	10	16	8.00	–	–	1
J.M.Anderson	11	16	4	23*	83	6.91	–	–	9
M.S.Panesar	4	5	1	13	18	4.50	–	–	–

Also played: R.S.Bopara (1 Test) 0, 22; G.Onions (1) did not bat; J.E.Root (1) 73, 20; J.W.A.Taylor (2) 34, 10, 4 (2 ct).

BOWLING

	O	M	R	W	Avge	Best	5wI	10wM
K.P.Pietersen	33	2	138	5	27.60	3-52	–	–
M.S.Panesar	230	61	557	19	29.31	6-81	2	1
J.M.Anderson	458.3	115	1167	39	29.92	5-72	1	–
G.P.Swann	519.3	107	1440	46	31.30	6-82	3	1
S.T.Finn	199.5	31	630	20	31.50	4-74	–	–
S.C.J.Broad	301.3	52	1002	27	37.11	7-72	2	1
T.T.Bresnan	287	59	887	16	55.43	4-37	–	–

Also bowled: R.S.Bopara 18-1-78-0; G.Onions 29.3-7-88-4; S.R.Patel 101-19-257-4; J.E.Root 1-0-5-0; I.J.L.Trott 41-3-114-0.

ICC TEST RANKINGS*

	Team	Matches	Points	Rating
1	South Africa (2)	29	3566	123
2	England (1)	41	4825	118
3	Australia (3=)	38	4332	114
4	Pakistan (5)	29	3148	109
5	India (3=)	37	3879	105
6	Sri Lanka (6)	32	3062	96
7	West Indies (7)	31	2809	91
8	New Zealand (8)	27	2126	79
9	Bangladesh (9)	15	0	0

Zimbabwe had not played sufficient games to secure a ranking.
* As of 21 December 2012.

INTERNATIONAL UMPIRES AND REFEREES 2013

ELITE PANEL OF UMPIRES 2013

The Elite Panel of ICC Umpires and Referees was introduced in April 2002 to raise standards and guarantee impartial adjudication. Two umpires from this panel stand in Test matches while one officiates with a home umpire from the Supplementary International Panel in limited-overs internationals.

Full Names	Birthdate	Birthplace	Tests	Debut	LOI	Debut
ALIM Sarwar DAR	06.06.68	Jhang, Pakistan	78	2003-04	152	1999-00
ASAD RAUF	12.05.56	Lahore, Pakistan	46	2004-05	98	1999-00
BOWDEN, Brent Fraser	11.04.63	Auckland, New Zealand	74	1999-00	176	1994-95
DAVIS, Stephen James	09.04.52	London, England	44	1997-98	116	1992-93
DHARMASENA, H.D.P.Kumar	24.04.71	Colombo, Sri Lanka	14	2010-11	43	2008-09
ERASMUS, Marais	27.02.64	George, South Africa	16	2009-10	45	2007-08
GOULD, Ian James	19.08.57	Taplow, England	33	2008-09	79	2006
HILL, Anthony Lloyd	26.06.51	Auckland, New Zealand	35	2001-02	94	1997-98
KETTLEBOROUGH, Richard Allan	15.03.73	Sheffield, England	12	2010-11	29	2009
LLONG, Nigel James	11.02.69	Ashford, England	16	2007-08	59	2006
OXENFORD, Bruce Nicholas James	05.03.60	Southport, Australia	12	2010-11	39	2007-08
TUCKER, Rodney James	28.08.64	Sydney, Australia	23	2009-10	27	2008-09

ELITE PANEL OF REFEREES 2013

Full Names	Birthdate	Birthplace	Tests	Debut	LOI	Debut
BOON, David Clarence	29.12.60	Launceston, Australia	14	2011	21	2011
BROAD, Brian Christopher	29.09.57	Bristol, England	21	2003-04	213	2003-04
CROWE, Jeffrey John	14.09.58	Auckland, New Zealand	60	2004-05	167	2003-04
MADUGALLE, Ranjan Senerath	22.04.59	Kandy, Sri Lanka	139	1993-94	270	1993-94
MAHANAMA, Roshan Siriwardena	31.05.66	Colombo, Sri Lanka	40	2004	187	2004
PYCROFT, Andrew John	06.06.56	Harare, Zimbabwe	22	2009	77	2009
SRINATH, Javagal	31.08.69	Mysore, India	24	2006	124	2006-07

INTERNATIONAL UMPIRES PANEL 2013

Nominated by their respective cricket boards, members from this panel officiate in home LOIs and supplement the Elite panel for Test matches. Specialist third umpires have been selected to undertake adjudication involving television replays. The number of Test matches/LOI in which they have stood is shown in brackets.

			Third Umpire
Australia	P.R.Reiffel (2/30)	S.D.Fry (-/7)	J.D.Ward (-/-)
Bangladesh	Nadir Shah (-/40)	Enamal Haque (1/45)	Sharfuddoula (-/5)
			Anisur Rahman (-/-)
England	R.K.Illingworth (2/15)	R.J.Bailey (-/3)	M.A.Gough (-/-)
			R.T.Robinson (-/-)
India	S.Asnani (-/10)	V.A.Kulkarni (-/2)	C.Shamsuddin (-/-)
			P.R.Sundaram (-/-)
New Zealand	G.A.V.Baxter (-/36)	C.B.Gaffaney (-/13)	D.J.Walker (-/-)
Pakistan	Zamir Haider (-/15)	Ahsan Raza (-/8)	Shozab Raza (-/-)
South Africa	J.D.Cloete (-/20)	S.George (-/5)	A.T.Holdstock (-/1)
Sri Lanka	R.E.S.Martinesz (-/4)	T.H.Wijewardena (-/-)	R.Palliyaguru (-/-)
West Indies	P.J.Nero (-/12)	J.S.Wilson (-/-)	G.O.Brathwaite (-/6)
			N.Duguid (-/-)
Zimbabwe	R.B.Tiffin (44/126)	O.Chirombe (-/8)	T.J.Matibiri (-/-)

Test Match and LOI statistics to 1 March 2013.

TEST MATCH CAREER RECORDS

These records, complete to 1 March 2013, contain all players registered for county cricket in 2011 at the time of going to press, plus those who have played Test cricket since 18 October 2011 (Test No. 2008). Records are for performances for the country shown, and do not include figures for multi-national teams.

ENGLAND – BATTING AND FIELDING

	M	I	NO	HS	Runs	Avge	100	50	Ct/St
K.Ali	1	2	–	9	10	5.00	–	–	–
T.R.Ambrose	11	16	1	102	447	29.80	1	3	31
J.M.Anderson	77	103	38	34	709	10.90	–	–	43
J.M.Bairstow	5	7	1	95	196	32.66	–	2	5
G.J.Batty	7	8	1	38	144	20.57	–	–	3
I.R.Bell	83	141	19	235	5699	46.71	17	34	64
R.S.Bopara	13	19	1	143	575	31.94	3	–	6
T.T.Bresnan	18	17	3	91	438	31.28	–	3	7
S.C.J.Broad	52	71	9	169	1612	26.00	1	9	14
M.A.Carberry	1	2	–	34	64	32.00	–	–	1
R.Clarke	2	3	–	55	96	32.00	–	1	1
P.D.Collingwood	68	115	10	206	4259	40.56	10	20	96
N.R.D.Compton	4	8	2	57	208	34.66	–	1	1
A.N.Cook	87	154	10	294	7117	49.42	23	29	75
S.T.Finn	17	19	13	19	51	8.50	–	–	4
J.S.Foster	7	12	3	48	226	25.11	–	–	17/1
S.J.Harmison	62	84	23	49*	742	12.16	–	–	7
M.J.Hoggard	67	92	27	38	473	7.27	–	–	24
G.O.Jones	34	53	4	100	1172	23.91	1	6	128/5
S.P.Jones	18	18	5	44	205	15.76	–	–	4
R.W.T.Key	15	26	1	221	775	31.00	1	3	11
A.Khan	1	–	–	–	–	–	–	–	–
J.Lewis	1	2	–	20	27	13.50	–	–	–
D.L.Maddy	3	4	–	24	46	11.50	–	–	4
S.I.Mahmood	8	11	1	34	81	8.10	–	–	–
E.J.G.Morgan	16	24	1	130	700	30.43	2	3	11
G.Onions	9	10	7	17*	30	10.00	–	–	–
M.S.Panesar	45	60	20	26	213	5.32	–	–	9
S.R.Patel	5	7	–	33	109	15.57	–	–	2
K.P.Pietersen	92	158	8	227	7414	49.42	22	29	54
L.E.Plunkett	9	13	2	44*	126	11.45	–	–	3
M.J.Prior	62	92	15	131*	3326	43.19	6	24	173/13
C.M.W.Read	15	23	4	55	360	18.94	–	1	48/6
J.E.Root	1	2	1	73	93	93.00	–	1	–
O.A.Shah	6	10	–	88	269	26.90	–	2	2
A.Shahzad	1	1	–	5	5	5.00	–	–	2
R.J.Sidebottom	22	31	11	31	313	15.65	–	–	5
A.J.Strauss	100	176	6	177	7037	40.91	21	27	121
G.P.Swann	50	60	10	85	1176	23.52	–	5	44
J.W.A.Taylor	2	3	–	34	48	16.00	–	–	2
J.C.Tredwell	1	1	–	37	37	37.00	–	–	1
C.T.Tremlett	11	13	4	25*	98	10.88	–	–	4
M.E.Trescothick	76	143	10	219	5825	43.79	14	29	95
I.J.L.Trott	38	66	6	226	2970	49.50	8	13	17

TEST　　　　　　　　**ENGLAND – BOWLING**

	O	M	R	W	Avge	Best	5wI	10wM
K.Ali	36	5	136	5	27.20	3- 80	–	–
J.M.Anderson	2823.5	654	8754	288	30.39	7- 43	12	1
G.J.Batty	232.2	34	733	11	66.63	3- 55	–	–
I.R.Bell	18	3	76	1	76.00	1- 33	–	–
R.S.Bopara	72.2	10	290	1	290.00	1- 39	–	–
T.T.Bresnan	625.3	151	1855	57	32.54	5- 48	1	–
S.C.J.Broad	1804	384	5493	172	31.93	7- 72	6	1
R.Clarke	29	11	60	4	15.00	2- 7	–	–
P.D.Collingwood	317.3	51	1018	17	59.88	3- 23	–	–
A.N.Cook	1	0	1	0	–	–	–	–
S.T.Finn	545.3	105	1976	70	28.22	6-125	3	–
S.J.Harmison	2198.4	426	7091	222	31.94	7- 12	8	1
M.J.Hoggard	2318.1	493	7564	248	30.50	7- 61	7	1
S.P.Jones	470.1	78	1666	59	28.23	6- 53	3	–
A.Khan	29	1	122	1	122.00	1-111	–	–
J.Lewis	41	9	122	3	40.66	3- 68	–	–
D.L.Maddy	14	1	40	0	–	–	–	–
S.I.Mahmood	188.2	25	762	20	38.10	4- 22	–	–
G.Onions	267.4	50	957	32	29.90	5- 38	1	–
M.S.Panesar	1878	413	5190	159	32.64	6- 37	12	2
S.R.Patel	101	19	257	4	64.25	2- 27	–	–
K.P.Pietersen	214.3	14	869	10	86.90	3- 52	–	–
L.E.Plunkett	256.2	40	916	23	39.82	3- 17	–	–
J.E.Root	1	0	5	0	–	–	–	–
O.A.Shah	5	0	31	0	–	–	–	–
A.Shahzad	17	4	63	4	15.75	3- 45	–	–
R.J.Sidebottom	802	188	2231	79	28.24	7- 47	5	1
G.P.Swann	2118.1	418	6176	212	29.13	6- 65	14	2
J.C.Tredwell	65	13	181	6	30.16	4- 82	–	–
C.T.Tremlett	447.4	109	1311	49	26.75	6- 48	2	–
M.E.Trescothick	50	6	155	1	155.00	1- 34	–	–
I.J.L.Trott	97	8	341	3	113.66	1- 5	–	–

TEST **AUSTRALIA – BATTING AND FIELDING**

	M	I	NO	HS	Runs	Avge	100	50	Ct/St
M.A.Beer	2	3	1	2*	6	3.00	–	–	1
J.M.Bird	2	2	1	6*	6	6.00	–	–	1
M.J.Clarke	90	150	15	329*	7150	52.96	23	25	105
T.A.Copeland	3	4	1	23*	39	13.00	–	–	2
E.J.M.Cowan	14	24	–	136	783	32.62	1	5	19
P.J.Cummins	1	2	1	13*	15	15.00	–	–	1
B.J.Haddin	43	71	8	169	2257	35.82	3	10	160/4
R.J.Harris	12	18	6	68*	212	17.66	–	1	4
J.W.Hastings	1	2	–	32	52	26.00	–	–	1
M.C.Henriques	1	2	1	81*	149	149.00	–	2	1
B.W.Hilfenhaus	27	38	12	56*	355	13.65	–	1	7
P.J.Hughes	21	39	1	160	1311	34.50	3	5	10
M.E.K.Hussey	79	137	16	195	6235	51.52	19	29	85
P.A.Jaques	11	19	–	150	902	47.47	3	6	7
M.G.Johnson	50	74	12	123*	1403	22.62	1	7	17
S.M.Katich	56	99	6	157	4188	45.03	10	25	39
U.T.Khawaja	6	11	2	65	263	29.22	–	1	3
N.M.Lyon	20	25	10	40*	192	12.80	–	–	5
S.E.Marsh	7	11	–	141	301	27.36	1	1	4
M.J.North	21	35	2	128	1171	35.48	5	4	17
J.L.Pattinson	8	10	4	42	217	36.16	–	–	–
R.T.Ponting	168	287	29	257	13378	51.85	41	62	196
C.J.L.Rogers	1	2	–	15	19	9.50	–	–	1
R.J.Quiney	2	3	–	9	9	3.00	–	–	5
P.M.Siddle	38	52	8	43	670	15.22	–	–	16
M.A.Starc	8	12	4	68*	193	24.12	–	1	3
S.W.Tait	3	5	2	8	20	6.66	–	–	1
M.S.Wade	10	18	4	106	530	37.85	2	2	30/2
D.A.Warner	16	28	2	180	1150	44.23	3	6	15
S.R.Watson	39	71	2	126	2526	36.60	2	19	25
C.L.White	4	7	2	46	146	29.20	–	–	1

AUSTRALIA – BOWLING

	O	M	R	W	Avge	Best	5wI	10wM
M.A.Beer	67.4	13	178	3	59.33	2- 56	–	–
J.M.Bird	63	21	178	11	16.18	4- 41	–	–
M.J.Clarke	382	58	1123	30	37.43	6- 9	2	–
T.A.Copeland	108	34	227	6	37.83	3- 87	–	–
P.J.Cummins	44	8	117	7	16.71	6- 79	1	–
R.J.Harris	385.2	95	1111	47	23.63	6- 47	2	–
J.W.Hastings	39	3	153	1	153.00	1- 51	–	–
M.C.Henriques	17	4	48	1	48.00	1- 48	–	–
B.W.Hilfenhaus	1013	258	2822	99	28.50	5- 75	2	–
M.E.K.Hussey	98	11	306	7	43.71	1- 0	–	–
M.G.Johnson	1870.4	331	6281	205	30.63	8- 61	7	2
S.M.Katich	173.1	21	635	21	30.23	6- 65	1	–
N.M.Lyon	732	152	2206	65	33.93	5- 34	2	–
M.J.North	209.4	37	591	14	42.21	6- 55	1	–
J.L.Pattinson	242	49	794	37	21.45	5- 27	3	–
R.T.Ponting	97.5	24	276	5	55.20	1- 0	–	–
R.J.Quiney	25	12	29	0	–	–	–	–
P.M.Siddle	1358.5	348	4091	142	28.80	6- 54	6	–
M.A.Starc	254.5	44	896	28	32.00	6-154	2	–
S.W.Tait	69	6	302	5	60.40	3- 97	–	–
M.S.Wade	1	1	9	0	–	–	–	–
D.A.Warner	43	1	191	4	47.75	2- 45	–	–
S.R.Watson	651	149	1864	62	30.06	6- 33	3	–
C.L.White	93	8	342	5	68.40	2- 71	–	–

TEST **SOUTH AFRICA – BATTING AND FIELDING**

	M	I	NO	HS	Runs	Avge	100	50	Ct/St
K.J.Abbott	1	1	–	13	13	13.00	–	–	–
H.M.Amla	70	121	10	311*	5785	52.11	19	27	58
M.V.Boucher	146	204	24	125	5515	30.30	5	35	530/23
Z.de Bruyn	3	5	1	83	155	38.75	–	1	–
M.de Lange	2	2	–	9	9	4.50	–	–	1
A.B.de Villiers	85	142	16	278*	6364	50.50	16	32	142/2
F.du Plessis	7	10	2	137	558	69.75	2	2	4
J.P.Duminy	17	26	5	166	789	37.57	2	4	14
D.Elgar	6	8	2	103*	192	32.00	1	–	6
A.J.Hall	21	33	4	163	760	26.20	1	3	16
C.W.Henderson	7	7	–	30	65	9.28	–	–	2
Imran Tahir	11	12	5	29*	88	12.57	–	–	4
J.H.Kallis	161	272	39	224	13045	55.98	44	58	190
R.K.Kleinveldt	4	5	2	17*	27	9.00	–	–	2
N.D.McKenzie	58	94	7	226	3253	37.39	5	16	54
M.Morkel	49	57	9	40	657	13.68	–	–	12
A.N.Petersen	24	43	2	182	1589	38.75	5	5	19
R.J.Peterson	12	15	2	84	320	24.61	–	2	8
V.D.Philander	16	19	3	74	364	22.75	–	2	5
A.G.Prince	66	104	16	162*	3665	41.64	11	11	47
J.A.Rudolph	48	83	9	222*	2622	35.43	6	11	29
G.C.Smith	109	190	12	277	8741	49.10	26	37	157
D.W.Steyn	65	80	18	76	866	13.96	–	1	18

SOUTH AFRICA – BOWLING

	O	M	R	W	Avge	Best	5wI	10wM
K.J.Abbott	28.4	11	68	9	7.55	7- 29	1	–
H.M.Amla	9	0	37	0	–	–	–	–
M.V.Boucher	1.2	0	6	1	6.00	1- 6	–	–
Z.de Bruyn	36	8	92	3	30.66	2- 32	–	–
M.de Lange	74.4	10	277	9	30.77	7- 81	1	–
A.B.de Villiers	33	6	99	2	49.50	2- 49	–	–
F.du Plessis	10	0	60	0	–	–	–	–
J.P.Duminy	145.5	15	510	12	42.50	3- 89	–	–
D.Elgar	3	0	18	0	–	–	–	–
A.J.Hall	500.1	95	1617	45	35.93	3- 1	–	–
C.W.Henderson	327	79	928	22	42.18	4-116	–	–
Imran Tahir	358.3	41	1305	26	50.19	3- 55	–	–
J.H.Kallis	3297	831	9303	287	32.41	6- 54	5	–
R.K.Kleinveldt	111.1	21	422	10	42.20	3- 65	–	–
N.D.McKenzie	15	0	68	0	–	–	–	–
M.Morkel	1607.4	324	5246	175	29.97	6- 23	6	–
A.N.Petersen	19	1	62	1	62.00	1- 2	–	–
R.J.Peterson	310.2	78	1006	31	32.45	5- 33	1	–
V.D.Philander	546.3	132	1525	89	17.13	6- 44	9	2
A.G.Prince	16	1	47	1	47.00	1- 2	–	–
J.A.Rudolph	110.4	13	432	4	108.00	1- 1	–	–
G.C.Smith	236.2	28	885	8	110.62	2-145	–	–
D.W.Steyn	2277.4	471	7523	332	22.65	7- 51	21	5

TEST	WEST INDIES – BATTING AND FIELDING								
	M	I	NO	HS	Runs	Avge	100	50	Ct/St
A.B.Barath	15	28	–	104	657	23.46	1	4	13
C.S.Baugh	21	36	2	68	610	17.94	–	3	43/5
T.L.Best	18	26	4	95	291	13.22	–	1	4
D.Bishoo	11	19	8	26	143	13.00	–	–	8
K.C.Brathwaite	9	17	–	68	363	21.35	–	4	5
D.M.Bravo	21	38	3	195	1637	46.77	4	8	16
G.R.Breese	1	2	–	5	5	2.50	–	–	1
S.Chanderpaul	146	249	42	203*	10696	51.67	27	61	62
C.D.Collymore	30	52	27	16*	197	7.88	–	–	6
N.Deonarine	14	22	2	82	588	29.40	–	4	12
F.H.Edwards	55	88	28	30	394	6.56	–	–	10
K.A.Edwards	9	18	1	121	665	39.11	2	4	7
A.B.Fudadin	3	5	1	55	122	30.50	–	1	4
S.T.Gabriel	1	2	–	13	13	6.50	–	–	–
C.H.Gayle	95	167	8	333	6691	42.08	14	34	88
S.P.Narine	5	5	1	22*	38	9.50	–	–	2
B.P.Nash	21	33	–	114	1103	33.42	2	8	6
V.Permaul	2	2	–	13	23	11.50	–	–	1
K.O.A.Powell	13	25	1	134	784	32.66	3	2	8
D.Ramdin	49	83	10	166	1825	25.00	3	8	144/3
R.Rampaul	18	31	8	40*	335	14.56	–	–	6
K.A.J.Roach	21	35	7	41	291	10.39	–	–	6
D.J.G.Sammy	31	51	1	106	1082	21.64	1	3	49
M.N.Samuels	44	78	6	260	2690	37.36	5	17	19
R.R.Sarwan	87	154	8	291	5842	40.01	15	31	53
S.Shillingford	8	12	2	31*	116	11.60	–	–	4
L.M.P.Simmons	8	16	–	49	278	17.37	–	–	5

WEST INDIES – BOWLING

	O	M	R	W	Avge	Best	5wI	10wM
A.B.Barath	1	0	4	0	–	–	–	–
T.L.Best	463.1	62	1656	46	36.00	6- 40	2	–
D.Bishoo	507.4	75	1582	40	39.55	5- 90	1	–
K.C.Brathwaite	7.4	0	50	1	50.00	1- 43	–	–
G.R.Breese	31.2	3	135	2	67.50	2-108	–	–
S.Chanderpaul	290	50	883	9	98.11	1- 2	–	–
C.D.Collymore	1056.1	245	3004	93	32.30	7- 57	4	1
N.Deonarine	194.5	47	531	19	27.94	4- 37	–	–
F.H.Edwards	1600.2	183	6249	165	37.87	7- 87	12	–
K.A.Edwards	4	0	19	0	–	–	–	–
A.B.Fudadin	5	1	11	0	–	–	–	–
S.T.Gabriel	26.3	3	86	4	21.50	3- 60	–	–
C.H.Gayle	1149.5	224	3024	72	42.00	5- 34	2	–
S.P.Narine	216.3	37	721	15	48.06	5-132	1	–
B.P.Nash	82	13	247	2	123.50	1- 21	–	–
V.Permaul	76	11	253	8	31.62	3- 32	–	–
R.Rampaul	573.2	111	1705	49	34.79	4- 48	–	–
K.A.J.Roach	697.1	133	2271	82	27.69	6- 48	5	1
D.J.G.Sammy	915.4	189	2608	76	34.31	7- 66	4	–
M.N.Samuels	490.3	55	1656	24	69.00	3- 74	–	–
R.R.Sarwan	337	33	1163	23	50.56	4- 37	–	–
S.Shillingford	430	66	1299	29	44.79	6-119	1	1
L.M.P.Simmons	32	1	147	1	147.00	1- 60	–	–

TEST

NEW ZEALAND – BATTING AND FIELDING

	M	I	NO	HS	Runs	Avge	100	50	Ct/St
A.R.Adams	1	2	–	11	18	9.00	–	–	1
B.J.Arnel	6	12	4	8*	45	5.62	–	–	3
T.D.Astle	1	2	–	35	38	19.00	–	–	–
T.A.Boult	10	18	10	33*	133	16.62	–	–	3
D.A.J.Bracewell	15	28	2	43	271	10.42	–	–	5
D.G.Brownlie	9	17	1	109	547	34.18	1	4	9
D.R.Flynn	24	45	5	95	1038	25.95	–	6	10
J.E.C.Franklin	31	46	7	122*	808	20.71	1	2	12
M.R.Gillespie	5	8	1	27	76	10.85	–	–	1
M.J.Guptill	30	57	1	189	1714	30.60	2	12	31
B.B.McCullum	72	126	7	225	4180	35.12	6	25	174/11
H.J.H.Marshall	13	19	2	160	652	38.35	2	2	1
C.S.Martin	71	104	52	12*	123	2.36	–	–	14
C.Munro	1	2	–	15	15	7.50	–	–	–
R.J.Nicol	2	4	–	19	28	7.00	–	–	2
J.S.Patel	19	30	7	27*	276	12.00	–	–	12
J.D.Ryder	18	33	2	201	1269	40.93	3	6	12
T.G.Southee	21	36	5	77*	581	18.74	–	2	8
S.B.Styris	29	48	4	170	1586	36.04	5	6	23
L.R.P.L.Taylor	43	79	4	154*	3268	43.57	8	17	68
C.F.K.van Wyk	9	17	1	71	341	21.31	–	1	23/1
D.L.Vettori	112	173	23	140	4516	30.10	6	23	58
N.Wagner	3	6	–	23	50	8.33	–	–	1
B.J.Watling	10	19	3	102*	528	33.00	1	3	19
K.S.Williamson	20	37	1	135	1090	30.27	3	5	16
R.A.Young	5	10	3	57	169	24.14	–	1	8

NEW ZEALAND – BOWLING

	O	M	R	W	Avge	Best	5wI	10wM
A.R.Adams	31.4	5	105	6	17.50	3- 44	–	–
B.J.Arnel	168	37	566	9	62.88	4- 95	–	–
T.D.Astle	31	6	97	1	97.00	1- 56	–	–
T.A.Boult	285	53	943	30	31.43	4- 42	–	–
D.A.J.Bracewell	440.4	79	1467	46	31.89	6- 40	2	–
D.G.Brownlie	11	0	52	1	52.00	1- 13	–	–
D.R.Flynn	1	1	0	0	–	–	–	–
J.E.C.Franklin	794.3	143	2786	82	33.97	6-119	3	–
M.R.Gillespie	144.4	24	631	22	28.68	6-113	3	–
M.J.Guptill	50.2	3	217	5	43.40	3- 37	–	–
B.B.McCullum	6	1	18	0	–	–	–	–
H.J.H.Marshall	1	0	4	0	–	–	–	–
C.S.Martin	2337.4	486	7878	233	33.81	6- 26	10	1
C.Munro	18	4	40	2	20.00	2- 40	–	–
R.J.Nicol	2.5	1	13	0	–	–	–	–
J.S.Patel	787.1	164	2520	52	48.46	5-110	1	–
J.D.Ryder	82	23	280	5	56.00	2- 7	–	–
T.G.Southee	676.2	134	2278	65	35.04	7- 64	3	–
S.B.Styris	326.4	77	1015	20	50.75	3- 28	–	–
L.R.P.L.Taylor	15	3	43	2	21.50	2- 4	–	–
D.L.Vettori	4778.2	1190	12392	360	34.42	7- 87	20	3
N.Wagner	93	18	344	5	68.80	2- 24	–	–
K.S.Williamson	114.5	10	424	8	53.00	2- 47	–	–

TEST   **INDIA – BATTING AND FIELDING**

	M	I	NO	HS	Runs	Avge	100	50	Ct/St
V.R.Aaron	1	2	1	4	6	6.00	–	–	–
R.Ashwin	13	19	5	103	599	42.78	1	3	2
P.P.Chawla	3	3	–	4	6	2.00	–	–	1
M.S.Dhoni	74	116	13	224	4107	39.87	6	28	203/32
R.S.Dravid	163	284	32	270	13265	52.63	36	63	209
G.Gambhir	54	96	5	206	4021	44.18	9	21	38
Harbhajan Singh	100	141	22	115	2202	18.50	2	9	42
R.A.Jadeja	2	2	–	16	28	14.00	–	–	–
Z.Khan	88	120	23	75	1146	11.81	–	3	19
V.Kohli	15	26	2	116	998	41.58	4	5	19
B.Kumar	1	1	–	38	38	38.00	–	–	1
V.V.S.Laxman	134	225	34	281	8781	45.97	17	56	135
P.P.Ojha	20	23	16	18*	86	12.28	–	–	8
C.A.Pujara	10	17	3	206*	813	58.07	3	1	9
S.K.Raina	17	29	2	120	768	28.44	1	7	22
W.P.Saha	2	4	–	36	74	18.50	–	–	2
V.Sehwag	102	177	6	319	8497	49.69	23	31	88
I.Sharma	48	71	27	31*	448	10.18	–	–	11
S.R.Tendulkar	195	322	33	248*	15739	54.46	51	67	115
R.Vinay Kumar	1	2	–	6	11	5.50	–	–	–
M.Vijay	13	22	–	139	625	28.40	1	2	11
U.T.Yadav	9	11	5	21	36	6.00	–	2	4
Yuvraj Singh	40	62	6	169	1900	33.92	3	11	31

INDIA – BOWLING

	O	M	R	W	Avge	Best	5wI	10wM
V.R.Aaron	32	4	129	3	43.00	3-106	–	–
R.Ashwin	738.1	128	2240	75	29.86	7-103	7	2
P.P.Chawla	82	13	270	7	38.57	4- 69	–	–
M.S.Dhoni	13	1	58	0	–	–	–	–
R.S.Dravid	20	4	39	1	39.00	1- 18	–	–
G.Gambhir	2	0	4	0	–	–	–	–
Harbhajan Singh	4683.3	857	13310	411	32.38	8- 84	25	5
R.A.Jadeja	137	52	260	8	32.50	3- 72	–	–
Z.Khan	2935.2	593	9545	295	32.35	7- 87	10	1
V.Kohli	11	0	35	0	–	–	–	–
B.Kumar	13	1	52	0	–	–	–	–
V.V.S.Laxman	54	12	126	2	63.00	1- 2	–	–
P.P.Ojha	1119.4	262	3004	95	31.62	6- 47	5	–
S.K.Raina	153.3	19	532	13	40.92	2- 1	–	–
V.Sehwag	621.5	74	1894	40	47.35	5-104	1	–
I.Sharma	1564.3	291	5267	137	38.44	6- 55	3	1
S.R.Tendulkar	697.4	82	2459	45	54.64	3- 10	–	–
R.Vinay Kumar	13	0	73	1	73.00	1- 73	–	–
U.T.Yadav	247.3	27	1040	32	32.50	5- 93	1	–
Yuvraj Singh	155.1	14	547	9	60.77	2- 9	–	–

TEST **PAKISTAN – BATTING AND FIELDING**

	M	I	NO	HS	Runs	Avge	100	50	Ct/St
Abdur Rehman	17	22	3	60	289	15.21	–	1	6
Adnan Akmal	16	21	5	61	440	27.50	–	2	47/8
Aizaz Cheema	7	5	5	1*	1	1.00	–	–	1
Asad Shafiq	19	30	3	111	1093	40.48	3	7	16
Azhar Ali	27	50	4	157	1944	42.26	4	14	17
Ehsan Adil	1	2	–	12	21	10.50	–	–	–
Imran Farhat	40	77	2	128	2400	32.00	3	14	40
Junaid Khan	9	10	4	9	36	6.00	–	–	1
Misbah-ul-Haq	39	67	11	161*	2419	43.19	3	18	35
Mohammad Ayub	1	2	–	25	47	23.50	–	–	1
Mohammad Hafeez	32	62	5	196	2002	35.12	5	8	21
Mohammad Irfan	2	4	1	6*	14	4.66	–	–	–
Mohammad Sami	36	56	14	49	487	11.59	–	–	7
Nasir Jamshed	2	4	–	46	51	12.75	–	–	1
Rahat Ali	2	4	2	22	25	12.50	–	–	–
Saeed Ajmal	26	38	10	50	318	11.35	–	1	9
Sarfraz Ahmed	4	8	–	40	89	11.12	–	–	12
Shahid Afridi	27	48	1	156	1716	36.51	5	8	10
Tanvir Ahmed	5	7	2	57	170	34.00	–	1	1
Taufiq Umar	43	81	5	236	2943	38.72	7	14	47
Umar Gul	47	67	9	65*	577	9.94	–	1	11
Younus Khan	82	144	11	313	6749	50.74	21	26	91

PAKISTAN – BOWLING

	O	M	R	W	Avge	Best	5wI	10wM
Abdur Rehman	892.2	202	2301	81	28.40	6- 25	2	–
Aizaz Cheema	200	39	638	20	31.90	4- 24	–	–
Azhar Ali	17	2	67	1	67.00	1- 4	–	–
Ehsan Adil	12.1	2	54	2	27.00	2- 54	–	–
Imran Farhat	71.1	4	284	3	94.66	2- 69	–	–
Junaid Khan	280.3	61	817	29	28.17	5- 38	3	–
Mohammad Hafeez	444.5	81	1122	34	33.00	4- 16	–	–
Mohammad Irfan	52.5	5	201	3	67.00	3- 86	–	–
Mohammad Sami	1249.5	193	4483	85	52.74	5- 36	2	–
Rahat Ali	52.2	2	227	6	37.83	6-127	1	–
Saeed Ajmal	1377	268	3671	133	27.60	7- 55	7	3
Shahid Afridi	532.2	69	1709	48	35.60	5- 52	1	–
Tanvir Ahmed	117.5	20	453	17	26.64	6-120	1	–
Taufiq Umar	13	2	44	0	–	–	–	–
Umar Gul	1599.5	256	5553	163	34.06	6-135	4	–
Younus Khan	127	17	465	9	51.66	2- 23	–	–

TEST **SRI LANKA – BATTING AND FIELDING**

	M	I	NO	HS	Runs	Avge	100	50	Ct/St
L.D.Chandimal	5	10	1	65	365	40.55	–	4	6/1
T.M.Dilshan	85	141	11	193	5255	40.42	15	21	88
R.M.S.Eranga	5	8	3	12	34	6.80	–	–	3
A.N.P.R.Fernando	4	6	1	17*	28	5.60	–	–	–
C.R.D.Fernando	40	47	17	39*	249	8.30	–	–	10
H.M.R.K.B.Herath	45	65	15	80*	704	14.08	–	1	10
D.P.M.D.Jayawardena	138	232	14	374	10806	49.56	31	45	194
H.A.P.W.Jayawardena	52	72	10	154*	1900	30.64	4	4	97/32
H.K.S.R.Kaluhalamulla	12	17	1	39	147	9.18	–	–	1
F.D.M.Karunaratne	4	8	1	85	200	28.57	–	2	2
C.K.B.Kulasekara	1	2	–	15	22	11.00	–	–	–
K.M.D.N.Kulasekara	18	25	1	64	359	14.95	–	1	8
R.A.S.Lakmal	13	18	6	18	77	6.41	–	–	2
A.D.Mathews	31	50	8	105*	1668	39.71	1	11	15
N.T.Paranavitana	32	60	5	111	1792	32.58	2	11	27
N.L.T.C.Perera	6	10	–	75	203	20.30	–	1	1
K.T.G.D.Prasad	12	16	1	47	275	18.33	–	–	5
T.T.Samaraweera	81	132	20	231	5462	48.76	14	30	45
K.C.Sangakkara	115	196	16	287	10045	55.80	30	41	169/20
J.K.Silva	3	6	–	39	84	14.00	–	–	5/1
H.D.R.L.Thirimanne	8	16	1	91	356	23.73	–	2	4
U.W.M.B.C.A.Welagedara	20	28	5	48	191	8.30	–	–	4

SRI LANKA – BOWLING

	O	M	R	W	Avge	Best	5wI	10wM
T.M.Dilshan	505.1	74	1544	36	42.88	4- 10	–	–
R.M.S.Eranga	157.2	23	570	15	38.00	4- 65	–	–
A.N.P.R.Fernando	106	11	473	3	157.66	2-114	–	–
C.R.D.Fernando	1030.1	143	3784	100	37.84	5- 42	3	–
H.M.R.K.B.Herath	1999.3	363	5571	186	29.95	7-157	14	2
D.P.M.D.Jayawardena	92.1	18	297	6	49.50	2- 32	–	–
H.K.S.R.Kaluhalamulla	524.2	70	1613	43	37.51	5- 82	1	–
C.K.B.Kulasekara	28	7	80	1	80.00	1- 65	–	–
K.M.D.N.Kulasekara	496.3	108	1456	41	35.51	4- 21	–	–
R.A.S.Lakmal	335.5	54	1245	20	62.25	3- 55	–	–
A.D.Mathews	249	44	775	11	70.45	2- 60	–	–
N.T.Paranavitana	17	0	86	1	86.00	1- 26	–	–
N.L.T.C.Perera	159	20	653	11	59.36	4- 63	–	–
K.T.G.D.Prasad	303.2	26	1298	22	59.00	3- 82	–	–
T.T.Samaraweera	221.1	36	689	15	45.93	4- 49	–	–
K.C.Sangakkara	13	0	42	0	–	–	–	–
H.D.R.L.Thirimanne	1	0	7	0	–	–	–	–
U.W.M.B.C.A.Welagedara	606.1	108	2186	54	40.48	5- 52	2	–

A.N.P.R.Fernando is also known as N.Pradeep; H.K.S.R.Kaluhalamulla is also known as S.Randiv.

TEST   **ZIMBABWE – BATTING AND FIELDING**

	M	I	NO	HS	Runs	Avge	100	50	Ct/St
R.W.Chakabva	2	4	–	63	108	27.00	–	1	2
A.G.Cremer	7	14	1	26	58	4.46	–	–	3
S.M.Ervine	5	8	–	86	261	32.62	–	3	7
M.W.Goodwin	19	37	4	166*	1414	42.84	3	8	10
K.M.Jarvis	4	7	4	25*	37	12.33	–	–	–
H.Masakadza	19	38	1	119	954	25.78	2	3	8
S.W.Masakadza	1	2	1	21	24	24.00	–	–	–
T.M.K.Mawoyo	4	8	1	163*	314	44.85	1	1	3
C.B.Mpofu	9	17	6	8	27	2.45	–	–	–
F.Mutizwa	1	2	–	18	24	12.00	–	–	–
N.Ncube	1	2	–	14	17	8.50	–	–	1
R.W.Price	21	36	7	36	242	8.34	–	–	4
V.Sibanda	6	12	–	93	320	26.66	–	2	4
T.Taibu	28	54	3	153	1546	30.31	1	12	57/5
B.R.M.Taylor	14	28	1	117	791	29.29	2	5	14
B.V.Vitori	3	5	–	14	33	6.60	–	–	1
M.N.Waller	2	4	1	72*	124	41.33	–	1	1

ZIMBABWE – BOWLING

	O	M	R	W	Avge	Best	5wI	10wM
A.G.Cremer	167	18	707	15	47.13	3- 86	–	–
S.M.Ervine	95	18	388	9	43.11	4-116	–	–
M.W.Goodwin	19.5	3	69	0	–	–	–	–
K.M.Jarvis	140.1	23	506	14	36.14	5- 64	1	–
H.Masakadza	60	16	117	5	23.40	1- 9	–	–
S.W.Masakadza	23	2	102	1	102.00	1-102	–	–
C.B.Mpofu	241.2	43	889	20	44.45	4- 92	–	–
N.Ncube	35	4	121	1	121.00	1- 80	–	–
R.W.Price	1004.3	240	2838	79	35.92	6- 73	5	1
T.Taibu	8	1	27	1	27.00	1- 27	–	–
B.R.M.Taylor	7	0	38	0	–	–	–	–
B.V.Vitori	90	12	334	6	55.66	4- 66	–	–
M.N.Waller	3	0	8	0	–	–	–	–

TEST   **BANGLADESH – BATTING AND FIELDING**

	M	I	NO	HS	Runs	Avge	100	50	Ct/St
Abul Hasan	1	2	1	113	120	120.00	1	–	–
Elias Sunny	3	5	1	20*	38	9.50	–	–	1
Imrul Kayes	16	32	–	75	549	17.15	–	1	16
Junaid Siddique	19	37	–	106	969	26.18	1	7	11
Mahmudullah	14	28	2	115	833	32.03	1	6	12
Mohammad Ashraful	57	111	4	158*	2419	22.60	5	8	24
Mushfiqur Rahim	30	59	4	101	1587	28.85	1	9	46/9
Naeem Islam	8	15	2	108	416	32.00	1	1	2
Nasir Hossain	6	11	–	96	472	42.90	–	4	2
Nazimuddin	3	6	–	78	125	20.83	–	1	1
Nazmul Hossain	2	4	2	8*	16	8.00	–	–	–
Raqibul Hasan	9	18	1	65	336	19.76	–	1	9
Robiul Islam	3	6	2	12	21	5.25	–	–	2
Rubel Hossain	14	25	14	17	103	9.36	–	–	6
Shahadat Hossain	34	64	17	40	476	10.12	–	–	8
Shahriar Nafees	23	46	–	138	1227	26.67	1	7	19
Shakib Al Hasan	28	53	2	144	1835	35.98	2	11	11
Sohag Gazi	2	4	–	19	30	7.50	–	–	2
Suhrawadi Shuvo	1	2	–	15	15	7.50	–	–	–
Tamim Iqbal	26	50	–	151	1835	37.70	4	11	8

BANGLADESH – BOWLING

	O	M	R	W	Avge	Best	5wI	10wM
Abul Hasan	24	0	113	0	–	–	–	–
Elias Sunny	103.5	11	353	12	29.41	6- 94	1	–
Imrul Kayes	2	0	8	0	–	–	–	–
Junaid Siddique	3	0	11	0	–	–	–	–
Mahmudullah	313.5	33	1072	24	44.66	5- 51	1	–
Mohammad Ashraful	269.1	11	1208	20	60.40	2- 42	–	–
Naeem Islam	95.4	8	303	1	303.00	1- 11	–	–
Nasir Hossain	86	13	233	3	77.66	2- 52	–	–
Nazmul Hossain	54.5	10	194	5	38.80	2- 61	–	–
Raqibul Hasan	7	1	17	1	17.00	1- 0	–	–
Robiul Islam	90	10	359	4	89.75	2-106	–	–
Rubel Hossain	407	35	1657	21	78.90	5-166	1	–
Shahadat Hossain	833.2	84	3505	69	50.79	6- 27	4	–
Shakib Al Hasan	1160.3	229	3322	102	32.56	7- 36	9	–
Sohag Gazi	128.5	13	394	12	32.83	6- 74	1	–
Suhrawadi Shuvo	49.3	6	146	4	36.50	3- 73	–	–
Tamim Iqbal	5	0	20	0	–	–	–	–

INTERNATIONAL TEST MATCH RESULTS

Matches completed by 1 March 2013.

	Opponents	Tests	Won by										Tied	Drawn
			E	A	SA	WI	NZ	I	P	SL	Z	B		
England	Australia	326	102	133	–	–	–	–	–	–	–	–	–	91
	South Africa	141	56	–	31	–	–	–	–	–	–	–	–	54
	West Indies	148	45	–	–	53	–	–	–	–	–	–	–	50
	New Zealand	94	45	–	–	–	8	–	–	–	–	–	–	41
	India	107	40	–	–	–	–	20	–	–	–	–	–	47
	Pakistan	74	22	–	–	–	–	–	16	–	–	–	–	36
	Sri Lanka	26	10	–	–	–	–	–	–	7	–	–	–	9
	Zimbabwe	6	3	–	–	–	–	–	–	–	0	–	–	3
	Bangladesh	8	8	–	–	–	–	–	–	–	–	0	–	0
Australia	South Africa	88	–	48	20	–	–	–	–	–	–	–	–	20
	West Indies	111	–	54	–	32	–	–	–	–	–	–	1	24
	New Zealand	52	–	27	–	–	8	–	–	–	–	–	–	17
	India	83	–	38	–	–	–	21	–	–	–	–	1	23
	Pakistan	57	–	28	–	–	–	–	12	–	–	–	–	17
	Sri Lanka	26	–	17	–	–	–	–	–	1	–	–	–	8
	Zimbabwe	3	–	3	–	–	–	–	–	–	0	–	–	0
	Bangladesh	4	–	4	–	–	–	–	–	–	–	0	–	0
South Africa	West Indies	25	–	–	16	3	–	–	–	–	–	–	–	6
	New Zealand	40	–	–	23	–	4	–	–	–	–	–	–	13
	India	27	–	–	12	–	–	7	–	–	–	–	–	8
	Pakistan	21	–	–	11	–	–	–	3	–	–	–	–	7
	Sri Lanka	20	–	–	10	–	–	–	–	5	–	–	–	5
	Zimbabwe	7	–	–	6	–	–	–	–	–	0	–	–	1
	Bangladesh	8	–	–	8	–	–	–	–	–	–	0	–	0
West Indies	New Zealand	39	–	–	–	12	9	–	–	–	–	–	–	18
	India	88	–	–	–	30	–	14	–	–	–	–	–	44
	Pakistan	46	–	–	–	15	–	–	16	–	–	–	–	15
	Sri Lanka	15	–	–	–	3	–	–	–	6	–	–	–	6
	Zimbabwe	6	–	–	–	4	–	–	–	–	0	–	–	2
	Bangladesh	10	–	–	–	6	–	–	–	–	–	2	–	2
New Zealand	India	52	–	–	–	–	9	18	–	–	–	–	–	25
	Pakistan	50	–	–	–	–	7	–	23	–	–	–	–	20
	Sri Lanka	28	–	–	–	–	10	–	–	8	–	–	–	10
	Zimbabwe	15	–	–	–	–	9	–	–	–	0	–	–	6
	Bangladesh	9	–	–	–	–	8	–	–	–	–	0	–	1
India	Pakistan	59	–	–	–	–	–	9	12	–	–	–	–	38
	Sri Lanka	35	–	–	–	–	–	14	–	6	–	–	–	15
	Zimbabwe	11	–	–	–	–	–	7	–	–	2	–	–	1
	Bangladesh	7	–	–	–	–	–	6	–	–	–	0	–	1
Pakistan	Sri Lanka	43	–	–	–	–	–	–	16	10	–	–	–	17
	Zimbabwe	15	–	–	–	–	–	–	9	–	2	–	–	4
	Bangladesh	8	–	–	–	–	–	–	8	–	–	0	–	0
Sri Lanka	Zimbabwe	15	–	–	–	–	–	–	–	10	0	–	–	5
	Bangladesh	12	–	–	–	–	–	–	–	12	–	0	–	0
Zimbabwe	Bangladesh	9	–	–	–	–	–	–	–	–	5	1	–	3
		2074	331	352	137	158	72	116	115	65	9	3	2	714

	Tests	Won	Lost	Drawn	Tied	Toss Won
England	930	331	268	331	–	448
Australia	750	352	196	200	2	379
South Africa	377	137	126	114	–	183
West Indies	488	158	162	167	1	255
New Zealand	379	72	156	151	–	194
India	469	116	149	203	1	235
Pakistan	373	115	104	154	–	174
Sri Lanka	220	65	80	75	–	118
Zimbabwe	87	9	52	26	–	49
Bangladesh	75	3	65	7	–	39

INTERNATIONAL TEST CRICKET RECORDS

(To 1 March 2013)

TEAM RECORDS

HIGHEST INNINGS TOTALS

952-6d	Sri Lanka v India	Colombo (RPS)	1997-98
903-7d	England v Australia	The Oval	1938
849	England v West Indies	Kingston	1929-30
790-3d	West Indies v Pakistan	Kingston	1957-58
765-6d	Pakistan v Sri Lanka	Karachi	2008-09
760-7d	Sri Lanka v India	Ahmedabad	2009-10
758-8d	Australia v West Indies	Kingston	1954-55
756-5d	Sri Lanka v South Africa	Colombo (SSC)	2006
751-5d	West Indies v England	St John's	2003-04
749-9d	West Indies v England	Bridgetown	2008-09
747	West Indies v South Africa	St John's	2004-05
735-6d	Australia v Zimbabwe	Perth	2003-04
729-6d	Australia v England	Lord's	1930
726-9d	India v Sri Lanka	Mumbai	2009-10
713-3d	Sri Lanka v Zimbabwe	Bulawayo	2003-04
710-7d	England v India	Birmingham	2011
708	Pakistan v England	The Oval	1987
707	India v Sri Lanka	Colombo (SSC)	2010
705-7d	India v Australia	Sydney	2003-04
701	Australia v England	The Oval	1934
699-5	Pakistan v India	Lahore	1989-90
695	Australia v England	The Oval	1930
692-8d	West Indies v England	The Oval	1995
687-8d	West Indies v England	The Oval	1976
682-6d	South Africa v England	Lord's	2003
681-8d	West Indies v England	Port-of-Spain	1953-54
679-7d	Pakistan v India	Lahore	2005-06
676-7	India v Sri Lanka	Kanpur	1986-87
675-5d	India v Pakistan	Multan	2003-04
674-6	Pakistan v India	Faisalabad	1984-85
674-6d	Australia v England	Cardiff	2009
674	Australia v India	Adelaide	1947-48
671-4	New Zealand v Sri Lanka	Wellington	1990-91
668	Australia v West Indies	Bridgetown	1954-55
664	India v England	The Oval	2007

660-5d	West Indies v New Zealand	Wellington	1994-95
659-4d	Australia v India	Sydney	2011-12
659-8d	Australia v England	Sydney	1946-47
658-8d	England v Australia	Nottingham	1938
658-9d	South Africa v West Indies	Durban	2003-04
657-7d	India v Australia	Calcutta	2000-01
657-8d	Pakistan v West Indies	Bridgetown	1957-58
656-8d	Australia v England	Manchester	1964
654-5	England v South Africa	Durban	1938-39
653-4d	England v India	Lord's	1990
653-4d	Australia v England	Leeds	1993
652-7d	England v India	Madras	1984-85
652-7d	Australia v South Africa	Johannesburg	2001-02
652-8d	West Indies v England	Lord's	1973
652	Pakistan v India	Faisalabad	1982-83
651	South Africa v Australia	Cape Town	2008-09
650-6d	Australia v West Indies	Bridgetown	1964-65

The highest for Zimbabwe is 563-9d (v WI, Harare, 2001), and for Bangladesh 556 (v WI, Mirpur, 2012-13).

LOWEST INNINGS TOTALS

† One batsman absent

26	New Zealand v England	Auckland	1954-55
30	South Africa v England	Port Elizabeth	1895-96
30	South Africa v England	Birmingham	1924
35	South Africa v England	Cape Town	1898-99
36	Australia v England	Birmingham	1902
36	South Africa v Australia	Melbourne	1931-32
42	Australia v England	Sydney	1887-88
42	New Zealand v Australia	Wellington	1945-46
42†	India v England	Lord's	1974
43	South Africa v England	Cape Town	1888-89
44	Australia v England	The Oval	1896
45	England v Australia	Sydney	1886-87
45	South Africa v Australia	Melbourne	1931-32
45	New Zealand v South Africa	Cape Town	2012-13
46	England v West Indies	Port-of-Spain	1993-94
47	South Africa v England	Cape Town	1888-89
47	New Zealand v England	Lord's	1958
47	West Indies v England	Kingston	2003-04
47	Australia v South Africa	Cape Town	2011-12
49	Pakistan v South Africa	Johannesburg	2012-13

The lowest for Sri Lanka is 71 (v P, Kandy, 1994-95), for Zimbabwe 51 (v NZ, Napier, 2011-12), and for Bangladesh 62 (v SL, Colombo PPS, 2006-07).

BATTING RECORDS

5000 RUNS IN TESTS

Runs			M	I	NO	HS	Avge	100	50
15739	S.R.Tendulkar	I	195	322	33	248*	54.46	51	67
13378	R.T.Ponting	A	168	287	29	257	51.85	41	62
13288	R.S.Dravid	I/ICC	164	286	32	270	52.31	36	63
13128	J.H.Kallis	SA/ICC	162	274	40	224	56.10	44	58
11953	B.C.Lara	WI/ICC	131	232	6	400*	52.88	34	48
11174	A.R.Border	A	156	265	44	205	50.56	27	63
10927	S.R.Waugh	A	168	260	46	200	51.06	32	50

Runs			M	I	NO	HS	Avge	100	50
10806	D.P.M.D.Jayawardena	SL	138	232	14	374	49.56	31	45
10696	S.Chanderpaul	WI	146	249	42	203*	51.67	27	61
10122	S.M.Gavaskar	I	125	214	16	236*	51.12	34	45
10045	K.C.Sangakkara	SL	115	196	16	287	55.80	30	41
8900	G.A.Gooch	E	118	215	6	333	42.58	20	46
8832	Javed Miandad	P	124	189	21	280*	52.57	23	43
8830	Inzamam-ul-Haq	P/ICC	120	200	22	329	49.60	25	46
8781	V.V.S.Laxman	I	134	225	34	281	45.97	17	56
8753	G.C.Smith	SA/ICC	110	192	12	277	48.62	26	37
8625	M.L.Hayden	A	103	184	14	380	50.73	30	29
8580	V.Sehwag	I/ICC	103	179	6	319	49.59	23	32
8540	I.V.A.Richards	WI	121	182	12	291	50.23	24	45
8463	A.J.Stewart	E	133	235	21	190	39.54	15	45
8231	D.I.Gower	E	117	204	18	215	44.25	18	39
8114	G.Boycott	E	108	193	23	246*	47.72	22	42
8032	G.St A.Sobers	WI	93	160	21	365*	57.78	26	30
8029	M.E.Waugh	A	128	209	17	153*	41.81	20	47
7728	M.A.Atherton	E	115	212	7	185*	37.70	16	46
7696	J.L.Langer	A	105	182	12	250	45.27	23	30
7624	M.C.Cowdrey	E	114	188	15	182	44.06	22	38
7558	C.G.Greenidge	WI	108	185	16	226	44.72	19	34
7530	Mohammad Yousuf	P	90	156	12	223	52.29	24	33
7525	M.A.Taylor	A	104	186	13	334*	43.49	19	40
7515	C.H.Lloyd	WI	110	175	14	242*	46.67	19	39
7487	D.L.Haynes	WI	116	202	25	184	42.29	18	39
7422	D.C.Boon	A	107	190	20	200	43.65	21	32
7414	K.P.Pietersen	E	92	158	8	227	49.42	22	29
7289	G.Kirsten	SA	101	176	15	275	45.27	21	34
7249	W.R.Hammond	E	85	140	16	336*	58.45	22	24
7212	S.C.Ganguly	I	113	188	17	239	42.17	16	35
7172	S.P.Fleming	NZ	111	189	10	274*	40.06	9	46
7150	M.J.Clarke	A	90	150	15	329*	52.96	23	25
7117	A.N.Cook	E	87	154	10	294	49.42	23	29
7110	G.S.Chappell	A	87	151	19	247*	53.86	24	31
7037	A.J.Strauss	E	100	178	6	177	40.91	21	27
6996	D.G.Bradman	A	52	80	10	334	99.94	29	13
6973	S.T.Jayasuriya	SL	110	188	14	340	40.07	14	31
6971	L.Hutton	E	79	138	15	364	56.67	19	33
6868	D.B.Vengsarkar	I	116	185	22	166	42.13	17	35
6806	K.F.Barrington	E	82	131	15	256	58.67	20	35
6749	Younus Khan	P	82	144	11	313	50.74	21	26
6744	G.P.Thorpe	E	100	179	28	200*	44.66	16	39
6691	C.H.Gayle	WI	95	167	8	333	42.04	14	34
6364	A.B.de Villiers	SA	85	142	16	278*	50.50	16	32
6361	P.A.de Silva	SL	93	159	11	267	42.97	20	22
6235	M.E.K.Hussey	A	79	137	16	195	51.52	19	29
6227	R.B.Kanhai	WI	79	137	6	256	47.53	15	28
6215	M.Azharuddin	I	99	147	9	199	45.03	22	21
6167	H.H.Gibbs	SA	90	154	7	228	41.95	14	26
6149	R.N.Harvey	A	79	137	10	205	48.41	21	24
6080	G.R.Viswanath	I	91	155	10	222	41.93	14	35
5949	R.B.Richardson	WI	86	146	12	194	44.39	16	27
5842	R.R.Sarwan	WI	87	154	8	291	40.01	15	31
5825	M.E.Trescothick	E	76	143	10	219	43.79	14	29
5807	D.C.S.Compton	E	78	131	15	278	50.06	17	28
5785	H.M.Amla	SA	70	121	10	311*	52.11	19	27

72

Runs			M	I	NO	HS	Avge	100	50
5768	Salim Malik	P	103	154	22	237	43.69	15	29
5764	N.Hussain	E	96	171	16	207	37.19	14	33
5762	C.L.Hooper	WI	102	173	15	233	36.46	13	27
5719	M.P.Vaughan	E	82	147	9	197	41.44	18	18
5699	I.R.Bell	E	83	141	19	235	46.71	17	34
5570	A.C.Gilchrist	A	96	137	20	204*	47.60	17	26
5515	M.V.Boucher	SA/ICC	147	206	24	125	30.30	5	35
5502	M.S.Atapattu	SL	90	156	15	249	39.02	16	17
5462	T.T.Samaraweera	SL	81	132	20	231	48.76	14	30
5444	M.D.Crowe	NZ	77	131	11	299	45.36	17	18
5410	J.B.Hobbs	E	61	102	7	211	56.94	15	28
5357	K.D.Walters	A	74	125	14	250	48.26	15	33
5345	I.M.Chappell	A	75	136	10	196	42.42	14	26
5334	J.G.Wright	NZ	82	148	7	185	37.82	12	23
5312	M.J.Slater	A	74	131	7	219	42.84	14	21
5255	T.M.Dilshan	SL	85	141	11	193	40.42	15	21
5248	Kapil Dev	I	131	184	15	163	31.05	8	27
5234	W.M.Lawry	A	67	123	12	210	47.15	13	27
5200	I.T.Botham	E	102	161	6	208	33.54	14	22
5138	J.H.Edrich	E	77	127	9	310*	43.54	12	24
5105	A.Ranatunga	SL	93	155	12	135*	35.69	4	38
5062	Zaheer Abbas	P	78	124	11	274	44.79	12	20

The most for Zimbabwe is 4794 (112 innings) by A.Flower, and for Bangladesh 3026 by Habibul Bashar (99 innings).

750 RUNS IN A SERIES

Runs			Series	M	I	NO	HS	Avge	100	50
974	D.G.Bradman	A v E	1930	5	7	–	334	139.14	4	–
905	W.R.Hammond	E v A	1928-29	5	9	1	251	113.12	4	–
839	M.A.Taylor	A v E	1989	6	11	1	219	83.90	2	5
834	R.N.Harvey	A v SA	1952-53	5	9	–	205	92.66	4	3
829	I.V.A.Richards	WI v E	1976	4	7	–	291	118.42	3	2
827	C.L.Walcott	WI v A	1954-55	5	10	–	155	82.70	5	2
824	G.St A.Sobers	WI v P	1957-58	5	8	2	365*	137.33	3	3
810	D.G.Bradman	A v E	1936-37	5	9	–	270	90.00	3	1
806	D.G.Bradman	A v SA	1931-32	5	5	1	299*	201.50	4	–
798	B.C.Lara	WI v E	1993-94	5	8	–	375	99.75	2	2
779	E.de C.Weekes	WI v I	1948-49	5	7	–	194	111.28	4	2
774	S.M.Gavaskar	I v WI	1970-71	4	8	3	220	154.80	4	3
766	A.N.Cook	E v A	2010-11	5	7	1	235*	127.66	3	2
765	B.C.Lara	WI v E	1995	6	10	1	179	85.00	3	3
761	Mudassar Nazar	P v I	1982-83	5	8	2	231	126.83	4	1
758	D.G.Bradman	A v E	1934	5	8	–	304	94.75	2	1
753	D.C.S.Compton	A v SA	1947	5	8	–	208	94.12	4	2
752	G.A.Gooch	E v I	1990	3	6	–	333	125.33	3	2

HIGHEST INDIVIDUAL INNINGS

400*	B.C.Lara	WI v E	St John's	2003-04
380	M.L.Hayden	A v Z	Perth	2003-04
375	B.C.Lara	WI v E	St John's	1993-94
374	D.P.M.D.Jayawardena	SL v SA	Colombo (SSC)	2006
365*	G.St A.Sobers	WI v P	Kingston	1957-58
364	L.Hutton	E v A	The Oval	1938
340	S.T.Jayasuriya	SL v I	Colombo (RPS)	1997-98
337	Hanif Mohammed	P v WI	Bridgetown	1957-58
336*	W.R.Hammond	E v NZ	Auckland	1932-33

334*	M.A.Taylor	A v P	Peshawar	1998-99
334	D.G.Bradman	A v E	Leeds	1930
333	G.A.Gooch	E v I	Lord's	1990
333	C.H.Gayle	WI v SL	Galle	2010-11
329*	M.J.Clarke	A v I	Sydney	2011-12
329	Inzamam-ul-Haq	P v NZ	Lahore	2001-02
325	A.Sandham	E v WI	Kingston	1929-30
319	V.Sehwag	I v SA	Chennai	2007-08
317	C.H.Gayle	WI v SA	St John's	2004-05
313	Younus Khan	P v SL	Karachi	2008-09
311*	H.M.Amla	SA v E	The Oval	2012
311	R.B.Simpson	A v E	Manchester	1964
310*	J.H.Edrich	E v NZ	Leeds	1965
309	V.Sehwag	I v P	Multan	2003-04
307	R.M.Cowper	A v E	Melbourne	1965-66
304	D.G.Bradman	A v E	Leeds	1934
302	L.G.Rowe	WI v E	Bridgetown	1973-74
299*	D.G.Bradman	A v SA	Adelaide	1931-32
299	M.D.Crowe	NZ v SL	Wellington	1990-91
294	A.N.Cook	E v I	Birmingham	2011
293	V.Sehwag	I v SL	Mumbai	2009-10
291	I.V.A.Richards	WI v E	The Oval	1976
291	R.R.Sarwan	WI v E	Bridgetown	2008-09
287	R.E.Foster	E v A	Sydney	1903-04
287	K.C.Sangakkara	SL v SA	Colombo (SSC)	2006
285*	P.B.H.May	E v WI	Birmingham	1957
281	V.V.S.Laxman	I v A	Calcutta	2000-01
280*	Javed Miandad	P v I	Hyderabad	1982-83
278*	A.B.de Villiers	SA v P	Abu Dhabi	2010-11
278	D.C.S.Compton	E v P	Nottingham	1954
277	B.C.Lara	WI v A	Sydney	1992-93
277	G.C.Smith	SA v E	Birmingham	2003
275*	D.J.Cullinan	SA v NZ	Auckland	1998-99
275	G.Kirsten	SA v E	Durban	1999-00
275	D.P.M.D.Jayawardena	SL v I	Ahmedabad	2009-10
274*	S.P.Fleming	NZ v SL	Colombo (SSC)	2002-03
274	R.G.Pollock	SA v A	Durban	1969-70
274	Zaheer Abbas	P v E	Birmingham	1971
271	Javed Miandad	P v NZ	Auckland	1988-89
270*	G.A.Headley	WI v E	Kingston	1934-35
270	D.G.Bradman	A v E	Melbourne	1936-37
270	R.S.Dravid	I v P	Rawalpindi	2003-04
270	K.C.Sangakkara	SL v Z	Bulawayo	2003-04
268	G.N.Yallop	A v P	Melbourne	1983-84
267*	B.A.Young	NZ v SL	Dunedin	1996-97
267	P.A.de Silva	SL v NZ	Wellington	1990-91
267	Younus Khan	P v I	Bangalore	2004-05
266	W.H.Ponsford	A v E	The Oval	1934
266	D.L.Houghton	Z v SL	Bulawayo	1994-95
262*	D.L.Amiss	E v WI	Kingston	1973-74
262	S.P.Fleming	NZ v SA	Cape Town	2005-06
261*	R.R.Sarwan	WI v B	Kingston	2004
261	F.M.M.Worrell	WI v E	Nottingham	1950
260	C.C.Hunte	WI v P	Kingston	1957-58
260	Javed Miandad	P v E	The Oval	1987
260	M.N.Samuels	WI v B	Khulna	2012-13
259*	M.J.Clarke	A v SA	Brisbane	2012-13

259	G.M.Turner	NZ v WI	Georgetown	1971-72
259	G.C.Smith	SA v E	Lord's	2003
258	T.W.Graveney	E v WI	Nottingham	1957
258	S.M.Nurse	WI v NZ	Christchurch	1968-69
257*	Wasim Akram	P v Z	Sheikhupura	1996-97
257	R.T.Ponting	A v I	Melbourne	2003-04
256	R.B.Kanhai	WI v I	Calcutta	1958-59
256	K.F.Barrington	E v A	Manchester	1964
255*	D.J.McGlew	SA v NZ	Wellington	1952-53
254	D.G.Bradman	A v E	Lord's	1930
254	V.Sehwag	I v P	Lahore	2005-06
253*	H.M.Amla	SA v I	Nagpur	2009-10
253	S.T.Jayasuriya	SL v P	Faisalabad	2004-05
251	W.R.Hammond	E v A	Sydney	1928-29
250	K.D.Walters	A v NZ	Christchurch	1976-77
250	S.F.A.F.Bacchus	WI v I	Kanpur	1978-79
250	J.L.Langer	A v E	Melbourne	2002-03

The highest for Bangladesh is 158* by Mohammad Ashraful (v I, Chittagong, 2004-05).

20 HUNDREDS

		200	Inn	E	A	SA	WI	NZ	I	P	SL	Z	B
51	S.R.Tendulkar	I	6	322	7	11	7	3	4	–	2	9	3	5
44	J.H.Kallis	SA	2	274	8	5	–	8	6	6	6	1	3	1
41	R.T.Ponting	A	6	287	8	–	8	7	2	8	5	1	1	1
36	R.S.Dravid	I	5	286	7	2	2	5	6	–	5	3	3	3
34	S.M.Gavaskar	I	4	214	4	8	–	13	2	–	5	2	–	–
34	B.C.Lara	WI	9	232	7	9	4	–	1	2	4	5	1	1
32	S.R.Waugh	A	1	260	10	–	2	7	2	2	3	3	1	2
31	D.P.M.D.Jayawardena	SL	6	232	8	2	5	1	3	6	1	–	1	4
30	M.L.Hayden †	A	2	184	5	–	6	5	1	6	1	3	2	–
30	K.C.Sangakkara	SL	8	196	2	1	3	3	3	5	9	–	2	2
29	D.G.Bradman	A	12	80	19	–	4	2	–	4	–	–	–	–
27	S.Chanderpaul	WI	2	249	5	5	5	–	3	1	4	1	–	3
27	A.R.Border	A	2	265	8	–	–	3	5	4	6	1	–	–
26	G.St A.Sobers	WI	2	160	10	4	–	–	1	8	3	–	–	–
26	G.C.Smith	SA	4	192	7	3	–	7	2	–	3	–	1	3
25	Inzamam-ul-Haq	P	2	200	5	1	–	4	3	3	–	–	5	2
24	G.S.Chappell	A	4	151	9	–	–	5	3	1	6	–	–	–
24	Mohammad Yousuf	P	4	156	6	1	–	7	1	4	–	1	3	2
24	I.V.A.Richards	WI	3	182	8	5	–	–	1	8	2	–	–	–
23	M.J.Clarke	A	4	150	4	–	4	4	–	6	1	3	–	–
23	A.N.Cook	E	2	154	–	4	2	4	–	5	3	3	–	2
23	V.Sehwag	I	6	179	2	3	5	2	2	–	4	5	–	–
23	J.L.Langer	A	3	182	5	–	2	3	4	4	2	–	–	–
23	Javed Miandad	P	6	189	2	6	–	2	7	5	–	1	1	–
22	W.R.Hammond	E	7	140	–	9	6	1	4	2	–	–	–	–
22	M.Azharuddin	I	–	147	6	2	4	–	2	3	5	1	–	–
22	K.P.Pietersen	E	3	158	–	3	3	3	2	6	2	1	–	–
22	M.C.Cowdrey	E	–	188	–	5	3	6	2	3	3	–	–	–
22	G.Boycott	E	1	193	–	7	1	5	2	4	3	–	–	–
22	R.N.Harvey	A	2	137	6	–	8	3	–	4	–	–	–	–
21	Younus Khan	P	3	144	2	–	4	2	1	5	–	5	–	2
21	G.Kirsten	SA	3	176	5	2	–	3	3	2	2	1	1	2
21	A.J.Strauss	E	–	178	–	4	3	6	3	3	2	–	–	–
21	D.C.Boon	A	1	190	7	–	3	3	6	1	1	–	–	–

75

			200	Inn	E	A	SA	WI	NZ	I	P	SL	Z	B
								Opponents						
20	K.F.Barrington	E	1	131	–	5	2	3	3	3	4	–	–	–
20	P.A.de Silva	SL	2	159	2	1	–	–	2	5	8	–	1	1
20	M.E.Waugh	A	–	209	6	–	4	4	1	1	3	1	–	–
20	G.A.Gooch	E	2	215	–	4	–	5	4	5	1	1	–	–

† Includes century scored for Australia v ICC in 2005-06.

The most for New Zealand is 17 by M.D.Crowe (131 innings), for Zimbabwe 12 by A.Flower (112), and for Bangladesh 5 by Mohammad Ashraful (107 innings).

The most double hundreds by batsmen not included above are 6 by M.S.Atapattu (16 hundreds for Sri Lanka), 4 by L.Hutton (19 for England), 4 by C.G.Greenidge (19 for West Indies), and 4 by Zaheer Abbas (12 for Pakistan).

HIGHEST PARTNERSHIP FOR EACH WICKET

1st	415	N.D.McKenzie/G.C.Smith	SA v B	Chittagong	2007-08
2nd	576	S.T.Jayasuriya/R.S.Mahanama	SL v I	Colombo (RPS)	1997-98
3rd	624	K.C.Sangakkara/D.P.M.D.Jayawardena	SL v SA	Colombo (SSC)	2006
4th	437	D.P.M.D.Jayawardena/T.T.Samaraweera	SL v P	Karachi	2008-09
5th	405	S.G.Barnes/D.G.Bradman	A v E	Sydney	1946-47
6th	351	D.P.M.D.Jayawardena/ H.A.P.W.Jayawardena	SL v I	Ahmedabad	2009-10
7th	347	D.St E.Atkinson/C.C.Depeiza	WI v A	Bridgetown	1954-55
8th	332	I.J.L.Trott/S.C.J.Broad	E v P	Lord's	2010
9th	195	M.V.Boucher/P.L.Symcox	SA v P	Johannesburg	1997-98
10th	151	B.F.Hastings/R.O.Collinge	NZ v P	Auckland	1972-73
	151	Azhar Mahmood/MUSHTAQ Ahmed	P v SA	Rawalpindi	1997-98

BOWLING RECORDS
200 WICKETS IN TESTS

Wkts			M	Balls	Runs	Avge	5 wI	10 wM
800	M.Muralitharan	SL/ICC	133	44039	18180	22.72	67	22
708	S.K.Warne	A	145	40705	17995	25.41	37	10
619	A.Kumble	I	132	40850	18355	29.65	35	8
563	G.D.McGrath	A	124	29248	12186	21.64	29	3
519	C.A.Walsh	WI	132	30019	12688	24.44	22	3
434	Kapil Dev	I	131	27740	12867	29.64	23	2
431	R.J.Hadlee	NZ	86	21918	9612	22.30	36	9
421	S.M.Pollock	SA	108	24453	9733	23.11	16	1
414	Wasim Akram	P	104	22627	9779	23.62	25	5
411	Harbhajan Singh	I	100	28101	13310	32.38	25	5
405	C.E.L.Ambrose	WI	98	22104	8500	20.98	22	3
390	M.Ntini	SA	101	20834	11242	28.82	18	4
383	I.T.Botham	E	102	21815	10878	28.40	27	4
376	M.D.Marshall	WI	81	17584	7876	20.94	22	4
373	Waqar Younis	P	87	16224	8788	23.56	22	5
362	Imran Khan	P	88	19458	8258	22.81	23	6
360	D.L.Vettori	NZ/ICC	112	28670	12392	34.42	20	3
355	D.K.Lillee	A	70	18467	8493	23.92	23	7
355	W.P.J.U.C.Vaas	SL	111	23438	10501	29.58	12	2
332	D.W.Steyn	SA	65	13666	7523	22.65	21	5
330	A.A.Donald	SA	72	15519	7344	22.25	20	3
325	R.G.D.Willis	E	90	17357	8190	25.20	16	–
310	B.Lee	A	76	16531	9554	30.81	10	–
309	L.R.Gibbs	WI	79	27115	8989	29.09	18	2
307	F.S.Trueman	E	67	15178	6625	21.57	17	3
297	D.L.Underwood	E	86	21862	7674	25.83	17	6
295	Z.Khan	I	88	17612	9545	32.35	10	1
291	C.J.McDermott	A	71	16586	8332	28.63	14	2
288	J.M.Anderson	E	77	16943	8754	30.39	12	1
288	J.H.Kallis	SA/ICC	162	19842	9341	32.43	5	–

Wkts			M	Balls	Runs	Avge	5 wI	10 wM
266	B.S.Bedi	I	67	21364	7637	28.71	14	1
261	Danish Kaneria	P	61	17697	9082	34.79	15	2
259	J.Garner	WI	58	13169	5433	20.97	7	–
259	J.N.Gillespie	A	71	14234	6770	26.13	8	–
252	J.B.Statham	E	70	16056	6261	24.84	9	1
249	M.A.Holding	WI	60	12680	5898	23.68	13	2
248	R.Benaud	A	63	19108	6704	27.03	16	1
248	M.J.Hoggard	E	67	13909	7564	30.50	7	1
246	G.D.McKenzie	A	60	17681	7328	29.78	16	3
242	B.S.Chandrasekhar	I	58	15963	7199	29.74	16	2
236	A.V.Bedser	E	51	15918	5876	24.89	15	5
236	J.Srinath	I	67	15104	7196	30.49	10	1
236	Abdul Qadir	P	67	17126	7742	32.80	15	5
235	G.St A.Sobers	WI	93	21599	7999	34.03	6	–
234	A.R.Caddick	E	62	13558	6999	29.91	13	1
233	C.S.Martin	NZ	71	14026	7878	33.81	10	1
229	D.Gough	E	58	11821	6503	28.39	9	–
228	R.R.Lindwall	A	61	13650	5251	23.03	12	–
226	S.J.Harmison	E/ICC	63	13375	7192	31.82	8	1
226	A.Flintoff	E/ICC	79	14951	7410	32.78	3	–
218	C.L.Cairns	NZ	62	11698	6410	29.40	13	1
216	C.V.Grimmett	A	37	14513	5231	24.21	21	7
216	H.H.Streak	Z	65	13559	6079	28.14	7	–
212	M.G.Hughes	A	53	12285	6017	28.38	7	1
212	G.P.Swann	E	50	12709	6176	29.13	14	2
208	S.C.G.MacGill	A	44	11237	6038	29.02	12	2
208	Saqlain Mushtaq	P	49	14070	6206	29.83	13	3
205	M.G.Johnson	A	50	11224	6281	30.63	7	2
202	A.M.E.Roberts	WI	47	11136	5174	25.61	11	2
202	J.A.Snow	E	49	12021	5387	26.66	8	1
200	J.R.Thomson	A	51	10535	5601	28.00	8	–

The most for Bangladesh is 102 in 28 Tests by Shakib Al Hasan.

35 OR MORE WICKETS IN A SERIES

Wkts			Series	M	Balls	Runs	Avge	5 wI	10 wM
49	S.F.Barnes	E v SA	1913-14	4	1356	536	10.93	7	3
46	J.C.Laker	E v A	1956	5	1703	442	9.60	4	2
44	C.V.Grimmett	A v SA	1935-36	5	2077	642	14.59	5	3
42	T.M.Alderman	A v E	1981	6	1950	893	21.26	4	–
41	R.M.Hogg	A v E	1978-79	6	1740	527	12.85	5	2
41	T.M.Alderman	A v E	1989	6	1616	712	17.36	6	1
40	Imran Khan	P v I	1982-83	6	1339	558	13.95	4	2
40	S.K.Warne	A v E	2005	5	1517	797	19.92	3	2
39	A.V.Bedser	E v A	1953	5	1591	682	17.48	5	1
39	D.K.Lillee	A v E	1981	6	1870	870	22.30	2	1
38	M.W.Tate	E v A	1924-25	5	2528	881	23.18	5	1
37	W.J.Whitty	A v SA	1910-11	5	1395	632	17.08	2	–
37	H.J.Tayfield	SA v E	1956-57	5	2280	636	17.18	4	1
36	A.E.E.Vogler	SA v E	1909-10	5	1349	783	21.75	4	1
36	A.A.Mailey	A v E	1920-21	5	1465	946	26.27	4	2
36	G.D.McGrath	A v E	1997	6	1499	701	19.47	2	–
35	G.A.Lohmann	E v SA	1895-96	3	520	203	5.80	4	2
35	B.S.Chandrasekhar	I v E	1972-73	5	1747	662	18.91	4	–
35	M.D.Marshall	WI v E	1988	5	1219	443	12.65	3	1

The most for New Zealand is 33 by R.J.Hadlee (3 Tests v A, 1985-86), for Sri Lanka 30 by M.Muralitharan (3 Tests v Z, 2001-02), for Zimbabwe 22 by H.H.Streak (3 Tests v P, 1994-95), and for Bangladesh 18 by Enamul Haque II (2 Tests v Z, 2004-05).

15 OR MORE WICKETS IN A TEST († On debut)

19- 90	J.C.Laker	E v A	Manchester	1956
17-159	S.F.Barnes	E v SA	Johannesburg	1913-14
16-136†	N.D.Hirwani	I v WI	Madras	1987-88
16-137†	R.A.L.Massie	A v E	Lord's	1972
16-220	M.Muralitharan	SL v E	The Oval	1998
15- 28	J.Briggs	E v SA	Cape Town	1888-89
15- 45	G.A.Lohmann	E v SA	Port Elizabeth	1895-96
15- 99	C.Blythe	E v SA	Leeds	1907
15-104	H.Verity	E v A	Lord's	1934
15-123	R.J.Hadlee	NZ v A	Brisbane	1985-86
15-124	W.Rhodes	E v A	Melbourne	1903-04
15-217	Harbhajan Singh	I v A	Madras	2000-01

The best analysis for South Africa is 13-132 by M.Ntini (v WI, Port-of-Spain, 2004-05), for West Indies 14-149 by M.A.Holding (v E, The Oval, 1976), for Pakistan 14-116 by Imran Khan (v SL, Lahore, 1981-82), for Zimbabwe 11-257 by A.G.Huckle (v NZ, Bulawayo, 1997-98), and for Bangladesh 12-200 by Enamul Haque II (v Z, Dhaka, 2004-05).

NINE OR MORE WICKETS IN AN INNINGS

10- 53	J.C.Laker	E v A	Manchester	1956
10- 74	A.Kumble	I v P	Delhi	1998-99
9- 28	G.A.Lohmann	E v SA	Johannesburg	1895-96
9- 37	J.C.Laker	E v A	Manchester	1956
9- 51	M.Muralitharan	SL v Z	Kandy	2001-02
9- 52	R.J.Hadlee	NZ v A	Brisbane	1985-86
9- 56	Abdul Qadir	P v E	Lahore	1987-88
9- 57	D.E.Malcolm	E v SA	The Oval	1994
9- 65	M.Muralitharan	SL v E	The Oval	1998
9- 69	J.M.Patel	I v A	Kanpur	1959-60
9- 83	Kapil Dev	I v WI	Ahmedabad	1983-84
9- 86	Sarfraz Nawaz	P v A	Melbourne	1978-79
9- 95	J.M.Noreiga	WI v I	Port-of-Spain	1970-71
9-102	S.P.Gupte	I v WI	Kanpur	1958-59
9-103	S.F.Barnes	E v SA	Johannesburg	1913-14
9-113	H.J.Tayfield	SA v E	Johannesburg	1956-57
9-121	A.A.Mailey	A v E	Melbourne	1920-21

The best analysis for Zimbabwe is 8-109 by P.A.Strang (v NZ, Bulawayo, 2000-01), and for Bangladesh 7-36 by Shakib Al Hasan (v NZ, Chittagong, 2008-09).

HAT-TRICKS

F.R.Spofforth	Australia v England	Melbourne	1878-79
W.Bates[7]	England v Australia	Melbourne	1882-83
J.Briggs[7]	England v Australia	Sydney	1891-92
G.A.Lohmann	England v South Africa	Port Elizabeth	1895-96
J.T.Hearne	England v Australia	Leeds	1899
H.Trumble	Australia v England	Melbourne	1901-02
H.Trumble	Australia v England	Melbourne	1903-04
T.J.Matthews (2)[2]	Australia v South Africa	Manchester	1912
M.J.C.Allom[1]	England v New Zealand	Christchurch	1929-30
T.W.J.Goddard	England v South Africa	Johannesburg	1938-39
P.J.Loader	England v West Indies	Leeds	1957
L.F.Kline	Australia v South Africa	Cape Town	1957-58
W.W.Hall	West Indies v Pakistan	Lahore	1958-59

G.M.Griffin[7]	South Africa v England	Lord's	1960
L.R.Gibbs	West Indies v Australia	Adelaide	1960-61
P.J.Petherick[1/7]	New Zealand v Pakistan	Lahore	1976-77
C.A.Walsh[3]	West Indies v Australia	Brisbane	1988-89
M.G.Hughes[3/7]	Australia v West Indies	Perth	1988-89
D.W.Fleming[1]	Australia v Pakistan	Rawalpindi	1994-95
S.K.Warne	Australia v England	Melbourne	1994-95
D.G.Cork	England v West Indies	Manchester	1995
D.Gough[7]	England v Australia	Sydney	1998-99
Wasim Akram[4]	Pakistan v Sri Lanka	Lahore	1998-99
Wasim Akram[4]	Pakistan v Sri Lanka	Dhaka	1998-99
D.N.T.Zoysa[5]	Sri Lanka v Zimbabwe	Harare	1999-00
Abdul Razzaq	Pakistan v Sri Lanka	Galle	2000-01
G.D.McGrath	Australia v West Indies	Perth	2000-01
Harbhajan Singh	India v Australia	Calcutta	2000-01
Mohammad Sami[7]	Pakistan v Sri Lanka	Lahore	2001-02
J.J.C.Lawson[7]	West Indies v Australia	Bridgetown	2002-03
Alok Kapali[7]	Bangladesh v Pakistan	Peshawar	2003
A.M.Blignaut	Zimbabwe v Bangladesh	Harare	2003-04
M.J.Hoggard	England v West Indies	Bridgetown	2003-04
J.E.C.Franklin	New Zealand v Bangladesh	Dhaka	2004-05
I.K.Pathan[6/7]	India v Pakistan	Karachi	2005-06
R.J.Sidebottom[7]	England v New Zealand	Hamilton	2007-08
P.M.Siddle	Australia v England	Brisbane	2010-11
S.C.J.Broad	England v India	Nottingham	2011

[1] On debut. [2] Hat-trick in each innings. [3] Involving both innings. [4] In successive Tests.
[5] His first 3 balls (second over of the match). [6] The fourth, fifth and sixth balls of the match.
[7] On losing side.

WICKET-KEEPING RECORDS

100 DISMISSALS IN TESTS†

Total			Tests	Ct	St
555	M.V.Boucher	South Africa/ICC	147	532	23
416	A.C.Gilchrist	Australia	96	379	37
395	I.A.Healy	Australia	119	366	29
355	R.W.Marsh	Australia	96	343	12
270†	P.J.L.Dujon	West Indies	79	265	5
269	A.P.E.Knott	England	95	250	19
241†	A.J.Stewart	England	82	227	14
235	M.S.Dhoni	India	74	203	32
228	Wasim Bari	Pakistan	81	201	27
219	R.D.Jacobs	West Indies	65	207	12
219	T.G.Evans	England	91	173	46
206	Kamran Akmal	Pakistan	53	184	22
201†	A.C.Parore	New Zealand	67	194	7
198	S.M.H.Kirmani	India	88	160	38
189	D.L.Murray	West Indies	62	181	8
187	A.T.W.Grout	Australia	51	163	24
186	M.J.Prior	England	62	173	13
176	I.D.S.Smith	New Zealand	63	168	8
174	R.W.Taylor	England	57	167	7
172†	B.B.McCullum	New Zealand	51	161	11
165	R.C.Russell	England	54	153	12
164	B.J.Haddin	Australia	43	160	4
152	D.J.Richardson	South Africa	42	150	2

Total			Tests	Ct	St
151†	K.C.Sangakkara	Sri Lanka	48	131	20
151†	A.Flower	Zimbabwe	55	142	9
147	D.Ramdin	West Indies	49	144	3
147†	Moin Khan	Pakistan	66	127	20
141	J.H.B.Waite	South Africa	49	124	17
133	G.O.Jones	England	34	128	5
130	Rashid Latif	Pakistan	37	119	11
130	K.S.More	India	49	110	20
130	W.A.S.Oldfield	Australia	54	78	52
129	H.A.P.W.Jayawardena	Sri Lanka	52	97	32
119	R.S.Kaluwitharana	Sri Lanka	49	93	26
112†	J.M.Parks	England	43	101	11
107	N.R.Mongia	India	44	99	8
104	Salim Yousuf	Pakistan	32	91	13
101†	J.R.Murray	West Indies	31	98	3

The most for Bangladesh is 87 (78 ct, 9 st) by Khaled Masud in 44 Tests.
† Excluding catches taken in the field

25 OR MORE DISMISSALS IN A SERIES

28	R.W.Marsh	Australia v England	1982-83
27 (inc 2st)	R.C.Russell	England v South Africa	1995-96
27 (inc 2st)	I.A.Healy	Australia v England (6 Tests)	1997
26 (inc 3st)	J.H.B.Waite	South Africa v New Zealand	1961-62
26	R.W.Marsh	Australia v West Indies (6 Tests)	1975-76
26 (inc 5st)	I.A.Healy	Australia v England (6 Tests)	1993
26 (inc 1st)	M.V.Boucher	South Africa v England	1998
26 (inc 2st)	A.C.Gilchrist	Australia v England	2001
26 (inc 2st)	A.C.Gilchrist	Australia v England	2006-07
25 (inc 2st)	I.A.Healy	Australia v England	1994-95
25 (inc 2st)	A.C.Gilchrist	Australia v England	2002-03
25	A.C.Gilchrist	Australia v India	2007-08

TEN OR MORE DISMISSALS IN A TEST

11	R.C.Russell	England v South Africa	Johannesburg	1995-96
11	A.B.de Villiers	South Africa v Pakistan	Johannesburg	2012-13
10	R.W.Taylor	England v India	Bombay	1979-80
10	A.C.Gilchrist	Australia v New Zealand	Hamilton	1999-00

SEVEN DISMISSALS IN AN INNINGS

7	Wasim Bari	Pakistan v New Zealand	Auckland	1978-79
7	R.W.Taylor	England v India	Bombay	1979-80
7	I.D.S.Smith	New Zealand v Sri Lanka	Hamilton	1990-91
7	R.D.Jacobs	West Indies v Australia	Melbourne	2000-01

FIVE STUMPINGS IN AN INNINGS

5	K.S.More	India v West Indies	Madras	1987-88

FIELDING RECORDS
100 CATCHES IN TESTS

Total			Tests	Total			Tests
210	R.S.Dravid	India/ICC	164	121	A.J.Strauss	England	100
196	R.T.Ponting	Australia	168	120	I.T.Botham	England	102
194	D.P.M.D.Jayawardena	Sri Lanka	138	120	M.C.Cowdrey	England	114
194	J.H.Kallis	South Africa/ICC	162	115	C.L.Hooper	West Indies	102
181	M.E.Waugh	Australia	128	115	S.R.Tendulkar	India	195
171	S.P.Fleming	New Zealand	111	112	S.R.Waugh	Australia	168
164	B.C.Lara	West Indies/ICC	131	110	R.B.Simpson	Australia	62
160	G.C.Smith	South Africa/ICC	110	110	W.R.Hammond	England	85
157	M.A.Taylor	Australia	104	109	G.St A.Sobers	West Indies	93
156	A.R.Border	Australia	156	108	S.M.Gavaskar	India	125
135	V.V.S.Laxman	India	134	105	I.M.Chappell	Australia	75
128	M.L.Hayden	Australia	103	105	M.J.Clarke	Australia	90
125	S.K.Warne	Australia	145	105	M.Azharuddin	India	99
122	G.S.Chappell	Australia	87	105	G.P.Thorpe	England	100
122	I.V.A.Richards	West Indies	121	103	G.A.Gooch	England	118

The most for Pakistan is 93 by Javed Miandad (124), for Zimbabwe 60 by A.D.R.Campbell (60) and for Bangladesh 24 by Mohammad Ashraful (57).

15 CATCHES IN A SERIES

15	J.M.Gregory	Australia v England	1920-21

SEVEN CATCHES IN A TEST

7	G.S.Chappell	Australia v England	Perth	1974-75
7	Yajurvindra Singh	India v England	Bangalore	1976-77
7	H.P.Tillekeratne	Sri Lanka v New Zealand	Colombo (SSC)	1992-93
7	S.P.Fleming	New Zealand v Zimbabwe	Harare	1997-98
7	M.L.Hayden	Australia v Sri Lanka	Galle	2003-04

FIVE CATCHES IN AN INNINGS

5	V.Y.Richardson	Australia v South Africa	Durban	1935-36
5	Yajurvindra Singh	India v England	Bangalore	1976-77
5	M.Azharuddin	India v Pakistan	Karachi	1989-90
5	K.Srikkanth	India v Australia	Perth	1991-92
5	S.P.Fleming	New Zealand v Zimbabwe	Harare	1997-98
5	G.C.Smith	South Africa v Australia	Perth	2012-13

APPEARANCE RECORDS
100 TEST MATCH APPEARANCES

			Opponents									
			E	A	SA	WI	NZ	I	P	SL	Z	B
195	S.R.Tendulkar	India	32	36	25	19	24	–	18	25	9	7
168	S.R.Waugh	Australia	46	–	16	32	23	18	20	8	3	2
168†	R.T.Ponting	Australia	35	–	26	24	17	29	15	14	3	4
164†	R.S.Dravid	India/ICC	21	32	21	23	15	–	15	20	9	7
162†	J.H.Kallis	South Africa/ICC	31	28	–	24	18	16	17	15	6	6
156	A.R.Border	Australia	47	–	6	31	23	20	22	7	–	–
147†	M.V.Boucher	South Africa/ICC	25	20	–	24	17	14	15	17	6	8
146	S.Chanderpaul	West Indies	32	20	21	–	15	23	14	7	6	8
145†	S.K.Warne	Australia	36	–	24	19	20	14	15	13	1	2

			E	A	SA	WI	NZ	I	P	SL	Z	B
138	D.P.M.D.Jayawardena	Sri Lanka	21	16	16	11	13	18	24	–	8	11
134	V.V.S.Laxman	India	17	29	19	22	10	–	15	13	6	3
133	A.J.Stewart	England	–	33	23	24	16	9	13	9	6	–
133†	M.Muralitharan	Sri Lanka/ICC	16	12	15	12	14	22	16	–	14	11
132	A.Kumble	India	19	20	21	17	11	–	15	18	7	4
132	C.A.Walsh	West Indies	36	38	10	–	10	15	18	3	2	–
131	Kapil Dev	India	27	20	4	25	10	–	29	14	2	–
131†	B.C.Lara	West Indies/ICC	30	30	18	–	11	17	12	8	2	2
128	M.E.Waugh	Australia	29	–	18	28	14	14	15	9	1	–
125	S.M.Gavaskar	India	38	20	–	27	9	–	24	7	–	–
124†	G.D.McGrath	Australia	30	–	17	23	14	11	17	8	1	2
124	Javed Miandad	Pakistan	22	24	–	17	18	28	–	12	3	–
121	I.V.A.Richards	West Indies	36	34	–	–	7	28	16	–	–	–
120†	Inzamam-ul-Haq	Pakistan/ICC	19	13	13	15	12	10	–	20	11	6
119	I.A.Healy	Australia	33	–	12	28	11	9	14	11	1	–
118	G.A.Gooch	England	–	42	3	26	15	19	10	3	–	–
117	D.I.Gower	England	–	42	–	19	13	24	17	2	–	–
116	D.L.Haynes	West Indies	36	33	1	–	10	19	16	1	–	–
116	D.B.Vengsarkar	India	26	24	–	25	11	–	22	8	–	–
115	M.A.Atherton	England	–	33	18	27	11	7	11	4	4	–
115	K.C.Sangakkara	Sri Lanka	20	11	15	12	10	15	16	–	5	11
114	M.C.Cowdrey	England	43	14	21	18	8	10	–	–	–	–
113	S.C.Ganguly	India	12	24	17	12	8	–	12	14	9	5
112†	D.L.Vettori	New Zealand/ICC	17	18	14	10	–	15	8	11	9	9
111	S.P.Fleming	New Zealand	19	14	15	11	–	13	9	13	11	6
111	W.P.J.U.C.Vaas	Sri Lanka	15	12	11	9	10	14	18	–	15	7
110	S.T.Jayasuriya	Sri Lanka	14	13	15	10	13	10	17	–	13	5
110	C.H.Lloyd	West Indies	34	29	–	–	8	28	11	–	–	–
110†	G.C.Smith	South Africa/ICC	21	18	–	14	13	13	14	7	2	8
108	G.Boycott	England	–	38	7	29	15	13	6	–	–	–
108	C.G.Greenidge	West Indies	29	32	–	–	10	23	14	–	–	–
108	S.M.Pollock	South Africa	23	13	–	16	11	12	12	13	5	3
107	D.C.Boon	Australia	31	–	6	22	17	11	11	9	–	–
105†	J.L.Langer	Australia	21	–	11	18	14	14	13	8	3	2
104	M.A.Taylor	Australia	33	–	11	20	11	9	12	8	–	–
104	Wasim Akram	Pakistan	18	13	4	17	9	12	–	19	10	2
103†	M.L.Hayden	Australia	20	–	19	15	11	18	6	7	2	4
103	Salim Malik	Pakistan	19	15	1	7	18	22	–	15	6	–
103†	V.Sehwag	India/ICC	17	22	15	10	12	–	9	11	3	4
102	I.T.Botham	England	–	36	–	20	15	14	14	3	–	–
102	C.L.Hooper	West Indies	24	25	10	–	2	19	14	6	2	–
101	G.Kirsten	South Africa	22	18	–	13	13	10	11	9	3	2
101	M.Ntini	South Africa	18	15	–	15	11	10	9	12	3	8
100	G.P.Thorpe	England	–	16	16	27	13	5	8	9	2	4
100	A.J.Strauss	England	–	20	16	18	9	12	13	8	–	4
100	Harbhajan Singh	India	14	17	11	11	13	–	9	15	7	3

† Includes appearance in the Australia v ICC 'Test' in 2005-06. The most for Zimbabwe is 67 by G.W.Flower, and for Bangladesh 57 by Mohammad Ashraful.

100 CONSECUTIVE TEST APPEARANCES

153	A.R.Border	Australia	March 1979 to March 1994
107	M.E.Waugh	Australia	June 1993 to October 2002
106	S.M.Gavaskar	India	January 1975 to February 1987

50 TESTS AS CAPTAIN

			Won	Lost	Drawn	Tied
102	G.C.Smith	South Africa	50	26	26	–
93	A.R.Border	Australia	32	22	38	1
80	S.P.Fleming	New Zealand	28	27	25	–
77	R.T.Ponting	Australia	48	16	13	–
74	C.H.Lloyd	West Indies	36	12	26	–
57	S.R.Waugh	Australia	41	9	7	–
56	A.Ranatunga	Sri Lanka	12	19	25	–
54	M.A.Atherton	England	13	21	20	–
53	W.J.Cronje	South Africa	27	11	15	–
51	M.P.Vaughan	England	26	11	14	–
50	I.V.A.Richards	West Indies	27	8	15	–
50	M.A.Taylor	Australia	26	13	11	–
50	A.J.Strauss	England	24	11	15	–

The most for India is 49 by S.C.Ganguly, for Pakistan 48 by Imran Khan, for Zimbabwe 21 by A.D.R.Campbell and H.H.Streak, and for Bangladesh 18 by Habibul Bashar.

50 TEST UMPIRING APPEARANCES

128	S.A.Bucknor	(West Indies)	28.04.1989 to 22.03.2009
108	R.E.Koertzen	(South Africa)	26.12.1992 to 24.07.2010
95	D.J.Harper	(Australia)	28.11.1998 to 23.06.2011
92	D.R.Shepherd	(England)	01.08.1985 to 07.06.2005
78	D.B.Hair	(Australia)	25.01.1992 to 08.06.2008
78	Alim Dar	(Pakistan)	21.10.2003 to 06.01.2013
74	S.J.A.Taufel	(Australia)	26.12.2000 to 20.08.2012
74	B.F.Bowden	(New Zealand)	11.03.2000 to 24.02.2013
73	S.Venkataraghavan	(India)	29.01.1993 to 20.01.2004
66	H.D.Bird	(England)	05.07.1973 to 24.06.1996

THE FIRST-CLASS COUNTIES REGISTER, RECORDS AND 2012 AVERAGES

All statistics are to 10 March 2013.

ABBREVIATIONS – General

*	not out/unbroken partnership	IT20	International Twenty20
b	born	l-o	limited-overs
BB	Best innings bowling analysis	LOI	Limited-Overs Internationals
Cap	Awarded 1st XI County Cap	Tests	International Test Matches
f-c	first-class	F-c Tours	Overseas tours involving first-class
HS	Highest Score		appearances

Awards

PCA 2012	Professional Cricketers' Association Player of 2012
Wisden 2011	One of *Wisden Cricketers' Almanack*'s Five Cricketers of 2011
YC 2012	Cricket Writers' Club Young Cricketer of 2012

ECB Competitions

BHC	Benson & Hedges Cup (1972-2002)
CB40	Clydesdale Bank 40 (2010-12)
CC	LV= County Championship
CGT	Cheltenham & Gloucester Trophy (2001-06)
FPT	Friends Provident Trophy (2007-09)
NL	National League (1999-2005)
NWT	NatWest Trophy (1981-2000)
P40	NatWest PRO 40 League (2006-09)
SL	Sunday League (1969-98)
T20	Twenty20 Competition

Education

ARU	Anglia Ruskin University
BHS	Boys' High School
C	College
CFE	College of Further Education
CHE	College of Higher Education
CS	Comprehensive School
GS	Grammar School
HS	High School
I	Institute
IHE	Institute of Higher Education
RGS	Royal Grammar School
S	School
SFC	Sixth Form College
SM	Secondary Modern School
SS	Secondary School
TC	Technical College
T(H)S	Technical (High) School
U	University
UMIST	University of Manchester Institute of Science and Technology
UWIC	University of Wales Institute, Cardiff

Playing Categories

LBG	Bowls right-arm leg-breaks and googlies
LF	Bowls left-arm fast
LFM	Bowls left-arm fast-medium
LHB	Bats left-handed
LM	Bowls left-arm medium pace
LMF	Bowls left-arm medium-fast
OB	Bowls right-arm off-breaks
RF	Bowls right-arm fast
RFM	Bowls right-arm fast-medium
RHB	Bats right-handed
RM	Bowls right-arm medium pace
RMF	Bowls right-arm medium-fast
RSM	Bowls right-arm slow-medium

SLA	Bowls left-arm leg-breaks
SLC	Bowls left-arm 'Chinamen'
WK	Wicket-keeper

Teams (see also p 219)

ACT	Australian Capital Territory
ADBP	Agricultural Development Bank of Pakistan
B	Bangladesh
BS	Basnahira South
CC&C	Combined Campuses & Colleges
CD	Central Districts
EL	England Lions
EP	Eastern Province
FS	Free State
GW	Griqualand West
HB	Habib Bank Limited
K	Kenya
KRL	Khan Research Laboratories
KZN	KwaZulu-Natal Inland
ME	Mashonaland Eagles
MT	Matabeleland Tuskers
MWR	Mid West Rhinos
NBP	National Bank of Pakistan
ND	Northern Districts
NSW	New South Wales
NT	Northern Transvaal
NW	North West
(O)FS	(Orange) Free State
PIA	Pakistan International Airlines
PNSC	Pakistan National Shipping Corporation
PTC	Pakistan Telecommunication Co
Q	Queensland
REDCO	Really Efficient Development Co
SAU	South African Universities
SNGPL	Sui Northern Gas Pipelines Limited
SR	Southern Rocks
SSGC	Sui Southern Gas Corporation
Tas	Tasmania
T&T	Trinidad & Tobago
Uni	Unicorns
UP	Uttar Pradesh
Vic	Victoria
WA	Western Australia
WAPDA	Water & Power Development Authority.
WP	Western Province
ZTB	Zarai Taraqiati Bank Limited

DERBYSHIRE

Formation of Present Club: 4 November 1870
Inaugural First-Class Match: 1871
Colours: Chocolate, Amber and Pale Blue
Badge: Rose and Crown
County Champions: (1) 1936
Gillette/NatWest/C&G/FP Trophy Winners: (1) 1981
Benson and Hedges Cup Winners: (1) 1993
Pro 40/National League (Div 1) Winners: (0); best –
4th (Div 2) 2002
Sunday League Winners: (1) 1990
Clydesdale Bank 40 Winners: (0); best – 3rd Group A 2011
Twenty20 Cup Winners: (0) best – Quarter-Finalist 2005

Chief Executive: Simon Storey, Derbyshire County Cricket Club, Grandstand Road, Derby
DE21 6AF • Tel: 01332 388101 • Fax: 0844 500 8322 • Email: info@derbyshireccc.com •
Web: www. derbyshireccc.com

Head Coach: K.M.Krikken. **Captain:** W.L.Madsen. **Vice-Captain:** none. **Overseas Player:**
S.Chanderpaul. **2013 Beneficiary:** none. **Head Groundsman:** Neil Godrich. **Scorer:** John
M.Brown. ‡ New registration. ^NQ Not qualified for England.

BORRINGTON, Paul Michael (Repton S; Chellarton S; Loughborough U), b Nottingham
24 May 1988. Son of A.J.Borrington (Derbyshire 1971-80). 5'10". RHB, OB. Debut
(Derbyshire) 2005. Loughborough UCCE 2008-09. HS 105 LU v Hants (Southampton)
2009. De HS 98 v Northants (Derby) 2012. BB – . LO HS 25 v Glam (Derby) 2009 (P40).

BURGOYNE, Peter Ian (St John Houghton S, Ilkeston; Derby SFC), b Nottingham 11 Nov
1993. 6'2". RHB, OB. Debut (Southern Rocks) 2012-13. Derbyshire 2nd XI debut 2011.
HS 104 and BB 3-27 SR v MWR (Kwekwe) 2012-13. LO HS 43 SR v MWR (Masvingo)
2012-13. LO BB 3-31 v Northants (Derby) 2012 (CB40). T20 HS 38. T20 BB 1-17.

‡^NQCHANDERPAUL, Shivnarine (Cove and John SS, Unity Village), b Unity Village,
Demerara, Guyana 16 Aug 1974. 5'6". LHB, LB. Guyana 1991-92 to date. Durham
2007-09. Lancashire 2010; cap 2010. Warwickshire 2011. *Wisden* 2007. **Tests** (WI): 146
(1993-94 to 2012-13, 14 as captain); HS 203* v SA (Georgetown) 2004-05; BB 1-2 v A
(Adelaide) 1996-97. **LOI** (WI): 268 (1994-95 to 2010-11, 16 as captain); HS 150 v SA (E
London) 1998-99; BB 3-18 v I (Sharjah) 1997-98. **IT20** (WI): 22 (2005-06 to 2010); HS 41
v E (Oval) 2007. F-c Tours (WI) (C=Captain): E 1995, 2000, 2004, 2007, 2009, 2012; A
1995-96, 1996-97, 2000-01, 2005-06C, 2009-10; SA 1998-99, 2003-04, 2007-08; NZ
1994-95, 1999-00, 2005-06C, 2008-09; I 1994-95, 2002-03, 2011-12; P 1997-98, 2001-02
(Sharjah), 2006-07; SL 2005C, 2010-11; Z 2001, 2003-04; B 1999-00, 2002-03, 2011-12,
2012-13; K 2001. 1000 runs (1+1); most – 1107 (2004-05). HS 303* Guyana v Jamaica
(Kingston) 1995-96. CC HS 201* Du v Worcs (Worcester) 2009. BB 4-48 Guyana v
Leeward Is (Basseterre) 1992-93. LO HS 150 (*see LOI*). LO BB 4-22 Guyana v Trinidad
(Hampton Court) 1995-96. T20 HS 87*.

CLARE, Jonathan Luke (St Theodore's HS), b Burnley, Lancs 14 Jun 1986. 6'4". RHB,
RMF. Debut (Derbyshire) 2007, taking 5-90 v Notts (Chesterfield); cap 2012. HS 130 v
Glamorgan (Derby) 2011. BB 7-74 v Northants (Northampton) 2008. LO HS 57 v Warwks
(Derby) 2012 (CB40). LO BB 3-39 v Scotland (Derby) 2008 (FPT). T20 HS 18. T20 BB 2-20.

DURHAM, Christopher Michael (Cheadle and Marple C), b Stockport, Cheshire 4 Mar 1992. 5'8½". RHB, WK. Debut (Derbyshire) 2012. Derbyshire 2nd XI debut 2009. HS 12* v Australia A (Derby) 2012. LO HS – . T20 HS 0.

DURSTON, Wesley John (Millfield S; University C, Worcester), b Taunton, Somerset 6 Oct 1980. 5'10". RHB, OB. Somerset 2002-09. Derbyshire debut 2010; cap 2012. Unicorns 2010 (l-o only). 1000 runs (1): 1138 (2011). HS 151 v Glos (Derby) 2011. BB 5-34 v Yorks (Leeds) 2012. LO HS 120* v Unicorns (Wormsley) 2012 (CB40). LO BB 3-7 v Worcs (Derby) 2011 (CB40). T20 HS 111 v Notts (Nottingham) 2010 – De record. T20 BB 3-25.

EVANS, Alasdair Campbell (George Watson's C, Edinburgh; Loughborough U), b Pembury, Kent 12 Jan 1989. 6'5". RHB, RMF. Debut Loughborough UCCE 2009. Loughborough UCCE 2009. Scotland 2009-11. Awaiting CC debut. **LOI** (Scot): 3 (2009 to 2012); HS – ; BB 1-13 v Canada (Ayr) 2012. HS 2 Scot v Ireland (Aberdeen) 2009. BB 2-41 LU v Leics (Leicester) 2009. LO HS 2* Scot v Somerset (Uddingston) 2012 (CB40). BB 2-34 v Northants (Derby) 2012 (CB40).

FOOTITT, Mark Harold Alan (Carlton le Willows S; West Notts C), b Nottingham 25 Nov 1985. 6'2". RHB, LFM. Nottinghamshire 2005-09. MCC 2006. No f-c appearances in 2008. Derbyshire debut 2010. HS 30 v Surrey (Oval) 2010. BB 5-45 Nt v West Indies A (Nottingham) 2006. De BB 5-53 v Northants (Chesterfield) 2011. LO HS 4 v Middx (Chesterfield) 2011 (CB40). LO BB 3-20 v Middx (Derby) 2010 (CB40). T20 HS – . T20 BB – .

‡GODLEMAN, Billy Ashley (Islington Green S), b Islington, London 11 Feb 1989. 6'3". LHB, LB. Middlesex 2005-09. Essex 2010-12. England U19s 2006 to 2007-08. HS 130 Ex v Leics (Leicester) 2011 and 130 Ex v Glos (Cheltenham) 2012. BB – . LO HS 82 M v Scotland (Lord's) 2009 (FPT). T20 HS 69.

GROENEWALD, Timothy Duncan (Maritzburg C; South Africa U), b Pietermaritzburg, South Africa 10 Jan 1984. 6'0". RHB, RFM. Debut Cambridge UCCE 2006. Warwickshire 2006-08. Derbyshire debut 2009; cap 2011. HS 78 Wa v Bangladesh A (Birmingham) 2008. CC HS 76 Wa v Durham (Chester-le-St) 2006. De HS 60* v Leics (Derby) 2011. BB 6-50 v Surrey (Croydon) 2009. LO HS 36 Wa v Lancs (Manchester) 2007 (FPT). LO BB 4-22 v Worcs (Worcester) 2011 (CB40). T20 HS 41. T20 BB 3-18.

HIGGINBOTTOM, Matthew (New Mills SFC; Leeds Met U), b Stockport, Cheshire 20 Oct 1990. 6'2". LHB, RMF. Debut (Leeds/Bradford MCCU) 2012. Bradford/Leeds MCCU 2009-12. Awaiting CC debut. Derbyshire 2nd XI debut 2009. HS 31* LBU v Yorks (Leeds) 2012. BB 2-22 LBU v Surrey (Oval) 2012. LO HS and LO BB – .

HUGHES, Alex Lloyd (Ounsdale HS, Wolverhampton), b Wordsley, Staffs 29 Sep 1991. 5'10". RHB, RM. Derbyshire 2nd XI debut 2009. Awaiting f-c debut. LO HS 37* v Yorks (Chesterfield) 2012 (CB40). LO BB 1-23 v Sussex (Derby) 2012 (CB40). T20 HS 11*. T20 BB – .

NQHUGHES, Chesney Francis (Albena Lake Hodge CS, Anguilla), b Anguilla 20 January 1991. 6'2". LHB, SLA. British passport. Debut (Derbyshire) 2010. Derbyshire 2nd XI debut 2009. Leeward Is 2009-10 to date (l-o only). HS 167 v Glamorgan (Derby) 2011. BB 2-9 v Middx (Derby) 2011. LO HS 81 Leeward Is v Windward Is (Kingston) 2010-11. LO BB 5-29 v Unicorns (Wormsley) 2012 (CB40). T20 HS 65. T20 BB 4-23.

JOHNSON, Richard Matthew, b Solihull, Warwicks 1 Sep 1988. RHB, WK. Warwickshire 2008-12. Derbyshire debut 2012. Herefordshire 2006. HS 72 Wa v Cambridge UCCE (Cambridge) 2008 – on debut. CC HS 49 Wa v Surrey (Birmingham) 2012. De HS 15* v Yorks (Chesterfield) 2012. LO HS 79 v Yorks (Chesterfield) 2012 (CB40). T20 HS 14.

KNIGHT, Thomas Craig (**'Tom'**) (Eckington C), b Sheffield, Yorks 28 Jun 1993. 6'0½''. RHB, SLA. Debut (Derbyshire) 2011. Derbyshire 2nd XI debut 2010 ,aged 16y 311d. HS 14 v Surrey (Oval) 2011. BB 2-32 v Glamorgan (Cardiff) 2011. LO HS 2* v Warwks (Derby) 2012 (CB40). LO BB 2-27 v Kent (Canterbury) 2011 (CB40). T20 HS 2*. T20 BB 3-16.

^{NQ}**MADSEN, Wayne** Lee (Kearsney C, Durban; U of South Africa), b Durban, South Africa 2 Jan 1984. Nephew of M.B.Madsen (Natal 1967-68 to 1978-79), T.R.Madsen (Natal 1976-77 to 1989-90) and H.R.Fotheringham (Natal, Transvaal 1971-72 to 1989-90) and cousin of G.S.Fotheringham (KwaZulu-Natal 2008-09 to 2009-10). 5'11''. RHB, OB. KwaZulu-Natal 2003-04 to 2007-08. Dolphins 2006-07 to 2007-08. Derbyshire debut 2009, scoring 170 v Glos (Cheltenham); cap 2011; captain 2012 to date. HS 231* v Northants (Northampton) 2012. BB 3-45 KZ-Natal v EP (Pt Elizabeth) 2007-08. De BB 1-68 v Glam (Cardiff) 2010. LO HS 75 v Netherlands (Derby) 2011 (CB40). LO BB 2-18 v Glamorgan (Derby) 2009 (P40). T20 HS 61*.

PALLADINO, Antonio Paul (Cardinal Pole SS; Anglia Polytechnic U), b Tower Hamlets, London 29 Jun 1983. 6'0''. RHB, RMF. Cambridge UCCE 2003-05. Essex 2003-10. Namibia 2009-10. Derbyshire debut 2011; cap 2012. HS 106 v Australia A (Derby) 2012. CC HS 66 Ex v Durham (Chelmsford) 2010. 50 wkts (2); most – 56 (2012). BB 7-53 v Kent (Derby) 2012. Hat-trick v Leics (Leicester) 2012. LO HS 31 Namibia v Boland (Windhoek) 2009-10. LO BB 4-32 v Kent (Canterbury) 2011 (CB40). T20 HS 8*. T20 BB 4-21.

POYNTON, Thomas (John Taylor HS, Barton-under-Needwood; Repton S), b Burton upon Trent, Staffs 25 Nov 1989. 5'10''. RHB, WK. Debut (Derbyshire) 2007. No f-c appearances in 2009 and 2011. HS 106 v Northants (Northampton) 2012. BB 2-96 v Glamorgan (Cardiff) 2010. LO HS 40 v Middx (Chesterfield) 2011 (CB40). T20 HS 8*.

REDFERN, Daniel James (Adam's GS, Newport, Shropshire), b Shrewsbury, Shropshire 18 Apr 1990. 5'9''. LHB, OB. Debut (Derbyshire) 2007; cap 2012. HS 133 v Hants (Southampton) 2012. BB 1-7 (twice). LO HS 57* v Yorks (Derby) 2007 (P40). LO BB 2-10 v Kent (Chesterfield) 2009 (P40). T20 HS 13.

SLATER, Benjamin Thomas (Netherthorpe S; Leeds Met U), b Chesterfield 26 Aug 1991. 5'10''. LHB, LB. Debut (Leeds/Bradford MCCU) 2012. Southern Rocks 2012-13. Derbyshire 2nd XI debut 2009. Awaiting 1st XI debut. HS 89 SR v ME (Harare) 2012-13. BB – . LO HS 46 SR v MWR (Masvingo) 2012-13. T20 HS 57.

TURNER, Mark Leif (Thornhill CS), b Sunderland, Co Durham 23 Oct 1984. 5'11''. RHB, RMF. Durham 2005-06. Somerset 2007-09, no f-c appearances in 2010. Derbyshire debut 2011. De HS 57 Sm v Derbys (Taunton) 2007. De HS 27* v Glamorgan (Derby) 2011. BB 5-32 v Northants (Northampton) 2011. LO HS 15* Sm v Essex (Taunton) 2009 (P40). LO BB 4-36 Sm v Worcs (Bath) 2010 (CB40). T20 HS 11*. T20 BB 3-22.

WAINWRIGHT, David John (Hemsworth HS and SFC; Loughborough U), b Pontefract, Yorks 21 Mar 1985. 5'9''. LHB, SLA. Yorkshire 2004-11; cap 2010. Derbyshire debut/cap 2012. Loughborough UCCE 2005-06. British U 2006. Police Sports Club 2011-12. HS 104* (batting at No 10) Y v Sussex (Hove) 2008. De HS 51* v Glamorgan (Cardiff) 2012. 50 wkts (1): 50 (2012). BB 6-33 v Northants (Derby) 2012. LO HS 26 Y v Surrey (Scarborough) 2007 (P40). LO BB 3-26 EL v Pakistan A (Dubai) 2009-10. T20 HS 15*. T20 BB 3-6.

WHITELEY, Ross Andrew (Repton S), b Sheffield, Yorks 13 Sep 1988. 6'2''. LHB, LM. Debut (Derbyshire) 2008. No f-c appearances in 2009-10. Derbyshire 2nd XI debut 2006. HS 130* v Kent (Derby) 2011. BB 2-6 v Hants (Derby) 2012. LO HS 40 v Kent (Canterbury) 2011 (CB40). LO BB 1-17 v Unicorns (Wormsley) 2012 (CB40). T20 HS 40*. T20 BB 1-12.

RELEASED/RETIRED

(Having made a County First-Class or List A appearance in 2012)

NQ**GUPTILL, Martin** James (Avondale C), b Auckland, New Zealand 30 Sep 1986. 6'3''. RHB, OB. Auckland 2005-06 to date. Derbyshire 2011-12; cap 2012. **Tests** (NZ): 30 (2008-09 to 2012-13); HS 189 v B (Hamilton) 2009-10; BB 3-37 v P (Napier) 2009-10. **LOI** (NZ): 69 (2008-09 to 2012-13); HS 122* v WI (Auckland) 2008-09 – on debut; BB 2-7 v B (Napier) 2009-10. **IT20** (NZ): 41 (2008-09 to 2012-13); HS 101* v SA (East London) 2012-13; BB – . F-c Tours (NZ): A 2011-12; SA 2012-13; WI 2012; I 2008-09 (NZ A), 2010-11, 2012; SL 2009, 2012-13; Z 2010-11 (NZ A), 2011-12. HS 195* Auck v Canterbury (Rangiora) 2011-12. De HS 143 v Glos (Derby) 2011. BB 3-37 (see Tests). De BB – . LO HS 156 Auck v Canterbury (Christchurch) 2009-10. LO BB 2-7 (see LOI). T20 HS 120*. T20 BB – .

NQ**KHAWAJA, Usman** Tariq (Westfield Sports HS; U of NSW), b Islamabad, Pakistan 18 Dec 1986. 5'9''. LHB, RM. NSW 2007-08 to 2011-12. Derbyshire 2011-12. Queensland 2012-13. **Tests** (A): 6 (2010-11 to 2011-12); HS 65 v SA (Johannesburg) 2011-12. **LOI** (A): 3 (2012-13); HS 8* v WI (Perth) 2012-13. F-c Tours (A): SA 2011-12; I 2012-13; SL 2011; Z 2011 (Aus A). HS 214 and BB 1-21 NSW v S Australia (Adelaide) 2010-11. De HS 135 v Kent (Canterbury) 2011. De BB – . LO HS 121 NSW v S Australia (Sydney) 2010-11. T20 HS 66*.

LINEKER, Matthew Steven (Swanwick Hall S), b Derby 22 Jan 1985. 6'5''. LHB, SLA. Derbyshire 2011-12. Derbyshire 2nd XI debut 2006. Nottinghamshire 2nd XI 2008. HS 71 v Kent (Derby) 2011. BB – . LO HS 13 v Kent (Canterbury) 2011.

NQ**NAVED-UL-HASAN**, Rana (Government HS, Sheikhupura), b Sheikhupura, Pakistan 28 Feb 1978. 5'11''. RHB, RMF. Debut Pakistan A v England A (Multan) 1995-96. Lahore 1999-00. Pakistan Customs 2000-01. Sheikhupura 2000-01 to 2001-02. Allied Bank 2001-02. WAPDA 2002-03 to date. Sialkot 2003-04 to 2005-06. Sussex 2005-07, 2010; cap 2005. Punjab 2006-07. Yorkshire 2008-09. MCC 2012. Herefordshire 2002. Derbyshire 2012 (l-o only). **Tests** (P): 9 (2004-05 to 2006-07); HS 42* v E (Lahore) 2005-06; BB 3-30 v E (Faisalabad) 2005-06. **LOI** (P): 74 (2002-03 to 2009-10); HS 33 v SL (Colombo, RPS) 2009 and v A (Adelaide) 2009-10; BB 6-27 v I (Jamshedpur) 2004-05. **IT20** (P): 4 (2006 to 2009-10); HS 17* v SA (Johannesburg) 2006-07; BB 3-19 v SL (Colombo, RPS) 2009. F-c Tours (P): A 2004-05; SA 2006-07; WI 2004-05; I 2004-05. HS 139 Sx v Middx (Lord's) 2005. 50 wkts (2+3); most – 91 (2000-01). BB 7-49 Sheikhupura v Sialkot (Muridke) 2001-02. CC BB 7-62 (11-148 match) Sx v Yorks (Leeds) 2006. LO HS 74 Y v Derbys (Derby) 2008. LO BB 6-27 (see LOI). T20 HS 95. T20 BB 5-17.

PARK, Garry Terence (Eshowe HS, Natal; Anglia Ruskin U), b Empangeni, Zululand, South Africa 19 Apr 1983. Elder brother of C.M.Park (Cambridge MCCU 2010-12) and younger brother of S.M.Park (Unicorns 2010). 5'7''. RHB, RM, occ WK. Cambridge UCCE 2003-05. Durham 2006-08. Derbyshire 2009-11. Cambridgeshire 2005, 2012. 1000 runs (1): 1059 (2009). HS 178* v Kent (Derby) 2009. BB 3-25 v Surrey (Derby) 2009. LO HS 64 v Surrey (Croydon) 2009 (P40). LO BB 2-21 v Yorks (Chesterfield) 2011 (CB40). T20 HS 66. T20 BB 3-11.

J.Needham and H.G.Siddique left the staff without making a County First-Class or List A appearance for Derbyshire in 2012.

DERBYSHIRE 2012

RESULTS SUMMARY

	Place	Won	Lost	Tied	Drew	NR
LV= County Championship (2nd Division)	1st	6	2		8	
All First-Class Matches		6	2		9	
Clydesdale Bank 40 (Group C)	4th	4	5			3
Friends Life t20 (North Group)	5th	2	6			2

LV= COUNTY CHAMPIONSHIP AVERAGES

BATTING AND FIELDING

Cap		M	I	NO	HS	Runs	Avge	100	50	Ct/St
2012	M.J.Guptill	8	14	2	137	594	49.50	2	2	13
	U.T.Khawaja	7	12	2	110*	415	41.50	1	4	7
2011	W.L.Madsen	16	25	2	231*	885	38.47	3	3	6
2012	D.J.Redfern	16	24	3	133	792	37.71	2	5	7
2012	W.J.Durston	16	25	2	121	801	34.82	2	4	24
	T.Poynton	14	17	4	106	393	30.23	1	2	42/1
	R.A.Whiteley	14	20	3	83	498	29.29	–	3	5
	P.M.Borrington	10	18	3	98	321	21.40	–	1	3
2012	J.L.Clare	11	13	1	48	247	20.58	–	–	2
2011	T.D.Groenewald	14	15	4	42	225	20.45	–	–	3
2012	D.J.Wainwright	16	22	4	51*	332	18.44	–	2	11
	M.S.Lineker	6	9	–	45	163	18.11	–	–	7
2012	A.P.Palladino	15	19	3	58	235	14.68	–	1	–
	M.L.Turner	6	6	2	13	42	10.50	–	–	6
	M.H.A.Footitt	4	5	2	8*	8	2.66	–	–	2

Also batted: C.F.Hughes (1 match) 28; R.M.Johnson (2) 15*, 1, 4 (4 ct).

BOWLING

	O	M	R	W	Avge	Best	5wI	10wM
J.L.Clare	204.3	40	642	30	21.40	6-40	2	1
A.P.Palladino	473.4	100	1352	56	24.14	7-53	3	–
T.D.Groenewald	399.4	89	1086	42	25.85	5-29	1	–
W.J.Durston	175.3	25	569	22	25.86	5-34	1	–
D.J.Wainwright	527.5	136	1380	44	31.36	6-33	3	–
R.A.Whiteley	163.1	23	658	20	32.90	2- 6	–	–
M.L.Turner	120.5	12	498	13	38.30	3-53	–	–
Also bowled:								
M.H.A.Footitt	90.2	20	240	9	26.66	3-43		

P.M.Borrington 1-0-1-0; M.J.Guptill 3-0-6-0; U.T.Khawaja 2-0-13-0; M.S.Lineker 2-0-2-0; W.L.Madsen 1-0-1-0; D.J.Redfern 12-2-47-0.

The First-Class Averages (pp 219–235) give the records of Derbyshire players in all first-class county matches (Derbyshire's other opponents being Australia A), with the exception of R.M.Johnson, whose first-class figures for Derbyshire are as above.

DERBYSHIRE RECORDS

FIRST-CLASS CRICKET

Highest Total	For 801-8d		v	Somerset	Taunton	2007
	V 662		by	Yorkshire	Chesterfield	1898
Lowest Total	For 16		v	Notts	Nottingham	1879
	V 23		by	Hampshire	Burton upon T	1958
Highest Innings	For 274	G.A.Davidson	v	Lancashire	Manchester	1896
	V 343*	P.A.Perrin	for	Essex	Chesterfield	1904

Highest Partnership for each Wicket

1st	322	H.Storer/J.Bowden	v	Essex	Derby	1929
2nd	417	K.J.Barnett/T.A.Tweats	v	Yorkshire	Derby	1997
3rd	316*	A.S.Rollins/K.J.Barnett	v	Leics	Leicester	1997
4th	328	P.Vaulkhard/D.Smith	v	Notts	Nottingham	1946
5th	302*†	J.E.Morris/D.G.Cork	v	Glos	Cheltenham	1993
6th	212	G.M.Lee/T.S.Worthington	v	Essex	Chesterfield	1932
7th	258	M.P.Dowman/D.G.Cork	v	Durham	Derby	2000
8th	198	K.M.Krikken/D.G.Cork	v	Lancashire	Manchester	1996
9th	283	A.Warren/J.Chapman	v	Warwicks	Blackwell	1910
10th	132	A.Hill/M.Jean-Jacques	v	Yorkshire	Sheffield	1986

† 346 runs were added for this wicket in two separate partnerships

Best Bowling	For 10- 40	W.Bestwick	v	Glamorgan	Cardiff	1921
(Innings)	V 10- 45	R.L.Johnson	for	Middlesex	Derby	1994
Best Bowling	For 17-103	W.Mycroft	v	Hampshire	Southampton	1876
(Match)	V 16-101	G.Giffen	for	Australians	Derby	1886

Most Runs – Season	2165	D.B.Carr	(av 48.11)		1959
Most Runs – Career	23854	K.J.Barnett	(av 41.12)		1979-98
Most 100s – Season	8	P.N.Kirsten			1982
Most 100s – Career	53	K.J.Barnett			1979-98
Most Wkts – Season	168	T.B.Mitchell	(av 19.55)		1935
Most Wkts – Career	1670	H.L.Jackson	(av 17.11)		1947-63
Most Career W-K Dismissals	1304	R.W.Taylor	(1157 ct; 147 st)		1961-84
Most Career Catches in the Field	563	D.C.Morgan			1950-69

LIMITED-OVERS CRICKET

Highest Total	50ov	365-3	v	Cornwall	Derby	1986
	40ov	304-3	v	Kent	Maidstone	2005
	T20	222-5	v	Yorkshire	Leeds	2010
Lowest Total	50ov	79	v	Surrey	The Oval	1967
	40ov	60	v	Kent	Canterbury	2008
	T20	81-8	v	Lancashire	Manchester	2011
Highest Innings	50ov	173*	M.J.Di Venuto	v	Derbys CB	Derby	2000
	40ov	141*	C.J.Adams	v	Kent	Chesterfield	1992
	T20	111	W.J.Durston	v	Notts	Nottingham	2010
Best Bowling	50ov	8-21	M.A.Holding	v	Sussex	Hove	1988
	40ov	6- 7	M.Hendrick	v	Notts	Nottingham	1972
	T20	5-27	T.Lungley	v	Leics	Leicester	2009

DURHAM

Formation of Present Club: 23 May 1882
Inaugural First-Class Match: 1992
Colours: Navy Blue, Yellow and Maroon
Badge: Coat of Arms of the County of Durham
County Champions: (2) 2008, 2009
Gillette/NatWest/C&G/FP Trophy Winners: (1) 2007
Benson and Hedges Cup Winners: (0); best –
Quarter-Finalist 1998, 2000, 2001
Pro 40/National League (Div 1) Winners: (0);
best – 6th 2009
Sunday League Winners: (0); best – 7th 1993
Clydesdale Bank 40 Winners: (0); best – Semi-Finalist 2011
Twenty20 Cup Winners: (0); best – Semi-Finalist 2008

Chief Executive: David Harker, Emirates Durham International Cricket Ground, Chester-le-Street, Co Durham DH3 3QR • Tel: 0191 387 1717 • Fax: 0191 387 1616 • Email: marketing@durhamccc.co.uk • Web: www.durhamccc.co.uk

Director of Cricket: G.Cook. **Assistant Coaches**: J.J.B.Lewis and A.Walker. **Captain**: P.D.Collingwood (f-c) and D.M.Benkenstein (l-o). **Vice-Captain**: none. **Overseas Player**: none. **2013 Beneficiary**: S.J.Harmison. **Head Groundsman**: David Measor. **Scorer**: Brian Hunt. ‡ New registration. ^NQ Not qualified for England.

Durham initially awarded caps immediately after their players joined the staff but revised this policy in 1998, again capping players on merit, past 'awards' having been nullified. Durham abolished both their capping and 'awards' systems after the 2005 season.

BENKENSTEIN, Dale Martin (Durban HS; Michaelhouse HS), b Salisbury, Rhodesia 9 Jun 1974. Son of M.M.Benkenstein (Rhodesia, Natal B 1970-71 to 1980-81); brother of twins B.R. (Natal B 1993-94) and B.N. Benkenstein (Natal B, GW 1994-95 to 1996-97). 5'9". RHB, RM/OB. Natal/KwaZulu-Natal 1993-94 to 2003-04. Dolphins 2004-05 to 2007-08. MCC 2004. British passport. Durham debut/cap 2005; captain 2006-08, l-o captain 2011 to date. *Wisden* 2008. **LOI** (SA): 23 (1998-99 to 2002-03); HS 69 v WI (Cape Town) 1998-99; BB 3-5 v Kenya (Colombo) 2002-03. F-c Tours (SA A): WI 2000; NZ 1998-99 (SA); SL 1995 (SA U-24), 1998. 1000 runs (5); most – 1500 (2006). HS 259 KZ-Natal v Northerns (Durban) 2001-02. Du HS 181 v Somerset (Taunton) 2009. BB 4-16 Dolphins v Warriors (Durban) 2005-06. Du BB 4-29 v Northants (Northampton) 2005. LO HS 107* Natal v North West (Fochville) 1997-98. LO BB 4-16 v Surrey (Chester-le-St) 2005 (NL). T20 HS 60. T20 BB 3-10.

BORTHWICK, Scott George (Farringdon Community Sports C, Sunderland), b Sunderland 19 Apr 1990. 5'9". LHB, LBG. Debut (Durham) 2009. England U19 2008-09 to 2009. **LOI**: 2 (2011 to 2011-12); HS 15 v Ireland (Dublin) 2011; BB – . **IT20**: 1 (2011); HS 14 and BB 1-15 v WI (Oval) 2011. HS 101 v Sri Lanka A (Chester-le-St) 2011. CC HS 68 v Notts (Chester-le-St) 2010. BB 5-80 v Sussex (Hove) 2011. LO HS 44 EL v Bangladesh A (Chittagong) 2011-12. LO BB 4-51 v Hants (Southampton) 2012 (CB40). T20 HS 30. T20 BB 3-19.

BRATHWAITE, Ruel Marlon Ricardo (Queen's C, Barbados; Dulwich C; Loughborough U; Queens' C, Cambridge), b Bridgetown, Barbados 6 Sep 1985. 6'2". RHB, RFM. British passport. Loughborough UCCE 2006-08. British U 2006. MCC 2007. Cambridge U 2009. Durham debut 2010. HS 76* LU v Worcs (Worcester) 2007. Du HS 16 v Australia A (Chester-le-St) 2012. CC HS 13 v Notts (Nottingham) 2011. BB 5-54 CU v Oxford U (Cambridge) 2009. Du BB 5-56 v Sussex (Chester-le-St) 2011. LO HS – . LO BB 1-19 WI v Eng Lions (Worcester) 2007. T20 HS 0. T20 BB 1-33.

BREESE, Gareth Rohan (Wolmer's BHS, Kingston; Kingston U of Technology, Jamaica), b Montego Bay, Jamaica 9 Jan 1976. 5'7". RHB, OB. Jamaica 1995-96 to 2005-06; captain/overseas player 2003-04 to 2005-06. British passport (Welsh father). Durham debut 2004; cap 2005. **Tests** (WI): 1 (2002-03); HS 5 and BB 2-108 v I (Madras) 2002-03. F-c Tours (WI): E 2002 (WI A); I 2002-03. HS 165* v Somerset (Taunton) 2004. BB 7-60 Jamaica v Barbados (Bridgetown) 2000-01. Du BB 5-41 (10-151 match) v Yorks (Scarborough) 2004 – scored 35 and 68 to complete match double. LO HS 68* v Notts (Chester-le-St) 2007 (FPT). LO BB 5-41 v Derbys (Chester-le-St) 2008 (FPT). T20 HS 37. T20 BB 4-14.

CLAYDON, Mitchell Eric (Westfield Sports HS, Sydney), b Fairfield, NSW, Australia 25 Nov 1982. 6'4". LHB, RFM. Yorkshire 2005-06. Durham debut 2007. Canterbury 2010-11. HS 55 v Notts (Chester-le-St) 2012. BB 6-104 v Somerset (Taunton) 2011. LO HS 19 v Glos (Bristol) 2009 (FPT). LO BB 4-39 Cant v Otago (Timaru) 2010-11. T20 HS 19. T20 BB 5-26.

COLLINGWOOD, Paul David (Blackfyne CS; Derwentside C), b Shotley Bridge 26 May 1976. 5'11". RHB, RM. Debut (Durham) 1996 v Northants (Chester-le-St) taking wicket of D.J.Capel with his first ball before scoring 91 and 16; cap 1998; benefit 2007; captain 2012 (*part*) to date. MBE 2005. *Wisden* 2007. **Tests**: 68 (2003-04 to 2010-11); HS 206 v A (Adelaide) 2006-07; BB 3-23 v NZ (Wellington) 2007-08. **LOI**: 197 (2001 to 2010-11, 25 as captain); HS 120* v A (Melbourne) 2006-07; BB 6-31 v B (Nottingham) 2005 – record analysis for E, and first to score a hundred (112*) and take six wickets in same LOI. **IT20**: 35 (2005 to 2010, as captain); HS 79 v WI (Oval) 2007; BB 4-22 v SL (Southampton) 2006. F-c Tours: A 2006-07, 2010-11; SA 2009-10; WI 2003-04, 2008-09; NZ 2007-08; I 2005-06, 2008-09; P 2005-06; SL 2003-04, 2007-08; B 2009-10. 1000 runs (2); most – 1120 (2005), inc six hundreds (Du record). HS 206 (*see Tests*). Du HS 190 v SL (Chester-le-St) 2002 and 190 v Derbys (Derby) 2005, sharing Du record 4th wkt partnership of 250 with D.M.Benkenstein. BB 5-52 v Somerset (Stockton) 2005. LO HS 120* (*see LOI*). LO BB 6-31 (*see LOI*). T20 HS 79. T20 BB 5-6 v Northants (Chester-le-St) 2011 – Du record.

COUGHLIN, Paul (St Robert of Newminster Catholic CS, Washington), b Sunderland 23 Oct 1992. RHB, RM. Debut (Durham) 2012. Northumberland 2011. HS 29* and BB 1-26 v Australia A (Chester-le-St) 2012 – only f-c appearance. LO HS 0 and LO BB – .

HARMISON, Stephen James (Ashington HS), b Ashington, Northumb 23 Oct 1978. Elder brother of B.W.Harmison (*see KENT*). 6'4". RHB, RF. Debut (Durham) 1996; cap 1999; benefit 2013. ICC World XI 2005-06. Lions 2007-08. Yorkshire 2012 (on loan). MCC 2007. *Wisden* 2005. MBE 2005. **Tests**: 63 (2002 to 2009); HS 49* v SA (Oval) 2008; BB 7-12 (9-73 match) v WI (Kingston) 2003-04. **LOI**: 58 (2002-03 to 2008-09); HS 18* v WI (Providence) 2008-09; BB 5-33 v A (Bristol) 2005; hat-trick v I (Nottingham) 2004. **IT20**: 2 (2005 to 2006); HS – ; BB 1-13 v A (Southampton) 2005. F-c Tours: A 2002-03, 2005-06 (RW), 2006-07; SA 1998-99 (Eng A), 2004-05; WI 2003-04, 2008-09; NZ 2007-08; I 2005-06, 2008-09; P 2005-06; SL 2007-08; Z 1998-99 (Eng A); B 2003-04. HS 49* (*see Tests*). Du HS 36* v Hants (Chester-le-St) 2008. 50 wkts (6); most – 65 (2008). BB 7-12 (*see Tests*). Du BB 7-29 (9-74 match) v Warwks (Chester-le-St) 2010. Hat-tricks (2): v Worcs (Chester-le-St) 2005 and v Sussex (Hove) 2008. LO HS 25* v Somerset (Chester-le-St) 2008 (P40). LO BB 5-33 (*see LOI*). T20 HS 6. T20 BB 5-41.

HARRISON, Jamie (Sedbergh S), b Whiston, Lancs 19 Nov 1990. 6'0". RHB, LMF. Debut (Durham) 2012. Durham 2nd XI debut 2009. Gloucestershire 2nd XI 2008. HS 23 v Warwks (Chester-le-St) 2012. BB 4-112 v Somerset (Taunton) 2012 – on debut. LO HS 7* and LO BB 2-51 v Somerset (Chester-le-St) 2012 (CB40).

JENNINGS, Keaton Karl (King Edward VII S, Johanneburg), b Johannesburg, South Africa 19 Jun 1992. Son of R.V.Jennings (Transvaal 1973-74 to 1992-93). Brother of D.Jennings (Gauteng and Easterns 1999 to 2003-04). Nephew of K.E.Jennings (Northern Transvaal 1981-82 to 1982-83). LHB, RMF. Debut (Gauteng) 2011-12. Durham debut 2012. HS 77 Gauteng v KZN (Johannesburg) 2011-12. Du HS 70 v Lancs (Liverpool) 2012. BB 2-8 Gauteng v WP (Cape Town) 2011-12. Du BB – . LO HS 71* Gauteng v KZN (Johannesburg) 2011-12. LO BB – .

MUCHALL, Gordon James (Durham S), b Newcastle upon Tyne, Northumb 2 Nov 1982. 6'0''. RHB, RM. Northumberland 1999. Older brother of P.B.Muchall (*see GLOUCESTER-SHIRE*). Debut (Durham) 2002; cap 2005. F-c Tour: SL 2002-03 (ECB Acad). HS 219 v Kent (Canterbury) 2006, sharing Du record 6th wkt partnership of 249 with P.Mustard (*see below*). BB 3-26 v Yorks (Leeds) 2003. LO HS 101* v Yorks (Leeds) 2005 (NL). LO BB 1-15 v Sussex (Hove) 2003 (NL). T20 HS 64*. T20 BB 1-8.

MUSTARD, Philip (Usworth CS), b Sunderland 8 Oct 1982. Cousin of C.Rushworth (*see below*). 5'11''. LHB, WK. Debut (Durham) 2002; captain 2010 (*part*) to 2012 (*part*). Mountaineers 2011-12. Auckland 2012-13. **LOI**: 10 (2007-08); HS 83 v NZ (Napier) 2007-08. **IT20**: 2 (2007-08); HS 40 v NZ (Christchurch) 2007-08. HS 130 v Kent (Canterbury) 2006. LO HS 143 v Surrey (Chester-le-St) 2012 (CB40). T20 HS 97*.

ONIONS, Graham (St Thomas More RC S, Blaydon), b Gateshead 9 Sep 1982. 6'1''. RHB, RFM. Debut (Durham) 2004. MCC 2007-08. *Wisden* 2009. Missed entire 2010 season through back injury. **Tests**: 9 (2009 to 2012); HS 17* v A (Lord's) 2009; BB 5-38 v WI (Lord's) 2009 – on debut. **LOI**: 4 (2009 to 2009-10); HS 1 v A (Centurion) 2009-10; BB 2-58 v SL (Johannesburg) 2009-10. F-c Tours: SA 2009-10; NZ 2012-13; I 2007-08 (EL), 2012-13; B 2006-07 (Eng A); UAE 2011-12 (*part*). HS 41 v Yorks (Leeds) 2007. 50 wkts (4); most – 72 (2012). BB 9-67 v Notts (Nottingham) 2012. LO HS 19 v Derbys (Derby) 2008 (FPT). LO BB 3-39 v Derbys (Derby) 2005 (NL). T20 HS 31. T20 BB 3-25.

PRINGLE, Ryan David (Durham SFC), b Sunderland 17 Apr 1992. RHB, OB. Awaiting f-c debut. Durham 2nd XI debut 2009. Northumberland 2011-12. LO HS – .

RAMANPREET SINGH (Gosforth HS), b Newcastle upon Tyne 19 Feb 1993. 5'11''. RHB, OB. Debut (Durham) 2012. Durham 2nd XI debut 2009, aged 16y 181d. Northumberland 2009. HS 22 v Australia A (Chester-le-St) 2012 – only f-c game.

RICHARDSON, Michael John (Rondebosch HS; Stonyhurst C, Nottingham U), b Pt Elizabeth, South Africa 4 Oct 1986. Son of D.J.Richardson (South Africa, EP and NT 1977-78 to 1997-98), grandson of J.H.Richardson (NE Transvaal and Transvaal B 1952-53 to 1960-61), nephew of R.P.Richardson (WP 1984-85 to 1988-89). 5'10''. RHB, WK. MCC Young Cricketer 2008-09. Debut (Durham) 2010. HS 73* v Yorks (Leeds) 2011. LO HS 45 v Glamorgan (Colwyn Bay) 2012 (CB40).

RUSHWORTH, Christopher (Castle View CS, Sunderland), b Sunderland 11 Jul 1986. Cousin of P.Mustard (*see above*). 6'2''. RHB, RMF. Debut (Durham) 2010. Northumberland 2004-05. HS 28 v Yorks (Chester-le-St) 2010. BB 5-38 v Sussex (Chester-le-St) 2012. LO HS 12* v Northants (Chester-le-St) 2011 (CB40). LO BB 5-31 v Notts (Chester-le-St) 2010 (CB40). T20 HS 2. T20 BB 3-20.

SMITH, William Rew (Bedford S; Collingwood C, Durham), b Luton, Beds 28 Sep 1982. 5'9''. RHB, OB. Nottinghamshire 2002-06. Durham UCCE 2003-05; captain 2004-05. British U 2004-05. Durham debut 2007; captain 2009-10 (*part*). Bedfordshire 1999-2002. HS 201* v Surrey (Guildford) 2008. BB 3-34 DU v Leics (Leicester) 2005. CC BB 1-5 v Lancs (Chester-le-St) 2007. LO HS 103 v Worcs (Chester-le-St) 2007 (FPT). LO BB 2-22 v Glamorgan (Colwyn Bay) 2012 (CB40). T20 HS 55. T20 BB 1-31.

STOKES, Benjamin Andrew (Cockermouth S), b Christchurch, Canterbury, New Zealand 4 Jun 1991. 6'1". LHB, RM. Debut (Durham) 2010. Durham 2nd XI debut 2007, aged 16y 99d. England U19s 2009 to 2009-10. **LOI:** 5 (2011); HS 20 v I (Oval) 2011. **IT20:** 2 (2011); HS 31 v WI (Oval) 2011. F-c Tours (EL): WI 2010-11. HS 185 v Lancs (Chester-le-St) 2011. BB 6-68 v Hants (Southampton) 2011. LO HS 150* v Warwks (Chester-le-St) 2011 (CB40) – Du record. LO BB 4-29 v Hants (Chester-le-St) 2011 (CB40). T20 HS 56. T20 BB 2-14.

STONEMAN, Mark Daniel (Whickham CS), b Newcastle upon Tyne, Northumb 26 Jun 1987. 5'11". LHB, RM. Debut (Durham) 2007. HS 128 v Sussex (Hove) 2011. LO HS 136* v Scotland (Chester-le-St) 2012 (CB40). T20 HS 46.

THORP, Callum David (Servite C, Tuart Hill, Perth), b Mount Lawley, Perth, Australia 11 Feb 1975. 6'3". British passport (English parents). RHB, RMF. W Australia 2002-03 to 2003-04. Durham debut 2005. HS 79* v MCC (Abu Dhabi) 2010. CC HS 75 v Hants (Southampton) 2006. 50 wkts (1): 50 (2008). BB 7-88 v Kent (Canterbury) 2008. LO HS 52 v Bangladeshis (Chester-le-St) 2005. LO BB 6-17 v Scotland (Edinburgh) 2006 (CGT). T20 HS 13. T20 BB 2-32.

WOOD, Mark Andrew (Ashington HS; Newcastle C), b Ashington 11 Jan 1990. 5'11". RHB, RMF. Debut (Durham) 2011. Durham 2nd XI debut 2009. Northumberland 2008-10. HS 48 v Sri Lanka A (Chester-le-St) 2011. CC HS 45* v Notts (Nottingham) 2011. BB 5-78 v Notts (Nottingham) 2012. LO HS 5 v Northants (Chester-le-St) 2011 (CB40). LO BB 3-32 v Surrey (Chester-le-St) 2012 (CB40).

RELEASED/RETIRED

(Having made a County First-Class or List A appearance in 2012)

BLACKWELL, Ian David (Brookfield Community S), b Chesterfield, Derbys 10 Jun 1978. 6'2". LHB, SLA. Derbyshire 1997-99. Somerset 2000-08; cap 2001; captain 2006 (*part*). Durham 2009-12. Warwickshire 2012 (on loan). MCC 2012. **Tests:** 1 (2005-06); HS 4 and BB- v I (Nagpur) 2005-06. **LOI:** 34 (2002-03 to 2005-06); HS 82 v I (Colombo) 2002-03; BB 3-26 v A (Adelaide) 2002-03. F-c Tour: I 2005-06. 1000 runs (3); most – 1256 (2005). HS 247* Sm v Derbys (Taunton) 2003 – off 156 balls and including 204 off 98 balls in reduced post-lunch session. Won Walter Lawrence Trophy 2005 for 67-ball hundred v Derbys (Taunton). Du HS 158 v Warwks (Birmingham) 2009 and v Durham MCCU (Durham) 2011. BB 7-52 v Australia A (Chester-le-St) 2012. CC BB 7-85 v Lancs (Manchester) 2009. LO HS 134* Sm v Sussex (Taunton) 2005 (NL). LO BB 5-26 Sm v Derbys (Taunton) 2005 (NL). T20 HS 82. T20 BB 4-26.

[NQ]**Di VENUTO, Michael** James (St Virgil's C; Hobart), b Hobart, Australia 12 Dec 1973. 6'0". LHB, RM/LBG. Tasmania 1991-92 to 2007-08. Sussex 1999; cap 1999. Derbyshire 2000-06; cap 2000; appointed captain for 2004 but missed entire season – back surgery. Durham 2007-12, carrying his bat for 155* v Warwks (Worcester) on debut. Italian passport 2008. **LOI** (A): 9 (1996-97 to 1997-98); HS 89 v SA (Johannesburg) 1996-97. F-c Tours: Z 1995-96 (Tas); Scotland/Ireland 1998 (Aus A). 1000 runs (10); most – 1654 (2009), inc six hundreds (Du record). HS 254* v Sussex (Chester-le-St) 2009. BB 1-0 Tas v Q (Brisbane) 1999-00. UK HB 1-3 Sx v Somerset (Taunton) 1999. LO HS 173* v Derbys CB (Derby) 2000 (NWT). LO BB 1-10 Tas v Q (Hobart) 1995-96. T20 HS 95*. T20 BB 3-19.

[NQ]**MYBURGH, Johannes** Gerhardus (Pretoria BHS; U of SA), b Pretoria, South Africa 22 Oct 1980. 5'7". Elder brother of S.J.Myburgh (Northerns, KwaZulu-Natal and Netherlands 2005-06 to date) and brother-in-law of F.de Wet (Northerns, NW, Lions, Hampshire, Dolphins and South Africa 2001-02 to 2011-12). RHB, OB. Northerns 1997-98 to 2006-07. Titans 2004-05. Canterbury 2007-08 to 2009-10. Hampshire 2011. Durham 2012. EU qualified through wife's visa. HS 203 Northerns B v Easterns (Pretoria) 1997-98. CC HS 80 H v Sussex (Southampton) 2011. Du HS 34 v Australia A (Chester-le-St) 2012. BB 4-56 Canterbury v ND (Hamilton) 2008-09. CC BB 1-30 v Durham (Southampton) 2011. LO HS 112 Canterbury v Auckland (Christchurch) 2009-10. LO BB 2-22 Canterbury v CD (Christchurch) 2009-10. T20 HS 88. T20 BB 3-16.

PLUNKETT, L.E. – *see YORKSHIRE.*

H.H.Gibbs and B.A.Raine left the staff without making a County First-Class or List A appearance in 2012.

COUNTY CAPS AWARDED IN 2012

Derbyshire	J.L.Clare, W.J.Durston, M.J.Guptill, A.P.Palladino, D.J.Redfern, D.J.Wainwright
Durham	–
Essex	–
Glamorgan	H.T.Waters
Gloucestershire	E.J.M.Cowan, D.M.Housego, B.A.C.Howell, G.J.McCarter, P.B.Muchall, R.J.Nicol
Hampshire	D.R.Briggs
Kent	M.T.Coles, S.A.Northeast
Lancashire	–
Leicestershire	W.A.White
Middlesex	J.L.Denly, T.S.Roland-Jones
Northamptonshire	J.A.Brooks, A.G.Wakely
Nottinghamshire	M.J.Lumb, J.W.A.Taylor
Somerset	–
Surrey	T.L.Maynard (posthumously), S.C.Meaker
Sussex	–
Warwickshire	V.Chopra, J.S.Patel
Worcestershire (colours)	B.L.D'Oliveira, N.L.Harrison, P.J.Hughes, M.Klinger, J.Leach, D.S.Lucas, C.J.Russell
Yorkshire	G.S.Ballance, S.A.Patterson, J.E.Root

Durham abolished their capping system after 2005. Gloucestershire award caps on first-class debut. Worcestershire award club colours on Championship debut. Glamorgan's capping system is now based on a player's number of appearances and not on his performances.

DURHAM 2012

RESULTS SUMMARY

	Place	Won	Lost	Tied	Drew	NR
LV= County Championship (1st Division)	6th	5	5		5	1
All First-Class Matches		7	5		5	1
Clydesdale Bank 40 (Group B)	5th	5	5			2
Friends Life t20 (North Group)	3rd	4	4	1		1

LV= COUNTY CHAMPIONSHIP AVERAGES

BATTING AND FIELDING

Cap		M	I	NO	HS	Runs	Avge	100	50	Ct/St
1998	P.D.Collingwood	13	24	3	114	697	33.19	1	4	19
	M.J.Di Venuto	5	10	–	96	291	29.10	–	1	11
	M.D.Stoneman	13	24	1	114	636	27.65	1	2	8
	B.A.Stokes	13	23	–	121	625	27.17	1	3	6
2005	D.M.Benkenstein	13	23	1	69	523	23.77	–	2	2
	C.Rushworth	9	11	7	24*	93	23.25	–	–	1
	M.J.Richardson	4	6	–	58	129	21.50	–	1	9
	S.G.Borthwick	13	21	4	60	358	21.05	–	2	18
	K.K.Jennings	5	8	–	70	168	21.00	–	1	–
	P.Mustard	14	24	2	80	443	20.13	–	1	44
	G.Onions	12	17	6	36	193	17.54	–	–	2
	I.D.Blackwell	5	10	1	38*	153	17.00	–	1	2
	W.R.Smith	13	25	1	100	395	16.45	1	–	5
	M.E.Claydon	6	10	2	55	112	14.00	–	–	–
	C.D.Thorp	13	20	2	36	218	12.11	–	–	9
	J.Harrison	3	6	1	23	60	12.00	–	–	–
2005	G.J.Muchall	6	11	–	25	104	9.45	–	–	3
1999	S.J.Harmison	3	5	3	3*	6	3.00	–	–	1

Also batted (1 match each): R.M.R.Brathwaite 0*, 0; L.E.Plunkett 24, 0; M.A.Wood, 34, 30 (1 ct).

BOWLING

	O	M	R	W	Avge	Best	5wI	10wM
G.Onions	373.4	101	959	64	14.98	9- 67	5	3
C.Rushworth	210.5	51	623	38	16.39	5- 38	3	–
C.D.Thorp	301.4	84	789	38	20.76	5- 59	1	–
B.A.Stokes	219.4	43	718	32	22.43	4- 40	–	–
J.Harrison	68	10	260	10	26.00	4-112	–	–
M.E.Claydon	101.2	15	412	14	29.42	4- 84	–	–
S.G.Borthwick	125.4	9	443	15	29.53	4- 37	–	–
Also bowled:								
M.A.Wood	28.4	2	97	5	19.40	5- 78	1	–
I.D.Blackwell	81	20	262	9	29.11	3- 74	–	–
S.J.Harmison	56.2	11	229	6	38.16	2- 38	–	–

D.M.Benkenstein 1-0-2-0; R.M.R.Brathwaite 5-0-31-1; P.D.Collingwood 19-3-60-1;
K.K.Jennings 5-2-9-0; L.E.Plunkett 12-0-69-0; W.R.Smith 7.2-1-35-1.

The First-Class Averages (pp 219–235) give the records of Durham players in all first-class
county matches (Durham's other opponents being Durham MCCU and Australia A), with
the exception of S.J.Harmison, whose first-class figures for Durham are as above, and:
I.D.Blackwell 7-14-1-62-229-17.61-0-1-3ct. 107-26-331-17-19.47-7/52-1-0.
G.Onions 13-18-7-36-216-19.63-0-0-1ct. 385.4-107-973-68-14.30-9/67-5-3.
B.A.Stokes 15-27-0-121-801-29.66-1-5-8ct. 241.4-49-800-37-21.62-4/3-0-0.

DURHAM RECORDS

FIRST-CLASS CRICKET

Highest Total	For 648-5d		v	Notts	Chester-le-St[2]	2009
	V 810-4d		by	Warwicks	Birmingham	1994
Lowest Total	For 67		v	Middlesex	Lord's	1996
	V 18		by	Durham MCCU	Chester-le-St[2]	2012
Highest Innings	For 273	M.L.Love	v	Hampshire	Chester-le-St[2]	2003
	V 501*	B.C.Lara	for	Warwicks	Birmingham	1994

Highest Partnership for each Wicket

1st	334*	S.Hutton/M.A.Roseberry	v	Oxford U	Oxford	1996
2nd	258	J.J.B.Lewis/M.L.Love	v	Notts	Chester-le-St[2]	2001
3rd	205	G.Fowler/S.Hutton	v	Yorkshire	Leeds	1993
4th	331	B.A.Stokes/D.M.Benkenstein	v	Lancashire	Chester-le-St[2]	2011
5th	247	G.J.Muchall/I.D.Blackwell	v	Worcs	Worcester	2011
6th	249	G.J.Muchall/P.Mustard	v	Kent	Canterbury	2006
7th	315	D.M.Benkenstein/O.D.Gibson	v	Yorkshire	Leeds	2006
8th	147	P.Mustard/L.E.Plunkett	v	Yorkshire	Leeds	2009
9th	127	D.G.C.Ligertwood/S.J.E.Brown	v	Surrey	Stockton	1996
10th	103	M.M.Betts/D.M.Cox	v	Sussex	Hove	1996

Best Bowling (Innings)	For 10- 47	O.D.Gibson	v	Hampshire	Chester-le-St[2]	2007
	V 9- 36	M.S.Kasprowicz	for	Glamorgan	Cardiff	2003
Best Bowling (Match)	For 14-177	A.Walker	v	Essex	Chelmsford	1995
	V 13-110	M.S.Kasprowicz	for	Glamorgan	Chester-le-St[2]	2003

Most Runs – Season	1654	M.J.Di Venuto	(av 78.76)	2009
Most Runs – Career	8788	D.M.Benkenstein	(av 46.74)	2005-12
Most 100s – Season	6	P.D.Collingwood		2005
	6	M.J.Di Venuto		2009
Most 100s – Career	21	D.M.Benkenstein		2005-11
Most Wkts – Season	80	O.D.Gibson	(av 20.75)	2007
Most Wkts – Career	518	S.J.E.Brown	(av 28.30)	1992-2002
Most Career W-K Dismissals	500	P.Mustard	(483 ct; 17 st)	2002-12
Most Career Catches in the Field	146	P.D.Collingwood		1996-2012

LIMITED-OVERS CRICKET

Highest Total	50ov	332-4		v	Worcs	Chester-le-St[2]	2007
	40ov	325-9		v	Surrey	The Oval	2011
	T20	225-2		v	Leics	Chester-le-St[2]	2010
Lowest Total	50ov	82		v	Worcs	Chester-le-St[1]	1968
	40ov	72		v	Warwicks	Birmingham	2002
	T20	93		v	Kent	Canterbury	2009
Highest Innings	50ov	138	M.J.Di Venuto	v	Derbyshire	Chester-le-St[2]	2008
	40ov	150*	B.A.Stokes	v	Warwicks	Birmingham	2011
	T20	83*	H.H.Gibbs	v	Derbyshire	Chester-le-St[2]	2012
Best Bowling	50ov	7-32	S.P.Davis	v	Lancashire	Chester-le-St[1]	1983
	40ov	6-31	N.Killeen	v	Derbyshire	Derby	2000
	T20	5- 6	P.D.Collingwood	v	Northants	Chester-le-St[2]	2011

[1] Chester-le-Street CC (Ropery Lane) [2] Emirates Durham International Cricket Ground

ESSEX

Formation of Present Club: 14 January 1876
Inaugural First-Class Match: 1894
Colours: Blue, Gold and Red
Badge: Three Seaxes above Scroll bearing 'Essex'
County Champions: (6) 1979, 1983, 1984, 1986, 1991, 1992
Gillette/NatWest/C&G/FP Trophy Winners: (3) 1985, 1997, 2008
Benson and Hedges Cup Winners: (2) 1979, 1998
Pro 40/National League (Div 1) Winners: (2) 2005, 2006
Sunday League Winners: (3) 1981, 1984, 1985
Clydesdale Bank 40 Winners: (0); best – Semi-Finalist 2010
Twenty20 Cup Winners: (0); best – Semi-Finalist 2006, 2008, 2010

Chief Executive: Derek Bowden, The Ford County Ground, New Writtle Street, Chelmsford CM2 0PG • Tel: 01245 252420 • Fax: 01245 254030 • Email: administration@essexcricket.org.uk • Web: www.essexcricket.org.uk

First Team Coach: A.P.Grayson. **Assistant Coach**: M.J.Walker. **Bowling Coach**: C.E.W.Silverwood. **Captain**: J.S.Foster. **Vice-Captain**: R.S.Bopara. **Overseas Players**: R.J.Quiney and S.W.Tait (T20 only). **2013 Beneficiary**: D.D.Masters. **Head Groundsman**: Stuart Kerrison. **Scorer**: A.E. (Tony) Choat. ‡ New registration. NQ Not qualified for England.

BOPARA, Ravinder Singh (Brampton Manor S; Barking Abbey Sports C), b Newham, London 4 May 1985. 5'8". RHB, RM. Debut (Essex) 2002; cap 2005. Auckland 2009-10. Dolphins 2010-11. MCC 2006, 2008. YC 2008. **Tests**: 13 (2007-08 to 2012); HS 143 v WI (Lord's) 2009; BB 1-39 v SL (Galle) 2007-08. **LOI**: 83 (2006-07 to 2012); HS 96 v I (Lord's) 2011; BB 4-38 v B (Birmingham) 2010. **IT20**: 22 (2008 to 2012-13); HS 59 v WI (Nottingham) 2012; BB 4-10 v WI (Oval) 2011 – England record. F-c Tours: WI 2008-09, 2010-11 (EL); SL 2007-08, 2011-12. 1000 runs (1): 1256 (2008). HS 229 v Northants (Chelmsford) 2007. BB 5-75 v Surrey (Chelmsford) 2006. LO HS 201* v Leics (Leicester) 2008 (FPT) – Ex record. LO BB 5-63 Dolphins v Warriors (Pietermaritzburg) 2010-11. T20 HS 105*. T20 BB 4-10.

CHAMBERS, Maurice Anthony (Homerton TC; Sir George Monoux C), b Port Antonio, Portland, Jamaica 14 Sep 1987. 6'3". RHB, RFM. Debut (Essex) 2005. No f-c appearances 2006-07 – stress fracture of the back. MCC YC 2004. F-c Tours (EL): WI 2010-11. HS 30 v Leics (Leicester) 2011. BB 6-68 (10-123 match) v Notts (Chelmsford) 2010. LO HS 2 v Lancs (Chelmsford) 2012 (CB40). LO BB 1-21 v Worcs (Worcester) 2012 (CB40). T20 HS 10*. T20 BB 3-31.

COOK, Alastair Nathan (Bedford S), b Gloucester 25 Dec 1984. 6'3". LHB, OB. Debut (Essex) 2003; cap 2005. MCC 2004-07. Essex 2nd XI debut 2000, aged 15y 235d. England U19 captain 2003-04. YC 2005. *Wisden* 2011. **ECB central contract 2012-13**. **Tests**: 88 (2005-06 to 2012-13, 7 as captain); HS 294 v I (Birmingham) 2011. Scored 60 and 104* v I (Nagpur) 2005-06 on debut. Third, after D.G.Bradman and S.R.Tendulkar, to score seven Test hundreds before his 23rd birthday. Second, after M.A.Taylor, to score 1000 runs in the calendar year of his debut. BB – . **LOI**: 64 (2006 to 2012-13, 41 as captain); HS 137 v P (Abu Dhabi) 2011-12. **IT20**: 4 (2007 to 2009-10); HS 26 v SA (Centurion) 2009-10. F-c Tours (C=captain): A 2006-07, 2010-11; SA 2009-10; WI 2005-06 (Eng A), 2008-09; NZ 2007-08, 2012-13C; I 2005-06, 2008-09, 2012-13C; SL 2004-05 (Eng A), 2007-08, 2011-12; B 2009-10C; UAE 2011-12 (v P). 1000 runs (5+1); most – 1466 (2005). HS (*see Tests*). CC HS 195 v Northants (Northampton) 2005. BB 3-13 v Northants (Chelmsford) 2005. LO HS 137 (*see LOI*). BB – . T20 HS 100*.

98

CRADDOCK, Thomas Richard (Holmfirth HS; Huddersfield New C; Leeds Met U), b Huddersfield, Yorks 13 Jul 1989. 5'10". RHB, LB. Debut (Essex) 2011. Leeds/Bradford MCCU (not f-c) 2010-11. Northamptonshire 2nd XI 2010. Gloucestershire 2nd XI 2011. HS 21 v Leics (Southend) 2011. BB 5-96 v Derbys (Chelmsford) 2012. LO HS 5* and LO BB 2-38 v Somerset (Taunton) 2011 (CB40). T20 HS – . T20 BB — .

FOAKES, Benjamin Thomas (Tendring TC), b Colchester 15 Feb 1993. 6'1". RHB, WK. Debut (Essex) 2011. Essex 2nd XI debut 2008, aged 15y 172d. England U19s 2010-11. HS 93 v Leics (Leicester) 2012. LO HS 56 EL v Australia A (Hobart) 2012-13.

FOSTER, James Savin (Forest S, Snaresbrook; Collingwood C, Durham U), b Whipps Cross 15 Apr 1980. 6'0". RHB, WK. British U 2000-01. Essex debut 2000; cap 2001; captain 2010 (*part*) to date; benefit 2011. Durham UCCE 2001. MCC 2004, 2008-10. **Tests**: 7 (2001-02 to 2002-03); HS 48 v I (Bangalore) 2001-02. **LOI**: 11 (2001-02); HS 13 v I (Bombay) 2001-02. **IT20**: 5 (2009); HS 14* v P (Oval) 2009. F-c Tours: A 2002-03; WI 2000-01 (Eng A); NZ 2001-02; I 2001-02, 2007-08 (Eng A). 1000 runs (1): 1037 (2004). HS 212 v Leics (Chelmsford) 2004. BB 1-122 v Northants (Northampton) 2008 – in contrived circumstances. LO HS 83* v Durham, inc 5 sixes in 5 balls off S.G.Borthwick (Chester-le-St) 2009 (P40). T20 HS 65*.

‡MAHMOOD, Sajid Iqbal (North C, Bolton), b Bolton, Lancs 21 Dec 1981. 6'4". RHB, RFM. Lancashire 2002-12; cap 2007. Somerset 2012 (on loan). MCC 2005, 2009. **Tests**: 8 (2006 to 2006-07); HS 34 and BB 4-22 v P (Leeds) 2006. **LOI**: 26 (2004 to 2009-10); HS 22* v P (Birmingham) 2006; BB 4-50 v SL (North Shore, Antigua) 2006-07. **IT20**: 4 (2006 to 2009-10); HS 1* v SA (Centurion) 2009-10; BB 1-31 v SA (Johannesburg) 2009-10. F-c Tours (Eng A): A 2006-07 (Eng); WI 2005-06; NZ 2008-09; I 2003-04; SL 2004-05. HS 94 La v Sussex (Manchester) 2004. BB 6-30 La v Durham (Chester-le-St) 2009. LO HS 29 La v Staffs (Stone) 2004 (CGT). LO BB 5-16 La v Sri Lanka A (Liverpool) 2007. T20 HS 34. T20 BB 4-21.

MASTERS, David Daniel (Fort Luton HS; Mid Kent CHE), b Chatham, Kent 22 Apr 1978. Son of K.D.Masters (Kent 1983-84), elder brother of D.Masters (Leicestershire 2009-10). 6'4". RHB, RMF. Kent 2000-02. Leicestershire 2003-07; cap 2007. Essex debut/cap 2008; benefit 2013. HS 119 Le v Sussex (Hove) 2003. Ex HS 67 v Leics (Chelmsford) 2009. 50 wkts (3); most – 93 (2011). BB 8-10 v Leics (Southend) 2011. LO HS 39 Le v Glos (Cheltenham) 2008 (P40). LO BB 5-17 v Surrey (Oval) 2008 (FPT). T20 HS 14. T20 BB 3-7.

MICKLEBURGH, Jaik Charles (Bungay HS), b Norwich, Norfolk 30 Mar 1990. 5'10". RHB, RM. Debut (Essex) 2008. Mid West Rhinos 2012-13. Essex 2nd XI debut, aged 16y 160d. Norfolk 2007. England U19s 2009. HS 174 v Durham (Chester-le-St) 2010. BB – . LO HS 73 MWR v ME (Kwekwe) 2012-13. T20 HS 47*.

MILLS, Tymal Solomon (Mildenhall C of T), b Dewsbury, Yorks 12 Aug 1992. 6'1". RHB, LMF. Debut (Essex) 2011. Essex 2nd XI debut 2010. England U19s 2010-11. HS 20* v Yorks (Chelmsford) 2012. BB 4-25 v Glamorgan (Cardiff) 2012. LO HS 2* v Australians (Chelmsford) 2012. LO BB 2-40 Eng Development XI v Sri Lanka A (Manchester) 2011 and 2-40 v Netherlands (Colchester) 2012 (CB40). T20 HS 3*. T20 BB – .

NAPIER, Graham Richard (The Gilberd S, Colchester), b Colchester 6 Jan 1980. 5'9½". RHB, RM. Debut (Essex) 1997; cap 2003; benefit 2012. Wellington 2008-09. MCC 2004. F-c Tour (Eng A): I 2003-04. HS 196 v Surrey (Croydon) 2011, hitting a world record-equalling 16 sixes and being dismissed just 28 balls after reaching his century. Won 2008 Walter Lawrence Trophy with 44-ball hundred v Sussex (Chelmsford) and in 2012 with 48-ball hundred v Cambridge MCCU (Cambridge). BB 6-53 v Surrey (Chelmsford) 2011. LO HS 79 Essex CB v Lancs CB (Chelmsford) 2000 (NWT). LO BB 6-29 v Worcs (Chelmsford) 2001 (NL). T20 HS 152* v Sussex (Chelmsford) 2008 – record T20 Cup score (58b, 10 fours, 16 sixes); 2nd highest score in all T20. T20 BB 4-10.

PETTINI, Mark Lewis (Comberton Village C; Hills Road SFC, Cambridge; Cardiff U), b Brighton, Sussex 7 Aug 1983. 5'10". RHB, RM. Debut (Essex) 2001; cap 2006; captain 2007 (*part*) to 2010 (*part*). Mountaineers 2011-12 to date. MCC 2005. 1000 runs (1): 1218 (2006). HS 208* v Derbys (Chelmsford) 2006. BB 1-72 v Leics (Leicester) 2012 – in contrived circumstances. LO 144 v Surrey (Oval) 2007 (FPT). T20 HS 87.

PHILLIPS, Timothy James (Felsted S; St Hild & St Bede C, Durham U), b Cambridge 13 Mar 1981. 6'1". LHB, SLA. Debut (Essex) 1999; cap 2006. Durham UCCE 2001-02. HS 89 v Worcs (Worcester) 2005. BB 5-41 v Derbys (Chelmsford) 2006. LO HS 58* v Glos (Cheltenham) 2011 (CB40). LO BB 5-28 v Unicorns (Bury St Edmunds) 2011 (CB40). T20 HS 57*. T20 BB 4-22.

‡NQ**QUINEY, Robert** John, b Brighton, Victoria, Australia 20 Aug 1982. 6'4". LHB, RM. Victoria 2006-07 to date. **Tests** (A): 2 (2012-13); HS 9 v SA (Brisbane) 2012-13; BB – . HS 153 Vic v Tas (Hobart) 2009-10. BB 2-22 Vic v WA (Melbourne) 2007-08. LO HS 122 Vic v EL (Melbourne) 2012-13. LO BB – . T20 HS 97. T20 BB – .

RAMSDEN, Henry Douglas ('Harry') (Oundle S), b Wandsworth, Surrey 11 Nov 1992. 6'4". LHB, OB. Essex 2nd XI debut 2012. Hertfordshire 2011. Awaiting 1st XI debut.

SHAH, Owais Alam (Isleworth & Syon S), b Karachi, Pakistan 22 Oct 1978. 6'0". RHB, OB. Middlesex 1996-2010; cap 2000; captain 2004 (*part*); benefit 2008. Cape Cobras 2010-11. Essex debut 2011. MCC 2002-08. YC 2001. **Tests**: 6 (2005-06 to 2008-09); HS 88 v I (Bombay) 2005-06; BB – . **LOI**: 71 (2001 to 2009-10); HS 107* v I (Oval) 2007; BB 3-15 v Ire (Belfast) 2009. **IT20**: 17 (2007 to 2009); HS 55* v WI (Oval) 2007. F-c Tours (Eng A): A 1996-97; WI 2005-06 (*part*), 2008-09 (Eng); I 2005-06 (Eng – *part*); SL 1997-98, 2004-05, 2007-08 (Eng). 1000 runs (8); most – 1728 (2005). HS 203 M v Derbys (Southgate) 2001. Ex HS 161 v Hants (Southampton) 2012. BB 3-33 M v Glos (Bristol) 1999. Ex BB – . LO HS 134 M v Sussex (Arundel) 1999 (NL). LO BB 4-11 M v Leics (Lord's) 2009 (P40). T20 HS 84. T20 BB 2-26.

NQ**SMITH, Gregory** Marc (St Stithins C), b Johannesburg, South Africa 20 Apr 1983. 5'9". RHB, RM/OB. Debut (SA Academy) 2003-04. Griqualand West 2003-04. Derbyshire 2006-11 (Kolpak registration); cap 2009; captain 2010 (*part*). Mountaineers 2010-11. Essex debut 2012. HS 165* De v Glamorgan (Derby) 2010. Ex HS 160 v Cambridge MCCU (Cambridge) 2012. BB 5-54 De v Northants (Chesterfield) 2010. Ex BB 2-31 v Yorks (Leeds) 2012. LO HS 88 De v Kent (Derby) 2007 (P40). LO BB 4-53 De v Lancs (Derby) 2009 (P40). T20 HS 100*. T20 BB 5-17.

‡NQ**TAIT, Shaun** William (Oakwood Area State S, S Aus), b Bedford Park, Adelaide, S Australia 22 Feb 1983. RHB, RF. S Australia 2002-03 to 2008-09. Durham 2004. Glamorgan 2010 (T20 only). Joins Essex in 2013 for T20 only. **Tests** (A): 3 (2005 to 2007-08); HS 8 v I (Perth) 2007-08; BB 3-97 v I (Nottingham) 2005. **LOI** (A): 35 (2006-07 to 2010-11); HS 11 v E (Sydney) 2006-07; BB 4-39 v SA (Gros Islet) 2006-07. **IT20** (A): 19 (2007-08 to 2010-11); HS 6 v P (Birmingham) 2010; BB 3-13 v P (Melbourne) 2009-10. F-c Tour (A): E 2005. HS 68 S Aus v Vic (Adelaide) 2005-06. CC HS 4. BB 7-29 (10-98 match) S Aus v Q (Brisbane) 2007-08. CC BB – . LO HS 22* Aus A v Z (Perth) 2003-04. LO BB 8-43 inc hat-trick S Aus v Tas (Adelaide) 2003-04, 8th best analysis in all l-o cricket. T20 HS 26. T20 BB 5-32.

^{NQ}**Ten DOESCHATE, Ryan** Neil (Fairbairn C; Cape Town U), b Port Elizabeth, South Africa 30 Jun 1980. 5'10½". RHB, RMF. Debut (Essex) 2003; cap 2006. EU passport – Dutch ancestry. Netherlands 2005 to date. Otago 2012-13. **LOI** (Ne): 33 (2006 to 2010-11); HS 119 v E (Nagpur) 2010-11; BB 4-31 v Canada (Nairobi) 2006-07. **IT20** (Ne): 9 (2008 to 2009-10); HS 56 v Kenya (Belfast) 2008; BB 3-23 v Scotland (Belfast) 2008. F-c Tours (Ne): SA 2006-07, 2007-08; K 2005-06, 2009-10; Ireland 2005. HS 259* and BB 6-20 (9-112 match) Netherlands v Canada (Pretoria) 2006. Ex HS 164 v Sri Lankans (Chelmsford) 2011. CC HS 159* v Surrey (Guildford) 2009. Ex BB 6-57 v NZ (Chelmsford) 2008. CC BB 5-13 v Hants (Chelmsford) 2010. LO HS 134* Ne v Namibia (Benoni) 2008-09. LO BB 5-50 v Glos (Bristol) 2007 (FPT). T20 HS 121*. T20 BB 4-24.

TOPLEY, Reece James William (Royal Hospital S, Ipswich), b Ipswich, Suffolk 21 February 1994. Son of T.D.Topley (Surrey, Essex, GW 1985-94) and nephew of P.A.Topley (Kent 1972-75). 6'7". RHB, LMF. Debut (Essex) 2011. Essex 2nd XI debut 2010, aged 16y 156d. HS 9 v Derbys (Chelmsford) 2011. BB 5-46 v Kent (Chelmsford) 2011 – on CC debut. LO HS 19 v Somerset (Taunton) 2011 (CB40). LO BB 4-46 v Australians (Chelmsford) 2012. T20 HS 1*. T20 BB 3-19. England U19s 2012-13.

VELANI, Kishen Shailesh (Brentwood S), b Newham, London 2 Sep 1994. 5'10". RHB, RM. Awaiting 1st XI debut. England U19s 2012-13.

WESTLEY, Thomas (Linton Village C; Hills Road SFC), b Cambridge 13 March 1989. 6'2". RHB, OB. Debut (Essex) 2007. MCC 2007, 2009. Durham MCCU 2010-11. Essex 2nd XI debut 2004, aged 15y 88d. Cambridgeshire 2005. HS 185 v Glamorgan (Colchester) 2012. BB 4-55 DU v Durham (Durham) 2010. CC BB 3-5 v Kent (Chelmsford) 2012. LO HS 82 v Glos (Chelmsford) 2012 (CB40). LO BB 1-9 v Worcs (Worcester) 2012 (CB40). T20 HS 13. T20 BB 1-7.

RELEASED/RETIRED

(Having made a County First-Class or List A appearance in 2012)

COMBER, Michael Andrew (Clacton County HS), b Colchester 26 Oct 1989. 6'3". RHB, RMF. Essex 2010. No f-c appearances in 2011-12. Essex 2nd XI debut 2007. Suffolk 2010-12. HS 19 and BB 2-34 v Bangladeshis (Chelmsford) 2010. LO 0. CC BB 1-4 v Durham (Chelmsford) 2010. LO HS 52* v Northants (Southend) 2010 (CB40). LO BB – . T20 HS 12.

^{NQ}**FRANKLIN, James** Edward Charles (Wellington C; Victoria U), Wellington, New Zealand 7 Nov 1980. 6'4½". LHB, LFM. Wellington 1998-99 to date. Gloucestershire 2004-10; cap 2004. Glamorgan 2006; cap 2006. Essex (l-o only) 2012. **Tests** (NZ): 31 (2000-01 to 2012-13); HS 122* v SA (Cape Town) 2006-07; BB 6-119 v A (Auckland) 2004-05. Hat-trick v B (Dhaka) 2004-05. **LOI** (NZ): 104 (2000-01 to 2012-13); HS 98* v I (Bangalore) 2010-11; BB 5-42 v E (Chester-le-St) 2004. **IT20** (NZ): 36 (2005-06 to 2012-13); HS 60 v Z (Hamilton) 2011-12; BB 4-15 v E (Hamilton) 2012-13. F-c Tours (NZ): E 2004; A 2004-05; SA 2004-05 (NZ A), 2005-06, 2012-13; I 2012; SL 2012-13; Z 2005, 2010-11 (NZ A); B 2004-05. HS 219 Wellington v Auckland (Auckland) 2008-09. CC HS 109 Gs v Derbys (Cheltenham) 2009; became only the second man for Gs to score a hundred and take a hat-trick in the same match. BB 7-14 Gs v Derbys (Bristol) 2010. Hat-trick (*see above*). LO HS 133* Gs v Derbys (Bristol) 2010 (CB40). LO BB 5-42 (*see LOI*). T20 HS 90. T20 BB 4-15.

GODLEMAN, B.A. – *see DERBYSHIRE.*

^{NO}**HARBHAJAN SINGH** PLAHA, b Jullundur City, India 3 Jul 1980. 6'0''. RHB, OB. Punjab 1997-98 to date. Surrey 2005-07. Essex 2012. **Tests** (I): 101 (1997-98 to 2012-13); HS 115 v NZ (Ahmedabad) 2010-11; BB 8-84 (15-217 match) v A (Madras) 2000-01. Took 28 wkts, inc a hat-trick, in 2 Tests v A in 2000-01. **LOI** (I): 229 (1997-98 to 2011); HS 49 v A (Vadodara) 2009-10; BB 5-31 v E (Delhi) 2005-06. **IT20** (I): 25 (2006-07 to 2012-13); HS 21 v NZ (Christchurch) 2008-09; BB 4-12 v E (Colombo, RPS) 2012-13. F-c Tours (I): E 2002, 2011; A 1999-00, 2003-04, 2007-08; SA 2001-02, 2006-07, 2010-11; WI 2001-02, 2006, 2011; NZ 1998-99, 2002-03, 2008-09; P 2005-06; SL 1998-99, 2001, 2008, 2010; Z 1998-99, 2001, 2005-06; B 2004-05, 2009-10. HS 115 (*see* Tests). CC HS 84 Sy v Glos (Bristol) 2005. Ex HS 40 v Hants (Chelmsford) 2012. BB 8-84 (*see* Tests). UK BB 7-83 I v Essex (Chelmsford) 2002. CC BB 6-36 v Hants (Southampton) 2005. Ex BB 4-91 v Glamorgan (Colchester) 2012. LO HS 79* Punjab v Maharashtra (Delhi) 2011-12. LO BB 5-31 (*see LOI*). T20 HS 49*. T20 BB 5-18.

PETERSEN, A.N. – *see SOMERSET.*

WHEATER, A.J. – *see HAMPSHIRE.*

WILLOUGHBY, Charl Myles (Wynberg BHS; Stellenbosch U), b Cape Town, South Africa 3 Dec 1974. 6'2''. LHB, LMF. Boland 1994-95 to 1999-00. W Province 2000-01 to 2003-04. WP-Boland 2004-05. Leicestershire 2005 (Kolpak). Cape Cobras 2005-06 to 2011-12. Somerset 2006-11; cap 2007. essex 2012. Qualified as UK resident in 2011. MCC 2001, 2004. Berkshire 2000. **Tests** (SA): 2 (2003); HS – ; BB 1-47 v B (Chittagong) 2002-03. **LOI** (SA): 3 (1999-00 to 2003); HS 0; BB 2-39 v P (Sharjah) 1999-00. F-c Tours (SA): E 2003; WI 2000 (SA A); Z 1998-99 (SA Acad), 2004 (SA A); B 2003. HS 47 Sm v Worcs (Taunton) 2006. Ex HS 1* v Glamorgan (Cardiff) 2012. 50 wkts (6+2); most – 66 (2006). BB 7-44 Sm v Glos (Taunton) 2006. Ex BB 5-70 v Kent (Chelmsford) 2012. LO HS 15 Sm v Kent (Canterbury) 2009 (FPT). LO BB 6-16 Le v Somerset (Leicester) 2005 (CGT) – Le record. T20 HS 11. T20 BB 4-9.

BENEFITS AWARDED IN 2013

Derbyshire	–
Durham	S.J.Harmison
Essex	D.D.Masters
Glamorgan	M.A.Wallace
Gloucestershire	–
Hampshire	–
Kent	–
Lancashire	–
Leicestershire	–
Middlesex	–
Northamptonshire	S.D.Peters
Nottinghamshire	G.P.Swann
Somerset	A.V.Suppiah
Surrey	–
Sussex	–
Warwickshire	J.O.Troughton
Worcestershire	–
Yorkshire	–

ESSEX 2012

RESULTS SUMMARY

	Place	Won	Lost	Tied	Drew	NR
LV= County Championship (2nd Division)	5th	3	3		10	
All First-Class Matches		3	3		11	
Clydesdale Bank 40 (Group A)	5th	4	6			2
Friends Life t20 (South Group)	3rd	5	4			1

LV= COUNTY CHAMPIONSHIP AVERAGES

BATTING AND FIELDING

Cap		M	I	NO	HS	Runs	Avge	100	50	Ct/St
2005	R.S.Bopara	5	7	2	174	331	66.20	2	–	–
	O.A.Shah	8	13	1	161	589	49.08	2	2	3
2006	R.N.ten Doeschate	9	12	3	69	412	45.77	–	4	7
2001	J.S.Foster	15	18	3	135	655	43.66	1	4	40/3
2006	M.L.Pettini	15	21	4	92	624	36.70	–	7	5
	T.Westley	16	23	2	185	755	35.95	2	3	9
	A.J.Wheater	11	13	2	98	391	35.54	–	3	7
	J.C.Mickleburgh	8	12	1	126	330	30.00	1	2	7
	B.A.Godleman	7	11	1	130	286	28.60	1	–	4
	B.T.Foakes	4	4	–	93	114	28.50	–	1	1
2003	G.R.Napier	11	11	1	43	235	23.50	–	–	4
	A.N.Petersen	7	11	–	145	235	21.36	1	–	8
	G.M.Smith	8	9	–	42	158	17.55	–	–	3
2008	D.D.Masters	13	11	–	35	113	10.27	–	–	3
	T.R.Craddock	6	8	3	16	46	9.20	–	–	2
	T.S.Mills	8	10	4	20*	30	5.00	–	–	5
	C.M.Willoughby	7	6	4	1*	2	1.00	–	–	3
	M.A.Chambers	7	7	1	2	2	0.33	–	–	4
	R.J.W.Topley	3	4	1	1	1	0.33	–	–	–

Also batted: A.N.Cook (2 matches – cap 2005) 9, 5, 1 (1 ct); Harbhajan Singh (5) 40, 5*, 13 (10 ct); T.J.Phillips (1 – cap 2006) 7.

BOWLING

	O	M	R	W	Avge	Best	5wI	10wM
D.D.Masters	371.3	114	873	46	18.97	7-60	3	–
G.R.Napier	295.2	49	974	41	23.75	5-58	2	–
M.A.Chambers	163.1	29	567	20	28.35	4-31	–	–
T.R.Craddock	125.5	23	438	15	29.20	5-96	1	–
T.S.Mills	129.1	19	425	14	30.35	4-25	–	–
R.J.W.Topley	112.1	24	350	11	31.81	3-59	–	–
C.M.Willoughby	174	31	609	19	32.05	5-70	1	–
Harbhajan Singh	176.3	38	431	13	33.15	4-91	–	–
T.Westley	143.3	24	470	10	47.00	3- 5	–	–

Also bowled:

	O	M	R	W	Avge	Best		
R.N.ten Doeschate	86	11	332	6	55.33	3-39		
G.M.Smith	107	21	353	6	58.83	2-31		

R.S.Bopara 2-0-5-0; A.N.Petersen 1-0-4-0; M.L.Pettini 3-1-0-72-1; A.J.Wheater 4-0-86-1.

The First-Class Averages (pp 219–235) give the records of Essex players in all first-class county matches (Essex's other opponents being Cambridge MCCU), with the exception of R.S.Bopara, A.N.Cook and A.N.Petersen, whose first-class figures for Essex are as above.

ESSEX RECORDS

FIRST-CLASS CRICKET

Highest Total	For	761-6d		v	Leics	Chelmsford	1990
	V	803-4d		by	Yorkshire	Brentwood	1934
Lowest Total	For	30		v	Yorkshire	Leyton	1901
	V	14		by	Surrey	Chelmsford	1983
Highest Innings	For	343*	P.A.Perrin	v	Derbyshire	Chesterfield	1904
	V	332	W.H.Ashdown	for	Kent	Brentwood	1934

Highest Partnership for each Wicket

1st	316	G.A.Gooch/P.J.Prichard	v	Kent	Chelmsford	1994
2nd	403	G.A.Gooch/P.J.Prichard	v	Leics	Chelmsford	1990
3rd	347*	M.E.Waugh/N.Hussain	v	Lancashire	Ilford	1992
4th	314	Salim Malik/N.Hussain	v	Surrey	The Oval	1991
5th	339	J.C.Mickleburgh/J.S.Foster	v	Durham	Chester-le-St[2]	2010
6th	253	A.J.Wheater/J.S.Foster	v	Northants	Chelmsford	2011
7th	261	J.W.H.T.Douglas/J.Freeman	v	Lancashire	Leyton	1914
8th	263	D.R.Wilcox/R.M.Taylor	v	Warwicks	Southend	1946
9th	251	J.W.H.T.Douglas/S.N.Hare	v	Derbyshire	Leyton	1921
10th	218	F.H.Vigar/T.P.B.Smith	v	Derbyshire	Chesterfield	1947

Best Bowling	For	10- 32	H.Pickett	v	Leics	Leyton	1895
(Innings)	V	10- 40	E.G.Dennett	for	Glos	Bristol	1906
Best Bowling	For	17-119	W.Mead	v	Hampshire	Southampton	1895
(Match)	V	17- 56	C.W.L.Parker	for	Glos	Gloucester	1925

Most Runs – Season	2559	G.A.Gooch	(av 67.34)	1984
Most Runs – Career	30701	G.A.Gooch	(av 51.77)	1973-97
Most 100s – Season	9	J.O'Connor		1929, 1934
	9	D.J.Insole		1955
Most 100s – Career	94	G.A.Gooch		1973-97
Most Wkts – Season	172	T.P.B Smith	(av 27.13)	1947
Most Wkts – Career	1610	T.P.B.Smith	(av 26.68)	1929-51
Most Career W-K Dismissals	1231	B.Taylor	(1040 ct; 191 st)	1949-73
Most Career Catches in the Field	519	K.W.R.Fletcher		1962-88

LIMITED-OVERS CRICKET

Highest Total	50ov	391-5		v	Surrey	The Oval	2008
	40ov	316-4		v	Glamorgan	Chelmsford	2004
	T20	242-3		v	Sussex	Chelmsford	2008
Lowest Total	50ov	57		v	Lancashire	Lord's	1996
	40ov	69		v	Derbyshire	Chesterfield	1974
	T20	82		v	Somerset	Chelmsford	2011
Highest Innings	50ov	201*	R.S.Bopara	v	Leics	Leicester	2008
	40ov	176	G.A.Gooch	v	Glamorgan	Southend	1983
	T20	152*	G.R.Napier	v	Sussex	Chelmsford	2008
Best Bowling	50ov	5- 8	J.K.Lever	v	Middlesex	Westcliff	1972
		5- 8	G.A.Gooch	v	Cheshire	Chester	1995
	40ov	8-26	K.D.Boyce	v	Lancashire	Manchester	1971
	T20	6-16	T.G.Southee	v	Glamorgan	Chelmsford	2011

GLAMORGAN

Formation of Present Club: 6 July 1888
Inaugural First-Class Match: 1921
Colours: Blue and Gold
Badge: Gold Daffodil
County Champions: (3) 1948, 1969, 1997
Gillette/NatWest/C&G/FP Trophy Winners: (0); best – Finalist 1977
Benson and Hedges Cup Winners: (0); best – Finalist 2000
Pro 40/National League (Div 1) Winners: (2) 2002, 2004
Sunday League Winners: (1) 1993
Clydesdale Bank 40 Winners: (0); best – 5th Group C 2011
Twenty20 Cup Winners: (0); best – Semi-Finalist 2004

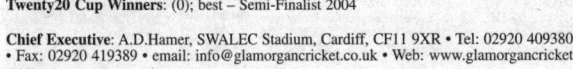

Chief Executive: A.D.Hamer, SWALEC Stadium, Cardiff, CF11 9XR • Tel: 02920 409380 • Fax: 02920 419389 • email: info@glamorgancricket.co.uk • Web: www.glamorgancricket.com

Head of Elite Performance: M.P.Mott. **Bowling Coach**: S.L.Watkin. **Player Development Manager**: R.V.Almond. **Captain**: M.A.Wallace (f-c) and M.J.North (l-o). **Vice-Captain**: tbc. **Overseas Players**: M.J.North and D.P.Nannes (T20 only). **2013 Beneficiary**: M.A.Wallace. **Head Groundsman**: Keith Exton. **Scorer**: Andrew K.Hignell. ‡ New registration. NQ Not qualified for England.

ALLENBY, James (Christ Church GS, Perth), b Perth, W Australia 12 Sep 1982. 6'0". RHB, RM. Leicestershire 2006-09. Glamorgan debut 2009; cap 2010. HS 138* Le v Bangladesh A (Leicester) 2008. CC HS 137 v Surrey (Oval) 2009. BB 5-44 v Derbys (Cardiff) 2011. LO HS 91* Le v Middx (Lord's) 2007 (P40). LO BB 5-43 Le v Derbys (Leicester) 2007 (FPT). T20 HS 110. T20 BB 5-21 Le v Lancs (Manchester) 2008, inc 4 wkts in 4 balls.

BRAGG, William David (Rougemont S, Newport; UWIC), b Newport, Monmouthshire 24 Oct 1986. 5'9". LHB, RM. Debut (Glamorgan) 2007. No f-c appearances in 2008. Wales MC 2004-09. 1000 runs (1): 1033 (2011). HS 110 v Leics (Colwyn Bay) 2011. BB 1-4 v Kent (Canterbury) 2011. LO HS 78 v Leics (Leicester) 2009 (P40). BB – . T20 HS 15.

COOKE, Christopher Barry (Bishops S, Cape Town; U of Cape Town), b Johannesburg, South Africa 30 May 1986. RHB, WK. W Province 2009-10. Awaiting Glamorgan f-c debut. Glamorgan 2nd XI debut 2010. HS 44* WP v EP (Cape Town) 2009-10. LO HS 137* v Somerset (Taunton) 2012 (CB40). T20 HS 47.

COSKER, Dean Andrew (Millfield S), b Weymouth, Dorset 7 Jan 1978. 5'11". RHB, SLA. Debut (Glamorgan) 1996; cap 2000; benefit 2010. MCC 2010. F-c Tours (Eng A): SA 1998-99; SL 1997-98; Z 1998-99; K 1997-98. HS 52 v Glos (Bristol) 2005. 50 wkts (1): 51 (2010). BB 6-91 (11-126 match) v Essex (Cardiff) 2009. LO HS 50* v Northants (Northampton) 2009 (FPT). LO BB 5-54 v Essex (Chelmsford) 2003 (NL). T20 HS 21*. T20 BB 3-11.

GLOVER, John Charles (Llantarnam CS; St Aidan's C, Durham), b Cardiff 29 Aug 1989. 6'4". RHB, RMF. Durham MCCU 2008-10. Glamorgan debut 2011. Glamorgan 2nd XI debut 2009. Wales MC 2008-11. HS 55 v Kent (Cardiff) 2012. CC BB 4-49 v Kent (Canterbury) 2011. BB 5-38 DU v Durham (Durham) 2009. LO HS 10 v Hants (Cardiff) 2012 (CB40). LO BB 3-34 v Scotland (Cardiff) 2012 (CB40).

‡[NQ]**GOODWIN, Murray** William (Newton Moore HS, Bunbury, WA), b Salisbury, Rhodesia 11 Dec 1972. Younger brother of D.G.Goodwin (Zimbabwe 1986-87 to 1989-90). Migrated to Australia in Nov 1986 and gained Australian citizenship in Sep 1997. Kolpak registration 2005 to date. 5'9". RHB, LB. WA 1994-95 to 1996-97, 2000-01 to 2005-06. Mashonaland 1997-98 to 1998-99. Sussex 2001-12; cap 2001. Warriors 2006-07. Netherlands 1997. **Tests** (Z): 19 (1997-98 to 2000); HS 166* v P (Bulawayo) 1997-98. **LOI** (Z): 71 (1997-98 to 2000); HS 112* v WI (Chester-le-St) 2000; BB 1-12 v SL (Sharjah) 1998-99. F-c Tours (Z): E 2000, SA 1999-00; WI 1999-00; NZ 1997-98; P 1998-99; SL 1997-98. 1000 runs (9+1); most – 1654 (2001). HS 344* Sx v Somerset (Taunton) 2009 (Sx record), sharing record Sx 4th wkt partnership of 363 with C.D.Hopkinson. BB 2-23 Z v Lahore City (Lahore) 1998-99. UK BB – . LO HS 167 WA v NSW (Perth) 2000-01. LO BB 1-9 Mashonaland v Eng A (Harare) 1998-99. T20 HS 102*.

‡**HOGAN, Michael** Garry, b Newcastle, New South Wales, Australia 31 May 1981. British passport. RHB, RFM. W Australia 2009-10 to date. HS 47* WA v SA (Adelaide) 2012-13. BB 6-70 WA v Tas (Hobart) 2010-11. LO HS 27 WA v Vic (Melbourne) 2011-12. LO BB 5-44 WA v Vic (Melbourne) 2010-11. T20 HS 5*. T20 BB 4-26.

JAMES, Nicholas Alexander (King Edward VI S, Aston), b Sandwell, Birmingham 17 Sep 1986. 5'9". LHB, SLA. Warwickshire 2008. Glamorgan debut 2010. Staffordshire 2006-07. England U19 2005 to 2005-06. HS 83 v Oxford MCCU (Oxford) 2012. CC HS 49 v Middx (Cardiff) 2011. BB 2-28 v Kent (Canterbury) 2011. LO HS 43 v Somerset (Cardiff) 2011 (CB40). LO BB 3-36 v Unicorns (Wormsley) 2011 (CB40). T20 HS 13. T20 BB 2-22.

JONES, Alexander John (Cowbridge CS), b Bridgend 10 Nov 1988. RHB, LMF. Debut (Glamorgan) 2011. Glamorgan 2nd XI debut 2008. Wales MC 2007-10. Cardiff MCCU 2009-10. HS 26 v Northants (Northampton) 2011. BB 1-50 v Surrey (Oval) 2011. LO HS 5 v Somerset (Taunton) 2010 (CB40). LO BB 1-31 v Hants (Southampton) 2012 (CB40). T20 HS 4*. T20 BB 3-16.

JONES, Simon Philip (Coedcae CS; Millfield S), b Morriston, Swansea 25 Dec 1978. Son of I.J.Jones (Glamorgan and England 1960-68). 6'3½". LHB, RFM. Glamorgan 1998-2007; cap 2002. Worcestershire 2008 (no 1st XI appearances in 2009). Hampshire 2010-11. MCC 2002-04. MBE 2005. *Wisden* 2005. **Tests**: 18 (2002 to 2005); HS 44 v I (Lord's) 2002 – on debut; BB 6-53 v A (Manchester) 2005. **LOI**: 8 (2004-05 to 2005); HS 1; BB 2-43 v Z (Bulawayo) 2004-05 – on debut. F-c Tours: A 2002-03 (*part*); SA 2004-05; WI 2003-04; I 2003-04 (Eng A – *part*). HS 46 v Yorks (Scarborough) 2001. BB 6-45 v Derbys (Cardiff) 2002. LO HS 26 v Hants (Swansea) 2007 (FPT). LO BB 5-32 Wo v Hants (Worcester) 2008 (FPT). T20 HS 11*. T20 BB 4-10.

‡[NQ]**NANNES, Dirk** Peter (Wesley C and Monash U, Melbourne), b Mount Waverley, Victoria, Australia 16 May 1976. 6'3". RHB, LFM. Victoria 2005-06 to 2009-10. Middlesex 2008; cap 2008. Dutch passport. Joins Glamorgan for T20 only in 2013. **LOI** (A): 1 (2009); HS 1 and BB 1-20 v Scotland (Edinburgh) 2009. **IT20** (Neth/A): 17 (2 for Neth 2009; 15 for A 2009 to 2010-11); HS 12* A v P (Birmingham) 2010; BB 4-18 A v B (Bridgetown) 2010. HS 31* Vic v S Australia (Adelaide) 2007-08. CC HS 5 and CC BB 6-32 M v Worcs (Kidderminster) 2008. BB 7-50 (11-95 match) Vic v Q (Brisbane) 2008-09. LO HS 5* M v Somerset (Lord's) 2008. LO BB 4-38 M v Worcs (Kidderminster) 2008 (P40). T20 HS 12*. T20 BB 5-40.

NQNORTH, Marcus James (Kent Street Sr HS), b Pakenham, Melbourne, Australia 28 Jul 1979. 6'1". LHB, OB. Debut (Aus Academy in Zim) 1998-99. W Australia 1999-00 to date. Durham 2004. Lancashire 2005. Derbyshire 2006. Gloucestershire 2007-08; cap 2007. Hampshire 2009 (one match only). Glamorgan debut 2012; 1-o captain in 2013. **Tests** (A): 21 (2008-09 to 2010-11); scored 117 v SA (Johannesburg) 2008-09 – on debut; HS 128 v I (Bangalore) 2010-11; BB 6-55 v P (Lord's) 2010. **LOI** (A): 2 (2009); HS 5 v P (Abu Dhabi) 2009; BB – . **IT20** (A): 1 (2009); HS 20 v P (Dubai) 2009. F-c Tours (Aus): E 2009, 2010 (v P; SA 2008-09; NZ 2009-10; I 2010-11; P 2005-06 (Aus A); Z 1998-99 (Aus Acad). 1000 runs (0+1): 1074 (2003-04). HS 239* WA v Vic (Perth) 2006-07. UK HS 219 Du v Glamorgan (Cardiff) 2004. Won Walter Lawrence Trophy 2007 for 73-ball hundred v Leics (Bristol). Gm HS 166 v Leics (Cardiff) 2012. BB 6-55 (see Tests). CC BB 3-40 v Derbys (Derby) 2004. LO HS 134* WA v Q (Perth) 2004-05. LO BB 4-26 Durham CB v Bucks (Beaconsfield) 2001 (CGT). T20 HS 70. T20 BB 2-19.

OWEN, William Thomas (Prestatyn HS; UWIC), b St Asaph, Flintshire 2 Sep 1988. 6'0". RHB, RMF. Debut (Glamorgan) 2007. Wales MC 2007-10. HS 69 v Derbys (Derby) 2011. BB 5-124 v Middx (Cardiff) 2011. LO HS 12 and LO BB 5-49 v Unicorns (Bournemouth) 2010 (CB40). T20 HS 8. T20 BB 3-21.

REED, Michael Thomas (De Lisle S, Leicester; Cardiff U), b Leicester 10 Sep 1988. RHB, RFM. Debut (Glamorgan) 2012. Glamorgan 2nd XI debut 2009. Wales MC 2009-10. Cardiff MCCU 2010-11 (not f-c). HS 5* v Derbys (Derby) 2012. BB 3-39 v Kent (Cardiff) 2012.

REES, Gareth Peter (Coedcae CS; Bath U), b Swansea 8 Apr 1985. 6'1". LHB, OB. Wales MC 2003-05. Debut (Glamorgan) 2006; cap 2009. MCC 2012. 1000 runs (2); most – 1088 (2008). HS 154 v Surrey (Oval) 2008. BB – . LO HS 123* v Essex (Chelmsford) 2009 (FPT). T20 HS 38.

SALTER, Andrew Graham (Milford Haven SFC; UWIC), b Haverfordwest 1 Jun 1993. RHB, OB. Cardiff MCCU 2012. Glamorgan 2nd XI debut 2010. Wales MC 2010-11. Awaiting Gm f-c debut. HS CfU v Warwks (Birmingham) 2012. BB 3-134 CfU v Somerset (Taunton Vale) 2012. LO HS 3 v Durham (Chester-le-St) 2012 (CB40). LO BB 2-41 v Notts (Nottingham) 2012 (CB40).

SMITH, Ruaidhri Alexander James (Llandaff Cathedral S; Shrewsbury S), b Glasgow, Scotland 5 Aug 1994. RHB, RM. Wales MC 2010-11. Glamorgan 2nd XI debut 2011. Awaiting 1st XI debut.

WAGG, Graham Grant (Ashlawn S, Rugby), b Rugby, Warwks 28 Apr 1983. 6'0". RHB, LM. Warwickshire 2002-04; contract terminated after ECB imposed a 15-month ban, expiring 1 Jan 2006, for taking cocaine. Derbyshire 2006-10; cap 2007. Glamorgan debut 2011. F-c Tour (Eng A): I 2003-04. HS 108 De v Northants (Northampton) 2008. Gm HS 70 v Glos (Bristol) 2011. 50 wkts (2); most – 59 (2008). BB 6-35 De v Surrey (Derby) 2009. Gm BB 6-44 v Derbys (Cardiff) 2012. LO HS 48* De v Middx (Lord's) 2010 (CB40). LO BB 4-35 De v Durham (Derby) 2008 (FPT). T20 HS 62. T20 BB 3-23.

WALLACE, Mark Alexander (Crickhowell HS), b Abergavenny, Monmouthshire 19 Nov 1981. 5'9". LHB, WK. Debut (Glamorgan) 1999; cap 2003; captain 2012 to date; benefit 2013. F-c Tour (ECB Acad): SL 2002-03. 1000 runs (1): 1020 (2011). HS 139 v Surrey (Oval) 2009. LO HS 105 v Durham (Chester-le-St) 2012 (CB40). T20 HS 42*.

NQWALTERS, Stewart Jonathan (Guildford GS, Perth, WA), b Mornington, Victoria, Australia 25 Jun 1983. 6'1". RHB, RM. Surrey 2006-10. Glamorgan debut 2011. HS 188 Sy v Leics (Oval) 2009. Gm HS 159 v Essex (Colchester) 2012. BB 1-4 Sy v Durham (Chester-le-St) 2007. LO HS 91 Sy v Northants (Oval) 2008 (P40). LO BB 1-12 Sy v Yorks (Scarborough) 2007 (P40). T20 HS 53*. T20 BB 1-9.

WATERS, Huw Thomas (Llantaram CS; Monmouth S), b Cardiff 26 Sep 1986. 6'2". RHB, RMF. Debut (Glamorgan) 2005; cap 2012. No f-c appearances in 2009. Wales MC 2004-07. HS 54 v Surrey (Cardiff) 2011. BB 7-53 v Hants (Cardiff) 2012. LO HS 8 v Hants (Swansea) 2007 (FPT). LO BB 3-47 v Durham (Chester-le-St) 2007 (P40). T20 HS 11*. T20 BB 3-30.

WRIGHT, Ben James (Cowbridge CS), b Preston, Lancs 5 Dec 1987. 5'9". RHB, RM. Debut (Glamorgan) 2006; cap 2011. No f-c appearances in 2008. HS 172 v Glos (Cardiff) 2010. BB 1-14 v Essex (Chelmsford) 2007. LO HS 79 v Lancs (Colwyn Bay) 2010 (CB40). LO BB 1-19 v Derbys (Derby) 2009 (FPT). T20 HS 55*. T20 BB 1-16.

RELEASED/RETIRED
(Having made a County First-Class or List A appearance in 2012)

CROFT, Robert Damien Bale (St John Lloyd Catholic CS, Llanelli; Neath Tertiary C; W Glamorgan IHE), b Morriston, Swansea 25 May 1970. 5'10½". RHB, OB. Glamorgan 1989-2012; cap 1992; benefit 2000; testimonial 2012; captain 2003 (part) to 2006 (part). MCC 1996. MBE 2012. **Tests**: 21 (1996 to 2001); HS 37* v SA (Manchester) 1998; BB 5-95 v NZ (Christchurch) 1996-97. **LOI**: 50 (1996 to 2001); HS 32 v SL (Perth) 1998-99; BB 3-51 v SA (Oval) 1998. F-c Tours: A 1998-99; SA 1993-94 (Eng A), 1995-96 (Gm); WI 1991-92 (Eng A), 1997-98; NZ 1996-97; SL 2000-01, 2003-04; Z 1990-91 (Gm), 1994-95 (Gm), 1996-97. HS 143 v Somerset (Taunton) 1995. 50 wkts (10); most – 76 (1996). Took 1,000th f-c wicket 2007. BB 8-66 (14-169 match) v Warwks (Swansea) 1992. LO HS 143 v Lincs (Lincoln) 2004 (CGT). LO BB 6-20 v Worcs (Cardiff) 1994 (SL). T20 HS 62*. T20 BB 3-9.

HARRIS, J.A.R. – *see MIDDLESEX*.

NQHENRIQUES, Moises Constantino, Funchal, Portugal 1 Feb 1987. 6'1½". RHB, RFM. NSW 2006-07 to date. Glamorgan 2012. **Tests** (A): 1 (2012-13); HS 81* and BB 1-48 v I (Chennai) 2012-13. **LOI** (A): 5 (2009-10 to 2012-13); HS 12 v I (Delhi) 2009-10; BB 3-32 v SL (Hobart) 2012-13. **IT20** (A): 1 (2008-09); HS 1 v NZ (Sydney) 2008-09. F-c Tour (A): I 2012-13. HS 161* NSW v Tas (Sydney) 2012-13. Gm HS 28 v Oxford MCCU (Oxford) 2012. CC HS 16 and Gm BB 4-54 v Derbys (Cardiff) 2012. BB 5-17 NSW v Q (Brisbane) 2006-07. LO HS 78 NSW v WA (Perth) 2012-13. LO BB 3-29 NSW v WA (Sydney) 2008-09. T20 HS 70. T20 BB 3-11.

NORMAN, Aneurin John (Millfield S), b Cardiff 22 Mar 1991. RHB, RM. Glamorgan 2011. Glamorgan 2nd XI debut 2008. Wales MC 2008-12. HS 34 v Kent (Canterbury) 2011. BB – . LO HS 15 v Unicorns (Wormsley) 2011. LO BB – .

O'SHEA, Michael Peter (Barry CS; Millfield S), b Cardiff 4 Sep 1987. 5'11". RHB, OB. Glamorgan 2005-09. Wales MC 2005-08. England U19s 2004-05 to 2006. HS 50 v Kent (Canterbury) 2009. LO HS 90 Unicorns v Worcs (Kidderminster) 2010 (CB40). LO BB 2-32 v Somerset (Cardiff) 2011 (CB40). T20 HS 11. T20 BB 1-25.

VAN JAARSVELD, Martin (Warmbaths S; Pretoria U), b Klerksdorp, South Africa 18 Jun 1974. 6'2". RHB, OB. N Transvaal/Northerns 1994-95 to 2003-04. Northamptonshire 2004. Titans 2004-05 to date. Kent 2005-11; cap 2005. Scored 118 and 111 v Warwks (Canterbury) on debut – second player after C.W.G.Bassano (Derbyshire) to score two hundreds on a county debut. Glamorgan (l-o only) 2012. PCA 2008. Qualified for England in 2010. **Tests** (SA): 9 (2002-03 to 2004-05); HS 73 v WI (Johannesburg) 2003-04. **LOI** (SA): 11 (2002-03 to 2004); HS 45 v E (Birmingham) 2003; BB 1-0 v B (Kimberley) 2002-03. Took wickets with his first and third balls in LOI. F-c Tours (SA): A 2002-03 (SA A); NZ 2003-04; I 2004-05; SL 1998-99 (SA A), 2004; Z 1998-99 (SA Acad). 1000 runs (6+1); most – 1509 (2009). HS 262* K v Glamorgan (Cardiff) 2005. BB 5-33 K v Surrey (Oval) 2008. LO HS 132* Titans v Eagles (Bloemfontein) 2008-09 and 132* K v Somerset (Canterbury) 2009 (FPT). LO BB 3-13 Titans v Cape Cobras (Centurion) 2008-09. T20 HS 82. T20 BB 3-20.

C.P.Ashling and S.E.Marsh left the staff without making a County First-Class or List A appearance for Glamorgan in 2012.

GLAMORGAN 2012

RESULTS SUMMARY

	Place	Won	Lost	Drew	NR	Aband
LV= County Championship (2nd Division)	6th	3	6	6		1
All First-Class Matches		4	6	6		1
Clydesdale Bank 40 (Group B)	6th	3	6		3	
Friends Life t20 (Mid/Wales/West Group)	5th	2	3		5	

LV= COUNTY CHAMPIONSHIP AVERAGES

BATTING AND FIELDING

Cap		M	I	NO	HS	Runs	Avge	100	50	Ct/St
2012	H.T.Waters	12	14	12	39	106	53.00	–	–	5
	M.J.North	9	13	–	116	577	44.38	1	5	2
2010	J.Allenby	14	21	4	125*	712	41.88	2	3	11
	S.J.Walters	13	21	1	159	750	37.50	1	6	12
2003	M.A.Wallace	15	23	4	118	653	34.36	2	1	37/4
2011	B.J.Wright	15	25	2	104	623	27.08	1	1	3
	W.D.Bragg	15	25	–	92	648	25.92	–	5	8
2009	G.P.Rees	11	18	–	66	358	19.88	–	1	9
	J.C.Glover	7	10	3	55	125	17.85	–	1	3
2000	D.A.Cosker	14	17	3	49*	243	17.35	–	–	7
	G.G.Wagg	8	12	–	54	203	16.91	–	1	3
	N.A.James	8	15	–	38	234	15.60	–	–	3
1992	R.D.B.Croft	6	8	1	23	79	11.28	–	–	2
	M.C.Henriques	4	7	–	16	36	5.14	–	–	–
	D.L.Lloyd	2	4	1	11*	11	3.66	–	–	–
	M.T.Reed	4	7	2	5*	18	3.60	–	–	–

Also batted: J.A.R.Harris (4 matches – cap 2010) 48, 6, 2; S.P.Jones (1 – cap 2002) 4, 1 (1 ct); W.T.Owen (3) 0, 7, 13* (2 ct).

BOWLING

	O	M	R	W	Avge	Best	5wI	10wM
R.D.B.Croft	123.2	20	367	21	17.47	5- 31	2	–
H.T.Waters	280.2	67	770	35	22.00	7- 53	2	–
M.C.Henriques	85	16	289	13	22.23	4- 54	–	–
G.G.Wagg	225.3	37	712	31	22.96	6- 44	1	–
J.Allenby	340.3	75	948	38	24.94	4- 39	–	–
J.C.Glover	176.4	40	585	19	30.78	4- 76	–	–
J.A.R.Harris	129	19	402	10	40.20	5-118	1	–
D.A.Cosker	337.3	72	945	11	85.90	3- 59	–	–

Also bowled:

	O	M	R	W	Avge	Best	5wI	10wM
M.J.North	73	8	223	7	31.85	3- 40		
W.T.Owen	56.2	5	238	7	34.00	4- 87		
M.T.Reed	88	10	310	8	38.75	3- 39		

W.D.Bragg 26.1-2-107-1; N.A.James 17-0-68-0; S.P.Jones 22-2-70-2; G.P.Rees 4.1-0-22-0; S.J.Walters 1-0-6-0; B.J.Wright 13-2-30-0.

The First-Class Averages (pp 219–235) give the records of Glamorgan players in all first-class county matches (Glamorgan's other opponents being Oxford MCCU), with the exception of J.A.R.Harris, whose first-class figures for Glamorgan are as above.

GLAMORGAN RECORDS

FIRST-CLASS CRICKET

Highest Total	For 718-3d		v	Sussex	Colwyn Bay	2000
	V 712		by	Northants	Northampton	1998
Lowest Total	For 22		v	Lancashire	Liverpool	1924
	V 33		by	Leics	Ebbw Vale	1965
Highest Innings	For 309*	S.P.James	v	Sussex	Colwyn Bay	2000
	V 322*	M.B.Loye	for	Northants	Northampton	1998

Highest Partnership for each Wicket

1st	374	M.T.G.Elliott/S.P.James	v	Sussex	Colwyn Bay	2000
2nd	252	M.P.Maynard/D.L.Hemp	v	Northants	Cardiff	2002
3rd	313	D.E.Davies/W.E.Jones	v	Essex	Brentwood	1948
4th	425*	A.Dale/I.V.A.Richards	v	Middlesex	Cardiff	1993
5th	264	M.Robinson/S.W.Montgomery	v	Hampshire	Bournemouth	1949
6th	240	J.Allenby/M.A.Wallace	v	Surrey	The Oval	2009
7th	211	P.A.Cottey/O.D.Gibson	v	Leics	Swansea	1996
8th	202	D.Davies/J.J.Hills	v	Sussex	Eastbourne	1928
9th	203*	J.J.Hills/J.C.Clay	v	Worcs	Swansea	1929
10th	143	T.Davies/S.A.B.Daniels	v	Glos	Swansea	1982

Best Bowling	For 10- 51	J.Mercer	v	Worcs	Worcester	1936
(Innings)	V 10- 18	G.Geary	for	Leics	Pontypridd	1929
Best Bowling	For 17-212	J.C.Clay	v	Worcs	Swansea	1937
(Match)	V 16- 96	G.Geary	for	Leics	Pontypridd	1929

Most Runs – Season	2276	H.Morris	(av 55.51)	1990
Most Runs – Career	34056	A.Jones	(av 33.03)	1957-83
Most 100s – Season	10	H.Morris		1990
Most 100s – Career	54	M.P.Maynard		1985-2005
Most Wkts – Season	176	J.C.Clay	(av 17.34)	1937
Most Wkts – Career	2174	D.J.Shepherd	(av 20.95)	1950-72
Most Career W-K Dismissals	933	E.W.Jones	(840 ct; 93 st)	1961-83
Most Career Catches in the Field	656	P.M.Walker		1956-72

LIMITED-OVERS CRICKET

Highest Total	50ov	429	v	Surrey	The Oval	2002
	40ov	328-4	v	Lancashire	Colwyn Bay	2011
	T20	206-6	v	Somerset	Taunton	2006
Lowest Total	50ov	76	v	Northants	Northampton	1968
	40ov	42	v	Derbyshire	Swansea	1979
	T20	94-9	v	Essex	Cardiff	2010
Highest Innings	50ov	162* I.V.A.Richards	v	Oxfordshire	Swansea	1993
	40ov	155* J.H.Kallis	v	Surrey	Pontypridd	1999
	T20	116* I.J.Thomas	v	Somerset	Taunton	2004
Best Bowling	50ov	5-13 R.J.Shastri	v	Scotland	Edinburgh	1988
	40ov	7-16 S.D.Thomas	v	Surrey	Swansea	1998
	T20	5-16 R.E.Watkins	v	Glos	Cardiff	2009

GLOUCESTERSHIRE

Formation of Present Club: 1871
Inaugural First-Class Match: 1870
Colours: Blue, Gold, Brown, Silver, Green and Red
Badge: Coat of Arms of the City and County of Bristol
County Champions (since 1890): (0); best – 2nd 1930, 1931, 1947, 1959, 1969, 1986
Gillette/NatWest/C&G/FP Trophy Winners: (5) 1973, 1999, 2000, 2003, 2004
Benson and Hedges Cup Winners: (3) 1977, 1999, 2000
Pro 40/National League (Div 1) Winners: (1) 2000
Sunday League Winners: (0); best – 2nd 1988
Clydesdale Bank 40 Winners: (0); best – 3rd in Group 2010, 2012
Twenty20 Cup Winners: (0); best – Finalist 2007

Chief Executive: Tom E.M.Richardson, County Ground, Nevil Road, Bristol BS7 9EJ • Tel: 0117 910 8000 • Fax: 0117 924 1193 • Email: info@glosccc.co.uk • Web: www.glosccc.co.uk

Director of Cricket: J.G.Bracewell. **Captain:** M.Klinger. **Vice-Captain:** H.J.H.Marshall. **Overseas Players:** D.T.Christian (T20 only) and M.Klinger. **2013 Beneficiary:** none. **Head Groundsman:** Sean Williams. **Scorer:** Adrian J.Bull. ‡ New registration. ^{NQ} Not qualified for England.

Gloucestershire revised their capping policy in 2004 and now award players with their County Caps when they make their first-class debut.

BEARD, Michael Adam (Lord Williams's S, Thame), b Oxford 24 Oct 1992. 6'5". LHB, LMF. Gloucestershire 2nd XI debut 2008, aged 15y 216d. Oxfordshire 2011. Awaiting 1st XI debut.

^{NQ}**CHRISTIAN, Daniel** Trevor, b Camperdown, NSW, Australia 4 May 1983. RHB, RFM. S Australia 2007-08 to date. Hampshire 2010. Joins Gloucestershire in 2013 for T20 only. **LOI** (A): 17 (2011-12 to 2012); HS 39 v I (Adelaide) 2011-12; BB 5-31 v SL (Melbourne) 2011-12. **IT20** (A): 11 (2009-10 to 2012-13); HS 4* v WI (Sydney) 2009-10; BB 3-27 v WI (Gros Islet) 2011-12. HS 131* S Aus v NSW (Adelaide) 2011-12. H HS 36 and H BB 2-115 v Somerset (Taunton) 2010. BB 5-24 (9-87 match) S Aus v WA (Perth) (2009-10). LO HS 100 S Aus v Queensland (Townsville) 2010-11. LO BB 6-48 S Aus v Vic (Geelong) 2010-11. T20 HS 75*. T20 BB 5-26.

COCKBAIN, Ian Andrew (Maghull HS), b Bootle, Liverpool 17 Feb 1987. Son of I.Cockbain (Lancs and Minor Cos 1979-94). 6'0". RHB, RM. Debut (Gloucestershire) 2011; cap 2011. Lancashire 2nd XI 2006-08. MCC YC 2008-10. Gloucestershire 2nd XI debut 2010. HS 127 v Middx (Uxbridge) 2011. LO HS 79 v Notts (Cheltenham) 2011 (CB40). T20 HS 78.

COUGHTRIE, Richard George (Newcastle RGS; Oxford Brookes U), b North Shields, Co Durham 1 Sep 1988. 5'10". RHB, WK. Oxford MCCU 2009-11. Gloucestershire debut/cap 2011. Gloucestershire 2nd XI debut 2009. Durham 2nd XI 2006-08. Northumberland 2008-09. HS 54* v Derbys (Derby) 2011. T20 HS 18.

DENT, Christopher David James (Backwell CS; Alton C), b Bristol 20 Jan 1991. 5'9". LHB, WK, occ SLA. Debut (Gloucestershire) 2010; cap 2010. Gloucestershire 2nd XI debut 2007, aged 16y 80d. England U19s Debut 2009-10. HS 114 v Hants (Southampton) 2012. BB – . LO HS 36 v Neth (Bristol) 2012 (CB40). LO BB 4-43 v Leics (Bristol) 2012 (CB40). T20 HS 63.

NQFULLER, James Kerr (Otago U, NZ), b Cape Town, South Africa 24 Jan 1990. British passport. 6'3". RHB, RFM. Otago 2009-10 to date. Gloucestershire debut/cap 2011. HS 57 v Leics (Cheltenham) 2012. BB 6-24 (10-79 match) Otago v Wellington (Dunedin) 2012-13. Gs BB 5-29 v Northants (Bristol) 2012. LO HS 43 v Lancs (Bristol) 2012 (CB40). LO BB 6-35 v Neth (Amstelveen) 2012 (CB40). T20 HS 36. T20 BB 4-24.

GIDMAN, Alex Peter Richard (Wycliffe C), b High Wycombe, Bucks 22 Jun 1981. Elder brother of W.R.S.Gidman (*see below*). 6'3". RHB, RM. Debut (Gloucestershire) 2002; cap 2004; captain 2009-12; benefit 2012. Otago 2007-08. MCC YC 2001. MCC 2004, 2007, 2010. F-c Tour (Eng A): SL 2004-05. Appointed captain of Eng A tour to India 2003-04 but withdrew because of hand injury. 1000 runs (4); most – 1244 (2006). HS 176 v Surrey (Bristol) 2009. BB 4-47 v Glamorgan (Cardiff) 2005. LO HS 116 v Sussex (Hove) 2009 (FPT). LO BB 5-42 Eng A v Bangladesh A (Mirpur) 2006-07. T20 HS 64. T20 BB 2-24.

GIDMAN, William Robert Simon (Wycliffe C; Berkshire C of Agriculture), b High Wycombe, Bucks 14 Feb 1985. Younger brother of A.P.R.Gidman (*see above*). 6'2". LHB, RM. Durham 2007. No f-c appearances in 2008-10. Gloucestershire debut/cap 2011, becoming first player for Gs to score 1000 runs and take 50 wkts in debut season. MCC YC 2004-06. 1000 runs (1): 1006 (2011). HS 116* v Northants (Bristol) 2011. 50 wkts (1): 51 (2011). BB 6-92 v Derbys (Bristol) 2011. LO HS 76 v Worcs (Worcester) 2012 (CB40). LO BB 4-36 Du v Hants (Chester-le-St) 2010 (CB40). T20 HS 40*. T20 BB 1-18.

HERRING, Cameron Lee (Tredegar CS), b Abergavenny, Monmouthshire 15 July 1994. 5'6". RHB, WK. Gloucestershire 2nd XI debut 2011. Awaiting 1st XI debut. Scholarship contract for 2013.

HOUSEGO, Daniel Mark (Oratory S, Reading), b Windsor, Berkshire 12 Oct 1988. 5'8". RHB, LB. Middlesex 2008-11. Glamorgan debut/cap 2012. Berkshire 2006. HS 104 M v Sri Lankans (Uxbridge) 2011. Gs HS 62 v Leics (Leicester) 2012. BB – . LO HS 132 v S Africans (Bristol) 2012. T20 HS 59*.

HOWELL, Benny Alexander Cameron (The Oratory S), b Bordeaux, France 5 Oct 1988. Son of J.B.Howell (Warwickshire 2nd XI 1978). 5'11". RHB, RM. Hampshire 2011. Gloucestershire debut/cap 2012. Hampshire 2nd XI debut 2005. Berkshire 2007. HS 83* v Yorks (Scarborough) 2012. BB 2-37 v Northants (Bristol) 2012. LO HS 122 v Surrey (Croydon) 2011 (CB40). LO BB 2-26 v Leics (Leicester) 2012 (CB40). T20 HS 55*. T20 BB 2-14.

‡NQKLINGER, Michael, b Kew, Melbourne, Australia 4 Jul 1980. 5'10½". RHB. Victoria 1999-00 to 2007-08. S Australia 2008-09 to date. Worcestershire 2012; cap 2012. Joins Gloucestershire in 2013 as captain. HS 255 S Aus v WA (Adelaide) 2008-09. UK HS 120 Wo v Oxford MCCU (Oxford) 2012. CC HS 69* Wo v Surrey (Oval) 2012. LO HS 133* S Aus v Tas (Adelaide) 2008-09. T20 HS 78.

McCARTER, Graeme John (Foyle and Londonderry C), b Londonderry, N.Ireland 10 Oct 1992. 6'2". RHB, RFM. Ireland 2011. Gloucestershire debut/cap 2012. Gloucestershire 2nd XI debut 2008, aged 15y 292d. HS 29* v Yorks (Bristol) 2012. BB 1-47 Ire v Namibia (Belfast) 2011. Gs BB – . LO HS – . LO BB 3-15 v Leics (Bristol) 2012 (CB40).

NOMARSHALL, Hamish John Hamilton (Mahurangi C, Warkworth; King C, Auckland), b Warkworth, New Zealand 15 Feb 1979. Twin brother of J.A.H.Marshall (ND and NZ 1997-98 to 2011-12). Irish passport, qualified to play in April 2011. 5'9''. RHB, RM. N Districts 1998-99 to date. Gloucestershire debut 2006 (scoring 102 v Worcs on UK debut); cap 2006; Kolpak registration 2008-11. MCC 2012. Buckinghamshire 2003. **Tests** (NZ): 13 (2000-01 to 2005-06); HS 160 v SL (Napier) 2004-05. **LOI** (NZ): 66 (2003-04 to 2006-07); HS 101* v P (Faisalabad) 2003-04. **IT20** (NZ): 3 (2004-05 to 2005-06); HS 8 v A (Auckland) 2004-05. F-c Tours (NZ): A 2004-05; SA 2000-01, 2005-06; Z 2005; B 2004-05. 1000 runs (1): 1218 (2006). HS 170 ND v Canterbury (Rangiora) 2009-10. Gs HS 168 v Leics (Cheltenham) 2006. BB 4-24 v Leics (Leicester) 2009. LO HS 122 v Sussex (Hove) 2007 (P40). LO BB 2-21 v Hants (Southampton) 2009 (P40). T20 HS 102.

MILES, Craig Neil (Bradon Forest S, Swindon; Filton C, Bristol), b Swindon, Wilts 20 July 1994. Brother of A.J.Miles (Cardiff MCCU 2012). 6'4''. RHB, RMF. Debut (Gloucestershire) 2011; cap 2011. Gloucestershire 2nd XI debut 2009, aged 14y 318d. HS 19 and BB 2-80 v Northants (Bristol) 2011 – only f-c game. LO BB 2-32 v Essex (Cheltenham) 2011 (CB40).

MUCHALL, Paul Bernard (Durham S), b Newcastle upon Tyne, Northumb 17 Mar 1987. Younger brother of G.J.Muchall (see *DURHAM*). 6'1''. RHB, RM. Debut (Gloucestershire) 2012; cap 2012. Kent 2010 (l-o only). Northumberland 2006-09. HS 23 v Kent (Canterbury) 2012. BB 2-60 v Essex (Chelmsford) 2012. LO HS 22 and LO BB 1-34 K v Durham (Chester-le-St) 2010 (CB40).

NORWELL, Liam Connor (Redruth SS), b Bournemouth, Dorset 27 Dec 1991. 6'3''. RHB, RMF. Debut (Gloucestershire) 2011; cap 2011. Gloucestershire 2nd XI debut 2009. HS 26 v Middx (Bristol) 2011. BB 6-46 v Derbys (Bristol) 2011 – on debut. LO HS 1* v Middx (Cheltenham) 2012 (CB40). LO BB 6-52 v Leics (Leicester) 2012. T20 HS 1*. T20 BB 2-41.

PAYNE, David Alan (Lytchett Minster S), b Poole, Dorset, 15 Feb 1991. 6'2''. RHB, LMF. Debut (Gloucestershire) 2011; cap 2011. Gloucestershire 2nd XI debut 2008. Dorset 2009. England U19s 2010. HS 62 v Glamorgan (Bristol) 2011. BB 6-26 v Leics (Bristol) 2011. LO HS 13 and LO BB 7-29 v Essex (Chelmsford) 2010 (CB40), inc 4 wkts in 4 balls and 6 wkts in 9 balls – Gs l-o record. T20 HS 10. T20 BB 3-20.

NORODERICK, Gareth Hugh (Maritzburg C), b Durban, South Africa 29 Aug 1991. 6'0''. RHB, WK. KwaZulu-Natal 2010-11 to 2011-12. Gloucestershire 2nd XI debut 2012. Northamptonshire 2nd XI 2011. Kolpak signing. HS 71* KZN v Boland (Chatsworth) 2011-12. LO HS 26 KZN v Gauteng (Durban) 2011-12. T20 HS 32.

SAXELBY, Ian David (Oakham S), b Nottingham 22 May 1989. 6'2''. RHB, RMF. Nephew of K.Saxelby (Nottinghamshire 1978-90) and M.Saxelby (Notts, Durham and Derbys 1989-2000). Debut (Gloucestershire) 2008; cap 2008. No 1st XI appearances in 2010. Nottinghamshire 2nd XI debut 2006. England U19s 2008. HS 60* v Northants (Northampton) 2009. BB 6-48 v Leics (Cheltenham) 2012. LO HS 7* and BB 4-31 v Surrey (Bristol) 2009 (FPT). T20 HS 7*. T20 BB 4-16 v Northants (Bristol) 2012 – joint Gs record.

TAYLOR, Jack Martin Robert (Chipping Norton S), b Banbury, Oxfordshire 12 Nov 1991. Elder brother of M.D.Taylor (see *below*). 5'11''. RHB, OB. Debut (Gloucestershire) 2010; cap 2010. Gloucestershire 2nd XI debut 2007, aged 15y 191d. Oxfordshire 2009-11. HS 63 and BB 2-28 v Glamorgan (Swansea) 2012. LO HS 22* v Essex (Chelmsford) 2012 (CB40). LO BB 3-37 v Unicorns (Exmouth) 2011 (CB40). T20 HS 38. T20 BB 4-16 v Somerset (Bristol) 2011 – joint Gs record.

TAYLOR, Matthew David (Chipping Norton S), b Banbury, Oxfordshire 8 Jul 1994. Younger brother of J.M.R.Taylor (*see above*). 6'0". RHB, LM. Gloucestershire 2nd XI debut 2011. Oxfordshire 2011-12. Awaiting f-c debut. Scholarship contract for 2013. LO HS 7* and LO BB 2-43 v Notts (Cheltenham) 2011 (CB40).

YOUNG, Edward George Christopher (Wellington C; Oxford Brookes U), b Chertsey, Surrey 21 May 1989. 6'1". RHB, SLA. Brother of P.J.W.Young (Oxford UCCE 2006-08). Oxford MCCU 2009-11. Gloucestershire debut/cap 2010. HS 133 OU v Lancs (Oxford) 2011. Gs HS 55* and BB 2-23 v Kent (Canterbury) 2012. LO HS 50 v Notts (Nottingham) 2011 (CB40). LO BB 3-25 v Lancs (Bristol) 2012 (CB40). T20 HS 28. T20 BB 2-14.

RELEASED/RETIRED

(Having made a County First-Class or List A appearance in 2012)

BATTY, Jonathan Neil (Wheatley Park S, Oxon; Repton S; Durham U; Keble C, Oxford), b Chesterfield, Derbys 18 Apr 1974. 5'10". RHB, WK. Comb U 1994-95. Oxford U 1996; blue 1996. Surrey 1997-2009; cap 2001; captain 2004; benefit 2009. Gloucestershire 2010-12; cap 2010. Oxfordshire 1993-96. Minor C 1996. 1000 runs (1): 1025 (2006). HS 168* Sy v Essex (Chelmsford) 2003. Gs HS 70 v Derbys (Bristol) 2011. BB 1-21 Sy v Lancs (Manchester) 2000. LO HS 158* Sy v Hants (Oval) 2005 (CGT). T20 HS 59.

COWAN, E.J.M. – *see NOTTINGHAMSHIRE.*

IRELAND, A.J. – *see LEICESTERSHIRE.*

[NQ]**NICOL, Robert** James, b Auckland, New Zealand 28 May 1983. RHB, RM/OB. Auckland 2001-02 to 2008-09. Canterbury 2009-10 to date. Gloucestershire 2012; cap 2012. **Tests** (NZ): 2 (2011-12); HS 19 v SA (Dunedin) 2011-12; BB – . **LOI** (NZ): 19 (2011-12 to 2012-13); HS 146 v Z (Whangarei) 2011-12; BB 4-19 v Z (Dunedin) 2011-12. **IT20** (NZ): 20 (2010 to 2012-13); HS 58 v SL (Pallekele) 2012-13; BB 2-20 v SA (Auckland) 2011-12. F-c Tour (NZ White): A 2006. HS 160 Auckland v Otago (Lincoln) 2006-07. Gs HS 75* v Yorks (Scarborough) 2012. BB 4-53 v Glamorgan (Swansea) 2012. LO HS 171* Canterbury v ND (Mt Maunganui) 2012-13. LO BB 5-54 Auckland v Canterbury (Rangiora) 2007-08. T20 HS 101*. T20 BB 5-22.

[NQ]**WILLIAMSON, Kane** Stuart (Tauranga Boys' C), b Tauranga, New Zealand 8 Aug 1990. Cousin of D.Cleaver (C Districts 2010-11 to date). 5'8". RHB, OB. N Districts 2007-08 to date. Gloucestershire 2011-12; cap 2011. **Tests** (NZ): 21 (2010-11 to 2012-13); HS 135 v SL (Colombo, PSS) 2012-13; scored 131 v I (Ahmedabad) 2010-11 on debut; BB 2-47 v WI (North Sound) 2012. **LOI** (NZ): 39 (2010 to 2012-13); HS 145* v SA (Kimberley) 2012-13; BB 4-22 v SA (Paarl) 2012-13. **IT20** (NZ): 13 (2011-12 to 2012-13); HS 48 and BB 1-6 v Z (Auckland) 2011-12. F-c Tours (NZ): A 2011-12; SA 2012-13; WI 2012; I 2010-11, 2012; SL 2012-13; Z 2011-12. HS 284* ND v Wellington (Lincoln) 2011-12. Gs HS 149 v Leics (Leicester) 2011. BB 5-75 ND v Canterbury (Christchurch) 2008-09. Gs BB 3-58 v Northants (Northampton) 2012. LO HS 145* (*see LOI*). LO BB 5-51 ND v Auckland (Auckland) 2009-10. T20 HS 53. T20 BB 3-33.

D.N.Wade left the staff without making a County First-Class or List A appearance for Gloucestershire in 2012.

GLOUCESTERSHIRE 2012

RESULTS SUMMARY

	Place	Won	Lost	Drew	NR	Aband
LV= County Championship (2nd Division)	9th	3	6	6		1
All First-Class Matches		3	6	6		1
Clydesdale Bank 40 (Group A)	3rd	5	5		2	
Friends Life t20 (Mid/Wales/West Group)	QF	4	3		4	

LV= COUNTY CHAMPIONSHIP AVERAGES

BATTING AND FIELDING

Cap†		M	I	NO	HS	Runs	Avge	100	50	Ct/St
2011	K.S.Williamson	4	7	–	128	366	52.28	2	1	3
2010	J.M.R.Taylor	3	5	1	63	151	37.75	–	1	1
2006	H.J.H.Marshall	15	25	3	117*	822	37.36	1	5	6
2011	I.A.Cockbain	15	24	2	112	764	34.72	1	5	12
2010	C.D.J.Dent	8	15	1	114	424	30.28	1	2	11
2012	E.J.M.Cowan	3	5	–	103	147	29.40	1	–	–
2010	J.N.Batty	8	11	2	55	256	28.44	–	1	24/1
2012	D.M.Housego	10	16	–	62	450	28.12	–	4	7
2011	W.R.S.Gidman	11	17	1	72	447	27.93	–	3	2
2012	R.J.Nicol	4	7	2	75*	128	25.60	–	1	6
2004	A.P.R.Gidman	13	22	1	129	528	25.14	1	3	10
2012	B.A.C.Howell	13	24	3	83*	497	23.66	–	3	5
2008	I.D.Saxelby	11	16	7	30	200	22.22	–	–	4
2010	E.G.C.Young	8	12	2	55*	186	18.60	–	1	3
2012	P.B.Muchall	4	7	2	23	82	16.40	–	–	1
2011	J.K.Fuller	8	12	1	57	134	12.18	–	1	3
2011	D.A.Payne	8	10	3	16	75	10.71	–	–	2
2011	R.G.Coughtrie	7	12	–	40	125	10.41	–	–	17
2011	L.C.Norwell	9	11	4	18	37	5.28	–	–	3

Also batted: A.J.Ireland (2 matches – cap 2007) 25*, 22, 0; G.J.McCarter (1 – cap 2012) 29* (1 ct).

BOWLING

	O	M	R	W	Avge	Best	5wI	10wM
W.R.S.Gidman	318	58	943	44	21.43	5-43	2	–
D.A.Payne	147	24	504	22	22.90	4-89	–	–
I.D.Saxelby	293.3	58	897	35	25.62	6-48	1	–
J.K.Fuller	174.2	27	653	24	27.20	5-29	1	–
L.C.Norwell	194.1	25	632	22	28.72	5-51	1	–
E.G.C.Young	137.5	28	414	10	41.40	2-23	–	–
Also bowled:								
R.J.Nicol	38.5	2	129	7	18.42	4-53	–	–
K.S.Williamson	34.3	4	121	5	24.20	3-58	–	–
J.M.R.Taylor	87	15	277	8	34.62	2-28	–	–
B.A.C.Howell	93.4	14	266	6	44.33	2-37	–	–

C.D.J.Dent 11-0-32-0; A.P.R.Gidman 14-3-50-2; A.J.Ireland 39.2-159-4; G.J.McCarter 19-3-67-0; P.B.Muchall 39.2-3-218-2.

Gloucestershire played no first-class fixtures outside the County Championship in 2012. The First-Class Averages (pp 219–235) give the records of their players in all first-class county matches, with the exception of E.J.M.Cowan, whose first-class figures for Gloucestershire are as above.

† Gloucestershire revised their capping policy in 2004 and now award players with their County Caps when they make their first-class debut.

GLOUCESTERSHIRE RECORDS

FIRST-CLASS CRICKET

Highest Total	For 695-8d		v	Middlesex	Gloucester	2004
	V 774-7d		by	Australians	Bristol	1948
Lowest Total	For 17		v	Australians	Cheltenham	1896
	V 12		by	Northants	Gloucester	1907
Highest Innings	For 341	C.M.Spearman	v	Middlesex	Gloucester	2004
	V 319	C.J.L.Rogers	for	Northants	Northampton	2006

Highest Partnership for each Wicket

1st	395	D.M.Young/R.B.Nicholls	v	Oxford U	Oxford	1962
2nd	256	C.T.M.Pugh/T.W.Graveney	v	Derbyshire	Chesterfield	1960
3rd	336	W.R.Hammond/B.H.Lyon	v	Leics	Leicester	1933
4th	321	W.R.Hammond/W.L.Neale	v	Leics	Gloucester	1937
5th	261	W.G.Grace/W.O.Moberley	v	Yorkshire	Cheltenham	1876
6th	320	G.L.Jessop/J.H.Board	v	Sussex	Hove	1903
7th	248	W.G.Grace/E.L.Thomas	v	Sussex	Hove	1896
8th	239	W.R.Hammond/A.E.Wilson	v	Lancashire	Bristol	1938
9th	193	W.G.Grace/S.A.P.Kitcat	v	Sussex	Bristol	1896
10th	131	W.R.Gouldsworthy/J.G.Bessant	v	Somerset	Bristol	1923

Best Bowling	For 10-40	E.G.Dennett	v	Essex	Bristol	1906
(Innings)	V 10-66	A.A.Mailey	for	Australians	Cheltenham	1921
	10-66	K.Smales	for	Notts	Stroud	1956
Best Bowling	For 17-56	C.W.L.Parker	v	Essex	Gloucester	1925
(Match)	V 15-87	A.J.Conway	for	Worcs	Moreton-in-M	1914

Most Runs – Season	2860	W.R.Hammond	(av 69.75)	1933
Most Runs – Career	33664	W.R.Hammond	(av 57.05)	1920-51
Most 100s – Season	13	W.R.Hammond		1938
Most 100s – Career	113	W.R.Hammond		1920-51
Most Wkts – Season	222	T.W.J.Goddard	(av 16.80)	1937
	222	T.W.J.Goddard	(av 16.37)	1947
Most Wkts – Career	3170	C.W.L.Parker	(av 19.43)	1903-35
Most Career W-K Dismissals	1054	R.C.Russell	(950 ct; 104 st)	1981-2004
Most Career Catches in the Field	719	C.A.Milton		1948-74

LIMITED-OVERS CRICKET

Highest Total	50ov	401-7	v	Bucks	Wing	2003
	40ov	344-6	v	Northants	Cheltenham	2001
	T20	254-3	v	Middlesex	Uxbridge	2011
Lowest Total	50ov	82	v	Notts	Bristol	1987
	40ov	49	v	Middlesex	Bristol	1978
	T20	68	v	Hampshire	Bristol	2010
Highest Innings	50ov	177	A.J.Wright	v	Scotland	Bristol	1997
	40ov	153	C.M.Spearman	v	Warwicks	Gloucester	2003
	T20	119	K.J.O'Brien	v	Middlesex	Uxbridge	2011
Best Bowling	50ov	6-21	C.A.Walsh	v	Kent	Bristol	1990
		6-21	C.A.Walsh	v	Cheshire	Bristol	1992
	40ov	7-29	D.A.Payne	v	Essex	Chelmsford	2010
	T20	4-16	J.M.R.Taylor	v	Somerset	Bristol	2011
		4-16	I.D.Saxelby	v	Northants	Bristol	2012

HAMPSHIRE

HAMPSHIRE
CRICKET

Formation of Present Club: 12 August 1863
Inaugural First-Class Match: 1864
Colours: Blue, Gold and White
Badge: Tudor Rose and Crown
County Champions: (2) 1961, 1973
Gillette/NatWest/C&G/FP Trophy Winners: (3) 1991, 2005, 2009
Benson and Hedges Cup Winners: (2) 1988, 1992
Pro 40/National League (Div 1) Winners: (0); best – 2nd 2008
Sunday League Winners: (3) 1975, 1978, 1986
Clydesdale Bank 40 Winners: (1) 2012
Twenty20 Cup Winners: (2) 2010, 2012

Chairman and CEO: Rod Bransgrove, The Ageas Bowl, Botley Road, West End, Southampton SO30 3XH • Tel: 023 8047 2002 • Fax: 023 8047 2122 • Email: enquiries@ageasbowl.com • Web: www.ageasbowl.com

Cricket Secretary: T.M.Tremlett. **First XI Manager**: G.W.White. **Coaches**: T.C.Middleton and C.White. **Captain**: J.H.K.Adams. **Vice-Captain**: none. **Overseas Players**: G.J.Bailey, Saeed Ajmal and Shahid Afridi (T20 only). **2013 Beneficiary**: none. **Head Groundsman**: Nigel Gray. **Scorer**: A.E. (Tony) Weld. ‡ New registration. ^{NQ} Not qualified for England.

ADAMS, James Henry Kenneth (Sherborne S; University C, London; Loughborough U), b Winchester 23 Sep 1980. 6'2". LHB, LM. British U 2002-04. Hampshire debut 2002; cap 2006; captain 2012 to date. Loughborough UCCE 2003-04 – scoring 107 v Somerset (Taunton) on debut. Dorset 1998. F-c Tour (EL): WI 2010-11. 1000 runs (3); most – 1351 (2009). HS 262* v Notts (Nottingham) 2006. BB 2-16 v Durham (Chester-le-St) 2004. LO HS 131 v Warwks (Birmingham) 2010 (CB40). LO BB 1-34 v Essex (Chelmsford) 2007 (FPT). T20 HS 101*. T20 BB – .

BALCOMBE, David John (St John's S, Leatherhead; St Hild & St Bede C, Durham), b City of London 24 Dec 1984. 6'4". RHB, RFM. Durham UCCE 2005-07. British U 2006. Hampshire debut 2007. Kent 2011 (on loan). HS 73 DU v Leics (Leicester) 2005 and 73 v Leics (Leicester) 2012. BB 8-71 (11-119 match) v Glos (Southampton) 2012. LO HS 6 K v Neth (Rotterdam) 2011 (CB40). LO BB 4-38 v Worcs (Worcester) 2011 (CB40). T20 HS 3. T20 BB 1-23.

‡^{NQ}BAILEY, George John, b Launceston, Tasmania, Australia 7 Sep 1982. 5'10". RHB, RM. Tasmania 2004-05 to date. **LOI** (A): 21 (2011-12 to 2012-13); HS 125* v WI (Perth) 2012-13. **IT20** (A): 16 (2011-12 to 2012-13); HS 63 v WI (Colombo, RPS) 2012-13. F-c Tours (Aus A): E 2012; I 2008-09. HS 160* Tas v Vic (Hobart) 2010-11. UK HS 81 Aus A v Derbys (Derby) 2012. BB – . LO HS 125* (*see LOI*). LO BB 1-19 Tas v Vic (Melbourne) 2004-05. T20 HS 63. T20 BB – .

BATES, Michael David (Lord Wandsworth C, Hook), b Frimley, Surrey 10 Oct 1990. 5'10". RHB, WK. Debut (Hampshire) 2010. Hampshire 2nd XI debut 2007. Berkshire 2009. England U19s 2009-10. HS 103 v Yorks (Leeds) 2012. LO HS 24* v Warwks (Birmingham) 2011 (CB40). T20 HS 10.

BRIGGS, Danny Richard (Isle of Wight C), b Newport, IoW, 30 Apr 1991. 6'2". RHB, SLA. Debut (Hampshire) 2009; cap 2012. Hampshire 2nd XI debut 2007, aged 16y 120d. **LOI**: 1 (2011-12); HS – ; BB 2-39 v P (Dubai) 2011-12. **IT20**: 3 (2012 to 2012-13); HS – ; BB 1-16 v SA (Birmingham) 2012. F-c Tour (EL): WI 2010-11. HS 38* EL v Barbados (Bridgetown) 2010-11. CC HS 36 v Somerset (Southampton) 2009 – on debut. BB 6-45 EL v Windward Is (Roseau) 2010-11. CC BB 6-65 v Notts (Southampton) 2011. LO HS 25 and LO BB 4-32 v Glamorgan (Cardiff) 2012 (CB40). T20 HS 10. T20 BB 5-19.

CARBERRY, Michael Alexander (St John Rigby Catholic C), b Croydon, Surrey 29 Sep 1980. 6'0". LHB, OB. Surrey 2001-02. Kent 2003-05. Hampshire debut/cap 2006. MCC 2008. **Tests**: 1 (2009-10); HS 34 v B (Chittagong) 2009-10. F-c Tours: B 2006-07 (Eng A), 2009-10. 1000 runs (2); most – 1251 (2009). HS 300* v Yorks (Southampton) 2011, sharing in UK 3rd highest and UK record 3rd-wkt partnership of 523 with N.D.McKenzie. BB 2-85 v Durham (Chester-le-St) 2006. LO HS 148* v Scotland (Southampton) 2012 (CB40). LO BB 2-11 v Notts (Nottingham) 2009 (FPT). T20 HS 90. T20 BB 1-16.

DAWSON, Liam Andrew (John Bentley S, Calne), b Swindon, Wilts 1 Mar 1990. 5'8". RHB, SLA. Debut (Hampshire) 2007. Mountaineers 2011-12. England U19s 2007 to 2008. Wiltshire 2006-07. HS 169 v Somerset (Southampton) 2011. BB 7-51 Mountaineers v ME (Mutare) 2011-12 (also scored 110* in same match). BB 5-29 v Leics (Southampton) 2012. LO HS 70 v Northants (Northampton) 2011 (CB40). LO BB 4-45 v Middx (Lord's) 2008 (P40). T20 HS 30. T20 BB 3-25.

ERVINE, Sean Michael (Lomagundi C, Chinhoyi), b Harare, Zimbabwe 6 Dec 1982. Elder brother of C.R.Ervine (Midlands, SR 2003-04 to date); son of R.M.Ervine (Rhodesia 1977-78); grandson of M.A.Den (Rhodesia 1935-36); nephew of N.B.Ervine (Rhodesia 1977-78) and G.M.Den (Rhodesia and Eastern Province 1963-64 to 1969-70). 6'2". LHB, RM. CFX Academy 2000-01 to 2001. Midlands 2001-02 to 2003-04. Hampshire debut/cap 2005; qualified for England in 2013 season. W Australia 2006-07 to 2007-08. Southern Rocks 2009-10. Matabeleland Tuskers 2011-12 to date. **Tests** (Z): 5 (2003 to 2003-04); HS 86 v B (Harare) 2003-04; BB 4-146 v A (Perth) 2003-04. **LOI** (Z): 42 (2001-02 to 2003-04); HS 100 v I (Adelaide) 2003-04; BB 3-29 v P (Sharjah) 2002-03. F-c Tours (Z): E 2003; A 2003-04. HS 237* v Somerset (Southampton) 2010. BB 6-82 Midlands v Mashonaland (Kwekwe) 2002-03. H BB 5-60 v Glamorgan (Cardiff) 2005. LO HS 167* v Ireland (Southampton) 2009 (FPT). LO BB 5-50 v Glamorgan (Cardiff) 2005 (CGT). T20 HS 82. T20 BB 4-12.

GEORGE, Jacob ('Jake') (Portsmouth GS), b Hammersmith, London 5 April 1994. 6'0". RHB, OB. Hampshire 2nd XI debut 2011. Awaiting 1st XI debut. Development contract in 2013.

GRIFFITHS, David Andrew (Sandown HS, IoW), b Newport, IoW 10 Sep 1985. 6'1". LHB, RFM. Debut (Hampshire) 2006. HS 31* v Surrey (Southampton) 2007. BB 6-85 v Notts (Nottingham) 2011. LO HS 7 v Durham (Southampton) 2011 (CB40). LO BB 4-29 v Glos (Southampton) 2009 (P40). T20 HS 4*. T20 BB 3-13.

NQMcKENZIE, Neil Douglas (King Edward VII HS; Rand Afrikaans U), b Johannesburg, South Africa 24 Nov 1975. 5'9½". Son of K.A.McKenzie (N-E Transvaal and Transvaal 1966-67 to 1986-87). RHB, RM. Transvaal/Gauteng 1994-95 to 1998-99. Northerns 1999-00 to 2003-04. Lions 2004-05 to date; captain 2004-05 to 2009-10 (part). Somerset 2007. Durham 2008 (part). Hampshire debut/cap 2010 (Kolpak registration). Wisden 2008. **Tests** (SA): 58 (2000 to 2008-09); HS 226 v B (Chittagong) 2007-08, sharing Test record 1st wkt partnership of 415 with G.C.Smith; BB – . **LOI** (SA): 64 (1999-00 to 2008-09); HS 131* v Kenya (Cape Town) 2001-02; BB – . **IT20** (SA): 2 (2005-06 to 2008-09); HS 7* v A (Brisbane) 2008-09. F-c Tours (SA): E 2003, 2008; A 2001-02, 2008-09; WI 2000-01; NZ 2003-04; I 2007-08; P 2003-04; SL 2000; Z 2001-02, 2004 (SA A); B 2003, 2007-08. 1000 runs (1): 1120 (2011). HS 237 v Yorks (Southampton) 2011, sharing in UK 3rd highest and UK record 3rd-wkt partnership of 523 with M.A.Carberry. BB 2-13 Lions v Eagles (Kimberley) 2007-08. H BB 2-30 v Lancs (Liverpool) 2010. LO HS 131* (see LOI). LO BB 2-19 Gauteng v GW (Kimberley) 1997-98. T20 HS 89*. T20 BB 1-4.

MASCARENHAS, Adrian Dimitri (Trinity C, Perth, Australia), b Hammersmith, London 30 Oct 1977. 6'2". Resident in Australia 1979-96. RHB, RMF. Debut (Hampshire) 1996, taking 6-88 v Glamorgan (Southampton); took 16 wickets in first two CC matches; cap 1998; benefit 2007; captain 2008-10. No f-c or l-o appearances in 2010 after Achilles injury. Dorset 1996. LOI: 20 (2007 to 2009); HS 52 v I (Bristol) 2007; hit sixes off five successive balls from Yuvraj Singh v I (Oval) 2007; BB 3-23 v I (Lord's) 2007. IT20: 14 (2007 to 2009); HS 31 v NZ (Auckland) 2007-08; BB 3-18 v Z (Cape Town) 2007-08. HS 131 v Kent (Canterbury) 2006. 50 wkts (1): 56 (2004). BB 6-25 v Derbys (Southampton) 2004. LO HS 79 v Worcs (Southampton) 1999 (NL) and 79 v Kent (Canterbury) 2004 (NL). LO BB 5-27 v Glos (Southampton) 2002 (NL). T20 HS 57*. T20 BB 5-14 v Sussex (Hove) 2004 – H record.

RIAZUDDIN, Hamza (Bradfield C), b Chelsea, London 19 Dec 1989. 5'11". RHB, RMF. Debut (Hampshire) 2008. England U19s 2009. Berkshire 2008. HS 55* v Loughborough MCCU (Southampton) 2012. CC HS 28 v Glos (Southampton) 2012. BB 5-61 v Glamorgan (Cardiff) 2012. LO HS 23* v Durham (Chester-le-St) 2010 (CB40). LO BB 3-37 v Scotland (Southampton) 2011 (CB40). T20 HS 13*. T20 BB 4-15.

ROBERTS, Michael David Tudor (Oratory S, Reading; Bath U), b Oxford 13 Mar 1989. 5'11". RHB, OB. Middlesex 2nd XI 2007-11. Hampshire 2nd XI debut 2011. Berkshire 2006-12. LO HS 4 Unicorns v Derbys (Wormsley) 2012 (CB40).

ROUSE, Adam Paul (Perrins Community Sports C; Peter Symonds C, Winchester), b Harare, Zimbabwe 30 Jun 1992. 5'8". RHB, WK. Hampshire 2nd XI debut 2008, aged 15y 331d. England U19s 2010. Awaiting 1st XI debut.

NQ**SAEED AJMAL**, b Faisalabad, Pakistan 14 Oct 1977. RHB, OB. Faisalabad 1996-97 to 2006-07. KRL 2000-01 to 2008-09. Islamabad 2001-02. Federal Areas 2007-08. ZT Bank 2009-10 to date. Worcestershire 2011. **Tests** (P): 26 (2009 to 2012-13); HS 50 v E (Birmingham) 2010; BB 7-55 (10-97 match) v E (Dubai) 2011-12. **LOI** (P): 74 (2008 to 2012-13); HS 33 v NZ (Abu Dhabi) 2009-10; BB 5-24 v I (Delhi) 2012-13. **IT20** (P): 51 (2009 to 2012-13); HS 21* v WI (Gros Islet) 2010-11; BB 4-19 v Ireland (Oval) 2009. F-c Tours (P): E 2010; A 2009-10; SA 2012-13; WI 2011; NZ 2009-10; SL 2009, 2012; Z 2011; B 2011-12; UAE 2010-11 (v SA), 2011-12 (v UAE), 2012-13 (v E). 50 wkts (0+1): 62 (2006-07). BB 7-55 (see Tests). CC BB 6-124 Wo v Sussex (Horsham) 2011. LO HS 33 (see LOI). LO BB 5-18 Faisalabad v Karachi (Karachi) 2003-04. T20 HS 21*. T20 BB 4-14.

NQ**SHAHID KHAN AFRIDI**, Sahibzada Mohammad (Ibrahim Alibhai S; Islamia Science C, Karachi) b Kohat, Pakistan, 1 Mar 1980. Brother of Tariq Afridi (Karachi 1999-00) and Ashfaq Afridi (Karachi Blues 2008-09). RHB, LBG. Debut Combined XI v Eng A 1995-96. Karachi 1995-96 to 2003-04. Habib Bank 1997-98 to 2008-09. Leicestershire 2001; cap 2001. Derbyshire 2003. GW 2003-04. Sind 2007-08 to 2008-09. MCC 2001. Hampshire T20 contract for 2013. **Tests** (P): 27 (1998-99 to 2010, 1 as captain); HS 156 v I (Faisalabad) 2005-06; BB 5-52 v A (Karachi) 1998-99 – on debut. **LOI** (P): 350 (1996-97 to 2012-13, 21 as captain); HS 124 v B (Dambulla) 2010; BB 6-38 v A (Dubai) 2009. Scored a 37-ball hundred (LOI record) which included then joint record 11 sixes v SL (Nairobi) 1996-97 in his first LOI innings. **IT20** (P): 59 (2006-07 to 2012-13, 19 as captain); HS 54* v SL (Lord's) 2009; BB 4-11 v Netherlands (Lord's) 2009. F-c Tours (P): E 2006, 2010; A 1996-97, 2004-05; WI 1999-00, 2005; I 1998-99, 2004-05; SL 2005-06; Z 2002-03; B 1998-99. HS 164 Le v Northants (Northampton) 2001. BB 6-101 Habib Bank v KRL (Rawalpindi) 1997-98. UK BB 5-84 Le v Essex (Chelmsford) 2001. LO HS 124 (see LOI). LO BB 6-38 (see LOI). T20 HS 80. T20 BB 5-20.

SHEPPARD, Jack David (Q Elizabeth GS, Wimborne), b Salisbury, Wilts 29 Dec 1992. 6'2". RHB, RMF. Hampshire 2nd XI debut 2010. Awaiting 1st XI debut.

TERRY, Sean Paul (Aquinas C, Perth; Notre Dame U, Perth), b Southampton 1 Aug 1991. Son of V.P.Terry (Hampshire, England 1978-96). RHB, OB. Debut (Hampshire) 2012. Hampshire 2nd XI debut 2011. HS 59* v Loughborough MCCU (Southampton) 2012 – on debut. CC HS 19 v Northants (Northampton) 2012. LO HS – .

TOMLINSON, James Andrew (Harrow Way S, Andover; Cardiff U), b Winchester 12 Jun 1982. 6'1''. LHB, LMF. British U 2002-03. Hampshire debut 2002; cap 2008. Wiltshire 2001. HS 42 v Somerset (Southampton) 2010. 50 wkts (1): 67 (2008). BB 8-46 (10-194 match) v Somerset (Taunton) 2008. LO HS 14 v Durham (Chester-le-St) 2010 (CB40). LO BB 4-47 v Glamorgan (Southampton) 2006 (CGT). T20 HS 5. T20 BB 1-20.

VINCE, James Michael (Warminster S), b Cuckfield, Sussex 14 Mar 1991. 6'2''. RHB, RM. Debut (Hampshire) 2009. Hampshire 2nd XI debut 2006. Wiltshire 2007-08. HS 180 v Yorks (Scarborough) 2010. LO HS 131 v Scotland (Southampton) 2011 (CB40). LO BB 1-18 EL v Australia A (Sydney) 2012-13. T20 HS 85*.

‡WHEATER, Adam Jack (Millfield S), b Whipps Cross, Essex 13 Feb 1990. 5'6''. RHB, WK. Essex 2008-12. Cambridge MCCU 2010. Matabeleland Tuskers 2010-11 to 2011-12. Badureliya Sports Club 2011-12. Northern Districts 2012-13. Essex 2nd XI debut, aged 16y 190d. HS 164 Ex v Northants (Chelmsford) 2011. BB 1-86 Ex v Leics (Leicester) 2012 – in contrived circumstances. LO HS 69 MT v SR (Bulawayo) 2010-11. T20 HS 29.

WOOD, Christopher Philip (Alton C), b Basingstoke 27 June 1990. 6'2''. RHB, LM. Debut (Hampshire) 2010. Hampshire 2nd XI debut 2007. England U19s 2009. HS 105* v Leics (Leicester) 2012. BB 5-41 v Loughborough MCCU (Southampton) 2012. CC BB 4-35 v Worcs (Southampton) 2011. LO HS 16 and LO BB 5-22 v Glamorgan (Cardiff) 2012 (CB40). T20 HS 18. T20 BB 3-26.

RELEASED/RETIRED

(Having made a County First-Class or List A appearance in 2012)

ALI, K. – *see LANCASHIRE.*

KATICH, S.M. – *see LANCASHIRE.*

SHAFAYAT, Bilal Mustapha (Greenwood Dale; Nottingham Bluecoat SFC), b Nottingham 10 Jul 1984. 5'7''. RHB, RMF. Nottinghamshire 2001-04, 2007-10. National Bank of Pakistan 2004-05. Northamptonshire 2005-06. Pakistan Customs 2007-08 to 2008-09. Habib Bank 2010-11. Hampshire 2012. Captained Eng U19 tour of Australia 2002-03. F-c Tour (Eng A): I 2003-04. 1000 runs (1): 1058 (2005). HS 161 Nh v Derbys (Derby) 2005. H HS 93 v Derbys (Southampton) 2012. BB 2-25 Nh v Pakistanis (Northampton) 2006. CC BB 1-24 Nt v Essex (Chelmsford) 2007. LO HS 104 Nt v Northants (Northampton) 2007 (FPT). LO BB 4-33 Nh v Worcs (Worcester) 2005 (NL). T20 HS 40. T20 BB 2-13.

G.J.Maxwell left the staff, without making a County First-Class or List A appearance in 2012.

HAMPSHIRE 2012

RESULTS SUMMARY

	Place	Won	Lost	Tied	Drew	NR
LV= County Championship (2nd Division)	4th	4	5		7	
All First-Class Matches		5	5		7	
Clydesdale Bank 40 (Group B)	Winners	9	2			2
Friends Life t20 (South Group)	Winners	8	2			3

LV= COUNTY CHAMPIONSHIP AVERAGES

BATTING AND FIELDING

Cap		M	I	NO	HS	Runs	Avge	100	50	Ct/St
2010	N.D.McKenzie	5	9	3	139	403	67.16	1	2	6
2006	J.H.K.Adams	14	25	5	149	987	49.35	3	4	15
2003	S.M.Katich	15	23	2	196	738	35.14	1	5	8
2005	S.M.Ervine	16	23	3	109*	696	34.80	1	4	7
	L.A.Dawson	16	25	2	134*	682	29.65	1	2	35
	B.M.Shafayat	8	10	–	93	289	28.90	–	2	–
2006	M.A.Carberry	10	18	2	84*	414	25.87	–	3	4
	J.M.Vince	11	18	1	114	417	24.52	1	–	13
	C.P.Wood	9	14	1	105*	318	24.46	1	1	1
	D.J.Balcombe	16	22	7	73	299	19.93	–	1	3
	M.D.Bates	16	22	–	103	437	19.86	1	1	51/1
	Kabir Ali	8	9	1	31	140	17.50	–	–	–
1998	A.D.Mascarenhas	5	5	–	27	79	15.80	–	–	2
	H.Riazuddin	4	6	1	28	68	13.60	–	–	1
2012	D.R.Briggs	4	6	2	20*	49	12.25	–	–	2
	S.P.Terry	3	4	–	19	34	8.50	–	–	1
2008	J.A.Tomlinson	12	14	7	11	45	6.42	–	–	4
	D.A.Griffiths	4	6	1	21	27	5.40	–	–	2

BOWLING

	O	M	R	W	Avge	Best	5wI	10wM
H.Riazuddin	78	17	240	10	24.00	5-61	1	–
J.A.Tomlinson	376.1	82	1131	43	26.30	5-69	2	–
S.M.Ervine	220.2	55	689	26	26.50	4-96	–	–
D.J.Balcombe	505.1	103	1589	59	26.93	8-71	3	1
Kabir Ali	216.3	36	769	22	34.95	3-42	–	–
C.P.Wood	252.5	68	683	19	35.94	4-52	–	–
L.A.Dawson	260.5	59	829	23	36.04	5-29	1	–
Also bowled:								
A.D.Mascarenhas	104	36	241	7	34.42	2-40	–	–
D.A.Griffiths	90.4	14	316	9	35.11	3-40	–	–
D.R.Briggs	82.1	15	249	5	49.80	2-79	–	–

J.H.K.Adams 3-2-4-1; M.A.Carberry 4-0-19-1; S.M.Katich 33-4-93-2; B.M.Shafayat 2-0-15-0; J.M.Vince 3-0-6-0.

The First-Class Average (pp 219–235) give the records of Hampshire players in all first-class county matches (Hampshire's other opponents being Loughborough MCCU), with the exception of:
M.A.Carberry 11-20-2-84*-468-26.00-0-3-4ct. 6-2-19-1-19.00-1/1-0-0.

HAMPSHIRE RECORDS

FIRST-CLASS CRICKET

Highest Total	For 714-5d		v	Notts	Southampton	2005
	V 742		by	Surrey	The Oval	1909
Lowest Total	For 15		v	Warwicks	Birmingham	1922
	V 23		by	Yorkshire	Middlesbrough	1965
Highest Innings	For 316	R.H.Moore	v	Warwicks	Bournemouth	1937
	V 303*	G.A.Hick	for	Worcs	Southampton	1997

Highest Partnership for each Wicket

1st	347	V.P.Terry/C.L.Smith	v	Warwicks	Birmingham	1987
2nd	373	J.H.K.Adams/M.A.Carberry	v	Somerset	Taunton	2011
3rd	523	M.A.Carberry/N.D.McKenzie	v	Yorkshire	Southampton	2011
4th	278	J.H.K.Adams/J.M.Vince	v	Yorkshire	Scarborough	2010
5th	235	G.Hill/D.F.Walker	v	Sussex	Portsmouth	1937
6th	411	R.M.Poore/E.G.Wynyard	v	Somerset	Taunton	1899
7th	325	G.Brown/C.H.Abercrombie	v	Essex	Leyton	1913
8th	257	N.Pothas/A.J.Bichel	v	Glos	Cheltenham	2005
9th	230	D.A.Livingstone/A.T.Castell	v	Surrey	Southampton	1962
10th	192	H.A.W.Bowell/W.H.Livsey	v	Worcs	Bournemouth	1921

Best Bowling	For 9- 25	R.M.H.Cottam	v	Lancashire	Manchester	1965
(Innings)	V 10- 46	W.Hickton	for	Lancashire	Manchester	1870
Best Bowling	For 16- 88	J.A.Newman	v	Somerset	Weston-s-Mare	1927
(Match)	V 17-103	W.Mycroft	for	Derbyshire	Southampton	1876

Most Runs – Season	2854	C.P.Mead	(av 79.27)	1928
Most Runs – Career	48892	C.P.Mead	(av 48.84)	1905-36
Most 100s – Season	12	C.P.Mead		1928
Most 100s – Career	138	C.P.Mead		1905-36
Most Wkts – Season	190	A.S.Kennedy	(av 15.61)	1922
Most Wkts – Career	2669	D.Shackleton	(av 18.23)	1948-69
Most Career W-K Dismissals	700	R.J.Parks	(630 ct; 70 st)	1980-92
Most Career Catches in the Field	629	C.P.Mead		1905-36

LIMITED-OVERS CRICKET

Highest Total	50ov	371-4		v	Glamorgan	Southampton	1975
	40ov	353-8		v	Middlesex	Lord's	2005
	T20	225-2		v	Middlesex	Southampton	2006
Lowest Total	50ov	75		v	Essex	Chelmsford	2007
	40ov	43		v	Essex	Basingstoke	1972
	T20	85		v	Sussex	Southampton	2008
Highest Innings	50ov	177	C.G.Greenidge	v	Glamorgan	Southampton	1975
	40ov	172	C.G.Greenidge	v	Surrey	Southampton	1987
	T20	124*	M.J.Lumb	v	Essex	Southampton	2009
Best Bowling	50ov	7-30	P.J.Sainsbury	v	Norfolk	Southampton	1965
	40ov	6-20	T.E.Jesty	v	Glamorgan	Cardiff	1975
	T20	5-14	A.D.Mascarenhas	v	Sussex	Hove	2004

KENT

Formation of Present Club: 1 March 1859
Substantial Reorganisation: 6 December 1870
Inaugural First-Class Match: 1864
Colours: Maroon and White
Badge: White Horse on a Red Ground
County Champions: (6) 1906, 1909, 1910, 1913, 1970, 1978
Joint Champions: (1) 1977
Gillette/NatWest/C&G/FP Trophy Winners: (2) 1967, 1974
Benson and Hedges Cup Winners: (3) 1973, 1976, 1978
Pro 40/National League (Div 1) Winners: (1) 2001
Sunday League Winners: (4) 1972, 1973, 1976, 1995
Clydesdale Bank 40 Winners: (0); best – 2nd Group C 2010
Twenty20 Cup Winners: (1) 2007

Cricket Chief Executive: Jamie Clifford, St Lawrence Ground, Old Dover Road, Canterbury, CT1 3NZ • Tel: 01227 456886 • Fax: 01227 762168 • Email: kent@ecb.co.uk • Web: www.kentcricket.co.uk

Head Coach: Jimmy C.Adams. **High Performance Director**: Simon Willis. **1st Team Assistant Coach**: Paul Relf. **Captain**: J.C.Tredwell. **Vice-Captain**: tba. **Overseas Player**: B.P.Nash. **2013 Beneficiary**: none. **Head Groundsman**: Andrew Peirson. **Scorer**: Lorne Hart. ‡ New registration. ^NQ Not qualified for England.

BALL, Adam James (Beths GS, Bexley) b Greenwich, London 1 March 1993. 6'1". RHB, LFM. Debut (Kent) 2011. No f-c appearances in 2012. Kent 2nd XI debut 2009, aged 16y 117d. England U19s 2010 to 2010-11. HS 46 v Glos (Canterbury) 2011. BB 3-36 v Leics (Leicester) 2011. LO HS 19 v Middx (Canterbury) 2011 (CB40). LO BB 2-31 v Sussex (Hove) 2011 (CB40). T20 HS 18. T20 BB 2-18.

BELL-DRUMMOND, Daniel James (Millfield S), b Lewisham, London 4 Aug 1993. 6'0". RHB, RMF. Debut (Kent) 2011. Kent 2nd XI debut 2009, aged 16y 21d. England U19s 2010 to 2010-11. HS 80 v Loughborough MCCU (Canterbury) 2011. CC HS 33 v Glamorgan (Cardiff) 2012. LO HS 42 v Worcs (Worcester) 2011 (CB40). T20 HS 11.

BILLINGS, Samuel William (Haileybury S; Loughborough U), b Pembury 15 Jun 1991. 5'11". RHB, WK. Loughborough MCCU 2011, scoring 131 v Northants (Loughborough) on f-c debut. Kent debut 2011. Kent 2nd XI debut 2007, aged 15y 349d. HS 131 (*see above*). K HS 19 v Loughborough MCCU (Canterbury) 2011. LO HS 143 v Derbys (Canterbury) 2012 (CB40). T20 HS 59.

BLAKE, Alexander (Hayes SS; Leeds Met U), b Farnborough 25 Jan 1989. 6'1". LHB, RMF. Debut (Kent) 2008. Kent 2nd XI debut 2005. Leeds/Bradford UCCE 2009-11 (not f-c). HS 105* v Yorks (Leeds) 2010. BB 2-9 v Pakistanis (Canterbury) 2010. CC BB 1-60 v Hants (Southampton) 2010. LO HS 81* v Scotland (Canterbury) 2010 (CB40). LO BB 2-13 v Yorks (Leeds) 2011 (CB40). T20 HS 35.

COLES, Matthew Thomas (Maplesden Noakes S; Mid-Kent C), b Maidstone 26 May 1990. 6'3". LHB, RMF. Debut (Kent) 2009; cap 2012. Kent 2nd XI debut 2007. HS 103* v Yorks (Leeds) 2012. 50 wkts (1): 59 (2012). BB 6-51 (9-83 match) v Northants (Northampton) 2012. LO HS 47 v Yorks (Leeds) 2011 (CB40). LO BB 6-32 v Yorks (Leeds) 2012 (CB40). T20 HS 16*. T20 BB 3-30.

COWDREY, Fabian Kruuse (Tonbridge S), b Canterbury 30 Jan 1993. Son of C.S.Cowdrey (Kent, Glamorgan, England 1977-92). Grandson of M.C.Cowdrey (Kent, Oxford U, England 1950-76). Nephew of G.R.Cowdrey (Kent 1984-97). 6'0". RHB, SLA. Kent 2nd XI debut 2009, aged 16y 207d. Awaiting 1st XI debut.

DAVIES, Mark (Northfield CS, Billingham; Stockton SFC), b Stockton-on-Tees, Durham 4 Oct 1980. 6'3". RHB, RMF. Durham 2002-10; cap 2005; no f-c appearances in 2011. Nottinghamshire 2007 (on loan). Kent debut 2012. F-c Tour (Eng A): NZ 2008-09. HS 62 Du v Somerset (Stockton) 2005. K HS 58 v Yorks (Leeds) 2012. 50 wkts (1): 50 (2004). BB 8-24 (11-75 match) Du v Hants (Basingstoke) 2008. K BB 5-27 v Derbys (Canterbury) 2012. LO HS 31* Du v Warwks (Chester-le-St) 2002 (NL). LO BB 4-13 Du v Sussex (Chester-le-St) 2001 (NL). T20 HS 13. T20 BB 2-14.

HAGGETT, Calum John (Millfield S), b Taunton, Somerset 30 Oct 1990. 6'3". LHB, RMF. Somerset 2nd XI 2009-11. Kent 2nd XI debut 2012. England U19s 2009-10. Awaiting f-c and l-o debut. T20 HS 2. T20 BB 1-15.

HARMISON, Ben William (Ashington HS), b Ashington, Northumb 9 Jan 1986. Younger brother of S.J.Harmison (*see DURHAM*). 6'5". LHB, RMF. Durham 2006-10, scoring 110 v Oxford U (Oxford) on debut. Scored 105 in his second match (v West Indies A) to emulate A.Fairbairn (Middlesex 1947) in scoring hundreds in first two f-c matches, those matches being in England. Kent debut 2012. HS 110 (*see above*). CC HS 101 Du v Warwks (Chester-le-St) 2007. K HS 46 v Northants (Northampton) 2012. BB 4-27 Du v Surrey (Guildford) 2008. K BB – . LO HS 67 Du v Notts (Chester-le-St) 2009 (P40). LO BB 3-43 Du v Scotland (Chester-le-St) 2008 (FPT). T20 HS 24. T20 BB 3-20.

JONES, Geraint Owen (Harristown State HS, Toowoomba and MacGregor State HS, Brisbane, Australia), b Kundiawa, Papua New Guinea 14 Jul 1976. Welsh parents. 5'10". RHB, WK. Debut (Kent) 2001; cap 2003; benefit 2012. MBE 2005. **Tests**: 34 (2003-04 to 2006-07); HS 100 v NZ (Leeds) 2004. **LOI**: 49 (2004 to 2006); HS 80 v Z (Bulawayo) 2004-05. **IT20**: 2 (2005 to 2006); HS 19 v A (Southampton) 2005. F-c Tours: A 2006-07; SA 2004-05; WI 2003-04; I 2005-06; P 2005-06; SL 2003-04. 1000 runs (2); most – 1345 (2009). HS 178 v Somerset (Canterbury) 2010. LO HS 86 v Surrey (Oval) 2008 (FPT). T20 HS 56.

KEMP, Benedict William (St Edmund's S, Canterbury; Oxford Brookes U), b Canterbury 26 May 1993. Son of N.J.Kemp (Kent, Middlesex 1977-82). 6'4". RHB, RFM. Debut (Oxford MCCU) 2012. Kent 2nd XI debut 2010. Awaiting Kent 1st XI debut. HS 3 and BB 1-71 OU v Worcs (Oxford) 2012 – only f-c match.

KEY, Robert William Trevor (Colfe's S), b East Dulwich, London 12 May 1979. 6'1". RHB, RM/OB. Debut (Kent) 1998; cap 2001; captain 2006-12; benefit 2011. MCC 2002-04, 2009. *Wisden* 2004. **Tests**: 15 (2002 to 2004-05); HS 221 v WI (Lord's) 2004. **LOI**: 5 (2003 to 2004); HS 19 v WI (Lord's) 2004. **IT20**: 1 (2009); HS 10* v Netherlands (Lord's) 2009. F-c Tours: A 2002-03; SA 1998-99 (Eng A), 2004-05; NZ 2008-09 (EL – captain); SL 2002-03 (ECB Acad); Z 1998-99 (Eng A). 1000 runs (6); most – 1896 (2004). HS 270* v Glamorgan (Cardiff) 2009. BB 2-31 v Somerset (Canterbury) 2010. LO HS 120* v Essex (Canterbury) 2008 (P40). T20 HS 98*.

^{NQ}**NASH, Brendan** Paul, b Attadale, Western Australia 14 Dec 1977. 5'8". LHB, LM. Queensland 2000-01 to 2006-07. Jamaica 2007-08 to 2011-12. Kent debut 2012. **Tests** (WI): 21 (2008-09 to 2011); HS 114 v SA (Basseterre) 2010; BB 1-21 v SL (Galle) 2010-11. **LOI** (WI): 9 (2008 to 2008-09); HS 39* and BB 3-56 v Canada (King City) 2008. F-c Tours (WI): E 2009; A 2009-10; NZ 2008-09; SL 2010-11; B 2010 (WI A). HS 207 Jamaica v T&T (St Augustine) 2010-11. K HS 132 v Yorks (Canterbury) 2012. BB 2-7 Jamaica v CC&C (Kingston) 2007-08. K BB 1-2 v Glamorgan (Canterbury) 2012. LO HS 71 WI A v South Africa A (Mirpur) 2010. LO BB 4-20 Jamaica v Guyana (Bridgetown) 2007-08. T20 HS 26. T20 BB 1-32.

NORTHEAST, Sam Alexander (Harrow S), b Ashford 16 Oct 1989. 5'11". RHB, OB. Debut (Kent) 2007; cap 2012. No 1st XI appearances in 2008. England U19s 2009. HS 176 v Loughborough MCCU (Canterbury) 2011. CC HS 165 v Derbys (Canterbury) 2012. BB – . LO HS 69 v Surrey (Canterbury) 2009 (P40) and 69 v Unicorns (Canterbury) 2012 (CB40). T20 HS 60.

PIESLEY, Christopher Damien (Fulston Manor S, Sittingbourne), b Chatham 12 Mar 1992. 5'11½". LHB, OB. Debut (Kent) 2010. No 1st XI appearances in 2012. Kent 2nd XI debut 2008, aged 16y 126d. HS 43 v Pakistanis (Canterbury) 2010. CC HS 4 v Glos (Cheltenham) 2011. LO HS 4 v Netherlands (Rotterdam) 2011 (CB40).

POWELL, Michael John (Crickhowell SS; Pontypool CFE), b Abergavenny, Monmouth-shire 3 Feb 1977. 6'1". RHB, OB, occ WK. Glamorgan 1997-2011, scoring 200* v Oxford U (Oxford) on debut; cap 2000; benefit 2011. Kent debut 2012. MCC 2005. 1000 runs (5); most – 1327 (2006). HS 299 Gm v Glos (Cheltenham) 2006 – record score for Glamorgan in England. K HS 134 v Leics (Canterbury) 2012. BB 2-39 Gm v Oxford U (Oxford) 1999. CC BB – . LO HS 114* Gm v Hants (Cardiff) 2008 (FPT). LO BB 1-26 Gm v Lincs (Lincoln) 2004 (CGT). T20 HS 68*.

RILEY, Adam Edward Nicholas (Beths GS, Bexley; Loughborough U), b Sidcup 23 Mar 1992. 6'2". RHB, OB. Debut (Kent) 2011. Loughborough MCCU 2012. Kent 2nd XI debut 2010. HS 18 LU v Notts (Nottingham) 2012. K HS 8 v Yorks (Leeds) 2012. BB 5-76 v Loughborough MCCU (Canterbury) 2011. CC BB 4-145 v Northants (Canterbury) 2011. LO HS 3* and LO BB 2-32 v Sussex (Hove) 2011 (CB40). T20 HS 5*. T20 BB 2-15.

SHAW, Stuart Ashley (Shavington HS, Crewe), b Crewe, Cheshire 14 Apr 1991. 5'11". RHB, LFM. Debut (Kent) 2011. Missed entire 2012 season with shin splints injury. Kent 2nd XI debut 2010. HS 22* and BB 5-118 v Derbys (Canterbury) 2011. LO HS 4* v Yorks (Leeds) 2011 (CB40). LO BB 3-26 v Middx (Lord's) 2011 (CB40). T20 HS 3*. T20 BB 1-10.

SHRECK, Charles Edward (Truro S), b Truro, Cornwall 6 Jan 1978. 6'7". RHB, RFM. Nottinghamshire 2003-11; cap 2006. Wellington 2005-06 to 2007-08. Kent 2012. MCC 2008. Cornwall 1997-2002. HS 19 Nt v Essex (Chelmsford) 2003. K HS 16 v Glamorgan (Cardiff) 2012. 50 wkts (3); most – 61 (2006, 2008). BB 8-31 (12-129 match) Nt v Middx (Nottingham) 2006. K BB 5-41 v Derbys (Derby) 2012. Hat-trick Nt v Middx (Lord's) 2006. LO HS 9* Wellington v CD (Palmerston N) 2005-06. LO BB 5-19 Cornwall v Worcs (Truro) 2002 (CGT). T20 HS 6*. T20 BB 4-22.

STEVENS, Darren Ian (Hinckley C), b Leicester 30 Apr 1976. 5'11". RHB, RM. Leicestershire 1997-2004; cap 2002. MCC 2002. Kent debut/cap 2005. F-c Tour (ECB Acad): SL 2002-03. 1000 runs (2); most – 1277 (2005). HS 208 v Glamorgan (Canterbury) 2005 and v Middx (Uxbridge) 2009. BB 7-21 (11-70 match) v Surrey (Canterbury) 2011. LO HS 133 Le v Northumb (Jesmond) 2000 (NWT). LO BB 5-32 v Scotland (Edinburgh) 2005 (NL). T20 HS 77. T20 BB 4-14.

THOMAS, Ivan Alfred Astley (John Roan S, Blackheath; Leeds U), b Greenwich, London 25 Sep 1991. 6'4". RHB, RMF. Debut (Leeds/Bradford MCCU) 2012. Kent debut 2012. Kent 2nd XI debut 2011. HS 11 and BB 2-24 LBU v Yorks (Leeds) 2012. K HS 0* and K BB 2-29 v Essex (Chelmsford) 2012.

TREDWELL, James Cullum (Southlands Community CS, New Romney), b Ashford 27 Feb 1982. 6'0". LHB, OB. Debut (Kent) 2001; cap 2007; captain 2013. MCC 2004, 2008. **Tests**: 1 (2009-10); HS 37 and BB 4-82 v B (Dhaka) 2009-10. **LOI**: 14 (2009-10 to 2012-13); HS 16 v A (Hobart) 2010-11; BB 4-44 v I (Rajkot) 2012-13. **IT20**: 5 (2012-13); HS 22 and BB 1-20 v NZ (Hamilton) 2012-13. F-c Tours: NZ 2012-13 (*part*); I 2003-04 (Eng A, captain); B 2009-10. HS 123* v New Zealanders (Canterbury) 2008. CC HS 116* v Yorks (Tunbridge W) 2007. 50 wkts (1): 69 (2009). BB 8-66 (11-120 match) v Glamorgan (Canterbury) 2009. LO HS 88 v Surrey (Oval) 2007 (FPT). LO BB 6-27 v Middx (Southgate) 2009 (FPT). T20 HS 34*. T20 BB 4-21.

RELEASED/RETIRED

(Having made a County First-Class or List A appearance in 2012)

[NQ]**AZHAR MAHMOOD** Sagar (F.G. No. 1 HS, Islamabad), b Rawalpindi, Pakistan 28 Feb 1975. 5'11". RHB, RFM. Islamabad 1993-94 to 2006-07. United Bank 1995-96 to 1996-97. Rawalpindi 1998-99 to 2004-05. PIA 2001-02. Surrey 2002-07; cap 2004. Habib Bank 2006-07 to 2010-11. Kent 2008-12; (British passport holder) scoring 116 v Notts (Canterbury) on debut; cap 2008. MCC 2001. **Tests** (P): 21 (1997-98 to 2001); HS 136 v SA (Johannesburg) 1997-98; BB 4-50 v E (Lord's) 2001. Scored 128* and 50* v SA (Rawalpindi) 1997-98 on debut. **LOI** (P): 143 (1996-97 to 2006-07); HS 67 v I (Adelaide) 1999-00; BB 6-18 v WI (Sharjah) 1999-00. F-c Tours (P): E 1997 (Pak A), 2001; A 1999-00; SA 1997-98; I 1998-99; SL 2000; Z 1997-98. HS 204* Sy v Middx (Oval) 2005. K HS 116 (*see above*). 50 wkts (0+1): 59 (1996-97). BB 8-61 Sy v Lancs (Oval) 2002. K BB 6-36 v Middx (Lord's) 2011. LO HS 101* Sy v Glamorgan (Oval) 2006 (CGT). LO BB 6-18 (*see LOI*). T20 HS 106*. T20 BB 5-24.

COOK, Simon James (Matthew Arnold S), b Oxford 15 Jan 1977. 6'4". RHB, RMF. Middlesex 1999-2004; cap 2003. Kent 2005-12; cap 2007. HS 93* M v Notts (Lord's) 2001. K HS 71 v Yorks (Leeds) 2006. BB 8-63 M v Northants (Northampton) 2002. K BB 6-35 v Sussex (Canterbury) 2007. LO HS 67* M v Durham (Lord's) 2003 (NL). LO BB 6-37 M v Leics (Leicester) 2004 (NL). T20 HS 25*. T20 BB 3-13.

KENT 2012

RESULTS SUMMARY

	Place	Won	Lost	Tied	Drew	NR
LV= County Championship (2nd Division)	3rd	4	3		9	
All First-Class Matches		4	3		10	
Clydesdale Bank 40 (Group C)	3rd	7	2			3
Friends Life t20 (South Group)	4th	4	5			1

LV= COUNTY CHAMPIONSHIP AVERAGES

BATTING AND FIELDING

Cap		M	I	NO	HS	Runs	Avge	100	50	Ct/St
2012	S.A.Northeast	11	17	1	165	880	55.00	3	5	6
	B.P.Nash	16	24	5	132*	908	47.78	3	4	6
2003	G.O.Jones	16	20	4	88	677	42.31	–	7	52
	M.J.Powell	16	20	3	134	647	38.05	2	3	6
2001	R.W.T.Key	15	24	3	119	797	37.95	1	5	7
2005	D.I.Stevens	16	20	–	123	619	30.95	2	2	7
	A.J.Blake	4	7	1	73	155	25.83	–	1	5
	S.A.Newman	6	9	–	64	215	23.88	–	1	3
2012	M.T.Coles	14	17	1	103*	371	23.18	1	1	4
	B.W.Harmison	11	16	1	46	311	20.73	–	–	3
2007	J.C.Tredwell	13	13	2	87	227	20.63	–	1	15
	M.Davies	15	16	4	58	227	18.91	–	1	4
	C.E.Shreck	16	16	11	16	84	16.80	–	–	1
	A.E.N.Riley	5	5	–	8	20	4.00	–	–	1

Also batted (1 match each): Azhar Mahmood (cap 2008) 49, 0 (1 ct); D.J.Bell-Drummond 33, 0; S.J.Cook (cap 2007) 15; I.A.A.Thomas 0*.

BOWLING

	O	M	R	W	Avge	Best	5wI	10wM
M.Davies	368.3	128	699	36	19.41	5-27	1	–
M.T.Coles	344.4	44	1146	52	22.03	6-51	2	–
D.I.Stevens	304.3	63	840	35	24.00	5-35	1	–
C.E.Shreck	502.3	110	1455	55	26.45	5-41	2	–
J.C.Tredwell	301	78	751	19	39.52	3-38	–	–

Also bowled:

| A.E.N.Riley | 63.4 | 17 | 231 | 5 | 46.20 | 2-43 | – | – |

Azhar Mahmood 21-5-71-2; B.W.Harmison 13-1-56-0; R.W.T.Key 4-1-27-0; B.P.Nash 28.5-1-72-4; S.A.Newman 6-0-31-0; I.A.A.Thomas 16-7-29-2.

The First-Class Averages (pp 219–235) give the records of Kent players in all first-class county matches (Kent's other opponents being the South Africans), with the exception of J.C.Tredwell, whose first-class figures for Kent are as above, and:

M.T.Coles 15-18-1-103*-392-23.05-1-1-4ct; 357.4-46-1197-53-22.58-6/51-2-0.
A.E.N.Riley 6-6-0-8-20-3.33-0-0-3ct. 81.4-19-301-7-43.00-2/43-0-0.
I.A.A.Thomas 2-2-1-0*-0-0.00-0-0-0ct. 35-11-88-3-29.33-2/29-0-0.

KENT RECORDS

FIRST-CLASS CRICKET

Highest Total	For 803-4d		v	Essex	Brentwood	1934
	V 676		by	Australians	Canterbury	1921
Lowest Total	For 18		v	Sussex	Gravesend	1867
	V 16		by	Warwicks	Tonbridge	1913
Highest Innings	For 332	W.H.Ashdown	v	Essex	Brentwood	1934
	V 344	W.G.Grace	for	MCC	Canterbury	1876

Highest Partnership for each Wicket

1st	300	N.R.Taylor/M.R.Benson	v	Derbyshire	Canterbury	1991
2nd	366	S.G.Hinks/N.R.Taylor	v	Middlesex	Canterbury	1990
3rd	323	R.W.T.Key/M.van Jaarsveld	v	Surrey	Tunbridge Wells	2005
4th	368	P.A.de Silva/G.R.Cowdrey	v	Derbyshire	Maidstone	1995
5th	277	F.E.Woolley/L.E.G.Ames	v	N Zealanders	Canterbury	1931
6th	315	P.A.de Silva/M.A.Ealham	v	Notts	Nottingham	1995
7th	248	A.P.Day/E.Humphreys	v	Somerset	Taunton	1908
8th	177	G.O.Jones/Yasir Arafat	v	Warwicks	Canterbury	2007
9th	171	M.A.Ealham/P.A.Strang	v	Notts	Nottingham	1997
10th	235	F.E.Woolley/A.Fielder	v	Worcs	Stourbridge	1909

Best Bowling	For 10- 30	C.Blythe	v	Northants	Northampton	1907
(Innings)	V 10- 48	C.H.G.Bland	for	Sussex	Tonbridge	1899
Best Bowling	For 17- 48	C.Blythe	v	Northants	Northampton	1907
(Match)	V 17-106	T.W.J.Goddard	for	Glos	Bristol	1939

Most Runs – Season	2894	F.E.Woolley	(av 59.06)	1928
Most Runs – Career	47868	F.E.Woolley	(av 41.77)	1906-38
Most 100s – Season	10	F.E.Woolley		1928, 1934
Most 100s – Career	122	F.E.Woolley		1906-38
Most Wkts – Season	262	A.P.Freeman	(av 14.74)	1933
Most Wkts – Career	3340	A.P.Freeman	(av 17.64)	1914-36
Most Career W-K Dismissals	1253	F.H.Huish	(901 ct; 352 st) 1895-1914	
Most Career Catches in the Field	773	F.E.Woolley		1906-38

LIMITED-OVERS CRICKET

Highest Total	50ov	384-6	v	Berkshire	Finchampstead	1994
	40ov	327-6	v	Leics	Canterbury	1993
	T20	217	v	Glos	Gloucester	2010
Lowest Total	50ov	60	v	Somerset	Taunton	1979
	40ov	83	v	Middlesex	Lord's	1984
	T20	72	v	Hampshire	Southampton	2011
Highest Innings	50ov	136*	C.L.Hooper	v	Berkshire	Finchampstead	1994
	40ov	146	A.Symonds	v	Lancashire	Tunbridge Wells	2004
	T20	112	A.Symonds	v	Middlesex	Maidstone	2004
Best Bowling	50ov	8-31	D.L.Underwood	v	Scotland	Edinburgh	1987
	40ov	6- 9	R.A.Woolmer	v	Derbyshire	Chesterfield	1979
	T20	5-17	Wahab Riaz	v	Glos	Beckenham	2011

LANCASHIRE

Formation of Present Club: 12 January 1864
Inaugural First-Class Match: 1865
Colours: Red, Green and Blue
Badge: Red Rose
County Champions (since 1890): (8) 1897, 1904, 1926, 1927, 1928, 1930, 1934, 2011
Joint Champions: (1) 1950
Gillette/NatWest/C&G/FP Trophy Winners: (7) 1970, 1971, 1972, 1975, 1990, 1996, 1998
Benson and Hedges Cup Winners: (4) 1984, 1990, 1995, 1996
Pro 40/National League (Div 1) Winners: (1) 1999.
Sunday League Winners: (4) 1969, 1970, 1989, 1998
Clydesdale Bank 40 Winners: (0); best – Semi-finalist 2012
Twenty20 Cup Winners: (0); best – Finalist 2005

Chief Executive: Daniel Gidney, Emirates Old Trafford, Talbot Road, Manchester M16 0PX • Tel: 0161 282 4000 • Fax: 0161 282 4100 • Email: enquiries@lccc.co.uk • Web: www.lccc.co.uk

Director of Cricket: Mike Watkinson. **Head Coach**: Peter Moores. **Assistant Coach**: Gary Yates. **Captain**: G.Chapple. **Vice-Captain**: none. **Overseas Player**: S.M.Katich. **2013 Beneficiary**: none. **Head Groundsman**: Matthew Merchant. **Scorer**: Alan West. ‡ New registration. [NQ] Not qualified for England.

AGATHANGELOU, Andrea Peter (Fields C, Rustenburg), b Rustenburg, South Africa 16 Nov 1989. 6'3". RHB, LB. North West 2007-08 to 2010-11. Lions 2008-09. Lancashire debut 2011. HS 158 NW v KZN (Potchefstroom) 2009-10. La HS 24 v Somerset (Taunton) 2012. BB 2-62 NW v KZN Inland (Potchefstroom) 2009-10. LO HS 94 NW v EP (Port Elizabeth) 2010-11.

‡ALI, Kabir (Moseley CS and SFC), b Moseley, Birmingham, Warwks 24 Nov 1980. 6'0". Cousin of A.K.Ali (*see LEICESTERSHIRE*) and M.M.Ali (*see WORCESTERSHIRE*). RHB, RMF. Worcestershire 1999-2009. Rajasthan 2006-07. Hampshire 2010-12. **Tests**: 1 (2003); HS 9 and BB 3-80 v SA (Leeds) 2003. **LOI**: 14 (2003 to 2006); HS 39* v P (Rawalpindi) 2005-06; BB 4-45 v I (Delhi) 2005-06. **F-c Tours**: WI 2005-06 (Eng A); SL 2002-03 (ECB Acad). HS 84* Wo v Durham (Stockton) 2003. 50 wkts (5); most – 71 (2002). BB 8-50 Wo v Lancs (Manchester) 2007. Took 8-53 before lunch first day Wo v Yorks (Scarborough) 2003. LO HS 92 Wo v Essex (Worcester) 2003 (NL). LO BB 5-36 Wo v Yorks (Leeds) 2002 (NL). T20 HS 50. T20 BB 4-44.

ANDERSON, James Michael (St Theodore RC HS and SFC, Burnley), b Burnley 30 Jul 1982. 6'2". LHB, RFM. Debut (Lancashire) 2002; cap 2003; benefit 2012. YC 2003. *Wisden* 2008. **ECB central contract 2012-13. Tests**: 78 (2003 to 2012-13); HS 34 v SA (Leeds) 2008; BB 7-43 v NZ (Nottingham) 2008. **LOI**: 167 (2002-03 to 2012-13); HS 20* v A (Brisbane) 2010-11; BB 5-23 v SA (Port Elizabeth) 2009-10. Hat-trick v P (Oval) 2003 – 1st for Eng in 373 LOI. **IT20**: 19 (2006-07 to 2009-10); HS 1* v A (Sydney) 2006-07; BB 3-23 v Netherlands (Lord's) 2009. **F-c Tours**: A (2006-07, 2010-11); SA 2004-05, 2009-10; WI 2003-04, 2005-06 (Eng A) (*part*), 2008-09; NZ 2007-08, 2012-13; SL 2003-04, 2007-08, 2011-12; UAE 2011-12 (v P). HS 37* v Durham (Manchester) 2005. 50 wkts (1); most – 60 (2005). BB 7-43 (*see Tests*). La BB 6-23 v Hants (Southampton) 2002. Hat-trick v Essex (Manchester) 2003. LO HS 20* (*see LOI*). LO BB 5-23 (*see LOI*). T20 HS 16. T20 BB 3-23.

129

BAILEY, Thomas Ernest (Our Lady's Catholic HS, Preston), b Preston 21 Apr 1991. 6'4". RHB, RFM. Debut (Lancashire) 2012. Lancashire 2nd XI debut 2011. HS- and BB 1-67 v Surrey (Liverpool) 2012 – only 1st XI game.

BROWN, Karl Robert (Hesketh Fletcher HS, Atherton), b Bolton 17 May 1988. 5'10". RHB, RMF. Debut (Lancashire) 2006. Moors Sports Club 2011-12. HS 114 v Sussex (Liverpool) 2011. BB 2-30 v Notts (Nottingham) 2009. LO HS 101* v Essex (Manchester) 2011 (CB40). T20 HS 51.

CHAPPLE, Glen (West Craven HS; Nelson & Colne C), b Skipton, Yorks 23 Jan 1974. 6'1". RHB, RMF. Debut (Lancashire) 1992; cap 1994; benefit 2004; captain 2009 to date. *Wisden* 2011. **LOI**: 1 (2006); HS 14 and BB – v Ireland (Belfast) 2006. F-c Tours (Eng A): A 1996-97; WI 1995-96 (La); I 1994-95. HS 155 v Somerset (Manchester) 2001. Scored 100 off 27 balls in contrived circumstances v Glamorgan (Manchester) 1993. 50 wkts (6); most – 57 (2011). BB 7-53 v Durham (Blackpool) 2007. LO HS 81* v Derbys (Manchester) 2002 (CGT). LO BB 6-18 v Essex (Lord's) 1996 (NWT) – La record. T20 HS 55*. T20 BB 3-36.

CLARK, Jordan (Sedbergh S), b Whitehaven, Cumbria 14 Oct 1990. 6'4". RHB, RM, occ WK. Awaiting f-c debut. Lancashire 2nd XI debut 2008. Cumberland 2007-08. LO HS 32 v Worcs (Liverpool) 2010 (CB40). T20 HS 38.

CROFT, Steven John (Highfield HS, Blackpool; Myerscough C), b Blackpool 11 Oct 1984. 5'10". RHB, RMF. Debut (Lancashire) 2005; cap 2010. Auckland 2008-09. HS 154* v Surrey (Guildford) 2012. BB 6-41 v Worcs (Manchester) 2012. LO HS 107 v Somerset (Taunton) 2011 (CB40). LO BB 4-24 v Scotland (Manchester) 2008 (FPT). T20 HS 88. T20 BB 3-6.

CROSS, Gareth David (Moorside S; Eccles C), b Bury 20 Jun 1984. 5'9". RHB, WK, occ RMF. Debut (Lancashire) 2005. No f-c appearances in 2009. HS 125 v Sussex (Hove) 2011. LO HS 76 v Warwks (Birmingham) 2007 (P40). LO BB 2-26 v Durham (Chester-le-St) 2008 (FPT). T20 HS 65*.

DAVIES, Alexander Luke (Queen Elizabeth GS, Blackburn), b Darwen 23 Aug 1994. 5'7". RHB, WK. Debut (Lancashire) 2012, without batting or bowling. Lancashire 2nd XI debut 2011. LO HS 6* v Glamorgan (Colwyn Bay) 2011 (CB40).

GRIFFITHS, Gavin Timothy (St Mary's C, Crosby), b Ormskirk 19 Nov 1993. 6'2". RHB, RFM. Lancashire 2nd XI debut 2011. Awaiting 1st XI debut. England U19s 2012-13.

HOGG, Kyle William (Saddleworth HS), b Birmingham, Warwks 2 Jul 1983. Son of W.Hogg (Lancashire, Warwickshire 1976-83); grandson of S.Ramadhin (Trinidad, Lancashire and West Indies 1949-50 to 1965). 6'4". LHB, RFM. Debut (Lancashire) 2001; cap 2010. Otago 2006-07. Worcestershire 2007 (on loan). Nottinghamshire 2007 (on loan). F-c Tour (ECB Acad). SL 2002-03. HS 88 v Yorks (Manchester) 2010. 50 wkts (1): 50 (2011). BB 7-28 (11-59 match) v Hants (Southampton) 2011. LO HS 66* v Scotland (Manchester) 2008 (FPT). LO BB 4-20 v Hants (Southampton) 2002 (NL). T20 HS 44. T20 BB 2-10.

HORTON, Paul James (St Margaret's HS, Liverpool), b Sydney, Australia 20 Sep 1982. 5'10". RHB, RM. UK resident since 1997. Debut (Lancashire) 2003; cap 2007. Matabeleland Tuskers 2011-12 to 2011-12. 1000 runs (3); most – 1116 (2007). HS 209 MT v SR (Masvingo) 2010-11. La HS 173 v Somerset (Taunton) 2009. LO HS 111* v Derbys (Manchester) 2009 (FPT). T20 HS 71.

NQKATICH, Simon Mathew (Trinity C, WA; U of WA), b Middle Swan, Midland, W Australia 21 Aug 1975. 6'0". LHB, SLC. W Australia 1996-97 to 2001-02. Durham 2000; cap 2000. Yorkshire (1 match) 2002. NSW 2002-03 to 2011-12. Hampshire 2003-05, 2012; cap 2003. Derbyshire 2007; cap/captain 2007. Lancashire (1 match) 2010. **Tests** (A): 56 (2001 to 2010-11); HS 157 v WI (Bridgetown) 2008; BB 6-65 v Z (Sydney) 2003-04. **LOI** (A): 45 (2000-01 to 2006-07); HS 107* v SL (Brisbane) 2005-06. **IT20** (A): 3 (2004-05 to 2005-06); HS 39 v SA (Johannesburg) 2005-06. F-c Tours (A): E 2001, 2005, 2009, 2010 (v P; SA 2008-09; WI 2008; NZ 2004-05, 2009-10; I 2004-05, 2008-09 (Aus A), 2008-09, 2010-11; SL 1999-00, 2003-04. 1000 runs (3+4); most – 1506 (2007-08). HS 306 NSW v Q (Sydney) 2007-08. UK HS 221 De v Somerset (Taunton) 2007. La HS 32 v Yorks (Manchester) 2010. BB 7-130 NSW v Vic (Melbourne) 2002-03. UK BB 4-21 H v Northants (Southampton) 2003. LO HS 136* NSW v Vic (Bowral) 2003-04. LO BB 3-21 Aus A v SA (Adelaide) 2001-02. T20 HS 75.

KERRIGAN, Simon Christopher (Corpus Christi RC HS, Preston), b Preston 10 May 1989. 5'9". RHB. SLA. Debut (Lancashire) 2010. Lancashire 2nd XI debut 2007. HS 40 v Somerset (Taunton) 2011. BB 9-51 (12-192 match) v Hants (Liverpool) 2011. LO HS 10 v Middx (Lord's) 2012 (CB40). LO BB 3-21 EL v Sri Lanka A (Northampton) 2011. T20 HS 4*. T20 BB 3-17.

LILLEY, Arron Mark (Mossley Hollins HS; Ashton SFC), b Tameside 1 Apr 1991. 6'1". RHB, OB. Lancashire 2nd XI debut 2010. Awaiting f-c debut. Made l-o debut in 2012, without batting or bowling.

MOORE, Stephen Colin (St Stithian's C, Johannesburg; Exeter U), b Johannesburg, South Africa 4 Nov 1980. 6'1". RHB, RM. Worcestershire 2003-09. Lancashire debut 2010; cap 2011. MCC 2009, 2011. F-c Tour (Eng A): NZ 2008-09. 1000 runs (4); most – 1451 (2008). HS 246 Wo v Derbys (Worcester) 2005. La HS 169* v Hants (Liverpool) 2011. BB 1-13 Wo v Lancs (Worcester) 2004. LO HS 118 v Surrey (Croydon) 2010 (CB40). LO BB 1-1 Wo v Scotland (Worcester) 2004 (NL). T20 HS 83*.

NEWBY, Oliver James (Ribblesdale HS; Myerscough C), b Blackburn 26 Aug 1984. 6'5". RHB, RMF. Debut (Lancashire) 2003. Nottinghamshire 2005 (on loan). Gloucestershire (on loan) 2008; cap 2008. No f-c appearances in 2010. HS 38* Nt v Kent (Nottingham) 2005 – on Notts debut. La HS 29* v Oxford MCCU (Oxford) 2011. BB 5-69 Gs v Northants (Bristol) 2008. La BB 4-21 v Durham MCCU (Durham) 2009. LO HS 36* v Glos (Bristol) 2012 (CB40). LO BB 5-35 v Essex (Chelmsford) 2012 (CB40). T20 HS 6*. T20 BB 2-34.

PARRY, Stephen David (Audenshaw HS), b Manchester 12 Jan 1986. 5'11". RHB, SLA. Debut (Lancashire) 2007, taking 5-23 v Durham U (Durham). No 1st XI appearances in 2008. Cumberland 2005-06. HS 2 and CC BB 2-51 v Durham (Manchester) 2009. BB 5-23 (see above). LO HS 31 v Essex (Chelmsford) 2009 (FPT). LO BB 4-21 v Middx (Manchester) 2012 (CB40). T20 HS 11. T20 BB 4-23.

PROCTER, Luke Anthony (Counthill S, Oldham), b Oldham 24 June 1988. 5'11". LHB, RM. Debut (Lancashire) 2010. Lancashire 2nd XI debut 2006. Cumberland 2007. HS 89 v Sussex (Hove) 2011. BB 7-71 v Surrey (Liverpool) 2012. LO HS 97 v West Indies A (Manchester) 2010. LO BB 3-29 v Unicorns (Colwyn Bay) 2010 (CB40). T20 HS 25*. T20 BB 3-22.

REECE, Luis Michael (St Michael's HS, Chorley; Leeds Met U), b Taunton, Somerset 4 Aug 1990. 6'1". LHB, LM. Debut (Leeds/Bradford MCCU) 2012. Lancashire 2nd XI debut 2008. Awaiting 1st XI debut. Unicorns 2011-12. HS 60 and BB 3-25 LBU v Yorks (Leeds) 2012. LO HS 59 Unicorns v Derbys (Chesterfield) 2012 (CB40). LO BB 4-35 Unicorns v Glos (Exmouth) 2011 (CB40).

SMITH, Thomas Christopher (Parkland HS, Chorley; Runshaw C, Leyland), b Liverpool 26 Dec 1985. 6'3". LHB, RMF. Debut (Lancashire) 2005; cap 2010. Leicestershire (on loan) 2008. F-c Tour (Eng A): B 2006-07. HS 128 v Hants (Southampton) 2010. BB 6-46 v Yorks (Manchester) 2009. LO HS 117 and LO BB 4-48 v Notts (Nottingham) 2011 (CB40). T20 HS 92*. T20 BB 3-12.

‡**WHITE, Wayne** Andrew (John Port S, Etwall; Nottingham Trent U), b Derby 22 Apr 1985. 6'2". RHB, RMF. Derbyshire 2005-08. Leicestershire 2009-12; cap 2010. HS 101* Le v Derbys (Derby) 2010. Scored 50* in 12 balls in contrived circumstances for Le v Essex (Leicester) 2012. BB 5-54 Le v Derbys (Derby) 2012. LO HS 46* Le v Glamorgan (Leicester) 2009 (P40). LO BB 6-29 Le v Notts (Leics) 2010 (CB40). T20 HS 26. T20 BB 3-27.

RELEASED/RETIRED

(Having made a County First-Class or List A appearance in 2012)

KEEDY, G. – *see SURREY.*

MAHMOOD, S.I. – *see ESSEX.*

NO**PRINCE, Ashwell** Gavin (St Thomas Senior SS, UPE), b Port Elizabeth, South Africa, 28 May 1977. LHB, OB. E Province 1995-96 to 1997-98. W Province 1997-98 to 2003-04. W Province-Boland 2004-05. Cape Cobras 2005-06 to 2007-08. Nottinghamshire 2008. Warriors 2008-09 to date. Lancashire 2009-12; cap 2010. **Tests** (SA): 66 (2001-02 to 2011-12, 2 as captain); HS 162* v B (Centurion) 2008-09; BB 1-2 v NZ (Cape Town) 2006. **LOI** (SA): 52 (2002-03 to 2007); HS 89* v WI (Port of Spain) 2005; BB – . **IT20** (SA): 1 (2005-06); HS 5 v NZ (Johannesburg) 2005-06. F-c Tours (SA): E 2008; A 2005-06; WI 2000 (SA A), 2005, 2010; I 2007-08, 2009-10; P 2007-08; SL 2006; Z 2007 (SA A); B 2007-08; UAE 2010-11 (v P). 1000 runs (1+1): 1180 (2008-09). HS 254 Warriors v Titans (Centurion) 2008-09. La HS 144 v Middx (Liverpool) 2012. BB 2-11 SA v Middx (Uxbridge) 2008. CC BB – . LO HS 128 Warriors v Dolphins (East London) 2009-10. LO BB – . T20 HS 74. T20 BB – .

SHAHZAD, A. – *see NOTTINGHAMSHIRE.*

TAHIR, Naqaash Sarosh (Moseley S; Spring Hill C), b Birmingham 14 Nov 1983. 5'10", RHB, RFM. Warwickshire 2004-11. Played one l-o game for Lancashire in 2012. HS 53 Wa v Durham (Birmingham) 2011. BB 7-107 Wa v Lancs (Blackpool) 2006. LO HS 13* Wa v Leics (Oakham) 2008 (FPT). LO BB 2-47 Wa v Notts (Nottingham) 2008 (FPT).

Yasir Arafat left the staff, without making a County First-Class or List A appearance in 2012.

LANCASHIRE 2012

RESULTS SUMMARY

	Place	Won	Lost	Tied	Drew	NR
LV= County Championship (1st Division)	8th	1	5		10	
All First-Class Matches		1	5		11	
Clydesdale Bank 40 (Group A)	SF	9	3			1
Friends Life t20 (North Group)	4th	3	4	1		2

LV= COUNTY CHAMPIONSHIP AVERAGES
BATTING AND FIELDING

Cap		M	I	NO	HS	Runs	Avge	100	50	Ct/St
2010	A.G.Prince	15	24	1	144	1008	43.82	2	8	15
2010	K.W.Hogg	13	18	8	61*	324	32.40	–	2	1
2007	P.J.Horton	16	25	3	137*	654	29.72	2	2	17
2010	T.C.Smith	6	9	–	91	267	29.66	–	3	4
2010	S.J.Croft	16	24	1	154*	666	28.95	2	2	15
	K.R.Brown	16	25	1	78	594	24.75	–	3	5
	L.A.Procter	13	20	3	46	414	24.35	–	–	–
	G.D.Cross	15	24	2	75*	498	22.63	–	3	28/3
2011	S.C.Moore	12	20	–	47	348	17.40	–	–	7
1994	G.Chapple	15	23	–	46	381	16.56	–	–	3
	A.Shahzad	10	15	5	28*	134	13.40	–	–	1
	S.C.Kerrigan	15	19	7	34*	96	8.00	–	–	3
2000	G.Keedy	4	4	–	5	8	2.00	–	–	–

Also played: A.P.Agathangelou (3 matches) 24, 5, 7 (1 ct); J.M.Anderson (1 – cap 2003) 0, 0 (1 ct); T.E.Bailey (1) did not bat; A.L.Davies (1) did not bat (2 ct); S.I.Mahmood (3 – cap 2007) 0, 1, 3; O.J.Newby (1) did not bat.

BOWLING

	O	M	R	W	Avge	Best	5wI	10wM
L.A.Procter	177.1	32	558	25	22.32	7- 71	2	–
G.Chapple	394.5	101	1010	42	24.04	5- 47	2	1
S.J.Croft	96.4	13	289	12	24.08	6- 41	1	–
S.C.Kerrigan	518.5	85	1532	44	34.81	4- 45	–	–
A.Shahzad	216.3	50	709	20	35.45	4- 40	–	–
K.W.Hogg	242.4	55	746	18	41.44	3- 23	–	–

Also bowled:

	O	M	R	W	Avge	Best	5wI	10wM
J.M.Anderson	36.2	7	105	5	21.00	5- 82	1	–
G.Keedy	130.2	17	401	7	57.28	3-101	–	–

T.E.Bailey 17-2-67-1; K.R.Brown 3-0-5-0; S.I.Mahmood 36-4-180-4; O.J.Newby 13-0-59-1; A.G.Prince 2-1-5-0; T.C.Smith 58-4-236-4.

The First-Class Averages (pp 219–235) give the records of Lancashire players in all first-class county matches (Lancashire's other opponents being Cambridge MCCU), with the exception of J.M.Anderson and A.Shahzad, whose first-class figures for Lancashire are as above, and:

S.C.Kerrigan 16-19-7-34*-96-8.00-0-0-4ct. 530.5-88-1562-44-35.50-4/45-0-0.

S.I.Mahmood 4-4-0-14-18-4.50-0-0-0ct. 53.4-7-247-8-30.87-4/38-0-0.

LANCASHIRE RECORDS

FIRST-CLASS CRICKET

Highest Total	For 863		v	Surrey	The Oval	1990
	V 707-9d		by	Surrey	The Oval	1990
Lowest Total	For 25		v	Derbyshire	Manchester	1871
	V 22		by	Glamorgan	Liverpool	1924
Highest Innings	For 424	A.C.MacLaren	v	Somerset	Taunton	1895
	V 315*	T.W.Hayward	for	Surrey	The Oval	1898

Highest Partnership for each Wicket

1st	368	A.C.MacLaren/R.H.Spooner	v	Glos	Liverpool	1903
2nd	371	F.B.Watson/G.E.Tyldesley	v	Surrey	Manchester	1928
3rd	364	M.A.Atherton/N.H.Fairbrother	v	Surrey	The Oval	1990
4th	358	S.P.Titchard/G.D.Lloyd	v	Essex	Chelmsford	1996
5th	360	S.G.Law/C.L.Hooper	v	Warwicks	Birmingham	2003
6th	278	J.Iddon/H.R.W.Butterworth	v	Sussex	Manchester	1932
7th	248	G.D.Lloyd/I.D.Austin	v	Yorkshire	Leeds	1997
8th	158	J.Lyon/R.M.Ratcliffe	v	Warwicks	Manchester	1979
9th	142	L.O.S.Poidevin/A.Kermode	v	Sussex	Eastbourne	1907
10th	173	J.Briggs/R.Pilling	v	Surrey	Liverpool	1885

Best Bowling	For	10-46	W.Hickton	v	Hampshire	Manchester	1870
(Innings)	V	10-40	G.O.B.Allen	for	Middlesex	Lord's	1929
Best Bowling	For	17-91	H.Dean	v	Yorkshire	Liverpool	1913
(Match)	V	16-65	G.Giffen	for	Australians	Manchester	1886

Most Runs – Season	2633	J.T.Tyldesley	(av 56.02)		1901
Most Runs – Career	34222	G.E.Tyldesley	(av 45.20)		1909-36
Most 100s – Season	11	C.Hallows			1928
Most 100s – Career	90	G.E.Tyldesley			1909-36
Most Wkts – Season	198	E.A.McDonald	(av 18.55)		1925
Most Wkts – Career	1816	J.B.Statham	(av 15.12)		1950-68
Most Career W-K Dismissals	925	G.Duckworth	(635 ct; 290 st)		1923-38
Most Career Catches in the Field	556	K.J.Grieves			1949-64

LIMITED-OVERS CRICKET

Highest Total	50ov	381-3		v	Herts	Radlett	1999
	40ov	324-4		v	Worcs	Worcester	2012
	T20	220-5		v	Derbyshire	Derby	2009
Lowest Total	50ov	59		v	Worcs	Worcester	1963
	40ov	68		v	Yorkshire	Leeds	2000
		68		v	Surrey	The Oval	2002
	T20	91		v	Derbyshire	Manchester	2003
Highest Innings	50ov	162*	A.R.Crook	v	Bucks	Wormsley	2005
	40ov	143	A.Flintoff	v	Essex	Chelmsford	1999
	T20	102*	L.Vincent	v	Derbyshire	Manchester	2008
Best Bowling	50ov	6-18	G.Chapple	v	Essex	Lord's	1996
	40ov	6-25	G.Chapple	v	Yorkshire	Leeds	1998
	T20	4-12	A.Flintoff	v	Durham	Chester-le-St[2]	2008

LEICESTERSHIRE

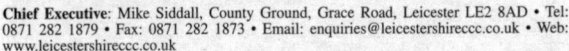

Formation of Present Club: 25 March 1879
Inaugural First-Class Match: 1894
Colours: Dark Green and Scarlet
Badge: Gold Running Fox on Green Ground
County Champions: (3) 1975, 1996, 1998
Gillette/NatWest/C&G/FP Trophy Winners: (0); best – Finalist 1992, 2001
Benson and Hedges Cup Winners: (3) 1972, 1975, 1985
Pro 40/National League (Div 1) Winners: (0); best – 2nd 2001
Sunday League Champions: (2) 1974, 1977
Clydesdale Bank 40 Winners: (0); best – 6th in Group 2010, 2011, 2012
Twenty20 Cup Winners: (3) 2004, 2006, 2011

Chief Executive: Mike Siddall, County Ground, Grace Road, Leicester LE2 8AD • Tel: 0871 282 1879 • Fax: 0871 282 1873 • Email: enquiries@leicestershireccc.co.uk • Web: www.leicestershireccc.co.uk

Head Coach/Academy Director: Phil Whitticase. **Captain**: R.R.Sarwan (f-c) and J.J.Cobb (l-o). **Vice-Captain**: none. **Overseas Players**: R.R.Sarwan and J.A.Burns. **2013 Beneficiary**: none. **Head Groundsman**: Andrew Ward. **Scorer**: Paul J.Rogers. ‡ New registration. [NQ] Not qualified for England.

BOYCE, Matthew Andrew Golding (Oakham S; Nottingham U), b Cheltenham, Glos 13 Aug 1985. 5'9". LHB, RM. Debut (Leicestershire) 2006. HS 122 v Yorks (Scarborough) 2012. BB – . LO HS 80 v Hants (Leicester) 2009 (FPT). T20 HS 63*.

BUCK, Nathan Liam (Newbridge HS; Ashby S), b Leicester 26 Apr 1991. 6'2" RHB, RMF. Debut (Leicestershire) 2009; cap 2011. Leicestershire 2nd XI debut 2008. England U19s 2009 to 2009-10. F-c Tour (EL): WI 2010-11. HS 27 v Kent (Canterbury) 2012. BB 5-99 v Glos (Bristol) 2011. LO HS 21 v Glamorgan (Leicester) 2009 (P40). LO BB 4-39 EL v Sri Lanka A (Dambulla) 2011-12. T20 HS 5*. T20 BB 3-16.

‡[NQ]BURNS, Joseph Antony, b Herston, Brisbane, Australia 6 Sep 1989. RHB, RM. Queensland 2010-11 to date. F-c Tour (Aus A): E 2012. HS 140* Q v S Australia (Adelaide) 2010-11 – on debut. UK HS 74* Aus A v Derbys (Derby) 2012. LO HS 114 Aus A v EL (Hobart) 2012-13. T20 HS 44.

COBB, Joshua James (Oakham S), b Leicester 17 Aug 1990. Son of R.A.Cobb (Leics and N Transvaal 1980-89). 5'11½". RHB, LB. Debut (Leicestershire) 2007. Leicestershire 2nd XI debut 2006, aged 16y 5d. England U19s 2009. HS 148* v Middx (Lord's) 2008. BB 2-11 v Glos (Bristol) 2008. LO HS 137 v Lancs (Manchester) 2012 (CB40). LO BB 2-35 v Surrey (Oval) 2011 (CB40). T20 HS 60. T20 BB 4-22.

ECKERSLEY, Edmund John Holden ('Ned') (St Benedict's GS, Ealing), b Oxford 9 Aug 1989. 6'0". RHB, WK. Debut (Leicestershire) 2011. Mountaineers 2011-12. Middlesex 2nd XI 2008. Northamptonshire 2nd XI 2010. HS 137* v Glamorgan (Cardiff) 2012. LO HS 72* v Worcs (Worcester) 2012 (CB40). T20 HS 13.

FRECKINGHAM, Oliver Henry (K Edward S, Melton Mowbray), b Oakham, Rutland 12 Nov 1988. RHB, RMF. Leicestershire 2nd XI debut 2010. Awaiting 1st XI debut.

NQ**HENDERSON, Claude** William (Worcester HS), b Worcester, Cape Province, South Africa 14 Jun 1972. Elder brother of J.M.Henderson (Boland, Transvaal, North West, Free State and Eagles 1994-95 to 2005-06). Applying for UK citizenship. 6'1½". RHB, SLA. Boland 1990-91 to 1997-98. W Province 1998-99 to 2003-04. Leicestershire debut/cap 2004 (the first Kolpak registration); benefit 2011. Lions 2006-07 to 2007-08. Cape Cobras 2008-09 to 2010-11. **Tests** (SA): 7 (2001-02 to 2002-03); HS 30 and BB 4-116 v A (Adelaide) 2001-02. **LOI** (SA): 4 (2001-02); HS – ; BB 4-17 v Z (Harare) 2001-02. F-c Tours (SA): A 2001-02; SL 1998 (SA A); Z 2001-02. HS 81 v Glos (Leicester) 2007. 50 wkts (1): 56 (2010). BB 7-57 Boland v EP (Paarl) 1994-95. Le BB 7-74 v Durham (Leicester) 2004. LO HS 45 Lions v Eagles (Johannesburg) 2006-07. LO BB 6-29 Boland v Easterns (Paarl) 1997-98. T20 HS 32. T20 BB 3-23.

HOGGARD, Matthew James (Grangefield S, Pudsey), b Leeds, Yorks 31 Dec 1976. 6'2". RHB, RMF. Yorkshire 1996-2009; cap 2000; benefit 2008. Free State 1998-99 to 1999-00. Leicestershire debut/cap 2010; captain 2010-12. MCC 2004-07. MBE 2005. *Wisden* 2005. **Tests**: 67 (2000 to 2007-08); HS 38 v WI (Oval) 2004; BB 7-61 (12-205 match) v SA (Johannesburg) 2004-05; hat-trick v WI (Bridgetown) 2003-04. **LOI**: 26 (2001-02 to 2005-06); HS 7 v I (Cochin) 2005-06; BB 5-49 v Z (Harare) 2001-02. F-c Tours: A 2002-03, 2006-07; SA 2004-05; WI 2003-04; NZ 2001-02, 2007-08; I 2001-02, 2005-06; P 2000-01, 2005-06; SL 2000-01, 2003-04, 2007-08; B 2003-04. HS 89* Y v Glamorgan (Leeds) 2004. Le HS 28 v Essex (Chelmsford) 2012. 50 wkts (3); most – 50 (2000, 2005, 2010). BB 7-49 Y v Somerset (Leeds) 2003. Le BB 6-63 v Middx (Lord's) 2010. Hat-tricks (3): (*see Tests*) and Y v Sussex (Hove) 2009; v Glamorgan (Leicester) 2011. LO HS 23 v Surrey (Oval) 2011 (CB40). LO BB 5-28 Y v Leics (Leicester) 2000 (NL). T20 HS 18. T20 BB 3-19.

‡NQ**IRELAND, Anthony** John (Plumtree HS), b Masvingo, Zimbabwe 30 Aug 1984. 6'2". RHB, RM. Midlands 2002-03 to 2004-05. Gloucestershire 2007-10, 2012; cap 2007. Middlesex 2011. Kolpak registration. **LOI** (Z): 26 (2005-06 to 2006-07); HS 8* v K (Bulawayo) 2005-06; BB 3-41 v B (Harare) (twice) – 2006 and 2006-07. **IT20** (Z): 1 (2006-07); HS 2* and BB 1-33 v B (Khulna) 2006-07. HS 29 M v Essex (Chelmsford) 2011. BB 7-36 Zimbabwe A v Bangladesh A (Mirpur) 2006-07. CC BB 6-31 Gs v Leics (Bristol) 2009. LO HS 22* M v Kent (Lord's) 2011 (CB40). LO BB 4-16 Zimbabwe A v Kenya (Harare) 2005-06. T20 HS 8*. T20 BB 3-7.

NAIK, Jigar Kumar Hakumatrai (Rushey Mead SS; Gateway SFC; Nottingham Trent U; Loughborough U), b Leicester 10 Aug 1984. 6'2". RHB, OB. Debut (Leicestershire) 2006. Loughborough UCCE 2007. Colombo CC 2010-11. HS 109* v Derbys (Leicester) 2009. BB 7-96 v Surrey (Oval) 2010. LO HS 18 v Derbys (Derby) 2009 (P40). LO BB 3-21 v Lancs (Leicester) 2009 (P40). T20 HS 7*. T20 BB 3-3.

‡**O'BRIEN, Niall** John (Marian C, Dublin), b Dublin, Ireland 8 Nov 1981. Son of B.A.O'Brien (Ireland 1966-81); elder brother of K.J.O'Brien (*see SOMERSET*). 5'6". LHB, WK. Kent 2004-06. Ireland 2005-06 to date. Northamptonshire 2007-12; cap 2011. MCC 2012. **LOI** (Ire): 51 (2006 to 2012); HS 72 v P (Kingston) 2006-07 and 72 v Scotland (Belfast) 2007. **IT20** (Ire): 20 (2008 to 2012-13); HS 50 v Canada (Colombo, SSC) 20090-10. HS 182 Nh v Glamorgan (Cardiff) 2012. BB 1-4 K v Cambridge UCCE (Cambridge) 2006. LO HS 121 Nh v Hants (Southampton) 2011 (CB40). T20 HS 84.

RADFORD, Luke Anthony (Bromsgrove S; Loughborough U), b Worcester 3 Jun 1988. Son of N.V.Radford (Transvaal, Lancs, Worcs, England 1978-79 to 1995), nephew of W.R.Radford (OFS, Boland, E Transvaal, Easterns 1977-78 to 1997-98) and G.Radford (Transvaal and NW 1991-92 to 1996-97). RHB, RFM. Debut (Leicestershire) 2011. Warwickshire 2nd XI debut 2007. HS- and BB 2-47 v Loughborough MCCU (Leicester) 2011 – only 1st XI appearance to date.

ROBSON, Angus James (Marcellin C, Randwick; Australian C of PE), b Darlinghurst, Sydney, Australia 19 Feb 1992. Younger brother of S.D.Robson (*see MIDDLESEX*). 5'9". RHB, LB. Leicestershire 2nd XI debut 2012. Awaiting 1st XI debut.

NQSARWAN, Ramnaresh Ronnie (North Gromuel S), b Wakenaam Island, Essequibo, Guyana 23 Jun 1980. 5'7½". RHB, LB. Guyana 1995-96 to date (youngest to play f-c cricket in WI). Gloucestershire 2005; cap 2005. Leicestershire debut 2013; captain 2013. **Tests** (WI): 87 (2000 to 2011); HS 291 v E (Bridgetown) 2008-09; BB 4-37 v B (St Lucia) 2004. **LOI** (WI): 179 (2000 to 2013); HS 120* v Z (St George's) 2012-13; BB 3-31 v NZ (Lord's) 2006. **IT20** (WI): 18 (2007 to 2010); HS 59 v E (Port of Spain) 2008-09; BB 2-10 v B (Johannesburg) 2007. F-c Tours (WI): E 2000, 2004, 2007, 2009; A 2000-01, 2005-06, 2009-10; SA 2003-04; NZ 2005-06, 2008-09; I 2002-03; P 2006-07; SL 2001-02; Z 2001, 2003-04; B 2002-03. HS 291 (see Tests). CC HS 117 Gs v Sussex (Hove) 2005 and 117 v Essex (Chelmsford) 2012. BB 6-62 Guyana v Leeward Is (Antigua) 2000-01. CC BB 2-38 Gs v Glamorgan (Bristol) 2005. Le BB – . LO HS 120* (see LOI). LO BB 5-10 Guyana v Bermuda (Hampton Court) 1998-99. T20 HS 70. T20 BB 2-10.

SMITH, Gregory Philip (Oundle S; St Hild & St Bede C, Durham U), b Leicester 16 Nov 1988. 6'0". RHB, LBG. Debut (Leicestershire) 2008. Durham MCCU 2009-11. England U19s 2008. HS 158* v Glos (Leicester) 2010. BB 1-64 v Glos (Leicester) 2008. LO HS 58 v Surrey (Oval) 2008 (P40). T20 HS 23.

SYKES, James Stuart (St Ives S, Huntingdon), b Hinchingbrooke, Cambs 26 Apr 1992. 6'2". LHB, SLA. Leicestershire 2nd XI debut 2009. Cambridgeshire 2010. Awaiting f-c debut. LO HS 12* v Worcs (Worcester) 2012 (CB40). LO BB 3-39 v Neth (Amstelveen) 2012 (CB40). T20 HS 2*. T20 BB 2-24.

TAYLOR, Robert Meadows Lombe (Harrow S; Loughborough U), b Northampton 21 Dec 1989. 6'3". LHB, LMF. Loughborough MCCU 2010-12. Leicestershire debut 2011. Leicestershire 2nd XI debut 2010. Northamptonshire 2nd XI 2010. LOI (Scot): 1 (2012-13); HS 9 and BB 1-47 v Afghanistan (Sharjah) 2012-13. HS 101* LU v Leics (Leicester) 2011. Le HS 70 v Surrey (Leicester) 2011. BB 5-91 v Kent (Leicester) 2012. LO HS 29* v Glos (Bristol) 2012 (CB40). LO BB 2-26 v Worcs (Leicester) 2012 (CB40). T20 HS 18*. T20 BB 2-7.

THAKOR, Shivsinh Jaysinh (Loughborough GS), b Leicester 22 Oct 1993: 6'1". RHB, RM. Debut (Leicestershire) 2011. Leicestershire 2nd XI debut 2008, aged 14y 218d. England U19s 2010-11. HS 134 v Loughborough MCCU (Leicester) 2011 – on debut. CC HS 85* v Hants (Leicester) 2012. BB 3-57 v Surrey (Leicester) 2011. LO HS 83* v Lancs (Leicester) 2012 (CB40). LO BB – .

THORNELY, Michael Alistair (Brighton C), b Camden, London 19 Oct 1987. 6'1". RHB, RM. Sussex 2007-10. Mashonaland Eagles 2011-12. Leicestershire debut 2012, scoring 97 and 131 v Glamorgan (Cardiff). HS 131 (see above). BB 2-14 v Worcs (Hove) 2010. Le BB 2-29 v Glos (Cheltenham) 2012. LO HS 105* Unicorns v Somerset (Taunton) 2011 (CB40). LO BB 1-20 v Australians (Leicester) 2012. T20 HS 1*. T20 BB – .

WELLS, Thomas Joshua (Gartree HS; Beauchamp C, Leicester), b Grantham, Lincs 15 Mar 1993. Father, John Wells, played rugby for Leicester. 6'2". RHB, RMF. Leicestershire 2nd XI debut 2010. Awaiting f-c debut. LO HS 4 v Glos (Leicester) 2012 (CB40) – only 1st XI appearance.

WILLIAMS, Robert Edward Morgan (Marlborough C; St Mary's C, Durham U), b Pembury, Kent 19 Jan 1987. 6'0". RHB, RMF. Durham UCCE 2007-09. Middlesex 2007. MCC 2007. HS 31 DU v Lancs (Durham) 2009. CC HS 15 and BB 5-112 M v Essex (Chelmsford) 2007 – on only M f-c appearance. BB 5-70 DU v Lancs (Durham) 2007. LO HS 2* and LO BB 2-60 v Bangladeshis (Lord's) 2010. T20 HS and BB – .

WYATT, Alexander Charles Frederick (Oakham S), b Roehampton 23 Jul 1990. 6'7". RHB, RMF. Debut (Leicestershire) 2009. Leicestershire 2nd XI debut 2007. HS 8 v Yorks (Scarborough) 2012. BB 3-35 v Hants (Leicester) 2012. LO HS 9* v Neth (Leicester) 2012 (CB40). LO BB 2-36 v Durham (Leicester) 2011 (CB40). T20 HS – . T20 BB 3-14.

RELEASED/RETIRED

(Having made a County First-Class or List A appearance in 2012)

^{NQ}**ABDUL RAZZAQ**, b Lahore, Pakistan 2 Dec 1979. 5'11". RHB, RFM. Lahore 1996-97 to 2006-07. Khan Research Labs 1997-98 to 1998-99. Pakistan Int Airlines 2001-02. Middlesex 2002-03; cap 2002. Zarai Taraqiati Bank Ltd 2003-04 to date. Worcestershire 2007; cap 2007. Surrey 2008. Leicestershire 1-o and T20 only 2011-12. **Tests** (P): 46 (1999-00 to 2006-07); HS 134 v B (Dhaka) 2001-02; BB 5-35 v SL (Karachi) 2004-05. **LOI** (P): 265 (1996-97 to 2011-12); HS 112 v SA (Port Elizabeth) 2002-03; BB 6-35 v B (Dhaka) 2001-02. **IT20** (P): 30 (2006 to 2012-13): HS 46* v E (Dubai) 2009-10; BB 3-13 v NZ (Christchurch) 2010-11. F-c Tours (P): E 1997 (P A), 2001, 2006; A 1999-00, 2004-05; SA 2002-03; WI 2000, 2005; NZ 1998-99 (P A), 2003-04; I 2004-05; SL 2000, 2005-06; B 2001-02; UAE 2001-02 (v WI). HS 203* M v Glamorgan (Cardiff) 2002. BB 7-51 Lahore City v Karachi Whites (Thatta) 1996-97 – on debut. CC BB 7-133 M v Essex (Southgate) 2002. LO HS 112 (*see LOI*). LO BB 6-35 (*see LOI*). T20 HS 109. T20 BB 4-13.

ALI, Abdul-Kadeer (Handsworth GS), b Moseley, Birmingham 7 Mar 1983. 6'1". Brother of M.M.Ali (*see WORCESTERSHIRE*), cousin of Kabir Ali (*see LANCASHIRE*). RHB, RM/LB. Worcestershire 2000-04. Gloucestershire 2005-10; cap 2005. Leicestershire 2012. F-c Tour (Eng A): I 2003-04. HS 161 Gs v Northants (Bristol) 2008. Le HS 48 v Derbys (Leicester) 2012. BB 1-4 Gs v Glamorgan (Bristol) 2005. LO HS 114 Gs v Hants (Southampton) 2007 (P40). LO BB 1-4 Wo v Worcs CB (Worcester) 2003 (CGT). T20 HS 53. T20 BB 2-28.

DIXEY, Paul Garrod (King's S, Canterbury; Hatfield C, Durham U), b Canterbury 2 Nov 1987. 5'8". RHB, WK. Kent 2005-10; no f-c appearances for K 2007-09. MCC 2007. Durham UCCE 2007-09. Leicestershire 2011-12. HS 103 DU v Lancs (Durham) 2009. Le HS 72* v Glos (Leicester) 2011. LO HS 42 v Surrey (Oval) 2011 (CB40).

Du TOIT, Jacques (Elspark S; Oosterlig C; Pretoria U), b Port Elizabeth, South Africa 2 Jan 1980. 6'2". RHB, RMF. British passport. Easterns 1998-99 to 2004-05. Leicestershire debut 2008. Colombo CC 2010-11. HS 154 v Cambridge MCCU (Cambridge) 2010. CC HS 122 v Surrey (Leicester) 2010. BB 3-31 v Glos (Leicester) 2008. LO HS 144 v Glamorgan (Colwyn Bay) 2008 (P40). LO BB 2-30 Easterns v KZ-Natal (Benoni) 2004-05. T20 HS 69. T20 BB 2-15.

JEFFERSON, William Ingleby (Beeston Hall S, Norfolk; Oundle S; St Hild & St Bede C, Durham U), b Derby 25 Oct 1979. Son of R.I.Jefferson (Cambridge U and Surrey 1961-66); grandson of J.Jefferson (Army 1919, Comb Services 1922). 6'10". RHB, RMF. British U 2000-02. Essex 2000-06; cap 2002. Durham UCCE 2001-02. Nottinghamshire 2007-09. Leicestershire 2010-12. F-c Tour (Eng A): B 2006-07. 1000 runs (2): most – 1555 (2004). HS 222 Ex v Hants (Southampton) 2004. Le HS 135 v Surrey (Oval) 2010. LO HS 1-16 Ex v Yorks (Leeds) 2005. LO HS 132 Ex v Essex CB (Chelmsford) 2003 (CGT). LO BB 2-9 Ex v Worcs (Worcester) 2005 (NL). T20 HS 83.

JONES, William Stephen (Harrow S; Cardiff U), b Perth, Australia 26 Mar 1990. British citizen. 6'1". RHB, LB. Leicestershire 2011-12. Cardiff MCCU 2012. Leicestershire 2nd XI debut 2010. Hertfordshire 2009. HS 48 v Kent (Leicester) 2012. BB 3-71 v Hants (Leicester) 2012. LO HS 3 v Surrey (Oval) 2011 (CB40).

JOSEPH, Robert ('Robbie') Hartman (Sutton Valence S; St Mary's C, Twickenham), b Antigua 20 Jan 1982. Resided in England since 1997. 6'1". RHB, RFM. Debut (First-Class Counties XI v NZ) 2000. Kent 2004-11. Leeward Is 2008-09. Leicestershire 2012. F-c Tour (EL): NZ 2008-09. HS 36* K v Sussex (Hove) 2007. Le HS 29 and Le BB 6-47 (12-113 match) v Glamorgan (Leicester) 2012 – on Le debut. 50 wkts (1): 55 (2008). BB 6-32 K v Durham (Chester-le-St) 2008. LO HS 15 K v (Canterbury) 2005 (NL). LO BB 5-13 K v Derbys (Canterbury) 2008 (P40). T20 HS 1*. T20 BB 2-14.

RELEASED/RETIRED continued on p 145

LEICESTERSHIRE 2012

RESULTS SUMMARY

	Place	Won	Lost	Tied	Drew	NR
LV= County Championship (2nd Division)	7th	3	3		10	
All First-Class Matches		3	3		10	
Clydesdale Bank 40 (Group A)	6th	3	6			3
Friends Life t20 (North Group)	6th	2	7			1

LV= COUNTY CHAMPIONSHIP AVERAGES
BATTING AND FIELDING

Cap		M	I	NO	HS	Runs	Avge	100	50	Ct/St
	S.J.Thakor	6	10	3	85*	427	61.00	–	4	2
	R.R.Sarwan	14	25	2	117	941	40.91	2	5	7
	J.J.Cobb	14	23	1	105	752	34.18	1	5	6
	M.A.Thornely	9	16	–	131	514	32.12	2	1	6
	M.A.G.Boyce	14	25	2	122	733	31.86	2	4	9
	E.J.H.Eckersley	16	28	4	137*	739	30.79	1	3	43/3
2012.	W.A.White	16	26	5	67	616	29.33	–	4	1
	W.S.Jones	3	6	–	48	138	23.00	–	–	2
2004	C.W.Henderson	12	19	4	57*	296	19.73	–	2	–
	W.I.Jefferson	2	4	–	49	75	18.75	–	–	1
	G.P.Smith	13	23	–	77	429	18.65	–	1	13
2010	M.J.Hoggard	10	12	7	28	81	16.20	–	–	1
	Kadeer Ali	3	4	–	48	63	15.75	–	–	1
	J.du Toit	6	10	–	48	127	12.70	–	–	4
2011	N.L.Buck	11	15	2	27	119	9.15	–	–	–
	R.H.Joseph	9	13	4	29	79	8.77	–	–	2
	M.N.Malik	5	7	1	21*	51	8.50	–	–	–
	P.G.Dixey	3	5	1	13	30	7.50	–	–	4/1
	A.C.F.Wyatt	5	6	2	8	14	3.50	–	–	1

Also batted: P.L.Mommsen (2 matches) 9, 5, 35 (2 ct); J.K.H.Naik (2) 33, 6, 1 (2 ct);
R.M.L.Taylor (1) 1.

BOWLING

	O	M	R	W	Avge	Best	5wI	10wM
M.J.Hoggard	220.4	42	691	24	28.79	4- 27	–	–
W.A.White	349	41	1286	43	29.90	5- 54	3	–
R.H.Joseph	202.3	36	762	24	31.75	6- 47	2	1
C.W.Henderson	390.1	82	1110	30	37.00	5-116	1	–
N.L.Buck	292	58	955	20	47.75	3- 50	–	–
Also bowled:								
R.M.L.Taylor	19	2	91	5	18.20	5- 91	1	–
W.S.Jones	26	2	129	5	25.80	3- 71	–	–
A.C.F.Wyatt	100	22	333	9	37.00	3- 35	–	–
M.N.Malik	87	10	309	6	51.50	2- 22	–	–

Kadeer Ali 11-2-33-0; M.A.G.Boyce 2-1-9-0; J.J.Cobb 56-4-208-3; J.du Toit 18-1-54-0;
P.L.Mommsen 10-0-43-0; J.K.H.Naik 56.2-5-205-3; R.R.Sarwan 16.1-0-75-0; G.P.Smith
1-0-9-0; S.J.Thakor 34-3-159-4; M.A.Thornely 40-3-150-3.

Leicestershire played no first-class fixtures outside the County Championship in 2012. The
First-Class Averages (pp 219–235) give the records of Leicestershire players in all first-class
county matches, with the exception of W.S.Jones and R.M.L.Taylor, whose first-class
figures for Leicestershire are as above.

LEICESTERSHIRE RECORDS

FIRST-CLASS CRICKET

Highest Total	For 701-4d		v	Worcs	Worcester	1906
	V 761-6d		by	Essex	Chelmsford	1990
Lowest Total	For 25		v	Kent	Leicester	1912
	V 24		by	Glamorgan	Leicester	1971
	24		by	Oxford U	Oxford	1985
Highest Innings	For 309*	H.D.Ackerman	v	Glamorgan	Cardiff	2006
	V 341	G.H.Hirst	for	Yorkshire	Leicester	1905

Highest Partnership for each Wicket

1st	390	B.Dudleston/J.F.Steele	v	Derbyshire	Leicester	1979
2nd	289*	J.C.Balderstone/D.I.Gower	v	Essex	Leicester	1981
3rd	436*	D.L.Maddy/B.J.Hodge	v	L'boro UCCE	Leicester	2003
4th	360*	J.W.A.Taylor/A.B.McDonald	v	Middlesex	Leicester	2010
5th	330	J.W.A.Taylor/S.J.Thakor	v	L'boro MCCU	Leicester	2011
6th	284	P.V.Simmons/P.A.Nixon	v	Durham	Chester-le-St[2]	1996
7th	219*	J.D.R.Benson/P.Whitticase	v	Hampshire	Bournemouth	1991
8th	195	J.W.A.Taylor/J.K.H.Naik	v	Derbyshire	Leicester	2009
9th	160	R.T.Crawford/W.W.Odell	v	Worcs	Leicester	1902
10th	228	R.Illingworth/K.Higgs	v	Northants	Leicester	1977

Best Bowling	For 10-18	G.Geary	v	Glamorgan	Pontypridd	1929
(Innings)	V 10-32	H.Pickett	for	Essex	Leyton	1895
Best Bowling	For 16-96	G.Geary	v	Glamorgan	Pontypridd	1929
(Match)	V 16-102	C.Blythe	for	Kent	Leicester	1909

Most Runs – Season	2446	L.G.Berry	(av 52.04)		1937
Most Runs – Career	30143	L.G.Berry	(av 30.32)		1924-51
Most 100s – Season	7	L.G.Berry			1937
	7	W.Watson			1959
	7	B.F.Davison			1982
Most 100s – Career	45	L.G.Berry			1924-51
Most Wkts – Season	170	J.E.Walsh	(av 18.96)		1948
Most Wkts – Career	2131	W.E.Astill	(av 23.18)		1906-39
Most Career W-K Dismissals	905	R.W.Tolchard	(794 ct; 111 st)		1965-83
Most Career Catches in the Field	426	M.R.Hallam			1950-70

LIMITED-OVERS CRICKET

Highest Total	50ov	406-5		v	Berkshire	Leicester	1996
	40ov	344-4		v	Durham	Chester-le-St[2]	1996
	T20	221-3		v	Yorkshire	Leeds	2004
Lowest Total	50ov	56		v	Northants	Leicester	1964
	40ov	36		v	Sussex	Leicester	1973
	T20	96		v	Notts	Leicester	2012
Highest Innings	50ov	201	V.J.Wells	v	Berkshire	Leicester	1996
	40ov	154*	B.J.Hodge	v	Sussex	Horsham	2004
	T20	111	D.L.Maddy	v	Yorkshire	Leeds	2004
Best Bowling	50ov	6-16	C.M.Willoughby	v	Somerset	Leicester	2005
	40ov	6-17	K.Higgs	v	Glamorgan	Leicester	1973
	T20	5-13	A.B.McDonald	v	Notts	Nottingham	2010

MIDDLESEX

Formation of Present Club: 2 February 1864
Inaugural First-Class Match: 1864
Colours: Blue
Badge: Three Seaxes
County Champions (since 1890): (10) 1903, 1920, 1921, 1947, 1976, 1980, 1982, 1985, 1990, 1993
Joint Champions: (2) 1949, 1977
Gillette/NatWest/C&G/FP Trophy Winners: (4) 1977, 1980, 1984, 1988
Benson and Hedges Cup Winners: (2) 1983, 1986
Pro 40/National League (Div 1) Winners: (0); best – 1st (Div 2) 2004
Sunday League Winners: (1) 1992
Clydesdale Bank 40 Winners: (0); best – 2nd in Group 2011, 2012
Twenty20 Cup Winners: (1) 2008

Secretary: Vincent J.Codrington, Lord's Cricket Ground, London NW8 8QN • Tel: 020 7289 1300 • Fax: 020 7289 5831 • Email: enquiries@middlesexccc.com • Web: www.middlesexccc.com

Managing Director of Cricket: Angus Fraser. **Head Coach**: Richard Scott. **Assistant Coach**: Richard Johnson. **Batting Coach**: Mark Ramprakash. **Club Captain**: N.J.Dexter. **First-class Captain**: C.J.L.Rogers. **Overseas Players**: C.J.L.Rogers and A.C.Voges (T20 only). **2013 Beneficiary**: none. **Head Groundsman**: Mick Hunt. **Scorer**: Don K.Shelley. ‡ New registration. NQ Not qualified for England.

NQBALBIRNIE, Andrew (St Andrew's C, Dublin; UWIC, b Dublin, Ireland 28 Dec 1990. 6'2". RHB, OB. Debut (Cardiff MCCU) 2012. Middlesex debut 2012. Middlesex 2nd XI debut 2011. MCC YCs 2010. **LOI** (Ire): 4 (2010); HS 17 v Canada (Amstelveen) 2010. HS 36* Ireland XI v South Africa A (Oak Hill) 2012. M HS 14 v Surrey (Oval) 2012. BB – . LO HS 17 (see LOI). LO BB – .

BERG, Gareth Kyle (South African College S), b Cape Town, South Africa 18 Jan 1981. 6'0". RHB, RMF. England qualified through residency. Debut (Middlesex) 2008; cap 2010. WP Academy (1999-00) and WP B (2001-02 to 2002-03). HS 130* v Leics (Leicester) 2011. BB 6-58 v Glamorgan (Cardiff) 2011. LO HS 65 v Surrey (Lord's) 2008 (FPT). LO BB 4-24 v Worcs (Worcester) 2011 (CB40). T20 HS 60*. T20 BB 4-20.

NQCOLLYMORE, Corey Dalanelo (Alexandra SS), b St Peter, Barbados 21 Dec 1977. 6'0". RHB, RFM. Barbados 1998-99 to 2008-09. Warwickshire 2003. Sussex 2008-10; cap 2008. Middlesex debut/cap 2011. Kolpak registration. **Tests** (WI): 30 (1998-99 to 2007); HS 16* v Z (Bulawayo) 2003-04 and 16* v E (Chester-le-St) 2007; BB 7-57 v SL (Kingston) 2003. **LOI** (WI): 84 (1999 to 2006-07); HS 13* v I (Toronto) 1999; BB 5-51 v SL (Colombo) 2001-02. F-c Tours (WI): E 2000, 2004, 2007; A 2005-06; SA 2003-04; P 2006-07; Z 2002, 2003-04; K 2000-01. HS 23 Sx v Notts (Horsham) 2009. M HS 8* v Derbys (Lord's) 2011. 50 wkts (1): 57 (2010). BB 7-57 (see Tests). CC BB 6-48 Sx v Leics (Leicester) 2010. M BB 4-28 v Surrey (Guildford) 2011. LO HS 13* (see LOI). LO BB 5-27 Barbados v Leeward Is (Weymouth) 2005-06. T20 HS 4. T20 BB 1-21.

DAVEY, Joshua Henry (Culford S), b Aberdeen, Scotland 3 Aug 1990. RHB, RM. Debut (Middlesex) 2010. Middlesex 2nd XI debut 2008. Suffolk 2009. **LOI** (Scot): 10 (2010 to 2012-13); HS 64 v Afghanistan (Sharjah) 2012-13; BB 5-9 v Afghanistan (Ayr) 2010. **IT20** (Scot): 1 (2012); HS 7 and BB 3-23 v B (The Hague) 2012. HS 72 and BB 2-41 v Oxford MCCU (Oxford) 2010 – on debut. CC HS 61 v Glos (Bristol) 2010. CC BB – . LO HS 91 Scot v Warwks (Birmingham) 2011 (CB40). LO BB 5-9 (see LOI). T20 HS 18*. T20 BB 3-23.

141

DENLY, Joseph Liam (Chaucer TC), b Canterbury, Kent 16 Mar 1986. 6'0". RHB, LB. Kent 2004-11; cap 2008. Middlesex debut/cap 2012. **LOI:** 9 (2009 to 2009-10); HS 67 v Ireland (Belfast) 2009 – on debut. **IT20:** 5 (2009 to 2009-10); HS 14 and BB 1-9 v SA (Centurion) 2009-10. F-c Tours (Eng A): NZ 2008-09; I 2007-08. 1000 runs (2); most – 1024 (2011). HS 199 K v Derbys (Derby) 2011. M HS 134* v Worcs (Lord's) 2012. BB 3-43 K v Surrey (Oval) 2011. M BB 1-18 v Somerset (Taunton) 2012. LO HS 115 K v Warwks (Birmingham) 2009 (FPT). LO BB 3-42 K v Netherlands (Rotterdam) 2011 (CB40). T20 HS 100. T20 BB 1-9.

DEXTER, Neil John (Northwood HS, Durban; Varsity C; U of South Africa), b Johannesburg, South Africa 21 Aug 1984. 6'0". RHB, RM. Kent 2005-08. Essex 2008. Middlesex debut 2009; cap 2010; captain 2010 (part) to date. Qualified for England in 2010. HS 146 (and 118) v Kent (Uxbridge) 2009. BB 3-23 v Surrey (Lord's) 2012. LO HS 135* K v Glamorgan (Cardiff) 2006 (CGT). LO BB 3-17 K v Leics (Canterbury) 2006 (P40). T20 HS 73. T20 BB 4-21.

FINN, Steven Thomas (Parmiter's S, Garston), b Watford, Herts 4 Apr 1989. 6'7½". RHB, RF. Middlesex debut 2005; cap 2009. Otago 2011-12. YC 2010. **ECB central contract 2012-13. Tests:** 18 (2009-10 to 2012-13); HS 56 v NZ (Dunedin) 2012-13; BB 6-125 v A (Brisbane) 2010-11. **LOI:** 33 (2010-11 to 2012-13); HS 35 v A (Brisbane) 2010-11; BB 4-34 v P (Abu Dhabi) 2011-12 (twice). **IT20:** 16 (2011 to 2012-13); HS 8* v I (Colombo, RPS) 2012-13; BB 3-16 v NZ (Pallekele) 2012-13. F-c Tours: A 2010-11; NZ 2012-13; I 2012-13; SL 2011-12; B 2009-10; UAE 2011-12 (v P). HS 56 (see Tests). M HS 32 v Essex (Lord's) 2011. 50 wkts (2); most – 64 (2010). BB 9-37 (14-106 match) v Worcs (Worcester) 2010. LO HS 35 (see LOI). LO BB 5-33 v Derbys (Lord's) 2011 (CB40). T20 HS 8*. T20 BB 3-16.

GUBBINS, Nicholas Richard Trail (Radley C; Leeds U), b Richmond, Surrey 31 Dec 1993. LHB, LB. Middlesex 2nd XI debut 2012. Awaiting 1st XI debut. Summer contract in 2013.

‡HARRIS, James Alexander Russell (Pontardulais CS; Gorseinon C), b Morriston, Swansea, Glamorgan 16 May 1990. 6'0". RHB, RFM. Glamorgan 2007-12, making debut aged 16y 351d – youngest Glamorgan player to take an f-c wicket; cap 2010. Glamorgan 2nd XI debut 2005, aged 14y 353d. Wales MC 2005-08. England U19s 2007. F-c Tour (Eng A): WI 2010-11. HS 87* Gm v Notts (Swansea) 2007. 50 wkts (1): 63 (2010). BB 7-66 (12-118 match) Gm v Glos (Bristol) 2007 – youngest (17y 3d) to take 10 wickets in any CC match. LO HS 29 EL v Sri Lanka A (Northampton) 2011. LO BB 4-48 Gm v Kent (Canterbury) 2008 (P40). T20 HS 18. T20 BB 4-23.

HELM, Thomas George (Misbourne S, Gt Missenden), b Stoke Mandeville Hospital, Bucks 7 May 1994. RHB, RMF. Middlesex 2nd XI debut 2011. Buckinghamshire 2011. Awaiting 1st XI debut.

LONDON, Adam Brian (Bishop Wand S, Sunbury), b Ashford 12 Oct 1988. 5'8". LHB, OB. Debut (Middlesex) 2009. No 1st XI appearances in 2011. Middlesex 2nd XI debut 2006. HS 77 v Northants (Northampton) 2010. BB 1-15 v Oxford MCCU (Oxford) 2010. CC BB – . LO HS 3 v West Indians (Lord's) 2012. BB – .

MALAN, Dawid Johannes (Paarl HS), b Roehampton, Surrey 3 Sep 1987. Son of D.J.Malan (WP B and Transvaal B 1978-79 to 1981-82), elder brother of C.C.Malan (Loughborough MCCU 2009-10). 6'0". LHB, LB. Boland 2005-06. MCC YC 2006-07. Middlesex debut 2008, scoring 132* v Northants (Uxbridge); cap 2010. MCC 2010-11. 1000 runs (1): 1001 runs (2010). HS 143 v Derbys (Derby) 2011. BB 5-61 v Lancs (Liverpool) 2012. LO HS 134 v Essex (Lord's) 2012 (CB40). LO BB 2-4 v Scotland (Edinburgh) 2009 (FPT). T20 HS 103. T20 BB 2-10.

MORGAN, Eoin Joseph Gerard (Catholic University S), b Dublin, Ireland 10 Sep 1986. 6'0". LHB, RM. British passport. Ireland 2004 to 2007-08. Middlesex debut 2006; cap 2008. *Wisden* 2010. **ECB central contract 2012-13. Tests**: 16 (2010 to 2011-12); HS 130 v P (Nottingham) 2010. **LOI** (E/Ire): 94 (23 for Ire 2006 to 2008-09; 71 for E 2009 to 2012-13); HS 115 Ire v Canada (Nairobi) 2006-07. **IT20**: 35 (2009 to 2012-13); HS 85* v SA (Johannesburg) 2009-10. F-c Tours (Ire): A 2010-11 (E); NZ 2008-09 (Eng A); Namibia 2005-06; UAE 2006-07, 2007-08, 2011-12 (v P). 1000 runs (1): 1085 (2008). HS 209* Ire v UAE (Abu Dhabi) 2006-07. CC HS 137* v Glos (Bristol) 2008. BB 2-24 v Notts (Lord's) 2007. LO HS 161 v Kent (Canterbury) 2009 (FPT). LO BB – . T20 HS 85*.

MURTAGH, Timothy James (John Fisher S; St Mary's C), b Lambeth, London 2 Aug 1981. Elder brother of C.P.Murtagh (Loughborough UCCE and Surrey 2005-09); nephew of A.J.Murtagh (Hampshire and EP 1973-77). 6'0". LHB, RFM. British U 2000-03. Surrey 2001-06. Middlesex debut 2007; cap 2008. MCC 2010. HS 74* Sy v Middx (Oval) 2004 and 74* Sy v Warwks (Croydon) 2005. M HS 55 v Leics (Leicester) 2011. 50 wkts (4); most – 85 (2011). BB 7-82 v Derbys (Derby) 2009. LO HS 35* v Surrey (Lord's) 2008 (FPT). LO BB 4-14 Sy v Derbys (Derby) 2005 (NL). T20 HS 40*. T20 BB 6-24 Sy v Middx (Lord's) 2005 – Sy record and 4th best UK figs.

PATEL, Ravi Hasmukh (Merchant Taylors' S, Northwood; Loughborough U), b Harrow 4 Aug 1991. RHB, SLA. Debut (Middlesex) 2010. No 1st XI appearances in 2011. Loughborough MCCU 2011. Middlesex 2nd XI debut 2008. HS 20 and BB 4-72 v Lancs (Lord's) 2012. LO HS and BB – .

RAYNER, Oliver Philip (St Bede's S, Sussex), b Fallingbostel, W Germany, 1 Nov 1985. 6'5". RHB, OB. Sussex 2006-11, scoring 101 v Sri Lankans (Hove) – first hundred on debut for Sussex since 1920. Middlesex debut 2011 (on loan). HS 143* v Notts (Nottingham) 2012. BB 5-49 Sx v Hants (Arundel) 2008. M BB 4-43 v Leics (Leicester) 2011. LO HS 61 Sx v Lancs (Hove) 2006 (P40). LO BB 2-20 v Netherlands (Deventer) 2011 (CB40). T20 HS 41*. T20 BB 5-18.

NO**ROBSON, Sam** David (Marcellin C, Randwick), b Paddington, Sydney, Australia 1 Jul 1989. Elder brother of A.J.Robson (*see LEICESTERSHIRE*). 6'0". RHB, LB. Debut (Middlesex) 2009. Middlesex 2nd XI debut 2008. HS 204 v Oxford MCCU (Oxford) 2010. CC HS 146 v Essex (Chelmsford) 2011. BB – . LO HS 65 v Sussex (Lord's) 2011 (CB40). T20 HS 28*.

NO**ROGERS, Christopher** John Llewellyn (Wesley C, Perth; Curtin U, Perth), b St George, Sydney, Australia 31 Aug 1977. Son of W.J.Rogers (NSW 1968-69 to 1969-70). 5'10". LHB, LBG. W Australia 1998-99 to 2007-08. Derbyshire 2004, 2008-10; cap 2008; captain 2008 (*part*) to 2010 (*part*). Leicestershire 2005. Northamptonshire 2006. Victoria 2008-09 to date. Middlesex debut/cap 2011; captain (f-c only) 2013. MCC 2011. Shropshire 2003. Wiltshire 2005. **Tests** (A): 1 (2007-08); HS 15 v I (Perth) 2007-08. F-c Tour (Aus A): P 2007-08. 1000 runs (6+2); most – 1461 (2009). HS 319 Nh v Glos (Northampton) 2006. M HS 173 v Somerset (Lord's) 2012. BB 1-16 Nh v Leics (Northampton) 2006. LO HS 140 Vic v S Aus (Melbourne) 2009-10. LO BB 2-22 Nh v Durham (Northampton) 2006. T20 HS 58.

ROLAND-JONES, Tobias Skelton ('**Toby**') (Hampton S; Leeds U), b Ashford 29 Jan 1988. 6'4". RHB, RMF. Debut (Middlesex) 2010; cap 2012. MCC 2011. Middlesex 2nd XI debut 2008. Leeds/Bradford UCCE 2009 (not f-c). Middlesex HS 52 v Sussex (Lord's) 2012. 50 wkts (1): 64 (2012). BB 6-66 v Sussex (Hove) 2012. LO HS 24 EL v Australia A (Sydney) 2012-13. LO BB 3-24 v Glos (Cheltenham) 2012 (CB40). T20 HS 12. T20 BB 4-25.

ROSSINGTON, Adam Matthew (Mill Hill S), b Edgware 5 May 1993. 5'11". RHB, WK. Debut (Middlesex) 2010. Middlesex 2nd XI debut 2010. England U19s 2010-11, scoring 113 v SL on debut. Summer contract. HS 29 v Warwks (Birmingham) 2012. LO HS 17 v West Indians (Lord's) 2012. T20 HS 25.

SANDHU, Gurjit Singh (Isleworth & Syon S; Heathland S), b W Middlesex Hospital 24 Mar 1992. 6'4". RHB, LMF. Middlesex 2nd XI debut 2008, aged 16y 85d. HS 8 and BB-v Sri Lankans (Uxbridge) 2011. LO HS 0 and LO BB 3-28 v Essex (Lord's) 2012 (CB40).

SIMPSON, John Andrew (St Gabriel's RC HS), b Bury, Lancs 3 Jul 1988. 5'10". LHB, WK. Debut (Middlesex) 2009, cap 2011. Lancashire 2nd XI debut 2004. Cumberland 2007. MCC YCs 2008. England U19s 2004-05 to 2005. HS 143 v Surrey (Lord's) 2011. LO HS 82 v Glos (Cheltenham) 2010 (CB40). T20 HS 60*.

SMITH, Thomas Michael John (Seaford Head Community C; Sussex Downs C), b Eastbourne, Sussex 29 Aug 1987. 5'9". RHB, SLA. Sussex 2007-09. No f-c appearances in 2008. Surrey 2009 (l-o only). Middlesex debut 2010. HS 33 v Derbys (Derby) 2010. BB 3-38 v Derbys (Lord's) 2011. LO HS 65 Sy v Leics (Leicester) 2009 (P40). LO BB 3-26 v Derbys (Lord's) 2010 (CB40). T20 HS 36*. T20 BB 5-24.

[NQ]**STIRLING, Paul** Robert (Belfast HS), b Belfast, N Ireland 3 Sep 1990. Father Brian Stirling was an international rugby referee. 5'10". RHB, OB. Ireland 2007-08 to date. ICC Combined XI 2011-12. Awaiting Middlesex f-c debut. **LOI** (Ire): 38 (2008 to 2012); HS 177 v Canada (Toronto) 2010; BB 4-11 v Netherlands (Amstelveen) 2010. **IT20** (Ire): 19 (2009 to 2012-13); HS 79 v Afghanistan (Dubai, DSC) 2011-12; BB 3-21 v B (Belfast) 2012. F-c Tours (Ire): WI 2009-10; Kenya 2011-12. HS 107 Ire v Canada (Dublin) 2011. BB 2-45 Ire v Jamaica (Spanish Town) 2009-10. LO HS 177 (*see LOI*). LO BB 4-11 (*see LOI*). T20 HS 82*. T20 BB 3-20.

‡[NQ]**VOGES, Adam** Charles (Edith Cowan U, Perth), b Perth, Australia 4 Oct 1979. 6'0". RHB, SLC. Western Australia 2002-03 to date. Nottinghamshire 2008-12; cap 2008. Joins Middlesex in 2013 for T20 only. **LOI** (A): 17 (2006-07 to 2012-13); HS 112* v WI (Melbourne) 2012-13. **IT20** (A): 7 (2007-08 to 2012-13); HS 51 v WI (Brisbane) 2012-13; BB 2-5 v I (Melbourne) 2007-08. F-c Tours (Aus A): I 2008-09; P 2007-08. HS 180 WA v Tas (Hobart) 2007-08. UK HS 165 v Oxford MCCU (Oxford) 2011. CC HS 139 Nt v Sussex (Horsham) 2009. BB 4-92 WA v S Aus (Adelaide) 2006-07. UK HS BB 3-21 Nt v Durham (Nottingham) 2008. LO HS 112* (*see LOI*). LO BB 3-25 Nt v Sussex (Hove) 2009 (P40). T20 HS 82*. T20 BB 2-4.

WILKIN, Oliver (Merchant Taylors' S, Northwood; Loughborough U), b Ealing 6 Apr 1992. RHB, RM. Loughborough MCCU 2011. Middlesex 2nd XI debut 2012. HS 38 LU v Northants (Loughborough) 2011. BB 2-63 v Kent (Canterbury) 2011. T20 HS 28. T20 BB 3-12.

RELEASED/RETIRED

(Having made a County First-Class or List A appearance in 2012)

CROOK, S.P. – *see NORTHAMPTONSHIRE.*

IRELAND, A.J. – *see GLOUCESTERSHIRE.*

[NQ]**SCOLLAY, Thomas** Edward (St Phillips C), b Alice Springs, Northern Territory, Australia 28 Nov 1987. RHB, OB. Awaiting f-c debut. Middlesex 2nd XI debut 2010. Hampshire 2nd XI 2008. LO HS 32 and LO BB 1-21 v Yorks (Lord's) 2010 (CB40). T20 HS 19.

STRAUSS, Andrew John (Radley C; Durham U), b Johannesburg, South Africa 2 Mar 1977. 5'11". LHB, LM. Middlesex 1998-2012; cap 2001; captain 2002 (part) to 2004 (part); benefit 2009. MCC 2002. N Districts 2007-08. Somerset (1 game) 2011. Oxfordshire 1996. British U (List A) 1997-98. *Wisden* 2004. MBE 2005. **Tests**: 100 (2004 to 2012, 50 as captain); HS 177 v NZ (Napier) 2007-08. Scored 112 & 83 (run out) v NZ (Lord's) on debut and 126 & 94* v SA (Port Elizabeth) 2004-05 on his debut overseas. **LOI**: 127 (2003-04 to 2010-11, 62 as captain); HS 158 v I (Bangalore) 2010-11; BB – . **IT20**: 4 (2005 to 2008-09); HS 33 v SL (Southampton) 2006. F-c Tours (C=captain): A 2006-07, 2010-11C; SA 2004-05, 2009-10C; WI 2008-09C; NZ 2007-08; I 2005-06, 2008-09; P 2005-06; SL 2011-12C; UAE 2011-12C (v P). 1000 runs (4); most – 1529 (2003). HS 241* v Leics (Lord's) 2011. BB 1-16 v Notts (Lord's) 2007. LO HS 163 v Surrey (Oval) 2008 (FPT) – M record. LO BB – . T20 HS 60.

WILLIAMS, R.E.M. – *see LEICESTERSHIRE.*

S.A.Newman left the staff without making a County First-Class or List A appearance in 2012.

LEICESTERSHIRE RELEASED/RETIRED (continued from p 138)

MALIK, Muhammad Nadeem (Wilford Meadows CS; Bilborough C), b Nottingham 6 Oct 1982. 6'5". RHB, RFM. Nottinghamshire 2001-03, 2007 – on loan. Worcestershire 2004-07. Leicestershire 2008-12, taking 5-51 v Middx (Leicester) on debut. HS 41 v Essex (Leicester) 2008. BB 6-46 v Essex (Chelmsford) 2008. LO HS 27* v Middx (Leicester) 2012 (CB40). LO BB 4-40 v Hants (Southampton) 2010 (CB40). T20 HS 3*. T20 BB 4-16.

MOMMSEN, Preston Luke (Hilton C, Durban), b Durban, South Africa 14 Oct 1987. RHB, OB. Scotland 2010 to date. Leicestershire 2012. **LOI** (Scot): 13 (2010 to 2012-13); HS 80 v Ireland (Amstelveen) 2010; BB 3-26 v Ireland (Edinburgh) 2011. **IT20** (Scot) 7 (2011-12 to 2012-13); HS 26 v Netherlands (Dubai) 2011-12; BB 1-23 v B (Hague) 2012 and 1-23 v Afghanistan (Sharjah) 2012-13. HS 102 Scot v Namibia (Windhoek) 2011-12. Le HS 35 v Glamorgan (Cardiff) 2012. BB 3-67 Scot v Netherlands (Aberdeen) 2011. Le BB – . LO HS 81* Scot v Northants (Northampton) 2011 (CB40). LO BB 3-26 (*see LOI*). T20 HS 39. T20 BB 3-12.

WHITE, W.A. – *see LANCASHIRE.*

NORTHAMPTONSHIRE RELEASED/RETIRED (continued from p 151)

WHITE, Robert Allan (Stowe S; Durham U; Loughborough U), b Chelmsford, Essex 15 Oct 1979. 5'11". RHB, LB. Northamptonshire 2000-12; cap 2008. Loughborough UCCE 2003. British U 2003. 1000 runs (1): 1037 (2008). HS 277 and BB 2-30 v Glos (Northampton) 2002 – highest maiden f-c hundred in UK; included 107 before lunch on first day. LO HS 111 v Warwks (Northampton) 2008 (FPT). LO BB 2-18 v Sussex (Northampton) 2002 (NL). T20 HS 94*.

MIDDLESEX 2012

RESULTS SUMMARY

	Place	Won	Lost	Tied	Drew	NR
LV= County Championship (1st Division)	3rd	5	4		7	
All First-Class Matches		5	4		8	
Clydesdale Bank 40 (Group A)	2nd	6	3	1		2
Friends Life t20 (South Group)	5th	3	7			

LV= COUNTY CHAMPIONSHIP AVERAGES

BATTING AND FIELDING

Cap		M	I	NO	HS	Runs	Avge	100	50	Ct/St
2001	A.J.Strauss	4	7	2	127*	277	55.40	1	1	7
2011	C.J.L.Rogers	16	29	2	173	1086	40.22	3	6	7
2012	J.L.Denly	16	28	4	134*	840	35.00	2	4	7
2010	N.J.Dexter	12	21	2	125	648	34.10	2	3	9
2010	D.J.Malan	16	26	–	140	827	31.80	2	3	23
	S.P.Crook	5	9	–	67	273	30.33	–	2	2
2010	O.P.Rayner	10	14	2	143*	338	28.16	1	1	12
	S.D.Robson	15	28	2	72	697	26.80	–	4	11
2008	T.J.Murtagh	15	21	6	45	360	24.00	–	–	5
2010	G.K.Berg	15	23	1	83	467	21.22	–	2	12
2012	T.S.Roland-Jones	14	20	5	52	294	19.60	–	1	3
2008	E.J.G.Morgan	5	7	1	71	109	18.16	–	1	6
2011	J.A.Simpson	13	19	1	47	279	15.50	–	–	42/5
	R.H.Patel	3	5	2	20	46	15.33	–	–	3
	A.M.Rossington	3	5	–	29	62	12.40	–	–	9/1
2011	C.D.Collymore	7	10	6	8	29	7.25	–	–	–
2009	S.T.Finn	5	6	4	1*	1	0.50	–	–	7

Also batted (1 match each): A.Balbirnie 14, 3; T.M.J.Smith 31, 0.

BOWLING

	O	M	R	W	Avge	Best	5wI	10wM
T.S.Roland-Jones	379	83	1167	61	19.13	6-66	4	1
S.T.Finn	170	39	538	28	19.21	4-43	–	–
T.J.Murtagh	496.3	117	1401	59	23.74	5-37	2	–
R.H.Patel	104	12	356	14	25.42	4-72	–	–
N.J.Dexter	102	20	317	12	26.41	3-23	–	–
G.K.Berg	329.4	73	1014	35	28.97	3-25	–	–
S.P.Crook	134.4	16	476	14	34.00	5-48	1	–
O.P.Rayner	205.5	27	529	15	35.26	4-67	–	–
C.D.Collymore	187.1	44	540	11	49.09	3-66	–	–

Also bowled:

D.J.Malan	47.2	7	199	7	28.42	5-61	1	–

A.Balbirnie 8-0-24-0; J.L.Denly 27-2-104-1; S.D.Robson 0.5-0-4-0; T.M.J.Smith 27.3-3-71-1.

The First-Class Averages (pp 219–235) give the records of Middlesex players in all first-class county matches (Middlesex's other opponents being Durham MCCU), with the exception of A.Balbirnie, S.T.Finn, E.J.G.Morgan and A.J.Strauss, whose first-class figures for Middlesex are as above.

MIDDLESEX RECORDS

FIRST-CLASS CRICKET

Highest Total	For 642-3d			v	Hampshire	Southampton	1923
	V 850-7d			by	Somerset	Taunton	2007
Lowest Total	For 20			v	MCC	Lord's	1864
	V 31			by	Glos	Bristol	1924
Highest Innings	For 331*	J.D.B.Robertson		v	Worcs	Worcester	1949
	V 341	C.M.Spearman		for	Glos	Gloucester	2004

Highest Partnership for each Wicket

1st	372	M.W.Gatting/J.L.Langer	v	Essex	Southgate	1998
2nd	380	F.A.Tarrant/J.W.Hearne	v	Lancashire	Lord's	1914
3rd	424*	W.J.Edrich/D.C.S.Compton	v	Somerset	Lord's	1948
4th	325	J.W.Hearne/E.H.Hendren	v	Hampshire	Lord's	1919
5th	338	R.S.Lucas/T.C.O'Brien	v	Sussex	Hove	1895
6th	270	J.D.Carr/P.N.Weekes	v	Glos	Lord's	1994
7th	271*	E.H.Hendren/F.T.Mann	v	Notts	Nottingham	1925
8th	182*	M.H.C.Doll/H.R.Murrell	v	Notts	Lord's	1913
9th	172	G.K.Berg/T.J.Murtagh	v	Leics	Leicester	2011
10th	230	R.W.Nicholls/W.Roche	v	Kent	Lord's	1899

Best Bowling	For 10- 40	G.O.B.Allen	v	Lancashire	Lord's	1929
(Innings)	V 9- 38	R.C.R-Glasgow†	for	Somerset	Lord's	1924
Best Bowling	For 16-114	G.Burton	v	Yorkshire	Sheffield	1888
(Match)	16-114	J.T.Hearne	v	Lancashire	Manchester	1898
	V 16-100	J.E.B.B.P.Q.C.Dwyer	for	Sussex	Hove	1906

Most Runs – Season	2669	E.H.Hendren	(av 83.41)	1923
Most Runs – Career	40302	E.H.Hendren	(av 48.81)	1907-37
Most 100s – Season	13	D.C.S.Compton		1947
Most 100s – Career	119	E.H.Hendren		1907-37
Most Wkts – Season	158	F.J.Titmus	(av 14.63)	1955
Most Wkts – Career	2361	F.J.Titmus	(av 21.27)	1949-82
Most Career W-K Dismissals	1223	J.T.Murray	(1024 ct; 199 st)	1952-75
Most Career Catches in the Field	561	E.H.Hendren		1907-37

LIMITED-OVERS CRICKET

Highest Total	50ov	341-7		v	Somerset	Lord's	2009
	40ov	350-6		v	Lancashire	Lord's	2012
	T20	213-4		v	Glamorgan	Richmond	2010
Lowest Total	50ov	41		v	Essex	Westcliff	1972
	40ov	23		v	Yorkshire	Leeds	1974
	T20	102		v	Glamorgan	Richmond	2011
Highest Innings	50ov	163	A.J.Strauss	v	Surrey	The Oval	2008
	40ov	147*	M.R.Ramprakash	v	Worcs	Lord's	1990
	T20	106	A.C.Gilchrist	v	Kent	Canterbury	2010
Best Bowling	50ov	6-15	W.W.Daniel	v	Sussex	Hove	1980
	40ov	6- 6	R.W.Hooker	v	Surrey	Lord's	1969
	T20	5-13	M.Kartik	v	Essex	Lord's	2007

† R.C.Robertson-Glasgow

NORTHAMPTONSHIRE

Formation of Present Club: 31 July 1878
Inaugural First-Class Match: 1905
Colours: Maroon
Badge: Tudor Rose
County Champions: (0); best – 2nd 1912, 1957, 1965, 1976
Gillette/NatWest/C&G/FP Trophy Winners: (2) 1976, 1992
Benson and Hedges Cup Winners: (1) 1980
Pro 40/National League (Div 1) Winners: (0); best – 2nd 2006, 2007
Sunday League Winners: (0); best – 3rd 1991
Clydesdale Bank 40 Winners: (0); best – 3rd Group B 2011
Twenty20 Cup Winners: (0); best – Semi-Finalist 2009

Chief Executive: K.David Smith, County Ground, Abington Avenue, Northampton, NN1 4PR • Tel: 01604 514455 • Fax: 01604 609288 • Email: post@nccc.co.uk • Web: www.nccc.co.uk

Head Coach: David Ripley. **Captain**: S.D.Peters (f-c) and A.G.Wakely (l-o). **Vice-Captain**: A.G.Wakely. **Overseas Players**: T.A.Copeland and C.L.White (T20 only). **2013 Beneficiary**: S.D.Peters. **Head Groundsman**: Paul Marshall. **Scorer**: A.C. (Tony) Kingston. ‡ New registration. NQ Not qualified for England.

‡**AZHAR ULLAH, Muhammad** b Burewala, Punjab, Pakistan 25 Dec 1983. RHB, RFM. Multan 2004-05 to 2006-07. WAPDA 2004-05 to date. Quetta 2005-06. Baluchistan 2007-08 to 2008-09. UK qualified through residency and British wife. HS 41 WAPDA v Karachi Whites (Karachi) 2007-08. BB 7-74 Quetta v Lahore Ravi (Quetta) 2005-06. LO HS 9 (twice). LO BB 5-56 WAPDA v Allied Bank (Karachi) 2004-05. T20 HS 5*. T20 BB 1-15.

COETZER, Kyle James (Aberdeen GS), b Aberdeen, Scotland 14 Apr 1984. 5'11''. RHB, RM. Durham 2004-10. Northamptonshire debut 2011. Scotland 2004 to date. **LOI** (Scot): 12 (2008 to 2012-13); HS 133 v Afghanistan (Sharjah) 2012-13; BB 1-35 v Netherlands (Aberdeen) 2011. **IT20** (Scot): 16 (2008 to 2012-13); HS 62 v Ireland (Dubai, DSC) 2011-12; BB 3-25 v Afghanistan (Abu Dhabi) 2009-10. F-c Tour (Scot): Kenya 2009-10. HS 172 Du v MCC (Abu Dhabi) 2010. CC HS 142 Du v Warwks (Chester-le-St) 2007. Nh HS 120 v Leics (Leicester) 2012. BB 2-16 Scot v Kenya (Nairobi) 2009-10. CC BB 1-9 v Glamorgan (Northampton) 2012. LO HS 133 (*see LOI*). LO BB 1-25 v Sussex (Arundel) 2012 (CB40). T20 HS 64. T20 BB 3-25.

‡**NQCOPELAND, Trent** Aaron, b Gosford, NSW, Australia 14 Mar 1986. RHB, RFM. New South Wales 2009-10 to date. **Tests** (A): 3 (2011); HS 23* v SL (Galle) 2011; BB 2-24 v SL (Pallekele) 2011. F-c Tours (A): SA 2011-12; SL 2011; Z 2011 (Aus A). HS 106 NSW v Tas (Hobart) 2012-13. BB 8-92 (10-149 match) NSW v Q (Sydney) 2009-10 – on debut. LO HS 21 NSW v WA (Sydney) 2011-12. LO BB 5-44 NSW v WA (Sydney) 2011-12. T20 HS 1. T20 BB – .

CROOK, Steven Paul (Rostrevor C; Magill U), b Modbury, S Australia 28 May 1983. Younger brother of A.R.Crook (S Australia, Aus Academy, Lancashire, Northamptonshire 1998-99 to 2008). 5'11''. RHB, RFM. British passport. Lancashire 2003-05. Northamptonshire 2005-09. Middlesex 2011-12. Aus Academy 2001-02. HS 97 v Yorks (Northampton) 2005. BB 5-48 M v Lancs (Lord's) 2012. Nh BB 5-71 v Essex (Northampton) 2009. LO HS 72 v Essex (Chelmsford) 2009 (FPT). LO BB 4-20 v Sussex (Northampton) 2006 (P40). T20 HS 29. T20 BB 3-21.

DAGGETT, Lee Martin (Woodhey HS, and Holy Cross C, Bury; Durham U) b Bury, Lancs 1 Oct 1982. 6'0". RHB, RMF. Durham UCCE 2003-05. British U 2004. Warwickshire 2006-08. Leicestershire 2008. Northamptonshire debut 2009. HS 50* v Leics (Leicester) 2011. BB 8-94 DU v Durham (Chester-le-St) 2004. CC BB 6-30 Wa v Durham (Birmingham) 2006. Nh BB 4-25 v Worcs (Worcester) 2010. LO HS 14* and BB 4-17 v Neth (Northampton) 2010 (CB40). T20 HS 3*. T20 BB 2-17.

DAVIS, Christian Arthur Linghorne (Bedford S), b Milton Keynes, Bucks 11 Oct 1992. 6'2". RHB, LFM. Northamptonshire 2nd XI debut 2010. Bedfordshire 2010. England U19s 2010-11. Awaiting f-c debut. LO HS 54 v Kent (Northampton) 2012 (CB40). LO BB – .

DE LANGE, Con de Wet (Worcester Gymnasium HS; UNISA), b Bellville, Cape Town, South Africa 11 Feb 1981. Cousin of A.D.de Lange (Free State, Boland 2006-07 to 2008-09) and nephew of C.P.L.de Lange (N Transvaal 1981-82 to 1986-87). 5'8". RHB, SLA. Boland 1997-98 to 2006-07. Cape Cobras 2005-06 to 2007-08. Eagles 2008-09 to 2009-10. Free State 2009-10 to 2010-11. Knights 2010-11. Northamptonshire debut 2012. Qualifies via UK residency. HS 109 Boland v Easterns (Paarl) 2003-04. Nh HS 40 and Nh BB 1-11 v Glos (Northampton) 2012. BB 7-48 (12-116 match) Boland v Gauteng (Randjesfontein) 2003-04. LO HS 66 Boland v EP (Pt Elizabeth) 2002-03. LO BB 4-8 Boland v EP (Pt Elizabeth) 2006-07. T20 HS 8. T20 BB 3-15.

DUCKETT, Ben Matthew (Stowe S), b Farnborough, Kent 17 Oct 1994. LHB, WK, occ OB. Northamptonshire 2nd XI debut 2011. England U19s 2012-13. Awaiting f-c debut. T20 HS 5*.

EVANS, Luke (St Aidan's S, Sunderland), b Sunderland 26 Apr 1987. 6'7". RHB, RMF. Durham 2007-10. No 1st XI appearances in 2008. Northamptonshire debut 2010 (on loan). HS 8* v Glos (Bristol) 2010. BB 4-38 v Hants (Southampton) 2012 and 4-38 v Glos (Bristol) 2012. LO HS 18 v Hants (Northampton) 2011 (CB40). LO BB 2-46 v Yorks (Northampton) 2012 (CB40). T20 HS -. T20 BB 1-15.

[NQ]**HALL, Andrew** James (Alberton HS), b Alberton, Johannesburg, South Africa 31 Jul 1975. 6'0". RHB, RFM. Transvaal/Gauteng 1995-96 to 2000-01. Easterns 2001-02 to 2003-04. Worcestershire 2003-04. Lions 2004-05 to 2005-06. Kent 2005-07; cap 2005. Northamptonshire debut 2008 (Kolpak registration); cap 2009; captain 2010 (*part*) to 2012. Dolphins 2009-10. Mashonaland Eagles 2010-11. Durham CB 1999. Suffolk 2002. **Tests** (SA): 21 (2001-02 to 2006-07); HS 163 v I (Kanpur) 2004-05; BB 3-1 v SL (Johannesburg) 2002-03. **LOI** (SA): 88 (1998-99 to 2007); HS 81 v SL (Galle) 2000-01; BB 5-18 v E (Bridgetown) 2006-07. **IT20** (SA): 2 (2005-06); HS 11 v A (Brisbane) 2005-06; BB 3-22 v A (Johannesburg) 2005-06. F-c Tours (SA): E 2003; WI 2004-05; I 2004-05; SL 2006; Z 1995-96 (Transvaal B), 2007-08 (SA A). 1000 runs (1): 1161 (2009). HS 163 (*see Tests*). UK HS 159 v Leics (Northampton) 2009. BB 6-77 (11-99 match) Easterns v WP (Pt Elizabeth) 2002-03. UK BB 5-29 v Essex (Northampton) 2009. LO HS 81* Gauteng v Border (E London) 1999-00. LO BB 5-18 (*see LOI*). T20 HS 66* and T20 BB 6-21 v Worcs (Northampton) 2008 (Nh record analysis, and 1st man in UK to score 50 and take 5 wkts in a game).

KEOGH, Robert Ian (Queensbury S; Dunstable C), b Luton, Beds 21 Oct 1991. 5'11". RHB, OB. Debut (Northamptonshire) 2012. Northamptonshire 2nd XI debut 2009. Bedfordshire 2009-10. Nh HS 6 and BB 1-69 v Glamorgan (Cardiff) 2012 – only f-c match. LO HS 30 v Sussex (Arundel) 2012 (CB40). LO BB – . T20 HS 1. T20 BB -.

KETTLEBOROUGH, James Michael (Bedford S), b Huntingdon 22 Oct 1992. 5'11". RHB, OB. Northamptonshire 2nd XI debut 2012. Middlesex 2nd XI 2011-12. Bedfordshire 2009-12. Awaiting 1st XI debut.

MIDDLEBROOK, James Daniel (Pudsey Crawshaw S), b Leeds, Yorks 13 May 1977. 6'1". RHB, OB. Yorkshire 1998-2001. Essex 2002-09; cap 2003. Northamptonshire debut 2010, cap 2011. MCC 2010. HS 127 Ex v Middx (Lord's) 2007. Nh HS 121 and Nh BB 5-63 v Glos (Northampton) 2012. 50 wkts (1): 56 (2003). BB 6-82 (10-170 match) Y v Hants (Southampton) 2000 – inc 4 wickets in 5 balls. Hat-trick Ex v Kent (Canterbury) 2003. LO HS 57* v Derbys (Derby) 2010 (CB40). LO BB 4-27 Ex v Somerset (Taunton) 2006 (CGT). T20 HS 43. T20 BB 3-13.

MURPHY, David (Richard Hale S, Hertford; Loughborough U), b Welwyn Garden City, Herts 24 June 1989. 5'11". RHB, WK. Loughborough MCCU 2009-11. Northamptonshire debut 2009. Northamptonshire 2nd XI debut 2007. **LOI** (Scot): 2 (2012-13); HS 13 v Afghanistan (Sharjah) 2012-13. **IT20** (Scot): 2 (2012-13); 6* v Afghanistan (Sharjah) 2012-13. Nh HS 79 v Glamorgan (Northampton) 2011. LO HS 31* v Neth (Northampton) 2010 (CB40). T20 HS 20.

NEWTON, Robert Irving (Framlingham C), b Taunton, Somerset 18 Jan 1990. 5'8". RHB, OB. Debut (Northamptonshire) 2010. Northamptonshire 2nd XI debut 2006. HS 119* v Derbys (Northampton) 2012. BB – . LO HS 66 v Essex (Northampton) 2010 (CB40). T20 HS 38.

PETERS, Stephen David (Coopers Coborn & Co S), b Harold Wood, Essex 10 Dec 1978. 5'11". RHB, occ LB. Essex 1996-2001, scoring 110 and 12* v Cambridge U (Cambridge) on debut. Worcestershire debut 2006; cap 2007; captain 2013. MCC 2011, 2012. 1000 runs (4); most – 1320 (2010). HS 222 v Glamorgan (Swansea) 2011. BB 1-19 Ex v Oxford U (Chelmsford) 1999. LO HS 107 v Yorks (Leeds) 2007 (FPT). T20 HS 61*.

SALES, David John Grimwood (Caterham S; Cumnor House S), b Carshalton, Surrey 3 Dec 1977. 6'0". RHB, RM. Debut (Northamptonshire) 1996 v Worcs (Kidderminster) scoring 0 and 210* – record Championship score on f-c debut; youngest (18y 237d) to score 200 in a Championship match; cap 1999; captain 2004-07; benefit 2007. Missed entire 2009 season with knee injury. Wellington 2001-02. MCC 2010. F-c Tours (Eng A): NZ 1999-00; SL 1997-98; K 1997-98; B 1999-00. 1000 runs (6); most – 1384 (2007). HS 303* v Essex (Northampton) 1999 – youngest Englishman (21y 240d) to score a f-c 300. BB 4-25 v Sri Lanka A (Northampton) 1999. CC BB 2-7 v Yorks (Scarborough) 1999. LO HS 161 v Yorks (Northampton) 2006 (CGT) – Nh record. LO BB – . T20 HS 78*. T20 BB 1-10.

‡SPRIEGEL, Matthew Neil William (Whitgift S; Loughborough U), b Epsom, Surrey 4 Mar 1987. 6'3". LHB, OB. Loughborough UCCE 2007-08; captain 2007-08. Surrey 2008-12. HS 108* Sy v Bangladeshis (Oval) 2010. CC HS 103 Sy v Northants (Oval) 2010. BB 2-28 Sy v Hants (Oval) 2008. LO HS 86 Sy v Durham (Oval) 2011 (CB40). LO BB 3-39 Sy v Warwks (Birmingham) 2011 (CB40). T20 HS 53*. T20 BB 4-33.

STONE, Oliver Peter (Thorpe St Andrew HS), b Norwich, Norfolk 9 Oct 1983. 6'1". RHB, RMF. Debut (Northamptonshire) 2012. Northamptonshire 2nd XI debut 2010. Norfolk 2011. Captained England U19s 2012-13. HS 26* and BB 1-6 v Yorks (Northampton) 2012. LO HS 7* v Yorks (Northampton) 2012 (CB40). LO BB 1-12 v Derbys (Northampton) 2012 (CB40). T20 HS 0. T20 BB 2-26.

SWEENEY, Samuel Alan (Parklands HS, Chorley; Myerscough C, Manchester), b Preston, Lancs 15 Mar 1990. RHB, RM. Northamptonshire 2nd XI debut 2011. Awaiting f-c debut. LO BB – .

WAKELY, Alexander George (Bedford S), b Hammersmith, London 3 Nov 1988. 6'2". RHB, OB. Debut (Northamptonshire) 2007; cap 2012; l-o captain 2013. Northamptonshire 2nd XI debut, aged 15y 295d. Bedfordshire 2004-05. HS 113* v Glamorgan (Cardiff) 2009. BB 2-62 v Somerset (Taunton) 2007 – on debut. LO HS 94 v Surrey (Northampton) 2011 (CB40). LO BB 2-14 v Lancs (Northampton) 2007 (P40). T20 HS 62. T20 BB – .

NQWHITE, Cameron Leon, b Bairnsdale, Victoria, Australia 18 Aug 1983. 6'1½". RHB, LBG. Victoria 2000-01 to date. Somerset 2006-07; captain 2006 (*part*); cap 2007. Northamptonshire (T20 only) debut 2012. **Tests** (A): 4 (2008-09); HS 46 v I (Nagpur) 2008-09; BB 2-71 v I (Chandigarh) 2008-09. **LOI** (A): 87 (2005-06 to 2010-11); HS 105 v E (Southampton) 2009 and 105 v P (Brisbane) 2009-10; BB 3-5 v B (Darwin) 2008. **IT20** (A): 38 (2006-07 to 2012-13); HS 85* v SL (Bridgetown) 2010; BB 1-11 v E (Sydney) 2006-07. F-c Tours (A): I 2008-09; P 2005-06 (Aus A), 2007-08 (Aus A). 1000 runs (2); most – 1190 (2006). HS 260* Sm v Derbys (Derby) 2006 – world record score in the fourth innings of a f-c match. BB 6-66 Vic v WA (Perth) 2002-03. CC BB 5-148 Sm v Surrey (Guildford) 2006. LO HS 126* Vic v NSW (Canberra) 2006-07. LO BB 4-15 Vic v Tas (Melbourne) 2004-05. T20 HS 141* Sm v Worcs (Worcester) 2006 – Sm record and 4th highest in all T20. T20 BB 4-10.

WILLEY, David Jonathan (Northampton S), b Northampton 28 Feb 1990. Son of P.Willey (Northants, Leics and England 1966-91). 6'1". LHB, LFM. Debut (Northamptonshire) 2009. Bedfordshire 2008. England U19s 2009. HS 76 v Yorks (Northampton) 2012. BB 5-29 (10-75 match) v Glos (Northampton) 2011. LO HS 74 v Surrey (Oval) 2011 (CB40). LO BB 3-49 v Scotland (Edinburgh) 2011 (CB40). T20 HS 30*. T20 BB 3-9.

RELEASED/RETIRED
(Having made a County First-Class or List A appearance in 2012)

BROOKS, J.A. – *see YORKSHIRE.*

BURTON, David Alexander (Sacred Heart RC SS; Lambeth C), b Dulwich, London 23 Aug 1985. 5'11". RHB, RMF. Gloucestershire 2006; cap 2006. Middlesex 2008-09. Northamptonshire 2010-12. MCC YC 2006. HS 52* Gs v Glamorgan (Cardiff) 2006 – on debut. Nh HS 11 v Glos (Northampton) 2012. BB 5-68 v Glos (Bristol) 2009. Nh BB 5-75 v Leics (Northampton) 2010. LO HS 5* v Derbys (Derby) 2012 (CB40). LO BB 3-25 v Warwks (Birmingham) 2011 (CB40). T20 HS – . T20 BB 2-13.

HOWGEGO, Benjamin Henry Nicholas (King's S, Ely; Stowe S; Exeter U), b King's Lynn, Norfolk 3 Mar 1988. 5'11". LHB, RM. Northamptonshire 2008-12. Northamptonshire 2nd XI debut 2005. HS 80 v Derbys (Chesterfield) 2010. BB – . LO HS 12 v Scotland (Edinburgh) 2011 (CB40). T20 HS 3.

O'BRIEN, N.J. – *see LEICESTERSHIRE.*

NQVAAS, Warnakulasuriya Patabendige Joseph Ushantha **Chaminda** (St Joseph's C, Maradana), b Mattumagala, Sri Lanka 27 Jan 1974. LHB, LFM. Colts 1990-91 to date. Hampshire 2003. Worcestershire 2005. Middlesex 2007; cap 2007. Northamptonshire 2010-12; cap 2011. **Tests** (SL): 111 (1994-95 to 2009); HS 100* v B (Colombo, SSC) 2007; BB 7-71 (14-191 match) v WI (Colombo, SSC) 2001-02. **LOI** (SL): 322 (1993-94 to 2008, 1 as captain); HS 50* v P (Sharjah) 2000-01; BB 8-19 v Z (Colombo, SSC) 2001-02, world record LOI analysis and inc first of two LOI hat-tricks. **IT20** (6): (2006-07 to 2007-08); HS 21 v A (Cape Town) 2007-08; BB 2-14 v B (Johannesburg) 2007-08. F-c Tours (SL): E 2002, 2006; A 1995-96, 2004, 2007-08; SA 1994-95, 1997-98, 2000-01, 2002-03; WI 2003, 2007-08; NZ 1994-95, 1996-97, 2004-05, 2006-07; I 1993-94, 1997-98, 2005-06; P 1995-96, 1999-00, 2001-02, 2004-05, 2008-09; Z 1994-95, 1999-00, 2004; B 1998-99 (v P), 2008-09. HS 134 Colts v Burgher (Colombo, SSC) 2004-05. Nh HS 96 v Essex (Northampton) 2011. 50 wkts (1+2); most – 70 (2011). BB 7-54 (11-93 match) WP v S Province (Colombo, RPS) 2004-05. Nh BB 6-46 v Essex (Chelmsford) 2011. LO HS 76* Colts v Nondescripts (Colombo, NCC) 2009-10. LO BB 8-19 (*see LOI*). T20 HS 73. T20 BB 3-16.

RELEASED/RETIRED continued on p 145

NORTHAMPTONSHIRE 2012

RESULTS SUMMARY

	Place	Won	Lost	Tied	Drew	NR
LV= County Championship (2nd Division)	8th	2	5		9	
All First-Class Matches		2	5		9	
Clydesdale Bank 40 (Group C)	6th	1	6			5
Friends Life t20 (Midlands/Wales/West Group)	6th	1	7			2

LV= COUNTY CHAMPIONSHIP AVERAGES
BATTING AND FIELDING

Cap		M	I	NO	HS	Runs	Avge	100	50	Ct/St
	C.D.de Lange	4	5	4	40*	156	156.00			
	R.I.Newton	13	20	3	119*	751	44.17	3	2	3
2011	J.D.Middlebrook	15	22	4	121	714	39.66	2	4	6
1999	D.J.G.Sales	14	21	3	140	706	39.22	2	3	6
2011	N.J.O'Brien	11	17	2	182	580	38.66	1	3	8/1
2007	S.D.Peters	15	23	2	148	763	36.33	2	3	10
2012	A.G.Wakely	14	21	2	96	690	36.31		5	9
	D.J.Willey	15	18	4	76	489	34.92		4	3
	K.J.Coetzer	13	19	—	120	563	29.63	1	2	5
	D.Murphy	10	11	1	54	252	25.20		1	23/2
2009	A.J.Hall	12	19	1	79	343	19.05		3	4
	L.M.Daggett	14	14	5	26*	110	12.22			5
2012	J.A.Brooks	10	10	3	22	54	7.71			
2011	W.P.J.U.C.Vaas	6	4	1	13*	19	6.33			

Also batted: D.A.Burton (1 match) 11; L.Evans (2) 0, 5, 0; B.H.N.Howgego (1) 1; R.I.Keogh (1) 6; O.P.Stone (3) 13, 26*, 8 (3 ct); R.A.White (2 – cap 2008) 12, 42, 8*.

BOWLING

	O	M	R	W	Avge	Best	5wI	10wM
L.Evans	65	16	214	12	17.83	4-38	–	–
A.J.Hall	293.5	73	812	34	23.88	5-50	1	–
D.J.Willey	440.1	90	1474	43	34.27	5-39	1	–
J.A.Brooks	259.4	66	821	23	35.69	5-61	2	–
J.D.Middlebrook	346.2	100	883	24	36.79	5-63	1	–
L.M.Daggett	372.1	95	1218	27	45.11	4-76	–	–

Also bowled:

	O	M	R	W	Avge	Best		
O.P.Stone	64	13	202	5	40.40	1- 6		
W.P.J.U.C.Vaas	107	23	280	6	46.66	2- 4		

D.A.Burton 13-1-52-1; K.J.Coetzer 19-1-74-1; C.D.de Lange 54-11-176-3; R.I.Keogh 20-5-69-1; N.J.O'Brien 1-0-3-0; A.G.Wakely 7-0-35-0.

Northamptonshire played no first-class fixtures outside the County Championship in 2012. The First-Class Averages (pp 219–235) give the records of their players in all first-class county matches.

NORTHAMPTONSHIRE RECORDS

FIRST-CLASS CRICKET

Highest Total	For	781-7d			v	Notts	Northampton	1995
	V	673-8d			by	Yorkshire	Leeds	2003
Lowest Total	For	12			v	Glos	Gloucester	1907
	V	33			by	Lancashire	Northampton	1977
Highest Innings	For	331*	M.E.K.Hussey		v	Somerset	Taunton	2003
	V	333	K.S.Duleepsinhji	for		Sussex	Hove	1930

Highest Partnership for each Wicket

1st	375	R.A.White/M.J.Powell	v	Glos	Northampton	2002
2nd	344	G.Cook/R.J.Boyd-Moss	v	Lancashire	Northampton	1986
3rd	393	A.Fordham/A.J.Lamb	v	Yorkshire	Leeds	1990
4th	370	R.T.Virgin/P.Willey	v	Somerset	Northampton	1976
5th	401	M.B.Loye/D.Ripley	v	Glamorgan	Northampton	1998
6th	376	R.Subba Row/A.Lightfoot	v	Surrey	The Oval	1958
7th	293	D.J.G.Sales/D.Ripley	v	Essex	Northampton	1999
8th	179	A.J.Hall/J.D.Middlebrook	v	Surrey	The Oval	2011
9th	156	R.Subba Row/S.Starkie	v	Lancashire	Northampton	1955
10th	148	B.W.Bellamy/J.V.Murdin	v	Glamorgan	Northampton	1925

Best Bowling	For	10-127	V.W.C.Jupp		v	Kent	Tunbridge W	1932
(Innings)	V	10- 30	C.Blythe	for		Kent	Northampton	1907
Best Bowling	For	15- 31	G.E.Tribe		v	Yorkshire	Northampton	1958
(Match)	V	17- 48	C.Blythe	for		Kent	Northampton	1907

Most Runs – Season	2198	D.Brookes	(av 51.11)	1952
Most Runs – Career	28980	D.Brookes	(av 36.13)	1934-59
Most 100s – Season	8	R.A.Haywood		1921
Most 100s – Career	67	D.Brookes		1934-59
Most Wkts – Season	175	G.E.Tribe	(av 18.70)	1955
Most Wkts – Career	1102	E.W.Clark	(av 21.26)	1922-47
Most Career W-K Dismissals	810	K.V.Andrew	(653 ct; 157 st)	1953-66
Most Career Catches in the Field	469	D.S.Steele		1963-84

LIMITED-OVERS CRICKET

Highest Total	50ov	360-2		v	Staffs	Northampton	1990
	40ov	319-7		v	Scotland	Northampton	2003
	T20	224-5		v	Glos	Milton Keynes	2005
Lowest Total	50ov	62		v	Leics	Leicester	1974
	40ov	41		v	Middlesex	Northampton	1972
	T20	47		v	Durham	Chester-le-St[2]	2011
Highest Innings	50ov	161	D.J.G.Sales	v	Yorkshire	Northampton	2006
	40ov	172*	W.Larkins	v	Warwicks	Luton	1983
	T20	111*	L.Klusener	v	Worcs	Kidderminster	2007
Best Bowling	50ov	7-10	C.Pietersen	v	Denmark	Brondby	2005
	40ov	7-39	A.Hodgson	v	Somerset	Northampton	1976
	T20	6-21	A.J.Hall	v	Worcs	Northampton	2008

NOTTINGHAMSHIRE

Formation of Present Club: March/April 1841
Substantial Reorganisation: 11 December 1866
Inaugural First-Class Match: 1864
Colours: Green and Gold
Badge: Badge of City of Nottingham
County Champions (since 1890): (6) 1907, 1929, 1981, 1987, 2005, 2010
Gillette/NatWest/C&G/FP Trophy Winners: (1) 1987
Benson and Hedges Cup Winners: (1) 1989
Pro 40/National League (Div 1) Winners: (0); best – 2nd 2007
Sunday League Winners: (1) 1991
Clydesdale Bank 40 Winners: (0); best – 2nd Group C 2011
Twenty20 Cup Winners: (0); best – Finalist 2006

Chief Executive: Lisa Pursehouse, Trent Bridge, Nottingham NG2 6AG • Tel: 0115 982 3000 • Fax: 0115 982 3037 • Email: administration@nottsccc.co.uk • Webs: www.nottsccc.co.uk • www.trentbridge.co.uk

Director of Cricket: Mick Newell. **Captain**: C.M.W.Read. **Vice-Captain**: tba. **Overseas Players**: E.J.M.Cowan and D.J.Hussey. **2013 Beneficiary**: G.P.Swann. **Head Groundsman**: Steve Birks. **Scorer**: Roger Marshall. ‡ New registration. NQ Not qualified for England.

NQ**ADAMS, Andre** Ryan (Westlake BHS, Auckland), b Mangere, Auckland, New Zealand 17 Jul 1975. 5'9''. RHB, RMF. Auckland 1997-98 to date. Essex 2004-06, scoring 124 on debut (*see below*); cap 2004. Nottinghamshire debut/cap 2007 (Kolpak registration). Herefordshire 2001. **Tests** (NZ): 1 (2001-02); HS 11 and BB 3-44 v E (Auckland) 2001-02. **LOI** (NZ): 42 (2001-02 to 2006-07); HS 45 v P (Rawalpindi) 2001-02; BB 5-22 v I (Queenstown) 2002-03. **IT20** (NZ): 4 (2004-05 to 2005-06); HS 7 v A (Auckland) 2004-05; BB 2-20 v SL (Auckland) 2006-07. HS 124 Ex v Leics (Leicester) 2004 (91 balls, 7 sixes, 13 fours; 100 off 80 balls) on UK debut. Nt HS 84 v Yorks (Scarborough) 2009. 50 wkts (3); most – 68 (2010). BB 7-32 (10-50 match) v Lancs (Manchester) 2012. Hat-trick Ex v Somerset (Taunton) 2005. LO HS 90* North Is Selection XI v Sri Lankans (New Plymouth) 2000-01. LO BB 5-7 Auckland v ND (Auckland) 1999-00. T20 HS 54*. T20 BB 5-20.

BALL, Jacob Timothy ('**Jake**') (Meden CS), b Mansfield 14 Mar 1991. Nephew of B.N.French (Notts and England 1976-95). 6'0''. RHB, RM. Debut (Nottinghamshire) 2011. Nottinghamshire 2nd XI debut 2008. England U19s 2010. HS 4 and BB 3-72 v MCC (Abu Dhabi) 2011 – only f-c match. LO HS 19* v Sri Lanka A (Nottingham) 2011. BB 3-32 v Leics (Nottingham) 2010 (CB40). T20 BB – .

BROAD, Stuart Christopher John (Oakham S), b Nottingham 24 Jun 1986. 6'6''. LHB, RFM. Son of B.C.Broad (Glos, Notts, OFS and England 1979-94). Debut (Leicestershire) 2005; cap 2007. Nottinghamshire debut/cap 2008. YC 2006. *Wisden* 2009. **ECB central contract 2012-13. Tests**: 53 (2007-08 to 2012-13); HS 169 v P (Lord's) 2010, sharing in record Test and UK f-c 8th-wkt partnership of 332 with I.J.L.Trott; BB 7-72 (11-165 match) v WI (Lord's) 2012. Hat-trick v I (Nottingham) 2011. **LOI**: 96 (2006 to 2012-13); HS 45* v I (Manchester) 2007; BB 5-23 v SA (Nottingham) 2008. **IT20**: 46 (2006 to 2012-13, 17 as captain); HS 18* v SA (Chester-le-St) 2012; BB4-24 v NZ (Auckland) 2012-13. F-c Tours: A 2010-11; SA 2009-10; WI 2005-06 (Eng A), 2008-09; NZ 2007-08, 2012-13; I 2008-09, 2012-13; SL 2007-08, 2011-12; B 2006-07 (Eng A), 2009-10; UAE 2011-12 (v P). HS 169 (*see Tests*). Nt HS 91* Le v Derbys (Leicester) 2007. Nt HS 60 v Worcs (Nottingham) 2009. BB 8-52 (11-131 match) v Warwks (Birmingham) 2010. LO HS 45* (*see LOI*). LO BB 5-23 (*see LOI*). T20 HS 18*. T20 BB 4-24.

CARTER, Andrew (Lincoln C), b Lincoln 27 Aug 1988. 6'4". RHB, RM. Debut (Nottinghamshire) 2009. Essex 2010 (on loan). Nottinghamshire 2nd XI debut 2006. Lincolnshire 2007-10. HS 17* v Sussex (Hove) 2012. BB 5-40 Ex v Kent (Canterbury) 2010. Nt BB 4-55 v Warwks (Nottingham) 2012. LO HS 12 v Sussex (Hove) 2009 (P40). LO BB 4-45 v Durham (Nottingham) 2012 (CB40). T20 HS – . T20 BB 4-20.

‡^{NQ}**COWAN, Edward** James McKenzie (Oxford Brookes U), b Paddington, Sydney, Australia 16 Jun 1982. Oxford UCCE 2003. British Us 2003. NSW 2004-05 to 2008-09. Tasmania 2009-10 to date. Gloucestershire 2012; cap 2012. 5'10". LHB, LB. **Tests** (A): 15 (2011-12 to 2012-13); HS 136 v SA (Brisbane) 2012-13. F-c Tours (A): WI 2011-12; I 2012-13. 1000 runs (0+1): 1299 (2011-12). HS 225 Tas v SA (Hobart) 2009-10. UK HS 137* Brit Us v Zimbabweans (Birmingham) 2003. CC HS Gs 103 v Essex (Cheltenham) 2012. BB – . LO HS 131* Tas v NSW (Sydney) 2010-11. T20 HS 70.

FLETCHER, Luke Jack (Henry Mellish S, Nottingham), b Nottingham 18 Sep 1988. 6'6". RHB, RMF. Debut (Nottinghamshire) 2008. Nottinghamshire 2nd XI debut 2007. HS 92 v Hants (Southampton) 2009. BB 5-82 v Lancs (Nottingham) 2011. LO HS 40* v Durham (Chester-le-St) 2009 (P40). LO BB 3-27 v Somerset (Taunton) 2011 (CB40). T20 HS 5. T20 BB 4-30.

FRANKS, Paul John (Southwell Minster CS), b Mansfield 3 Feb 1979. 6'2". LHB, RMF. Debut (Nottinghamshire) 1996; cap 1999; benefit 2007. Canterbury 2002-03. MW Rhinos 2010-11. YC 2000. **LOI**: 1 (2000); HS 4 v WI (Nottingham) 2000. F-c Tours (Eng A): SA 1998-99; WI 2000-01; NZ 1999-00; SL 2004-05; B 1999-00. HS 123* v Leics (Leicester) 2003. 50 wkts (2); most – 63 (1999). BB 7-56 v Middx (Lord's) 2000. Hat-trick v Warwks (Nottingham) 1997. LO HS 84* v Lincs (Lincoln) 2003 (CGT). LO BB 6-27 v Durham (Chester-le-St) 2000 (NL). T20 HS 29*. T20 BB 2-12.

GURNEY, Harry Frederick (Garendon HS; Loughborough GS; Leeds U), b Nottingham 25 Oct 1986. 6'2". RHB, LFM. Leicestershire 2007-11. Nottinghamshire debut 2012. Bradford/Leeds UCCE 2006-07 (not f-c). HS 24* Le v Middx (Leicester) 2009. Nt HS 6 v Somerset (Nottingham) 2012. BB 5-82 Le v Surrey (Leicester) 2009. Nt BB 4-40 v Worcs (Worcester) 2012. LO HS 13* v Durham (Chester-le-St) 2012 (CB40). LO BB 5-24 Le v Hants (Leicester) 2010 (CB40). T20 HS 5*. T20 BB 3-21.

HALES, Alexander Daniel (Chesham S), b Hillingdon, Middx 3 Jan 1989. 6'5". RHB, RM, occ WK. Debut (Nottinghamshire) 2008; cap 2011. Nottinghamshire 2nd XI debut 2007. Buckinghamshire 2006-07. MCC YCs 2006-07. England U19s 2008. **IT20**: 12 (2011 to 2012-13); HS 99 v WI (Nottingham) 2012. 1000 runs (1): 1127 (2011). HS 184 v Somerset (Nottingham) 2011. BB 2-63 v Yorks (Nottingham) 2009. LO HS 150* v Worcs (Nottingham) 2009 (P40). T20 HS 99.

^{NQ}**HUSSEY, David** John (Prendiville Catholic C; Edith Cowan U), b Morley, Perth, Australia 15 Jul 1977. Younger brother of M.E.K.Hussey (WA, Northants, Glos, Durham and Australia 1994-95 to date). 5'11". RHB, OB. Victoria 2002-03 to date. Nottinghamshire debut/cap 2004; scored 107* v Oxford U (Oxford) – on UK debut. **LOI** (A): 69 (2008 to 2012-13); HS 111 v Scotland (Edinburgh) 2009; BB 4-21 v E (Adelaide) 2010-11. **IT20** (A): 39 (2007-08 to 2012-13); HS 88* v SA (Johannesburg) 2008-09; BB 3-25 v SA (Melbourne) 2008-09. F-c Tour (Aus A): P 2007-08. 1000 runs (4+1); most – 1315 (2004). HS 275 v Essex (Nottingham) 2007. Scored 170, 116 and 140 in successive innings 2004. BB 4-105 v Hants (Nottingham) 2005. LO HS 140* Vic v NSW (Sydney) 2012-13. LO BB 4-21 (see LOI). T20 HS 100*. T20 BB 3-25.

HUTTON, Brett Alan (Worksop C), b Doncaster, Yorks 6 Feb 1993. 6'2". RHB, RM. Debut (Nottinghamshire) 2011. Nottinghamshire 2nd XI debut 2010. HS 9 and BB- v MCC (Abu Dhabi) 2011. LO HS 17* and LO BB 1-60 v Sri Lanka A (Nottingham) 2011.

KELSALL, Samuel (Trentham HS, Stoke), b Stoke-on-Trent, Staffs 14 Mar 1993. 5'7". RHB, RM. Debut (Nottinghamshire) 2011. Nottinghamshire 2nd XI debut 2008, aged 15y 158d. HS 35 v Warwks (Nottingham) 2012. LO HS 40 v Sri Lanka A (Nottingham) 2011.

LUMB, Michael John (St Stithians C, Johannesburg), b Johannesburg, South Africa 12 Feb 1980. Son of R.G.Lumb (Yorkshire 1970-84); nephew of A.J.S.Smith (SAU and Natal 1972-73 to 1983-84). 6'0". LHB, RM. Yorkshire 2000-06; ECB qualified and CC debut 2001; cap 2003. Hampshire 2007-11; cap 2008. Nottinghamshire debut/cap 2012. **IT20**: 14 (2009-10 to 2012-13); HS 53* v NZ (Wellington) 2012-13. F-c Tour (Eng A): I 2003-04. 1000 runs (2); most – 1038 (2003). HS 221 v Notts (Nottingham) 2009. Nt HS 171 v Sussex (Nottingham) 2012. BB 2-10 Y v Kent (Canterbury) 2001. LO HS 110 EL v Pakistan A (Dubai) 2009-10. LO BB – . T20 HS 124* H v Essex (Southampton) 2009 – H record. T20 BB 3-32.

MULLANEY, Steven John (St Mary's RC S, Astley), b Warrington, Cheshire 19 Nov 1986. 5'9". RHB, RM. Lancashire 2006-08. No f-c appearances in 2009. Nottinghamshire debut 2010, scoring 100* v Hants (Southampton). HS 165* La v Durham UCCE (Durham) 2007. Nt HS (*see above*). BB 4-31 v Essex (Nottingham) 2010. LO HS 61 v Sri Lanka A (Nottingham) 2011. LO BB 3-13 La v Derbys (Derby) 2007 (FPT). T20 HS 53. T20 BB 4-19.

PATEL, Samit Rohit (Worksop C), b Leicester 30 Nov 1984. Elder brother of A.Patel (Derbyshire and Notts 2007-11). 5'8". RHB, SLA. Debut (Nottinghamshire) 2002; cap 2008. Nottinghamshire 2nd XI debut 1999, aged 14y 274d. **Tests**: 5 (2011-12 to 2012-13); HS 33 v I (Kolkata) 2012-13; BB 2-27 v SL (Galle) 2011-12. **LOI**: 36 (2008 to 2012-13); HS 70* v I (Mohali) 2011-12; BB 5-41 v SA (Oval) 2008. **IT20**: 18 (2011 to 2012-13); HS 67 v SL (Pallekele) 2012-13; BB 2-6 v Afghanistan (Colombo, RPS) 2012-13. F-c Tours: I 2012-13; SL 2011-12; NZ 2008-09 (Eng A). HS 176 v Glos (Nottingham) 2007. BB 7-68 (11-111 match) v Hants (Southampton) 2011. LO HS 114 v Durham (Chester-le-St) 2008 (FPT). LO BB 6-13 v Ireland (Dublin) 2009 (FPT). T20 HS 84*. T20 BB 3-11.

PHILLIPS, Ben James (Langley Park S and SFC, Beckenham), b Lewisham, London 30 Sep 1974. 6'6". RHB, RFM. Kent 1996-98. Northamptonshire 2002-06; cap 2005. Somerset 2008-10, having joined staff in 2007 but missed entire season through injury. Nottinghamshire debut 2011. HS 100* K v Lancs (Manchester) 1997. Nt HS 71 v Yorks (Nottingham) 2011. BB 6-29 Nh v Cambridge UCCE (Cambridge) 2006. CC BB 5-47 K v Sussex (Horsham) 1997. Nt BB 4-33 v Durham (Chester-le-St) 2012. LO HS 51* Sm v Worcs (Bath) 2010 (CB40). LO BB 4-25 K v Northants (Canterbury) 2000 (NL). T20 HS 41*. T20 BB 4-18.

READ, Christopher Mark Wells (Torquay GS; Bath U), b Paignton, Devon 10 Aug 1978. 5'8". RHB, WK. Gloucestershire (l-o only) 1997. Debut 1997-98 for England A in Kenya. Nottinghamshire debut 1998; cap 1999; captain 2008 to date; benefit 2009. MCC 2002. Devon 1995-97. *Wisden* 2010. **Tests**: 15 (1999 to 2006-07); HS 55 v P (Leeds) 2006. Made six dismissals twice in successive innings 2006-07 to establish an Ashes record. **LOI**: 36 (1999-00 to 2006-07); HS 30* v SA (Manchester) 2003. **IT20**: 1 (2006); HS 13 v P (Bristol) 2006. F-c Tours: A 2006-07; SA 1998-99 (Eng A), 1999-00; WI 2000-01 (Eng A), 2003-04, 2005-06 (Eng A); SL 1997-98 (Eng A), 2002-03 (ECB Acad), 2003-04; Z 1998-99 (Eng A); B 2003-04; K 1997-98 (Eng A). 1000 runs (3); most – 1203 (2009). HS 240 v Essex (Chelmsford) 2007. BB – . LO HS 135 v Durham (Nottingham) 2006 (CGT). T20 HS 58*.

‡**SHAHZAD, Ajmal** (Woodhouse Grove S; Bradford U), b Huddersfield, Yorkshire 27 Jul 1985. 6'0". RHB, RFM. Yorkshire 2006-12 (first British-born Asian to play for Yorkshire); cap 2010. Lancashire 2012 (on loan). **Tests:** 1 (2010); HS 5 and BB 3-45 v B (Manchester) 2010. **LOI:** 11 (2009-10 to 2010-11); HS 9 v A (Brisbane) 2010-11; BB 3-41 v B (Bristol) 2010. **IT20:** 3 (2009-10 to 2010-11); HS 0*; BB 2-38 v P (Dubai) 2009-10. F-c Tours: A 2010-11; B 2009-10. HS 88 Y v Sussex (Hove) 2009. BB 5-51 Y v Durham (Chester-le-St) 2010. LO HS 59* Y v Kent (Leeds) 2011 (CB40). LO BB 5-51 Y v Sri Lanka A (Leeds) 2007. T20 HS 20. T20 BB 3-30.

SWANN, Graeme Peter (Sponne S, Towcester), b Northampton 24 Mar 1979. Son of R.Swann (Northumberland 1969-72; Bedfordshire 1988-95); younger brother of A.J.Swann (Northamptonshire and Lancashire 1996-2004). 6'0". RHB, OB. Northamptonshire 1998-2004; cap 1999. Nottinghamshire debut/cap 2005; benefit 2013. MCC 2005. Bedfordshire 1996. *Wisden* 2009. **ECB central contract 2012-13. Tests:** 50 (2008-09 to 2012-13); HS 85 v SA (Centurion) 2009-10; BB 6-65 v P (Birmingham) 2010. **LOI:** 76 (1999-00 to 2012-13); HS 34 v SL (Dambulla) 2007-08; BB 5-28 v A (Chester-le-St) 2009. **IT20:** 39 (2007-08 to 2012-13); HS 34 v SL (Pallekele) 2012-13; BB 3-13 v P (Dubai) 2011-12. F-c Tours: A 2010-11; SA 1998-99 (Eng A), 1999-00, 2009-10; WI 2000-01 (Eng A *part*), 2008-09; NZ 2012-13 (*part*); I 2008-09, 2012-13; SL 2004-05 (Eng A) 2011-12; Z 1998-99 (Eng A); B 2009-10; UAE 2011-12 (v P). HS 183 Nh v Glos (Bristol) 2002 – including 114 before lunch on third day. Nt HS 97 v Essex (Chelmsford) 2007. 50 wkts (1): 57 (1999). BB 7-33 Nh v Derbys (Northampton) 2003. Nt BB 7-100 v Glamorgan (Swansea) 2007. LO HS 83 Nh v Leics (Northampton) 2001 (NL). LO BB 5-17 v Glos (Nottingham) 2007 (P40). T20 HS 90*. T20 BB 3-13.

TAYLOR, James William Arthur (Shrewsbury S), b Nottingham 6 Jan 1990. 5'6". RHB, LB. Leicestershire 2008-11; cap 2009. Nottinghamshire debut/cap 2012. MCC 2010. Shropshire 2007. England U19s 2008 to 2009. YC 2009. **Tests:** 2 (2012); HS 34 v SA (Leeds) 2012. **LOI:** 1 (2011); HS 1 v Ireland (Dublin) 2011. F-c Tour (EL): WI 2010-11. 1000 runs (3); most – 1602 (2011). HS 237 Le v Loughborough MCCU (Leicester) 2011. CC HS 207* Le v Surrey (Oval) 2009. Nt HS 163* v Sussex (Nottingham) 2012. BB – . LO HS 115* v Hants (Southampton) 2012 (CB40). LO BB 4-61 Le v Warwks (Leicester) 2010 (CB40). T20 HS 62*. T20 BB 1-10.

^NQ**WESSELS, Mattheus** Hendrik ('**Riki**') (Woodridge C, Pt Elizabeth; Northampton U), b Marogudoore, Queensland, Australia 12 Nov 1985. Left Australia when 2 months old. Son of K.C.Wessels (OFS, Sussex, WP, NT, Q, EP, GW, Australia and South Africa 1973-74 to 1999-00). 5'11". RHB, WK. MCC 2004. Northamptonshire 2005-09 (Kolpak registration). Nondescripts 2007-08. Mid West Rhinos 2009-10 to 2011-12. Nottinghamshire debut 2011. HS 199 v Sussex (Hove) 2012. BB 1-10 MWR v MT (Bulawayo) 2009-10. LO HS 100 Nh v Surrey (Oval) 2008 (P40). LO BB 1-0 MWR v MT (Bulawayo) 2009-10. T20 HS 86*.

WHITE, Graeme Geoffrey (Stowe S), b Milton Keynes, Bucks 18 Apr 1987. 5'11". RHB, SLA. Northamptonshire 2006-09. Nottinghamshire debut 2010. HS 65 Nh v Glamorgan (Colwyn Bay) 2007. Nt HS 54* v Lancs (Southport) 2011. BB 4-72 v Durham (Nottingham) 2011. LO HS 39* v Somerset (Taunton) 2012 (CB40). LO BB 5-35 v Scotland (Edinburgh) 2010 (CB40). T20 HS 26*. T20 BB 3-22.

WOOD, Samuel Kenneth William (Colonel Frank Seely S, Nottingham), b Nottingham 3 Apr 1993. 5'11". LHB, OB. Debut Nottinghamshire 2011. Nottinghamshire 2nd XI debut 2008, aged 15y 40d. England U19s 2010-11. HS 45 and BB 3-64 v Surrey (Oval) 2012. LO HS 8 and LO BB 2-24 v Lancs (Manchester) 2011 (CB40).

(Having made a County First-Class or List A appearance in 2012)

EDWARDS, Neil James (Cape Cornwall CS; Richard Huish C), b Treliske, Truro, Cornwall 14 Oct 1983. 6'3". LHB, RM. Somerset 2002-08. Nottinghamshire 2010-12. Cornwall 2000-06. 1000 runs (1): 1251 (2007). HS 212 Sm v Loughborough UCCE (Taunton) 2007. Nt HS 195 v Loughborough MCCU (Nottingham) 2012. CC HS 160 Sm v Hants (Taunton) 2003. BB 1-16 Sm v Derbys (Taunton) 2004. LO HS 65 Sm v Yorks (Taunton) 2006 (P40). T20 HS 1.

ELSTONE, Scott Liam (Friary Grange C), b Burton-on-Trent, Staffs 10 Jun 1990. 5'8". RHB, OB. Awaiting f-c debut. Nottinghamshire 2nd XI debut 2006, aged 16y 81d. LO HS 40 v Glamorgan (Nottingham) 2011 (CB40). LO BB 1-22 v Scotland (Nottingham) 2010 (CB40). T20 HS 21*.

PATTINSON, Darren John, b Grimsby, Lincs 2 Aug 1979. Elder brother of J.L.Pattinson (Victoria and Australia 2008-09 to date). 6'1". RHB, RFM. Victoria 2006-07 to date. Nottinghamshire 2008-11, taking 5-22 v Kent (Canterbury) on debut; cap 2008. **Tests**: 1 (2008); HS 13 and BB 2-95 v SA (Leeds) 2008. HS 59 v Durham (Chester-le-St) 2009. BB 8-35 Vic v WA (Perth) 2010-11. Nt BB 6-30 v Lancs (Nottingham) 2008. LO HS 16* Vic v S Australia (Adelaide) 2012-13. LO BB 4-29 v Warwks (Nottingham) 2008. T20 HS 12*. T20 BB 5-25 v Warwks (Birmingham) 2011 – Nt record.

VOGES, A.C. – *see MIDDLESEX.*

K.Turner left the staff without making a County First-Class or List A appearance in 2012.

NOTTINGHAMSHIRE 2012

RESULTS SUMMARY

	Place	Won	Lost	Tied	Drew	NR
LV= County Championship (1st Division)	5th	4	2		10	
All First-Class Matches		4	2		11	
Clydesdale Bank 40 (Group B)	4th	6	5			1
Friends Life t20 (North Group)	QF	5	2			4

LV= COUNTY CHAMPIONSHIP AVERAGES
BATTING AND FIELDING

Cap		M	I	NO	HS	Runs	Avge	100	50	Ct/St
1999	C.M.W.Read	16	24	4	104*	975	48.75	1	8	43/1
	S.J.Mullaney	6	10	1	94	391	43.44	–	4	5
2012	M.J.Lumb	14	23	–	171	910	39.56	3	3	7
	M.H.Wessels	12	19	–	199	733	38.57	2	1	7/1
1999	P.J.Franks	10	17	7	86*	354	35.40	–	3	1
2011	A.D.Hales	15	24	1	155*	797	34.65	2	4	16
2012	J.W.A.Taylor	14	22	3	163*	608	32.00	1	1	8
2008	A.C.Voges	9	12	2	105	313	31.30	1	2	12
2008	S.R.Patel	9	14	2	69	329	27.41	–	2	7
	N.J.Edwards	8	15	1	53	317	22.64	–	1	5
	B.J.Phillips	13	18	4	47	257	18.35	–	–	5
	L.J.Fletcher	8	13	5	42*	93	11.62	–	–	2
2007	A.R.Adams	12	14	–	29	151	10.78	–	–	8
2008	S.C.J.Broad	2	4	1	12	30	10.00	–	–	1
	A.Carter	9	8	4	17*	32	8.00	–	–	2
	G.G.White	5	9	–	14	60	6.66	–	–	2
2005	G.P.Swann	3	5	–	12	23	4.60	–	–	1
	H.F.Gurney	10	9	1	6	10	1.25	–	–	–

Also played (1 match each): S.Kelsall 0, 35; S.K.W.Wood 45, 2.

BOWLING

	O	M	R	W	Avge	Best	5wI	10wM
G.P.Swann	87.2	21	188	10	18.80	3-26	–	–
A.R.Adams	344.3	63	1035	54	19.16	7-32	4	1
B.J.Phillips	328.3	97	813	30	27.10	4-33	–	–
L.J.Fletcher	247.5	70	671	24	27.95	4-53	–	–
H.F.Gurney	234.3	52	713	21	33.95	4-40	–	–
A.Carter	251.2	40	900	25	36.00	4-55	–	–
S.R.Patel	164.4	30	536	14	38.28	4-67	–	–
P.J.Franks	187.5	27	618	16	38.62	4-47	–	–
G.G.White	144.1	26	519	13	39.92	4-97	–	–

Also bowled: S.C.J.Broad 62-8-225-4; M.J.Lumb 2-0-13-0; S.J.Mullaney 16-2-41-0; J.W.A.Taylor 2-0-16-0; A.C.Voges 7-2-6-1; M.H.Wessels 15-3-43-1; S.K.W.Wood 28-2-84-3.

The First-Class Averages (pp 219–235) give the records of Nottinghamshire players in all first-class county matches (Nottinghamshire's other opponents being Loughborough MCCU), with the exception of S.C.J.Broad, S.R.Patel and G.P.Swann, whose first-class figures for Nottinghamshire are as above, and:
J.W.A.Taylor 15-24-4-163*-709-35.45-2-1-8ct. 2-0-16-0.

NOTTINGHAMSHIRE RECORDS

FIRST-CLASS CRICKET

Highest Total	For 791		v	Essex	Chelmsford	2007
	V 781-7d		by	Northants	Northampton	1995
Lowest Total	For 13		v	Yorkshire	Nottingham	1901
	V 16		by	Derbyshire	Nottingham	1879
	16		by	Surrey	The Oval	1880
Highest Innings	For 312*	W.W.Keeton	v	Middlesex	The Oval	1939
	V 345	C.G.Macartney	for	Australians	Nottingham	1921

Highest Partnership for each Wicket

1st	406*	D.J.Bicknell/G.E.Welton	v	Warwicks	Birmingham	2000
2nd	398	A.Shrewsbury/W.Gunn	v	Sussex	Nottingham	1890
3rd	367	W.Gunn/J.R.Gunn	v	Leics	Nottingham	1903
4th	361	A.O.Jones/J.R.Gunn	v	Essex	Leyton	1905
5th	359	D.J.Hussey/C.M.W.Read	v	Essex	Nottingham	2007
6th	372*	K.P.Pietersen/J.E.Morris	v	Derbyshire	Derby	2001
7th	301	C.C.Lewis/B.N.French	v	Durham	Chester-le-St[2]	1993
8th	220	G.F.H.Heane/R.Winrow	v	Somerset	Nottingham	1935
9th	170	J.C.Adams/K.P.Evans	v	Somerset	Taunton	1994
10th	152	E.B.Alletson/W.Riley	v	Sussex	Hove	1911
	152	U.Afzaal/A.J.Harris	v	Worcs	Nottingham	2000

Best Bowling	For	10-66	K.Smales	v	Glos	Stroud	1956
(Innings)	V	10-10	H.Verity	for	Yorkshire	Leeds	1932
Best Bowling	For	17-89	F.C.L.Matthews	v	Northants	Nottingham	1923
(Match)	V	17-89	W.G.Grace	for	Glos	Cheltenham	1877

Most Runs – Season	2620	W.W.Whysall	(av 53.46)	1929
Most Runs – Career	31592	G.Gunn	(av 35.69)	1902-32
Most 100s – Season	9	W.W.Whysall		1928
	9	M.J.Harris		1971
	9	B.C.Broad		1990
Most 100s – Career	65	J.Hardstaff jr		1930-55
Most Wkts – Season	181	B.Dooland	(av 14.96)	1954
Most Wkts – Career	1653	T.G.Wass	(av 20.34)	1896-1920
Most Career W-K Dismissals	957	T.W.Oates	(733 ct; 224 st)	1897-1925
Most Career Catches in the Field	466	A.O.Jones		1892-1914

LIMITED-OVERS CRICKET

Highest Total	50ov	346-9		v	Ireland	Nottingham	2009
	40ov	294-8		v	Durham	Nottingham	2012
	T20	215-6		v	Yorkshire	Nottingham	2011
Lowest Total	50ov	123		v	Yorkshire	Scarborough	1969
	40ov	57		v	Glos	Nottingham	2009
	T20	91		v	Lancashire	Manchester	2006
Highest Innings	50ov	149*	D.W.Randall	v	Devon	Torquay	1988
	40ov	167*	P.Johnson	v	Kent	Nottingham	1993
	T20	91	M.A.Ealham	v	Yorkshire	Nottingham	2004
Best Bowling	50ov	6-10	K.P.Evans	v	Northumb	Jesmond	1994
	40ov	6-12	R.J.Hadlee	v	Lancashire	Nottingham	1980
	T20	5-25	D.J.Pattinson	v	Warwicks	Birmingham	2011

SOMERSET

Formation of Present Club: 18 August 1875
Inaugural First-Class Match: 1882
Colours: Black, White and Maroon
Badge: Somerset Dragon
County Champions: (0); best – 2nd (Div 1) 2001, 2010, 2012
Gillette/NatWest/C&G/FP Trophy Winners: (3) 1979, 1983, 2001
Benson and Hedges Cup Winners: (2) 1981, 1982
Pro 40/National League (Div 1) Winners: (0); best – 4th 2001
Sunday League Winners: (1) 1979
Clydesdale Bank 40 Winners: (0); best – Finalist 2010, 2011
Twenty20 Cup Winners: (1) 2005

Chief Executive: Guy Lavender, County Ground, Taunton TA1 1JT • Tel: 0845 337 1875 • Fax: 01823 332395 • Email: enquiries@somersetcountycc.co.uk • Web: www.somerset-cricketclub.co.uk

Director of Cricket: Dave Nosworthy. **Head Coach**: Andy Hurry. **Captain**: M.E.Trescothick. **Vice-Captain**: A.C.Thomas. **Overseas Players**: Abdur Rehman and A.N.Petersen. **2013 Beneficiary**: A.V.Suppiah. **Groundsman**: Simon Lee. **Scorer**: Gerald A.Stickley. ‡ New registration. ^{NQ} Not qualified for England.

ABDUR REHMAN, b Sialkot, Pakistan 1 Mar 1980. LHB, SLA. Gujranwala 1997-98 to 2001-02. Habib Bank 1999-00 to date. Sialkot 2003-04 to date. Somerset debut 2012. **Tests** (P): 17 (2007-08 to 2012); HS 60 v SA (Abu Dhabi) 2010-11; BB 6-25 v E (Abu Dhabi) 2011-12. **LOI** (P): 25 (2006-07 to 2012); HS 31 v SA (Multan) 2007-08; BB 2-20 v WI (Faisalabad) 2006-07. **IT20** (P): 7 (2006-07 to 2010-11); HS 7 v WI (Gros Islet) 2010-11; BB 2-7 v Kenya (Nairobi) 2007. F-c Tours (P): E 2010; A 2006 (Pak A), 2009 (Pak A); WI 2011; NZ 2010-11; SL 2009 (Pak A), 2012; B 2011-12; UAE 2010-11 (v SA), 2011-12 (v SL and E). HS 96 HB v NBP (Multan) 2005-06. Sm HS 17 v Notts (Taunton) 2012. BB 9-65 (14-101 match) v Worcs (Taunton) 2012. LO HS 50 HB v KRL (Rawalpindi) 2007-08. LO BB 6-16 v Notts (Taunton) 2012 (CB40) — Sm record. T20 HS 21. T20 BB 3-17.

BARROW, Alexander William Rodgerson (King's C, Taunton), b Frome 6 May 1992. 5'7". RHB, RM/OB. Debut (Somerset) 2011. Somerset 2nd XI debut 2009. HS 69 v Yorks (Leeds) 2011. BB 1-4 v Hants (Southampton) 2011. LO HS 72 v Durham (Chester-le-St) 2012 (CB40).

BUTTLER, Joseph Charles (King's C, Taunton), b Taunton 8 Sep 1990. 6'0". RHB, WK. Debut (Somerset) 2009. Somerset 2nd XI debut 2006. **LOI**: 6 (2011-12 to 2012-13); HS 21 v NZ (Hamilton) 2012-13. **IT20**: 21 (2011 to 2012-13); HS 54 v NZ (Hamilton) 2012-13. HS 144 v Hants (Southampton) 2010. LO HS 119 EL v Sri Lanka A (Kurunegala) 2011-12. T20 HS 72*.

COMPTON, Nicholas Richard Denis (Harrow S; Durham U), b Durban, South Africa 26 Jun 1983. Son of R.Compton (Natal 1978-79 to 1980-81). Grandson of D.C.S.Compton (Middlesex, England, Holkar, Europeans, Commonwealth and Cavaliers 1936-64); great-nephew of L.H.Compton (Middlesex 1938-56). 6'1". RHB, OB. Middlesex 2004-09; cap 2006. Somerset debut 2010; cap 2011. Mashonaland Eagles 2010-11. PCA 2012. MCC 2007. **Tests**: 5 (2012-13); HS 117 v NZ (Dunedin) 2012-13. F-c Tours: NZ 2012-13; I 2012-13; B 2006-07 (Eng A). 1000 runs (3); most – 1494 (2012). Scored 685 runs in April 2012 – a record for April. HS 254* v Durham (Chester-le-St) 2011. BB 1-1 v Hants (Southampton) 2010. LO HS 131 M v Kent (Canterbury) 2009 (FPT). LO BB 1-0 M v Scotland (Lord's) 2009 (FPT). T20 HS 74.

DIBBLE, Adam John (Taunton S), b Exeter, Devon 9 Mar 1991. 6'4". RHB, RMF. Debut (Somerset) 2011. Missed most of 2012 through injury. Somerset 2nd XI debut 2009. Devon 2009. HS 43 and BB 3-42 v Warwks (Birmingham) 2012. LO HS – . LO BB 3-52 v Glos (Taunton) 2011 (CB40). T20 HS – . T20 BB 1-20.

DOCKRELL, George Henry (Gonzaga C, Dublin), b Dublin, Ireland 22 Jul 1992. 6'3". RHB, SLA. Ireland 2010 to date. Somerset debut 2011. **LOI** (Ire): 30 (2009-10 to 2012); HS 19 v WI (Mohali) 2010-11; BB 4-35 v Netherlands (Amstelveen) 2010. **IT20** (Ire): 19 (2009-10 to 2012-13); HS 2* v Kenya (Mombasa) 2011-12; BB 4-20 v Netherlands (Dubai) 2009-10. HS 53 Ire v Namibia (Belfast) 2011. Sm HS 14 v Notts (Taunton) 2011. BB 6-27 v Middx (Taunton) 2012. LO HS 22* Ire v Namibia (Belfast) 2011. LO BB 4-35 (*see LOI*). T20 HS 2*. T20 BB 4-20.

GREGORY, Lewis (Hele's S, Plympton), b Plymouth, Devon 24 May 1992. 6'0". RHB, RMF. Debut (Somerset) 2011. Somerset 2nd XI debut 2008, aged 16y and 87d. Devon 2008. England U19s 2010 to 2010-11. HS 48 v Warwks (Birmingham) 2011. BB 2-22 v Notts (Taunton) 2012. LO HS 39 v Glamorgan (Taunton) 2012 (CB40). LO BB 4-27 v Glos (Taunton) 2011 (CB40). T20 HS 22. T20 BB 4-15.

HILDRETH, James Charles (Millfield S), b Milton Keynes, Bucks 9 Sep 1984. 5'10", RHB, RMF. Debut (Somerset) 2003; cap 2007. F-c Tour (EL): WI 2010-11. 1000 runs (3); most – 1440 (2010). HS 303* v Warwks (Taunton) 2009. BB 2-39 v Hants (Taunton) 2004. LO HS 151 v Scotland (Taunton) 2009 (FPT). LO BB 2-26 v Worcs (Worcester) 2008 (FPT). T20 HS 107*. T20 BB 3-24.

HUSSAIN, Gemaal Maqsood (Top Valley CS, Nottingham; High Pavement SFC, Nottingham), b Whipps Cross, London, 10 Oct 1983. 6'5". RHB, RMF. Gloucestershire 2009-10; cap 2009. Somerset debut 2011. Bradford/Leeds UCCE 2003 (not f-c). HS 42 v Lancs (Liverpool) 2011. 50 wkts (1): 67 (2010). BB 6-33 v Worcs (Taunton) 2011. LO HS 18* v Hants (Southampton) 2012 (CB40). BB 2-17 Gs v Notts (Nottingham) 2009 (P40). T20 HS 8. T20 BB 3-22.

JONES, Chris Robert (Poole GS; Richard Huish C, Taunton; Grey C, Durham U), b Harold Wood, Essex 5 Nov 1990. 6'3". RHB, RM. Debut (Somerset) 2010. Durham MCCU 2011-12. Somerset 2nd XI debut 2006, aged 15y 290d. Dorset 2008-11. HS 69 DU v Yorks (Durham) 2011. Sm HS 55 v Notts (Nottingham) 2011. BB 1-17 v Surrey (Taunton) 2012. LO HS 45* v Essex (Taunton) 2011 (CB40). T20 HS 16.

KIESWETTER, Craig (Diocesan C; Millfield S), b Johannesburg, South Africa 18 Nov 1987. 6'1". RHB, WK. Debut (Somerset) 2007; cap 2009. Represented South Africa in U19 World Cup 2006. Qualified for England Feb 2010. **LOI**: 46 (2009-10 to 2012-13); HS 107 v B (Chittagong) 2009-10. **IT20**: 25 (2009-10 to 2012-13); HS 63 v A (Bridgetown) 2009-10. F-c Tour (EL): WI 2010-11. 1000 runs (1): 1242 (2009). HS 164 v Notts (Nottingham) 2011. LO HS 143 England XI v Bangladesh CB (Fatullah) 2009-10. T20 HS 84.

KIRBY, Steven Paul (Elton HS; Bury C), b Ainsworth, nr Bolton, Lancs 4 Oct 1977. 6'3½". RHB, RFM. Leicestershire staff 1998 – no f-c appearances. Yorkshire 2001-04, debut as sub for M.J.Hoggard (England duty) taking 7-50; cap 2003. Gloucestershire 2005-10; cap 2005. Somerset debut 2011. MCC 2008, 2010-11. F-c Tour (Eng A): I 2003-04 (*part*). HS 57 Y v Hants (Leeds) 2002. Sm HS 19 v Durham (Taunton) 2011. 50 wkts (3); most – 67 (2003). BB 8-80 (13-154 match) Y v Somerset (Taunton) 2003. Sm BB 6-115 v Lancs (Liverpool) 2011. LO HS 15 Y v Leics (Leicester) 2003 (NL). LO BB 5-36 Gs v Middx (Lord's) 2007 (FPT). T20 HS 25. T20 BB 3-17.

LEACH, Matthew Jack (Bishop Fox's Community S, Taunton; Richard Huish C; UWIC), b Taunton 22 Jun 1991. 6'0". LHB, SLA. Debut (Cardiff MCCU) 2012. Somerset debut 2012. Somerset 2nd XI debut 2009. Dorset 2011. HS 0*. BB 2-37 v Lancs (Liverpool) 2012. LO HS 2 v Hants (Southampton) 2012 (CB40). LO BB 1-30 v Scotland (Uddingston) 2012 (CB40).

MESCHEDE, Craig Anthony Joseph (King's C, Taunton), b Johannesburg, South Africa 21 Nov 1991. 6'1". RHB, RMF. Debut (Somerset) 2011. Somerset 2nd XI debut 2008, aged 16y 244d. HS 62 and BB 3-26 v Durham (Chester-le-St) 2012. LO HS 33 v Notts (Nottingham) 2012 (CB40). LO BB 4-27 v Scotland (Taunton) 2012 (CB40). T20 HS 53. T20 BB 3-9.

OVERTON, Craig (West Buckland S), b Barnstaple, Devon 10 Apr 1994. 6'5". RHB, RMF. Debut (Somerset) 2012. Somerset 2nd XI debut 2011. Devon 2010-11. HS 50 v Durham (Taunton) 2012. BB 4-38 v Durham (Chester-le-St) 2012. LO HS 20 v Hants (Taunton) 2012 (CB40). LO BB 2-30 EL v Australia A (Melbourne) 2012-13.

OVERTON, Jamie (West Buckland S), b Barnstaple, Devon 10 Apr 1994. 6'5". RHB, RFM. Debut (Somerset) 2012. Somerset 2nd XI debut 2011. Devon 2011. HS 34* v Surrey (Oval) 2012. BB 2-61 v Durham (Taunton) 2012. LO HS 10 v Scotland (Taunton) 2012 (CB40). LO BB 4-42 v Durham (Chester-le-St) 2012 (CB40).

‡NOPETERSEN, Alviro** Nathan, b Port Elizabeth, South Africa 25 November 1980. RHB, RM/OB. Northerns 2000-01 to 2005-06. Titans 2004-05 to 2005-06. Lions 2005-06 to date. North West 2008-09. Glamorgan 2011; cap/captain 2011. Essex 2012. **Tests** (SA): 24 (2009-10 to 2012-13); HS 182 v E (Leeds) 2012; scored 100 v I (Kolkata) on debut; BB 1-2 v WI (Port-of-Spain) 2010. **LOI** (SA): 17 (2006-07 to 2011-12); HS 80 v Z (Potchefstroom) 2006-07; BB – . **IT20** (SA): 2 (2010); HS 8 v WI (North Sound) 2010. F-c Tours (SA): E 2012; A 2012-13; WI 2010; NZ 2011-12; I 2007-08 (SA A), 2009-10; Z 2007 (SA A); B 2010 (SA A); UAE (v P) 2010-11. 1000 runs (1+2); most – 1376 (2008-09). HS 210 Gm v Surrey (Oval) 2011. BB 2-7 Northerns v Easterns (Benoni) 2001-02. CC BB 1-37 Gm v Glos (Cardiff) 2011. LO HS 145* Lions v Dolphins (Potchefstroom) 2011-12. LO BB 2-48 Lions v Cape Cobras (Johannesburg) 2011-12. T20 HS 84*. T20 BB 1-5.

REGAN, James Alan (All Hallows Catholic S; Farnborough SFC), b Frimley, Surrey 30 May 1994. RHB, WK. Debut (Somerset) 2012, without batting or bowling. Somerset 2nd XI debut 2010, aged 16y 81d.

NOSUPPIAH, Arul** Vivasvan (Millfield S; Exeter U), b Kuala Lumpur, Malaysia 30 Aug 1983. Son of R.Suppiah (Kuala Lumpur). Brother of R.V.Suppiah (Malaysia 1997-98 to 2006; f-c 2004). 6'0". RHB, SLA. Debut (Somerset) 2002; cap 2009; benefit 2013. Malaysia 2000-01 to 2005 (not f-c). Devon 2003-05. 1000 runs (1): 1201 (2009). HS 156 v Indians (Taunton) 2011. CC HS 151 v Notts (Taunton) 2009. BB 3-46 v West Indies A (Taunton) 2002. CC BB 3-58 v Hants (Taunton) 2009. LO HS 80 v Lancs (Manchester) 2010 (CB40). LO BB 4-39 v Surrey (Oval) 2006 (CGT). T20 HS 32*. T20 BB 6-5 v Glamorgan (Cardiff) 2011 – world record T20 analysis.

NOTHOMAS, Alfonso** Clive (Ravensmead SS; Parow HS), b Cape Town, South Africa 9 Feb 1977. 5'10". RHB, RFM. W Province 1998-99. North West 2000-01 to 2002-03. Northerns 2003-04 to 2005-06. Titans 2004-05 to 2007-08. Warwickshire 2007. Somerset debut 2008; cap 2008 (Kolpak registration). **IT20** (SA): 1 (2006-07); HS-and BB 3-25 v P (Johannesburg) 2006-07. F-c Tour (SA A): Z 2004. HS 119* North West v Northerns (Pretoria) 2002-03. UK HS 94 v Hants (Taunton) 2011. BB 7-54 Titans v Cape Cobras (Cape Town) 2005-06. UK BB 6-60 (10-88 match) v Sussex (Taunton) 2011 and 6-60 v Warwks (Taunton) 2012. LO HS 28* v Scotland (Edinburgh) 2009 (FPT). LO BB 4-18 v Glos (Bristol) 2009 (P40). T20 HS 30*. T20 BB 4-8.

TREGO, Peter David (Wyvern CS, W-s-M), b Weston-super-Mare 12 Jun 1981. 6'0". RHB, RMF. Somerset 2000-02, 2006 to date; cap 2007. Kent 2003. Middlesex 2005. Herefordshire 2005. HS 140 v West Indies A (Taunton) 2002. CC HS 135 v Derbys (Taunton) 2006. 50 wkts (1): 50 (2012). BB 6-59 M v Notts (Nottingham) 2005. Sm BB 5-53 v Notts (Nottingham) 2012. LO HS 147 v Glamorgan (Taunton) 2010 (CB40). LO BB 5-40 EL v West Indies A (Worcester) 2010. T20 HS 79. T20 BB 4-27.

TRESCOTHICK, Marcus Edward (Sir Bernard Lovell S), b Keynsham 25 Dec 1975. 6'2". LHB, RM, occ WK. Debut (Somerset) 1993; cap 1999; joint captain 2002; benefit 2008; captain 2010 to date. PCA 2000, 2009, 2011. *Wisden* 2004. MBE 2005. **Tests:** 76 (2000 to 2006, 2 as captain); HS 219 v SA (Oval) 2003; BB 1-34 v P (Karachi) 2000-01. **LOI:** 123 (2000 to 2006, 10 as captain); HS 137 v P (Lord's) 2001; BB 2-7 v Z (Manchester) 2000. **IT20:** 3 (2005 to 2006); HS 72 v SL (Southampton) 2006. F-c Tours: A 2002-03; SA 2004-05; WI 2003-04; NZ 1999-00 (Eng A), 2001-02; I 2001-02, 2005-06 (*part*); P 2000-01, 2005-06; SL 2000-01, 2003-04; B 1999-00 (Eng A), 2003-04. 1000 runs (5); most – 1817 (2009). HS 284 v Northants (Northampton) 2007. BB 4-36 (inc hat-trick) v Young A (Taunton) 1995. CC BB 4-82 v Yorks (Leeds) 1998. Hat-trick 1995 (*see above*). LO HS 184 v Glos (Taunton) 2008 (P40) – Sm record. LO BB 4-50 v Northants (Northampton) 2000 (NL). T20 HS 108*.

WALLER, Maximilian Thomas Charles (Millfield S; Bournemouth U), b Salisbury, Wiltshire 3 March 1988. 6'0". RHB, LB. Debut (Somerset) 2009. Somerset 2nd XI debut 2006. Dorset 2007-08. HS 28 v Hants (Southampton) 2009. BB 3-33 v Cardiff MCCU (Taunton Vale) 2012. CC BB 2-27 v Sussex (Hove) 2009. LO HS 13 v Durham (Chester-le-St) 2012 (CB40). LO BB 2-24 v Unicorns (Exmouth) 2010 (CB40). T20 HS 3. T20 BB 4-16.

RELEASED/RETIRED

(Having made a County First-Class or List A appearance in 2012)

BURKE, James Edward (Plymouth C), b Plymouth, Devon 25 Jan 1991. 6'3". RHB, RMF. Somerset 2012. Somerset 2nd XI debut 2008. Devon 2008-12. HS – . BB 2-51 v Cardiff MCCU (Taunton) 2012 – only 1st XI appearance.

MUTCH, Robert Grant, b 3 Sep 1984. LHB, LMF. Easterns 2005-06 to 2008-09. Played one l-o match for Somerset in 2012. HS 34* Easterns v Gauteng (Benoni) 2005-06. BB 4-49 Easterns v Gauteng (Johannesburg) 2008-09. LO HS – . LO BB 4-28 Easterns v Gauteng (Johannesburg) 2008-09.

NQPHILANDER, Vernon Darryl, b Bellville, Cape Province, South Africa 24 Jun 1985. RHB, RMF. Western Province 2003-04 to 2009-10. WP Boland 2004-05. Cape Cobras 2005-06 to date. Middlesex 2008. Somerset 2012. Devon 2004. **Tests** (SA): 16 (2011-12 to 2012-13); HS 74 v P (Centurion) 2012-13; BB 6-44 (10-114 match) v NZ (Hamilton) 2011-12. **LOI** (SA): 8 (2007 to 2011-12); HS 23 v E (Leeds) 2008; BB 4-12 v Ireland (Belfast) 2007 – on debut. **IT20** (SA): 7 (2007-08); HS 6 v E (Cape Town) 2007-08; BB 2-23 v B (Cape Town) 2007-08. F-c Tours: A 2012; A 2012-13; NZ 2011-12; SL 2010 (SA A); B 2010 (SA A). HS 168 WP v GW (Kimberley) 2004-05. UK HS 61 and UK BB 5-30 SA v E (Lord's) 2012. CC HS 38 v Warwks (Birmingham) 2012. 50 wkts (0+2); most – 59 (2009-10). BB 7-61 Cape Cobras v Knights (Cape Town) 2011-12. CC BB 5-43 v Middx (Taunton) 2012. LO HS 79* SA A v Bangladesh A (East London) 2010-11. LO BB 4-12 (*see LOI*). T20 HS 56*. T20 BB 5-17.

SNELL, Stephen David (Sandown HS), b Winchester, Hampshire 27 Feb 1983. 6'0". RHB, WK. Gloucestershire 2005-10; cap 2005. Somerset 2012. MCC YC 2002-04. HS 127 Gs v Worcs (Worcester) 2008. Sm HS 10 v Worcs (Taunton) 2012. LO HS 95 v Middx (Cheltenham) 2010 (CB40). T20 HS 50.

SUTTON, Andrew Peter (Hanley Castle HS; Worcester TC), b Cheltenham, Glos 29 Nov 1985. RHB, RMF. Somerset 2012. Herefordshire 2004-09. Wiltshire 2010. MCC YC 2005-07. BB 1-31 v Cardiff MCCU (Taunton Vale) 2012 – only 1st XI appearance.

J.A.Morkel and K.J.O'Brien left the staff, without making a County First-Class or List A appearance in 2012.

SOMERSET 2012
RESULTS SUMMARY

	Place	Won	Lost	Tied	Drew	NR
LV= County Championship (1st Division)	2nd	5	1		10	
All First-Class Matches		5	1		11	
Clydesdale Bank 40 (Group B)	3rd	6	4			2
Friends Life t20 (Mid/Wales/West Group)	SF	6	3			3

LV= COUNTY CHAMPIONSHIP AVERAGES
BATTING AND FIELDING

Cap		M	I	NO	HS	Runs	Avge	100	50	Ct/St
2011	N.R.D.Compton	11	18	6	204*	1191	99.25	4	7	7
2009	C.Kieswetter	11	17	4	152	654	50.30	1	2	29/1
2007	J.C.Hildreth	16	25	3	120	946	43.00	3	5	16
1999	M.E.Trescothick	9	13	–	146	506	38.92	2	1	26
2007	P.D.Trego	16	21	3	92	600	33.33	–	4	12
2009	A.V.Suppiah	16	25	–	124	728	29.12	2	5	9
	J.Overton	3	4	2	34*	55	27.50	–	–	1
	J.C.Buttler	12	16	1	93	400	26.66	–	2	12/1
	C.A.J.Meschede	6	6	–	62	135	22.50	–	1	2
	C.R.Jones	5	7	–	50	150	21.42	–	1	2
	G.M.Hussain	5	7	4	29	55	18.33	–	–	
	A.W.R.Barrow	9	15	–	47	186	12.40	–	–	14
	C.Overton	7	8	1	50	75	10.71	–	1	4
	V.D.Philander	5	6	–	38	62	10.33	–	–	2
	L.Gregory	4	4	–	18	40	10.00	–	–	
2008	A.C.Thomas	9	11	1	39*	96	9.60	–	–	5
	G.H.Dockrell	10	10	4	13*	54	9.00	–	–	5
	Abdur Rehman	4	5	–	17	43	8.60	–	–	2
	S.I.Mahmood	3	4	1	13	25	8.33	–	–	1
	S.P.Kirby	9	11	5	6*	20	3.33	–	–	3

Also batted: A.J.Dibble (1 match) 1, 43; M.J.Leach (2) 0*; S.D.Snell (2) 8, 10 (8 ct); M.T.C.Waller (2) 4, 17, 3 (4 ct).

BOWLING

	O	M	R	W	Avge	Best	5wI	10wM
Abdur Rehman	174	50	383	27	14.18	9-65	3	1
V.D.Philander	181.1	42	491	23	21.34	5-43	2	
A.C.Thomas	252.4	50	740	33	22.42	6-60	2	
G.H.Dockrell	309.5	67	950	34	27.94	6-27	1	
G.M.Hussain	92.4	17	353	12	29.41	5-48	1	
C.Overton	113.1	23	363	12	30.25	4-38	–	
S.P.Kirby	225.1	47	735	24	30.62	3-34	–	
P.D.Trego	508.5	123	1554	50	31.08	5-53	–	
C.A.J.Meschede	98	18	350	10	35.00	3-26	–	

Also bowled:

	O	M	R	W	Avge	Best	5wI	10wM
S.I.Mahmood	66.1	10	241	8	30.12	4-62		
J.Overton	66	7	229	6	38.16	2-61		

J.C.Buttler 2-0-11-0; A.J.Dibble 13-2-42-3; L.Gregory 24-2-127-4; J.C.Hildreth 2-0-30-0; C.R.Jones 2-0-17-1; C.Kieswetter 3-0-3-2; M.J.Leach 20-4-43-2; A.V.Suppiah 73-18-211-3; M.T.C.Waller 19-2-81-3.

The First-Class Averages (pp 219–235) give the records of Somerset players in all first-class county matches (Somerset's other opponents being Cardiff MCCU), with the exception of C.R.Jones, C.Kieswetter, M.J.Leach, S.I.Mahmood and V.D.Philander, whose first-class figures for Somerset are as above, and:
N.R.D.Compton 12-19-6-236-1427-109.76-5-7-8ct.

SOMERSET RECORDS

FIRST-CLASS CRICKET

Highest Total	For 850-7d		v	Middlesex	Taunton	2007
	V 811		by	Surrey	The Oval	1899
Lowest Total	For 25		v	Glos	Bristol	1947
	V 22		by	Glos	Bristol	1920
Highest Innings	For 342	J.L.Langer	v	Surrey	Guildford	2006
	V 424	A.C.MacLaren	for	Lancashire	Taunton	1895

Highest Partnership for each Wicket

1st	346	L.C.H.Palairet/ H.T.Hewett	v	Yorkshire	Taunton	1892
2nd	450	N.R.D.Compton/J.C.Hildreth	v	Cardiff MCCU	Taunton Vale	2012
3rd	319	P.M.Roebuck/M.D.Crowe	v	Leics	Taunton	1984
4th	310	P.W.Denning/I.T.Botham	v	Glos	Taunton	1980
5th	320	J.D.Francis/I.D.Blackwell	v	Durham UCCE	Taunton	2005
6th	265	W.E.Alley/K.E.Palmer	v	Northants	Northampton	1961
7th	279	R.J.Harden/G.D.Rose	v	Sussex	Taunton	1997
8th	172	I.V.A.Richards/I.T.Botham	v	Leics	Leicester	1983
	172	A.R.K.Pierson/P.S.Jones	v	N Zealanders	Taunton	1999
9th	183	C.H.M.Greetham/H.W.Stephenson	v	Leics	Weston-s-Mare	1963
	183	C.J.Tavaré/N.A.Mallender	v	Sussex	Hove	1990
10th	163	I.D.Blackwell/N.A.M.McLean	v	Derbyshire	Taunton	2003

Best Bowling	For 10- 49	E.J.Tyler	v	Surrey	Taunton	1895
(Innings)	V 10- 35	A.Drake	for	Yorkshire	Weston-s-Mare	1914
Best Bowling	For 16- 83	J.C.White	v	Worcs	Bath	1919
(Match)	V 17-137	W.Brearley	for	Lancashire	Manchester	1905

Most Runs – Season	2761	W.E.Alley	(av 58.74)		1961
Most Runs – Career	21142	H.Gimblett	(av 36.96)		1935-54
Most 100s – Season	11	S.J.Cook			1991
Most 100s – Career	49	H.Gimblett			1935-54
Most Wkts – Season	169	A.W.Wellard	(av 19.24)		1938
Most Wkts – Career	2165	J.C.White	(av 18.03)		1909-37
Most Career W-K Dismissals	1007	H.W.Stephenson	(698 ct; 309 st)		1948-64
Most Career Catches in the Field	381	J.C.White			1909-37

LIMITED-OVERS CRICKET

Highest Total	50ov	413-4	v	Devon	Torquay	1990
	40ov	377-9	v	Sussex	Hove	2003
	T20	250-3	v	Glos	Taunton	2006
Lowest Total	50ov	58	v	Middlesex	Southgate	2000
	40ov	58	v	Essex	Chelmsford	1977
	T20	82	v	Kent	Taunton	2010
Highest Innings	50ov	162*	C.J.Tavaré	v	Devon	Torquay	1990
	40ov	184	M.E.Trescothick	v	Glos	Taunton	2008
	T20	141*	C.L.White	v	Worcs	Worcester	2006
Best Bowling	50ov	8-66	S.R.G.Francis	v	Derbyshire	Derby	2004
	40ov	6-16	Abdur Rehman	v	Notts	Taunton	2012
	T20	6- 5	A.V.Suppiah	v	Glamorgan	Cardiff	2011

SURREY

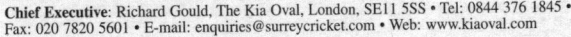

Formation of Present Club: 22 August 1845
Inaugural First-Class Match: 1864
Colours: Chocolate
Badge: Prince of Wales' Feathers
County Champions (since 1890): (18) 1890, 1891, 1892, 1894, 1895, 1899, 1914, 1952, 1953, 1954, 1955, 1956, 1957, 1958, 1971, 1999, 2000, 2002
Joint Champions: (1) 1950
Gillette/NatWest/C&G/FP Trophy Winners: (1) 1982
Benson and Hedges Cup Winners: (3) 1974, 1997, 2001
Pro 40/National League (Div 1) Winners: (1) 2003
Sunday League Winners: (1) 1996
Clydesdale Bank 40 Winners: (1) 2011
Twenty20 Cup Winners: (1) 2003

Chief Executive: Richard Gould, The Kia Oval, London, SE11 5SS • Tel: 0844 376 1845 • Fax: 020 7820 5601 • E-mail: enquiries@surreycricket.com • Web: www.kiaoval.com

Team Director: Chris Adams. **First XI Coach**: Ian Salisbury. **Captain**: G.C.Smith. **Vice-Captain**: tba. **Overseas Players**: R.T.Ponting and G.C.Smith. **2013 Beneficiary**: none. **Head Groundsman**: Lee Fortiss. **Scorer**: Keith R.Booth. ‡ New registration. NQ Not qualified for England.

ANSARI, Zafar Shahaan (Hampton S; Cambridge U), b Ascot, Berks 10 Dec 1991. Younger brother of A.S.Ansari (Cambridge U 2008-12). 5'11". LHB, SLA. Cambridge MCCU 2011-12. Surrey debut 2011. Surrey 2nd XI debut 2008, aged 16y 133d. Summer contract. HS 83* v Warwks (Birmingham) 2012. BB 5-33 CU v Surrey (Cambridge) 2011. Sy BB 2-39 v Glos (Cheltenham) 2011. LO HS 60* v Durham (Oval) 2012 (CB40). LO BB 3-28 v Somerset (Oval) 2012 (CB40). T20 HS 38*. T20 BB 2-26.

BATTY, Gareth Jon (Bingley GS), b Bradford, Yorks 13 Oct 1977. Younger brother of J.D.Batty (Yorkshire and Somerset 1989-96). 5'11". RHB, OB. Yorkshire 1997. Surrey 1999-2001, rejoined in 2010; cap 2011. Worcestershire 2002-09. MCC 2012. **Tests**: 7 (2003-04 to 2005); HS 38 v SL (Kandy) 2003-04; BB 3-55 v SL (Galle) 2003-04. Took wicket with his third ball in Test cricket. **LOI**: 10 (2002-03 to 2008-09); HS 17 v WI (Bridgetown) 2008-09; BB 2-40 v WI (Gros Islet, St Lucia) 2003-04. **IT20**: 1 (2008-09); HS 4 v WI (Port-of-Spain) 2008-09. F-c Tours: WI 2003-04, 2005-06; NZ 2008-09 (Eng A); SL 2002-03 (ECB Acad); SL 2003-04; B 2003-04. HS 133 Wo v Surrey (Oval) 2004. Sy HS 79 v Essex (Croydon) 2011. 50 wkts (2); most – 60 (2003). BB 7-52 (10-113 match) Wo v Northants (Northampton) 2004. Sy BB 6-73 (10-142 match) v Warwks (Oval) 2012. LO HS 83* v Yorks (Oval) 2001 (NL). LO BB 5-35 Wo v Hants (Southampton) 2009 (FPT). T20 HS 87. T20 BB 4-13.

BURNS, Rory Joseph (City of London Freemen's S), b Epsom 26 Aug 1990. 5'9". LHB, WK. Debut (Surrey) 2011. Surrey 2nd XI debut 2009. MCC Univs 2010. Hampshire 2nd XI 2010. HS 121 v Middx (Oval) 2012. LO HS 32 v Durham (Chester-le-St) 2012 (CB40). T20 HS 23.

DAVIES, Steven Michael (King Charles I S, Kidderminster), b Bromsgrove, Worcs 17 Jun 1986. 5'10". LHB, WK. Worcestershire 2005-09. Surrey debut 2010; cap 2011. Worcs 2nd XI debut 2001, aged 15y 8d. MCC 2006-07, 2011. **LOI**: 8 (2009-10 to 2010-11); HS 87 v P (Chester-le-St) 2010. **IT20**: 5 (2008-09 to 2010-11); HS 33 v P (Cardiff) 2010. F-c Tours: A 2010-11; B 2006-07 (Eng A); UAE 2011-12 (v P). 1000 runs (4); most – 1090 (2010). HS 192 Wo v Glos (Bristol) 2006. Sy HS 156 v Northants (Northampton) 2011. LO HS 119 Wo v Glos (Worcester) 2008 (P40). T20 HS 99*.

NODE BRUYN, Zander (Helpmekaar HS; Randburg HS; Rand Afrikaans U, Jo'burg), b Johannesburg, South Africa 5 Jul 1975. 6'0". RHB, RMF. Transvaal B 1995-96 to 1996-97. Gauteng 1996-97 to 2001-02. Easterns 2002-03 to 2005-06. Titans 2004-05 to 2005-06. Worcestershire 2005. Warriors 2006-07 to 2008-09. Somerset 2008-10; cap 2008. Lions 2009-10 to date. Surrey debut 2011 (Kolpak registration). **Tests** (SA): 3 (2004-05); HS 83 v I (Kanpur) 2004-05 – on debut; BB 2-32 v I (Calcutta) 2004-05. F-c Tours (SA): I 2004-05; SL 2005-06 (SA A). 1000 runs (1+1): 1383 (2011). HS 266* Easterns v GW (Kimberley) 2003-04. UK HS 179 v Kent (Oval) 2011. BB 7-67 Warriors v Titans (Pt Elizabeth) 2007-08. UK BB 4-23 Sm v Essex (Colchester) 2010. Sy BB 3-39 v Glos (Oval) 2011. LO HS 122* Sm v Pakistanis (Taunton) 2010. LO BB 5-44 Easterns v WP (Cape Town) 2003-04. T20 HS 95*. T20 BB 4-18.

DERNBACH, Jade Winston (St John the Baptist S), b Johannesburg, South Africa 3 Mar 1986. 6'1½". RHB, RFM. Italian passport. UK resident since 1998. Debut (Surrey) 2003; cap 2011. **LOI**: 22 (2011 to 2012-13); HS 5 v SL (Leeds) 2011; BB 4-45 v P (Dubai) 2011-12. **IT20**: 21 (2011 to 2012-13); HS 12 v I (Colombo, RPS) 2012-13; BB 4-22 v I (Manchester) 2011. F-c Tour (Eng A): WI 2010-11. HS 56* v Northants (Northampton) 2010. 50 wkts (1): 51 (2010). BB 6-47 v Leics (Leicester) 2009. LO HS 31 v Somerset (Taunton) 2010 (CB40). LO BB 5-31 v Derbys (Chesterfield) 2008 (P40). T20 HS 12. T20 BB 4-22.

DUNN, Matthew Peter (Bearwood C, Wokingham), b Egham 5 May 1992. 6'2". LHB, RFM. Debut (Surrey) 2010. Surrey 2nd XI debut 2009. England U19s 2010. HS 2* v Cambridge MCCU (Cambridge) 2011. CC HS 0*. BB 5-56 v Derbys (Derby) 2011. LO BB 2-32 England Dev XI v Sri Lanka A (Manchester) 2011.

EDWARDS, George Alexander (St Joseph C, Croydon), b King's College H, Camberwell, London 29 Jul 1992. 6'3". RHB, RFM. Debut (Surrey) 2011. Surrey 2nd XI debut 2009, aged 16y 322d. HS 19 v Cambridge MCCU (Cambridge) 2011. CC HS 17 and BB 4-44 v Worcs (Worcester) 2012.

HARINATH, Arun (Whitgift S; Loughborough U), b Sutton 26 Mar 1987. 5'11". LHB, OB. Loughborough UCCE 2007-09. MCC 2008. Surrey debut 2009. Surrey 2nd XI debut 2003. Buckinghamshire 2007-08. HS 109 v Middx (Oval) 2012. BB – . LO HS 21* v Warwks (Oval) 2009 (P40).

JEWELL, Thomas Melvin (Bradfield C), b Reading, Berkshire 13 Jan 1991. 6'1". RHB, RMF. Debut (Surrey) 2008. Surrey 2nd XI debut 2007. HS 70 and CC BB 1-24 v Lancs (Liverpool) 2012. BB 5-49 v Cambridge MCCU (Cambridge) 2011. LO HS 1 v Northants (Northampton) 2009 (P40). LO BB – .

‡KEEDY, Gary (Garforth CS), b Wakefield, Yorks 27 Nov 1974. 6'0". LHB, SLA. Yorkshire 1994 (one match). Lancashire debut 1995; cap 2000; benefit 2009. MCC 2011. F-c Tour: WI 1995-96 (La). HS 64 La v Sussex (Hove) 2008. 50 wkts (4); most – 72 (2004). BB 7-68 (10-128 match) La v Durham (Manchester) 2010. LO HS 33 La v Derbys (Derby) 2008. LO BB 5-30 La v Sussex (Manchester) 2000 (NL). T20 HS 9*. T20 BB 4-15.

LEWIS, Jonathan (Churchfields S, Swindon; Swindon C), b Aylesbury, Bucks 26 Aug 1975. 6'2". RHB, RMF. Gloucestershire 1995-2011; cap 1998; captain 2006-08; benefit 2007. Surrey debut 2012. MCC 2005, 2010. Wiltshire 1993, 1995. **Tests**: 1 (2006); HS 20 and BB 3-68 v SL (Nottingham) 2006. **LOI**: 13 (2005 to 2007); HS 17 v I (Leeds) 2007; BB 4-36 v A (Brisbane) 2006-07. **IT20**: 2 (2005 to 2006-07); HS 1 v A (Sydney) 2006-07; BB 4-24 v A (Southampton) 2005. F-c Tours (Eng A): WI 2000-01; SL 2004-05. HS 71 Gs v Middx (Uxbridge) 2011. Sy HS 42 v Somerset (Oval) 2012. 50 wkts (9); most – 74 (2003). BB 8-95 Gs v Z (Gloucester) 2000. CC BB 7-38 (10-75 match) Gs v Somerset (Bristol) 2006. Sy BB 5-41 v Middx (Lord's) 2012. Hat-trick Gs v Notts (Nottingham) 2000. LO HS 54 Gs v Durham (Cheltenham) 2009 (P40). LO BB 5-19 Gs v Hants (Southampton) 2005 (NL). T20 HS 43. T20 BB 4-24.

LINLEY, Timothy Edward (St Mary's RC CS, Menston; Notre Dame SFC; Oxford Brookes U), b Leeds, Yorks 23 Mar 1982. 6'2". RHB, RFM. Oxford UCCE 2003-05. British U 2004. Sussex 2006 (1 match). Surrey debut 2009. HS 42 OU v Derbys (Oxford) 2005. Sy HS 36 v Kent (Canterbury) 2009. 50 wkts (1): 73 (2011). BB 6-57 (9-79 match) v Leics (Leicester) 2011. LO HS 20* v Warwks (Oval) 2009 (P40). LO BB 3-50 v Hants (Croydon) 2011 (CB40). T20 HS 8. T20 BB 2-28.

MEAKER, Stuart Christopher (Cranleigh S), b Durban, South Africa 21 Jan 1989. Moved to UK in 2001. 6'1". RHB, RFM. Debut (Surrey) 2008; cap 2012. England U19s 2007 to 2008. Surrey 2nd XI debut 2007. **LOI:** 2 (2011-12); HS 1 and BB 1-45 v I (Mumbai) 2011-12. HS 94 v Bangladeshis (Oval) 2010. CC HS 72 v Essex (Colchester) 2009. BB 8-52 (11-167 match) v Somerst (Oval) 2012. LO HS 21* v Glamorgan (Oval) 2012 (CB40). LO BB 4-47 EL v Bangladesh A (Chittagong) 2011-12. T20 HS 17. T20 BB 2-16.

PIETERSEN, Kevin Peter (Maritzburg C; Natal U), b Pietermaritzburg, South Africa 27 Jun 1980. British passport (English mother) – qualified for England Oct 2004. 6'4". RHB, OB. MBE 2005. *Wisden* 2005. Natal/KwaZulu-Natal 1997-98 to 1999-00. Nottinghamshire 2001-04; cap 2002. Hampshire 2005-08; cap 2005 (no f-c appearances 2006-07, 2009-10). Surrey debut 2010 (initially on loan). Dolphins 2010-11. MCC 2004. **ECB central contract 2012-13. Tests:** 93 (2005 to 2012-13, 3 as captain); HS 227 v A (Adelaide) 2010-11; BB 3-52 v SA (Leeds) 2012. **LOI:** 132 (2004-05 to 2012-13, 12 as captain); HS 130 v P (Dubai) 2011-12; scored 454 runs (av 151.33) in 7-match series, including fastest England 100 off 69 balls (E London), v SA 2004-05; BB 2-22 v SA (Leeds) 2008. **IT20:** 36 (2005 to 2011-12); HS 79 v Z (Cape Town) 2007-08; BB 1-27 v SA (Centurion) 2009-10. F-c Tours: A 2006-07, 2010-11; SA 2009-10; WI 2008-09; NZ 2007-08, 2012-13; I 2003-04 (Eng A), 2005-06, 2008-09 (Captain), 2012-13; P 2005-06; SL 2007-08, 2011-12; B 2009-10; UAE 2011-12 (v P). 1000 runs (2): most – 1546 (2005). HS 254* Nt v Middx (Nottingham) 2003. Sy HS 234* v Lancs (Guildford) 2012. BB 4-31 Nt v Durham U (Nottingham) 2003. CC BB 3-72 Nt v Hants (Nottingham) 2004. Sy BB 2-24 v Notts (Oval) 2012. LO HS 147 Nt v Somerset (Taunton) 2002 (NL). LO BB 3-14 Nt v Middx (Lord's) 2004 (NL). T20 HS 103*. T20 BB 3-33.

‡[NQ]**PONTING, Ricky** Thomas, b Launceston, Tasmania, Australia 19 Dec 1974. 5'10". RHB, RM. Tasmania 1992-93 to date. Somerset 2004. **Tests** (A): 168 (1995-96 to 2012-13, 77 as captain); HS 257 v I (Melbourne) 2003-04; BB 1-0 v WI (Brisbane) 1996-97. **LOI** (A): 375 (1994-95 to 2011-12, 230 as captain); HS 164 v SA (Johannesburg) 2005-06; BB 1-12 v Z (Sydney) 2000-01. **IT20** (A): 17 (2004-05 to 2009, 17 as captain); HS 98* v NZ (Auckland) 2004-05. F-c Tours (A)(C=captain): E 1995 (Young A), 1997, 2001, 2005C, 2009C, 2010C (v P); SA 2001-02, 2005-06C, 2008-09C, 2011-12; WI 1994-95, 1998-99, 2003, 2008C; NZ 2004-05C, 2009-10C, 2012; I 1996-97; 1997-98, 2000-01, 2004-05C, 2008-09C, 2010-11C; P 1998-99; SL 1999-00, 2003-04C, 2011; Z 1995-96 (Tas), 1999-00; B 2005-06C; UAE 2002-03 (v P). HS 257 (*see Tests*). CC HS 117 Sm v Glamorgan (Taunton) 2004. BB 2-10 A v Mumbai (Mumbai) 2000-01. LO HS 164 (*see LOI*). LO BB 3-34 Tas v WA (Hobart) 1996-97. T20 HS 98*. T20 BB 1-11.

ROY, Jason Jonathan (Whitgift S), b Durban, South Africa 21 Jul 1990. 6'0". RHB, RM. Debut (Surrey) 2010. Surrey 2nd XI debut 2008. HS 106* and BB 2-29 v Glamorgan (Oval) 2011. LO HS 131 v Leics (Leicester) 2011 (CB40). LO BB – . T20 HS 101* v Kent (Beckenham) 2010 – Sy record.

SIBLEY, Dominic Peter (Whitgift S, Croydon), b Epsom 5 Sep 1995. 6'3". RHB, LB. Surrey 2nd XI debut 2011, aged 15y 302d. England U19s 2012-13. Awaiting 1st XI debut.

‡**NQSMITH, Graeme** Craig (K Edward VII S, Johannesburg), b Johannesburg, South Africa 1 Feb 1981. 6'3" LHB, OB. W Province 2000-01 to 2003-04. W Province Boland 2004-05. Somerset 2005. Cape Cobras 2010-11. **Tests** (SA): 110 (2001-02 to 2012-13; inc 1 for ICC, 102 as captain); HS 277 v E (Birmingham) 2003; BB 2-145 v WI (St John's) 2004-05. **LOI** (SA): 190 (2001-02 to 2012-13; inc 1 for Africa XI, 150 as captain); HS 141 v E (Centurion) 2009-10; BB 3-30 v SL (Perth) 2005-06. **IT20** (SA): 33 (2005-06 to 2011-12, 27 as captain); HS 89* v A (Johannesburg) 2005-06. F-c Tours (SA) (C=captain): E 2003C, 2008C, 2012C; A 2005-06C, 2008-09C, 2012-13C; WI 2004-05C, 2010C; NZ 2003-04C, 2011-12C; I 2004-05C, 2007-08C, 2009-10C; P 2003-04C, 2007-08C; SL 2004C; B 2002-03C, 2007-08C; UAE 2010-11C (v P). HS 311 Sm v Leics (Taunton) 2005. BB 2-145 (*see Tests*). CC BB 1-34 Sm v Durham (Taunton) 2005. LO HS 141 (*see LOI*). LO BB 3-30 (*see LOI*). T20 HS 105. T20 BB 3-23.

‡**SOLANKI, Vikram** Singh (Regis S, Wolverhampton), b Udaipur, India 1 Apr 1976. 6'0". RHB, OB, occ WK. Worcestershire 1995-2012; cap 1998; captain 2005-10; benefit 2007. Rajasthan 2006-07. **LOI**: 51 (1999-00 to 2006); HS 106 v SA (Oval) 2003; BB 1-17 v SL (Leeds) 2006. **IT20**: 3 (2005 to 2007-08); HS 43 v I (Durban) 2007-08. F-c Tours (Eng A): SA 1998-99, 1999-00 (Eng – *part*); WI 2000-01, 2005-06 (Captain); NZ 1999-00; SL 2004-05; Z 1996-97 (Wo), 1998-99; B 1999-00. 1000 runs (6); most – 1339 (1999). HS 270 Wo v Glos (Cheltenham) 2008, sharing Wo 2nd wkt record partnership of 318 with S.C.Moore. Won Walter Lawrence Trophy in 2009 with 49-ball hundred v Glamorgan (Worcester). BB 5-40 Wo v Middx (Lord's) 2004. LO HS 164* Wo v Worcs CB (Worcester) 2003 (CGT). LO BB 4-14 Wo v Somerset (Taunton) 2006 (P40). T20 HS 100. T20 BB 1-6.

TREMLETT, Christopher Timothy (Thornden S, Chandler's Ford; Taunton's C, Southampton), b Southampton, Hampshire 2 Sep 1981. Son of T.M.Tremlett (Hampshire 1976-91); grandson of M.F.Tremlett (Somerset, CD and England 1947-60). 6'7". RHB, RFM. Hampshire 2000-09, taking wicket of M.H.Richardson (NZ A) with his first ball; cap 2004. Surrey debut 2010. **Tests**: 11 (2007 to 2011-12); HS 25* v I (Oval) 2007; BB 6-48 v SL (Southampton) 2011. **LOI**: 15 (2005 to 2010-11); HS 19* v I (Birmingham) 2007; BB 4-32 v B (Nottingham) 2005 – on debut (hat-trick ball hit stump without dislodging bails). **IT20**: 1 (2007-08); BB 2-45 v I (Durban) 2007-08. F-c Tours: A 2010-11; SL 2002-03 (ECB Acad); UAE 2011-12 (v P). HS 64 H v Glos (Southampton) 2010. Sy HS 53* v Middx (Lord's) 2010. BB 6-44 H v Sussex (Hove) 2005. Sy BB 4-29 v Glos (Bristol) 2010. Hat-trick: H v Notts (Nottingham) 2005. LO HS 38* H v Cheshire (Alderley Edge) 2004 (CGT). LO BB 4-25 H v Essex (Southend) 2002 (NL). T20 HS 13. T20 BB 4-16.

VAN DEN BERGH, Frederick Oliver Edward (Whitgift S, Croydon; Durham U), b Farnborough, Kent 14 Jun 1992. 6'2". RHB, SLA. Debut (Surrey) 2011. Surrey 2nd XI debut, aged 16y 326d. Summer contract. HS 16* v Leeds/Bradford MCCU (Oval) 2012. BB 3-79 v Cambridge MCCU (Cambridge) 2011.

NQWILSON, Gary Craig (Methodist C, Belfast; Manchester Met), b Dundonald, N Ireland 5 Feb 1986. 5'10". RHB, WK. Ireland 2005 to date. Surrey debut 2010. MCC YC 2005. Surrey 2nd XI debut 2010. **LOI** (Ire): 39 (2007 to 2012); HS 113 v Netherlands (Dublin) 2010. **IT20** (Ire): 27 (2008 to 2012-13); HS 41* v B (Belfast) 2012. HS 125 v Leics (Leicester) 2010. BB – . LO HS 113 (*see LOI*). T20 HS 54*.

RELEASED/RETIRED

(Having made a County First-Class or List A appearance in 2012)

HAMILTON-BROWN, R.J. – *see SUSSEX*.

JORDAN, C.J. – *see SUSSEX*.

[NQ]**KARTIK, Murali** (educated in New Delhi), b Madras, India 11 Sep 1976. 6'0". LHB, SLA. Railways 1996-97 to date. Central Zone 1997-98 to date. Lancashire 2005-06. Middlesex 2007-09; cap 2007. Somerset 2010-11. Surrey 2012. **Tests** (I): 8 (1999-00 to 2004-05); HS 43 v B (Dhaka) 2000-01; BB 4-44 v A (Mumbai) 2004-05. **LOI** (I): 37 (2001-02 to 2007-08); HS 32* v A (Perth) 2003-04; BB 6-27 v A (Mumbai) 2007-08. **IT20** (I): 1 (2007-08); HS and BB-v P (Jaipur) 2007-08. F-c Tours (I A): E 2003; A 2003-04 (I); SA 2001-02; WI 1999-00, 2002-03; P 1997-98; SL 2002; B 2000-01 (I). HS 96 Railways v Rest of India (Delhi) 2005-06. CC HS 65* Sm v Lancs (Taunton) 2011. Sy HS 23* v Lancs (Guildford) 2012 and 23* v Somerset (Taunton) 2012. 50 wkts (1): 51 (2007). BB 9-70 Rest of India v Bombay (Bombay) 2000-01. CC BB 6-21 M v Glamorgan (Lord's) 2007. Sy BB 5-69 v Middx (Oval) 2012. LO HS 44 Railways v Rajasthan (Indore) 2008-09. LO BB 6-27 (*see LOI*). T20 HS 28. T20 BB 5-13 M v Essex (Lord's) 2007 – M record.

MAYNARD, Thomas Lloyd (Millfield S; Whitchurch HS, Cardiff), b Cardiff 25 Mar 1989; d Wimbledon Park 18 Jun 2012. Son of M.P.Maynard (Glamorgan and England 1985-2005). 6'3". RHB, OB. Glamorgan 2007-10. Surrey 2011-12; cap 2012 – awarded posthumously. Wales MC 2006-08. 1000 runs (1): 1022 (2011). HS 143 v Worcs (Worcester) 2012. BB – . LO HS 108 Gm v Northants (Colwyn Bay) 2009 (P40). LO BB – . T20 HS 78*.

RAMPRAKASH, Mark Ravin (Gayton HS; Harrow Weald SFC), b Bushey, Herts 5 Sep 1969. 5'9". RHB, OB. Middlesex 1987-2000; cap 1990; captain 1997-99. Surrey 2001-12, scoring 146 v Kent (Oval) on debut; cap 2002; joint Testimonial 2008. MCC 2012. YC 1991. *Wisden* 2006. PCA 2006. MBE 2012. **Tests**: 52 (1991 to 2001-02); HS 154 v WI (Bridgetown) 1997-98; BB 1-2 v WI (Georgetown) 1997-98. **LOI**: 18 (1991 to 2001-02); HS 51 v WI (Port-of-Spain) 1997-98; BB 3-28 v Z (Harare) 2001-02. F-c Tours: A 1994-95 (*part*), 1998-99; SA 1995-96; WI 1991-92 (Eng A), 1993-94, 1997-98; NZ 1991-92, 2001-02; I 1994-95 (Eng A), 2001-02; P 1990-91 (Eng A); SL 1990-91 (Eng A). 1000 runs (20, inc 2000 (3): 2258 (1995), 2278 (2006), 2026 (2007)). Averaged 103.54 in f-c matches 2006, the second-highest average by any batsman scoring 1000 runs in a season (105.28 in CC), setting world records by scoring 2000 runs in only 20 innings, posting scores of at least 150 in five successive matches and reaching double figures in each of his 24 innings. In 2007 he became the first to score 2000 f-c runs in a season and average over 100 (101.30) twice. Ten hundreds in a season (2): 1995, 2007. HS 301* v Northants (Oval) 2006. BB 3-32 M v Glamorgan (Lord's) 1998. Sy BB 2-35 v Northants (Northampton) 2004. LO HS 147* M v Worcs (Lord's) 1990 (SL) – M record. LO BB 5-38 M v Leics (Lord's) 1993 (SL). T20 HS 85*.

[NQ]**RUDOLPH**, Jacobus Andries ('**Jacques**') (Afrikaanse Hoer Seunskool), b Springs, Transvaal, South Africa 4 May 1981. Elder brother of G.J.Rudolph (Limpopo and Namibia 2006-07 to date). 5'11". LHB, LBG. Northerns 1997-98 to 2003-04. Titans 2004-05, 2008-09 to date. Eagles 2005-06 to 2007-08. Yorkshire 2007-11 (Kolpak registration); scored 122 v Surrey (Oval) on debut; cap 2007. Surrey 2012. **Tests** (SA): 48 (2003 to 2012-13); HS 222* v B (Chittagong) 2003 – on debut; BB 1-1 v E (Leeds) 2003. **LOI** (SA): 45 (2003 to 2005-06); HS 81 v B (Dhaka) 2003. **IT20** (SA): 1 (2005-06); HS 6* v A (Brisbane) 2005-06. F-c Tours (SA): E 2003, 2012; A 2001-02, 2005-06, 2012-13; WI 2004-05; NZ 2003-04, 2011-12; I 2004-05; SL 2004, 2005-06, 2006; B 2003. 1000 runs (4+1); most – 1375 (2010). HS 228* Y v Durham (Leeds) 2010. Sy HS 68 v Worcs (Worcester) 2012. BB 5-80 Eagles v Cape Cobras (Cape Town) 2007-08. CC BB 1-13 Y v Somerset (Scarborough) 2008. LO HS 134* South Africa A v Kenya (Laudium) 2001-02. LO BB 4-41 South Africa A v New Zealand A (Colombo) 2005-06. T20 HS 83*. T20 BB 3-16.

SPRIEGEL, M.N.W. – *see NORTHAMPTONSHIRE.*

T.J.Lancefield and D.P.Nannes left the staff without making a County First-Class or List A appearance for Surrey in 2012.

SURREY 2012

RESULTS SUMMARY

	Place	Won	Lost	Drew	NR	Aband
LV= County Championship (1st Division)	7th	3	4	8		1
All First-Class Matches		4	4	8		1
Clydesdale Bank 40 (Group B)	2nd	6	3		3	
Friends Life t20 (South Group)	6th	3	7			

LV= COUNTY CHAMPIONSHIP AVERAGES

BATTING AND FIELDING

Cap		M	I	NO	HS	Runs	Avge	100	50	Ct/St
	K.P.Pietersen	4	7	1	234*	572	95.33	2	2	1
	G.C.Wilson	3	4	1	68	182	60.66	–	2	4
	R.J.Burns	9	15	–	121	640	42.66	1	4	6
2012	T.L.Maynard	7	14	1	143	525	40.38	1	2	10
2011	R.J.Hamilton-Brown	8	16	1	115	555	37.00	1	4	4
	A.Harinath	6	11	1	109	368	36.80	2	–	–
	J.J.Roy	12	21	2	83	612	32.21	–	3	11
	Z.de Bruyn	15	27	–	125	709	26.25	1	5	5
	J.Lewis	13	19	6	42	326	25.07	–	–	3
	J.A.Rudolph	5	10	–	68	229	22.90	–	1	2
2011	S.M.Davies	12	20	–	104	438	21.90	1	1	24/1
	Z.S.Ansari	8	13	1	83*	234	19.50	–	1	3
	M.Kartik	7	8	2	23*	113	18.83	–	–	3
2012	S.C.Meaker	10	14	4	41	177	17.70	–	–	1
2011	G.J.Batty	14	24	2	36	287	13.04	–	–	15
	C.J.Jordan	7	12	1	40	141	12.81	–	–	3
2002	M.R.Ramprakash	5	10	–	37	107	10.70	–	–	2
2011	J.W.Dernbach	7	14	4	22	55	5.50	–	–	2
	T.E.Linley	7	10	4	14	28	4.66	–	–	2

Also played: M.P.Dunn (1 match) 0*; G.A.Edwards (2) 17, 10*; T.M.Jewell (1) 70;
M.N.W.Spriegel (2) 17, 1, 17; C.T.Tremlett (1) did not bat.

BOWLING

	O	M	R	W	Avge	Best	5wI	10wM
M.Kartik	251.1	58	597	27	22.11	5-69	1	–
S.C.Meaker	284.3	51	993	44	22.56	8-52	3	1
G.J.Batty	305	71	789	30	26.30	6-73	2	1
J.W.Dernbach	172	39	522	19	27.47	3-39	–	–
T.E.Linley	150.3	34	464	16	29.00	5-62	1	–
J.Lewis	335	77	980	31	31.61	5-41	1	–
C.J.Jordan	125.3	16	517	10	51.70	3-29	–	–
Also bowled:								
G.A.Edwards	44.5	6	184	5	36.80	4-44	–	–
Z.de Bruyn	130	24	383	6	63.83	2-16	–	–

Z.S.Ansari 16-2-55-0; M.P.Dunn 10-1-50-1; R.J.Hamilton-Brown 13-0-38-1; T.M.Jewell
11-3-24-1; K.P.Pietersen 11-3-27-2; J.J.Roy 1-0-1-0; C.T.Tremlett 27-6-82-1.

The First-Class Averages (pp 219–235) give the records of Surrey players in all first-class
county matches (Surrey's other opponents being Leeds/Bradford MCCU), with the exception of Z.S.Ansari, J.W.Dernbach, S.C.Meaker, K.P.Pietersen and J.A.Rudolph, whose
first-class figures for Surrey are as above.

SURREY RECORDS

FIRST-CLASS CRICKET

Highest Total	For 811		v	Somerset	The Oval	1899
	V 863		by	Lancashire	The Oval	1990
Lowest Total	For 14		v	Essex	Chelmsford	1983
	V 16		by	MCC	Lord's	1872
Highest Innings	For 357*	R.Abel	v	Somerset	The Oval	1899
	V 366	N.H.Fairbrother	for	Lancashire	The Oval	1990

Highest Partnership for each Wicket

1st	428	J.B.Hobbs/A.Sandham	v	Oxford U	The Oval	1926
2nd	371	J.B.Hobbs/E.G.Hayes	v	Hampshire	The Oval	1909
3rd	413	D.J.Bicknell/D.M.Ward	v	Kent	Canterbury	1990
4th	448	R.Abel/T.W.Hayward	v	Yorkshire	The Oval	1899
5th	318	M.R.Ramprakash/Azhar Mahmood	v	Middlesex	The Oval	2005
6th	298	A.Sandham/H.S.Harrison	v	Sussex	The Oval	1913
7th	262	C.J.Richards/K.T.Medlycott	v	Kent	The Oval	1987
8th	205	I.A.Greig/M.P.Bicknell	v	Lancashire	The Oval	1990
9th	168	E.R.T.Holmes/E.W.J.Brooks	v	Hampshire	The Oval	1936
10th	173	A.Ducat/A.Sandham	v	Essex	Leyton	1921

Best Bowling	For	10-43	T.Rushby	v	Somerset	Taunton	1921
(Innings)	V	10-28	W.P.Howell	for	Australians	The Oval	1899
Best Bowling	For	16-83	G.A.R.Lock	v	Kent	Blackheath	1956
(Match)	V	15-57	W.P.Howell	for	Australians	The Oval	1899

Most Runs – Season	3246	T.W.Hayward	(av 72.13)		1906
Most Runs – Career	43554	J.B.Hobbs	(av 49.72)		1905-34
Most 100s – Season	13	T.W.Hayward			1906
	13	J.B.Hobbs			1925
Most 100s – Career	144	J.B.Hobbs			1905-34
Most Wkts – Season	252	T.Richardson	(av 13.94)		1895
Most Wkts – Career	1775	T.Richardson	(av 17.87)		1892-1904
Most Career W-K Dismissals	1221	H.Strudwick	(1035 ct; 186 st)		1902-27
Most Career Catches in the Field	605	M.J.Stewart			1954-72

LIMITED-OVERS CRICKET

Highest Total	50ov	496-4		v	Glos	The Oval	2007
	40ov	386-3		v	Glamorgan	The Oval	2010
	T20	224-5		v	Glos	Bristol	2006
Lowest Total	50ov	74		v	Kent	The Oval	1967
	40ov	64		v	Worcs	Worcester	1978
	T20	88		v	Kent	The Oval	2012
Highest Innings	50ov	268	A.D.Brown	v	Glamorgan	The Oval	2002
	40ov	203	A.D.Brown	v	Hampshire	Guildford	1997
	T20	101*	J.J.Roy	v	Kent	Beckenham	2010
Best Bowling	50ov	7-33	R.D.Jackman	v	Yorkshire	Harrogate	1970
	40ov	7-30	M.P.Bicknell	v	Glamorgan	The Oval	1999
	T20	6-24	T.J.Murtagh	v	Middlesex	Lord's	2005

SUSSEX

Formation of Present Club: 1 March 1839
Substantial Reorganisation: August 1857
Inaugural First-Class Match: 1864
Colours: Dark Blue, Light Blue and Gold
Badge: County Arms of Six Martlets
County Champions: (3) 2003, 2006, 2007
Gillette/NatWest/C&G/FP Trophy Winners: (5) 1963,
1964, 1978, 1986, 2006
Benson and Hedges Cup Winners: (0); best – Semi-Finalist 1982, 1999
Pro 40/National League (Div 1) Winners: (2) 2008, 2009
Sunday League Winners: (1) 1982
Clydesdale Bank Winners: (0); best – Semi-Finalist 2011, 2012
Twenty20 Cup Winners: (1) 2009

Chief Executive: Zac Toumazi, The BrightonandHoveJobs.com County Ground, Eaton Road, Hove BN3 3AN • Tel: 0844 264 0202 • Fax: 01273 771549 • Email: info@sussexcricket.co.uk • Web: www.sussexcricket.co.uk

Professional Cricket Manager: Mark Robinson. **Club Coaches**: Mark Davis and Carl Robinson. **Captain**: E.C.Joyce. **Vice-Captain**: C.D.Nash. **Overseas Players**: J.W.Hastings, (T20 only), S.J.Magoffin and S.B.Styris (T20 only). **2013 Beneficiary**: none. **Head Groundsman**: Andy Mackay. **Scorer**: M.J. (Mike) Charman. ‡ New registration. NQ Not qualified for England.

ANYON, James Edward (Garstang HS; Preston C; Loughborough U), b Lancaster, Lancs 5 May 1983. 6'1". LHB, RFM. Loughborough U 2003-04. Warwickshire 2005-09. Surrey 2009 (on loan). Sussex debut 2010; cap 2011. Cumberland 2003. HS 64* v Surrey (Horsham) 2012. 50 wkts (1): 55 (2011). BB 6-82 Wa v Glamorgan (Cardiff) 2008. Sx BB 5-36 v Lancs (Liverpool) 2012. LO HS 12 Wa v Worcs (Birmingham) 2006 (CGT). LO BB 3-6 Wa v Notts (Nottingham) 2008 (FPT). T20 HS 8*. T20 BB 3-6.

BEER, William Andrew Thomas (Reigate GS; Collyer's C, Horsham), b Crawley 8 Oct 1988. RHB, LB. Debut (Sussex) 2008. No f-c appearances in 2009. HS 37* and BB 3-31 v Worcs (Worcester) 2010. LO HS 27* v Derbys (Derby) 2011 (CB40). LO BB 3-27 v Warwks (Hove) 2012 (CB40). T20 HS 22. T20 BB 3-19.

BROWN, Ben Christopher (Ardingly C), b Crawley 23 Nov 1988. RHB, WK. Debut (Sussex) 2007. No f-c appearances in 2008 or 2009. HS 112 v Derbys (Horsham) 2010 and 112 v Oxford MCCU (Oxford) 2011. LO HS 60 v Yorks (Scarborough) 2011 (CB40). T20 HS 68.

GATTING, Joe Stephen (Cardinal Newman C; Brighton C), b Brighton 25 Nov 1987. Son of S.P.Gatting (Middlesex 2nd XI, football for Arsenal, Brighton & Hove Albion, Charlton Athletic), nephew of M.W.Gatting (Middlesex and England 1975-95). 6'0". RHB, OB. Debut (Sussex) 2009, scoring 152 v Cambridge UCCE (Cambridge). HS 152 (*see above*). CC HS 116* v Worcs (Worcester) 2011. BB 1-8 v Notts (Nottingham) 2011. LO HS 122 v Worcs (Horsham) 2011 (CB40). LO BB – . T20 HS 45*. LO BB 1-12.

GLOVER, John Andrew (Hove Park S; Brighton & Hove SFC), b Shoreham-by-Sea 10 Oct 1992. 6'2". RHB, RFM. Debut (Sussex) 2011. Sussex 2nd XI debut 2010. Expected to miss 2013 season with injury. HS- and BB 1-52 v Oxford MCCU (Oxford) 2011 – only 1st XI game.

HAMILTON-BROWN, Rory James (Millfield S), b St John's Wood, London 3 Sep 1987. 6'0". RHB, OB. Surrey 2005, 2010-12; captain 2010-12 (*part*); cap 2011. No f-c appearances 2006-07. Sussex 2008-09. 1000 runs (1): 1639 (2011). HS 171* and BB 2-49 v Yorks (Hove) 2010. LO HS 115 Sy v Glamorgan (Oval) 2010 (CB40). LO BB 3-28 Sy v Leics (Leicester) 2007 (P40). T20 HS 87*. T20 BB 4-15.

‡**NOHASTINGS, John** Wayne, b Nepean, NSW, Australia 4 Nov 1985. 6'5". RHB, RFM. Victoria 2007-08 to date. Joins Sussex in 2013 for T20 only. **Tests** (A): 1 (2012-13); HS 32 and BB 1-51 v SA (Perth) 2012-13. **LOI** (A): 11 (2010-11 to 2011); HS 21* v B (Dhaka) 2010-11; BB 2-35 v E (Brisbane) 2010-11. **IT20** (A): 3 (2010-11 to 2011); HS 15 v SL (Perth) 2010-11; BB 3-14 v SL (Pallekele) 2011. HS 93 Vic v Tas (Hobart) 2009-10. BB 5-30 Vic v WA (Perth) 2012-13. LO HS 69* Vic v S Australia (Adelaide) 2012-13. LO BB 4-28 Aus A v South Africa A (Harare) 2011. T20 HS 23*. T20 BB 3-14.

HATCHETT, Lewis James (Steyning GS), b Shoreham-by-Sea 21 Jan 1990. 6'3". LHB, LMF. Debut (Sussex) 2010. Sussex 2nd XI debut 2009. HS 20 v Middx (Uxbridge) 2010. BB 5-47 v Leics (Leicester) 2010.

‡**NOJORDAN, Christopher** James (Comber Mere S, Barbados; Dulwich C), b Christ Church, Barbados 4 Oct 1988. 6'0". RHB, RFM. Surrey 2007-12. Missed entire 2010 season with back injury. Barbados 2011-12 to date. HS 79* and CC BB 4-57 Sy v Essex (Chelmsford) 2011. BB 7-43 Barbados v CC&C (Bridgetown) 2012-13. LO HS 38 Sy v Yorks (Guildford) 2008 (P40). LO BB 3-24 Barbados v Guyana (Bridgetown) 2012-13. T20 HS 31. T20 BB 2-34.

JOYCE, Edmund Christopher (Presentation C, Bray, Co Wicklow; Trinity C, Dublin), b Dublin, Ireland 22 Sep 1978. Brother of four Ireland cricketers: Augustine (2000), Dominick (2004-06), Cecilia (2001-07) and Isobel, her twin (1999-2007). 5'11". LHB, RM. Ireland 1997-98. Middlesex 1999-2008; cap 2002. Sussex debut/cap 2009; captain 2013. Qualified for England 2005. MCC 2006, 2008. **LOI** (E/Ire): 32 (17 for E 2006 to 2006-07; 13 for Ire 2010-11 to 2012); HS 107 E v A (Sydney) 2006-07. **IT20** (E/Ire): 13 (2 for E 2006 to 2006-07; 11 for Ire 2011-12 to 2012-13); HS 38 Ire v Scotland (Dubai, DSC) 2011-12. F-c Tour (Eng A): WI 2005-06. 1000 runs (6); most – 1668 (2005). HS 211 M v Warwks (Birmingham) 2006. Sx HS 183 v Notts (Horsham) 2009. BB M 2-34 v Cambridge U (Cambridge) 2004. CC BB 1-4 M v Glamorgan (Cardiff) 2005. Sx BB 1-9 v Hants (Southampton) 2009. LO HS 146 v Glos (Hove) 2009 (FPT). LO BB 2-10 M v Notts (Nottingham) 2003 (NL). T20 HS 78*.

KHAN, Amjad (Skolenpa Duevej, Denmark), b Copenhagen, Denmark 14 Oct 1980. 6'0". RHB, RFM. Kent 2001-10. Sussex debut 2011. Denmark 1998-2000. Qualified for England Dec 2006. Missed 2007 season following reconstructive knee surgery. **Tests**: 1 (2008-09); HS-and BB 1-111 v WI (Port-of-Spain) 2008-09. **IT20**: 1 (2008-09); HS 2 and BB 2-34 v WI (Port-of-Spain) 2008-09. F-c Tours: WI 2008-09 (part); NZ 2008-09 (Eng A – part). HS 78 K v Middx (Lord's) 2003. Sx HS 65 v Notts (Nottingham) 2011. 50 wkts (2); most – 63 (2002). BB 6-52 K v Yorks (Canterbury) 2002. Sx BB 5-25 v Middx (Hove) 2012. LO HS 65* Denmark v Ireland (Harare) 1999-00. LO BB 4-26 K v Leics (Leicester) 2003 (NL). T20 HS 15. T20 BB 3-11.

LIDDLE, Christopher John (Nunthorpe CS), b Middlesbrough, Yorks 1 Feb 1984. 6'5". RHB, LFM. Leicestershire 2005-06. Sussex debut 2007. Missed entire 2009 season with a stress fracture of the right ankle. HS 53 v Worcs (Hove) 2007. BB 3-42 Le v Somerset (Leicester) 2006. Sx BB 2-43 v Sri Lanka A (Hove) 2007. LO HS 15 v Derbys (Derby) 2012 (CB40). LO BB 5-18 v Netherlands (Amstelveen) 2011 (CB40). T20 HS 16. T20 BB 5-17.

MACHAN, Matthew William (Brighton C), b Brighton 15 Feb 1991. 5'8". LHB, RM/OB. Debut (Sussex) 2010. Sussex 2nd XI debut 2006, aged 15y 153d. **LOI** (Scot): 2 (2012-13); HS 44 and BB 1-29 v Afghanistan (Sharjah) 2012-13. **IT20** (Scot): 2 (2012-13); HS 42* and BB 3-23 v Afghanistan (Sharjah) 2012-13. HS 99 v Oxford MCCU (Oxford) 2011. CC HS 71 v Notts (Nottingham) 2011. LO HS 126* v Unicorns (Hove) 2012 (CB40). LO BB 1-29 (see LOI). T20 HS 42*. T20 BB 3-23.

^{NQ}**MAGOFFIN, Stephen** James (Indooroopilly HS; Curtin U, Perth), b Corinda, Queensland, Australia 17 Dec 1979. 6'3". LHB, RFM. W Australia 2004-05 to 2010-11. Surrey 2007 (one f-c match). Worcestershire 2008. Queensland 2011-12. Sussex debut 2012; cap 2013. HS 79 WA v Tas (Perth) 2008-09. UK HS 41* v Worcs (Worcester) 2012. 50 wkts (1): 57 (2012). BB 8-47 WA v S Australia (Perth) 2005-06. UK BB 7-34 v Lancs (Liverpool) 2012. LO HS 24* Wo v Hants (Southampton) 2008 (FPT). LO BB 4-58 Sy v Kent (Oval) 2007 (FPT). T20 HS 11*. T20 BB 2-15.

NASH, Christopher David (Collyer's SFC; Loughborough U), b Cuckfield 19 May 1983. 5'11". RHB, OB. Debut (Sussex) 2002 – no f-c appearances 2003-04; cap 2008. Loughborough UCCE 2003-04. British U 2004. 1000 runs (1): 1321 (2009). HS 184 v Leics (Leicester) 2010. BB 4-12 v Glamorgan (Cardiff) 2010. LO HS 124* v Kent (Canterbury) 2011 (CB40). LO BB 4-40 v Yorks (Hove) 2009 (FPT). T20 HS 80*. T20 BB 4-7.

PANESAR, Mudhsuden Singh ('Monty') (Stopsley HS; Bedford Modern S; Loughborough U), b Luton, Beds 25 Apr 1982. 6'0". LHB, SLA. Northamptonshire 2001-09; cap 2006. British U 2002-05. Loughborough UCCE 2004. Lions 2009-10. Sussex debut/cap 2010. MCC 2006. Bedfordshire 1998-99. *Wisden* 2007. **Tests**: 46 (2005-06 to 2012-13); HS 26 v SL (Nottingham) 2006; BB 6-37 v NZ (Manchester) 2008. **LOI**: 26 (2006-07 to 2007-08); HS 13 v WI (Nottingham) 2007; BB 3-25 v B (Bridgetown) 2006-07. **IT20**: 1 (2006-07); HS 1 and BB 2-40 v A (Sydney) 2006-07. F-c Tours: A 2006-07, 2010-11; WI 2008-09; NZ 2007-08, 2012-13; I 2005-06, 2008-09, 2012-13; SL 2002-03 (ECB Acad), 2007-08, 2011-12; UAE 2011-12 (v P). HS 46* v Middx (Hove) 2010. 50 wkts (6); most – 71 (2006). BB 7-60 (13-137 match) v Somerset (Taunton) 2012. LO HS 17* Nh v Leics (Northampton) 2008 (FPT). LO BB 5-20 ECB Acad v SL Acad XI (Colombo) 2002-03. T20 HS 3*. T20 BB 3-14.

PRIOR, Matthew James (Brighton C), b Johannesburg, South Africa 26 Feb 1982. 5'11". RHB, WK. Debut (Sussex) 2001; cap 2003; benefit 2012. MCC 2005. *Wisden* 2009. **ECB central contract 2012-13.** Tests: 63 (2007 to 2012-13); HS 131* v WI (Port-of-Spain) 2008-09 (scored 126* v WI on debut – first instance while keeping wicket for England). **LOI**: 68 (2004-05 to 2010-11); HS 87 v WI (Birmingham) 2009. **IT20**: 10 (2007 to 2009-10); HS 32 v SA (Cape Town) 2007-08. F-c Tours: A 2010-11; SA 2009-10; WI 2008-09; NZ 2012-13; I 2003-04 (Eng A), 2008-09, 2012-13; SL 2004-05 (Eng A), 2007-08, 2011-12; B 2006-07 (Eng A), 2009-10; UAE 2011-12 (v P). 1000 runs (3); most – 1158 (2004). HS 201* v Loughborough U (Hove) 2004. CC HS 153* v Essex (Colchester) 2003. LO HS 144 v Warwks (Hove) 2005 (NL). T20 HS 117 v Glamorgan (Hove) 2010 – Sx record.

^{NQ}**RIPPON, Michael** James (Rondebosch BHS, Cape Town), b Cape Town, South Africa 14 Sep 1991. RHB, SLC. Dutch passport. Western Province 2011-12. Awaiting Sussex f-c and l-o debut. HS 40 and BB 3-34 WP v KZN Inland (Pietermaritzburg) 2011-12 – on debut. LO HS 10 WP v Boland (Paarl) 2011-12. LO BB – . T20 HS 3*. T20 BB 4-23.

^{NQ}**STYRIS, Scott** Bernard (Hamilton BHS), b Brisbane, Australia 10 Jul 1975. 5'10". RHB, RMF. N Districts 1994-95 to date. Middlesex 2005-06; cap 2006. Auckland 2005-06 to 2009-10. Durham 2007. Essex l-o and T20 only 2010-11. Sussex debut (l-o and T20 only) 2012. **Tests**: 29 (2002 to 2007-08); HS 170 v SA (Auckland) 2003-04; BB 3-28 v I (Wellington) 2002-03. **LOI** (NZ): 188 (1999-00 to 2010-11); HS 141 v SL (Bloemfontein) 2002-03; BB 6-25 v WI (Port-of-Spain) 2002. **IT20** (NZ): 31 (2004-05 to 2010-11); HS 66 v A (Auckland) 2004-05; BB 3-5 v Z (Providence) 2009-10. F-c Tours (NZ): E 2000 (NZ A), 2004; A 2004-05; SA 2000-01, 2005-06, 2007-08; WI 2002; I 2003-04; SL 2002-03; Z 2005; B 2004-05. HS 212* ND v Otago (Hamilton) 2001-02. UK HS 133 and UK BB 6-71 M v Lancs (Lord's) 2006. LO HS 141 (*see LOI*). LO BB 6-25 (*see LOI*). T20 HS 106*. T20 BB 3-5.

WELLS, Luke William Peter (St Bede's S), b Eastbourne 29 Dec 1990. Son of A.P.Wells (Border, Kent, Sussex and England 1981-2000) and nephew of C.M.Wells (Border, Derbyshire, Sussex and WP 1979-96). 6'4". LHB, OB. Debut (Sussex) 2010. Colombo CC 2011-12. Sussex 2nd XI debut 2008. England U19s 2009 to 2010. HS 174 v Yorks (Hove) 2011. BB 2-28 v Worcs (Horsham) 2011. LO HS 17 v Yorks (Hove) 2011 (CB40). BB 3-19 v Netherlands (Amstelveen) 2011 (CB40). T20 HS 3.

WRIGHT, Luke James (Belvoir HS; Ratcliffe C; Loughborough U), b Grantham, Lincs 7 Mar 1985. Younger brother of A.S.Wright (Leicestershire 2001-02). 5'11". RHB, RMF. Leicestershire 2003 (one f-c match). Sussex debut 2004; cap 2007. **LOI**: 46 (2007 to 2010-11); HS 52 v NZ (Birmingham) 2008; BB 2-34 v NZ (Bristol) 2008. **IT20**: 42 (2007-08 to 2012-13); HS 99* v Afghanistan (Colombo, RPS) 2012-13 – Eng record; BB 2-24 v NZ (Hamilton) 2012-13. F-c Tour (EL): NZ 2008-09. HS 155* v MCC (Lord's) 2008. CC HS 134 v Middx (Uxbridge) 2010. BB 5-65 v Derbys (Derby) 2010. LO HS 125 v Glos (Hove) 2007 (P40). LO BB 4-12 v Middx (Hove) 2004 (NL). T20 HS 117. T20 BB 3-17.

YARDY, Michael Howard (William Parker S, Hastings), b Pembury, Kent 27 Nov 1980. 6'0". LHB, LM/SLA. Debut (Sussex) 2000; cap 2005; captain 2009-12. **LOI**: 28 (2006 to 2010-11); HS 60* v A (Perth) 2010-11; BB 3-24 v P (Nottingham) 2006 – on debut. **IT20**: 14 (2006 to 2010-11); HS 35* v P (Cardiff) 2010; BB 2-19 v P (Bridgetown) 2009-10. F-c Tours (Eng A, C=Captain): WI 2005-06; I 2007-08C; B 2006-07C. 1000 runs (2); most – 1520 (2005). HS 257 (record Sx score v touring team) and BB 5-83 v Bangladeshis (Hove) 2005. CC HS 179 v Middx (Lord's) 2005. CC BB 3-15 v Yorks (Leeds) 2009. LO HS 98* v Surrey (Oval) 2006 (CGT). LO BB 6-27 v Warwks (Birmingham) 2005 (NL). T20 HS 76*. T20 BB 3-21.

RELEASED/RETIRED

(Having made a County First-Class or List A appearance in 2012)

ADKIN, William Anthony (Sackville S, E Grinstead; Southampton Solent C), b Redhill, Surrey 9 Apr 1990. 6'8½". LHB, RM. Sussex 2010-12. Sussex 2nd XI debut 2006, aged 16y 88d. HS 45 v Surrey (Guildford) 2010. BB 1-28 v Worcs (Worcester) 2011. LO HS 30 and LO BB 1-16 v Bangladeshis (Hove) 2010. T20 HS 8*. T20 BB 1-28.

NQ**GONDAL, Naveed** Arif (Mandi Baha u Din S), Mandi Baha u Din, Pakistan 2 Nov 1981. EU qualification via Danish wife. 5'10½". LHB, LMF. Gujranwala 2001-02 to 2002-03. Sialkot 2008-09 to date. Sussex 2011-12. F-c Tours (Pak A): A 2009; SL 2009. HS 100* v Lancs (Hove) 2011. BB 7-66 v Sialkot v Abbottabad (Abbottabad) 2009-10. Sx BB 4-41 v Notts (Nottingham) 2011. LO HS 49 v Gujranwala v Sargodha (Sargodha) 2002-03. LO BB 3-19 Sialkot v Peshawar (Sialkot) 2008-09. T20 HS 12. T20 BB 3-12.

GOODWIN, M.W. – see GLAMORGAN.

HODD, A.J. – see YORKSHIRE.

NQ**WERNARS, Kirk** Ogilvy, b Constantiaberg, Cape Town, South Africa 14 Jun 1991. EU passport. 6'3". LHB, RMF. W Province 2009-10 to 2010-11. Sussex 2011. BB 2-11 WP v Boland (Cape Town) 2009-10. Sx BB 2-13 v Yorks (Hove) 2011. LO HS 37* WP v Namibia (Windhoek) 2010-11 and 37* v Warwks (Hove) 2012 (CB40). LO BB 6-27 WP v Gauteng (Johannesburg) 2010-11. T20 HS 9. T20 BB 1-21.

SUSSEX 2012

RESULTS SUMMARY

	Place	Won	Lost	Tied	Drew	NR
LV= County Championship (1st Division)	4th	5	5		6	
All First-Class Matches		5	5		7	
Clydesdale Bank 40 (Group C)	SF	7	2			4
Friends Life t20 (South Group)	SF	7	2			3

LV= COUNTY CHAMPIONSHIP AVERAGES
BATTING AND FIELDING

Cap		M	I	NO	HS	Runs	Avge	100	50	Ct/St
2009	E.C.Joyce	14	24	3	108*	829	39.47	2	5	9
2008	C.D.Nash	16	28	2	162	984	37.84	3	2	8
	L.W.P.Wells	14	21	2	127	713	37.52	2	3	12
	A.Khan	7	7	3	57*	142	35.50	–	1	–
2011	J.E.Anyon	15	19	8	64*	316	28.72	–	2	6
	B.C.Brown	13	22	3	76*	521	27.42	–	5	38/3
2007	L.J.Wright	9	14	1	81	356	27.38	–	3	7
2005	M.H.Yardy	16	25	2	110	574	24.95	1	3	32
2003	M.J.Prior	4	5	–	86	114	22.80	–	1	7
2013	S.J.Magoffin	15	19	3	41*	363	22.68	–	–	4
	J.S.Gatting	10	16	3	72*	279	21.46	–	1	4
	N.A.Gondal	7	10	–	46	184	18.40	–	–	2
2001	M.W.Goodwin	14	23	1	77	360	16.36	–	2	5
	K.O.Wernars	2	4	–	50	65	16.25	–	1	1
	L.J.Hatchett	3	6	3	18*	32	10.66	–	–	1
2010	M.S.Panesar	15	16	4	31	88	7.33	–	–	3

Also batted (1 match each): W.A.Adkin 9, 6 (1 ct); M.W.Machan 4, 6.

BOWLING

	O	M	R	W	Avge	Best	5wI	10wM
S.J.Magoffin	480.2	161	1143	57	20.05	7-34	2	–
C.D.Nash	135.2	23	446	21	21.23	3-23	–	–
M.S.Panesar	514.1	157	1227	53	23.15	7-60	2	1
A.Khan	156.4	30	522	22	23.72	5-25	2	–
N.A.Gondal	151	23	512	17	30.11	3-34	–	–
J.E.Anyon	429.5	73	1645	42	39.16	5-36	2	–
Also bowled:								
L.J.Hatchett	64.5	12	280	8	35.00	3-25	–	–
L.J.Wright	79	6	327	5	65.40	1-14	–	–

W.A.Adkin 5-1-20-0; J.S.Gatting 12-0-56-0; L.W.P.Wells 10-4-37-1; K.O.Wernars 36-11-100-4; M.H.Yardy 12-1-68-2.

The First-Class Averages (pp 219–235) give the records of Sussex players in all first-class county matches (Sussex's other opponents being the West Indians), with the exception of: M.J.Prior 5-5-0-86-114-22.80-0-1-8ct.

SUSSEX RECORDS

FIRST-CLASS CRICKET

Highest Total	For 742-5d		v	Somerset	Taunton	2009
	V 726		by	Notts	Nottingham	1895
Lowest Total	For 19		v	Surrey	Godalming	1830
	19		v	Notts	Hove	1873
	V 18		by	Kent	Gravesend	1867
Highest Innings	For 344*	M.W.Goodwin	v	Somerset	Taunton	2009
	V 322	E.Paynter	for	Lancashire	Hove	1937

Highest Partnership for each Wicket

1st	490	E.H.Bowley/J.G.Langridge	v	Middlesex	Hove	1933
2nd	385	E.H.Bowley/M.W.Tate	v	Northants	Hove	1921
3rd	385*	M.H.Yardy/M.W.Goodwin	v	Warwicks	Hove	2006
4th	363	M.W.Goodwin/C.D.Hopkinson	v	Somerset	Taunton	2009
5th	297	J.H.Parks/H.W.Parks	v	Hampshire	Portsmouth	1937
6th	255	K.S.Duleepsinhji/M.W.Tate	v	Northants	Hove	1930
7th	344	K.S.Ranjitsinhji/W.Newham	v	Essex	Leyton	1902
8th	291	R.S.C.Martin-Jenkins/M.J.G.Davis	v	Somerset	Taunton	2002
9th	178	H.W.Parks/A.F.Wensley	v	Derbyshire	Horsham	1930
10th	156	G.R.Cox/H.R.Butt	v	Cambridge U	Cambridge	1908

Best Bowling	For 10- 48	C.H.G.Bland	v	Kent	Tonbridge	1899
(Innings)	V 9- 11	A.P.Freeman	for	Kent	Hove	1922
Best Bowling	For 17-106	G.R.Cox	v	Warwicks	Horsham	1926
(Match)	V 17- 67	A.P.Freeman	for	Kent	Hove	1922

Most Runs – Season	2850	J.G.Langridge	(av 64.77)		1949
Most Runs – Career	34150	J.G.Langridge	(av 37.69)		1928-55
Most 100s – Season	12	J.G.Langridge			1949
Most 100s – Career	76	J.G.Langridge			1928-55
Most Wkts – Season	198	M.W.Tate	(av 13.47)		1925
Most Wkts – Career	2211	M.W.Tate	(av 17.41)		1912-37
Most Career W-K Dismissals	1176	H R Butt	(911 ct; 265 st)		1890-1912
Most Career Catches in the Field	779	J.G.Langridge			1928-55

LIMITED-OVERS CRICKET

Highest Total	50ov	384-9		v	Ireland	Belfast	1996
	40ov	399-4		v	Worcs	Horsham	2011
	T20	239-5		v	Glamorgan	Hove	2010
Lowest Total	50ov	49		v	Derbyshire	Chesterfield	1969
	40ov	59		v	Glamorgan	Hove	1996
	T20	67		v	Hampshire	Hove	2004
Highest Innings	50ov	158*	M.W.Goodwin	v	Essex	Chelmsford	2006
	40ov	163	C.J.Adams	v	Middlesex	Arundel	1999
	T20	117	M.J.Prior	v	Glamorgan	Hove	2010
Best Bowling	50ov	6- 9	A.I.C.Dodemaide	v	Ireland	Downpatrick	1990
	40ov	7-41	A.N.Jones	v	Notts	Nottingham	1986
	T20	5-11	Mushtaq Ahmed	v	Essex	Hove	2005

WARWICKSHIRE

Formation of Present Club: 8 April 1882
Substantial Reorganisation: 19 January 1884
Inaugural First-Class Match: 1894
Colours: Dark Blue, Gold and Silver
Badge: Bear and Ragged Staff
County Champions: (7) 1911, 1951, 1972, 1994, 1995, 2004, 2012
Gillette/NatWest/C&G/FP Trophy Winners: (5) 1966, 1968, 1989, 1993, 1995
Benson and Hedges Cup Winners: (2) 1994, 2002
Pro 40/National League (Div 1) Winners: (0); best – 3rd 2001, 2002
Sunday League Winners: (3) 1980, 1994, 1997
Clydesdale Bank 40 Winners: (1) 2010
Twenty20 Cup Winners: (0); best – Finalist 2003

Chief Executive: Colin Povey, County Ground, Edgbaston, Birmingham, B5 7QU • Tel: 0844 635 1902 • Fax: 0121 446 4544 • Email: info@edgbaston.com • Web: www.edgbaston.com

Director of Cricket: Dougie Brown. **Assistant Coach**: Graeme Welch. **Captain**: J.O.Troughton. **Vice-Captain**: tba. **Overseas Player**: J.S.Patel. **2013 Beneficiary**: J.O.Troughton. **Head Groundsman**: Gary Barwell. **Scorer**: Melvin Smith. ‡ New registration. ^{NQ} Not qualified for England.

ALLIN, Thomas William (Bideford C; N Devon C; UWIC), b Bideford, Devon 27 Nov 1987. Son of A.W.Allin (Glamorgan 1976) and brother of M.L.Allin (Devon 2003). RHB, RMF. Cardiff UCCE (not f-c) 2008-10. Warwickshire 2nd XI debut 2008. Devon 2007. Awaiting f-c debut. LO HS 2* and BB- v Surrey (Birmingham) 2011 (CB40) – only 1st XI game.

AMBROSE, Timothy Raymond (Merewether HS, NSW; TAFE C), b Newcastle, NSW, Australia 1 Dec 1982. ECB qualified – British/EU passport. 5'7". RHB, WK. Sussex 2001-05; cap 2003. Warwickshire debut 2006; cap 2007. **Tests**: 11 (2007-08 to 2008-09); HS 102 v NZ (Wellington) 2007-08. **LOI**: 5 (2008); HS 6 v NZ (Oval) 2008. **IT20**: 1 (2008); HS – . F-c Tours: WI 2008-09; NZ 2007-08. HS 251* v Worcs (Worcester) 2007. LO HS 135 v Durham (Birmingham) 2007 (FPT). T20 HS 77.

BARKER, Keith Hubert Douglas (Moorhead HS; Fulwood C, Preston), b Manchester 21 Oct 1986. Son of K.H.Barker (British Guiana 1960-61 to 1963-64). Played football for Blackburn Rovers and Rochdale. 6'3". LHB, LM. Debut (Warwickshire) 2009. HS 118 v Sussex (Birmingham) 2011. 50 wkts (1): 56 (2012). BB 6-40 v Somerset (Taunton) 2012. LO HS 56 v Scotland (Birmingham) 2011. LO BB 4-33 v Scotland (Birmingham) 2010 (CB40). T20 HS 46. T20 BB 4-19.

BELL, Ian Ronald (Princethorpe C), b Walsgrave-on-Sowe 11 Apr 1982. 5'9". RHB, RM. Debut (Warwickshire) 1999; cap 2001; benefit 2011. MCC 2004. YC 2004. MBE 2005. *Wisden* 2007. **ECB central contract 2012-13. Tests**: 84 (2004 to 2012-13); HS 235 v I (Oval) 2011; BB 1-33 v P (Faisalabad) 2005-06. **LOI**: 127 (2004-05 to 2012-13); HS 126* v I (Southampton) 2007; BB 3-9 v Z (Bulawayo) 2004-05 – taking a wicket with his third ball in LOI. **IT20**: 7 (2006 to 2010-11); HS 60* v NZ (Manchester) 2008. F-c Tours: A 2006-07, 2010-11; SA 2009-10; WI 2000-01 (Eng A – *part*), 2008-09; NZ 2007-08, 2012-13; I 2005-06, 2008-09, 2012-13; P 2005-06; SL 2002-03 (ECB Acad), 2004-05, 2007-08, 2011-12; B 2009-10; UAE 2011-12 (v P). 1000 runs (4); most – 1714 (2004). HS 262* v Sussex (Horsham) 2004. BB 4-4 v Middx (Lord's) 2004. LO HS 158 EL v India A (Worcester) 2010. LO BB 5-41 v Essex (Chelmsford) 2003 (NL). T20 HS 85. T20 BB 1-12.

BEST, Paul Merwood (Bablake S, Coventry; Homerton C, Cambridge), b Nuneaton 8 Mar 1991. LHB, SLA. Cambridge MCCU 2011-12 (blue 2011-12). Warwickshire debut 2011. Northamptonshire 2011. Warwickshire 2nd XI debut 2010. England U19s 2009-10 to 2010. HS 150 CU v Surrey (Cambridge) 2011. CC HS 31* Nh v Glamorgan (Swansea) 2011. Wa HS 2 and CC BB 2-69 v Durham (Chester-le-St) 2011. BB 6-86 (9-131 match) CU v Oxford U (Cambridge) 2011. LO HS 16* and LO BB 3-43 v Yorks (Birmingham) 2012 (CB40). T20 HS – . T20 BB 3-19.

CHOPRA, Varun (Ilford County HS), b Barking, Essex 21 Jun 1987. 6'1". RHB, LB. Essex 2006-09, scoring 106 v Glos (Chelmsford) on CC Debut. Warwickshire debut 2010; cap 2012. Tamil Union 2011-12. England U19s 2005 to 2006. 1000 runs (2): most – 1203 (2011). HS 233* Tamil Union v Sinhalese (Colombo, PSS) 2011-12. Wa HS 228 v Worcs (Worcester) 2011 (in 2nd CC game of season, having scored 210 v Somerset in 1st). BB – . LO HS 115 v Leics (Birmingham) 2011 (CB40). T20 HS 56*.

CLARKE, Rikki (Broadwater SS; Godalming C), b Orsett, Essex 29 Sep 1981. 6'4". RHB, RFM. Surrey 2002-07, scoring 107* v Cambridge U (Cambridge) on debut; cap 2005. Derbyshire cap/captain 2008. Warwickshire debut 2008; cap 2011. MCC 2006. YC 2002. **Tests**: 2 (2003-04); HS 55 and BB 2-7 v B (Chittagong) 2003-04. **LOI**: 20 (2003 to 2006); HS 39 v P (Lord's) 2006; BB 2-28 v B (Dhaka) 2003-04. F-c Tours: WI 2003-04, 2005-06; SL 2002-03 (ECB Acad), 2004-05; B 2003-04. 1000 runs (1): 1027 (2006). HS 214 Sy v Somerset (Guildford) 2006. Wa HS 140 v Lancs (Liverpool) 2012. BB 6-63 v Kent (Canterbury) 2010. Took seven catches in an innings v Lancs (Liverpool) 2011 to equal world record. LO HS 98* Sy v Derbys (Derby) 2002 (NL). LO BB 4-28 v Northants (Birmingham) 2011 (CB40). T20 HS 79*. T20 BB 3-11.

COLEMAN, Frederick Robert John (Strathallan S; Oxford Brookes U), b Edinburgh, Scotland 15 Dec 1991. RHB, OB. Debut (Scotland) 2011-12. Oxford MCCU 2012. Awaiting Warwickshire 1st XI debut. Warwickshire 2nd XI debut 2010. HS 110 OU v Worcs (Oxford) 2012 – on UK debut. LO HS 5 Scot v Hants (Southampton) 2012 (CB40).

EVANS, Laurie John (Whitgift S; The John Fisher S; St Mary's C, Durham U), b Lambeth, London 12 Oct 1987. 6'0". RHB, RFM. Durham UCCE 2007. MCC 2007. Surrey 2009-10. Warwickshire debut 2010. HS 133* DU v Lancs (Durham) 2007. Wa HS 52 v Sussex (Birmingham) 2011. BB 1-30 Sy v Bangladeshis (Oval) 2010. LO HS 36* v Derbys (Croydon) 2009 (P40). T20 HS 68*.

GORDON, Recordo Olton (Aston Manor S; Hamstead Hall SFC), b St Elizabeth, Jamaica 12 Oct 1991. RHB, RFM. Warwickshire 2nd XI debut 2011. Awaiting 1st XI debut.

HAIN, Samuel Robert (Southport S, Gold Coast), b Hong Kong 16 July 1995. UK passport (British parents). RHB, RM. Warwickshire 2nd XI debut 2011. Awaiting 1st XI debut.

‡**HANNON-DALBY, Oliver** James (Brooksbank S, Leeds Met U), b Halifax, Yorkshire 20 Jun 1989. 6'7". LHB, RMF. Yorkshire 2008-12. No 1st XI appearances in 2009. HS 11* Y v Lancs (Manchester) 2010. BB 5-68 v Warwks (Birmingham) and 5-68 v Somerset (Leeds) 2010 – in consecutive matches. LO HS 21* Y v Warwks (Scarborough) 2012 (CB40). LO BB 2-22 Y v Worcs (Worcester) 2011 (CB40). T20 HS – . T20 BB 2-23.

JAVID, Ateeq (Aston Manor S), b Birmingham 15 Oct 1991. RHB, RM. Debut (Warwickshire) 2009. Warwickshire 2nd XI debut 2008. England U19s 2010 to 2010-11. HS 48 v Yorks (Leeds) 2010. BB – . LO HS 34 v Northants (Birmingham) 2011 (CB40). BB – .

MADDY, Darren Lee (Wreake Valley C), b Leicester 23 May 1974. 5'9". RHB, RM/OB. Leicestershire 1994-2006; cap 1996; benefit 2006. Warwickshire debut/cap 2007; captain 2007-08. **Tests**: 3 (1999 to 1999-00); HS 24 v SA (Durban) 1999-00; BB – . **LOI**: 8 (1998 to 1999-00); HS 53 v Z (Harare) 1999-00. **IT20**: 4 (2007-08); HS 50 and BB 2-6 v NZ (Durban) 2007-08. F-c Tours (Eng A): SA 1996-97 (Le), 1998-99, 1999-00 (Eng); SL 1997-98; Z 1998-99; K 1997-98. 1000 runs (4); most – 1187 (2002). HS 229* Le v Loughborough U (Leicester) 2003. CC HS 162 Le v Durham (Darlington) 1998. Wa HS 148* v Kent (Canterbury) 2007. BB 5-37 Le v Hants (Southampton) 2002. Wa BB 5-63 v Durham (Chester-le-St) 2007. LO HS 167* Le v Scotland (Edinburgh) 2006 (CGT). LO BB 4-16 Le v Somerset (Taunton) 2000 (NL). T20 HS 111 Le v Yorks (Leeds) 2004 – Le record. T20 BB 3-10.

METTERS, Christopher Liam (Coombeshead C; Exeter C), b Torquay, Devon 12 Sep 1990. 6'2". RHB, SLA. Debut (Warwickshire) 2011, taking 6-65 v Worcs (Birmingham). Missed entire 2012 season with shoulder injury. Warwickshire 2nd XI debut 2010. Essex 2nd XI 2010. Devon 2008-10. HS 30 v Hants (Southampton) 2011. BB (see above). LO HS 2 v Northants (Birmingham) 2011 (CB40). LO BB 2-41 v Durham (Chester-le-St) 2011 (CB40).

MILNES, Thomas Patrick (Heart of England S, Coventry), b Stourbridge, Worcs 6 Oct 1992. RHB, RFM. Debut (Warwickshire) 2011. Warwickshire 2nd XI debut 2009. England U19s 2010-11. HS 24 and CC BB 1-14 v Durham (Chester-le-St) 2012. BB 4-15 v Durham MCCU (Durham) 2011.

^{NQ}**PATEL, Jeetan** Shashi, b Wellington, New Zealand 7 May 1980. RHB, OB. Wellington 1999-00 to date. Warwickshire debut 2009; cap 2012. **Tests** (NZ): 19 (2006-07 to 2012-13); HS 27* v SA (Cape Town) 2006-07; BB 5-110 v WI (Napier) 2008-09. **LOI** (NZ): 39 (2005 to 2009-10); HS 34 v SL (Kingston) 2006-07; BB 3-11 v SA (Mumbai, BS) 2006-07. **IT20** (NZ): 11 (2005-06 to 2008-09); HS 5 v E (Auckland) 2007-08; BB 3-20 v SA (Johannesburg) 2005-06. F-c Tours (NZ): E 2008; SA 2005-06, 2012-13; I 2010-11, 2012; SL 2009, 2012-13; Z 2010-11, 2011-12; B 2008-09. HS 120 v Yorks (Birmingham) 2009. 50 wkts (1): 51 (2012). BB 7-75 v Somerset (Taunton) 2012. LO HS 34 (see LOI). LO BB 4-16 NZ A v Aus A (Hyderabad) 2008-09. T20 HS 12. T20 BB 4-27.

PIOLET, Steffan Andrew (Warden Park S; Central Sussex C), b Redhill, Surrey 8 Aug 1988. 6'1". RHB, RM. Debut (Warwickshire) 2009. Sussex 2nd XI 2006-08. Warwickshire 2nd XI debut 2008. HS 26* and BB 6-17 (10-43 match) v Durham UCCE (Durham) 2009 – on debut. CC HS 6 and CC BB 1-67 v Yorks (Leeds) 2010. LO HS 39 v Yorks (Birmingham) 2011 (CB40). LO BB 4-31 v Derbys (Derby) 2012 (CB40). T20 HS 26*. T20 BB 3-25.

PORTERFIELD, William Thomas Stuart (Strabane GS; Leeds Met U), b Londonderry, N.Ireland 6 Sep 1984. 5'11". LHB, OB. Ireland 2006 to date. MCC 2007. Gloucestershire 2008-10; cap 2008. Warwickshire debut 2011. **LOI** (Ire): 60 (2006 to 2012); HS 112* v Bermuda (Nairobi) 2006-07. **IT20** (Ire): 30 (2008 to 2012-13); HS 56* v Kenya (Dubai, DSC) 2011-12. F-c Tour (Ire, C=captain): WI 2009-10C. HS 175 Gs v Worcs (Cheltenham) 2010. Wa HS 87 v Durham (Chester-le-St) 2011. BB 1-29 Ire v Jamaica (Spanish Town) 2009-10. UK BB 1-57 Gs v Loughborough UCCE (Bristol) 2008. LO HS 112* (see LOI). T20 HS 83.

RANKIN, William Boyd (Strabane GS; Harper Adams UC), b Londonderry, Co Derry, N Ireland 5 Jul 1984. 6'8". LHB, RMF. Brother of R.J.Rankin. Ireland U19 2003-04). Ireland 2006-07 to 2008. Derbyshire 2007. Warwickshire debut 2008. Middlesex summer contract 2004-05. **LOI** (Ireland): 37 (2006-07 to 2011-12); HS 7* v SL (St George's) 2006-07; BB 3-32 v P (Kingston) 2006-07. **IT20** (Ire): 15 (2009 to 2012-13); HS 7* v Kenya (Mombasa) 2011-12; BB 3-20 v Kenya (Dubai, DSC) 2011-12. HS 43 ICC Combined XI v England XI (Dubai) 2011-12. Wa HS 28 v Durham (Chester-le-St) 2011. 50 wkts (1): 55 (2011). BB 5-16 v Essex (Birmingham) 2010. LO HS 9 v Kent (Canterbury) 2009 (FPT). LO BB 4-34 v Kent (Birmingham) 2010 (CB40). T20 HS 7*. T20 BB 4-9.

TROTT, Ian Jonathan Leonard (Rondebosch BHC; Stellenbosch U), b Cape Town, South Africa 22 Apr 1981. Stepbrother of K.C.Jackson (WP and Boland 1988-89 to 2001-02). 6'0". RHB, RM. Boland 2000-01. W Province 2001-02. EU/British passport. Warwickshire debut 2003, scoring 134 v Sussex (Birmingham); cap 2005. Otago 2005-06. *Wisden* 2010. **ECB central contract 2012-13. Tests**: 39 (2009 to 2012-13); HS 226 v B (Lord's) 2010; scored 119 v A (Oval) 2009 on debut. BB 1-5 v SL (Lord's) 2011. **LOI**: 57 (2009 to 2012-13); HS 137 v A (Sydney) 2010-11; BB 2-31 v A (Adelaide) 2010-11. **IT20**: 7 (2007 to 2009-10); HS 51 v SA (Centurion) 2009-10. F-c Tours: A 2010-11; SA 2009-10; NZ 2008-09 (EL), 2012-13; I 2007-08 (EL), 2012-13; SL 2011-12; B 2009-10; UAE 2011-12 (v P). 1000 runs (6); most – 1400 (2009). HS 226 (*see Tests*). CC HS 210 v Sussex (Birmingham) 2005. BB 7-39 v Kent (Canterbury) 2003. LO HS 137 (*see LOI*). LO BB 4-55 v Hants (Lord's) 2005 (CGT). T20 HS 86*. T20 BB 2-19.

TROUGHTON, Jamie Oliver (**'Jim'**) (Trinity S; Leamington Spa; Birmingham U), b Camden, London 2 Mar 1979. Great-grandson of H.T.Crichton (Warwicks 1908). 5'11". LHB, SLA. Debut (Warwickshire) 2001; cap 2002; captain 2011 to date; benefit 2013. **LOI**: 6 (2003); HS 20 v P (Lord's) 2003. F-c Tour (ECB Acad): SL 2002-03. 1000 runs (1): 1067 (2002). HS 223 v Hants (Birmingham) 2009. BB 3-1 v Cambridge U (Cambridge) 2004. CC BB 2-26 v Lancs (Birmingham) 2006. LO HS 115* and BB 4-23 Wa CB v Cumberland (Millom) 2001 (CGT). T20 HS 68*. T20 BB 2-10.

WESTWOOD, Ian James (Wheelers Lane S; Solihull SFC), b Birmingham 13 Jul 1982. 5'7½". LHB, OB. Debut (Warwickshire) 2003; cap 2008; captain 2009-10. HS 178 v West Indies A (Birmingham) 2006. CC HS 176 v Glamorgan (Cardiff) 2008. BB 2-39 v Hants (Southampton) 2009. LO HS 65 v Northants (Northampton) 2008 (FPT). BB 1-28 Wa CB v Cambs (March) 2001 (CGT). T20 HS 49*. T20 BB 3-29.

WOAKES, Christopher Roger (Barr Beacon Language S, Walsall), b Birmingham 2 March 1989. 6'2". RHB, RMF. Debut (Warwickshire) 2006; cap 2009. MCC 2009. Herefordshire 2006-07. **LOI**: 11 (2010-11 to 2012-13); HS 33* v SA (Nottingham) 2012; BB 6-45 v A (Brisbane) 2010-11. **IT20**: 3 (2010-11 to 2011); HS 19* v A (Adelaide) 2010-11; BB 1-29 v A (Melbourne) 2010-11. F-c Tour (EL): WI 2010-11. HS 136* v Hants (Birmingham) 2010. 50 wkts (2); most – 58 (2010). BB 7-20 (10-123 match) v Hants (Birmingham) 2011. LO HS 49* v Leics (Birmingham) 2010 (CB40). LO BB 6-45 (*see LOI*). T20 HS 55*. T20 BB 4-21.

WRIGHT, Christopher Julian Clement (Eggars S, Alton; Anglia Ruskin U), b Chipping Norton, Oxon 14 Jul 1985. 6'3". RHB, RFM. Cambridge UCCE 2004-05. Middlesex 2004-07. Tamil Union 2005-06. Essex 2008-11. Warwickshire debut (on loan) 2011. HS 77 Ex v Cambridge MCCU (Cambridge) 2011. CC HS 71* Ex v Middx (Chelmsford) 2008. Wa HS 53 v Notts (Birmingham) 2012. 50 wkts (1): 67 (2012). BB 6-22 Ex v Leics (Leicester) 2008. Wa BB 5-24 v Worcs (Worcester) 2012. LO HS 42 Ex v Glos (Cheltenham) 2011 (CB40). LO BB 4-20 Ex v Unicorns (Chelmsford) 2011 (CB40). T20 HS 6*. T20 BB 4-24.

RELEASED/RETIRED on p 189

WARWICKSHIRE 2012

RESULTS SUMMARY

	Place	Won	Lost	Tied	Drew	NR
LV= County Championship (1st Division)	**1st**	6	1		9	
All First-Class Matches		6	1		10	
Clydesdale Bank 40 (Group B)	Finalist	9	4			1
Friends Life t20 (Mid/Wales/West Group)	4th	4	3			3

LV= COUNTY CHAMPIONSHIP AVERAGES

BATTING AND FIELDING

Cap		M	I	NO	HS	Runs	Avge	100	50	Ct/St
2009	C.R.Woakes	8	10	4	118*	431	71.83	2	1	3
	I.D.Blackwell	4	6	1	84	265	53.00	–	2	–
2011	R.Clarke	16	21	4	140	760	44.70	3	2	29
2007	T.R.Ambrose	13	18	4	151*	623	44.50	1	3	42/1
2001	I.R.Bell	4	6	1	120	215	43.00	1	1	6
2008	I.J.Westwood	12	19	1	120	771	42.83	2	5	5
2012	V.Chopra	16	26	1	195	1028	41.12	3	5	26
2002	J.O.Troughton	15	24	3	132	733	34.90	2	4	9
2007	D.L.Maddy	14	21	2	112	473	24.89	1	–	10
	W.T.S.Porterfield	14	22	2	84	482	24.10	–	2	20
	K.H.D.Barker	15	17	4	46	304	23.38	–	–	5
2012	J.S.Patel	13	14	3	76	221	20.09	–	1	3
	C.J.C.Wright	15	15	5	53	194	19.40	–	1	2
	R.M.Johnson	3	4	–	49	72	18.00	–	–	6
2005	N.M.Carter	2	4	–	26	51	12.75	–	–	2
	W.B.Rankin	6	4	2	5	9	4.50	–	–	2

Also batted: L.J.Evans (1 match) 4, 9 (1 ct); T.P.Milnes (3) 24, 7*; I.J.L.Trott (2 – cap 2005) 178, 2 (1 ct).

BOWLING

	O	M	R	W	Avge	Best	5wI	10wM
K.H.D.Barker	392.1	94	1166	56	20.82	6-40	5	1
J.S.Patel	395.1	87	1161	51	22.76	7-75	4	–
C.J.C.Wright	450.3	74	1492	62	24.06	5-24	2	–
C.R.Woakes	225.5	47	681	27	25.22	4-67	–	–
R.Clarke	189	43	554	20	27.70	4-46	–	–
D.L.Maddy	139	44	344	12	28.66	4-39	–	–
W.B.Rankin	138.1	15	515	16	32.18	5-78	1	–
Also bowled:								
I.D.Blackwell	90.2	15	279	6	46.50	4-47	–	–

N.M.Carter 36-4-149-2; V.Chopra 2-0-5-0; T.P.Milnes 32-1-142-2; I.J.Westwood 9-4-26-0.

The First-Class Averages (pp 219–235) give the records of Warwickshire players in all first-class county matches (Warwickshire's other opponents being Cardiff MCCU), with the exception of I.R.Bell, I.D.Blackwell, R.M.Johnson, I.J.L.Trott and C.R.Woakes, whose full first-class figures for Warwickshire are as above, and:
V.Chopra 17-27-1-195-1052-40.46-3-5-27ct. 2-0-5-0.

WARWICKSHIRE RECORDS

FIRST-CLASS CRICKET

Highest Total	For	810-4d		v	Durham	Birmingham	1994
	V	887		by	Yorkshire	Birmingham	1896
Lowest Total	For	16		v	Kent	Tonbridge	1913
	V	15		by	Hampshire	Birmingham	1922
Highest Innings	For	501*	B.C.Lara	v	Durham	Birmingham	1994
	V	322	I.V.A.Richards	for	Somerset	Taunton	1985

Highest Partnership for each Wicket

1st	377*	N.F.Horner/K.Ibadulla	v	Surrey	The Oval	1960
2nd	465*	J.A.Jameson/R.B.Kanhai	v	Glos	Birmingham	1974
3rd	327	S.P.Kinneir/W.G.Quaife	v	Lancashire	Birmingham	1901
4th	470	A.I.Kallicharran/G.W.Humpage	v	Lancashire	Southport	1982
5th	335	J.O.Troughton/T.R.Ambrose	v	Hampshire	Birmingham	2009
6th	226	T.R.Ambrose/H.H.Streak	v	Worcs	Worcester	2007
7th	289*	I.R.Bell/T.Frost	v	Sussex	Horsham	2004
8th	228	A.J.W.Croom/R.E.S.Wyatt	v	Worcs	Dudley	1925
9th	233	I.J.L.Trott/J.S.Patel	v	Yorkshire	Birmingham	2009
10th	214	N.V.Knight/A.Richardson	v	Hampshire	Birmingham	2002

Best Bowling	For	10-41	J.D.Bannister	v	Comb Servs	Birmingham	1959
(Innings)	V	10-36	H.Verity	for	Yorkshire	Leeds	1931
Best Bowling	For	15-76	S.Hargreave	v	Surrey	The Oval	1903
(Match)	V	17-92	A.P.Freeman	for	Kent	Folkestone	1932

Most Runs – Season		2417	M.J.K.Smith	(av 60.42)	1959
Most Runs – Career		35146	D.L.Amiss	(av 41.64)	1960-87
Most 100s – Season		9	A.I.Kallicharran		1984
		9	B.C.Lara		1994
Most 100s – Career		78	D.L.Amiss		1960-87
Most Wkts – Season		180	W.E.Hollies	(av 15.13)	1946
Most Wkts – Career		2201	W.E.Hollies	(av 20.45)	1932-57
Most Career W-K Dismissals		800	E.J.Smith	(662 ct; 138 st)	1904-30
Most Career Catches in the Field		422	M.J.K.Smith		1956-75

LIMITED-OVERS CRICKET

Highest Total	50ov	392-5		v	Oxfordshire	Birmingham	1984
	40ov	321-7		v	Leics	Birmingham	2010
	T20	205-2		v	Northants	Birmingham	2005
		205-7		v	Glamorgan	Swansea	2005
Lowest Total	50ov	98		v	Leics	Leicester	1998
	40ov	59		v	Yorkshire	Leeds	2001
	T20	106-8		v	Worcs	Worcester	2011
Highest Innings	50ov	206	A.I.Kallicharran	v	Oxfordshire	Birmingham	1984
	40ov	137	I.R.Bell	v	Yorkshire	Birmingham	2005
	T20	89	N.V.Knight	v	Worcs	Worcester	2003
Best Bowling	50ov	6-32	K.Ibadulla	v	Hampshire	Birmingham	1965
		6-32	A.I.Kallicharran	v	Oxfordshire	Birmingham	1984
	40ov	6-15	A.A.Donald	v	Yorkshire	Birmingham	1995
	T20	5-19	N.M.Carter	v	Worcs	Birmingham	2005

WORCESTERSHIRE

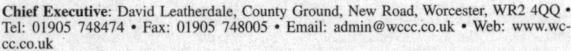

Formation of Present Club: 11 March 1865
Inaugural First-Class Match: 1899
Colours: Dark Green and Black
Badge: Shield Argent a Fess between three Pears Sable
County Championships: (5) 1964, 1965, 1974, 1988, 1989
Gillette/NatWest/C&G/FP Trophy Winners: (1) 1994
Benson and Hedges Cup Winners: (1) 1991
Pro 40/National League (Div 1) Winners: (1) 2007
Sunday League Winners: (3) 1971, 1987, 1988
Clydesdale Bank 40 Winners: (0); best – 5th in Group 2010
Twenty20 Cup Winners: (0); best – Quarter-Finalist 2004, 2007, 2012

Chief Executive: David Leatherdale, County Ground, New Road, Worcester, WR2 4QQ •
Tel: 01905 748474 • Fax: 01905 748005 • Email: admin@wccc.co.uk • Web: www.wc-cc.co.uk

Director of Cricket: Steve J.Rhodes. **Assistant Coach**: Damian D'Oliveira. **Bowling Coach**: Matt Mason. **Captain**: D.K.H.Mitchell. **Vice-Captain**: tba. **Overseas Players**: J.D.P.Oram (T20 only) and T.T.Samaraweera. **2013 Beneficiary**: none. **Head Groundsman**: Tim Packwood. **Scorer**: Dawn Pugh. ‡ New registration. NQ Not qualified for England.

Worcestershire revised their capping policy in 2002 and now award players with their County Colours when they make their Championship debut.

ALI, Moeen Munir (Moseley S), b Birmingham, Warwks 18 Jun 1987. Brother of A.K.Ali (*see LEICESTERSHIRE*) and cousin of Kabir Ali (*see LANCASHIRE*). 6'0". LHB, OB. Warwickshire 2005-06, having joined staff when aged 15. Worcestershire debut 2007. MCC 2012. HS 158 v Somerset (Worcester) 2011. BB 6-29 (12-96 match) v Lancs (Manchester) 2012. LO HS 158 v Sussex (Horsham) 2011 (CB40). LO BB 3-32 v Yorks (Worcester) 2009 (P40). T20 HS 82. T20 BB 3-19.

ANDREW, Gareth Mark (Ansford Community S; Richard Huish C), b Yeovil, Somerset 27 Dec 1983. 6'0". LHB, RMF. Somerset 2003-05. Worcestershire debut 2008. Canterbury 2012-13. HS 180* Canterbury v Auckland (Auckland) 2012-13. HS 92* v Notts (Worcester) 2009. 50 wkts (1): 52 (2011). BB 5-58 v Middx (Kidderminster) 2008. LO HS 104 v Surrey (Oval) 2010 (CB40). LO BB 5-31 v Yorks (Worcester) 2009 (P40). T20 HS 65*. T20 BB 4-22.

CESSFORD, Graeme (Queen Elizabeth HS, Hexham; Newcastle C), b Hexham, Northumberland 4 Oct 1983. 6'2". RHB, RFM. Worcestershire 2nd XI debut 2012. Awaiting 1st XI debut.

CHOUDHRY, Shaaiq Hussain (Fir Vale S; Bradford U), b Rotherham, Yorkshire 3 Nov 1985. 5'10". RHB, SLA. MCC 2007. Warwickshire 2009. Worcestershire debut 2010. Bradford/Leeds UCCE 2006-08 (not f-c). HS 75 Wa v Durham UCCE (Durham) 2009. CC HS 63 v Sussex (Hove) 2010. BB 4-38 v Lancs (Manchester) 2012. LO HS 39 v Sussex (Hove) 2010 (CB40). LO BB 4-54 v Surrey (Oval) 2010 (CB40). T20 HS 26*. T20 BB 2-24.

COX, Oliver Ben (Bromsgrove S), b Wordsley, Stourbridge 2 Feb 1992. 5'10". RHB, WK. Debut (Worcestershire) 2009. Worcestershire 2nd XI debut 2009. HS 61 v Somerset (Taunton) 2009 – on debut. LO HS 9* v Somerset (Worcester) 2010 (CB40). T20 HS 6*.

D'OLIVEIRA, Brett Louis (Worcester SFC), b Worcester 28 Feb 1992. Son of D.B.D'Oliveira (Worcs 1982-95), grandson of B.L.D'Oliveira (Worcs, EP and England 1964-80). RHB, LB. Debut (Worcestershire) 2012. Worcestershire 2nd XI debut 2010. HS 19 v Warwks (Birmingham) 2012. BB – . LO HS 16* v Essex (Worcester) 2012 (CB40). LO BB 2-35 v Glos (Cheltenham) 2012 (CB40) and 2-35 v Leics (Worcester) 2012 (CB40). T20 HS 6*. T20 BB 3-20.

HARRISON, Nicholas Luke (Hardenhuish S, Chippenham), b Bath, Somerset 3 Feb 1992. RHB, RMF. Debut (Worcestershire) 2012. Worcestershire 2nd XI debut 2010. Wiltshire 2009-10. HS 10 v Somerset (Taunton) 2012. BB 2-78 v Oxford MCCU (Oxford) 2012. CC BB 1-62 v Warwks (Worcester) 2012. LO HS 5* v Leics (Worcester) 2012 (CB40). LO BB 2-43 v Yorks (Leeds) 2011 (CB40).

‡NOJOHNSON, Michael Anthony, b Perth, Australia 11 Aug 1988. RHB, WK. W Australia 2008-09 to 2011-12. Has played 2nd XI cricket for Somerset, Hampshire, Northamptonshire, Surrey and Kent. Awaiting UK 1st XI debut. HS 53 WA v Q (Perth) 2011-12. LO HS 14 WA v NSW (Sydney) 2008-09. T20 HS 8*.

JONES, Richard Alan (Grange HS and King Edward VI C, Stourbridge; Loughborough U), b Wordsley, Stourbridge 6 Nov 1986. 6'2". RHB, RMF. Debut (Worcestershire) 2007. Matabeleland Tuskers 2011-12. HS 62 MT v SR (Bulawayo) 2011-12. Wo HS 53* v Durham (Worcester) 2009. BB 7-115 v Sussex (Hove) 2010. LO HS 11* v Sussex (Worcester) 2010 (CB40). LO BB 1-25 MT v ME (Bulawayo) 2011-12. T20 HS 9. T20 BB 1-17.

KAPIL, Aneesh (Denstone C), b Wolverhampton 3 Aug 1993. 5'8". RHB, RFM. Debut (Worcestershire) 2011. Worcestershire 2nd XI debut 2008, aged 15y 10d. HS 54 v Sussex (Horsham) 2011 – on debut. BB 3-17 v Notts (Worcester) 2012. LO HS 44 v Yorks (Worcester) 2011 (CB40). LO BB 1-18 v Netherlands (Worcester) 2011 (CB40). T20 HS 13. T20 BB 3-9.

NOKERVEZEE, Alexei Nicolaas (Duneside HS, Namibia; Grenoobi HS, SA; Segbroek C, Holland), b Walvis Bay, Namibia 11 Sep 1989. 5'8". RHB, OB. Netherlands 2005 to 2009-10. Worcestershire debut 2008. LOI (Ne): 39 (2006 to 2011-12); HS 92 v Kenya (Voorburg) 2010; BB – . IT20 (Ne): 10 (2009 to 2011-12); HS 58* v Afghanistan (Dubai, DSC) 2011-12. HS 155 v Derbys (Derby) 2010. BB 1-14 Netherlands v Namibia (Windhoek) 2007-08. LO HS 121* Netherlands v Denmark (Potchefstroom) 2008-09. LO BB – . T20 HS 58*.

LEACH, Joseph (Shrewsbury S; Leeds U), b Stafford 30 Oct 1990. 6'1". RHB, RMF. Debut (Leeds/Bradford MCCU) 2012. Worcestershire 2nd XI debut 2008. Worcestershire 2nd XI debut 2008. Staffordshire 2008-09. HS 50 and BB 4-73 LBU v Surrey (Oval) 2012 – on debut. CC HS 46 v Lancs (Worcester) 2012. CC BB 2-49 v Warwks (Worcester) 2012. LO BB – .

LUCAS, David Scott (Djanogly CTC, Nottingham), b Nottingham 19 Aug 1978. 6'2". RHB, LMF. Nottinghamshire 1999-2002. Yorkshire 2005. Northamptonshire 2007-11; cap 2009. Worcestershire debut 2012. Lincolnshire 2006. HS 60 Nh v Leics (Leicester) 2011. Wo HS 19 and Wo BB 4-37 v Surrey (Worcester) 2012. 50 wkts (1): 60 (2009). BB 7-24 (12-73 match) Nh v Glos (Cheltenham) 2009. LO HS 32* Nh v Lancs (Manchester) 2009 (FPT). LO BB 5-48 Nh v Hants (Northampton) 2011 (CB40). T20 HS 5*. T20 BB 3-19.

MITCHELL, Daryl Keith Henry (Prince Henry's HS; University C, Worcester), b Badsey, near Evesham 25 Nov 1983. 5'10". RHB, RM. Debut (Worcestershire) 2005; captain 2011 to date. Mountaineers 2011-12. 1000 runs (2); most – 1180 (2010). HS 298 v Somerset (Taunton) 2009. BB 4-49 v Yorks (Leeds) 2009. LO HS 92 v Somerset (Taunton) 2008 (FPT). LO BB 4-42 v Lancs (Worcester) 2006 (CGT). T20 HS 45. T20 BB 4-11 v Glos (Bristol) 2008 – Wo record.

‡NOORAM, Jacob David Philip, b Palmerston North, New Zealand 28 Jul 1978. 6'6". LHB, RMF. Central Districts 1997-98 to date. Joins Worcestershire in 2013 for T20 only. **Tests** (NZ): 33 (2002-03 to 2009); HS 133 v SA (Centurion) 2005-06; BB 4-41 v I (Hamilton) 2002-03. **LOI** (NZ): 160 (2000-01 to 2012-13); HS 101* v A (Perth) 2006-07; BB 5-26 v I (Auckland) 2002-03. **IT20** (NZ): 36 (2005-06 to 2012-13); HS 66* v A (Perth) 2007-08; BB 3-33 v SL (Colombo, RPS) 2009. F-c Tours (NZ): E 2000 (NZ A), 2004, 2008; A 2004-05; SA 2005-06; I 2003-04; SL 2003, 2009; B 2004-05, 2008-09. HS 155 CD v Canterbury (Christchurch) 1998-99. BB 6-45 CD v ND (Hamilton) 2005-06. LO HS 127 CD v Auckland (Auckland) 1997-98. LO BB 5-26 (see LOI). T20 HS 66*. T20 BB 5-14.

PARDOE, Matthew Graham (Haybridge HS), b Stourbridge 5 Jan 1991. 6'1". LHB, LM. Debut (Worcestershire) 2011. Southern Rocks 2012-13. Worcestershire 2nd XI debut 2007. HS 90 SR v ME (Masvingo) 2012-13. CC HS 74 v Notts (Nottingham) 2011. BB 2-34 SR v Mountaineers (Mutare) 2012-13. LO HS 42 SR v MT (Bulawayo) 2012-13. T20 HS 1.

PINNER, Neil Douglas (RGS Worcester), b Wordsley, Stourbridge 29 Sep 1990. 5'11". RHB, OB. Debut (Worcestershire) 2011. Worcestershire 2nd XI debut 2008. HS 82 v Lancs (Worcester) 2012. BB – . LO HS 37 v Kent (Canterbury) 2011 (CB40). LO BB – .

RICHARDSON, Alan (Alleyne's HS, Stone; Stafford CFE; Durham U), b Newcastle-under-Lyme, Staffs 6 May 1975. 6'2". RHB, RMF. Derbyshire 1995 (one match). Warwickshire 1999-2004; cap 2002. Middlesex 2005-09; cap 2005, taking 7-113 v Notts (Lord's) on debut. Worcestershire debut 2010. MCC 2012. Wisden 2011. Staffordshire 1996-98. Minor Counties 1998. HS 91 Wa v Hants (Birmingham) 2002 – adding Wa record 214 for 10th wicket with N.V.Knight. Wo HS 41 v Sussex (Horsham) 2011. 50 wkts (4); most – 73 (2011). BB 8-46 Wa v Sussex (Birmingham) 2002. Wo BB 6-22 v Lancs (Worcester) 2011. LO HS 21* M v Lancs (Lord's) 2005 (NL). LO BB 5-35 Wa v Staffs (Stone) 2002 (CGT). T20 HS 6*. T20 BB 3-13.

RUSSELL, Christopher James (Medina HS), b Newport, IoW 16 Feb 1989. 6'1". RHB, RMF. Debut (Worcestershire) 2012. Worcestershire 2nd XI debut 2008. HS 22 v Middx (Worcester) 2012. BB 4-43 v Warwks (Birmingham) 2012. LO HS – . LO BB 1-23 v Unicorns (Worcester) 2010 (CB40).

‡NOSAMARAWEERA, Thilan Thusara, b Colombo, Sri Lanka 22 Sep 1976. Younger brother of D.P.Samaraweera (Colts and Sri Lanka 1991-92 to 2003-04). RHB, OB. Colts CC 1996-97 to 1997-98. Sinhalese SC 1998-99. Kandurata 2009-10. **Tests** (SL): 81 (2001 to 2012-13); HS 231 v P (Karachi) 2008-09; BB 4-49 v B (Colombo, SSC) 2002. **LOI** (SL): 53 (1998-99 to 2010-11); HS 105* v I (Dhaka) 2009; BB 3-34 v E (Sydney) 1998-99. F-c Tours (SL): E 2002, 2006, 2007 (SL A), 2011; A 2004, 2007-08, 2012-13; SA 1999-00 (SL A), 2011-12; WI 2003, 2006-07 (SL A), 2007-08; NZ 2004-05; I 2001-02 (Colombo CA), 2005-06, 2006-07 (SL A), 2009-10; P 2001-02, 2002-03 (SL A), 2004-05, 2008-09; Z 2004; B 2005-06, 2008-09. 1000 runs (1): 1236 (2003-04). HS 231 (see Tests). BB 6-55 SSC v Singha SC (Colombo, SSC) 2000-01 and 6-55 SL A v Pakistan A (Dambulla) 2001. LO HS 105* (see LOI). LO BB 7-30 SL A v ECB Nat Academy (Kurunegala) 2002-03. T20 HS 71. T20 BB 3-17.

SHANTRY, Jack David (Priory SS; Shrewsbury SFC; Liverpool U), b Shrewsbury, Shropshire 29 Jan 1988. Son of B.K.Shantry (Gloucestershire 1978-79) and brother of A.J.Shantry (Northants, Warwicks, Glamorgan 2003-11). 6'4". LHB, LM. Debut (Worcestershire) 2009. Shropshire 2007-09. HS 47* v Yorks (Scarborough) 2011. BB 5-49 v Leics (Leicester) 2010. LO HS 18 v Sussex (Hove) 2010 (CB40). LO BB 4-32 v Middx (Worcester) 2012 (CB40). T20 HS 6*. T20 BB 4-33.

RELEASED/RETIRED
(Having made a County First-Class or List A appearance in 2012)

CAMERON, James Gair (St George's C, Harare; U of WA), b Harare, Zimbabwe 31 Jan 1986. LHB, RM. British passport holder. Worcestershire 2010-12. HS 105 v Sussex (Worcester) 2010. BB 2-18 v Northants (Worcester) 2010. LO HS 69 v Derbys (Worcester) 2011 (CB40). LO BB 4-44 v Glamorgan (Cardiff) 2010 (CB40). T20 HS 57. T20 BB 3-22.

[NO]**HUGHES, Phillip** Joel, b Macksville, NSW, Australia 30 Nov 1988. LHB, OB. NSW 2007-08 to 2011-12. Middlesex 2009, scoring 118 and 65* on debut. Hampshire 2010. Worcestershire 2012. S Australia 2012-13. **Tests** (A): 22 (2008-09 to 2012-13); HS 160 (and 115) v SA (Durban) 2008-09. **LOI** (A): 10 (2012-13); HS 138* v SL (Hobart) 2012-13. Scored 112 v SL (Melbourne) on LOI debut. F-c Tours (A): E 2009; SA 2008-09, 2011-12; NZ 2009-10; I 2008-09 (Aus A). 2012-13; SL 2011. HS 198 NSW v S Australia (Adelaide) 2008-09. UK HS 195 M v Surrey (Oval) 2009. Wo HS 135* v Warwks (Birmingham) 2012. LO HS 138* (*see LOI*). T20 HS 87*.

KLINGER, M. – *see GLOUCESTERSHIRE.*

SCOTT, Ben James Matthew (Whitton S, Richmond; Richmond C), b Isleworth 4 Aug 1981. 5'8". RHB, WK. Surrey 2003. Middlesex 2004-09; cap 2007. Worcestershire 2010-12. MCC YC 2000. F-c Tour (Eng A): NZ 2008-09. HS 164* M v Northants (Uxbridge) 2008. Wo HS 106 v Lancs (Manchester) 2012. LO HS 73* M v Surrey (Southgate) 2006 (CGT). T20 HS 43*.

SOLANKI, V. – *see SURREY.*

A.D.Blofield and J.K.Manuel left the staff, without making a First-Class County or List A appearance in 2012.

WARWICKSHIRE RELEASED/RETIRED (continued from p 183)
(Having made a County First-Class or List A appearance in 2012)

CARTER, Neil Miller (Hottentots Holland HS; Cape Technicon), b Cape Town, South Africa 29 Jan 1975. British passport. 6'2". LHB, LMF. Boland 1999-00 to 2000-01. Warwickshire 2001-12; cap 2005; benefit 2012. PCA 2010. **IT20** (Scot): 1 (2012-13); HS 3 and BB 2-27 v Afghanistan (Sharjah) 2012-13. HS 103 v Sussex (Hove) 2002 – completed maiden hundred off 67 balls. 50 wkts (1): 51 (2010). BB 6-30 v Lancs (Liverpool) 2011. LO HS 135 v Scotland (Birmingham) 2006 (CGT). LO BB 5-31 v Durham (Birmingham) 2002 (NL). T20 HS 58. T20 BB 5-19 v Worcs (Birmingham) 2005 – Wa record.

JOHNSON, R.M. – *see DERBYSHIRE.*

MILLER, Andrew Stephen (St Cecilia's RC HS; Preston C), b Preston, Lancs 27 Sep 1987. 6'4". RHB, RFM. Warwickshire 2008-12. HS 35 v Durham (Birmingham) 2010. BB 5-58 v Lancs (Birmingham) 2010. LO HS 2* v Scotland (Birmingham) 2011 (CB40). LO BB 2-31 v Durham (Birmingham) 2011 (CB40). T20 HS 0*. T20 BB 2-16.

WORCESTERSHIRE 2012

RESULTS SUMMARY

	Place	Won	Lost	Tied	Drew	NR
LV= County Championship (1st Division)	9th	1	8		7	
All First-Class Matches		1	8		8	
Clydesdale Bank 40 (Group A)	7th	3	7	1		1
Friends Life t20 (Mid/Wales/West Group)	QF	4	4			3

LV= COUNTY CHAMPIONSHIP AVERAGES
BATTING AND FIELDING

Cap†		M	I	NO	HS	Runs	Avge	100	50	Ct/St
2012	P.J.Hughes	9	17	1	135*	560	35.00	2	2	2
2009	A.N.Kervezee	6	10	1	76	283	31.44	–	3	7
2012	M.Klinger	6	11	1	69*	293	29.30	–	2	7
2005	D.K.H.Mitchell	16	30	2	133*	766	27.35	2	1	22
2008	M.M.Ali	16	28	3	94	652	26.08	–	4	5
1998	V.S.Solanki	13	23	3	106	472	23.60	1	2	18
2009	J.D.Shantry	4	5	2	22*	67	22.33	–	–	1
2010	J.G.Cameron	11	17	3	52	300	21.42	–	1	3
2011	M.G.Pardoe	12	22	2	55	407	20.35	–	1	10
2011	N.D.Pinner	4	7	–	82	132	18.85	–	1	1
2011	A.Kapil	4	6	1	41	93	18.60	–	–	–
2007	R.A.Jones	10	15	5	32	151	15.10	–	–	5
2009	O.B.Cox	3	6	1	25*	67	13.40	–	–	5
2010	B.J.M.Scott	13	20	1	106	228	12.00	1	–	28/5
2008	G.M.Andrew	9	16	2	29	159	11.35	–	–	3
2012	C.J.Russell	6	10	2	22	83	10.37	–	–	2
2012	J.Leach	5	9	–	46	93	10.33	–	–	–
2012	B.L.D'Oliveira	3	6	–	19	62	10.33	–	–	–
2012	D.S.Lucas	7	9	–	19	74	8.22	–	–	2
2010	A.Richardson	14	21	9	18	79	6.58	–	–	3
2010	S.H.Choudhry	3	5	–	20	29	5.80	–	–	3
2012	N.L.Harrison	2	4	–	10	12	3.00	–	–	–

BOWLING

	O	M	R	W	Avge	Best	5wI	10wM
A.Richardson	461.3	137	1113	57	19.52	6-47	4	1
M.M.Ali	284.1	40	901	33	27.30	6-29	2	1
R.A.Jones	200.1	26	857	31	27.64	6-32	1	–
J.D.Shantry	100	19	321	11	29.18	5-58	1	–
C.J.Russell	134.4	23	563	17	33.11	4-43	–	–
G.M.Andrew	179	27	685	18	38.05	5-86	1	–
D.S.Lucas	239	40	852	22	38.72	4-37	–	–

Also bowled:

S.H.Choudhry	41.2	9	83	7	11.85	4-38	–	–

J.G.Cameron 37-1-160-2; B.L.D'Oliveira 43-2-198-0; N.L.Harrison 23-3-98-1; A.Kapil 35-4-136-4; J.Leach 40-8-127-4; D.K.H.Mitchell 8-0-24-0; N.D.Pinner 4-0-13-0.

The First-Class Averages (pp 219–235) give the records of Worcestershire players in all first-class county matches (Worcestershire's other opponents being Oxford MCCU), with the exception of P.J.Hughes and J.Leach, whose full first-class figures for Worcestershire are as above, and:

M.Klinger 7-12-1-120-413-37.54-1-2-8ct.

† Worcestershire revised their capping policy in 2002 and now award players with their County Colours when they make their Championship debut.

WORCESTERSHIRE RECORDS

FIRST-CLASS CRICKET

Highest Total	For	701-6d		v	Surrey	Worcester	2007
	V	701-4d		by	Leics	Worcester	1906
Lowest Total	For	24		v	Yorkshire	Huddersfield	1903
	V	30		by	Hampshire	Worcester	1903
Highest Innings	For	405*	G.A.Hick	v	Somerset	Taunton	1988
	V	331*	J.D.B.Robertson	for	Middlesex	Worcester	1949

Highest Partnership for each Wicket

1st	309	H.K.Foster/F.L.Bowley	v	Derbyshire	Derby	1901
2nd	316	S.C.Moore/V.S.Solanki	v	Glos	Cheltenham	2008
3rd	438*	G.A.Hick/T.M.Moody	v	Hampshire	Southampton	1997
4th	330	B.F.Smith/G.A.Hick	v	Somerset	Taunton	2006
5th	393	E.G.Arnold/W.B.Burns	v	Warwicks	Birmingham	1909
6th	265	G.A.Hick/S.J.Rhodes	v	Somerset	Taunton	1988
7th	256	D.A.Leatherdale/S.J.Rhodes	v	Notts	Nottingham	2002
8th	184	S.J.Rhodes/S.R.Lampitt	v	Derbyshire	Kidderminster	1991
9th	181	J.A.Cuffe/R.D.Burrows	v	Glos	Worcester	1907
10th	119	W.B.Burns/G.A.Wilson	v	Somerset	Worcester	1906

Best Bowling	For	9- 23	C.F.Root	v	Lancashire	Worcester	1931
(Innings)	V	10- 51	J.Mercer	for	Glamorgan	Worcester	1936
Best Bowling	For	15- 87	A.J.Conway	v	Glos	Moreton-in-M	1914
(Match)	V	17-212	J.C.Clay	for	Glamorgan	Swansea	1937

Most Runs – Season	2654	H.H.I.H.Gibbons	(av 52.03)	1934
Most Runs – Career	34490	D.Kenyon	(av 34.18)	1946-67
Most 100s – Season	10	G.M.Turner		1970
	10	G.A.Hick		1988
Most 100s – Career	106	G.A.Hick		1984-2008
Most Wkts – Season	207	C.F.Root	(av 17.52)	1925
Most Wkts – Career	2143	R.T.D.Perks	(av 23.73)	1930-55
Most Career W-K Dismissals	1095	S.J.Rhodes	(991 ct; 104 st)	1985-2004
Most Career Catches in the Field	528	G.A.Hick		1984-2008

LIMITED-OVERS CRICKET

Highest Total	50ov	404-3		v	Devon	Worcester	1987
	40ov	376-6		v	Surrey	Oval	2010
	T20	227-6		v	Northants	Kidderminster	2007
Lowest Total	50ov	58		v	Ireland	Worcester	2009
	40ov	86		v	Yorkshire	Leeds	1969
	T20	86		v	Northants	Worcester	2006
Highest Innings	50ov	180*	T.M.Moody	v	Surrey	The Oval	1994
	40ov	160	T.M.Moody	v	Kent	Worcester	1991
	T20	116*	G.A.Hick	v	Northants	Luton	2004
Best Bowling	50ov	7-19	N.V.Radford	v	Beds	Bedford	1991
	40ov	6-16	Shoaib Akhtar	v	Glos	Worcester	2005
	T20	4-11	D.K.H.Mitchell	v	Glos	Bristol	2008

YORKSHIRE

Formation of Present Club: 8 January 1863
Substantial Reorganisation: 10 December 1891
Inaugural First-Class Match: 1864
Colours: Dark Blue, Light Blue and Gold
Badge: White Rose
County Championships (since 1890): (30) 1893, 1896,
1898, 1900, 1901, 1902, 1905, 1908, 1912, 1919, 1922,
1923, 1924, 1925, 1931, 1932, 1933, 1935, 1937, 1938,
1939, 1946, 1959, 1960, 1962, 1963, 1966, 1967, 1968, 2001
Joint Champions: (1) 1949
Gillette/NatWest/C&G/FP Trophy Winners: (3) 1965, 1969, 2002
Benson and Hedges Cup Winners: (1) 1987
Pro 40/National League (Div 1) Winners: (0); best – 2nd 2000
Sunday League Winners: (1) 1983
Clydesdale Bank 40 Winners: (0); best – Semi-Finalist 2010
Twenty20 Cup Winners: (0); best – Finalist 2012

Chairman: Colin Graves, Headingley Carnegie, Kirkstall Lane, Headingley, Leeds, LS6
3DP • Tel: 0871 971 1222 • Fax: 0113 278 4099 • Email: cricket@yorkshireccc.com • Web:
www.yorkshireccc.com

Director of Professional Cricket: Martyn Moxon. **Senior 1st XI Coach**: Jason Gillespie.
Senior 2nd XI Coach: Paul Farbrace. **Captain**: A.W.Gale. **Vice-Captain**: tba. **Overseas
Players**: none. **2013Beneficiary**: none. **Head Groundsman**: Andy Fogarty. **Scorer**: John
T.Potter. ‡ New registration. ^{NQ} Not qualified for England.

ASHRAF, Moin Aqeeb (Dixons City Academy, Bradford), b Bradford 5 Jan 1992. 6'4".
RHB, RMF. Debut (Yorkshire) 2010. Yorkshire 2nd XI debut 2009. HS 10 and BB 5-32 v
Kent (Leeds) 2010. LO HS 3* v Kent (Leeds) 2012 (CB40). LO BB 2-25 England Dev XI v
Sri Lanka A (Manchester) 2011. T20 HS – . T20 BB 4-18.

AZEEM Muhammad RAFIQ (Holgate S Sports C; Barnsley C), b Karachi, Pakistan 27 Feb
1991. 5'11". RHB, OB. Debut (Yorkshire) 2009. Derbyshire (on loan) 2011. Yorkshire 2nd
XI debut 2008. England U19s 2009 to 2010. HS 100 v Worcs (Worcester) 2009. BB 5-50 v
Essex (Chelmsford) 2012. LO HS 34* v Unicorns (Leeds) 2012 (CB40). LO BB 3-22 v
Kent (Leeds) 2012 (CB40). T20 HS 21*. T20 BB 3-15.

BAIRSTOW, Jonathan Marc (St Peter's S, York; Leeds Met U), b Bradford 26 Sep 1989.
Son of D.L.Bairstow (Yorkshire, GW and England 1970-90) and brother of A.D.Bairstow
(Derbyshire 1995). 6'0". RHB, WK. Debut (Yorkshire) 2009. Inaugural winner of
Young Wisden Schools Cricketer of the Year 2008. YC 2011. **Tests**: 5 (2012 to 2012-13);
HS 95 v SA (Lord's) 2012. **LOI**: 7 (2011 to 2012); HS 41* v I (Cardiff) 2011. **IT20**: 18 (2011
to 2012-13); HS 60* v P (Dubai) 2011-12. F-c Tours: I 2012-13; WI 2010-11 (EL). 1000
runs (1): 1213 (2011). HS 205 v Notts (Nottingham) 2011. LO HS 114 v Middx (Lord's)
2011 (CB40). T20 HS 68*.

BALLANCE, Gary Simon (Peterhouse S, Marondera, Zimbabwe; Harrow S; Leeds Met
U), b Harare, Zimbabwe 22 Nov 1989. Nephew of G.S.Ballance (Rhodesia B 1978-79) and
D.L.Houghton (Rhodesia/Zimbabwe 1978-79 to 1997-98). 6'0". LHB, LB. Debut (York-
shire) 2008; cap 2012. Mid West Rhinos 2010-11 to 2011-12. Derbyshire (List A) 2006-07.
HS 210 MWR v SR (Masvingo) 2011-12. Y HS 121* v Glos (Bristol) 2012. BB – . LO HS
135* MWR v ME (Kwekwe) 2010-11. T20 HS 67.

BRESNAN, Timothy Thomas (Castleford HS and TC; Pontefract New C), b Pontefract 28 Feb 1985. 6'0". RHB, RFM. Debut (Yorkshire) 2003; cap 2006. MCC 2006, 2009. *Wisden* 2011. **ECB central contract 2012-13. Tests**: 18 (2009 to 2012-13); HS 91 v B (Dhaka) 2009-10; BB 5-48 v I (Nottingham) 2011. **LOI**: 69 (2006 to 2012-13); HS 80 v SA (Centurion) 2009-10; BB 5-48 v I (Bangalore) 2010-11. **IT20**: 25 (2006 to 2012-13); HS 23* v NZ (Gros Islet) 2009-10; BB 3-10 v P (Cardiff) 2010. F-c Tours: A 2010-11; I 2012-13; SL 2011-12; B 2006-07 (Eng A), 2009-10. HS 126* Eng A v Indians (Chelmsford) 2007. Y HS 116 v Surrey (Oval) 2007, sharing in Y record 9th wicket partnership of 246 with J.N.Gillespie. BB 5-42 v Worcs (Worcester) 2005. LO HS 80 (*see LOI*). BB 5-48 (*see LOI*). T20 HS 42. T20 BB 3-10.

‡**BROOKS, Jack** Alexander (Wheatley Park S), b Oxford 4 Jun 1984. 6'2". RHB, RFM. Northamptonshire 2009-12; cap 2012. Oxfordshire 2004-09. HS 53 Nh v Glos (Bristol) 2010. BB 5-23 Nh v Leics (Leicester) 2011. LO HS 10 Nh v Middx (Uxbridge) 2009 (P40). LO BB 3-35 EL v Bangladesh A (Sylhet) 2011-12. T20 HS 33*. T20 BB 3-24.

GALE, Andrew William (Whitcliffe Mount S; Heckmondwike GS), b Dewsbury 28 Nov 1983. 6'2". LHB, LB. Debut (Yorkshire) 2004, 2006 to date; cap 2008; captain 2010 to date. F-c Tour (EL): WI 2010-11. HS 151* v Notts (Nottingham) 2010. BB 1-33 v Loughborough UCCE (Leeds) 2007. LO HS 125* v Essex (Chelmsford) 2010 (CB40). T20 HS 91.

GIBSON, Barney Peter (Crawshaw HS, Pudsey), b Leeds 31 Mar 1996. 5'8½". RHB, WK. Debut (Yorkshire) 2011, aged 15y 27d, becoming youngest player to play f-c cricket, beating a record set in 1867. HS 1* v Durham MCCU (Durham) 2011.

HODD, Andrew John (Bexhill C), b Chichester, Sussex 12 Jan 1984. 5'9". RHB, WK. Sussex 2003-11. Surrey 2005 (1 match). Yorkshire debut 2012 (on loan). HS 123 Sx v Yorks (Hove) 2004. Y HS 58 v Derbys (Leeds) 2012. LO HS 91 Sx v Lancs (Hove) 2010 (CB40). T20 HS 26.

HODGSON, Daniel Mark (Richmond S; Leeds U), b Northallerton 26 Feb 1990. RHB, WK. Debut (Leeds/Bradford MCCU) 2012, scoring 64 v Surrey (Oval). Mountaineers 2012-13. Yorkshire 2nd XI debut 2011. Awaiting Y f-c debut. HS 94* Mountaineers v SR (Mutare) 2012-13. LO HS 24 Mountaineers v MT (Mutare) 2012-13. T20 HS 18.

JAQUES, Philip Anthony (Fig Tree HS, Wollongong; Australian C of PE, Homebush), b Wollongong, NSW, Australia 3 May 1979. 6'1". LHB, SLC. British passport (English parents) and now UK qualified. New South Wales 2000-01 to date. Northamptonshire 2003; cap 2003. Yorkshire debut 2004; cap 2005. Worcestershire 2006-07, 2010. **Tests** (A): 11 (2005-06 to 2008); HS 150 v SL (Hobart) 2007-08. **LOI** (A): 6 (2005-06 to 2006-07); HS 94 v SA (Melbourne) 2005-06. F-c Tours (A): WI 2008; P 2005-06 (Aus A), 2007-08 (Aus A); B 2005-06. 1000 runs (4+2); most – 1409 (2003). HS 244 Wo v Essex (Chelmsford) 2006. BB – . Y HS 243 v Hants (Southampton) 2004. LO HS 171* NSW v Q (Sydney) 2009-10. T20 HS 92.

LEANING, Jack Andrew (Archbishop Holgate's S, York; York C), b Bristol, Glos 18 Oct 1993. RHB, RMF. Yorkshire 2nd XI debut 2011. Awaiting f-c debut. LO HS 11 v Warwks (Scarborough) 2012 (CB40) – only 1st XI appearance.

LEES, Alexander Zak (Holy Trinity SS, Halifax), b Halifax 14 Apr 1993. 6'3". LHB, LB. Debut (Yorkshire) 2010. Awaiting CC debut. Yorkshire 2nd XI debut 2010. HS 38 v India A (Leeds) 2010. LO HS 23 v Warwks (Scarborough) 2012 (CB40).

LILLEY, Alexander Edward (St Aidan's C of E HS, Harrogate), b Halifax 17 Apr 1992. 5'10". RHB, LM. Debut (Yorkshire) 2011. Yorkshire 2nd XI debut 2010. HS 0 and BB- v Durham MCCU (Durham) 2011 – only 1st XI game.

LYTH, Adam (Caedmon S, Whitby; Whitby Community C), b Whitby 25 Sep 1987. 5'8". LHB, RM. Debut (Yorkshire) 2007; cap 2010. F-c Tour (EL): WI 2010-11. 1000 runs (1): 1509 (2010). HS 248* v Leics (Leicester) 2012. BB 1-12 v Loughborough UCCE (Leeds) 2007. CC BB 1-20 v Somerset (Scarborough) 2008. LO HS 109* v Sussex (Scarborough) 2009 (P40). LO BB – . T20 HS 78.

PATTERSON, Steven Andrew (Malet Lambert CS; St Mary's SFC, Hull; Leeds U), b Hull 3 Oct 1983. 6'4". RHB, RMF. Debut (Yorkshire) 2005; cap 2012. Bradford/Leeds UCCE 2003 (not f-c). HS 53 v Sussex (Hove) 2011. 50 wkts (1): 53 (2012). BB 5-50 v Essex (Scarborough) 2010. LO HS 25* v Worcs (Leeds) 2006 (P40). LO BB 6-32 v Derbys (Leeds) 2010. T20 HS 3*. T20 BB 4-30.

‡PLUNKETT, Liam Edward (Nunthorpe SS; Teesside Tertiary C), b Middlesbrough, Yorks 6 Apr 1985. 6'3". RHB, RFM. Durham 2003-12. Dolphins 2007-08. **Tests**: 9-(2005-06 to 2007); HS 44* v WI (Leeds) 2007; BB 3-17 v SL (Birmingham) 2006. **LOI**: 29 (2005-06 to 2010-11); HS 56 v P (Lahore) 2005-06; BB 3-24 v A (Sydney) 2006-07. **IT20**: 1 (2006); HS – ; BB 1-37 v SL (Southampton) 2006. F-c Tours: WI 2010-11 (EL); NZ 2008-09 (EL); I 2005-06, 2007-08 (EL); P 2005-06. HS 107* Du v Durham MCCU (Durham) 2011. CC HS 94* Du v Sussex (Hove) 2009. 50 wkts (3); most – 60 (2009). BB 6-63 (11-119 match) Du v Worcs (Chester-le-St) 2009. LO HS 72 Du v Somerset (Chester-le-St) 2008 (P40). LO BB 4-15 Du v Essex (Chester-le-St) 2007 (FPT). T20 HS 41. T20 BB 5-31.

PYRAH, Richard Michael (Ossett S; Wakefield C), b Dewsbury 1 Nov 1982. 6'0". RHB, RM. Debut (Yorkshire) 2004; cap 2010. HS 134* v Loughborough MCCU (Leeds) 2010. CC HS 117 v Lancs (Leeds) 2011. BB 5-58 v Notts (Leeds) 2011. LO HS 69 v Netherlands (Leeds) 2011 (CB40). LO BB 5-50 Yorks CB v Somerset (Scarborough) 2002 (CGT). T20 HS 35. T20 BB 5-16 v Durham (Scarborough) 2011 – Y record.

RANDHAWA, Gurman Singh (Newsome HS; Huddersfield New C), b Huddersfield 25 Jan 1992. 5'10". LHB, SLA. Debut (Yorkshire) 2011. Yorkshire 2nd XI debut 2009. England U19s 2010-11. HS 5 and BB 2-54 v Durham MCCU (Durham) 2011 – only 1st XI game.

RASHID, Adil Usman (Belle Vue S, Bradford), b Bradford 17 Feb 1988. 5'8". RHB, LBG. Debut (Yorkshire) 2006; cap 2008. MCC 2007-09. YC 2007. Match double (114, 48, 8-157 and 2-45) for England U19 v India U19 (Taunton) 2006. **LOI**: 5 (2009 to 2009-10); HS 31* v A (Oval) 2009; BB 1-16 v Ireland (Belfast) 2009. **IT20**: 5 (2009 to 2009-10); HS 9* v SA (Nottingham) 2009; BB 1-11 v WI (Oval) 2009. F-c Tours (EL): WI 2010-11; I 2007-08; B 2006-07 (Eng A). HS 157* v Lancs (Leeds) 2009. 50 wkts (2); most – 65 (2008). BB 7-107 v Hants (Southampton) 2008. LO HS 43 v Netherlands (Amstelveen) 2011 (CB40). LO BB 4-38 v Northants (Northampton) 2012 (CB40). T20 HS 36*. T20 BB 4-20.

ROOT, Joseph Edward (King Ecgbert S, Sheffield; Worksop C), b Sheffield 30 Dec 1990. 6'0". RHB, OB. Debut (Yorkshire) 2010; cap 2012. Yorkshire 2nd XI debut 2007. England U19s 2009-10 to 2010. YC 2012. **Tests**: 2 (2012-13); HS 73 v I (Nagpur) 2012-13 – on debut; BB – . **LOI**: 8 (2012-13); HS 79* v NZ (Napier) 2012-13; BB – . F-c Tours: NZ 2012-13; I 2012-13. 1000 runs (1): 1013 (2011). HS 222 v Hants (Southampton) 2012. BB 3-33 v Warwks (Leeds) 2011. LO HS 110* EL v Sri Lanka A (Colombo, RPS) 2011-12. LO BB 2-10 EL v Bangladesh A (Sylhet) 2011-12. T20 HS 65. T20 BB 1-12.

SAYERS, Joseph John (St Mary's RC CS, Menston; Worcester C, Oxford) b Leeds 5 Nov 1983. 6'0". LHB, OB. Oxford U 2002-04; blue 2002-03-04. Yorkshire debut 2004; cap 2007. 1000 runs (1): 1150 (2009). HS 187 v Kent (Tunbridge W) 2007. BB 3-15 v Durham MCCU (Durham) 2011. CC BB 3-20 v Warwks (Scarborough) 2009. LO HS 62 v Glos (Leeds) 2003 (NL). LO BB 1-31 v Warwks (Birmingham) 2005 (NL). T20 HS 44.

SIDEBOTTOM, Ryan Jay (King James's GS, Almondbury), b Huddersfield 15 Jan 1978. Son of A.Sidebottom (Yorks, OFS and England 1973-91). 6'3". LHB, LFM. Yorkshire 1997-2003; cap 2000. Returned to Yorkshire in 2011. Nottinghamshire 2004-10; cap 2004; benefit 2010. *Wisden* 2007. Tests: 22 (2001 to 2009-10); HS 31 v SL (Kandy) 2007-08; BB 7-47 v NZ (Napier) 2007-08. Hat-trick v NZ (Hamilton) 2007-08. LOI: 25 (2001-02 to 2009-10); HS 24 v A (Southampton) 2009; BB 3-19 v SL (Dambulla) 2007-08. IT20: 18 (2007 to 2010); HS 5* and BB 3-16 v NZ (Auckland) 2007-08. F-c Tours: SA 2009-10; WI 2000-01 (Eng A), 2008-09; NZ 2007-08; SL 2007-08. HS 61 v Worcs (Worcester) 2011. 50 wkts (3); most – 62 (2011). BB 7-37 (11-98 match) v Somerset (Leeds) 2011. LO HS 32 Nt v Middx (Nottingham) 2005 (NL). LO BB 6-40 v Glamorgan (Cardiff) 1998 (SL). T20 HS 17*. T20 BB 4-25.

WAINMAN, James Charles (Leeds GS), b Harrogate 25 Jan 1993. 6'4". LHB, LMF. Yorkshire 2nd XI debut 2010. Awaiting 1st XI debut.

WARDLAW, Iain (Whitcliffe Mount HS, Cleckheaton; Huddersfield U), b Dewsbury 29 Jun 1985. 6'2". RHB, RMF. Debut (Yorkshire) 2011. LOI (Scot): 2 (2012-13); HS 2* and BB 2-52 v Afghanistan (Sharjah) 2012-13. IT20 (Scot): 2 (2012-13); HS – ; BB 2-30 v Afghanistan (Sharjah) 2012-13. HS 17* and BB 1-37 v Hants (Leeds) 2012. LO HS 6* v Kent (Leeds) 2012 (CB40). LO BB 3-60 v Derbys (Chesterfield) 2012 (CB40). T20 HS – . T20 BB 2-17.

RELEASED/RETIRED
(Having made a County First-Class or List A appearance in 2012)

BROPHY, Gerard Louis (Christian Brothers C, Boksburg; Witwatersrand TC), b Welkom, OFS, South Africa 26 Nov 1975. British/EU passport. Qualified for England 2006. 5'11". RHB, WK, RM. Transvaal/Gauteng 1996-97 to 1998-99. Free State 1999-00 to 2000-01. Northamptonshire 2002-05. Yorkshire 2006-12; cap 2008; benefit 2011. F-c Tour (SA Acad): Z 1998. HS 185 SA Academy v Zim President's XI (Harare) 1998-99. UK HS 181 Nh v Sussex (Hove) 2014. Y HS 177* v Worcs (Worcester) 2011. LO HS 93* v Derbys (Leeds) 2010 (CB40). T20 HS 57*.

HANNON-DALBY, O.J. – *see WARWICKSHIRE*.

McGRATH, Anthony (Yorkshire Martyrs Collegiate S), b Bradford 6 Oct 1975. 6'2". RHB, RM. Yorkshire 1995-2012; cap 1999; captain 2003, 2009; benefit 2009. MCC 1999-00. Tests: 4 (2003); HS 81 v Z (Chester-le-St) 2003; BB 3-16 v Z (Lord's) 2003. LOI: 14 (2003 to 2004); HS 52 v SA (Manchester) 2003; BB 1-13 v WI (Nottingham) 2004. F-c Tours (Eng A): A 1996-97; P 1995-96; Z 1995-96 (Y); B 1999-00 (MCC). 1000 runs (3); most – 1425 (2005). HS 211 v Warwks (Birmingham) 2009. BB 5-39 v Derbys (Derby) 2004. LO HS 148 v Somerset (Taunton) 2006 (P40). LO BB 4-41 v Surrey (Leeds) 2003 (NL). T20 HS 73*. T20 BB 3-17.

[NO]**MILLER, David** Andrew (Maritzburg C), b Pietermaritzburg, South Africa 10 Jun 1989. 5'11". LHB, OB. Dolphins 2007-08 to date. KwaZulu-Natal 2008-09 to date. Yorkshire l-o and T20 only 2012. LOI (SA): 18 (2010 to 2012-13); HS 59 v A (Pt Elizabeth) 2011-12. IT20 (SA): 12 (2010 to 2012-13); HS 36* v Z (Bloemfontein) 2010-11. HS 149 Dolphins v Lions (Durban) 2010-11. LO HS SA A v Bangladesh A (Mirpur) 2010. T20 HS 90*.

SHAHZAD, A. – *see NOTTINGHAMSHIRE*.

[NO]**STARC, Mitchell** Aaron, b Baulkham Hills, Sydney, Australia 13 Jan 1990. LHB, LFM. New South Wales 2008-09 to date. Yorkshire 2012. Tests (A): 8 (2011-12 to 2012-13); HS 68* and BB 6-154 v SA (Perth) 2012-13. LOI (A): 18 (2010-11 to 2012-13); HS 52* v SL (Sydney) 2012-13; BB 5-20 v WI (Perth) 2012-13. IT20 (A): 10 (2012 to 2012-13); HS 2 v WI (Colombo, RPS) 2012-13; BB 3-11 v P (Dubai, DSC) 2012. F-c Tours: E 2012 (Aus A); WI 2011-12; I 2012-13. HS 68* (*see Tests*). UK HS Aus A v Derbys (Derby) 2012. Y HS 28* v Northants (Leeds) 2012. BB 6-154 (*see Tests*). UK BB 3-50 v Northants (Leeds) 2012. LO HS 52* (*see LOI*). LO BB 5-20 (*see LOI*). T20 HS 8*. T20 BB 3-11.

YORKSHIRE 2012

RESULTS SUMMARY

	Place	Won	Lost	Tied	Drew	NR
LV= County Championship (2nd Division)	2nd	5			11	
All First-Class Matches		5			12	
Clydesdale Bank 40 (Group C)	5th	4	7			1
Friends Life t20 (North Group)	Finalist	9	2			2

LV= COUNTY CHAMPIONSHIP AVERAGES
BATTING AND FIELDING

Cap		M	I	NO	HS	Runs	Avge	100	50	Ct/St
2010	A.Lyth	12	15	1	248*	751	53.64	1	5	12
2011	J.M.Bairstow	9	12	1	182	588	53.45	3	1	14
1999	A.McGrath	13	15	3	106*	584	48.66	2	3	4
2005	P.A.Jaques	15	19	1	160	792	44.00	2	4	16
2012	J.E.Root	14	19	2	222*	738	43.41	2	2	8
2012	G.S.Ballance	16	19	4	121*	613	40.86	1	2	10
2008	A.W.Gale	14	18	3	80	481	32.06	–	2	4
	Azeem Rafiq	10	10	1	75*	265	29.44	–	2	5
2007	J.J.Sayers	5	7	–	45	165	23.57	–	–	2
2000	R.J.Sidebottom	11	10	2	37	164	20.50	–	–	1
2012	S.A.Patterson	15	14	5	37	174	19.33	–	–	1
2006	T.T.Bresnan	4	–		38	73	18.25	–	–	2
	A.J.Hodd	4	5	–	58	91	18.20	–	1	18
2008	A.U.Rashid	10	8	–	58	129	16.12	–	1	–
	M.A.Ashraf	8	6	4	6*	14	7.00	–	–	1
2010	R.M.Pyrah	4	4	–	9	9	2.25	–	–	–

Also played: G.L.Brophy (3 matches – cap 2008) 2*, 22 (6 ct); S.J.Harmison 2, 23, 0 (1 ct); A.Shahzad (3 – cap 2010) 25, 5, 4; M.A.Starc (2) 28*; I.Wardlaw (2) 13*, 17* (1 ct).

BOWLING

	O	M	R	W	Avge	Best	5wI	10wM
S.A.Patterson	389.2	116	999	48	20.81	5- 77	1	–
M.A.Ashraf	117.5	27	376	17	22.11	4- 36	–	–
Azeem Rafiq	222.5	58	633	26	24.34	5- 50	1	–
T.T.Bresnan	130.2	31	397	14	28.35	5- 81	1	–
R.J.Sidebottom	297	72	798	24	33.25	5- 30	1	–
A.McGrath	171.1	50	424	12	35.33	4- 21	–	–
A.U.Rashid	202.5	26	656	16	41.00	5-105	1	–

Also bowled:

M.A.Starc	42.1	13	153	7	21.85	3- 50		
S.J.Harmison	42	4	195	8	24.37	3- 49		
A.Shahzad	68.1	14	210	8	26.25	3- 86		

G.S.Ballance 6-1-23-0; A.W.Gale 6.1-0-97-0; A.Lyth 12-3-116-0; R.M.Pyrah 38-9-128-2; J.E.Root 48-14-130-1; I.Wardlaw 52-1-225-2.

The First-Class Averages (pp 219–235) give the records of Yorkshire players in all first-class county matches (Yorkshire's other opponents being Leeds/Bradford MCCU), with the exception of J.M.Bairstow, T.T.Bresnan, S.J.Harmison, A.Shahzad and M.A.Starc, whose first-class figures for Yorkshire are as above, and:
J.E.Root 15-21-2-222*-746-39.26-2-2-9ct. 48-14-130-1-130.00-1/39-0-0.

YORKSHIRE RECORDS

FIRST-CLASS CRICKET

Highest Total   For 887   v   Warwicks   Birmingham   1896

Highest Total	For 887		v	Warwicks	Birmingham	1896
	V 681-7d		by	Leics	Bradford	1996
Lowest Total	For 23		v	Hampshire	Middlesbrough	1965
	V 13		by	Notts	Nottingham	1901
Highest Innings	For 341	G.H.Hirst	v	Leics	Leicester	1905
	V 318*	W.G.Grace	for	Glos	Cheltenham	1876

Highest Partnership for each Wicket

1st	555	P.Holmes/H.Sutcliffe	v	Essex	Leyton	1932
2nd	346	W.Barber/M.Leyland	v	Middlesex	Sheffield	1932
3rd	346	J.J.Sayers/A.McGrath	v	Warwicks	Birmingham	2009
4th	358	D.S.Lehmann/M.J.Lumb	v	Durham	Leeds	2006
5th	340	E.Wainwright/G.H.Hirst	v	Surrey	The Oval	1899
6th	276	M.Leyland/E.Robinson	v	Glamorgan	Swansea	1926
7th	254	W.Rhodes/D.C.F.Burton	v	Hampshire	Dewsbury	1919
8th	292	R.Peel/Lord Hawke	v	Warwicks	Birmingham	1896
9th	192	T.T.Bresnan/J.N.Gillespie	v	Surrey	The Oval	2007
10th	149	G.Boycott/G.B.Stevenson	v	Warwicks	Birmingham	1982

Best Bowling	For 10-10	H.Verity	v	Notts	Leeds	1932
(Innings)	V 10-37	C.V.Grimmett	for	Australians	Sheffield	1930
Best Bowling	For 17-91	H.Verity	v	Essex	Leyton	1933
(Match)	V 17-91	H.Dean	for	Lancashire	Liverpool	1913

Most Runs – Season	2883	H.Sutcliffe	(av 80.08)		1932
Most Runs – Career	38558	H.Sutcliffe	(av 50.20)		1919-45
Most 100s – Season	12	H.Sutcliffe			1932
Most 100s – Career	112	H.Sutcliffe			1919-45
Most Wkts – Season	240	W.Rhodes	(av 12.72)		1900
Most Wkts – Career	3597	W.Rhodes	(av 16.02)		1898-1930
Most Career W-K Dismissals	1186	D.Hunter	(863 ct; 323 st)		1888-1909
Most Career Catches in the Field	665	J.Tunnicliffe			1891-1907

LIMITED-OVERS CRICKET

Highest Total	50ov	411-6		v	Devon	Exmouth	2004
	40ov	352-6		v	Notts	Scarborough	2001
	T20	213-7		v	Worcs	Leeds	2010

Lowest Total	50ov	76		v	Surrey	Harrogate	1970
	40ov	54		v	Essex	Leeds	2003
	T20	90-9		v	Durham	Chester-le-St[2]	2009

Highest Innings	50ov	160	M.J.Wood	v	Devon	Exmouth	2004
	40ov	191	D.S.Lehmann	v	Notts	Scarborough	2001
	T20	109	I.J.Harvey	v	Derbyshire	Leeds	2005

Best Bowling	50ov	7-27	D.Gough	v	Ireland	Leeds	1997
	40ov	7-15	R.A.Hutton	v	Worcs	Leeds	1969
	T20	5-16	R.M.Pyrah	v	Durham	Scarborough	2011

FIRST-CLASS UMPIRES 2013

† New appointment. See page 84 for key to abbreviations.

BAILEY, Robert John (Biddulph HS), b Biddulph, Staffs 28 Oct 1963. 6'3''. RHB, OB. Northamptonshire 1982-99; cap 1985; benefit 1993; captain 1996-97. Derbyshire 2000-01; cap 2000. Staffordshire 1980. YC 1984. **Tests:** 4 (1988 to 1989-90); HS 43 v WI (Oval) 1988. **LOI:** 4 (1984-85 to 1989-90); HS 43* v SL (Oval) 1988. F-c Tours: SA 1991-92 (Nh); WI 1989-90; Z 1994-95 (Nh). 1000 runs (13); most – 1987 (1990). HS 224* Nh v Glamorgan (Swansea) 1986. BB 5-54 Nh v Notts (Northampton) 1993. F-c career: 374 matches; 21844 runs @ 40.52, 47 hundreds; 121 wickets @ 42.51; 272 ct. Appointed 2006. Umpired 3 LOI (2011 to 2012). **ICC International Panel (Third Umpire) 2011 to date.**

BAINTON, Neil Laurence, b Romford, Essex 2 October 1970. No f-c appearances. Appointed 2006.

BENSON, Mark Richard (Sutton Valence S), b Shoreham, Sussex 6 Jul 1958. 5'10''. LHB, OB. Kent 1980-95; cap 1981; captain 1991-96 (did not play in 1996); benefit 1991. **Tests:** 1 (1986); HS 30 v I (Birmingham) 1986. **LOI:** 1 (1986); HS 24 v NZ (Leeds) 1986. 1000 runs (11); most – 1725 (1987). HS 257 K v Hants (Southampton) 1991. BB 2-55 K v Surrey (Dartford) 1986. F-c career: 292 matches; 18387 runs @ 40.23, 48 hundreds; 5 wickets @ 98.60; 140 ct. Appointed 2000. Umpired 27 Tests (2004-05 to 2009-10) and 72 LOI (2004 to 2008-09). **ICC Elite Panel 2006-09.**

BODENHAM, Martin John Dale (Brighton, Sussex 23 Apr 1950. No f-c appearances. Former football referee who officiated at the 1997 League Cup final and four internationals. Appointed 2009.

COOK, Nicholas Grant Billson (Lutterworth GS), b Leicester 17 Jun 1956. 6'0''. RHB, SLA. Leicestershire 1978-85; cap 1982. Northamptonshire 1986-94; cap 1987; benefit 1995. **Tests:** 15 (1983 to 1989); HS 31 v A (Oval) 1989; BB 6-65 (11-83 match) v P (Karachi) 1983-84. **LOI:** 3 (1983-84 to 1989-90); HS – ; BB 2-18 v P (Peshawar) 1987-88. F-c Tours: NZ 1979-80 (DHR), 1983-84; P 1983-84, 1987-88; SL 1985-86 (Eng B); Z 1980-81 (Le), 1984-85 (EC). HS 75 Le v Somerset (Taunton) 1980. 50 wkts (8); most – 90 (1982). BB 7-34 (10-97 match) Nh v Essex (Chelmsford) 1992. F-c career: 356 matches; 3137 runs @ 11.66; 879 wickets @ 29.01; 197 ct. Appointed 2009.

COWLEY, Nigel Geoffrey (Dutchy Manor SS, Mere), b Shaftesbury, Dorset 1 Mar 1953. 5'7''. RHB, OB. Dorset 1972. Hampshire 1974-89; cap 1978; benefit 1988. Glamorgan 1990. 1000 runs (1): 1042 (1984). HS 109* H v Somerset (Taunton) 1977. BB 6-48 H v Leics (Southampton) 1982. F-c career: 271 matches; 7309 runs @ 23.35, 2 hundreds; 437 wickets @ 34.04; 105 ct. Appointed 2000.

EVANS, Jeffery Howard, b Llanelli, Carms 7 Aug 1954. No f-c appearances. Appointed 2001. Umpired in Indian Cricket League 2007-08.

GALE, Stephen Clifford, b Shrewsbury, Shropshire 3 Jun 1952. No f-c appearances. Shropshire (list A only) 1976-85. Reserve List 2008-10. Appointed 2011.

GARRATT, Steven Arthur, b Nottingham 5 Jul 1953. No f-c appearances. Reserve List 2003-07 standing in 20 f-c matches. Appointed 2008.

GOUGH, Michael Andrew (English Martyrs RCS; Hartlepool SFC), b Hartlepool, Co Durham 18 Dec 1979. Son of M.P.Gough (Durham 1974-77). 6'5''. RHB, OB. Durham 1998-2003. F-c Tours (Eng A): NZ 1999-00; B 1999-00. HS 123 Du v CU (Cambridge) 1998. CC HS 103 Du v Essex (Colchester) 2002. BB 5-56 Du v Middx (Chester-le-St) 2001. F-c career: 67 matches; 2952 runs @ 25.44, 2 hundreds; 30 wickets @ 45.00; 57 ct. Reserve List 2006-08. Appointed 2009.

GOULD, Ian James (Westgate SS, Slough), b Taplow, Bucks 19 Aug 1957. 5'8''. LHB, WK. Middlesex 1975-81, 1996; cap 1977. Auckland 1979-80. Sussex 1981-90; cap 1981; captain 1987; benefit 1990. MCC YC. **LOI:** 18 (1982-83 to 1983); HS 42 v A (Sydney) 1982-83. F-c Tours: A 1982-83; P 1980-81 (Int); Z 1980-81 (M). HS 128 M v

Worcs (Worcester) 1978. BB 3-10 Sx v Surrey (Oval) 1989. Middlesex coach 1991-2000. Reappeared in one match (v OU) 1996. F-c career: 298 matches; 8756 runs @ 26.05, 4 hundreds; 7 wickets @ 52.14; 603 dismissals (536 ct, 67 st). Appointed 2002. Umpired 33 Tests (2008-09 to 2012-13) and 79 LOI (2006 to 2012-13), including 2010-11 World Cup. **ICC Elite Panel 2009 to date.**

HARTLEY, Peter John (Greenhead GS; Bradford C), b Keighley, Yorks 18 Apr 1960. 6'0". RHB, RMF. Warwickshire 1982. Yorkshire 1985-97; cap 1987; benefit 1996. Hampshire 1998-2000; cap 1998. F-c Tours (Y): SA 1991-92; WI 1986-87; Z 1995-96. HS 127* Y v Lancs (Manchester) 1988. 50 wkts (7); most – 81 (1995). BB 9-41 (inc hat-trick, 4 wkts in 5 balls and 5 in 9; 11-68 match) Y v Derbys (Chesterfield) 1995. Hat-trick 1995. F-c career: 232 matches; 4321 runs @ 19.91, 2 hundreds; 683 wickets @ 30.21; 68 ct. Appointed 2003. Umpired 6 LOI (2007 to 2009). **ICC International Panel 2006-09.**

ILLINGWORTH, Richard Keith (Salts GS), b Bradford, Yorks 23 Aug 1963. 5'11". RHB, SLA. Worcestershire 1982-2000; cap 1986; benefit 1997. Natal 1988-89. Derbyshire 2001. Wiltshire 2005. **Tests:** 9 (1991 to 1995-96); HS 28 v SA (Pt Elizabeth) 1995-96; BB 4-96 v WI (Nottingham) 1995. Took wicket of P.V.Simmons with his first ball in Tests – v WI (Nottingham) 1991. **LOI:** 25 (1991 to 1995-96); HS 14 v P (Melbourne) 1991-92; BB 3-33 v Z (Albury) 1991-92. F-c Tours: SA 1995-96; NZ 1991-92; P 1990-91 (Eng A); SL 1990-91 (Eng A); Z 1989-90 (Eng A), 1990-91 (Wo), 1993-94 (Wo), 1996-97 (Wo). HS 120* Wo v Warwks (Worcester) 1987 – as night-watchman. Scored 106 for England A v Z (Harare) 1989-90 – also as night-watchman. 50 wkts (5); most – 75 (1990). BB 7-50 Wo v OU (Oxford) 1985. F-c career: 376 matches; 7027 runs @ 22.45, 4 hundreds; 831 wickets @ 31.54; 161 ct. Appointed 2006. Umpired 2 Tests (2012-13) and 15 LOI (2010 to 2012). **ICC International Panel 2011 to date.**

JESTY, Trevor Edward (Privet County SS, Gosport), b Gosport, Hants 2 Jun 1948. 5'8½". RHB, RM. Hampshire 1966-84; cap 1971; benefit 1982. Surrey 1985-87; cap 1985; captain 1985. Lancashire 1987-88 to 1991; cap 1989. Border 1973-74. GW 1974-75 to 1980-81. Canterbury 1979-80. **Wisden** 1982. **LOI:** 10 (1982-83); HS 52* v NZ (Adelaide) 1982-83; BB 1-23 v A (Sydney) 1982-83. F-c Tours (La): WI 1987-88, 1982-83 (Int); Z 1988-89. 1000 runs (10); most – 1645 (1982). HS 248 H v CU (Cambridge) 1984. Scored 122* La v OU (Oxford) 1991 in his final f-c innings. 50 wkts (2); most – 52 (1981). BB 7-75 H v Worcs (Southampton) 1976. F-c career: 490 matches; 21916 runs @ 32.71, 35 hundreds; 585 wickets @ 27.47; 265 ct, 1 st. Appointed 1994. Umpired in Indian Cricket League 2007-08.

KETTLEBOROUGH, Richard Allan (Worksop C), b Sheffield, Yorks 15 Mar 1973. 6'0". LHB, RM. Yorkshire 1994-97. Middlesex 1998-99. F-c Tour (Y): Z 1995-96. HS 108 Y v Essex (Leeds) 1996. BB 2-26 Y v Notts (Scarborough) 1996. F-c career: 33 matches; 1258 runs @ 25.16, 1 hundred; 3 wickets @ 81.00; 20 ct. Appointed 2006. Umpired 12 Tests (2010-11 to 2012-13) and 29 LOI (2009 to 2012-13), including 2010-11 World Cup. **ICC Elite Panel 2011 to date.**

LLONG, Nigel James (Ashford North S), b Ashford, Kent 11 Feb 1969. 6'0". LHB, OB. Kent 1990-98; cap 1993. F-c Tour (K): Z 1992-93. HS 130 K v Hants (Canterbury) 1996. BB 5-21 K v Middx (Canterbury) 1996. F-c career: 68 matches; 3024 runs @ 31.17, 6 hundreds; 35 wickets @ 35.97; 59 ct. Appointed 2002. Umpired 16 Tests (2007-08 to 2012-13) and 59 LOI (2006 to 2012-13), including 2010-11 World Cup. **ICC International Panel 2004 to date.**

LLOYDS, Jeremy William (Blundell's S), b Penang, Malaya 17 Nov 1954. 6'0". LHB, OB. Somerset 1979-84; cap 1982. Gloucestershire 1985-91; cap 1985. OFS 1983-84 to 1987-88. F-c Tour (Gl): SL 1986-87. 1000 runs (3); most – 1295 (1986). HS 132* Sm v Northants (Northampton) 1982. BB 7-88 Sm v Essex (Chelmsford) 1982. F-c career: 267 matches; 10679 runs @ 31.04, 10 hundreds; 333 wickets @ 38.86; 229 ct. Appointed 1998. Umpired 5 Tests (2003-04 to 2004-05) and 18 LOI (2000 to 2005-06). **ICC International Panel 2003-06.**

MALLENDER, Neil Alan (Beverley GS), b Kirk Sandall, Yorks 13 Aug 1961. 6'0". RHB, RFM. Northamptonshire 1980-86 and 1995-96; cap 1984. Somerset 1987-94; cap 1987;

benefit 1994. Otago 1983-84 to 1992-93; captain 1990-91 to 1992-93. **Tests:** 2 (1992); HS 4 v P (Oval) 1992; BB 5-50 v P (Leeds) 1992 – on debut. F-c Tour (Nh): Z 1994-95. HS 100* Otago v CD (Palmerston N) 1991-92. UK HS 87* Nh v Sussex (Hove) 1990. 50 wkts (6); most – 56 (1983). BB 7-27 Otago v Auckland (Auckland) 1984-85. UK BB 7-41 Nh v Derbys (Northampton) 1982. F-c career: 345 matches; 4709 runs @ 17.18, 1 hundred; 937 wickets @ 26.31; 111 ct. Appointed 1999. Umpired 3 Tests (2003-04) and 22 LOI (2001 to 2003-04), including 2002-03 World Cup. **ICC Elite Panel 2004.**

MILLNS, David James (Garibaldi CS; N Notts C; Nottingham Trent U), b Clipstone, Notts 27 Feb 1965. 6'3". LHB, RF. Nottinghamshire 1988-89, 2000-01; cap 2000. Leicestershire 1990-99; cap 1991; benefit 1999. Tasmania 1994-95. Boland 1996-97. F-c Tours: A 1992-93 (Eng A); SA 1996-97 (Le). HS 121 Le v Northants (Northampton) 1997. 50 wkts (4); most – 76 (1994). BB 9-37 (12-91 match) Le v Derbys (Derby) 1991. F-c career: 171 matches; 3082 runs @ 22.01, 3 hundreds; 553 wickets @ 27.35; 76 ct. Reserve List 2007-08. Appointed 2009.

O'SHAUGHNESSY, Steven Joseph (Harper Green SS, Franworth), b Bury, Lancs 9 Sep 1961. 5'10½". RHB, RM. Lancashire 1980-87; cap 1985. Worcestershire 1988-89. Scored 100 in 35 min to equal world record for La v Leics (Manchester) 1983. 1000 runs (1): 1167 (1984). HS 159* La v Somerset (Bath) 1984. BB 4-66 La v Notts (Nottingham) 1982. F-c career: 112 matches; 3720 runs @ 24.31, 5 hundreds; 114 wickets @ 36.03; 57 ct. Reserve list 2009-10. Appointed 2011.

ROBINSON, Robert Timothy (Dunstable GS; High Pavement SFC; Sheffield U), b Sutton in Ashfield, Notts 21 Nov 1958. 6'0". RHB, RM. Nottinghamshire 1978-99; cap 1983; captain 1988-95; benefit 1992. *Wisden* 1985. **Tests:** 29 (1984-85 to 1989); HS 175 v A (Leeds) 1985. **LOI:** 26 (1984-85 to 1988); HS 83 v P (Sharjah) 1986-87. F-c Tours: A 1987-88; SA 1989-90 (Eng XI), 1996-97 (Nt); NZ 1987-88; WI 1985-86; I/SL 1984-85; P 1987-88. 1000 runs (14) inc 2000 (1): 2032 (1984). HS 220* Nt v Yorks (Nottingham) 1990. BB 1-22. F-c career: 425 matches; 27571 runs @ 42.15, 63 hundreds; 4 wickets @ 72.25; 257 ct. Appointed 2007.

SAGGERS, Martin John (Springwood HS; King's Lynn; Huddersfield U), b King's Lynn, Norfolk 23 May 1972. 6'2". RHB, RMF. Durham 1996-98. Kent 1999-2009; cap 2001; benefit 2009. MCC 2004. Essex 2007 (on loan). Norfolk 1995-96. **Tests:** 3 (2003-04 to 2004); HS 1 and BB 2-29 v B (Chittagong) 2003-04 – on debut. F-c Tour: B 2003-04. HS 64 K v Worcs (Canterbury) 2004. 50 wkts (4); most – 83 (2002). BB 7-79 K v Durham (Chester-le-St) 2000. F-c career: 119 matches; 1165 runs @ 11.20; 415 wickets @ 25.33; 27 ct. Reserve list 2010-11. Appointed 2012.

SHARP, George (Elwick Road SS, Hartlepool), b West Hartlepool, Co Durham 12 Mar 1950. 5'11". RHB, WK, occ LM. Northamptonshire 1968-85; cap 1973; benefit 1982. HS 98 Nh v Yorks (Northampton) 1983. BB 1-47. F-c career: 306 matches; 6254 runs @ 19.85; 1 wicket @ 70.00; 655 dismissals (565 ct, 90 st). Appointed 1992. Umpired 15 Tests (1996 to 2001-02) and 31 LOI (1995-96 to 2001-02). **ICC International Panel 1996 to 2001-02.**

WILLEY, Peter (Seaham SS), b Sedgefield, Co Durham 6 Dec 1949. 6'1". RHB, OB. Northamptonshire 1966-83; cap 1971; benefit 1981. Leicestershire 1984-91; cap 1984; captain 1987. EP 1982-83 to 1984-85. Northumberland 1992. **Tests:** 26 (1976 to 1986); HS 102* v WI (St John's) 1980-81; BB 2-73 v WI (Lord's) 1980. **LOI:** 26 (1977 to 1985-86); HS 64 v A (Sydney) 1979-80; BB 3-33 v A (Melbourne) 1979-80. F-c Tours: A 1979-80; SA 1972-73 (DHR), 1981-82 (SAB); WI 1980-81, 1985-86; I 1979-80; SL 1977-78 (DHR). 1000 runs (10); most – 1783 (1982). HS 227 Nh v Somerset (Northampton) 1976. 50 wkts (3); most – 52 (1979). BB 7-37 Nh v OU (Oxford) 1975. F-c career: 559 matches; 24361 runs @ 30.56, 44 hundreds; 756 wickets @ 30.95; 235 ct. Appointed 1993. Umpired 25 Tests (1995-96 to 2003-04) and 34 LOI (1996 to 2003), including 1999 and 2002-03 World Cups. **ICC International Panel 1996 to 2001-02 and 2003-04.**

RESERVE FIRST-CLASS LIST: Paul K.Baldwin, Mike Burns, Ismail Dawood, Ben J.Debenham, Mark A.Eggleston, Russell J.Evans, Graham D.Lloyd, Paul R.Pollard, Billy V.Taylor, Alex G.Wharf.

Test Match and LOI statistics to 1 March 2013.

UNIVERSITIES REGISTER 2012

CAMBRIDGE († = Blue)

Full Names	Birthdate	Birthplace	College	Bat/Bowl	F-C Debut
ACKLAND, Ben James	26.10.89	Nuneaton	Anglia RU	RHB/OB	2010
†ANSARI, Akbar Shahzaman	03.07.88	Ascot	Trinity Hall	RHB/LB	2008
ANSARI, Zafar Shahaan	10.12.91	Ascot	Trinity Hall	LHB/SLA	2011
BELL, Dean William	03.05.92	Blackpool	Anglia RU	RHB/WK	2011
†BEST, Paul Merwood	08.03.91	Nuneaton	Homerton	LHB/SLA	2011
†ELLIOTT, Tom Christopher	21.11.91	Epsom	Sidney Sussex	RHB/RM	2012
†EVANS, Jonathan James	11.02.88	Oxford	Darwin	RHB/WK	2012
†HICKEY, Matthew Robert	23.09.91	Wandsworth	Trinity Hall	LHB/LM	2012
†HUGHES, Philip Heywood	17.06.91	Southampton	Downing	RHB/RM	2010
JOHNSON, James Alexander Michael	25.11.91	Haywards Heath	Anglia RU	RHB/OB	2012
†KENNEDY, Augustus Damian John	10.08.90	London	Corpus Christi	RHB/WK	2010
†LODWICK, Jonathon Andrew	14.10.89	Reading		RHB/RM	2010
PARK, Craig Mitchell	01.03.86	Natal, SA	Anglia RU	RHB/RFM	2010
POYSDEN, Joshua Edward	08.08.91	Shoreham-by-Sea	Anglia RU	LHB/LB	2011
†PROBERT, Thomas John William	26.09.86	Pembury	Peterhouse	LHB/RM	2009
†SADLER, Patrick Thomas	28.09.91	Waltham Forest	Churchill	RHB/RFM	2011
SALISBURY, Matthew Edward Thomas	18.04.93	Chelmsford	Anglia RU	RHB/RMF	2012
†TIMMS, Richard Thomas	09.09.84	Bristol	Gonville & Caius	RHB/RFM	2005
TURNBULL, Peter Thomas	20.05.89	Pontypridd	Anglia RU	RHB/RMF	2009
WOOLLEY, Robert James Joseph	06.08.90	Manchester	Anglia RU	RHB/RM	2009

CARDIFF

Full Names	Birthdate	Birthplace	College	Bat/Bowl	F-C Debut
BALBIRNIE, Andrew	28.12.90	Dublin, Ireland	Cardiff Met	RHB/OB	2012
BENDON, Daniel Steven	12.01.89	Kettering	Cardiff	RHB/LBG	2012
DAVIES, Samuel Llyr	30.01.92	Neath	UWIC	RHB/LM	2012
ELKIN, Zachary	21.06.91	Cape Town, SA	Cardiff	RHB/WK	2012
FRIEND, Thomas Toby	03.05.91	Newport, IoW	UWIC	RHB/RFM	2012
HARRIS, Philip Graham	12.05.90	Worcester	UWIC	RHB/RFM	2012
HOBDEN, Matthew Edward	27.03.93	Eastbourne	UWIC	RHB/RFM	2012
JONES, William Stephen	26.03.90	Perth, Australia	Cardiff	RHB/LB	2011
LEACH, Matthew Jack	22.06.91	Taunton	UWIC	LHB/SLA	2012
MILES, Adam James	19.09.89	Swindon		RHB/WK	2012
QURESHI, Uzair Asad	23.02.93	Lambeth	UWIC	RHB/OB	2012
SALTER, Andrew Graham	01.06.93	Haverfordwest	UWIC	RHB/OB	2012
SIDDIQUE, Hamza Ghani	19.01.91	Stoke-on-Trent	Cardiff	RHB/OB	2012

DURHAM

Full Names	Birthdate	Birthplace	College	Bat/Bowl	F-C Debut
BLACKABY, Luke Alexander	01.02.91	Farnborough	Grey	LHB/LM	2010
GREEN, Matthew James Emrys	19.04.93	Wakefield	St Cuthbert's	RHB/RM	2012
JONES, Christopher Robert	05.11.90	Harold Wood	Grey	RHB/RM	2010
PATEL, Luke Adam	06.10.90	Wakefield	Grey	LHB/OB	2012
SALT, Jonathan David	06.01.91	Chester	Van Mildert	RHB/RM	2011
SANGHA, Ajay Singh	06.06.92	Windsor		RHB/OB	2012
SHAH, Rishabh Arjun Chandra	11.09.90	Whipps Cross		RHB/LB	2011
SMITH, Joshua William George	30.05.92	Oxford	Grey	LHB/WK	2012
WALLIS, Charles Alexander	14.10.91	Westminster	Hatfield	RHB/RM	2012
WATERS, Seren Robert	11.04.90	Nairobi, Kenya	St Cuthbert's	RHB/LB	2008-09
WATKINS, Nathaniel Ashley Thomas	07.11.91	Oxford	Hatfield	RHB/SLA	2011

LEEDS/BRADFORD

Full Names	Birthdate	Birthplace	College	Bat/Bowl	F-C Debut
BUSH, Harry	06.11.89	Los Angeles, USA	Leeds	RHB/OB	2012
HARDMAN, Thomas Richard	03.12.90	Bury	Leeds Met	RHB/RMF	2012
HIGGINBOTTOM, Matthew	20.10.90	Stockport	Leeds Met	LHB/RMF	2012
HODGSON, Daniel Mark	26.02.90	Northallerton	Leeds	RHB/WK	2012
LEACH, Joseph	30.10.90	Stafford	Leeds	RHB/RM	2012
MacQUEEN, Alexander	12.01.93	Chertsey	Leeds	RHB/OB	2012
MOORE, Richard Andrew Leigh	11.05.89	Crewe	Leeds Met	RHB/RM	2012
REECE, Luis Michael	04.08.90	Taunton	Leeds Met	LHB/LM	2012
ROEBUCK, Charles George	14.08.91	Huddersfield	Bradford	RHB/RM	2010
SLATER, Benjamin Thomas	26.08.91	Chesterfield	Leeds Met	LHB/OB	2012
THOMAS, Ivan Alfred Astley	25.09.91	Greenwich	Leeds	RHB/RMF	2012
WEBB, Jonathon Patrick	12.01.92	Solihull	Leeds	RHB/RM	2012

LOUGHBOROUGH

Full Names	Birthdate	Birthplace	College	Bat/Bowl	F-C Debut
BILLINGS, Samuel William	15.06.91	Pembury	Loughborough	RHB/WK	2011
DAECHE-MARSHALL, Frederick William	10.08.91	Enfield	Loughborough	RHB/RM	2012
ENDERSBY, Devon Malcolm	12.05.92	East London, SA	Loughborough	RHB/RMF	2012
EVANS, Rhodri Francis	06.12.89	Swansea	Loughborough	LHB/RM	2009
LESTER, Toby James	05.04.93	Blackpool	Loughborough	LHB/LFM	2012
MORRIS, Aiden Joseph	25.04.93	Nottingham	Loughborough	RHB/RMF	2012
PATEL, Nitesh	31.10.89	Stourbridge	Loughborough	RHB/OB	2011
RILEY, Adam Edward Nicholas	23.03.92	Sidcup	Loughborough	RHB/OB	2011
SOILLEUX, Adam Charles	29.11.91	Southend	Loughborough	RHB/RM	2011
STURMER, Ian William	23.08.91	Chiddingly	Loughborough	RHB/RM	2011
TAVARÉ, William Andrew	01.01.90	Bristol	Loughborough	RHB/RM	2010
TAYLOR, Robert Meadows Lombe	21.12.89	Northampton	Loughborough	LHB/LM	2010
WILSON, Adam David	10.10.88	Sheffield	Loughborough	RHB/RFM	2012

OXFORD († = Blue)

Full Names	Birthdate	Birthplace	College	Bat/Bowl	F-C Debut
†AGARWAL, Samridh Sunil	13.07.90	Agra, India	Queen's	RHB/OB	2010
†CHADWICK, Thomas Robert	21.10.91	Norwich	Worcester	RHB/RM	2011
COLEMAN, Frederick Robert John	15.12.91	Edinburgh	Brookes U	RHB/OB	2011-12
CONWAY, Danny Oliver	01.05.85	Stockton-on-Tees	Brookes U	RHB/RM	2010
†DAVIES, Joseph Matthew	05.09.92	Salford	St Catherine's	RHB/WK	2012
ELLISON, Charles Peter	26.01.91	Canterbury	Brookes U	RHB/RMF	2011
FLEMING, Joshua David	29.06.89	Crawley	Brookes U	RHB/RM	2011
†JEFFERY, Benjamin Anthony	31.07.91	Camden	St John's	RHB/LB	2011
JOHN, Frederick Robert Harold	06.09.91	Newport	Brookes U	RHB/WK	2012
†JOHNSON, Frederick Francis Jeremy	26.03.90	Lambeth	Queen's	RHB/RMF	2012
†JONES, Owain James	24.09.92	Brighton	St Edmund Hall	LHB/RM	2012
KEMP, Benedict William	26.05.93	Canterbury	Brookes U	RHB/RM	2012
MORRIS, Charles Andrew John	06.07.92	Hereford	Brookes U	RHB/RMF	2012
†PASCOE, Daniel Charles	14.05.83	Canberra, Aus	Lincoln	RHB/SLA	2009
†SCOTT, Alex James Denis	04.05.90	Hong Kong	Keble	RHB/OB	2010
†SHARMA, Rajiv	10.06.84	Auckland, NZ	Mansfield	RHB/RMF	2009
STEBBINGS, Benjamin Robert William	04.10.89	Oxford	Brookes U	RHB/RM	2010
THOMPSON, James Scott	11.03.91	Shrewsbury	Brookes U	RHB/RMF	2012
WALKER, Charles Aubrey Mark	21.05.92	Bristol	Brookes U	RHB/OB	2011
†WESTAWAY, Samuel Alexander	29.07.92	Welwyn Garden City	Pembroke	RHB/WK	2011
†WILLIAMS, Ben	24.06.92	Whiston	Hertford	RHB/RSM	2011

TOURING TEAMS REGISTER 2012

AUSTRALIA A

Full Names	Birthdate	Birthplace	Team	Type	F-C Debut
BAILEY, George John	07.09.82	Launceston	Tasmania	RHB/RM	2004-05
BIRD, Jackson Munro	11.12.86	Sydney	Tasmania	RHB/RFM	2011-12
BURNS, Joseph Anthony	06.09.89	Brisbane	Queensland	RHB/RM	2010-11
COOPER, Tom Lexley William	26.11.86	Wollongong	S Australia	RHB/OB	2008-09
COULTER-NILE, Nathan Mitchell	11.10.87	Osborne Park	W Australia	RHB/RF	2009-10
COWAN, Edward James McKenzie	16.06.82	Paddington	Tasmania	LHB/LB	2003
DAVIS, Liam Murray	02.08.84	Perth	W Australia	RHB/RFM	2007-08
FORREST, Peter James	15.11.85	Windsor	Queensland	RHB/RM	2006-07
HOLLAND, Jonathan Mark	29.05.87	Sandringham	Victoria	RHB/SLA	2008-09
HUGHES, Phillip Joel	30.11.88	Macksville	S Australia	LHB/OB	2007-08
JOHNSON, Mitchell Guy	02.11.81	Townsville	W Australia	LHB/LF	2001-02
KLINGER, Michael	04.07.80	Kew, Melbourne	S Australia	RHB	1998-99
LYON, Nathan Michael	20.11.87	Young	S Australia	RHB/OB	2010-11
McDERMOTT, Alister Craig	07.06.91	Brisbane	Queensland	RHB/RFM	2009-10
PAINE, Timothy David	08.12.84	Hobart	Tasmania	RHB/WK	2005-06
SMITH, Steven Peter Devereux	02.06.89	Sydney	NSW	RHB/LBG	2007-08
STARC, Mitchell Aaron	30.01.90	Sydney	NSW	LHB/LFM	2008-09

SOUTH AFRICA

Full Names	Birthdate	Birthplace	Team	Type	F-C Debut
AMLA, Hashim Mahomed	31.03.83	Durban	Dolphins	RHB/RM	1999-00
DE VILLIERS, Abraham Benjamin	17.02.84	Pretoria	Titans	RHB/WK	2003-04
DUMINY, Jean-Paul	14.04.84	Cape Town	Cape Cobras	LHB/OB	2001-02
IMRAN TAHIR, Mohammad	27.03.79	Lahore	Dolphins	RHB/LBG	1996-97
KALLIS, Jacques Henry	16.10.75	Cape Town	Cape Cobras	RHB/RMF	1993-94
MORKEL, Morne	06.10.84	Vereeniging	Titans	RHB/RFM	2003-04
PETERSEN, Alviro Nathan	25.10.80	Port Elizabeth	Lions	RHB/OB	2000-01
PHILANDER, Vernon Darryl	24.06.85	Bellville	Cape Cobras	RHB/RMF	2004-04
RUDOLPH, Jacobus Andries	04.05.81	Springs	Titans	LHB/LBG	1997-98
SMITH, Graeme Craig	01.02.81	Johannesburg	Cape Cobras	LHB/OB	1999-00
STEYN, Dale Willem	27.06.83	Phalaborwa	Cape Cobras	RHB/RF	2003-04

WEST INDIES

Full Names	Birthdate	Birthplace	Team	Type	F-C Debut
BARATH, Adrian Boris	14.04.90	Chaguanas, Tr	Trinidad	RHB/OB	2006-07
BEST, Tino la Bertram	26.08.81	St Michael	Barbados	RHB/RF	2001-02
BRAVO, Darren Michael	06.02.89	Trinidad	Trinidad	LHB/RMF	2006-07
CHANDERPAUL, Shivnarine	16.08.74	Unity Village	Guyana	LHB/LB	1991-92
DEONARINE, Narsingh	16.08.83	Berbice	Guyana	LHB/OB	1999-00
EDWARDS, Fidel Henderson	06.02.82	St Peter	Barbados	RHB/RF	2001-02
EDWARDS, Kirk Anton	03.11.84	Barbados	Barbados	RHB/OB	2005-06
FUDADIN, Assad Badyr	01.08.85	Guyana	Guyana	LHB/RMF	2003-04
GABRIEL, Shannon Terry	28.04.88	Trinidad	Trinidad	RHB/RFM	2009-10
NARINE, Sunil Philip	26.05.88	Trinidad	Trinidad	LHB/OB	2008-09
POWELL, Kieran Omar Akeem	06.03.90	Nevis	Leeward Is	LHB/RM	2007-08
RAMDIN, Denesh	13.03.85	Couva	Trinidad	RHB/WK	2003-04
RAMPAUL, Ravindranath	15.10.84	Preysal	Trinidad	LHB/RFM	2001-02
ROACH, Kemar Andre Jamal	30.06.88	St Lucy	Barbados	RHB/RF	2007-08
SAMMY, Darren Julius Garvey	20.12.83	Micoud, St Lucia	Windward Is	RHB/RM	2002-03
SAMUELS, Marlon Nathaniel	05.01.81	Kingston	Jamaica	RHB/OB	1996-97
SHILLINGFORD, Shane	22.02.83	Dominica	Windward Is	RHB/OB	2000-01

THE 2012 FIRST-CLASS SEASON STATISTICAL HIGHLIGHTS

FIRST TO INDIVIDUAL TARGETS

1000 RUNS	N.R.D.Compton	Somerset	1 June
2000 RUNS	–	Most 1494 – N.R.D.Compton (Somerset, England Lions)	
50 WICKETS	G.Onions	Durham, England	8 August
100 WICKETS	–	Most 72 – G.Onions (Durham, England)	

TEAM HIGHLIGHTS

HIGHEST INNINGS TOTALS

642-3d	Somerset v Cardiff MCCU	Taunton Vale
637-2d	South Africa v England (*1st Test*)	The Oval

HIGHEST FOURTH INNINGS TOTAL

397-5	Somerset (set 396) v Sussex	Hove

LOWEST INNINGS TOTALS († *One man absent hurt*)

18†	Durham MCCU v Durham	Chester-le-Street
60	Worcestershire v Warwickshire	Worcester
63	Lancashire v Worcestershire	Manchester
93	Durham v Sussex	Arundel
95	Derbyshire v Gloucestershire	Bristol
95	Glamorgan v Derbyshire	Cardiff
98	Middlesex v Nottinghamshire	Uxbridge

LARGE MARGINS OF VICTORY

Inns & 279 runs	Kent (533) beat Leicestershire (141 & 113)	Canterbury
Inns & 202 runs	Warwickshire (471-8d) beat Worcs (60 & 209)	Worcester
373 runs	Durham (315-4d & 193-7d) beat Durham MCCU (117 & 18)	Chester-le-Street

NARROW MARGINS OF VICTORY

2 runs	Surrey (385-8d & 134-5d) beat Leeds/Brad MCCU (205 & 312)	The Oval
2 runs	Hampshire (323 & 54-0d) beat Essex (18-0d & 357)	Chelmsford
3 runs	Middlesex (256 & 106) beat Surrey (222 & 137)	Lord's
8 runs	Surrey (144 & 341) beat Middlesex (232 & 245)	The Oval
1 wkt	Somerset (254 & 273-9) beat Warwicks (400 & 124)	Taunton

60 EXTRAS IN AN INNINGS

	B	LB	W	NB		
61	15	11	3	32	Glamorgan (558-9d) v Leicestershire	Cardiff
60	8	14	4	34	Warwickshire (571) v Surrey	Birmingham

Under ECB regulations, Test matches excluded, two penalty extras were scored for each no-ball.

BATTING HIGHLIGHTS
TRIPLE HUNDREDS

H.M.Amla	311*	South Africa v England (*1st Test*)	The Oval

DOUBLE HUNDREDS

N.R.D.Compton (2)	236	Somerset v Cardiff MCCU	Taunton Vale
	204*	Somerset v Nottinghamshire	Nottingham
J.C.Hildreth	268	Somerset v Cardiff MCCU	Taunton Vale
A.Lyth	248*	Yorkshire v Leicestershire	Leicester
W.L.Madsen	231*	Derbyshire v Northamptonshire	Northampton
K.P.Pietersen	234*	Surrey v Lancashire	Guildford
J.E.Root	222*	Yorkshire v Hampshire	Southampton

HUNDRED IN EACH INNINGS OF A MATCH

R.I.Newton	115 119*	Northamptonshire v Derbyshire	Northampton

FASTEST HUNDRED AGAINST GENUINE BOWLING

G.R.Napier (100*)	48 balls Essex v Cambridge MCCU	Cambridge

MOST SIXES IN AN INNINGS

8	G.R.Napier (100*)	Essex v Cambridge MCCU	Cambridge
8	K.P.Pietersen (234*)	Surrey v Lancashire	Guildford

150 OR MORE RUNS FROM BOUNDARIES IN AN INNINGS

Runs	6s	4s		
168	8	30	K.P.Pietersen	Surrey v Lancashire	Guildford

HUNDRED ON FIRST-CLASS DEBUT

Z.Elkin	138	Cardiff MCCU v Somerset	Taunton Vale

HUNDRED ON FIRST-CLASS DEBUT IN BRITAIN

F.R.J.Coleman	110	Oxford MCCU v Worcestershire	Oxford

CARRYING BAT THROUGH COMPLETED INNINGS

J.H.K.Adams	139*	Hampshire (302) v Essex	Southampton
P.J.Horton	49*	Lancashire (170) v Durham	Chester-le-Street
P.J.Hughes	135*	Worcestershire (246) v Warwickshire	Birmingham
A.Lyth	248*	Yorkshire (486) v Leicestershire	Leicester
D.K.H.Mitchell	133*	Worcestershire (323) v Middlesex	Worcester

LONG INNINGS (Qualification 600 mins and/or 400 balls)

Mins	Balls			
790	529	H.M.Amla (311*)	South Africa v England (*1st Test*)	The Oval
514	400	W.L.Madsen (231*)	Derbyshire v Northamptonshire	Northampton
549	462	N.J.O'Brien (182)	Northamptonshire v Glamorgan	Cardiff

FIRST-WICKET PARTNERSHIP OF 100 IN EACH INNINGS

126/139	S.D.Peters/N.J.O'Brien	Northamptonshire v Leics	Northampton
120/120	A.N.Petersen/G.C.Smith/J.A.Rudolph	South Africa v England (2nd Test)	Leeds

OTHER NOTABLE PARTNERSHIPS († *County record*)

Qualifications: 1st-4th wkts: 250 runs; 5th-6th: 225; 7th: 200; 8th: 175; 9th: 150; 10th: 100.

First Wicket

252	S.A.Northeast/R.W.T.Key	Kent v Hampshire	Southampton

Second Wicket

450†	N.R.D.Compton/J.C.Hildreth	Somerset v Cardiff MCCU	Taunton Vale
259	G.C.Smith/H.M.Amla	South Africa v England (*1st Test*)	The Oval

Third Wicket

377*	H.M.Amla/J.H.Kallis	South Africa v England (*1st Test*)	The Oval

Fourth Wicket

303	N.J.Edwards/M.H.Wessels	Notts v Loughborough MCCU	Nottingham

Fifth Wicket

294	R.S.Bopara/J.S.Foster	Essex v Northamptonshire	Northampton
225	R.J.Hamilton-Brown/T.L.Maynard	Surrey v Worcestershire	Worcester

Seventh Wicket

204	M.N.Samuels/D.J.G.Sammy	West Indies v England (*2nd Test*)	Nottingham
204	J.O.Troughton/C.R.Woakes	Warwickshire v Somerset	Taunton

Eighth Wicket

224	D.L.Maddy/R.Clarke	Warwickshire v Lancashire	Liverpool

Ninth Wicket

261	W.L.Madsen/T.Poynton	Derbyshire v Northamptonshire	Northampton
153	M.T.Coles/M.Davies	Kent v Yorkshire	Leeds

Tenth Wicket

168	C.P.Wood/D.J.Balcombe	Hampshire v Leicestershire	Leicester
143	D.Ramdin/T.L.Best	West Indies v England (*3rd Test*)	Birmingham

BOWLING HIGHLIGHTS
EIGHT OR MORE WICKETS IN AN INNINGS

Abdur Rehman	9-65	Somerset v Worcestershire	Taunton
D.J.Balcombe	8-71	Hampshire v Gloucestershire	Southampton
S.C.Meaker	8-52	Surrey v Somerset	The Oval
G.Onions	9-67	Durham v Nottinghamshire	Nottingham

TEN OR MORE WICKETS IN A MATCH

Abdur Rehman		14-101 Somerset v Worcestershire	Taunton
A.R.Adams		10- 50 Nottinghamshire v Lancashire	Manchester
M.M.Ali		12- 96 Worcestershire v Lancashire	Manchester
D.J.Balcombe		11-119 Hampshire v Gloucestershire	Southampton
K.H.D.Barker		10- 70 Warwickshire v Durham	Birmingham
G.J.Batty		10-142 Surrey v Warwickshire	The Oval
S.C.J.Broad		11-165 England v West Indies (*1st Test*)	Lord's
G.Chapple		10-133 Lancashire v Middlesex	Lord's
J.L.Clare		11- 57 Derbyshire v Glamorgan	Cardiff
R.H.Joseph		12-111 Leicestershire v Glamorgan	Leicester
S.C.Meaker		11-167 Surrey v Somerset	The Oval
G.Onions	(3)	10- 73 Durham v Middlesex	Lord's
		11- 95 Durham v Lancashire	Chester-le-Street
		10-125 Durham v Nottinghamshire	Nottingham
M.S.Panesar		13-137 Sussex v Somerset	Taunton
A.Richardson		10-128 Worcestershire v Surrey	The Oval
T.S.Roland-Jones		10-118 Middlesex v Worcestershire	Worcester

BOWLING UNCHANGED THROUGHOUT INNINGS

C.J.C.Wright (14.4-5-24-5)/K.H.B.Barker (14-4-36-5) Warwicks v Worcs   Worcester

HAT-TRICKS

A.P.Palladino	Derbyshire v Leicestershire	Leicester

MOST RUNS CONCEDED IN AN INNINGS

S.C.Kerrigan	49-4-178-3 Lancashire v Warwickshire	Birmingham

MOST OVERS BOWLED IN AN INNINGS

G.P.Swann	52-10-151-0 England v South Africa (*1st Test*)	The Oval

MATCH DOUBLE (CENTURY AND FIVE WICKETS IN AN INNINGS)

J.D.Middlebrook (121 & 5-63) Northamptonshire v Gloucestershire   Northampton

WICKET-KEEPING HIGHLIGHTS
SIX WICKET-KEEPING DISMISSALS IN AN INNINGS

M.D.Bates	6ct	Hampshire v Gloucestershire	Southampton
B.C.Brown	6ct	Sussex v Middlesex	Hove
E.J.H.Eckersley	5ct, 1st	Leicestershire v Gloucestershire	Leicester
M.J.Prior	5ct, 1st	England v South Africa (*3rd Test*)	Lord's

FIELDING HIGHLIGHTS
FIVE CATCHES IN THE FIELD IN AN INNINGS

R.Clarke	5ct	Warwickshire v Durham	Chester-le-Street
M.E.Trescothick (2)	5ct	Somerset v Nottinghamshire	Taunton
	5ct	Somerset v Sussex	Hove

SIX OR MORE CATCHES IN THE FIELD IN A MATCH

L.A.Dawson	7ct	Hampshire v Northamptonshire	Northampton
M.E.Trescothick	6ct	Somerset v Nottinghamshire	Taunton

COUNTY CHAMPIONSHIP 2012
LV= FINAL TABLES

DIVISION 1

	P	W	L	D	Bonus Points Bat	Points Bowl	Deduct Points	Total Points
1 WARWICKSHIRE (2)	16	6	1	9	43	45	–	211
2 Somerset (4)	16	5	1	10	32	45	–	187
3 Middlesex (-)	16	5	4	7	33	38	–	172
4 Sussex (5)	16	5	5	6	28	41	–	167
5 Nottinghamshire (6)	16	4	2	10	26	43	–	163
6 Durham (3)	16	5	5	6*	18	45	4	157
7 Surrey (-)	16	3	4	9*	26	40	2	139
8 Lancashire (1)	16	1	5	10	25	35	–	106
9 Worcestershire (7)	16	1	8	7	17	42	–	96

DIVISION 2

	P	W	L	D	Bonus Points Bat	Points Bowl	Deduct Points	Total Points
1 Derbyshire (5)	16	6	2	8	31	43	–	194
2 Yorkshire (-)	16	5	–	11	41	40	–	194
3 Kent (8)	16	4	3	9	39	40	–	170
4 Hampshire (-)	16	4	5	7	28	40	–	153
5 Essex (3)	16	3	3	10	27	40	–	145
6 Glamorgan (6)	16	3	6	7*	28	35	1	131
7 Leicestershire (9)	16	3	3	10	24	33	5	130
8 Northamptonshire (3)	16	2	5	9	37	34	–	130
9 Gloucestershire (4)	16	3	6	7*	22	35	–	126

* includes one match abandoned without a ball being bowled.

SCORING OF CHAMPIONSHIP POINTS 2012 and 2013

(a) For a win, 16 points, plus any points scored in the first innings.

(b) In a tie, each side to score eight points, plus any points scored in the first innings.

(c) In a drawn match, each side to score three points, plus any points scored in the first innings (see also paragraph (f) below).

(d) If the scores are equal in a drawn match, the side batting in the fourth innings to score eight points plus any points scored in the first innings, and the opposing side to score three points plus any points scored in the first innings.

(e) **First Innings Points** (awarded only for performances **in the first 110 overs** of each first innings and retained whatever the result of the match).
   (i) A maximum of five batting points to be available as under:
      200 to 249 runs – 1 point; 250 to 299 runs – 2 points; 300 to 349 runs – 3 points; 350 to 399 runs – 4 points; 400 runs or over – 5 points.
   (ii) A maximum of three bowling points to be available as under:
      3 to 5 wickets taken – 1 point; 6 to 8 wickets taken – 2 points; 9 to 10 wickets taken – 3 points.

(f) If a match is abandoned without a ball being bowled, each side to score three points.

(g) The side which has the highest aggregate of points gained at the end of the season shall be the Champion County of their respective Division. Should any sides in the Championship table be equal on points, the following tie-breakers will be applied in the order stated: most wins, fewest losses, team achieving most points in contests between teams level on points, most wickets taken, most runs scored. At the end of the season, the top two teams from the Second Division will be promoted and the bottom two teams from the First Division will be relegated.

COUNTY CHAMPIONS

The English County Championship was not officially constituted until December 1889. Prior to that date there was no generally accepted method of awarding the title; although the 'least matches lost' method existed, it was not consistently applied. Rules governing playing qualifications were agreed in 1873 and the first unofficial points system 15 years later.

Research has produced a list of champions dating back to 1826, but at least seven different versions exist for the period from 1864 to 1889 (see *The Wisden Book of Cricket Records*). Only from 1890 can any authorised list of county champions commence.

That first official Championship was contested between eight counties: Gloucestershire, Kent, Lancashire, Middlesex, Nottinghamshire, Surrey, Sussex and Yorkshire. The remaining counties were admitted in the following seasons: 1891 – Somerset, 1895 – Derbyshire, Essex, Hampshire, Leicestershire and Warwickshire, 1899 – Worcestershire, 1905 – Northamptonshire, 1921 – Glamorgan, and 1992 – Durham.

The Championship pennant was introduced by the 1951 champions, Warwickshire, and the Lord's Taverners' Trophy was first presented in 1973. The first sponsors, Schweppes (1977-83), were succeeded by Britannic Assurance (1984-98), PPP Healthcare (1999-2000), CricInfo (2001), Frizzell (2002-05) and Liverpool Victoria (2006 to date). Based on their previous season's positions, the 18 counties were separated into two divisions in 2000. From 2000 to 2005 the bottom three Division 1 teams were relegated and the top three Division 2 sides promoted. This was reduced to two teams from the end of the 2006 season.

1890	Surrey	1933	Yorkshire	1973	Hampshire
1891	Surrey	1934	Lancashire	1974	Worcestershire
1892	Surrey	1935	Yorkshire	1975	Leicestershire
1893	Yorkshire	1936	Derbyshire	1976	Middlesex
1894	Surrey	1937	Yorkshire	1977	Kent
1895	Surrey	1938	Yorkshire		Middlesex
1896	Yorkshire	1939	Yorkshire	1978	Kent
1897	Lancashire	1946	Yorkshire	1979	Essex
1898	Yorkshire	1947	Middlesex	1980	Middlesex
1899	Surrey	1948	Glamorgan	1981	Nottinghamshire
1900	Yorkshire	1949	Middlesex	1982	Middlesex
1901	Yorkshire		Yorkshire	1983	Essex
1902	Yorkshire	1950	Lancashire	1984	Essex
1903	Middlesex		Surrey	1985	Middlesex
1904	Lancashire	1951	Warwickshire	1986	Essex
1905	Yorkshire	1952	Surrey	1987	Nottinghamshire
1906	Kent	1953	Surrey	1988	Worcestershire
1907	Nottinghamshire	1954	Surrey	1992	Essex
1908	Yorkshire	1955	Surrey	1993	Middlesex
1909	Kent	1956	Surrey	1994	Warwickshire
1910	Kent	1957	Surrey	1995	Warwickshire
1911	Warwickshire	1958	Surrey	1996	Leicestershire
1912	Yorkshire	1959	Yorkshire	1997	Glamorgan
1913	Kent	1989	Worcestershire	1998	Leicestershire
1914	Surrey	1990	Middlesex	1999	Surrey
1919	Yorkshire	1991	Essex	2000	Surrey
1920	Middlesex	1960	Yorkshire	2001	Yorkshire
1921	Middlesex	1961	Hampshire	2002	Surrey
1922	Yorkshire	1962	Yorkshire	2003	Sussex
1923	Yorkshire	1963	Yorkshire	2004	Warwickshire
1924	Yorkshire	1964	Worcestershire	2005	Nottinghamshire
1925	Yorkshire	1965	Worcestershire	2006	Sussex
1926	Lancashire	1966	Yorkshire	2007	Sussex
1927	Lancashire	1967	Yorkshire	2008	Durham
1928	Lancashire	1968	Yorkshire	2009	Durham
1929	Nottinghamshire	1969	Glamorgan	2010	Nottinghamshire
1930	Lancashire	1970	Kent	2011	Lancashire
1931	Yorkshire	1971	Surrey	2012	Warwickshire
1932	Yorkshire	1972	Warwickshire		

COUNTY CHAMPIONSHIP RESULTS 2012

DIVISION 1

	DURHAM	LANCS	MIDDX	NOTTS	SOM'T	SURREY	SUSSEX	WARWKS	WORCS
DURHAM	–	C-le-St L 2w	C-le-St D 15	C-le-St N 114	C-le-St Drawn	C-le-St D I/38	C-le-St D 5w	C-le-St Drawn	C-le-St D 6w
LANCS	L'pool Drawn	–	L'pool Drawn	Man N 185	L'pool Drawn	L'pool Drawn	L'pool Sx 10w	L'pool Wa 5w	Man Wo 205
MIDDX	Lord's Drawn	Lord's M 109	–	Uxbridge Drawn	Lord's Drawn	Lord's M 3	Lord's M 10w	Uxbridge Drawn	Lord's M 132
NOTTS	N'ham D 16	N'ham Drawn	N'ham Drawn	–	N'ham Drawn	N'ham Drawn	N'ham Drawn	N'ham Drawn	N'ham N 92
SOM'T	Taunton Sm 5w	Taunton Drawn	Taunton Sm 6w	Taunton Drawn	–	Taunton Drawn	Taunton Drawn	Taunton Sm 1w	Taunton Sm I/148
SURREY	Oval Aband	Guildford Drawn	Oval Sy 8	Oval Sy 195	Oval	–	Oval Sy 86	Oval Wa 5w	Oval Drawn
SUSSEX	Arundel Sx 2w	Hove Drawn	Hove Sx 8w	Hove N 7w	Hove Sm 5w	Horsham Sx 10w	–	Hove Drawn	Hove Sx I/117
WARWKS	B'ham Wa 9w	B'ham Drawn	B'ham Drawn	B'ham Drawn	B'ham Wa 2w	B'ham Drawn	B'ham Drawn	–	B'ham Wa 7w
WORCS	Worcs Drawn	Worcs Drawn	Worcs M 5w	Worcs Drawn	Worcs Drawn	Worcs Drawn	Worcs Drawn	Worcs Wa I/202	–

DIVISION 2

	DERBYS	ESSEX	GLAM	GLOS	HANTS	KENT	LEICS	N'HANTS	YORKS
DERBYS	–	Derby Drawn	Derby D 8w	Derby Drawn	Derby D 6w	Derby Drawn	Derby Drawn	Derby Drawn	C'field D 202
ESSEX	C'ford D 10w	–	Colch'r Drawn	C'ford E I/38	C'ford H 2	C'ford Drawn	C'ford Drawn	C'ford Drawn	C'ford Y 239
GLAM	Cardiff D 130	Cardiff Drawn	–	Swansea Gm 26	Cardiff H 2w	Cardiff Gm 7w	Cardiff Drawn	Cardiff Drawn	Col B Drawn
GLOS	Bristol Gs 7w	Chelt'm Drawn	Bristol Aband	–	Bristol Drawn	Bristol Drawn	Chelt'm Drawn	Bristol Gs 207	Bristol Y 4w
HANTS	So'ton Drawn	So'ton E 122	So'ton H 31	So'ton Gs 33	–	So'ton Drawn	So'ton Drawn	So'ton H 8w	So'ton Drawn
KENT	Cant K 222	Cant E 7w	Cant Drawn	Cant Drawn	Tun W Drawn	–	Cant K I/279	Cant Drawn	Cant Drawn
LEICS	Leics Drawn	Leics Drawn	Leics L 52	Leics L 2w	Leics L 126	Leics K 147	–	Leics Drawn	Leics Drawn
N'HANTS	No'ton Drawn	No'ton Drawn	No'ton Gm 3w	No'ton Nh 121	No'ton Nh 117	No'ton K I/120	No'ton Drawn	–	No'ton Drawn
YORKS	Leeds Drawn	Leeds Drawn	Leeds Y 8w	Scar Y 2w	Leeds Drawn	Leeds Drawn	Scar Y I/22	Leeds Drawn	–

COUNTY CHAMPIONSHIP RESULTS 2013

KEEP YOUR OWN RECORD (see page 210)

DIVISION 1

	DERBYS	DURHAM	MIDDX	NOTTS	SOM'T	SURREY	SUSSEX	WARWKS	YORKS
DERBYS	–	Derby	Derby	Derby	Derby	Derby	Derby	Derby	C'field
DURHAM	C-le-St	–	C-le-St	C-le-St	C-le-St	C-le-St	C-le-St	C-le-St	C-le-St
MIDDX	Lord's	Lord's	–	Uxbridge	Lord's	Lord's	Lord's	Uxbridge	Lord's
NOTTS	N'ham	N'ham	N'ham	–	N'ham	N'ham	N'ham	N'ham	N'ham-
SOM'T	Taunton	Taunton	Taunton	Taunton	–	Taunton	Taunton	Taunton	Taunton
SURREY	Oval	Oval	Oval	Oval	Oval	–	Oval	Guildford	Oval
SUSSEX	Hove	Hove	Hove	Hove	Horsham	Arundel	–	Hove	Hove
WARWKS	B'ham	B'ham	B'ham	B'ham	B'ham	B'ham	B'ham	–	B'ham
YORKS	Leeds	Scar	Leeds	Scar	Leeds	Leeds	Leeds	Leeds	–

DIVISION 2

	ESSEX	GLAM	GLOS	HANTS	KENT	LANCS	LEICS	N'HANTS	WORCS
ESSEX	–	C'ford	C'ford	C'ford	C'ford	C'ford	C'ford	Colch'r	C'ford
GLAM	Cardiff	–	Cardiff	Cardiff	Cardiff	Col B	Swansea	Cardiff	Cardiff
GLOS	Bristol	Bristol	–	Bristol	Chelt'm	Bristol	Bristol	Bristol	Chelt'm
HANTS	So'ton	So'ton	So'ton	–	So'ton	So'ton	So'ton	So'ton	So'ton
KENT	Cant	Cant	Cant	Cant	–	Cant	Tun W	Cant	Cant
LANCS	Man	Man	L'pool	S'port	Man	–	Man	Man	Man
LEICS	Leics	Leics	Leics	Leics	Leics	Leics	–	Leics	Leics
N'HANTS	No'ton	No'ton	No'ton	No'ton	No'ton	No'ton	No'ton	–	No'ton
WORCS	Worcs	Worcs	Worcs	Worcs	Worcs	Worcs	Worcs	Worcs	–

CLYDESDALE BANK 40 2012

This latest format of the 40-over competition was launched in 2010, and is now the only List-A tournament played in the UK. The three Group winners, plus the runner-up with the most points, met in the semi-finals, with the winner decided in the final at Lord's.

GROUP A	P	W	L	T	NR	Pts	Net RR
1 Lancashire (4)	12	9	2	–	1	19	+0.05
2 Middlesex (2)	12	6	3	1	2	15	+0.77
3 Gloucestershire (6)	12	5	5	–	2	12	+0.99
4 Netherlands (5)	12	5	6	–	1	11	–0.91
5 Essex (3)	12	4	6	–	2	10	–0.18
6 Leicestershire (6)	12	3	6	–	3	9	–0.73
7 Worcestershire (7)	12	3	7	1	1	8	–0.01

GROUP B	P	W	L	T	NR	Pts	Net RR
1 Hampshire (4)	12	7	3	–	2	16	+0.75
2 Surrey (1)	12	6	3	–	3	15	+0.46
3 Somerset (3)	12	6	4	–	2	14	+0.38
4 Nottinghamshire (2)	12	6	5	–	1	13	+0.10
5 Durham (2)	12	5	5	–	2	12	+0.26
6 Glamorgan (5)	12	3	6	–	3	9	–0.97
7 Scotland (7)	12	1	8	–	3	5	–1.35

GROUP C	P	W	L	T	NR	Pts	Net RR
1 Sussex (1)	12	7	1	–	4	18	+1.01
2 Warwickshire (5)	12	8	3	–	1	17	+0.66
3 Kent (4)	12	7	2	–	3	17	+0.87
4 Derbyshire (3)	12	4	5	–	3	11	–0.43
5 Yorkshire (3)	12	4	7	–	1	9	+0.01
6 Northamptonshire (3)	12	1	6	–	5	7	–0.56
7 Unicorns (7)	12	1	8	–	3	5	–1.54

Win = 2 points. Tie (T)/No Result (NR) = 1 point. (Last year's positions in brackets.)
Positions of counties finishing equal on points are decided by most wins or, if equal, the team that achieved the most points in the matches played between them; if still equal, the team with the higher net run rate (ie deducting from the average runs per over scored by that team in matches where a result was achieved, the average runs per over scored against that team).

Statistical Highlights in 2012

Highest total	350-6	Middlesex v Lancashire	Lord's
Biggest victory (runs)	167	Gloucestershire beat Leics	Bristol
Biggest victory (wkts)	10	Kent beat Warwickshire	Canterbury
	10	Middlesex beat Gloucestershire	Cheltenham
	10	Warwickshire beat Unicorns	Wormsley
Most runs	598 (ave 85.42)	M.A.Carberry (Hampshire)	
Highest innings	148*	M.A.Carberry	Hampshire v Scotland	Southampton
Most sixes	11	E.J.G.Morgan	Middlesex v Scotland	Lord's
Highest partnership	222	M.J.Guptill/W.J.Durston	Derbyshire v Unicorns	Wormsley
Most wickets	21 (ave 20.52)	A.Shahzad (Lancashire)	
Best bowling	6-16	Abdur Rehman	Somerset v Nottinghamshire	Taunton
Most economical	8-3-10-3	M.Davies	Kent v Warwickshire	Canterbury
Most expensive	7-0-83-2	N.L.Harrison	Worcestershire v Lancashire	Worcester
Most w/k dismissals	19	J.N.Batty (Gloucestershire)	
	19	G.D.Cross (Lancashire)	
Most catches	13	S.J.Croft (Lancashire)	

2012 CLYDESDALE BANK 40 FINAL

HAMPSHIRE v WARWICKSHIRE

At Lord's, London, on 15 September (floodlit).
Result: HAMPSHIRE won by losing fewer wickets.
Toss: Warwickshire. Award: J.H.K.Adams.

HAMPSHIRE		Runs	Balls	4/6	Fall
M.A.Carberry	c Patel b Wright	35	31	4/2	2- 70
J.M.Vince	c Patel b Carter	18	20	4	1- 48
* J.H.K.Adams	b Woakes	66	70	4/1	4-171
N.D.McKenzie	b Blackwell	19	36	2	3-127
S.M.Ervine	c Ambrose b Maddy	57	55	6/1	5-240
S.M.Katich	not out	35	26	5	
L.A.Dawson	not out	2	3	–	
† M.D.Bates					
C.P.Wood					
Kabir Ali					
D.A.Griffiths					
Extras	(B 1, LB 2, W 7, NB 2)	12			
Total	(5 wkts; 40 overs)	**244**			

WARWICKSHIRE		Runs	Balls	4/6	Fall
D.L.Maddy	c Wood b Dawson	35	44	3	2- 89
V.Chopra	c Adams b Wood	26	36	2/1	1- 53
I.R.Bell	c Carberry b Griffiths	81	81	9/1	6-218
† T.R.Ambrose	c Bates b Wood	26	30	2	3-137
* J.O.Troughton	c Adams b Ervine	5	5	1	4-144
R.Clarke	b Wood	24	23	–/1	5-193
C.R.Woakes	not out	24	16	4	
I.D.Blackwell	b Ali	2	3	–	7-240
N.M.Carter	not out	4	3	1	
J.S.Patel					
C.J.C.Wright					
Extras	(B 1, LB 6, W 7, NB 3)	17			
Total	(7 wkts; 40 overs)	**244**			

WARWICKSHIRE	O	M	R	W	HAMPSHIRE	O	M	R	W
Carter	8	0	63	1	Dawson	8	0	39	1
Woakes	8	0	59	1	Kabir Ali	8	0	50	1
Blackwell	8	0	42	1	Wood	8	0	39	3
Wright	3	0	14	1	Ervine	6	0	46	1
Patel	8	0	32	0	Griffiths	8	0	43	1
Maddy	5	0	31	1	Katich	2	0	20	0

Umpires: R.K.Illingworth and N.A.Mallender

SEMI-FINALS

At Old Trafford, Manchester, on 1 September. Toss: Warwickshire. **WARWICKSHIRE** won by 23 runs. Warwickshire 250-6 (40; V.Chopra 110, W.T.S.Porterfield 67, A.Shahzad 3-52). Lancashire 227 (39.4; P.J.Horton 78, N.M.Carter 4-38, C.J.C.Wright 3-48). Award: V.Chopra.

At County Ground, Hove, on 1 September. Toss: Sussex. **HAMPSHIRE** won by eight wickets. Sussex 219-8 (40; L.J.Wright 122, S.M.Ervine 3-36). Hampshire 222-2 (33; M.A.Carberry 68, J.M.Vince 58). Award: M.A.Carberry.

CLYDESDALE BANK/PRO40/NATIONAL/SUNDAY LEAGUE CHAMPIONS

1969	Lancashire	1984	Essex	1999	Lancashire
1970	Lancashire	1985	Essex	2000	Gloucestershire
1971	Worcestershire	1986	Hampshire	2001	Kent
1972	Kent	1987	Worcestershire	2002	Glamorgan
1973	Kent	1988	Worcestershire	2003	Surrey
1974	Leicestershire	1989	Lancashire	2004	Glamorgan
1975	Hampshire	1990	Derbyshire	2005	Essex
1976	Kent	1991	Nottinghamshire	2006	Essex
1977	Leicestershire	1992	Middlesex	2007	Worcestershire
1978	Hampshire	1993	Glamorgan	2008	Sussex
1979	Somerset	1994	Warwickshire	2009	Sussex
1980	Warwickshire	1995	Kent	2010	Warwickshire
1981	Essex	1996	Surrey	2011	Surrey
1982	Sussex	1997	Warwickshire	2012	Hampshire
1983	Yorkshire	1998	Lancashire		

PRINCIPAL 40-OVER RECORDS 1969-2012

Highest Total		399-4	Sussex v Worcs	Horsham	2011
Highest Total Batting Second		327-4	Unicorns v Sussex	Arundel	2010
Lowest Total		23	Middlesex v Yorks	Leeds	1974
Largest Victory (Runs)		249	Somerset beat Glamorgan	Taunton	2010
Highest Scores	203	A.D.Brown	Surrey v Hampshire	Guildford	1997
	191	D.S.Lehmann	Yorkshire v Notts	Scarborough	2001
	184	M.E.Trescothick	Somerset v Glos	Taunton	2008
	176	G.A.Gooch	Essex v Glamorgan	Southend	1983
	175*	I.T.Botham	Somerset v Northants	Wellingborough	1986
Fastest Hundred	44 balls	M.A.Ealham	Kent v Derbyshire	Maidstone	1995
	44 balls	T.C.Smith	Lancashire v Worcestershire	Worcester	2012
Most Sixes (Inns)	13	I.T.Botham	Somerset v Northants	Wellingborough	1986

Highest Partnership for each Wicket

1st	239	G.A.Gooch/B.R.Hardie	Essex v Notts	Nottingham	1985
2nd	302	M.E.Trescothick/C.Kieswetter	Somerset v Glos	Taunton	2008
3rd	228*	M.W.Goodwin/C.J.Adams	Sussex v Middlesex	Hove	2003
4th	219	C.G.Greenidge/C.L.Smith	Hampshire v Surrey	Southampton	1987
5th	221*	R.R.Sarwan/M.A.Hardinges	Glos v Lancashire	Manchester	2005
6th	167	C.L.Cairns/C.M.W.Read	Notts v Sussex	Nottingham	2003
7th	164	J.N.Snape/M.A.Hardinges	Glos v Notts	Nottingham	2003
8th	116*	N.D.Burns/P.A.J.DeFreitas	Leics v Northants	Leicester	2001
9th	105	D.G.Moir/R.W.Taylor	Derbyshire v Kent	Derby	1984
10th	82	G.Chapple/P.J.Martin	Lancashire v Worcs	Manchester	1996

Best Bowling	8-26	K.D.Boyce	Essex v Lancashire	Manchester	1971
	7-15	R.A.Hutton	Yorkshire v Worcs	Leeds	1969
	7-16	S.D.Thomas	Glamorgan v Surrey	Swansea	1998
	7-29	D.A.Payne	Gloucestershire v Essex	Chelmsford	2010
	7-30	M.P.Bicknell	Surrey v Glamorgan	The Oval	1999
	7-39	A.Hodgson	Northants v Somerset	Northampton	1976
	7-41	A.N.Jones	Sussex v Notts	Nottingham	1986
Four Wkts in Four Balls		A.Ward	Derbyshire v Sussex	Derby	1970
		V.C.Drakes	Notts v Derbys	Nottingham	1999
		D.A.Payne	Gloucestershire v Essex	Chelmsford	2010
Most Economical Analysis					
	8-8-0-0	B.A.Langford	Somerset v Essex	Yeovil	1969
Most Expensive Analysis					
	8-0-100-0	D.S.Harrison	Glamorgan v Somerset	Taunton	2010
Most Wicket-Keeping Dismissals in an Innings					
	7 (6 ct, 1 st)	R.W.Taylor	Derbyshire v Lancs	Manchester	1975
Most Catches in an Innings by a Fielder					
	5	J.M.Rice	Hampshire v Warwicks	Southampton	1978
	5	D.J.G.Sales	Northants v Essex	Northampton	2007

FRIENDS LIFE t20 2012

In 2012, the Twenty20 competition was sponsored by Friends Life. Between 2003 and 2009, three regional leagues competed to qualify for the knockout stages, but this was reduced to two leagues in 2010, before returning to the three-division format in 2012. (2011's positions in brackets.)

MIDLANDS/WALES/WEST GROUP

	P	W	L	T	NR	Pts	Net RR
Somerset (4)	10	5	2	–	3	13	+0.27
Gloucestershire (8)	10	4	2	–	4	12	+0.24
Worcestershire (5)	10	4	3	–	3	11	+0.57
Warwickshire (8)	10	4	3	–	3	11	–0.03
Glamorgan (7)	10	2	3	–	5	9	–0.70
Northamptonshire (9)	10	1	7	–	2	4	–0.61

NORTH GROUP

	P	W	L	T	NR	Pts	Net RR
Yorkshire (6)	10	7	1	–	2	16	+0.86
Nottinghamshire (1)	10	5	1	–	4	14	+1.87
Durham (4)	10	4	4	1	1	10	–0.25
Lancashire (3)	10	3	4	1	2	9	+0.10
Derbyshire (7)	10	2	6	–	2	6	–0.56
Leicestershire (2)	10	2	7	–	1	5	–1.35

SOUTH GROUP

	P	W	L	T	NR	Pts	Net RR
Sussex (2)	10	6	1	–	3	15	+1.38
Hampshire (1)	10	5	2	–	3	13	+0.69
Essex (6)	10	5	4	–	1	11	–0.03
Kent (4)	10	4	5	–	1	9	–0.46
Middlesex (9)	10	3	7	–	–	6	–0.21
Surrey (5)	10	3	7	–	–	6	–0.70

QUARTER-FINALS: SOMERSET beat Essex by 27 runs at Taunton.
SUSSEX beat Gloucestershire by 39 runs at Hove.
YORKSHIRE beat Worcestershire by 29 runs at Leeds.
HAMPSHIRE beat Nottinghamshire by four wickets at Nottingham.

SEMI-FINALS: YORKSHIRE beat Sussex by 36 runs at Cardiff.
HAMPSHIRE beat Somerset by six wickets at Cardiff.

LEADING AGGREGATES AND RECORDS 2012

BATTING (350 runs)		M	I	NO	HS	Runs	Avg	100	50	R/100b	Sixes
P.J.Hughes	(Worcs)	8	8	4	87*	402	100.50	–	4	126.8	7
D.A.Miller	(Yorkshire)	12	11	3	74*	390	48.75	–	4	153.5	21

BOWLING (17 wkts)		O	M	R	W	Avge	BB	4w	R/Over
M.A.Starc	(Yorkshire)	36.5	–	218	21	10.38	3-24	–	5.91
C.J.Liddle	(Sussex)	27.4	–	203	17	11.94	5-17	1	7.33
R.J.W.Topley	(Essex)	32.0	–	246	17	14.47	3-19	–	7.68

Highest total	230-4		Sussex v Gloucestershire	Hove
Highest innings	107*	J.C.Hildreth	Somerset v Glamorgan	Taunton
Most sixes	9	S.B.Styris	Sussex v Gloucestershire	Hove
Best bowling	5-17	C.J.Liddle	Sussex v Middlesex	Lord's
	5-17	G.M.Smith	Essex v Kent	Chelmsford
Most economical	4-0-10-2	G.Chapple	Lancashire v Leicestershire	Manchester
	4-1-10-1	G.Chapple	Lancashire v Durham	Chester-le-Street
Most expensive	4-0-61-1	Azhar Mahmood	Kent v Middlesex	Canterbury
Most w/k dismissals	4	J.N.Batty	Gloucestershire v Somerset	Taunton

2012 FRIENDS LIFE t20 FINAL

YORKSHIRE v HAMPSHIRE

At Sophia Gardens, Cardiff, on 25 August.
Result: HAMPSHIRE won by 10 runs.
Toss: Hampshire. Award: D.A.Miller.

HAMPSHIRE		Runs	Balls	4/6	Fall
M.A.Carberry	b Sidebottom	8	10	2	1- 23
J.H.K.Adams	c Ballance b Pyrah	43	37	2/1	2- 70
J.M.Vince	b Ashraf	36	33	3	4-113
N.D.McKenzie	lbw b Rafiq	4	4	–	3- 76
S.M.Ervine	c Root b Sidebottom	21	15	–/1	5-131
S.M.Katich	run out	25	16	3	6-150
L.A.Dawson	not out	8	5	–	
* A.D.Mascarenhas					
C.P.Wood					
† M.D.Bates					
D.R.Briggs					
Extras	(LB 1, W 4)	5			
Total	(6 wkts; 20 overs)	**150**			

YORKSHIRE		Runs	Balls	4/6	Fall
* A.W.Gale	b Mascarenhas	15	14	3	1- 24
P.A.Jaques	b Dawson	11	13	1	3- 38
J.E.Root	b Mascarenhas	7	9	–	2- 34
† J.M.Bairstow	c Bates b Briggs	3	5	–	4- 47
D.A.Miller	not out	72	46	5/5	
G.S.Ballance	c Briggs b Ervine	7	16	-	5- 87
T.T.Bresnan	c Ervine b Wood	18	14	2	6-137
R.M.Pyrah	b Wood	1	2	–	7-140
Azeem Rafiq	c Ervine b Wood	0	1	–	8-140
R.J.Sidebottom					
M.A.Ashraf					
Extras	(B 1, LB 3, W 2)	6			
Total	(8 wkts; 20 overs)	**140**			

YORKSHIRE	O	M	R	W	HAMPSHIRE	O	M	R	W
Root	1	0	9	0	Dawson	4	0	21	1
Sidebottom	4	0	20	2	Mascarenhas	4	0	20	2
Bresnan	3	0	18	0	Wood	4	0	26	3
Pyrah	4	0	37	1	Briggs	4	0	27	1
Ashraf	4	0	43	1	Ervine	4	0	42	1
Azeem Rafiq	4	0	22	1					

Umpires: R.J.Bailey and M.A.Gough

TWENTY20 CUP WINNERS

2003	Surrey	2007	Kent	2011	Leicestershire
2004	Leicestershire	2008	Middlesex	2012	Hampshire
2005	Somerset	2009	Sussex		
2006	Leicestershire	2010	Hampshire		

PRINCIPAL TWENTY20 CUP RECORDS 2003-12

Highest Total	254-3		Gloucestershire v Middx	Uxbridge	2011
Highest Total Batting 2nd	222-3		Northants v Worcs	Kidderminster	2007
Lowest Total	47		Northants v Durham	Chester-le-St	2011
Largest Victory (Runs)	143		Somerset v Essex	Chelmsford	2011
Largest Victory (Balls)	75		Hampshire v Glos	Bristol	2010
Highest Scores	152*	G.R.Napier	Essex v Sussex	Chelmsford	2008
	141*	C.L.White	Somerset v Worcs	Worcester	2006
	124*	M.J.Lumb	Hampshire v Essex	Southampton	2009
	119	K.J.O'Brien	Gloucestershire v Middx	Uxbridge	2011
Fastest Hundred	34 balls	A.Symonds	Kent v Middlesex	Maidstone	2004
Most Sixes (Innings)	16	G.R.Napier	Essex v Sussex	Chelmsford	2008
Most Runs in Career	2209	D.I.Stevens	Kent, Leicestershire		2003-12

Highest Partnership for each Wicket

1st	192	K.J.O'Brien/H.J.H.Marshall	Gloucestershire v Middx	Uxbridge	2011
2nd	186	J.L.Langer/C.L.White	Somerset v Glos	Taunton	2006
3rd	144*	J.H.K.Adams/S.M.Ervine	Hampshire v Surrey	Southampton	2010
4th	139	M.R.Ramprakash/R.Clarke	Surrey v Glos	Bristol	2006
5th	117*	M.N.W.Spiegel/G.C.Wilson	Surrey v Middlesex	Lord's	2012
6th	98*	R.W.T.Key/M.J.Walker	Kent v Middlesex	Beckenham	2006
7th	67	O.A.C.Banks/B.J.Phillips	Somerset v Northants	Northampton	2008
8th	68	M.W.Alleyne/J.Lewis	Glos v Glamorgan	Cardiff	2005
9th	59*	G.Chapple/P.J.Martin	Lancashire v Leics	Leicester	2003
9th	59*	D.J.Willey/J.A.Brooks	Northants v Warwickshire	Birmingham	2011
10th	59	H.H.Streak/J.E.Anyon	Warwickshire v Worcs	Birmingham	2005

Best Bowling	6-5	A.V.Suppiah	Somerset v Glamorgan	Cardiff	2011
	6-16	T.G.Southee	Essex v Glamorgan	Chelmsford	2011
	6-21	A.J.Hall	Northants v Worcs	Northampton	2008
	6-24	T.J.Murtagh	Surrey v Middlesex	Lord's	2005
Most Wkts in Career	103	Azhar Mahmood	Kent, Surrey		2003-12

Most Economical Innings Analyses (Qualification: 4 overs)

4-2-5-2	A.C.Thomas	Somerset v Hampshire	Southampton	2010
4-0-5-3	D.R.Briggs	Hampshire v Kent	Canterbury	2010
4-1-6-2	J.Louw	Northants v Warwicks	Birmingham	2004
4-0-6-1	M.W.Alleyne	Glos v Worcs	Worcester	2005

Most Maiden Overs in an Innings

4-2-9-1	M.Morkel	Kent v Surrey	Beckenham	2007
4-2-5-2	A.C.Thomas	Somerset v Hampshire	Southampton	2010

Most Expensive Innings Analyses

4-0-67-1	R.J.Kirtley	Sussex v Essex	Chelmsford	2008
4-0-65-2	M.J.Hoggard	Yorkshire v Lancs	Leeds	2005
4-0-64-0	Abdul Razzaq	Hampshire v Somerset	Taunton	2010
4-0-63-1	R.J.Kirtley	Sussex v Surrey	Hove	2004

Most Wicket-Keeping Dismissals in an Innings

5 (5 ct)	M.J.Prior	Sussex v Middlesex	Richmond	2006
5 (4 ct, 1 st)	G.L.Brophy	Yorkshire v Durham	Chester-le-St	2008
5 (3 ct, 2 st)	B.J.M.Scott	Worcs v Yorkshire	Worcester	2011

Most Catches in an Innings by a Fielder

4	D.Pretorius	Warwicks v Glamorgan	Swansea	2005
4	W.R.Smith	Notts v Surrey	Nottingham	2006
4	D.J.G.Sales	Northants v Worcs	Northampton	2008
4	G.D.Elliott	Surrey v Kent	The Oval	2009
4	G.R.Breese	Durham v Yorkshire	Scarborough	2011

YOUNG CRICKETER OF THE YEAR

This annual award, made by The Cricket Writers' Club, is currently restricted to players qualified for England, Andrew Symonds meeting that requirement at the time of his award, and under the age of 23 on 1st May. In 1986 their ballot resulted in a dead heat. Up to 5 March 2013 their selections have gained a tally of 2,235 international Test match caps (shown in brackets).

1950	R.Tattersall (16)	1972	D.R.Owen-Thomas	1993	M.N.Lathwell (2)
1951	P.B.H.May (66)	1973	M.Hendrick (30)	1994	J.P.Crawley (37)
1952	F.S.Trueman (67)	1974	P.H.Edmonds (51)	1995	A.Symonds (26 – Australia)
1953	M.C.Cowdrey (114)	1975	A.Kennedy	1996	C.E.W.Silverwood (6)
1954	P.J.Loader (13)	1976	G.Miller (34)	1997	B.C.Hollioake
1955	K.F.Barrington (82)	1977	I.T.Botham (102)	1998	A.Flintoff (79)
1956	B.Taylor	1978	D.I.Gower (117)	1999	A.J.Tudor (10)
1957	M.J.Stewart (8)	1979	P.W.G.Parker (1)	2000	P.J.Franks
1958	A.C.D.Ingleby-Mackenzie	1980	G.R.Dilley (41)	2001	O.A.Shah (6)
1959	G.Pullar (28)	1981	M.W.Gatting (79)	2002	R.Clarke (2)
1960	D.A.Allen (39)	1982	N.G.Cowans (19)	2003	J.M.Anderson (77)
1961	P.H.Parfitt (37)	1983	N.A.Foster (29)	2004	I.R.Bell (83)
1962	P.J.Sharpe (12)	1984	R.J.Bailey (4)	2005	A.N.Cook (87)
1963	G.Boycott (108)	1985	D.V.Lawrence (5)	2006	S.C.J.Broad (52)
1964	J.M.Brearley (39)	1986 {	A.A.Metcalfe	2007	A.U.Rashid
1965	A.P.E.Knott (95)		J.J.Whitaker (1)	2008	R.S.Bopara (13)
1966	D.L.Underwood (86)	1987	R.J.Blakey (2)	2009	J.W.A.Taylor (2)
1967	A.W.Greig (58)	1988	M.P.Maynard (4)	2010	S.T.Finn (17)
1968	R.M.H.Cottam (4)	1989	N.Hussain (96)	2011	J.M.Bairstow (7)
1969	A.Ward (5)	1990	M.A.Atherton (115)	2012	J.E.Root (1)
1970	C.M.Old (46)	1991	M.R.Ramprakash (52)		
1971	J.Whitehouse	1992	I.D.K.Salisbury (15)		

THE PROFESSIONAL CRICKETERS' ASSOCIATION

PLAYER OF THE YEAR

Founded in 1967, the Professional Cricketers' Association introduced this award, decided by their membership, in 1970. The NatWest-sponsored award is presented at the PCA's Annual Awards Dinner in London.

1970 {	M.J.Procter	1984	R.J.Hadlee	1999	S.G.Law
	J.D.Bond	1985	N.V.Radford	2000	M.E.Trescothick
1971	L.R.Gibbs	1986	C.A.Walsh	2001	D.P.Fulton
1972	A.M.E.Roberts	1987	R.J.Hadlee	2002	M.P.Vaughan
1973	P.G.Lee	1988	G.A.Hick	2003	Mushtaq Ahmed
1974	B.Stead	1989	S.J.Cook	2004	A.Flintoff
1975	Zaheer Abbas	1990	G.A.Gooch	2005	A.Flintoff
1976	P.G.Lee	1991	Waqar Younis	2006	M.R.Ramprakash
1977	M.J.Procter	1992	C.A.Walsh	2007	O.D.Gibson
1978	J.K.Lever	1993	S.L.Watkin	2008	M.van Jaarsveld
1979	J.K.Lever	1994	B.C.Lara	2009	M.E.Trescothick
1980	R.D.Jackman	1995	D.G.Cork	2010	N.M.Carter
1981	R.J.Hadlee	1996	P.V.Simmons	2011	M.E.Trescothick
1982	M.D.Marshall	1997	S.P.James	2012	N.R.D.Compton
1983	K.S.McEwan	1998	M.B.Loye		

2012 FIRST-CLASS AVERAGES

These averages involve the 493 players who appeared in the 168 first-class matches played by 29 teams in England and Wales during the 2012 season.

'Cap' denotes the season in which the player was awarded a 1st XI cap by the county he represented in 2012. If he played for more than one county in 2012, the county(ies) who awarded him his cap is (are) underlined. Durham abolished both their capping and 'awards' system after the 2005 season. Glamorgan's capping system is based on a player's number of appearances. Gloucestershire now cap players on first-class debut. Worcestershire now award county colours when players make their Championship debut.

Team abbreviations: AA – Australia A; CU – Cambridge University/Cambridge MCCU; CfU – Cardiff MCCU; De – Derbyshire; Du – Durham; DU – Durham MCCU; E – England; EL – England Lions; Ex – Essex; Gm – Glamorgan; Gs – Gloucestershire; H – Hampshire; K – Kent; La – Lancashire; LBU – Leeds/Bradford MCCU; Le – Leicestershire; LU – Loughborough MCCU; M – Middlesex; Nh – Northamptonshire; Nt – Nottinghamshire; OU – Oxford University/Oxford MCCU; SA – South Africa(ns); Sm – Somerset; Sy – Surrey; Sx – Sussex; Wa – Warwickshire; WI – West Indies/Indians; Wo – Worcestershire; Y – Yorkshire.

† Left-handed batsman. Cap: a dash (–) denotes a non-county player. A blank denotes uncapped by his current county.

BATTING AND FIELDING

	Cap	M	I	NO	HS	Runs	Avge	100	50	Ct/St
† Abdur Rehman (Sm)		4	5	–	17	43	8.60	–	–	2
B.J.Ackland (CU)	–	2	4	–	52	72	18.00	–	1	–
A.R.Adams (Nt)	2007	12	14	–	29	151	10.78	–	–	8
† J.H.K.Adams (H)	2006	15	27	6	149	1024	48.76	3	4	15
† W.A.Adkin (Sx)		1	2	–	9	15	7.50	–	–	1
S.S.Agarwal (OU)	–	3	5	–	76	167	33.40	–	2	–
A.P.Agathangelou (La)		3	3	–	24	36	12.00	–	–	1
A.K.Ali (Le)		3	4	–	48	63	15.75	–	–	1
Kabir Ali (H)		8	9	1	31	140	17.50	–	–	–
† M.M.Ali (Wo)	2007	17	30	4	94	672	25.84	–	4	7
J.Allenby (Gm)	2010	15	22	4	125*	733	40.72	2	3	11
T.R.Ambrose (Wa)	2007	14	19	4	151*	660	44.00	1	3	46/1
M.M.Amla (SA)	–	4	6	1	311*	559	111.80	2	1	2
† J.M.Anderson (E/La)	2003	6	10	2	12	36	4.50	–	–	7
† G.M.Andrew (Wo)	2008	10	17	3	29	161	11.50	–	–	3
A.S.Ansari (CU)	–	3	4	1	48*	89	29.66	–	–	1
Z.S.Ansari (CU/Sy)		9	15	2	83*	318	24.46	–	2	4
† J.E.Anyon (Sx)	2011	15	19	8	64*	316	28.72	–	2	6
M.A.Ashraf (Y)		8	6	4	6*	14	7.00	–	–	1
Azeem Rafiq (Y)		11	11	1	75*	293	29.30	–	2	7
Azhar Mahmood (K)	2008	1	2	–	49	49	24.50	–	–	1
G.J.Bailey (AA)	–	2	4	–	81	125	31.25	–	1	3
T.E.Bailey (La)		1	–	–	–	–	–	–	–	–
J.M.Bairstow (E/EL/Y)	2011	15	21	2	182	972	51.15	4	4	24
A.Balbirnie (CfU/M)		3	5	1	19	38	9.50	–	–	–
D.J.Balcombe (H)		17	22	7	73	299	19.93	–	1	4
† G.S.Ballance (Y)	2012	17	20	4	121*	617	38.56	1	2	11
A.B.Barath (WI)		5	8	–	42	152	19.00	–	–	1
† K.H.D.Barker (Wa)		15	17	4	46	304	23.38	–	–	5
A.W.R.Barrow (Sm)		9	15	–	47	186	12.40	–	–	14
M.D.Bates (H)		17	23	–	103	530	23.04	1	2	56/1

	Cap	M	I	NO	HS	Runs	Avge	100	50	Ct/St
G.J.Batty (Sy)	2011	14	24	2	36	287	13.04	–	–	15
J.N.Batty (Gs)	2010	8	11	2	55	256	28.44	–	1	24/1
D.W.Bell (CU)	–	2	3	–	10	26	8.66	–	–	3
I.R.Bell (E/EL/Wa)	2001	11	17	4	120	610	46.92	1	6	11
D.J.Bell-Drummond (K)		2	4	1	48*	123	41.00	–	–	1
D.S.Bendon (CfU)		1	2	–	5	5	2.50	–	–	–
D.M.Benkenstein (Du)	2005	14	25	3	69	583	26.50	–	3	4
G.K.Berg (M)	2010	16	24	1	83	526	22.86	–	3	13
† P.M.Best (CU)		3	3	–	36	73	24.33	–	–	1
T.L.Best (WI)	–	1	1	–	95	95	95.00	–	1	–
S.W.Billings (K/LU)		3	4	–	69	131	32.75	–	1	4
J.M.Bird (AA)		3	2	1	4*	8	8.00	–	–	1
L.A.Blackaby (DU)	–	2	3	1	45	107	53.50	–	–	–
† I.D.Blackwell (Du/Wa)		11	20	2	84	494	27.44	–	3	3
† A.J.Blake (K)		5	8	1	73	164	23.42	–	1	5
R.S.Bopara (E/Ex)	2005	6	9	2	174	353	50.42	2	–	4
P.M.Borrington (De)		10	18	3	98	321	21.40	–	1	3
S.G.Borthwick (Du)		14	22	4	60	380	21.11	–	2	21
† M.A.G.Boyce (Le)		14	25	2	122	733	31.86	2	4	9
† W.D.Bragg (Gm)		15	25	–	92	648	25.92	–	5	8
R.M.R.Brathwaite (Du)		3	5	2	16	29	9.66	–	–	1
† D.M.Bravo (WI)	–	5	8	1	57	208	29.71	–	2	2
T.T.Bresnan (E/Y)	2006	9	9	2	39*	149	21.28	–	1	5
D.R.Briggs (H)	2012	4	6	2	20*	49	12.25	–	–	2
† S.C.J.Broad (E/Nt)	2008	7	11	1	37	135	13.50	–	–	1
J.A.Brooks (EL/Nh)	2012	11	11	3	22	72	9.00	–	–	3
G.L.Brophy (Y)	2008	4	3	1	23	47	23.50	–	–	8
B.C.Brown (Sx)		14	22	3	76*	521	27.42	–	5	38/3
† K.R.Brown (La)		17	27	2	78	636	25.44	–	3	5
N.L.Buck (Le)	2011	11	15	2	27	119	9.15	–	–	4
J.E.Burke (Sm)		1								–
J.A.Burns (AA)	–	3	4	2	74*	113	56.50	–	1	–
† R.J.Burns (Sy)		10	17	2	121	741	49.40	2	4	7
D.A.Burton (Nh)		1	1	–	11	11	11.00	–	–	–
H.Bush (LBU)	–	2	4	–	70	118	29.50	–	1	–
J.C.Buttler (Sm)		12	16	1	93	400	26.66	–	2	12/1
J.G.Cameron (Wo)	2010	12	19	4	88	399	26.60	–	2	3
† M.A.Carberry (EL/H)	2006	12	22	3	84*	572	30.10	–	4	4
A.Carter (Nt)		10	9	4	17*	36	7.20	–	–	2
† N.M.Carter (Wa)	2005	2	4	–	26	51	12.75	–	–	2
T.R.Chadwick (OU)		1	1	–	21	21	21.00	–	–	–
M.A.Chambers (Ex)		7	7	1	2	2	0.33	–	–	–
† S.Chanderpaul (WI)	–	4	7	2	91	327	65.40	–	3	2
G.Chapple (La)	1994	15	23	–	46	381	16.56	–	–	3
V.Chopra (EL/Wa)	2012	18	28	1	195	1062	39.33	3	5	27
S.H.Choudhry (Wo)	2010	4	7	1	20	31	5.16	–	–	3
J.L.Clare (De)	2012	11	13	1	48	247	20.58	–	–	2
R.Clarke (Wa)	2011	17	22	4	140	826	45.88	3	3	31
† M.E.Claydon (Du)		8	13	2	55	139	12.63	–	1	–
J.J.Cobb (Le)		14	23	1	105	752	34.18	1	5	6
I.A.Cockbain (Gs)	2011	15	24	2	112	764	34.72	1	5	12
† K.J.Coetzer (Nh)		13	19	–	120	563	29.63	1	2	5

	Cap	M	I	NO	HS	Runs	Avge	100	50	Ct/St
F.R.J.Coleman (OU)	–	1	1	–	110	110	110.00	1	–	
M.T.Coles (EL/K)	2012	17	19	1	103*	392	21.77	1	1	4
P.D.Collingwood (Du)	1998	14	25	3	114	744	33.81	1	4	19
C.D.Collymore (M)	2011	7	10	6	8	29	7.25	–	–	
N.R.D.Compton (EL/Sm)	2011	14	21	6	236	1494	99.60	5	7	9
D.O.Conway (OU)	–	1	2	2	9*	9	–	–	–	
† A.N.Cook (E/Ex)	2005	8	14	1	115	386	29.69	1	1	7
S.J.Cook (K)	2007	2	2	–	15	28	14.00	–	–	
T.L.W.Cooper (AA)	–	3	5	1	26*	38	9.50	–	–	
D.A.Cosker (Gm)	2000	15	17	3	49*	243	17.35	–	–	10
P.Coughlin (Du)		1	2	1	29*	32	32.00	–	–	1
R.G.Coughtrie (Gs)	2011	7	12	–	40	125	10.41	–	–	17
N.M.Coulter-Nile (AA)		2	3	–	24	34	11.33	–	–	
† E.J.M.Cowan (AA/Gs)	2012	7	12	1	109	513	46.63	2	2	9
O.B.Cox (Wo)	2009	3	6	1	25*	67	13.40	–	–	5
T.R.Craddock (Ex)		6	8	3	16	46	9.20	–	–	2
R.D.B.Croft (Gm)	1992	7	9	2	23	89	12.71	–	–	2
S.J.Croft (La)	2010	17	25	1	154*	749	31.20	2	3	15
S.P.Crook (M)		6	10	–	67	285	28.50	–	2	2
G.D.Cross (La)		16	25	3	75*	547	24.86	–	3	31/3
F.W.Daeche-Marshall (LU)		2	3	–	32	36	12.00	–	–	
L.M.Daggett (Nh)		14	14	5	26*	110	12.22	–	–	5
A.L.Davies (La)		1	–	–	–	–	–	–	–	2
J.M.Davies (OU)		1	1	–	31	31	31.00	–	–	
M.Davies (K)		15	16	4	58	227	18.91	–	1	4
S.L.Davies (CfU)		1	2	–	42	56	28.00	–	–	1
† S.M.Davies (Sy)	2011	12	20	–	104	438	21.90	1	1	24/1
L.M.Davis (AA)		3	5	–	62	173	34.60	–	1	4
L.A.Dawson (H)		17	27	2	134*	684	27.36	1	2	37
Z.de Bruyn (Sy)		15	27	–	125	709	26.25	1	5	5
C.D.de Lange (Nh)		4	5	4	40*	156	156.00	–	–	–
A.B.de Villiers (SA)		4	5	–	47	175	35.00	–	–	11
J.L.Denly (M)	2012	16	28	4	134*	840	35.00	2	4	7
† C.D.J.Dent (Gs)	2010	8	15	1	114	424	30.28	1	2	11
† N.Deonarine (WI)		1	1	–	7	7	7.00	–	–	
J.W.Dernbach (EL/Sy)	2011	18	15	5	28*	83	8.30	–	–	2
N.J.Dexter (M)	2010	13	23	2	125	701	33.38	2	4	10
† M.J.Di Venuto (Du)		5	10	–	96	291	29.10	–	1	11
A.J.Dibble (Sm)		1	2	–	43	44	22.00	–	–	
P.G.Dixey (Le)		3	5	1	13	30	7.50	–	–	4/1
G.H.Dockrell (Sm)		11	10	4	13*	54	9.00	–	–	5
B.L.D'Oliveira (Wo)	2012	3	6	–	19	62	10.33	–	–	4
J.du Toit (Le)		6	10	–	48	127	12.70	–	–	4
† J.P.Duminy (SA)		4	5	2	61	169	56.33	–	1	2
† M.P.Dunn (Sy)		2	1	1	0*	0	–	–	–	
C.M.Durham (De)		1	1	1	12*	12	–	–	–	1/1
W.J.Durston (De)	2012	17	27	3	121	878	36.58	2	4	26
E.J.H.Eckersley (Le)		16	28	4	137*	739	30.79	1	3	43/3
F.H.Edwards (WI)		2	4	2	10*	12	6.00	–	–	
G.A.Edwards (Sy)		2	2	1	17	27	27.00	–	–	1
K.A.Edwards (WI)		4	7	–	8	20	2.85	–	–	1
N.J.Edwards (Nt)		9	16	1	195	512	34.13	1	1	6

	Cap	M	I	NO	HS	Runs	Avge	100	50	Ct/St
Z.Elkin (CfU)	–	2	4	–	138	169	42.25	1	–	1
T.C.Elliott (CU)	–	2	2	–	44	74	37.00	–	–	–
C.P.Ellison (OU)	–	1	1	–	1	1	1.00	–	–	–
D.M.Endersby (LU)	–	2	3	–	9	13	4.33	–	–	4
† S.M.Ervine (H)	2005	17	25	4	109*	763	36.33	1	4	10
J.J.Evans (CU)	–	1	1	–	12	12	12.00	–	–	1
L.Evans (Nh)		2	3	–	5	5	1.66	–	–	–
L.J.Evans (Wa)		1	2	–	9	13	6.50	–	–	1
† R.F.Evans (LU)	–	2	4	1	20	56	18.66	–	–	–
S.T.Finn (E/M)	2009	8	10	6	10	11	2.75	–	–	8
J.D.Fleming (OU)	–	1	2	–	7	7	3.50	–	–	–
L.J.Fletcher (Nt)		9	14	5	42*	116	12.88	–	–	2
B.T.Foakes (Ex)		4	4	–	93	114	28.50	–	1	1
M.H.A.Footitt (De)		5	6	3	8*	11	3.66	–	–	2
P.J.Forrest (AA)	–	3	5	–	52	87	17.40	–	1	5
J.S.Foster (Ex)	2001	16	19	4	135	769	51.25	2	4	43/3
† P.J.Franks (Nt)	1999	11	19	7	86*	389	32.41	–	3	1
T.T.Friend (CfU)	–	2	4	1	48	85	28.33	–	–	2
† A.B.Fudadin (WI)	–	1	1	–	28	28	28.00	–	–	1
J.K.Fuller (Gs)	2011	8	12	1	57	134	12.18	–	1	3
S.T.Gabriel (WI)	–	2	2	–	13	13	6.50	–	–	–
† A.W.Gale (Y)	2008	15	20	4	80	487	30.43	–	2	4
J.S.Gatting (Sx)		11	16	3	72*	279	21.46	–	1	4
A.P.R.Gidman (Gs)	2004	13	22	1	129	528	25.14	1	3	10
† W.R.S.Gidman (Gs)	2011	11	17	1	72	447	27.93	–	3	2
J.C.Glover (Gm)		7	10	3	55	125	17.85	–	1	3
† B.A.Godleman (Ex)		8	13	1	130	437	36.41	1	2	5
† N.A.Gondal (Sx)		8	10	–	46	184	18.40	–	–	2
M.W.Goodwin (Sx)	2001	14	23	1	77	360	16.36	–	2	5
M.J.E.Green (DU)	–	2	3	1	4	4	2.00	–	–	–
L.Gregory (Sm)		4	4	–	18	40	10.00	–	–	1
† D.A.Griffiths (H)		5	6	1	21	27	5.40	–	–	2
T.D.Groenewald (De)	2011	14	15	4	42	225	20.45	–	–	3
† M.J.Guptill (De)	2012	8	14	2	137	594	49.50	2	3	13
H.F.Gurney (Nt)		10	9	1	6	10	1.25	–	–	–
A.D.Hales (Nt)	2011	16	26	1	155*	857	34.28	2	4	18
A.J.Hall (Nh)	2009	12	19	1	79	343	19.05	–	3	4
R.J.Hamilton-Brown (Sy)	2011	9	18	1	115	577	33.94	1	4	4
† O.J.Hannon-Dalby (Y)		1	1	1	5*	5	–	–	–	1
Harbhajan Singh (Ex)		5	3	1	40	58	29.00	–	–	10
T.R.Hardman (LBU)	–	2	4	–	44	65	16.25	–	–	1
† A.Harinath (Sy)		6	11	1	109	368	36.80	2	–	–
† B.W.Harmison (K)		12	17	1	46	325	20.31	–	–	3
S.J.Harmison (Du/Y)	1999	6	8	3	23	31	6.20	–	–	2
J.A.R.Harris (EL/Gm)	2010	6	5	1	48	58	14.50	–	–	–
P.G.Harris (CfU)	–	2	2	1	20	23	23.00	–	–	–
J.Harrison (Du)		3	6	1	23	60	12.00	–	–	–
N.L.Harrison (Wo)		3	4	–	10	12	3.00	–	–	1
† L.J.Hatchett (Sx)		3	6	3	18*	32	10.66	–	–	1
C.W.Henderson (Le)	2004	12	19	4	57*	296	19.73	–	2	6
M.C.Henriques (Gm)		5	8	–	28	64	8.00	–	–	1
M.R.Hickey (CU)	–	1	1	1	19*	19	–	–	–	–

222

	Cap	M	I	NO	HS	Runs	Avge	100	50	Ct/St
† M.Higginbottom (LBU)	–	2	4	3	31*	79	79.00	–	–	–
J.C.Hildreth (Sm)	2007	17	26	3	268	1214	52.78	4	5	17
M.E.Hobden (CfU)	–	2	1	1	15*	15	–	–	–	–
A.J.Hodd (Y)		4	5	–	58	91	18.20	–	1	18
D.M.Hodgson (LBU)	–	2	4	–	64	77	19.25	–	1	6
K.W.Hogg (La)	2010	14	19	9	61*	366	36.60	–	2	1
M.J.Hoggard (Le)	2010	10	12	7	28	81	16.20	–	–	–
J.M.Holland (AA)	–	2	3	–	17	33	11.00	–	–	1
P.J.Horton (La)	2007	17	27	4	137*	742	32.26	2	2	18
D.M.Housego (Gs)	2012	10	16	–	62	450	28.12	–	4	7
B.A.C.Howell (Gs)	2012	13	24	3	83*	497	23.66	–	3	5
† B.H.N.Howgego (Nh)		1	1	–	1	1	1.00	–	–	–
† C.F.Hughes (De)		1	1	–	28	28	28.00	–	–	–
P.H.Hughes (CU)		1	1	–	13	13	13.00	–	–	–
† P.J.Hughes (AA/Wo)	2012	10	18	1	135*	611	35.94	2	3	2
G.M.Hussain (Sm)		6	7	4	29	55	18.33	–	–	–
Imran Tahir (SA)		4	4	2	2*	3	1.50	–	–	1
A.J.Ireland (Gs)	2007	2	3	1	25*	47	23.50	–	–	–
N.A.James (Gm)		9	17	–	83	327	19.23	–	1	3
P.A.Jaques (Y)	2005	13	19	1	160	792	44.00	2	4	16
A.Javid (Wa)		1	1	–	31	31	31.00	–	–	–
W.I.Jefferson (Le)		2	4	–	49	75	18.75	–	–	1
B.A.Jeffery (OU)	–	3	5	–	39	93	18.60	–	–	2
K.K.Jennings (Du)		5	8	–	70	168	21.00	–	1	–
T.M.Jewell (Sy)		2	2	–	70	88	44.00	–	1	2
F.R.H.John (OU)	–	2	3	1	27	55	27.50	–	–	3
F.F.J.Johnson (OU)	–	1	1	–	0	0	0.00	–	–	–
J.A.M.Johnson (CU)	–	2	3	1	61	93	46.50	–	1	–
† M.G.Johnson (AA)	–	3	3	–	21	27	9.00	–	–	–
R.M.Johnson (De/Wa)		5	7	1	49	92	15.33	–	–	10
C.R.Jones (DU/Sm)		7	11	–	50	185	16.81	–	1	4
G.O.Jones (K)	2003	16	20	4	88	677	42.31	–	7	52
† O.J.Jones (OU)	–	2	3	1	83	216	108.00	–	3	–
R.A.Jones (Wo)	2007	10	15	5	32	151	15.10	–	–	5
† S.P.Jones (Gm)	2002	1	2	–	4	5	2.50	–	–	1
W.S.Jones (CfU/Le)		5	10	–	48	215	21.50	–	–	5
C.J.Jordan (Sy)		8	14	1	54	213	16.38	–	1	4
R.H.Joseph (Le)		3	4	1	29	79	8.77	–	–	2
† E.C.Joyce (Sx)	2009	14	24	3	108*	829	39.47	2	5	9
J.H.Kallis (SA)	–	4	6	1	182*	316	63.20	1	1	8
A.Kapil (Wo)	2011	4	6	1	41	93	18.60	–	–	–
† M.Kartik (Sy)		7	8	2	23*	113	18.83	–	–	3
† S.M.Katich (H)	2003	15	23	2	196	738	35.14	1	5	8
† G.Keedy (La)	2000	5	7	3	11	8	2.00	–	–	1
S.Kelsall (Nt)		1	2	–	35	35	17.50	–	–	–
B.W.Kemp (OU)	–	1	1	–	3	3	3.00	–	–	1
A.D.J.Kennedy (CU)	–	1	1	–	15	15	15.00	–	–	3
R.I.Keogh (Nh)		1	1	–	6	6	6.00	–	–	–
S.C.Kerrigan (EL/La)		17	20	8	34*	97	8.08	–	–	4
A.N.Kervezee (Wo)	2009	7	12	1	76	283	25.72	–	3	7
R.W.T.Key (K)	2001	15	24	3	119	797	37.95	1	5	7
A.Khan (Sx)		8	7	3	57*	142	35.50	–	1	–

	Cap	M	I	NO	HS	Runs	Avge	100	50	Ct/St
† U.T.Khawaja (De)		8	14	3	110*	537	48.81	1	6	10
C.Kieswetter (EL/Sm)	2009	13	20	6	152	848	60.57	3	4	33/2
S.P.Kirby (Sm)		9	11	5	6*	20	3.33	–	–	3
M.Klinger (AA/Wo)	2012	11	19	2	120	606	35.64	1	4	10
J.Leach (LBU/Wo)	2012	7	13	–	50	159	12.23	–	1	2
† M.J.Leach (CfU/Sm)		3	1	1	0*	0	–	–	–	–
† T.Lester (LU)	–	2	3	2	0*	0	0.00	–	–	–
J.Lewis (Sy)		13	19	6	42	326	25.07	–	–	3
C.J.Liddle (Sx)		1	–	–	–	–	–	–	–	–
† M.S.Lineker (De)		7	11	–	45	219	19.90	–	–	7
T.E.Linley (Sy)		8	11	4	15	43	6.14	–	–	4
D.L.Lloyd (Gm)		2	4	1	11*	11	3.66	–	–	–
J.A.Lodwick (CU)		1	1	–	32	32	32.00	–	–	–
† A.B.London (M)		1	2	1	30	40	40.00	–	–	–
D.S.Lucas (Wo)	2012	7	9	–	19	74	8.22	–	–	2
† M.J.Lumb (Nt)	2012	15	25	–	171	971	38.84	3	3	7
N.M.Lyon (AA)		3	3	2	15*	23	23.00	–	–	2
† A.Lyth (Y)	2010	13	16	1	248*	751	50.06	1	5	13
G.J.McCarter (Gs)	2012	1	1	1	29*	29	–	–	–	–
A.C.McDermott (AA)	–	1	2	1	12	12	12.00	–	–	1
A.McGrath (Y)	1999	14	17	3	106*	648	46.28	2	3	5
N.D.McKenzie (H)	2010	5	9	3	139	403	67.16	1	2	6
A.MacQueen (LBU)	–	1	2	–	69	72	36.00	–	1	–
† M.W.Machan (Sx)		2	2	–	6	10	5.00	–	–	–
D.L.Maddy (Wa)	2007	15	22	2	112	478	23.90	1	–	12
W.L.Madsen (De)	2011	17	27	2	231*	928	37.12	3	3	7
† S.J.Magoffin (Sx)	2013	15	19	3	41*	363	22.68	–	–	4
S.I.Mahmood (La/Sm)	2007	7	8	1	14	43	6.14	–	–	1
† D.J.Malan (M)	2010	17	27	–	140	897	33.22	2	4	25
M.N.Malik (Le)		5	7	1	21*	51	8.50	–	–	–
H.J.H.Marshall (Gs)	2006	15	25	3	117*	822	37.36	1	5	6
A.D.Mascarenhas (H)	1998	5	5	–	27	79	15.80	–	–	2
D.D.Masters (Ex)	2008	14	12	–	52	165	13.75	–	1	3
T.L.Maynard (Sy)	2012	8	16	2	143	635	45.35	1	3	12
S.C.Meaker (EL/Sy)	2012	13	16	4	41	211	17.58	–	–	1
C.A.J.Meschede (Sm)		7	7	1	62	172	28.66	–	1	3
J.C.Mickleburgh (Ex)		9	14	1	126	359	27.61	1	2	7
J.D.Middlebrook (Nh)	2011	15	22	4	121	714	39.66	2	4	6
A.J.Miles (CfU)		1	2	1	6	6	6.00	–	–	–
A.S.Miller (Wa)		1	1	1	0*	0	–	–	–	1
T.S.Mills (Ex)		8	10	4	20*	30	5.00	–	–	5
T.P.Milnes (Wa)		4	3	1	24	40	13.33	–	–	–
D.K.H.Mitchell (Wo)	2005	17	32	2	133*	833	27.76	2	2	23
P.L.Mommsen (Le)		2	3	–	35	49	16.33	–	–	2
R.A.L.Moore (LBU)	–	2	4	–	37	76	19.00	–	–	1
S.C.Moore (La)	2011	13	22	–	47	363	16.50	–	–	7
† E.J.G.Morgan (EL/M)	2008	7	10	1	71	171	19.00	–	2	6
† M.Morkel (SA)	–	4	5	–	25	79	15.80	–	–	–
A.J.Morris (LU)	–	1	2	–	7	7	3.50	–	–	–
C.A.J.Morris (OU)	–	2	3	–	7	8	2.66	–	–	1
G.J.Muchall (Du)	2005	7	13	–	25	125	9.61	–	–	5
P.B.Muchall (Gs)	2012	4	7	2	23	82	16.40	–	–	1

224

	Cap	M	I	NO	HS	Runs	Avge	100	50	Ct/St
S.J.Mullaney (Nt)		6	10	1	94	391	43.44	–	4	5
D.Murphy (Nh)		10	11	1	54	252	25.20	–	1	23/2
† T.J.Murtagh (M)	2008	16	22	7	45	391	26.06	–	–	5
† P.Mustard (Du)		15	25	3	80	482	21.90	–	1	46
J.G.Myburgh (Du)		1	2	–	34	42	21.00	–	–	–
J.K.H.Naik (Le)		2	3	–	33	40	13.33	–	–	2
G.R.Napier (Ex)	2003	12	12	2	100*	335	33.50	1	–	4
† S.P.Narine (WI)		–	1	1	–	11	11.00	–	–	–
B.P.Nash (K)		16	24	5	132*	908	47.78	3	4	6
C.D.Nash (Sx)	2008	17	28	2	162	984	37.84	3	2	9
O.J.Newby (La)		1	–	–	–	–	–	–	–	–
† S.A.Newman (K)	2011	6	9	–	64	215	23.88	–	1	3
R.I.Newton (Nh)		13	20	3	119*	751	44.17	3	2	3
R.J.Nicol (Gs)	2012	4	7	2	75*	128	25.60	–	1	6
M.J.North (Gm)		9	13	–	116	577	44.38	1	5	2
S.A.Northeast (K)	2012	12	19	2	165	969	57.00	3	6	6
L.C.Norwell (Gs)	2011	9	11	4	18	37	5.28	–	–	3
† N.J.O'Brien (K)	2011	11	17	2	182	580	38.66	1	3	8/1
G.Onions (Du/E)		14	18	7	36	216	19.63	–	–	1
C.Overton (Sm)		7	8	1	50	75	10.71	–	1	4
J.Overton (Sm)		3	4	2	34*	55	27.50	–	–	1
W.T.Owen (Gm)		3	3	1	13*	20	10.00	–	–	2
T.D.Paine (AA)		4	6	1	59	170	34.00	–	1	13/2
A.P.Palladino (De)	2012	16	21	3	106	344	19.11	1	1	4
† M.S.Panesar (Sx)	2010	16	16	4	31	88	7.33	–	–	3
† M.G.Pardoe (Wo)	2011	12	22	2	55	407	20.35	–	1	10
C.M.Park (CU)		2	3	1	71*	81	40.50	–	1	3
D.C.Pascoe (OU)		3	4	–	38	63	15.75	–	–	1
J.S.Patel (Wa)	2012	13	14	3	76	221	20.09	–	1	3
† L.A.Patel (DU)		2	3	–	3	5	1.66	–	–	–
N.Patel (LU)		2	3	–	46	46	15.33	–	–	–
R.H.Patel (M)		3	5	2	20	46	15.33	–	–	3
S.R.Patel (EL/Nt)	2008	12	18	2	69	402	25.12	–	3	10
S.A.Patterson (Y)	2012	16	15	5	37	180	18.00	–	–	1
D.A.Payne (Gs)	2011	8	10	3	16	75	10.71	–	–	2
S.D.Peters (Nh)	2007	15	23	2	148	763	36.33	2	3	10
A.N.Petersen (Ex/SA)		11	17	1	182	500	31.25	2	–	10
M.L.Pettini (Ex)	2006	16	23	4	92	644	33.89	–	7	5
V.D.Philander (Sm/SA)		9	11	–	61	177	16.09	–	1	3
B.J.Phillips (Nt)		14	20	4	47	286	17.87	–	–	5
† T.J.Phillips (Ex)	2006	2	2	1	73*	80	80.00	–	1	1
K.P.Pietersen (E/Sy)		9	15	1	234*	994	71.00	3	4	2
N.D.Pinner (Wo)	2011	4	7	–	82	132	18.85	–	1	1
L.E.Plunkett (Du)		1	2	–	24	24	12.00	–	–	–
† W.T.S.Porterfield (Wa)		15	23	2	84	558	26.57	–	3	21
† K.O.A.Powell (WI)	–	5	8	–	108	216	27.00	1	–	2
M.J.Powell (Gm)		17	21	4	134	695	40.88	2	3	6
T.Poynton (De)		14	17	4	106	393	30.23	1	2	42/1
J.E.Poysden (CU)		1	1	–	7	7	7.00	–	–	–
† A.G.Prince (La)	2010	15	24	4	144	1008	43.82	2	8	15
M.J.Prior (E/Sx)	2003	11	13	–	86	424	32.61	–	4	20/4
† T.J.W.Probert (CU)	–	1	1	–	0	0	0.00	–	–	1

	Cap	M	I	NO	HS	Runs	Avge	100	50	Ct/St
† L.A.Procter (La)		14	21	3	77	491	27.27	–	1	–
R.M.Pyrah (Y)	2010	4	4	–	9	9	2.25	–	–	–
U.A.Qureshi (CfU)	–	2	4	–	47	79	19.75	–	–	–
Ramanpreet Singh (Du)		1	2	–	22	34	17.00	–	–	1
D.Ramdin (WI)	–	5	7	1	107*	213	35.50	1	–	10
† R.Rampaul (WI)	–	4	5	1	6*	14	3.50	–	–	1
M.R.Ramprakash (Sy)	2002	5	10	–	37	107	10.70	–	–	2
† W.B.Rankin (Wa)		6	4	2	5	9	4.50	–	–	2
A.U.Rashid (Y)	2008	10	8	–	58	129	16.12	–	1	–
O.P.Rayner (M)		11	15	2	143*	359	27.61	1	1	12
C.M.W.Read (Nt)	1999	17	26	4	104*	1014	46.09	1	8	45/1
† D.J.Redfern (De)	2012	17	25	3	133	848	38.54	2	6	8
† L.M.Reece (LBU)	–	2	4	–	60	134	33.50	–	1	1
M.T.Reed (Gm)		4	7	2	5*	18	3.60	–	–	–
† G.P.Rees (Gm)	2009	12	20	–	66	413	20.65	–	1	10
J.A.Regan (Sm)		1								
H.Riazuddin (H)		5	7	2	55*	123	24.60	–	1	1
A.Richardson (Wo)	2010	14	21	9	18	79	6.58	–	–	3
M.J.Richardson (Du)		5	8	–	58	184	23.00	–	1	13
A.E.N.Riley (K/LU)		7	7	–	18	38	5.42	–	–	4
K.A.J.Roach (WI)	–	4	6	1	14	53	10.60	–	–	–
S.D.Robson (M)		16	29	2	117	814	30.14	1	4	12
C.G.Roebuck (LBU)	–	1	2	–	0	0	0.00	–	–	–
C.J.L.Rogers (M)	2011	17	31	2	173	1108	38.20	3	6	15
T.S.Roland-Jones (M)	2012	15	21	6	52	296	19.73	–	1	3
J.E.Root (EL/Y)	2012	18	26	3	222*	964	41.91	3	3	13
A.M.Rossington (M)		3	5	–	29	62	12.40	–	–	9/1
J.J.Roy (Sy)		13	23	2	83	644	30.66	–	3	11
† J.A.Rudolph (SA/Sy)		9	15	–	69	420	28.00	–	3	4
C.Rushworth (Du)		9	11	7	24*	93	23.25	–	–	1
C.J.Russell (Wo)	2012	6	10	2	22	83	10.37	–	–	2
P.T.Sadler (CU)	–	2	2	–	9	11	5.50	–	–	1
D.J.G.Sales (Nh)	1999	14	21	3	140	706	39.22	2	3	6
M.E.T.Salisbury (CU)	–	2	2	1	1*	1	–	–	–	1
J.D.Salt (DU)	–	2	3	–	16	17	5.66	–	–	2
A.G.Salter (CfU)	–	2	4	3	21	41	41.00	–	–	1
D.G.Sammy (WI)	–	4	5	–	106	201	40.20	1	–	4
M.N.Samuels (WI)	–	4	7	1	117	462	77.00	1	3	–
A.S.Sangha (DU)	–	2	4	–	32	63	15.75	–	–	–
R.R.Sarwan (Le)		14	25	2	117	941	40.91	2	5	7
I.D.Saxelby (Gs)	2008	11	16	7	30	200	22.22	–	–	4
† J.J.Sayers (Y)	2007	6	9	1	45	241	30.12	–	–	3
A.J.D.Scott (OU)	–	1	2	1	11*	11	11.00	–	–	–
B.J.M.Scott (Wo)	2010	14	21	1	106	301	15.05	1	1	29/5
B.M.Shafayat (H)		8	10	–	93	289	28.90	–	2	–
O.A.Shah (Ex)		8	13	1	161	589	49.08	2	2	3
R.A.C.Shah (DU)	–	2	4	1	56*	76	25.33	–	1	1
A.Shahzad (L/Y)	2010	13	18	5	28*	168	12.92	–	–	1
† J.D.Shantry (Wo)	2009	5	5	2	22*	67	22.33	–	–	2
R.Sharma (OU)	–	1	2	–	39	73	36.50	–	–	–
S.Shillingford (WI)	–	3	4	–	16	28	7.00	–	–	1
C.E.Shreck (K)		17	17	11	16	86	14.33	–	–	–

	Cap	M	I	NO	HS	Runs	Avge	100	50	Ct/St
H.G.Siddique (CfU)	–	2	4	–	37	53	13.25	–	–	1
† R.J.Sidebottom (Y)	2000	11	10	2	37	164	20.50	–	–	1
J.A.Simpson (M)	2011	14	21	2	49*	343	18.05	–	–	43/5
† B.T.Slater (LBU)	–	2	4	–	15	39	9.75	–	–	–
† G.C.Smith (SA)	–	4	6	–	131	293	48.83	1	2	8
G.M.Smith (Ex)	2009	9	10	–	160	318	31.80	1	–	4
G.P.Smith (Le)		13	23	–	77	429	18.65	–	2	13
† J.W.G.Smith (DU)	–	2	3	–	0	0	0.00	–	–	5/1
S.P.D.Smith (AA)	–	1	2	1	78	84	84.00	–	1	3
† T.C.Smith (La)	2010	7	11	1	91	352	35.20	–	4	6
T.M.J.Smith (M)		1	2	–	31	31	15.50	–	–	–
W.R.Smith (Du)		14	27	1	100	509	19.57	1	1	5
S.D.Snell (Sm)		2	2	–	10	18	9.00	–	–	8
A.C.Soilleux (LU)	–	2	3	1	22	26	13.00	–	–	–
V.S.Solanki (Wo)	1998	14	25	3	106	556	25.27	1	3	18
† M.N.W.Spriegel (Sy)		3	5	–	25	73	14.60	–	–	–
† M.A.Starc (AA/Y)		4	4	1	36	92	30.66	–	–	1
B.R.W.Stebbings (OU)	–	2	3	–	24	39	13.00	–	–	4
D.I.Stevens (K)	2005	16	20	–	123	619	30.95	2	2	7
D.W.Steyn (SA)	–	4	5	–	26	42	8.40	–	–	1
B.A.Stokes (Du/EL)		16	28	–	121	827	29.53	1	5	8
O.P.Stone (Nh)		3	3	1	26*	47	23.50	–	–	3
† M.D.Stoneman (Du)		14	26	1	114	661	26.44	1	2	9
† A.J.Strauss (E/M)	2001	10	18	2	141	710	44.37	3	1	13
I.W.Sturmer (LU)	–	1	1	–	5	5	5.00	–	–	2
A.V.Suppiah (Sm)	2009	17	26	–	124	769	29.57	2	5	9
A.P.Sutton (Sm)		1	–	–	–	–	–	–	–	–
G.P.Swann (E/Nt)	2005	8	11	2	41	154	17.11	–	–	6
W.A.Tavaré (LU)	–	2	4	1	61	90	30.00	–	1	–
J.M.R.Taylor (Gs)	2010	3	5	1	63	151	37.75	–	1	1
J.W.A.Taylor (E/EL/Nt)	2012	18	28	4	163*	875	36.45	3	1	10
† R.M.L.Taylor (Le/LU)		3	4	–	1	2	0.50	–	–	1
R.N.ten Doeschate (Ex)	2006	9	12	3	69	412	45.77	–	4	7
S.P.Terry (H)		4	5	1	59*	93	23.25	–	1	3
S.J.Thakor (Le)		6	10	3	85*	427	61.00	–	4	2
A.C.Thomas (Sm)	2008	9	11	1	39*	96	9.60	–	–	1
I.A.A.Thomas (K/LBU)		4	6	2	11	30	7.50	–	–	–
J.S.Thompson (OU)		1	2	–	9	9	4.50	–	–	–
M.A.Thornely (Le)	–	1	2	–	9	9	4.50	–	–	–
C.D.Thorp (Du)		9	16	–	131	514	32.12	2	1	6
R.T.Timms (CU)		14	21	2	36	221	11.63	–	–	9
† J.A.Tomlinson (H)	2008	1	1	–	52	52	52.00	–	1	–
R.J.W.Topley (Ex)		12	14	7	11	45	6.42	–	–	4
J.C.Tredwell (EL/K)	2007	3	4	1	1	1	0.33	–	–	–
P.D.Trego (Sm)	2007	15	15	2	87	232	17.84	–	1	16
C.T.Tremlett (Sy)		17	22	4	92	630	35.00	–	4	13
† M.E.Trescothick (Sm)	1999	1	–	–	–	–	–	–	–	–
I.J.L.Trott (E/Wa)	2005	9	13	–	146	506	38.92	2	1	26
J.O.Troughton (Wa)	2002	8	13	2	178	537	48.81	1	3	2
P.T.Turnbull (CU)		16	25	3	132	800	36.36	2	5	9
M.L.Turner (De)	–	2	2	–	20	20	10.00	–	–	–
† W.P.J.U.C.Vaas (Nh)	2011	7	7	2	13	43	8.60	–	–	7
		6	4	1	13*	19	6.33	–	–	–

	Cap	M	I	NO	HS	Runs	Avge	100	50	Ct/St
F.O.E.van den Bergh (Sy)		1	1	1	16*	16	–	–	–	–
J.M.Vince (H)		12	19	1	128	545	30.27	2	–	13
A.C.Voges (Nt)	2008	9	12	2	105	313	31.30	1	2	12
G.G.Wagg (Gm)		9	13	–	60	263	20.23	–	2	3
† D.J.Wainwright (De)	2012	17	23	4	51*	350	18.42	–	2	11
A.G.Wakely (Nh)	2012	14	21	2	96	690	36.31	–	5	9
C.A.M.Walker (OU)	–	1	2	–	8	9	4.50	–	–	–
† M.A.Wallace (Gm)	2003	16	24	5	122*	775	40.78	3	1	42/4
M.T.C.Waller (Sm)		3	3	–	17	24	8.00	–	–	4
C.A.Wallis (DU)	–	2	3	1	8	10	5.00	–	–	2
S.J.Walters (Gm)		14	23	2	159	813	38.71	1	7	13
I.Wardlaw (Y)		3	3	2	17*	31	31.00	–	–	2
H.T.Waters (Gm)	2012	13	14	12	39	106	53.00	–	–	5
S.R.Waters (DU)	–	2	4	–	30	49	12.25	–	–	–
N.A.T.Watkins (DU)	–	2	3	1	38*	50	25.00	–	–	1
J.P.Webb (LBU)	–	2	4	–	38	62	15.50	–	–	1
† L.W.P.Wells (Sx)		15	21	2	127	713	37.52	2	3	12
† K.D.Wernars (Sx)		3	4	–	50	65	16.25	–	1	1
M.H.Wessels (Nt)		13	20	–	199	905	45.25	3	1	8/1
S.A.Westaway (OU)	–	1	2	1	26*	40	40.00	–	–	3
T.Westley (Ex)		17	25	2	185	786	34.17	2	3	9
† I.J.Westwood (Wa)	2008	13	20	1	120	771	40.57	2	5	5
A.J.Wheater (Ex)		12	15	2	98	462	35.53	–	4	7
G.G.White (Nt)		6	11	2	30*	109	12.11	–	–	2
R.A.White (Nh)	2008	2	3	1	42	62	31.00	–	–	–
W.A.White (Le)	2012	16	26	5	67	616	29.33	–	4	1
R.A.Whiteley (De)		15	21	3	83	509	28.27	–	3	5
D.J.Willey (Nh)		15	18	4	76	489	34.92	–	4	3
B.Williams (OU)	–	3	5	–	92	163	32.60	–	2	1
K.S.Williamson (Gs)	2011	4	7	–	128	366	52.28	2	1	3
† C.M.Willoughby (Ex)		8	6	4	1*	2	1.00	–	–	2
A.D.Wilson (LU)	–	1	2	–	6	6	3.00	–	–	–
G.C.Wilson (Sy)		4	6	1	68	206	41.20	–	2	8
C.R.Woakes (EL/Wa)	2009	10	13	5	118*	588	73.50	2	2	3
C.P.Wood (H)		10	15	1	105*	324	23.14	1	1	1
M.A.Wood (Du)		2	4	–	34	76	19.00	–	–	4
† S.K.W.Wood (Nt)		1	2	–	45	47	23.50	–	–	–
R.J.J.Woolley (CU)	–	2	2	–	1	1	0.50	–	–	–
B.J.Wright (Gm)	2011	16	27	3	104	661	27.54	1	1	3
C.J.C.Wright (Wa)		16	16	5	53	201	18.27	–	1	2
L.J.Wright (Sx)	2007	9	14	1	81	356	27.38	–	3	7
A.C.F.Wyatt (Le)		5	6	2	8	14	3.50	–	–	1
† M.H.Yardy (Sx)	2005	16	25	2	110	574	24.95	1	3	32
E.G.C.Young (Gs)	2010	8	12	2	55*	186	18.60	–	1	3

BOWLING

See BATTING AND FIELDING section for details of matches and caps

	Cat	O	M	R	W	Avge	Best	5wI	10wM
Abdur Rehman (Sm)	SLA	174	50	383	27	14.18	9- 65	3	1
A.R.Adams (Nt)	RMF	344.3	63	1035	54	19.16	7- 32	4	1
J.H.K.Adams (H)	LM	3	2	4	1	4.00	1- 4	–	–
W.A.Adkin (Sx)	RM	5	1	20	0				
S.S.Agarwal (OU)	OB	84.5	13	235	6	39.16	3- 46	–	–
A.K.Ali (Le)	RM/LB	11	2	33	0				
Kabir Ali (H)	RMF	216.3	36	769	22	34.95	3- 42	–	–
M.M.Ali (Wo)	OB	296.1	42	957	33	29.00	6- 29	2	1
J.Allenby (Gm)	RM	359.3	80	992	42	23.61	4- 39	–	–
J.M.Anderson (E/La)	RFM	295.1	77	713	23	31.00	5- 82	1	–
G.M.Andrew (Wo)	RMF	194	28	745	19	39.21	5- 86	1	–
A.S.Ansari (CU)	LB	7	2	15	0				
Z.S.Ansari (CU/Sy)	SLA	41	6	150	0				
J.E.Anyon (Sx)	RFM	429.5	73	1645	42	39.16	5- 36	2	–
M.A.Ashraf (Y)	RMF	117.5	27	376	17	22.11	4- 36	–	–
Azeem Rafiq (Y)	OB	246.5	63	711	28	25.39	5- 50	1	–
Azhar Mahmood (K)	RFM	21	5	71	2	35.50	2- 25	–	–
T.E.Bailey (La)	RFM	17	2	67	1	67.00	1- 67	–	–
A.Balbirnie (CfU/M)	OB	8	0	24	0				
D.J.Balcombe (H)	RFM	533.1	111	1671	64	26.10	8- 71	3	1
G.S.Ballance (Y)	LB	6	1	23	0				
K.H.D.Barker (Wa)	LM	392.1	94	1166	56	20.82	6- 40	5	1
G.J.Batty (Sy)	OB	305	71	789	30	26.30	6- 73	2	1
D.S.Bendon (CfU)	LBG	6	1	33	1	33.00	1- 33	–	–
D.M.Benkenstein (Du)	RM/OB	1	0	2	0				
G.K.Berg (M)	RMF	329.4	73	1014	35	28.97	3- 25	–	–
P.M.Best (CU)	SLA	114	20	439	5	87.80	2- 86	–	–
T.L.Best (WI)	RF	12	2	37	2	18.50	2- 37	–	–
J.M.Bird (AA)	RFM	97	21	313	7	44.71	2- 65	–	–
L.A.Blackaby (DU)	LM	31	6	103	4	25.75	4- 51	–	–
I.D.Blackwell (Du/Wa)	SLA	197.2	41	610	23	26.52	7- 52	1	–
A.J.Blake (K)	RMF	1	0	1	0				
R.S.Bopara (E/Ex)	RM	20	1	83	0				
P.M.Borrington (De)	RMF	1	0	2	0				
S.G.Borthwick (Du)	LBG	130.4	12	446	15	29.73	4- 37	–	–
M.A.G.Boyce (Le)	RM	2	1	9	0				
W.D.Bragg (Gm)	RM	26.1	0	107	1	107.00	1- 10	–	–
R.M.R.Brathwaite (Du)	RFM	33.3	4	137	9	15.22	3- 32	–	–
D.M.Bravo (WI)	RMF	5	0	39	0				
T.T.Bresnan (E/Y)	RFM	337.2	75	1071	28	38.25	5- 81	1	–
D.R.Briggs (H)	SLA	82.1	15	249	5	49.80	2- 79	–	–
S.C.J.Broad (E/Nt)	RFM	295.3	53	966	29	33.31	7- 72	2	1
J.A.Brooks (Nh)	RFM	295.4	81	890	29	30.68	5- 61	2	–
K.R.Brown (La)	RM	3	0	5	0				
N.L.Buck (Le)	RMF	292	58	955	20	47.75	3- 50	–	–
J.E.Burke (Sm)	RMF	18	3	68	2	34.00	2- 51	–	–
D.A.Burton (Nh)	RMF	13	1	52	1	52.00	1- 44	–	–
H.Bush (LBU)	OB	7	0	28	0				
J.C.Buttler (Sm)	(WK)	2	0	11	0				

	Cat	O	M	R	W	Avge	Best	5wl	10wM
J.G.Cameron (Wo)	RM	48	3	192	2	96.00	1- 19	–	–
M.A.Carberry (EL/H)	OB	6	2	19	1	19.00	1- 1.	–	–
A.Carter (Nt)	RM	261.2	43	938	26	36.07	4- 55	–	–
N.M.Carter (Wa)	LMF	36	4	149	2	74.50	2- 86	–	–
M.A.Chambers (Ex)	RFM	163.1	29	567	20	28.35	4- 31	–	–
G.Chapple (La)	RMF	394.5	101	1010	42	24.04	5- 47	2	1
V.Chopra (EL/Wa)	LB	2	0	5	0			–	–
S.H.Choudhry (Wo)	SLA	70.4	13	165	10	16.50	4- 38	–	–
J.L.Clare (De)	RMF	204.3	40	642	30	21.40	6- 40	2	1
R.Clarke (Wa)	RFM	204	54	569	26	21.88	4- 46	–	–
M.E.Claydon (Du)	RMF	126.2	23	495	16	30.93	4- 84	–	–
J.J.Cobb (Le)	LB	56	4	208	3	69.33	1- 5	–	–
K.J.Coetzer (Nh)	RM	19	1	74	1	74.00	1- 9	–	–
M.T.Coles (K)	RMF	400.1	51	1341	59	22.72	6- 51	2	–
P.D.Collingwood (Du)	RM	19	3	60	1	60.00	1- 8	–	–
C.D.Collymore (M)	RFM	187.1	44	540	11	49.09	3- 66	–	–
D.O.Conway (OU)	RMF	35	8	125	4	31.25	3- 67	–	–
S.J.Cook (K)	RMF	12	5	19	1	19.00	1- 19	–	–
T.L.W.Cooper (AA)	OB	8	0	32	1	32.00	1- 2	–	–
D.A.Cosker (Gm)	SLA	361.3	83	991	16	61.93	4- 22	–	–
P.Coughlin (Du)	RM	10	0	46	1	46.00	1- 26	–	–
N.M.Coulter-Nile (AA)	RF	40	9	145	7	20.71	3- 32	–	–
T.R.Craddock (Ex)	LB	125.3	23	438	15	29.20	5- 96	1	–
R.D.B.Croft (Gm)	OB	141.3	27	403	23	17.52	5- 31	2	–
S.J.Croft (La)	RMF	96.4	13	289	12	24.08	6- 41	1	–
S.P.Crook (M)	RFM	158.3	25	534	18	29.66	5- 48	1	–
L.M.Daggett (Nh)	RMF	372.1	95	1218	27	45.11	4- 76	–	–
M.Davies (K)	RMF	368.3	128	699	36	19.41	5- 27	1	–
L.A.Dawson (H)	SLA	265.2	62	837	26	32.19	5- 29	1	–
Z.de Bruyn (Sy)	RMF	130	24	383	6	63.83	2- 16	–	–
C.D.de Lange (Nh)	SLA	54	11	176	3	58.66	1- 11	–	–
J.L.Denly (M)	LB	27	2	104	1	104.00	1- 18	–	–
C.D.J.Dent (Gs)	SLA	11	0	32	0			–	–
J.W.Dernbach (EL/Sy)	RFM	201.5	48	611	21	29.09	3- 39	–	–
N.J.Dexter (M)	RM	115	25	332	12	27.66	3- 23	–	–
A.J.Dibble (Sm)	RMF	13	2	42	3	14.00	3- 42	–	–
G.H.Dockrell (Sm)	SLA	340.5	80	996	35	28.45	6- 27	2	–
B.L.D'Oliveira (Wo)	LB	43	2	198	0			–	–
J.du Toit (Le)	RMF	18	1	54	0			–	–
J.P.Duminy (SA)	OB	20	2	58	2	29.00	1- 10	–	–
M.P.Dunn (Sy)	RFM	24.1	1	136	4	34.00	3- 41	–	–
W.J.Durston (De)	OB	177.3	25	574	22	26.09	5- 34	1	–
F.H.Edwards (WI)	RF	60	8	212	3	70.66	2- 79	–	–
G.A.Edwards (Sy)	RFM	44.5	6	184	5	36.80	4- 44	–	–
C.P.Ellison (OU)	RM	31	12	88	3	29.33	3- 42	–	–
D.M.Endersby (LU)	RMF	29	2	121	3	40.33	1- 38	–	–
S.M.Ervine (H)	RM	232.2	59	716	27	26.51	4- 96	–	–
L.Evans (Nh)	RMF	65	16	214	12	17.83	4- 38	–	–
R.F.Evans (LU)	RM	4	1	12	0			–	–
S.T.Finn (E/M)	RF	293	57	969	41	23.63	4- 43	–	–
L.J.Fletcher (Nt)	RMF	266.5	77	708	28	25.28	4- 21	–	–
M.H.A.Footitt (De)	LFM	108.2	21	332	11	30.18	3- 43	–	–

	Cat	O	M	R	W	Avge	Best	5wI	10wM
P.J.Forrest (AA)	RM	3	1	7	1	7.00	1- 7	–	–
P.J.Franks (Nt)	RMF	204.5	32	667	16	41.68	4- 47	–	–
T.T.Friend (CfU)	RFM	38	3	187	2	93.50	2- 96	–	–
J.K.Fuller (Gs)	RFM	174.2	27	653	24	27.20	5- 29	1	–
S.T.Gabriel (WI)	RFM	26.3	3	86	4	21.50	3- 60	–	–
A.W.Gale (Y)	LB	6.1	0	97	0			–	–
J.S.Gatting (Sx)	OB	12	0	56	0				
A.P.R.Gidman (Gs)	RM	14	3	50	2	25.00	2- 50	–	–
W.R.S.Gidman (Gs)	RM	318	58	943	44	21.43	5- 43	2	–
J.C.Glover (Gm)	RMF	176.4	40	585	19	30.78	4- 76	–	–
N.A.Gondal (Sx)	LMF	160	26	529	18	29.38	3- 34	–	–
M.J.E.Green (DU)	RM	42	3	137	1	137.00	1- 53	–	–
L.Gregory (Sm)	RMF	24	2	127	4	31.75	2- 22	–	–
D.A.Griffiths (H)	RFM	110.3	18	382	11	34.72	3- 40	–	–
T.D.Groenewald (De)	RFM	399.4	89	1086	42	25.85	5- 29	1	–
M.J.Guptill (De)	OB	3	0	6	0			–	–
H.F.Gurney (Nt)	LFM	234.3	52	713	21	33.95	4- 40	–	–
A.J.Hall (Nh)	RFM	293.5	73	812	34	23.88	5- 50	1	–
R.J.Hamilton-Brown (Sy)	OB	13	0	38	1	38.00	1- 14	–	–
O.J.Hannon-Dalby (Y)	RMF	25.1	4	54	4	13.50	3- 36	–	–
Harbhajan Singh (Ex)	OB	176.3	38	431	13	33.15	4- 91	–	–
T.R.Hardman (LBU)	RM	36	3	179	3	59.66	2- 51	–	–
B.W.Harmison (K)	RMF	19	2	66	0				
S.J.Harmison (Du/Y)	RF	98.2	15	424	14	30.28	3- 49	–	–
J.A.R.Harris (EL/Gm)	RFM	173	29	553	17	32.52	6-102	2	–
P.G.Harris (CfU)	RM	38	7	137	1	137.00	1- 63	–	–
J.Harrison (Du)	LMF	68	10	260	10	26.00	4-112	–	–
N.L.Harrison (Wo)	RMF	46	8	176	3	58.66	2- 78	–	–
L.J.Hatchett (Sx)	LMF	64.5	12	280	8	35.00	3- 25	–	–
C.W.Henderson (Le)	SLA	390.1	82	1110	30	37.00	5-116	1	–
M.C.Henriques (Gm)	RFM	95	18	323	16	20.18	4- 54	–	–
M.R.Hickey (CU)	LM	4	0	17	0				
M.Higginbottom (LBU)	RMF	29	7	120	4	30.00	2- 22	–	–
J.C.Hildreth (Sm)	RMF	2	0	30	0				
M.E.Hobden (CfU)	RFM	49.3	5	195	5	39.00	5- 62	1	–
K.W.Hogg (La)	RMF	262.4	62	795	19	41.84	3- 23	–	–
M.J.Hoggard (Le)	RMF	220.4	42	691	24	28.79	4- 27	–	–
J.M.Holland (AA)	SLA	93	19	273	10	27.30	3- 49	–	–
B.A.C.Howell (Gs)	RMF	93.4	14	266	6	44.33	2- 37	–	–
G.M.Hussain (Sm)	RMF	101.4	17	385	13	29.61	5- 48	1	–
Imran Tahir (SA)	LBG	134	16	424	12	35.33	4- 31	–	–
A.J.Ireland (Gs)	RM	39	2	159	4	39.75	2- 20	–	–
N.A.James (Gm)	SLA	17	0	68	0				
K.K.Jennings (Du)	RMF	5	2	9	0				
T.M.Jewell (Sy)	RMF	39	11	114	6	19.00	3- 39	–	–
F.F.J.Johnson (OU)	RMF	11	3	42	1	42.00	1- 42	–	–
M.G.Johnson (AA)	LF	82.1	13	276	8	34.50	4- 47	–	–
C.R.Jones (DU/Sm)	RM	2	0	17	1	17.00	1- 17	–	–
O.J.Jones (OU)	RM	30	3	107	2	53.50	1- 7	–	–
R.A.Jones (Wo)	RMF	200.1	26	857	31	27.64	6- 32	1	–
S.P.Jones (Gm)	RFM	22	2	70	2	35.00	2- 70	–	–
W.S.Jones (CfU/Le)	LB	33	2	174	5	34.80	3- 71	–	–

	Cat	O	M	R	W	Avge	Best	5wI	10wM
C.J.Jordan (Sy)	RFM	160.3	23	599	15	39.93	3- 29	–	–
R.H.Joseph (Le)	RFM	202.3	36	762	24	31.75	6- 47	2	1
J.H.Kallis (SA)	RFM	76	22	213	4	53.25	2- 38	–	–
A.Kapil (Wo)	RFM	35	4	136	4	34.00	3- 28	–	–
M.Kartik (Sy)	SLA	251.1	58	597	27	22.11	5- 69	1	–
S.M.Katich (H)	SLC	33	4	93	2	46.50	1- 22	–	–
G.Keedy (La)	SLA	139.5	18	421	8	52.62	3-101	–	–
B.W.Kemp (OU)	RFM	20	3	81	1	81.00	1- 71	–	–
R.I.Keogh (Nh)	OB	20	5	69	1	69.00	1- 69	–	–
S.C.Kerrigan (EL/La)	SLA	573.2	98	1674	50	33.48	6- 59	1	–
R.W.T.Key (K)	RM/OB	4	1	27	0				
A.Khan (Sx)	RFM	167.4	30	564	22	25.63	5- 25	2	–
U.T.Khawaja (De)	RM	4	1	15	0				
C.Kieswetter (EL/Sm)	OB	3	0	3	2	1.50	2- 3	–	–
S.P.Kirby (Sm)	RFM	225.1	47	735	24	30.62	3- 34	–	–
J.Leach (LBU/Wo)	RMF	68.4	14	226	12	18.83	4- 73	–	–
M.J.Leach (CfU/Sm)	SLA	61	5	194	2	97.00	2- 37	–	–
T.Lester (LU)	LFM	49.1	6	213	2	106.50	1- 59	–	–
J.Lewis (Sy)	RMF	335	77	980	31	31.61	5- 41	1	–
C.J.Liddle (Sx)	LFM	6	2	10	1	10.00	1- 10	–	–
M.S.Lineker (De)	SLA	2	0	2	0				
T.E.Linley (Sy)	RFM	188.5	39	570	22	25.90	5- 45	2	–
J.A.Lodwick (CU)	RM	46.5	12	99	7	14.14	4- 55	–	–
D.S.Lucas (Wo)	LMF	239	40	852	22	38.72	4- 37	–	–
M.J.Lumb (Nt)	RM	2	0	13	0				
N.M.Lyon (AA)	OB	104	18	390	8	48.75	4-115	–	–
A.Lyth (Y)	RM	12	3	116	0				
G.J.McCarter (Gs)	RFM	19	3	67	0				
A.C.McDermott (AA)	RFM	28	6	76	6	12.66	4- 38	–	–
A.McGrath (Y)	RM	196.1	59	489	19	25.73	4- 21	–	–
A.MacQueen (LBU)	OB	1	0	5	0				
D.L.Maddy (Wa)	RM/OB	147	50	354	14	25.28	4- 39	–	–
W.L.Madsen (De)	OB	1	0	1	0				
S.J.Magoffin (Sx)	RFM	480.2	161	1143	57	20.05	7- 34	2	–
S.I.Mahmood (La/Sm)	RFM	119.5	17	488	16	30.50	4- 38	–	–
D.J.Malan (M)	LB	63.2	13	227	7	32.42	5- 61	1	–
M.M.Malik (Le)	RFM	87	10	309	6	51.50	2- 22	–	–
A.D.Mascarenhas (H)	RMF	104	36	241	7	34.42	2- 40	–	–
D.D.Masters (Ex)	RMF	395.1	119	941	53	17.75	7- 60	4	–
S.C.Meaker (EL/Sy)	RMF	355.3	62	1225	51	24.01	8- 52	3	1
C.A.J.Meschede (Sm)	RMF	119	22	418	12	34.83	3- 26	–	–
J.D.Middlebrook (Nh)	OB	346.2	100	883	24	36.79	5- 63	1	–
A.S.Miller (Wa)	RFM	16	3	46	1	46.00	1- 24	–	–
T.S.Mills (Ex)	LMF	129.1	19	425	14	30.35	4- 25	–	–
T.P.Milnes (Wa)	RFM	49	5	202	5	40.40	2- 31	–	–
D.K.H.Mitchell (Wo)	RM	9	0	27	0				
P.L.Mommsen (Le)	OB	10	0	43	0				
R.A.L.Moore (LBU)	RMF	13	3	56	0				
M.Morkel (SA)	RFM	150.2	30	451	14	32.21	4- 72	–	–
A.J.Morris (LU)	RMF	9	0	47	1	47.00	1- 47	–	–
C.A.J.Morris (OU)	RMF	61.5	19	206	4	51.50	2- 7	–	–
P.B.Muchall (Gs)	RMF	39.2	3	218	2	109.00	2- 60	–	–

	Cat	O	M	R	W	Avge	Best	5wI	10wM
S.J.Mullaney (Nt)	RM	16	2	41	0			–	–
T.J.Murtagh (M)	RFM	526.3	127	1455	61	23.85	5- 37	2	–
J.K.H.Naik (Le)	OB	56.2	5	205	3	68.33	2- 36	–	–
G.R.Napier (Ex)	RM	317.2	56	1033	45	22.95	5- 58	2	–
S.P.Narine (WI)	OB	15	1	70	0			–	–
B.P.Nash (K)	LM	28.5	1	72	4	18.00	1- 2	–	–
C.D.Nash (Sx)	OB	135.2	23	446	21	21.23	3- 23	–	–
O.J.Newby (La)	RMF	13	0	59	1	59.00	1- 59	–	–
S.A.Newman (K)	RM	6	0	31	0			–	–
R.J.Nicol (Gs)	RM/OB	38.5	2	129	7	18.42	4- 53	–	–
M.J.North (Gm)	OB	73	8	223	7	31.85	3- 40	–	–
L.C.Norwell (Gs)	RMF	194.1	25	632	22	28.72	5- 51	1	–
N.J.O'Brien (Nh)	(WK)	1	0	3	0			–	–
G.Onions (Du/EL)	RFM	415.1	114	1061	72	14.73	9- 67	5	3
C.Overton (Sm)	RMF	113.1	23	363	12	30.25	4- 38	–	–
J.Overton (Sm)	RFM	66	7	229	6	38.16	2- 61	–	–
W.T.Owen (Gm)	RMF	56.2	5	238	7	34.00	4- 87	–	–
A.P.Palladino (De)	RMF	499.4	107	1431	56	25.55	7- 53	3	–
M.S.Panesar (Sx)	SLA	514.1	157	1227	53	23.15	7- 60	2	1
D.C.Pascoe (OU)	SLA	79	21	195	5	39.00	3- 53	–	–
J.S.Patel (Wa)	OB	395.1	87	1161	51	22.76	7- 75	4	–
L.A.Patel (DU)	OB	15	0	90	1	90.00	1- 64	–	–
R.H.Patel (M)	SLA	104	12	356	14	25.42	4- 72	–	–
S.R.Patel (EL/Nt)	SLA	194.4	35	642	16	40.12	4- 67	–	–
S.A.Patterson (Y)	RMF	427.2	125	1115	53	21.03	5- 77	1	–
D.A.Payne (Gs)	LMF	147	24	504	22	22.90	4- 89	–	–
A.N.Petersen (Ex/SA)	RM/OB	1	0	4	0			–	–
M.L.Pettini (Ex)	RM	3.1	0	72	1	72.00	1- 72	–	–
V.D.Philander (Sm/SA)	RFM	321	77	843	36	23.41	5- 30	3	–
B.J.Phillips (Nt)	RFM	345.3	105	841	32	26.28	4- 33	–	–
T.J.Phillips (Ex)	SLA	19.4	0	95	1	95.00	1- 49	–	–
K.P.Pietersen (E/Sy)	OB	30	4	118	6	19.66	3- 52	–	–
N.D.Pinner (Wo)	OB	4	0	13	0			–	–
L.E.Plunkett (Du)	RFM	12	0	69	0			–	–
J.E.Poysden (CU)	LB	25	1	147	1	147.00	1- 96	–	–
A.G.Prince (La)	OB	2	1	5	0			–	–
T.J.W.Probert (CU)	RM	50	13	145	4	36.25	3- 68	–	–
L.A.Procter (La)	RM	190.1	33	631	28	22.53	7- 71	2	–
R.M.Pyrah (Y)	RM	38	9	128	2	64.00	1- 9	–	–
R.Rampaul (WI)	RFM	80	17	233	7	33.28	3- 75	–	–
W.B.Rankin (Wa)	RMF	138.1	15	515	16	32.18	5- 78	1	–
A.U.Rashid (Y)	LB	202.5	26	656	16	41.00	5-105	1	–
O.P.Rayner (M)	OB	240.5	38	590	18	32.77	4- 67	–	–
D.J.Redfern (De)	OB	19	3	72	1	72.00	1- 25	–	–
L.M.Reece (LBU)	LM	34	6	120	5	24.00	3- 25	–	–
M.T.Reed (Gm)	RFM	88	10	310	8	38.75	3- 39	–	–
G.P.Rees (Gm)	LM	4.1	0	22	0			–	–
H.Riazuddin (H)	RMF	92	23	269	12	22.41	5- 61	1	–
A.Richardson (Wo)	RMF	461.3	137	1113	57	19.52	6- 47	4	1
A.E.N.Riley (K/LU)	OB	106.4	21	413	9	45.88	2- 43	–	–
K.A.J.Roach (WI)	RF	89	10	364	11	33.09	3- 60	–	–
S.D.Robson (M)	LBG	4.5	0	17	0			–	–

	Cat	O	M	R	W	Avge	Best	5wI	10wM
T.S.Roland-Jones (M)	RMF	405	87	1245	64	19.45	6- 66	4	1
J.E.Root (EL/Y)	OB	58	16	164	1	164.00	1- 39	–	–
J.J.Roy (Sy)	RM	1	0	1	0				
C.Rushworth (Du)	RMF	210.5	51	623	38	16.39	5- 38	3	–
C.J.Russell (Wo)	RMF	134.4	23	563	17	33.11	4- 43	–	–
P.T.Sadler (CU)	RFM	60	20	142	1	142.00	1- 50	–	–
M.E.T.Salisbury (CU)	RMF	47	7	225	4	56.25	2- 54	–	–
J.D.Salt (DU)	RMF	36	4	127	6	21.16	2- 25	–	–
A.G.Salter (CfU)	OB	55	5	211	4	52.75	3-134	–	–
D.J.G.Sammy (WI)	RM	86	6	291	6	48.50	2- 92	–	–
M.N.Samuels (WI)	OB	61.3	6	213	5	42.60	2- 14	–	–
A.S.Sangha (DU)	OB	35	0	162	3	54.00	1- 36	–	–
R.R.Sarwan (Le)	LB	16.1	0	75	0				
I.D.Saxelby (Gs)	RMF	293.3	58	897	35	25.62	6- 48	1	–
A.J.D.Scott (OU)	LB	4	1	5	1	5.00	1- 5	–	–
B.M.Shafayat (H)	RMF	2	0	15	0				
A.Shahzad (La/Y)	RFM	284.4	64	919	28	32.82	4- 40	–	–
J.D.Shantry (Wo)	LM	135	24	423	15	28.20	5- 58	1	–
R.Sharma (OU)	RMF	26	9	62	1	62.00	1- 62	–	–
S.Shillingford (WI)	OB	75.5	13	299	3	99.66	2- 75	–	–
C.E.Shreck (K)	RFM	526.3	112	1545	58	26.63	5- 41	2	–
R.J.Sidebottom (Y)	LFM	297	72	798	24	33.25	5- 30	1	–
G.M.Smith (Ex)	OB/RM	122	22	407	6	67.83	2- 31	–	–
G.P.Smith (Le)	LBG	1	0	9	0				
T.C.Smith (La)	RMF	66	7	248	6	41.33	2- 12	–	–
T.M.J.Smith (M)	SLA	27.3	3	71	1	71.00	1- 71	–	–
W.R.Smith (Du)	OB	7.2	1	35	1	35.00	1- 32	–	–
A.C.Soilleux (LU)	RMF	57	9	263	7	37.57	3- 67	–	–
M.N.W.Spriegel (Sy)	OB	12	2	36	0				
M.A.Starc (AA/Y)	LFM	97.4	23	351	12	29.25	3- 50	–	–
B.R.W.Stebbings (OU)	RMF	1	0	3	0				
D.I.Stevens (K)	RM	304.3	63	840	35	24.00	5- 35	1	–
D.W.Steyn (SA)	RF	149	36	496	16	31.00	5- 56	1	–
B.A.Stokes (Du/EL)	RM	245.4	50	816	37	22.05	4- 3	–	–
I.W.Sturmer (LU)	RM	23	3	118	2	59.00	1- 35	–	–
A.V.Suppiah (Sm)	SLA	80	18	232	3	77.33	1- 8	–	–
A.P.Sutton (Sm)	RMF	30	6	99	2	49.50	1- 31	–	–
G.P.Swann (E/Nt)	OB	299.5	71	778	20	38.90	3- 26	–	–
J.M.R.Taylor (Gs)	OB	87	15	277	8	34.62	2- 28	–	–
J.W.A.Taylor (E/ELNt)	LB	2	0	16	0				
R.M.L.Taylor (Le/LU)	LM	80	10	408	10	40.80	5- 91	1	–
R.N.ten Doeschate (Ex)	RMF	86	11	332	6	55.33	3- 39	–	–
S.J.Thakor (Le)	RM	34	3	159	4	39.75	2- 24	–	–
A.C.Thomas (Sm)	RFM	252.4	50	740	33	22.42	6- 60	2	–
I.A.A.Thomas (K/LBU)	RMF	85.3	32	188	8	23.50	2- 24	–	–
J.S.Thompson (OU)	RMF	9	6	13	1	13.00	1- 13	–	–
M.A.Thornely (Le)	RM	40	3	150	3	50.00	2- 9	–	–
C.D.Thorp (Du)	RMF	320.3	90	818	44	18.59	5- 59	1	–
R.T.Timms (CU)	RFM	2	0	13	0				
J.A.Tomlinson (H)	LMF	376.1	82	1131	43	26.30	5- 69	2	–
R.J.W.Topley (Ex)	LMF	112.1	24	350	11	31.81	3- 59	–	–
J.C.Tredwell (EL/K)	OB	371	99	911	26	35.03	3- 35	–	–

	Cat	O	M	R	W	Avge	Best	5wI	10wM
P.D.Trego (Sm)	RMF	523.5	125	1609	50	32.18	5- 53	2	–
C.T.Tremlett (Sy)	RFM	27	6	82	1	82.00	1- 82	–	–
I.J.L.Trott (E/Wa)	RM	40	3	112	0			–	–
P.T.Turnbull (CU)	RMF	70	17	237	10	23.70	6-108	1	–
M.L.Turner (De)	RMF	140.5	12	619	15	41.26	3- 53	–	–
W.P.J.U.C.Vaas (Nh)	LMF	107	28	280	6	46.66	2- 43	–	–
F.O.E.van den Bergh (Sy)	SLA	23	5	69	1	69.00	1- 69	–	–
J.M.Vince (H)	RM	3	0	6	0			–	–
A.C.Voges (Nt)	SLC	7	2	6	1	6.00	1- 2	–	–
G.G.Wagg (Gm)	LM	246.3	45	769	32	24.03	6- 44	1	–
D.J.Wainwright (De)	SLA	565.5	141	1542	50	30.84	6- 33	3	–
A.G.Wakely (Nh)	OB	7	0	35	0			–	–
C.A.M.Walker (OU)	OB	10	0	35	0			–	–
M.T.C.Waller (Sm)	LB	52	14	145	4	36.25	3- 33	–	–
C.A.Wallis (DU)	RM	31	1	189	1	189.00	1- 43	–	–
S.J.Walters (Gm)	RM	1	0	6	0			–	–
I.Wardlaw (Y)	RMF	65	2	300	3	100.00	1- 37	–	–
H.T.Waters (Gm)	RMF	304.2	79	798	39	20.46	7- 53	2	–
N.A.T.Watkins (DU)	SLA	52	2	199	5	39.80	3- 24	–	–
L.W.P.Wells (Sx)	OB	10	4	37	1	37.00	1- 24	–	–
K.O.Wernars (Sx)	RMF	44	14	121	5	24.20	2- 16	–	–
M.H.Wessels (Nt)	(WK)	15	3	43	1	43.00	1- 40	–	–
T.Westley (Ex)	OB	152.3	24	504	10	50.40	3- 5	–	–
I.J.Westwood (Wa)	OB	9	4	26	0			–	–
A.J.Wheater (Ex)	(WK)	4	0	86	1	86.00	1- 86	–	–
G.G.White (Nt)	SLA	157.4	34	532	15	35.46	4- 97	–	–
W.A.White (Le)	RMF	349	41	1286	43	29.90	5- 54	3	–
R.A.Whiteley (De)	LMF	177.1	23	736	20	36.80	2- 6	–	–
D.J.Willey (Nh)	LFM	440.1	90	1474	43	34.27	5- 39	1	–
B.Williams (OU)	RSM	3	0	15	0			–	–
K.S.Williamson (Gs)	OB	34.3	4	121	5	24.20	3- 58	–	–
C.M.Willoughby (Sm)	LMF	180	34	621	19	32.68	5- 70	1	–
A.D.Wilson (LU)	RM	28	7	97	1	97.00	1- 24	–	–
C.R.Woakes (EL/Wa)	RMF	267.5	55	776	27	28.74	4- 67	–	–
C.P.Wood (H)	LM	273.5	73	732	26	28.15	5- 41	1	–
M.A.Wood (Du)	RMF	46.4	6	147	9	16.33	5- 78	1	–
S.K.W.Wood (Nt)	OB	28	2	84	3	28.00	3- 64	–	–
R.J.J.Woolley (CU)	RM	58.1	11	202	3	67.33	1- 39	–	–
B.J.Wright (Gm)	RM	13	2	30	0			–	–
C.J.C.Wright (Wa)	RFM	471.3	77	1562	67	23.31	5- 24	2	–
L.J.Wright (Sx)	RM	79	6	327	5	65.40	1- 14	–	–
A.C.F.Wyatt (Le)	RMF	100	22	333	9	37.00	3- 35	–	–
M.H.Yardy (Sx)	LM/SLA	12	1	68	2	34.00	1- 12	–	–
E.G.C.Young (Gs)	SLA	137.5	28	414	10	41.40	2- 23	–	–

FIRST-CLASS CAREER RECORDS

Compiled by Philip Bailey

The following career records are for all players who appeared in first-class cricket during the 2012 season, and are complete to the end of that season. Some players who did not appear in 2012 but may do so in 2013 are included.

BATTING AND FIELDING

'1000' denotes instances of scoring 1000 runs in a season. Where these have been achieved outside the British Isles they are shown after a plus sign.

	M	I	NO	HS	Runs	Avge	100	50	1000	Ct/St
Abdul Razzaq	117	183	27	203*	5254	33.67	8	28	–	32
Abdur Rehman	124	168	19	96	2593	17.40	–	12	–	54
Ackland, B.J.	7	14	3	74	365	33.18	–	4	–	2
Adams, A.R.	149	205	21	124	4067	22.10	3	18	–	100
Adams, J.H.K.	141	251	22	262*	8796	38.41	16	46	4	128
Adkin, W.A.	6	9	2	45	134	19.14	–	–	–	5
Agarwal, S.S.	10	16	2	117	439	31.35	1	3	–	2
Agathangelou, A.P.	30	56	2	158	1867	34.57	4	11	0+1	42
Ali, A.K.	103	186	10	161	5003	28.42	6	26	–	55
Ali, Kabir	130	182	28	84*	2621	17.01	–	7	–	55
Ali, M.M.	86	150	12	158	4669	33.83	7	29	1	33
Allenby, J.	87	135	20	138*	4425	38.47	7	32	–	77
Ambrose, T.R.	150	226	22	251*	6937	34.00	10	42	–	364/22
Amla, H.M.	153	254	24	311*	11690	50.82	36	57	0+2	121
Anderson, J.M.	139	167	64	37*	1038	10.07	–	–	–	75
Andrew, G.M.	68	105	15	92*	2005	22.27	–	11	–	23
Ansari, A.S.	14	21	5	193	603	37.68	2	1	–	4
Ansari, Z.S.	15	25	2	83*	408	17.73	–	2	–	8
Anyon, J.E.	88	115	36	64*	1123	14.21	–	4	–	29
Ashraf, M.A.	19	19	5	10	56	4.00	–	–	–	8
Azeem Rafiq	21	23	3	100	491	24.55	1	2	–	8
Azhar Mahmood	176	274	32	204*	7703	31.83	9	42	–	142
Azharullah	49	63	35	41	432	15.42	–	–	–	12
Bailey, G.J.	83	149	15	160*	5417	40.42	14	27	–	77
Bailey, T.E.	1	–	–	–	–	–	–	–	–	–/–
Bairstow, J.M.	61	102	19	205	3861	46.51	7	26	1	123/5
Balbirnie, A.	5	8	1	36*	99	14.14	–	–	–	2
Balcombe, D.J.	51	66	16	73	761	15.22	–	2	–	13
Ball, A.J.	9	15	1	46	184	13.14	–	–	–	5
Ball, J.T.	1	2	1	4	4	4.00	–	–	–	–
Ballance, G.S.	50	79	13	210	3380	51.21	12	16	0+1	49
Barath, A.B.	46	81	4	192	2714	35.24	7	14	–	32
Barker, K.H.D.	32	38	6	118	862	26.93	2	2	–	11
Barrow, A.W.R.	16	26	–	69	404	15.53	–	1	–	18
Bates, M.D.	33	46	4	103	836	19.66	1	3	–	102/5
Batty, G.J.	181	278	44	133	5677	24.26	2	28	–	139
Batty, J.N.	220	345	38	168*	9673	31.50	20	41	1	605/68
Beer, W.A.T.	5	4	2	37*	76	38.00	–	–	–	1
Bell, D.W.	5	7	1	23*	76	12.66	–	–	–	8/6
Bell, I.R.	210	351	39	262*	14191	45.48	39	74	4	149
Bell-Drummond, D.J.	6	11	1	80	270	27.00	–	1	–	4
Bendon, D.S.	1	2	–	5	5	2.50	–	–	–	–
Benkenstein, D.M.	257	395	45	259	15690	44.82	38	84	5	164

F-C	M	I	NO	HS	Runs	Avge	100	50	1000	Ct/St
Berg, G.K.	55	89	10	130*	2479	31.37	2	15	–	37
Best, P.M.	9	12	2	150	378	37.80	1	1	–	5
Best, T.L.	92	122	22	95	1272	12.72	–	2	–	30
Billings, S.W.	6	9	–	131	353	39.22	1	1	–	6
Bird, J.M.	11	11	6	12	40	8.00	–	–	–	6
Blackaby, L.A.	7	10	1	45	223	24.77	–	–	–	1
Blackwell, I.D.	210	319	26	247*	11595	39.57	27	64	4	66
Blake, A.J.	28	47	2	105*	993	22.06	1	4	–	17
Bopara, R.S.	129	215	27	229	7895	41.99	22	30	1	74
Borrington, P.M.	38	64	8	105	1544	27.57	2	7	–	22
Borthwick, S.G.	42	61	13	101	1201	25.02	1	6	–	44
Boyce, M.A.G.	78	140	8	122	3736	28.30	5	19	–	48
Bragg, W.D.	45	77	–	110	2155	27.98	1	15	1	21/1
Brathwaite, R.M.R.	23	26	10	76*	200	12.50	–	1	–	2
Bravo, D.M.	47	80	5	195	2895	38.60	6	15	–	42
Breese, G.R.	117	187	20	165*	4401	26.35	4	27	–	99
Bresnan, T.T.	117	150	26	126*	3473	28.00	3	17	–	49
Briggs, D.R.	37	46	8	371	371	9.76	–	–	–	11
Broad, S.C.J.	100	131	24	169	2635	24.62	1	16	–	30
Brooks, J.A.	37	42	14	53	327	11.67	–	1	–	8
Brophy, G.L.	126	198	26	185	5520	32.09	8	27	–	301/22
Brown, B.C.	35	56	7	112	1586	32.36	4	9	–	61/7
Brown, K.R.	45	76	5	114	1862	26.22	1	10	–	20
Buck, N.L.	47	64	16	27	384	8.00	–	–	–	6
Burke, J.E.	1	–	–	–	–	–	–	–	–	–
Burns, J.A.	17	28	3	140*	1175	47.00	3	6	–	12
Burns, R.J.	11	19	2	121	776	45.64	2	4	–	9
Burton, D.A.	7	11	4	52*	77	11.00	–	1	–	1
Bush, H.	2	4	–	70	118	29.50	–	1	–	–
Buttler, J.C.	39	55	5	144	1523	30.46	2	7	–	66/2
Cameron, J.G.	34	59	6	105	1553	29.30	1	8	–	17
Carberry, M.A.	133	235	22	300*	9197	43.17	26	41	3	60
Carter, A.	17	17	6	17*	107	9.72	–	–	–	4
Carter, N.M.	111	155	24	103	2989	22.81	1	13	–	27
Chadwick, T.R.	2	3	–	21	22	7.33	–	–	–	12
Chambers, M.A.	43	56	21	30	197	5.62	–	–	–	12
Chanderpaul, S.	290	471	87	303*	21332	55.55	62	108	1+1	164
Chapple, G.	281	392	67	155	7907	24.32	6	34	–	89
Chopra, V.	96	160	9	233*	5380	35.62	10	26	2	96
Choudhry, S.H.	9	15	3	75	253	21.08	–	3	–	5
Clare, J.L.	49	68	8	130	1590	26.50	2	8	–	19
Clarke, R.	150	232	24	214	7407	35.61	16	33	1	231
Claydon, M.E.	49	61	12	55	693	14.14	–	1	–	6
Cobb, J.J.	51	89	6	148*	2072	24.96	2	12	–	24
Cockbain, I.A.	27	45	3	127	1306	31.09	2	8	–	22
Coetzer, K.J.	63	107	10	172	3238	33.38	6	14	–	33
Coleman, F.R.J.	2	2	–	110	130	65.00	1	–	–	2
Coles, M.T.	43	60	11	103*	1042	21.26	1	3	–	11
Collingwood, P.D.	218	375	31	206	12493	36.31	26	64	2	251
Collymore, C.D.	157	212	98	23	891	7.81	–	–	–	46
Comber, M.A.	2	3	–	19	19	6.33	–	–	–	1
Compton, N.R.D.	96	164	23	254*	6254	44.35	16	27	3	49
Conway, D.O.	7	7	3	20	43	10.75	–	–	–	4
Cook, A.N.	172	304	24	294	13194	47.12	38	64	5+1	159
Cook, S.J.	141	186	31	93*	2577	16.62	–	7	–	34
Cooke, C.B.	6	11	1	44*	186	18.60	–	–	–	12/1

F-C	M	I	NO	HS	Runs	Avge	100	50	1000	Ct/St
Cooper, T.L.W.	24	41	3	203*	1295	34.07	1	8	–	16
Copeland, T.A.	29	35	7	53	364	13.00	–	1	–	22
Cosker, D.A.	209	273	78	52	2731	14.00	–	1	–	126
Coughlin, P.	1	2	1	29*	32	32.00	–	–	–	1
Coughtrie, R.G.	30	52	6	54*	909	19.76	–	2	–	59/1
Coulter-Nile, N.M.	15	26	2	46	417	17.37	–	–	–	13
Cowan, E.J.M.	74	132	9	225	5064	41.17	15	19	0+1	58
Cox, O.B.	17	31	6	61	432	17.28	–	2	–	42/2
Craddock, T.R.	14	19	7	21	111	9.25	–	–	–	3
Croft, R.D.B.	407	599	107	143	12880	26.17	8	54	–	177
Croft, S.J.	94	146	12	154*	4128	30.80	5	25	–	84
Crook, S.P.	51	66	8	97	1610	27.75	–	11	–	18
Cross, G.D.	49	77	5	125	1787	24.81	2	9	–	120/21
Daeche-Marshall, F.W.	2	3	–	32	36	12.00	–	–	–	–
Daggett, L.M.	68	81	35	50*	601	13.06	–	1	–	12
Davey, J.H.	5	9	1	72	269	33.62	–	3	–	3
Davies, A.L.	1	–	–	–	–	–	–	–	–	2
Davies, J.M.	1	1	–	31	31	31.00	–	–	–	–
Davies, M.	98	123	45	63	960	12.30	–	2	–	21
Davies, S.L.	1	2	–	42	56	28.00	–	–	–	1
Davies, S.M.	122	204	20	192	7005	38.07	11	35	4	360/17
Davis, L.M.	31	59	1	303*	2074	35.75	4	7	–	26
Dawson, L.A.	62	99	10	169	2829	31.78	5	14	–	72
de Bruyn, Z.	213	359	34.	266*	13154	40.47	28	74	1+1	122
de Lange, C.D.	87	139	16	109	2879	23.40	1	13	–	45
de Villiers, A.B.	102	173	19	278*	7481	48.57	16	43	0+1	156/2
Denly, J.L.	100	177	10	199	5770	34.55	14	28	2	44
Dent, C.D.J.	36	67	6	114	1798	29.47	2	9	–	52
Deonarine, N.	100	171	19	198	5673	37.32	8	38	0+1	66
Dernbach, J.W.	73	93	34	56*	561	9.50	–	1	–	10
Dexter, N.J.	77	126	17	146	4217	38.68	10	22	–	65
Di Venuto, M.J.	336	591	42	254*	25200	45.90	60	146	10	417
Dibble, A.J.	3	6	2	43	84	21.00	–	–	–	–
Dixey, P.G.	22	37	3	103	592	17.41	1	2	–	46/8
Dockrell, G.H.	19	19	5	53	171	12.21	–	1	–	9
D'Oliveira, B.L.	3	6	–	19	62	10.33	–	–	–	–
du Toit, J.	41	65	3	154	1944	31.35	4	10	–	32
Duminy, J.P.	73	119	21	200*	4998	51.00	15	25	–	55
Dunn, M.P.	6	6	6	2*	3	–	–	–	–	–
Durham, C.M.	1	1	1	12*	12	–	–	–	–	1/1
Durston, W.J.	73	126	18	151	3982	36.87	6	24	1	76
Eckersley, E.J.H.	23	40	4	137*	1186	32.94	2	6	–	71
Edwards, F.H.	83	128	46	40	593	7.23	–	–	–	14
Edwards, G.A.	3	4	1	19	56	18.66	–	–	–	1
Edwards, K.A.	43	78	4	171	2789	37.68	4	19	–	24
Edwards, N.J.	73	125	4	212	3849	31.80	4	18	1	67
Elkin, Z.	2	4	–	138	169	42.25	1	–	–	1
Elliott, T.C.	2	2	–	44	74	37.00	–	–	–	–
Ellison, C.P.	3	3	–	1	3	1.00	–	–	–	–
Endersby, D.M.	2	3	–	9	13	4.33	–	–	–	4
Ervine, S.M.	149	236	26	237*	7320	34.85	13	37	–	113
Evans, A.C.	4	2	–	2	3	1.50	–	–	–	1
Evans, J.J.	1	1	–	12	12	12.00	–	–	–	1
Evans, L.	8	10	4	8*	31	5.16	–	–	–	1
Evans, L.J.	13	24	1	133*	680	29.56	1	4	–	8
Evans, R.F.	6	8	1	44	123	17.57	–	–	–	2

238

F-C	M	I	NO	HS	Runs	Avge	100	50	1000	Ct/St
Finn, S.T.	77	92	31	32	415	6.80	–	–	–	25
Fleming, J.D.	2	4	–	13	30	7.50	–	–	–	–
Fletcher, L.J.	38	54	16	92	522	13.73	–	1	–	7
Foakes, B.T.	5	5	–	93	119	23.80	–	1	–	4
Footitt, M.H.A.	27	32	12	30	165	8.25	–	–	–	9
Forrest, P.J.	40	71	5	177	2302	34.87	6	9	–	43
Foster, J.S.	206	310	41	212	9946	36.97	18	49	1	575/51
Franklin, J.E.C.	145	223	32	219	6801	35.60	14	29	–	55
Franks, P.J.	206	301	56	123*	6862	28.00	4	38	–	66
Friend, T.T.	2	4	1	48	85	28.33	–	–	–	2
Fudadin, A.B.	52	86	7	108	2519	31.88	2	12	–	41
Fuller, J.K.	11	16	1	57	169	11.26	–	1	–	5
Gabriel, S.T.	25	33	11	14	110	5.00	–	–	–	3
Gale, A.W.	94	148	12	151*	4957	36.44	12	22	–	36
Gatting, J.S.	30	44	4	152	1257	31.42	3	5	–	13
Gidman, A.P.R.	158	276	24	176	8779	34.83	17	49	4	102
Gidman, W.R.S.	28	47	7	116*	1461	36.52	1	11	1	6
Glover, J.C.	18	24	7	55	201	11.82	–	1	–	6
Godleman, B.A.	69	118	4	130	3447	30.23	5	17	–	52
Gondal, N.A.	43	56	14	100*	759	18.07	1	–	–	13
Goodwin, M.W.	296	513	42	344*	22113	46.94	67	90	9+1	155
Green, M.J.E.	2	3	1	4	4	2.00	–	–	–	–
Gregory, L.	10	14	2	48	141	11.75	–	–	–	–
Griffiths, D.A.	33	48	19	31*	187	6.44	–	–	–	4
Groenewald, T.D.	67	87	26	78	1284	21.04	–	4	–	22
Guptill, M.J.	69	125	8	195*	4174	35.67	7	24	–	65
Gurney, H.F.	27	27	9	24*	73	4.05	–	–	–	2
Hales, A.D.	51	86	5	184	3116	38.46	6	20	1	47
Hall, A.J.	210	311	40	163	9443	34.84	12	57	1	200
Hamilton-Brown, R.J.	51	91	6	171*	2893	34.03	6	13	1	36
Hannon-Dalby, O.J.	24	25	10	11*	45	3.00	–	–	–	2
Harbhajan Singh	170	227	41	115	3678	19.77	2	13	–	87
Hardman, T.R.	2	4	–	44	65	16.25	–	–	–	1
Harinath, A.	32	55	2	109	1497	28.24	2	8	–	7
Harmison, B.W.	49	79	6	110	1813	24.83	3	7	–	26
Harmison, S.J.	211	270	77	49*	1888	9.78	–	–	–	31
Harris, J.A.R.	65	89	17	87*	1532	21.27	–	7	–	16
Harris, P.G.	2	2	1	20	23	23.00	–	–	–	–
Harrison, J.	3	6	1	23	60	12.00	–	–	–	–
Harrison, N.L.	3	4	–	10	12	3.00	–	–	–	1
Hastings, J.W.	20	25	3	93	524	23.81	–	2	–	7
Hatchett, L.J.	8	10	3	20	62	8.85	–	–	–	2
Henderson, C.W.	271	373	78	81	5589	18.94	–	20	–	88
Henriques, M.C.	32	56	6	82	1321	26.42	–	8	–	15
Hickey, M.R.	3	5	1	53	120	30.00	–	1	–	–
Higginbottom, M.	2	4	3	31*	79	79.00	–	–	–	–
Hildreth, J.C.	151	243	20	303*	9872	44.26	27	46	3	128
Hobden, M.E.	2	1	1	15*	15	–	–	–	–	–
Hodd, A.J.	61	89	15	123	2097	28.33	4	10	–	131/12
Hodgson, D.M.	2	4	–	64	77	19.25	–	1	–	6
Hogan, M.G.	27	40	11	41	389	13.41	–	–	–	8
Hogg, K.W.	90	116	21	88	2355	24.78	–	15	–	19
Hoggard, M.J.	232	294	91	89*	1833	9.02	–	4	–	62
Holland, J.M.	27	33	11	55	284	12.90	–	1	–	7
Horton, P.J.	126	211	19	209	7374	38.40	15	40	3	135/1
Housego, D.M.	25	45	3	104	1153	27.45	2	4	–	12

F-C	M	I	NO	HS	Runs	Avge	100	50	1000	Ct/St
Howell, B.A.C.	14	26	3	83*	568	24.69	–	4	–	5
Howgego, B.H.N.	21	35	4	80	670	21.61	–	1	–	11
Hughes, C.F.	27	49	2	167	1553	33.04	4	6	–	25
Hughes, P.H.	7	13	2	87	283	25.72	–	2	–	1
Hughes, P.J.	80	146	8	198	6259	45.35	19	32	–	47
Hussain, G.M.	31	49	16	42	299	9.06	–	–	–	4
Hussey, D.J.	160	251	26	275	12339	54.84	41	55	4+1	216
Imran Tahir	153	189	43	77*	2026	13.87	–	3	–	68
Ireland, A.J.	41	61	17	29	257	5.84	–	–	–	9
James, N.A.	15	27	1	83	622	23.92	–	2	–	4
Jaques, P.A.	175	305	12	244	14371	49.04	40	67	4+2	141
Javid, A.	8	14	–	48	177	12.64	–	–	–	6
Jefferson, W.I.	119	212	14	222	7096	35.83	17	27	2	127
Jeffery, B.A.	4	7	–	39	110	15.71	–	–	–	5
Jennings, K.K.	11	18	–	77	441	24.50	–	4	–	2
Jewell, T.M.	8	7	1	70	185	30.83	–	2	–	2
John, F.R.H.	2	3	1	27	55	27.50	–	–	–	3
Johnson, F.F.J.	1	1	–	0	0	0.00	–	–	–	–
Johnson, J.A.M.	2	3	1	61	93	46.50	–	1	–	–
Johnson, M.A.	10	16	–	53	200	12.50	–	1	–	34/2
Johnson, M.G.	83	116	22	123*	2122	22.57	2	10	–	20
Johnson, R.M.	13	20	2	72	325	18.05	–	1	–	36/2
Jones, A.J.	2	3	–	26	34	11.33	–	–	–	1
Jones, C.R.	19	29	1	69	489	17.46	–	4	–	10
Jones, G.O.	175	269	25	178	8075	33.09	15	43	2	540/35
Jones, O.J.	2	3	1	83	216	108.00	–	3	–	–
Jones, R.A.	42	65	12	62	622	11.73	–	–	–	17
Jones, S.P.	91	113	37	46	904	11.89	–	–	–	18
Jones, W.S.	7	14	–	48	227	16.21	–	–	–	5
Jordan, C.J.	40	53	10	79*	939	21.83	–	4	–	22
Joseph, R.H.	62	84	32	36*	535	10.28	–	–	–	12
Joyce, E.C.	183	306	25	211	12522	44.56	28	71	6	157
Kallis, J.H.	246	403	57	224	19047	55.04	60	94	1	252
Kapil, A.	9	14	1	54	232	17.84	–	1	–	2
Kartik, M.	188	238	38	96	3979	19.89	–	19	–	132
Katich, S.M.	254	432	51	306	19829	52.04	54	105	3+4	220
Keedy, B.	217	250	121	64	1427	11.06	–	2	–	52
Kelsall, S.	2	4	–	35	50	12.50	–	–	–	1
Kemp, B.W.	1	1	–	3	3	3.00	–	–	–	1
Kennedy, A.D.J.	3	5	1	61	158	39.50	–	1	–	11
Keogh, R.I.	1	1	–	6	6	6.00	–	–	–	–
Kerrigan, S.C.	36	43	16	40	230	8.51	–	–	–	8
Kervezee, A.N.	59	103	7	155	3209	33.42	4	20	1	32
Key, R.W.T.	253	438	33	270*	16731	41.31	46	66	6	145
Khan, A.	108	127	40	78	1466	16.85	–	6	–	25
Khawaja, U.T.	54	92	9	214	3607	43.45	10	17	–	37
Kieswetter, C.	89	131	19	164	4613	41.18	10	23	1	252/5
Kirby, S.P.	156	217	66	57	1232	8.15	–	1	–	32
Klinger, M.	93	165	17	255	5612	37.91	11	27	0+1	84
Knight, T.C.	2	3	1	14	15	7.50	–	–	–	1
Leach, J.	7	13	–	50	159	12.23	–	1	–	2
Leach, M.J.	3	1	1	0*	0	–	–	–	–	–
Lees, A.Z.	2	2	–	38	38	19.00	–	–	–	–
Lester, T.J.	2	3	2	0*	0	0.00	–	–	–	–
Levi, R.E.	37	58	7	150*	1925	37.74	4	12	–	26
Lewis, J.	241	346	69	71	4517	16.30	–	13	–	61

F-C	M	I	NO	HS	Runs	Avge	100	50	1000	Ct/St
Liddle, C.J.	16	14	5	53	113	12.55	–	1	–	5
Lineker, M.S.	10	17	–	71	326	19.17	–	1	–	8
Linley, T.E.	42	59	14	42	393	8.73	–	–	–	14
Lloyd, D.L.	2	4	1	11*	11	3.66	–	–	–	–
Lodwick, J.A.	2	1	–	32	32	32.00	–	–	–	1
London, A.B.	9	17	3	77	367	26.21	–	3	–	4
Lucas, D.S.	92	119	27	60	1664	18.08	–	2	–	17
Lumb, M.J.	150	251	15	219	8254	34.97	15	48	2	99
Lyon, N.M.	24	32	12	40*	260	13.00	–	–	–	6
Lyth, A.	65	104	2	248*	3927	38.50	5	29	1	57
McCarter, G.J.	2	2	1	29*	39	39.00	–	–	–	1
McDermott, A.C.	9	13	6	22	74	10.57	–	–	–	2
McGrath, A.	257	429	30	211	14698	36.83	35	70	3	181
McKenzie, N.D.	247	419	52	237	16647	45.35	46	77	1	221
MacQueen, A.	1	2	–	69	72	36.00	–	1	–	–
Machan, M.W.	5	6	–	99	191	31.83	–	2	–	–
Maddy, D.L.	281	455	31	229*	13639	32.16	27	62	4	289
Madsen, W.L.	80	140	9	231*	4712	35.96	13	21	–	67
Magoffin, S.J.	88	124	33	79	1820	20.00	–	4	–	25
Mahmood, S.I.	115	148	19	94	2036	15.78	–	9	–	26
Malan, S.E.	81	139	10	143	4614	35.76	9	25	1	97
Malik, M.N.	90	120	42	41	768	9.84	–	–	–	11
Marsh, S.E.	73	132	16	166*	4284	36.93	7	24	–	60
Marshall, H.J.H.	192	325	22	170	10824	35.72	20	56	1	105
Mascarenhas, A.D.	194	290	32	131	6454	25.01	8	23	–	76
Masters, D.D.	162	201	29	119	2438	14.17	1	6	–	52
Maxwell, G.J.	11	19	2	103*	770	45.29	1	6	–	13
Maynard, T.L.	48	79	6	143	2384	32.65	4	11	1	48
Meaker, S.C.	42	54	7	94	777	16.53	–	4	–	6
Meschede, C.A.J.	12	15	2	62	321	24.69	–	2	–	3
Mickleburgh, J.C.	50	90	1	174	2439	27.40	3	13	–	35
Middlebrook, J.D.	187	267	41	127	6242	27.61	9	24	–	92
Miles, A.J.	1	2	1	6	6	6.00	–	–	–	–
Miller, A.S.	18	26	12	35	85	6.07	–	–	–	5
Miller, D.A.	35	56	5	149	1466	28.74	2	6	–	34
Mills, T.S.	12	16	6	20*	49	4.90	–	–	–	7
Milnes, T.P.	5	4	1	24	63	21.00	–	–	–	–
Mitchell, D.K.H.	97	179	21	298	5925	37.50	12	26	2	136
Mommsen, P.L.	7	12	–	102	226	18.83	1	–	–	10
Moore, R.A.L.	2	4	–	37	76	19.00	–	–	–	1
Moore, S.C.	143	258	19	246	8762	36.66	17	41	4	72
Morgan, E.J.G.	76	123	14	209*	3763	34.52	9	18	1	61/1
Morkel, M.	78	96	13	82*	1326	15.97	–	4	–	32
Morris, A.J.	1	2	–	7	7	3.50	–	–	–	–
Morris, C.A.J.	2	3	–	7	8	2.66	–	–	–	1
Muchall, G.J.	137	237	11	219	6537	28.92	11	33	–	93
Muchall, P.B.	4	7	2	23	82	16.40	–	–	–	1
Mullaney, S.J.	39	64	6	165*	1809	31.18	2	10	–	30
Murphy, D.	33	45	10	79	1035	29.57	–	8	–	88/5
Murtagh, T.J.	130	180	55	74*	2828	22.62	–	10	–	38
Mustard, P.	147	226	27	130	6074	30.52	6	34	–	484/17
Mutch, R.G.	5	8	4	34*	116	29.00	–	–	–	1
Myburgh, J.G.	80	145	18	203	5509	43.37	13	32	–	52
Naik, J.K.H.	43	67	16	109*	1205	23.62	1	3	–	20
Napier, G.R.	122	166	33	196	4068	30.58	5	21	–	46
Narine, S.P.	9	13	4	40*	165	18.33	–	–	–	7

F-C	M	I	NO	HS	Runs	Avge	100	50	1000	Ct/St
Nash, B.P.	102	168	24	207	5487	38.10	12	22	–	38
Nash, C.D.	111	190	13	184	6646	37.54	13	33	2	50
Naved-ul-Hasan	148	211	22	139	4269	22.58	5	12	–	68
Newby, O.J.	48	42	11	38*	313	10.09	–	–	–	8
Newman, S.A.	135	230	4	219	8630	38.18	16	51	4	99
Newton, R.I.	27	45	4	119*	1586	38.68	5	6	–	7
Nicol, R.J.	93	153	16	160	4665	34.05	10	25	–	72
Norman, A.J.	1	1	–	34	34	34.00	–	–	–	–
North, M.J.	182	315	28	239*	12153	42.34	34	62	0+1	138
Northeast, S.A.	58	103	4	176	3240	32.72	6	17	–	31
Norwell, L.C.	12	16	6	26	96	9.60	–	–	–	3
O'Brien, K.J.	24	32	2	171*	946	31.53	1	7	–	20
O'Brien, N.J.	110	169	20	182	5317	35.68	11	23	–	300/31
Onions, G.	99	128	44	41	1085	12.91	–	–	–	22
Oram, J.D.P.	85	136	18	155	3992	33.83	8	18	–	36
O'Shea, M.P.	6	9	–	50	137	15.22	–	1	–	1
Overton, C.	7	8	1	50	75	10.71	–	1	–	4
Overton, J.	3	4	2	34*	55	27.50	–	–	–	1
Owen, W.T.	16	18	6	69	225	18.75	–	1	–	3
Paine, T.D.	50	90	7	215	2637	31.77	1	19	–	143/8
Palladino, A.P.	82	109	26	106	1205	14.51	1	4	–	25
Panesar, M.S.	170	214	68	46*	1263	8.65	–	–	–	35
Pardoe, M.G.	25	48	2	74	914	19.86	–	5	–	13
Park, C.M.	8	11	1	81	360	36.00	–	4	–	7
Park, G.T.	47	79	10	178*	2354	34.11	4	14	1	43
Parry, S.D.	3	2	–	2	3	1.50	–	–	–	1
Pascoe, D.C.	8	11	2	38	229	25.44	–	–	–	6
Patel, J.S.	128	157	42	120	2317	20.14	1	10	–	46
Patel, L.A.	5	8	–	32	95	11.87	–	–	–	1
Patel, N.	5	9	–	46	101	11.22	–	–	–	2
Patel, R.H.	7	11	5	20	88	14.66	–	–	–	3
Patel, S.R.	107	168	13	176	6076	39.20	13	35	1	60
Patterson, S.A.	56	64	20	53	660	15.00	–	1	–	11
Pattinson, D.J.	62	75	16	59	763	12.93	–	1	–	7
Payne, D.A.	22	31	9	62	330	15.00	–	1	–	7
Peters, S.D.	226	382	30	222	12433	35.32	29	59	4	180
Petersen, A.N.	146	261	14	210	9774	39.57	29	39	1+2	112
Pettini, M.L.	120	200	25	208*	5727	33.10	5	37	1	78
Philander, V.D.	87	116	15	168	2559	25.33	2	7	–	23
Phillips, B.J.	123	171	31	100*	2938	20.98	1	15	–	37
Phillips, T.J.	73	103	16	89	1789	20.56	–	7	–	48
Pietersen, K.P.	191	313	21	254*	14545	49.81	45	61	3	139
Pinner, N.D.	5	8	1	82	132	16.50	–	1	–	2
Piolet, S.A.	3	5	1	26*	47	11.75	–	–	–	3
Plunkett, L.E.	107	146	28	107*	2645	22.41	1	12	–	64
Ponting, R.T.	273	467	56	257	22714	55.26	77	101	0+1	289
Porterfield, W.T.S.	77	129	5	175	3708	29.90	4	23	–	88
Powell, K.O.A.	42	73	4	139	2425	35.14	4	12	–	19
Powell, M.J.	229	379	37	299	13156	38.46	27	67	5	136
Poynton, T.	21	28	4	106	498	20.75	1	2	–	54/3
Poysden, J.E.	3	2	–	47	54	27.00	–	–	–	2
Prince, A.G.	223	359	45	254	13719	43.69	33	70	1+1	160
Prior, M.J.	213	324	37	201*	11502	40.07	26	66	3	536/39
Probert, T.J.W.	3	4	3	4*	6	6.00	–	–	–	2
Procter, L.A.	24	36	4	89	986	30.81	–	3	–	2
Pyrah, R.M.	37	48	5	134*	1186	27.58	3	5	–	15

242

F-C	M	I	NO	HS	Runs	Avge	100	50	1000	Ct/St
Quiney, R.J.	49	83	5	153	2928	37.53	7	15	–	37
Qureshi, U.A.	2	4	–	47	79	19.75	–	–	–	–
Ramanpreet Singh	1	2	–	22	34	17.00	–	–	–	1
Ramdin, D.	102	167	23	166*	4403	30.57	10	19	–	269/24
Rampaul, R.	58	85	14	64*	963	13.56	–	2	–	18
Ramprakash, M.R.	461	764	93	301*	35659	53.14	114	147	20	261
Rankin, W.B.	54	64	26	43	313	8.23	–	–	–	18
Rashid, A.U.	99	137	24	157*	3709	32.82	4	23	–	47
Rayner, O.P.	63	79	17	143*	1650	26.61	2	9	–	72
Read, C.M.W.	274	412	69	240	12707	37.04	21	70	3	804/45
Redfern, D.J.	62	101	7	133	2961	31.50	2	21	–	31
Reece, L.M.	2	4	–	60	134	33.50	–	1	–	1
Reed, M.T.	4	7	2	5*	18	3.60	–	–	–	–
Rees, G.P.	92	159	8	154	4950	32.78	11	27	2	74
Regan, J.A.	1	–	–	–	–	–	–	–	–	–
Riazuddin, H.	8	9	2	55*	130	18.57	–	1	–	1
Richardson, A.	153	176	73	91	1067	10.35	–	1	–	46
Richardson, M.J.	11	17	1	73*	353	22.06	–	3	–	40/1
Riley, A.E.N.	13	15	4	18	55	5.00	–	–	–	6
Rippon, M.J.	3	2	–	40	40	20.00	–	–	–	1
Roach, K.A.J.	50	71	13	52*	591	10.18	–	1	–	19
Robson, S.D.	43	77	5	204	2671	37.09	5	12	–	44
Roderick, G.H.	12	17	5	71*	452	37.66	–	3	–	10/1
Roebuck, C.G.	2	3	–	23	23	7.66	–	–	–	–
Rogers, C.J.L.	221	392	27	319	18220	49.91	55	85	6+2	192
Roland-Jones, T.S.	31	43	10	52	559	16.93	–	1	–	9
Root, J.E.	36	61	8	222*	2015	38.01	4	8	1	19
Rossington, A.M.	5	8	–	29	67	8.37	–	–	–	11/1
Roy, J.J.	28	50	3	106*	1437	30.57	1	6	–	22
Rudolph, J.A.	225	383	25	228*	16096	44.96	46	73	4+1	204
Rushworth, C.	21	28	10	28	248	13.77	–	–	–	3
Russell, C.J.	6	10	2	22	83	10.37	–	–	–	2
Sadler, P.T.	4	5	1	34	47	11.75	–	–	–	2
Saeed Ajmal	110	146	45	53	1222	12.09	–	3	–	36
Sales, D.J.G.	230	366	32	303*	13118	39.27	26	63	6	208
Salisbury, M.E.T.	2	2	1	1*	1	1.00	–	–	–	1
Salt, J.D.	3	5	2	16	18	6.00	–	–	–	2
Salter, A.G.	2	4	3	21	41	41.00	–	–	–	1
Samaraweera, T.T.	247	352	65	231	14156	49.32	38	70	0+1	189
Sammy, D.J.G.	85	140	8	121	3269	24.76	2	20	–	116
Samuels, M.N.	90	153	11	257	5658	39.84	11	32	–	58
Sandhu, G.S.	1	2	1	8	15	15.00	–	–	–	–
Sangha, A.S.	2	4	–	32	63	15.75	–	–	–	–
Sarwan, R.R.	208	352	25	291	12882	39.39	33	68	–	144
Saxelby, I.D.	38	55	17	60*	626	16.47	–	1	–	12
Sayers, J.J.	102	170	13	187	5374	34.22	11	28	1	59
Scott, A.J.D.	4	5	1	27	60	15.00	–	–	–	1
Scott, B.J.M.	103	160	28	164*	3474	26.31	4	19	–	271/31
Shafayat, B.M.	140	233	9	161	6650	29.68	10	36	1	116/10
Shah, O.A.	245	417	37	203	16050	42.23	44	78	8	190
Shah, R.A.C.	5	10	1	56*	175	19.44	–	1	–	3
Shahid Afridi	111	183	4	164	5631	31.45	12	30	–	75
Shahzad, A.	59	77	21	88	1323	23.62	–	3	–	9
Shantry, J.D.	27	36	12	47*	282	11.75	–	–	–	8
Sharma, R.	12	18	2	114	518	32.37	1	1	–	4
Shillingford, S.	74	121	21	63	1341	13.41	–	4	–	42

243

F-C	M	I	NO	HS	Runs	Avge	100	50	1000	Ct/St
Shreck, C.E.	113	129	76	19	269	5.07	–	–	–	33
Siddique, H.G.	2	4	–	37	53	13.25	–	–	–	1
Sidebottom, R.J.	174	219	67	61	2145	14.11	–	3	–	52
Simpson, J.A.	51	80	10	143	2039	29.12	2	10	–	157/8
Slater, B.T.	2	4	–	15	39	9.75	–	–	–	–
Smith, G.C.	141	244	17	311	11522	50.75	34	44	–	194
Smith, G.M.	97	162	13	165*	4617	30.98	6	29	–	31
Smith, G.P.	47	87	6	158*	2300	28.39	4	11	–	33
Smith, J.W.G.	3	5	–	3	4	0.80	–	–	–	5/1
Smith, S.P.D.	32	57	7	177	2100	42.00	5	10	–	43
Smith, T.C.	76	110	19	128	2454	26.96	3	13	–	82
Smith, T.M.J.	11	18	1	33	196	11.52	–	–	–	3
Smith, W.R.	105	174	9	201*	5115	31.00	12	17	–	52
Snell, S.D.	44	72	7	127	1701	26.16	1	13	–	104/3
Soilleux, A.C.	3	5	1	22	35	8.75	–	–	–	–
Solanki, V.S.	297	501	32	270	16743	35.69	31	88	6	317
Spriegel, M.N.W.	35	57	3	108*	1310	24.25	3	3	–	24
Starc, M.A.	26	29	13	54*	379	23.68	–	1	–	11
Stebbings, B.R.W.	6	8	–	29	129	16.12	–	–	–	6
Stevens, D.I.	202	327	20	208	10274	33.46	24	48	2	148
Steyn, D.W.	99	118	28	82	1316	14.62	–	3	–	21
Stirling, P.R.	14	22	–	107	589	26.77	2	2	–	11
Stokes, B.A.	44	70	5	185	2442	37.56	6	11	–	25
Stone, O.P.	3	3	1	26*	47	23.50	–	–	–	3
Stoneman, M.D.	66	112	4	128	3006	27.83	4	16	–	43
Strauss, A.J.	241	424	25	241*	17046	42.72	46	74	5	228
Sturmer, I.W.	2	3	1	5	12	6.00	–	–	–	2
Styris, S.B.	128	213	20	212*	6048	31.33	10	30	–	103
Suppiah, A.V.	94	156	8	156	5026	33.95	8	29	1	54
Sutton, A.P.	1	–	–	–	–	–	–	–	–	–
Swann, G.P.	233	316	29	183	7369	25.67	4	35	–	176
Tahir, N.S.	56	65	16	53	751	15.32	–	1	–	7
Tait, S.W.	50	70	29	68	509	12.41	–	2	–	15
Tavaré, W.A.	5	9	1	61	262	32.75	–	3	–	–
Taylor, J.M.R.	8	14	1	63	273	21.00	–	1	–	4
Taylor, J.W.A.	81	134	19	237	5409	47.03	13	24	3	58
Taylor, R.M.L.	12	20	1	101*	399	21.00	1	1	–	5
ten Doeschate, R.N.	99	144	19	259*	5863	46.90	18	23	–	61
Terry, S.P.	4	5	1	59*	93	23.25	–	1	–	3
Thakor, S.J.	9	15	3	134	617	51.41	1	4	–	2
Thomas, A.C.	129	179	34	119*	3587	24.73	2	12	–	32
Thomas, I.A.A.	4	6	2	11	30	7.50	–	–	–	–
Thompson, J.S.	1	2	–	9	9	4.50	–	–	–	–
Thornely, M.A.	28	50	2	131	1152	24.00	2	5	–	22
Thorp, C.D.	86	115	14	79*	1507	14.92	–	3	–	51
Timms, R.T.	10	18	–	57	371	20.61	–	3	–	6
Tomlinson, J.A.	83	109	48	42	611	10.01	–	–	–	21
Topley, R.J.W.	12	15	6	9	22	2.44	–	–	–	1
Tredwell, J.C.	128	182	23	123*	3598	22.62	3	14	–	136
Trego, P.D.	133	191	29	140	5658	34.92	9	35	–	60
Tremlett, C.T.	119	152	41	64	1979	17.82	–	7	–	32
Trescothick, M.E.	293	502	29	284	20221	42.75	51	98	5	395
Trott, I.J.L.	186	311	36	226	12343	44.88	29	60	6	163
Troughton, J.O.	156	242	20	223	7932	35.72	19	39	1	80
Turnbull, P.T.	9	11	1	33	88	8.80	–	–	–	1
Turner, M.L.	23	26	12	57	245	17.50	–	1	–	10

F-C	M	I	NO	HS	Runs	Avge	100	50	1000	Ct/St
Vaas, W.P.J.U.C.	227	300	59	134	6223	25.82	4	29	–	57
van den Bergh, F.O.E.	2	2	1	16*	16	16.00	–	–	–	–
van Jaarsveld, M.	262	447	41	262*	18090	44.55	52	92	6+1	400
Vince, J.M.	53	86	8	180	2460	31.53	5	7	–	36
Voges, A.C.	123	207	27	180	7433	41.29	15	42	–	162
Wagg, G.G.	91	130	12	108	2733	23.16	1	15	–	31
Wainwright, D.J.	54	70	16	104*	1465	27.12	2	5	–	24
Wakely, A.G.	64	101	4	113*	2930	30.20	2	19	–	38
Walker, C.A.M.	3	4	–	43	78	19.50	–	–	–	–
Wallace, M.A.	199	318	26	139	8643	29.59	14	40	1	499/46
Waller, M.T.C.	8	9	1	28	91	11.37	–	–	–	5
Wallis, C.A.	2	3	1	8	10	5.00	–	–	–	2
Walters, S.J.	55	91	7	188	2657	31.63	5	12	–	56
Wardlaw, I.	4	3	2	17*	31	31.00	–	–	–	2
Waters, H.T.	50	69	36	54	411	12.45	–	1	–	12
Waters, S.R.	9	17	2	157*	484	32.26	1	2	–	5
Watkins, N.A.T.	3	5	1	38*	54	13.50	–	–	–	2
Webb, J.P.	2	4	–	38	62	15.50	–	–	–	1
Wells, L.W.P.	33	56	6	174	1664	33.28	5	4	–	20
Wernars, K.O.	8	12	3	53	246	27.33	–	2	–	5
Wessels, M.H.	112	185	15	199	6005	35.32	14	29	–	196/13
Westaway, S.A.	2	4	2	63*	103	51.50	–	1	–	7
Westley, T.	65	110	11	185	3003	30.33	5	15	–	36
Westwood, I.J.	108	183	18	178	5613	34.01	12	30	–	60
Wheater, A.J.	44	62	8	164	2319	42.94	3	16	–	56
White, C.L.	120	203	26	260*	7184	40.58	16	32	2	121
White, G.G.	21	32	5	65	418	15.48	–	2	–	8
White, R.A.	112	190	17	277	5706	32.98	8	28	1	67
White, W.A.	62	100	13	101*	2285	26.26	1	12	–	20
Whiteley, R.A.	27	43	7	130*	1198	33.27	2	5	–	14
Wilkin, O.	3	6	–	38	138	23.00	–	–	–	1
Willey, D.J.	30	41	8	76	979	29.66	–	7	–	7
Williams, B.	7	12	2	92	279	27.90	–	2	–	5
Williams, R.E.M.	9	15	5	31	119	11.90	–	–	–	4
Williamson, K.S.	56	97	4	284*	3890	41.82	10	18	–	50
Willoughby, C.M.	233	259	115	47	874	6.06	–	–	–	46
Wilson, A.D.	1	2	–	6	6	3.00	–	–	–	–
Wilson, G.C.	31	46	4	125	1178	28.04	1	6	–	53/1
Woakes, C.R.	71	94	26	136*	2590	38.08	6	10	–	35
Wood, C.P.	21	30	2	105*	651	23.25	1	2	–	5
Wood, M.A.	5	9	1	48	194	24.25	–	–	–	6
Wood, S.K.W.	2	2	–	45	47	23.50	–	–	–	–
Woolley, R.J.J.	11	12	3	89*	284	31.55	–	2	–	8
Wright, B.J.	63	103	7	172	2648	27.58	5	11	–	31
Wright, C.J.C.	79	98	25	77	1353	18.53	–	5	–	15
Wright, L.J.	79	114	16	155*	3460	35.30	9	18	–	36
Wyatt, A.C.F.	12	13	5	8	28	3.50	–	–	–	2
Yardy, M.H.	155	258	25	257	8797	37.75	18	44	2	148
Yasir Arafat	189	276	40	170	6547	27.74	5	34	–	51
Young, E.G.C.	20	30	5	133	844	33.76	1	5	–	11

BOWLING

'50wS' denotes instances of taking 50 or more wickets in a season. Where these have been achieved outside the British Isles they are shown after a plus sign.

	Runs	Wkts	Avge	Best	5wI	10wM	50wS
Abdul Razzaq	10818	340	31.81	7-51	11	2	–
Abdur Rehman	11941	463	25.79	9-65	23	5	0+1
Ackland, B.J.	3	0	–				
Adams, A.R.	14219	614	23.15	7-32	31	6	3
Adams, J.H.K.	666	12	55.50	2-16	–	–	–
Adkin, W.A.	232	2	116.00	1-28	–	–	–
Agarwal, S.S.	797	15	53.13	5-78	1	–	–
Agathangelou, A.P.	311	6	51.83	2-62	–	–	–
Ali, A.K.	337	3	112.33	1- 4	–	–	–
Ali, Kabir	13214	483	27.35	8-50	23	4	5
Ali, M.M.	3739	82	45.59	6-29	3	1	–
Allenby, J.	4423	166	26.64	5-44	3	–	–
Ambrose, T.R.	1	0	–				
Amla, H.M.	236	1	236.00	1-10	–	–	–
Anderson, J.M.	14351	524	27.38	7-43	25	3	2
Andrew, G.M.	5944	172	34.55	5-58	4	–	1
Ansari, A.S.	476	12	39.66	4-50	–	–	–
Ansari, Z.S.	552	12	46.00	5-33	1	–	–
Anyon, J.E.	8706	238	36.57	6-82	5	–	1
Ashraf, M.A.	1149	39	29.46	5-32	1	–	–
Azeem Rafiq	1759	51	34.49	5-50	1	–	–
Azhar Mahmood	15337	611	25.10	8-61	27	3	0+1
Azharullah	4714	182	25.90	7-74	11	1	0+1
Bailey, G.J.	46	0	–				
Bailey, T.E.	67	1	67.00	1-67	–	–	–
Balbirnie, A.	24	0	–				
Balcombe, D.J.	5091	169	30.12	8-71	8	2	1
Ball, A.J.	560	15	37.33	3-36	–	–	–
Ball, J.T.	106	3	35.33	3-72	–	–	–
Ballance, G.S.	40	0	–				
Barath, A.B.	3	0	–				
Barker, K.H.D.	2279	84	27.13	6-40	6	1	1
Barrow, A.W.R.	36	1	36.00	1- 4	–	–	–
Batty, G.J.	16130	478	33.74	7-52	19	2	2
Batty, J.N.	61	1	61.00	1-21	–	–	–
Beer, W.A.T.	228	9	25.33	3-31	–	–	–
Bell, I.R.	1598	47	34.00	4- 4	–	–	–
Bendon, D.S.	33	1	33.00	1-33			
Benkenstein, D.M.	3570	100	35.70	4-16	–	–	–
Berg, G.K.	3512	115	30.53	6-58	3	–	–
Best, P.M.	1340	31	43.22	6-86	2	–	–
Best, T.L.	7599	275	27.63	7-33	10	2	–
Bird, J.M.	1161	60	19.35	6-62	5	2	0+1
Blackaby, L.A.	236	5	47.20	4-51	–	–	–
Blackwell, I.D.	14295	398	35.91	7-52	14	–	–
Blake, A.J.	129	3	43.00	2- 9	–	–	–
Bopara, R.S.	5836	134	43.55	5-75	1	–	–
Borrington, P.M.	7	0	–				
Borthwick, S.G.	2302	76	30.28	5-80	1	–	–
Boyce, M.A.G.	72	0	–				
Bragg, W.D.	157	2	78.50	1- 4	–	–	–
Brathwaite, R.M.R.	2087	65	32.10	5-54	3	–	–

F-C	Runs	Wkts	Avge	Best	5wI	10wM	50wS
Bravo, D.M.	28	1	28.00	1- 9	–	–	–
Breese, G.R.	8390	281	29.85	7- 60	12	3	–
Bresnan, T.T.	10289	328	31.36	5- 42	6	–	–
Briggs, D.R.	3854	118	32.66	6- 45	5	–	–
Broad, S.C.J.	10245	360	28.45	8- 52	16	2	–
Brooks, J.A.	3417	118	28.95	5- 23	4	–	–
Brophy, G.L.	7	0	–				
Brown, K.R.	49	2	24.50	2- 30	–	–	–
Buck, N.L.	4012	102	39.33	5- 99	1	–	–
Burke, J.E.	68	2	34.00	2- 51	–	–	–
Burton, D.A.	744	17	43.76	5- 68	2	–	–
Bush, H.	28	0	–				
Buttler, J.C.	11	0	–				
Cameron, J.G.	566	10	56.60	2- 18	–	–	–
Carberry, M.A.	910	14	65.00	2- 85	–	–	–
Carter, A.	1509	47	32.10	5- 40	1	–	–
Carter, N.M.	10604	309	34.31	6- 30	14	–	1
Chambers, M.A.	3573	110	32.48	6- 68	2	1	–
Chanderpaul, S.	2491	57	43.70	4- 48	–	–	–
Chapple, G.	23311	883	26.39	7- 53	36	3	6
Chopra, V.	95	0	–				
Choudhry, S.H.	321	12	26.75	4- 38	–	–	–
Clare, J.L.	3612	135	26.75	7- 74	5	1	–
Clarke, R.	8392	240	34.96	6- 63	2	–	–
Claydon, M.E.	3867	120	32.22	6-104	2	–	–
Cobb, J.J.	530	9	58.88	2- 11	–	–	–
Coetzer, K.J.	231	4	57.75	2- 16	–	–	–
Coles, M.T.	3531	120	29.42	6- 51	4	–	1
Collingwood, P.D.	5244	133	39.42	5- 52	1	–	–
Collymore, C.D.	12546	466	26.92	7- 57	12	2	1
Comber, M.A.	94	4	23.50	2- 34	–	–	–
Compton, N.R.D.	215	3	71.66	1- 1	–	–	–
Conway, D.O.	684	18	38.00	4- 48	–	–	–
Cook, A.N.	205	6	34.16	3- 13	–	–	–
Cook, S.J.	10993	342	32.14	8- 63	12	–	–
Cooper, T.L.W.	332	5	66.40	1- 2	–	–	–
Copeland, T.A.	2870	111	25.85	8- 92	5	1	–
Cosker, D.A.	18531	510	36.33	6- 91	8	1	1
Coughlin, P.	46	1	46.00	1- 26	–	–	–
Coulter-Nile, N.M.	1561	61	25.59	5- 57	1	–	–
Cowan, E.J.M.	33	0	–				
Craddock, T.R.	1066	37	28.81	5- 96	1	–	–
Croft, R.D.B.	41229	1175	35.08	8- 66	51	9	10
Croft, S.J.	1915	50	38.30	6- 41	1	–	–
Crook, S.P.	4188	103	40.66	5- 48	3	–	–
Daggett, L.M.	6097	164	37.17	8- 94	2	–	–
Davey, J.H.	133	3	44.33	2- 41	–	–	–
Davis, L.M.	6	1	6.00	1- 6	–	–	–
Davies, M.	6425	289	22.23	8- 24	13	2	1
Dawson, L.A.	1893	53	35.71	7- 51	2	–	–
de Bruyn, Z.	9578	242	39.57	7- 67	3	–	–
de Lange, C.D.	6917	178	38.85	7- 48	5	1	–
de Villiers, A.B.	133	2	66.50	2- 49	–	–	–
Denly, J.L.	1071	21	51.00	3- 43	–	–	–
Dent, C.D.J.	83	0	–				
Deonarine, N.	3677	122	30.13	7- 26	3	–	–

F-C	Runs	Wkts	Avge	Best	5wI	10wM	50wS
Dernbach, J.W.	6538	203	32.20	6- 47	9	–	1
Dexter, N.J.	1910	49	38.97	3- 23	–	–	–
Di Venuto, M.J.	484	5	96.80	1- 0	–	–	–
Dibble, A.J.	184	5	36.80	3- 42	–	–	–
Dockrell, G.H.	1641	64	25.64	6- 27	4	–	–
D'Oliveira, B.L.	198	0	–				
du Toit, J.	436	6	72.66	3- 31	–	–	–
Duminy, J.P.	1757	43	40.86	5-108	1	–	–
Dunn, M.P.	377	13	29.00	5- 56	1	–	–
Durston, W.J.	2415	55	43.90	5- 34	1	–	–
Edwards, F.H.	8632	255	33.85	7- 87	15	1	–
Edwards, G.A.	266	5	53.20	4- 44	–	–	–
Edwards, K.A.	19	0	–				
Edwards, N.J.	194	2	97.00	1- 16	–	–	–
Ellison, C.P.	224	7	32.00	3- 69	–	–	–
Endersby, D.M.	121	3	40.33	1- 38	–	–	–
Ervine, S.M.	9475	224	42.29	6- 82	5	–	–
Evans, A.C.	247	4	61.75	2- 41	–	–	–
Evans, L.	666	26	25.61	4- 38	–	–	–
Evans, L.J.	30	1	30.00	1- 30	–	–	–
Evans, R.F.	229	2	114.50	1- 57	–	–	–
Finn, S.T.	7855	285	27.56	9- 37	7	1	2
Fletcher, L.J.	3519	118	29.82	5- 82	1	–	–
Footitt, M.H.A.	2234	72	31.02	5- 45	3	–	–
Forrest, P.J.	27	1	27.00	1- 7	–	–	–
Foster, J.S.	128	1	128.00	1-122	–	–	–
Franklin, J.E.C.	11453	431	26.57	7- 14	14	1	–
Franks, P.J.	16828	512	32.86	7- 56	11	–	2
Friend, T.T.	187	2	93.50	2- 96	–	–	–
Fudadin, A.B.	586	19	30.84	4- 42	–	–	–
Fuller, J.K.	946	27	35.03	5- 29	1	–	–
Gabriel, S.T.	1965	67	29.32	5- 78	1	–	–
Gale, A.W.	144	1	144.00	1- 33	–	–	–
Gatting, J.S.	111	2	55.50	1- 8	–	–	–
Gidman, A.P.R.	4428	101	43.84	4- 47	–	–	–
Gidman, W.R.S.	2117	99	21.38	6- 92	5	–	1
Glover, J.C.	1387	39	35.56	5- 38	1	–	–
Godleman, B.A.	35	0	–				
Gondal, N.A.	4414	181	24.38	7- 66	10	1	0+1
Goodwin, M.W.	376	7	53.71	2- 23	–	–	–
Green, M.J.E.	137	1	137.00	1- 53	–	–	–
Gregory, L.	412	11	37.45	2- 22	–	–	–
Griffiths, D.A.	3292	94	35.02	6- 85	2	–	–
Groenewald, T.D.	5853	188	31.13	6- 50	6	–	–
Guptill, M.J.	346	6	57.66	3- 37	–	–	–
Gurney, H.F.	2160	52	41.53	5- 82	1	–	–
Hales, A.D.	167	3	55.66	2- 63	–	–	–
Hall, A.J.	15400	567	27.16	6- 77	16	1	–
Hamilton-Brown, R.J.	542	9	60.22	2- 49	–	–	–
Hannon-Dalby, O.J.	1938	43	45.06	5- 68	2	–	–
Harbhajan Singh	20240	698	28.99	8- 84	39	7	0+2
Hardman, T.R.	179	3	59.66	2- 51	–	–	–
Harinath, A.	30	0	–				
Harmison, B.W.	1210	33	36.66	4- 27	–	–	–
Harmison, S.J.	20805	744	27.96	7- 12	27	1	6
Harris, J.A.R.	6294	228	27.60	7- 66	9	1	1

F-C	Runs	Wkts	Avge	Best	5wI	10wM	50wS
Harris, P.G.	137	1	137.00	1- 63	–	–	–
Harrison, J.	260	10	26.00	4-112	–	–	–
Harrison, N.L.	176	3	58.66	2- 78	–	–	–
Hastings, J.W.	1572	63	24.95	5- 61	1	–	–
Hatchett, L.J.	581	22	26.40	5- 47	1	–	–
Henderson, C.W.	27707	899	30.81	7- 57	34	2	1
Henriques, M.C.	1798	63	28.53	5- 17	2	–	–
Hickey, M.R.	155	4	38.75	2- 63	–	–	–
Higginbottom, M.	120	4	30.00	2- 22	–	–	–
Hildreth, J.C.	444	5	88.80	2- 39	–	–	–
Hobden, M.E.	195	5	39.00	5- 62	1	–	–
Hodd, A.J.	7	0	–				
Hogan, M.G.	2846	100	28.46	6- 70	4	–	–
Hogg, K.W.	6154	193	31.88	7- 28	4	1	1
Hoggard, M.J.	21194	770	27.52	7- 49	25	1	3
Holland, J.M.	2905	75	38.73	4- 61	–	–	–
Horton, P.J.	16	0	–				
Housego, D.M.	17	0	–				
Howell, B.A.C.	266	6	44.33	2- 37	–	–	–
Howgego, B.H.N.	16	0	–				
Hughes, C.F.	451	10	45.10	2- 9	–	–	–
Hughes, P.J.	9	0	–				
Hussain, G.M.	2976	104	28.61	6- 33	4	–	1
Hussey, D.J.	1639	25	65.56	4-105	–	–	–
Imran Tahir	16429	634	25.91	8- 76	44	9	2+2
Ireland, A.J.	3715	122	30.45	7- 36	4	1	–
James, N.A.	154	6	25.66	2- 28	–	–	–
Jaques, P.A.	87	0	–				
Javid, A.	78	0	–				
Jefferson, W.I.	60	1	60.00	1- 16	–	–	–
Jennings, K.K.	36	2	18.00	2- 8	–	–	–
Jewell, T.M.	374	16	23.37	5- 49	1	–	–
Johnson, F.F.J.	42	1	42.00	1- 42	–	–	–
Johnson, M.G.	9567	310	30.86	8- 61	12	3	–
Jones, A.J.	158	2	79.00	1- 50	–	–	–
Jones, C.R.	17	1	17.00	1- 17	–	–	–
Jones, G.O.	26	0	–				
Jones, O.J.	107	2	53.50	1- 7	–	–	–
Jones, R.A.	4003	126	31.76	7-115	4	–	–
Jones, S.P.	8142	267	30.49	6- 45	15	1	–
Jones, W.S.	180	5	36.00	3- 71	–	–	–
Jordan, C.J.	3232	84	38.47	5- 77	1	–	–
Joseph, R.H.	5572	174	32.02	6- 32	7	1	1
Joyce, E.C.	1025	11	93.18	2- 34	–	–	–
Kallis, J.H.	13134	415	31.64	6- 54	8	–	–
Kapil, A.	274	8	34.25	3- 17	–	–	–
Kartik, M.	16316	626	26.06	9- 70	36	5	1
Katich, S.M.	3778	107	35.30	7-130	3	–	–
Keedy, G.	20483	656	31.22	7- 68	32	7	4
Kemp, B.W.	81	1	81.00	1- 71	–	–	–
Keogh, R.I.	69	1	69.00	1- 69	–	–	–
Kerrigan, S.C.	3231	114	28.34	9- 51	6	1	1
Kervezee, A.N.	145	2	72.50	1- 14	–	–	–
Key, R.W.T.	233	3	77.66	2- 31	–	–	–
Khan, A.	10974	347	31.62	6- 52	10	–	2
Khawaja, U.T.	62	1	62.00	1- 21	–	–	–

F-C	Runs	Wkts	Avge	Best	5wI	10wM	50wS
Kieswetter, C.	3	2	1.50	2- 3	–	–	–
Kirby, S.P.	15444	546	28.28	8-80	17	4	3
Klinger, M.	3	0	–				
Knight, T.C.	143	2	71.50	2-32	–	–	–
Leach, J.	226	12	18.83	4-73	–	–	–
Leach, M.J.	194	2	97.00	2-37	–	–	–
Lester, T.J.	213	2	106.50	1-59	–	–	–
Lewis, J.	21603	829	26.05	8-95	35	5	9
Liddle, C.J.	986	19	51.89	3-42	–	–	–
Lineker, M.S.	2	0	–				
Linley, T.E.	3370	133	25.33	6-57	5	1	1
Lodwick, J.A.	159	7	22.71	4-55	–	–	–
London, A.B.	54	1	54.00	1-15	–	–	–
Lucas, D.S.	8381	261	32.11	7-24	9	1	1
Lumb, M.J.	255	6	42.50	2-10	–	–	–
Lyon, N.M.	2540	71	35.77	5-34	2	–	–
Lyth, A.	297	3	99.00	1-12	–	–	–
McCarter, G.J.	157	1	157.00	1-47	–	–	–
McDermott, A.C.	828	42	19.71	7-24	2	–	–
McGrath, A.	4779	134	35.66	5-39	1	–	–
McKenzie, N.D.	519	10	51.90	2-13	–	–	–
MacQueen, A.	5	0	–				
Machan, M.W.	4	0	–				
Maddy, D.L.	7898	252	31.34	5-37	5	–	–
Madsen, W.L.	373	7	53.28	3-45	–	–	–
Magoffin, S.J.	7719	304	25.39	8-47	10	1	1
Mahmood, S.I.	10397	323	32.18	6-30	9	2	–
Malan, D.J.	1591	38	41.86	5-61	1	–	–
Malik, M.N.	8381	235	35.66	6-46	7	–	–
Marsh, S.E.	131	2	65.50	2-20	–	–	–
Marshall, H.J.H.	1768	37	47.78	4-24	–	–	–
Mascarenhas, A.D.	12640	446	28.34	6-25	17	–	1
Masters, D.D.	13520	522	25.90	8-10	24	–	3
Maxwell, G.J.	665	18	36.94	3-36	–	–	–
Maynard, T.L.	45	0	–				
Meaker, S.C.	3932	141	27.88	8-52	8	1	1
Meschede, C.A.J.	559	14	39.92	3-26	–	–	–
Mickleburgh, J.C.	50	0	–				
Middlebrook, J.D.	15503	408	37.99	6-82	11	1	1
Miller, A.S.	1262	35	36.05	5-58	2	–	–
Miller, D.A.	23	0	–				
Mills, T.S.	666	21	31.71	4-25	–	–	–
Milnes, T.P.	241	9	26.77	4-15	–	–	–
Mitchell, D.K.H.	710	17	41.76	4-49	–	–	–
Mommsen, P.L.	170	4	42.50	3-67	–	–	–
Moore, R.A.L.	56	0	–				
Moore, S.C.	321	5	64.20	1-13	–	–	–
Morgan, E.J.G.	83	2	41.50	2-24	–	–	–
Morkel, M.	7830	285	27.47	6-23	12	2	–
Morris, A.J.	47	1	47.00	1-47	–	–	–
Morris, C.A.J.	206	4	51.50	2- 7	–	–	–
Muchall, G.J.	617	15	41.13	3-26	–	–	–
Muchall, P.B.	218	2	109.00	2-60	–	–	–
Mullaney, S.J.	882	16	55.12	4-31	–	–	–
Murphy, D.	3	0	–				
Murtagh, T.J.	11870	426	27.86	7-82	18	2	4

250

F-C	Runs	Wkts	Avge	Best	5wI	10wM	50wS
Mutch, R.G.	485	20	24.25	4- 49	–	–	–
Myburgh, J.G.	1392	31	44.90	4- 56	–	–	–
Naik, J.K.H.	3351	104	32.22	7- 96	3	–	–
Napier, G.R.	9857	283	34.83	6- 53	7	–	–
Narine, S.P.	782	46	17.00	8- 17	6	2	–
Nash, B.P.	652	21	31.04	2- 7	–	–	–
Nash, C.D.	1904	59	32.27	4- 12	–	–	–
Naved-ul-Hasan	15302	628	24.36	7- 49	33	6	2+3
Newby, O.J.	3887	118	32.94	5- 69	1	–	–
Newman, S.A.	90	0	–				
Newton, R.I.	19	0	–				
Nicol, R.J.	2080	34	61.17	4- 53	–	–	–
Norman, A.J.	49	0	–				
North, M.J.	5504	136	40.47	6- 55	2	–	–
Northeast, S.A.	10	0	–				
Norwell, L.C.	973	34	28.61	6- 46	2	–	–
O'Brien, K.J.	643	25	25.72	5- 39	1	–	–
O'Brien, N.J.	19	2	9.50	1- 4	–	–	–
Onions, G.	9553	359	26.61	9- 67	16	3	4
Oram, J.D.P.	4172	155	26.91	6- 45	3	–	–
Overton, C.	363	12	30.25	4- 38	–	–	–
Overton, J.	229	6	38.16	2- 61	–	–	–
Owen, W.T.	1548	40	38.70	5-124	1	–	–
Paine, T.D.	3	0	–				
Palladino, A.P.	6804	225	30.24	7- 53	8	–	2
Panesar, M.S.	17491	577	30.31	7- 60	30	4	6
Park, C.M.	295	2	147.50	1- 34	–	–	–
Park, G.T.	974	18	54.11	3- 25	–	–	–
Parry, S.D.	256	9	28.44	5- 23	1	–	–
Pascoe, D.C.	645	25	25.80	6- 68	2	–	–
Patel, J.S.	12210	319	38.27	7- 75	12	1	1
Patel, L.A.	165	2	82.50	1- 57	–	–	–
Patel, R.H.	724	26	27.84	4- 72	–	–	–
Patel, S.R.	5840	151	38.67	7- 68	3	1	–
Patterson, S.A.	4272	141	30.29	5- 50	2	–	1
Pattinson, D.J.	5642	171	32.99	8- 35	8	–	–
Payne, D.A.	1802	64	28.15	6- 26	2	–	–
Peters, S.D.	31	1	31.00	1- 19	–	–	–
Petersen, A.N.	556	11	50.54	2- 7	–	–	–
Pettini, M.L.	263	1	263.00	1- 72	–	–	–
Philander, V.D.	6760	349	19.36	7- 61	18	2	0+2
Phillips, B.J.	8101	270	30.00	6- 29	5	–	–
Phillips, T.J.	5798	122	47.52	5- 41	1	–	–
Pietersen, K.P.	3657	71	51.50	4- 31	–	–	–
Pinner, N.D.	13	0	–				
Piolet, S.A.	182	13	14.00	6- 17	1	1	–
Plunkett, L.E.	10192	321	31.75	6- 63	8	1	3
Ponting, R.T.	799	14	57.07	2- 10	–	–	–
Porterfield, W.T.S.	138	2	69.00	1- 29	–	–	–
Powell, K.O.A.	34	0	–				
Powell, M.J.	132	2	66.00	2- 39	–	–	–
Poynton, T.	96	2	48.00	2- 96	–	–	–
Poysden, J.E.	216	5	43.20	3- 20	–	–	–
Prince, A.G.	171	4	42.75	2- 11	–	–	–
Probert, T.J.W.	258	10	25.80	4- 20	–	–	–
Procter, L.A.	1045	38	27.50	7- 71	2	–	–

F-C	Runs	Wkts	Avge	Best	5wI	10wM	50wS
Pyrah, R.M.	1901	47	40.44	5- 58	1	–	–
Quiney, R.J.	387	3	129.00	2- 22	–	–	–
Rampaul, R.	5123	168	30.49	7- 51	6	1	–
Ramprakash, M.R.	2202	34	64.76	3- 32	–	–	–
Rankin, W.B.	4908	175	28.04	5- 16	6	–	1
Rashid, A.U.	10306	296	34.81	7-107	16	1	2
Rayner, O.P.	4483	126	35.57	5- 49	3	–	–
Read, C.M.W.	90	0	–				
Redfern, D.J.	341	6	56.83	1- 7	–	–	–
Reece, L.M.	120	5	24.00	3- 25	–	–	–
Reed, M.T.	310	8	38.75	3- 39	–	–	–
Rees, G.P.	25	0	–				
Riazuddin, H.	469	17	27.58	5- 61	1	–	–
Richardson, A.	13639	500	27.27	8- 46	18	2	4
Riley, A.E.N.	960	23	41.73	5- 76	1	–	–
Rippon, M.J.	272	6	45.33	3- 34	–	–	–
Roach, K.A.J.	4786	166	28.83	7- 23	8	1	–
Robson, S.D.	47	0	–				
Rogers, C.J.L.	131	1	131.00	1- 16	–	–	–
Roland-Jones, T.S.	2743	132	20.78	6- 66	7	1	1
Root, J.E.	510	8	63.75	3- 33	–	–	–
Roy, J.J.	62	2	31.00	2- 29	–	–	–
Rudolph, J.A.	2572	58	44.34	5- 80	3	–	–
Rushworth, C.	1613	64	25.20	5- 38	3	–	–
Russell, C.J.	563	17	33.11	4- 43	–	–	–
Sadler, P.T.	248	3	82.66	2- 38	–	–	–
Saeed Ajmal	11124	410	27.13	7- 55	25	3	0+1
Sales, D.J.G.	184	9	20.44	4- 25	–	–	–
Salisbury, M.E.T.	225	4	56.25	2- 54	–	–	–
Salt, J.D.	220	7	31.42	2- 25	–	–	–
Salter, A.G.	211	4	52.75	3-134	–	–	–
Samaraweera, T.T.	8366	356	23.50	6- 55	15	2	0+1
Sammy, D.J.G.	5620	196	28.67	7- 66	10	–	–
Samuels, M.N.	3075	54	56.94	5- 87	1	–	–
Sandhu, G.S.	69	0	–				
Sangha, A.S.	162	3	54.00	1- 36	–	–	–
Sarwan, R.R.	2328	56	41.57	6- 62	1	–	–
Saxelby, I.D.	3264	106	30.79	6- 48	3	1	–
Sayers, J.J.	178	6	29.66	3- 15	–	–	–
Scott, A.J.D.	308	16	19.25	4- 52	–	–	–
Scott, B.J.M.	1	0	–				
Shafayat, B.M.	663	8	82.87	2- 25	–	–	–
Shah, O.A.	1493	26	57.42	3- 33	–	–	–
Shahid Afridi	7023	258	27.22	6-101	8	–	–
Shahzad, A.	5273	155	34.01	5- 51	3	–	–
Shantry, J.D.	2384	64	37.25	5- 49	2	–	–
Sharma, R.	592	15	39.46	5- 81	1	–	–
Shillingford, S.	7488	290	25.82	8- 33	14	3	0+2
Shreck, C.E.	11949	399	29.94	8- 31	21	2	3
Sidebottom, R.J.	14268	561	25.43	7- 37	24	3	3
Smith, G.C.	1086	11	98.72	2-145	–	–	–
Smith, G.M.	5636	152	37.07	5- 54	2	–	–
Smith, G.P.	73	1	73.00	1- 64	–	–	–
Smith, S.P.D.	2495	45	55.44	7- 64	1	–	–
Smith, T.C.	4830	150	32.20	6- 46	2	–	–
Smith, T.M.J.	851	12	70.91	3- 38	–	–	–

F-C	Runs	Wkts	Avge	Best	5wI	10wM	50wS
Smith, W.R.	592	9	65.77	3- 34	–	–	–
Snell, S.D.	15	0	–				
Soilleux, A.C.	319	9	35.44	3- 67	–	–	–
Solanki, V.S.	4120	86	47.90	5- 40	4	1	–
Spriegel, M.N.W.	859	19	45.21	2- 28	–	–	–
Starc, M.A.	2332	71	32.84	5- 66	2	–	–
Stebbings, B.R.W.	3	0	–				
Stevens, D.I.	5109	170	30.05	7- 21	3	1	–
Steyn, D.W.	10797	442	24.42	8- 41	26	6	0+2
Stirling, P.R.	214	4	53.50	2- 45	–	–	–
Stokes, B.A.	1862	65	28.64	6- 68	1	–	–
Stone, O.P.	202	5	40.40	1- 6	–	–	–
Strauss, A.J.	142	3	47.33	1- 16	–	–	–
Sturmer, I.W.	161	2	80.50	1- 35	–	–	–
Styris, S.B.	6440	204	31.56	6- 32	9	1	–
Suppiah, A.V.	2611	45	58.02	3- 46	–	–	–
Sutton, A.P.	99	2	49.50	1- 31	–	–	–
Swann, G.P.	21266	663	32.07	7- 33	28	5	1
Tahir, N.S.	4163	139	29.94	7-107	2	–	–
Tait, S.W.	5661	198	28.59	7- 29	7	1	0+1
Taylor, J.M.R.	645	15	43.00	2- 28	–	–	–
Taylor, J.W.A.	176	0	–				
Taylor, R.M.L.	1142	26	43.92	5- 91	1	–	–
ten Doeschate, R.N.	5860	173	33.87	6- 20	7	–	–
Thakor, S.J.	233	7	33.28	3- 57	–	–	–
Thomas, A.C.	11235	419	26.81	7- 54	20	2	–
Thomas, I.A.A.	188	8	23.50	2- 24	–	–	–
Thompson, J.S.	13	1	13.00	1- 13	–	–	–
Thornely, M.A.	250	7	35.71	2- 14	–	–	–
Thorp, C.D.	6398	249	25.69	7- 88	9	1	1
Timms, R.T.	139	0	–				
Tomlinson, J.A.	8439	248	34.02	8- 46	10	1	1
Topley, R.J.W.	1151	45	25.57	5- 46	2	–	–
Tredwell, J.C.	11620	335	34.68	8- 66	11	3	1
Trego, P.D.	8943	244	36.65	6- 59	3	–	1
Tremlett, C.T.	10805	391	27.63	6- 44	9	–	–
Trescothick, M.E.	1551	36	43.08	4- 36	–	–	–
Trott, I.J.L.	2777	58	47.87	7- 39	1	–	–
Troughton, J.O.	1416	22	64.36	3- 1	–	–	–
Turnbull, P.T.	961	31	31.00	6-108	2	–	–
Turner, M.L.	2119	53	39.98	5- 32	1	–	–
Vaas, W.P.J.U.C.	19027	772	24.64	7- 28	34	4	1+2
van den Bergh, F.O.E.	148	4	37.00	3- 79	–	–	–
van Jaarsveld, M.	1947	50	38.94	5- 33	1	–	–
Vince, J.M.	67	0	–				
Voges, A.C.	1439	42	34.26	4- 92	–	–	–
Wagg, G.G.	9173	281	32.64	6- 35	9	1	2
Wainwright, D.J.	4648	134	34.68	6- 33	5	–	1
Wakely, A.G.	319	6	53.16	2- 62	–	–	–
Walker, C.A.M.	35	0	–				
Wallace, M.A.	3	0	–				
Waller, M.T.C.	493	10	49.30	3- 33	–	–	–
Wallis, C.A.	189	1	189.00	1- 43	–	–	–
Walters, S.J.	245	3	81.66	1- 4	–	–	–
Wardlaw, I.	368	4	92.00	1- 37	–	–	–
Waters, H.T.	3336	107	31.17	7- 53	3	–	–

F-C	Runs	Wkts	Avge	Best	5wI	10wM	50wS
Waters, S.R.	68	2	34.00	1-18	–	–	–
Watkins, N.A.T.	328	10	32.80	5-88	1	–	–
Wells, L.W.P.	297	5	59.40	2-28	–	–	–
Wernars, K.O.	274	12	22.83	2-11	–	–	–
Wessels, M.H.	85	3	28.33	1-10	–	–	–
Westley, T.	1264	30	42.13	4-55	–	–	–
Westwood, I.J.	264	6	44.00	2-39	–	–	–
Wheater, A.J.	86	1	86.00	1-86	–	–	–
White, C.L.	7174	180	39.85	6-66	3	1	–
White, G.G.	1493	34	43.91	4-72	–	–	–
White, R.A.	1071	18	59.50	2-30	–	–	–
White, W.A.	5003	139	35.99	5-54	4	–	–
Whiteley, R.A.	1159	26	44.57	2- 6	–	–	–
Wilkin, O.	213	4	53.25	2-63	–	–	–
Willey, D.J.	2155	68	31.69	5-29	3	1	–
Williams, B.	100	1	100.00	1-55	–	–	–
Williams, R.E.M.	755	23	32.82	5-70	2	–	–
Williamson, K.S.	2233	51	43.78	5-75	1	–	–
Willoughby, C.M.	22038	848	25.98	7-44	33	3	6+2
Wilson, A.D.	97	1	97.00	1-24	–	–	–
Wilson, G.C.	46	0	–				
Woakes, C.R.	6266	250	25.06	7-20	12	3	2
Wood, C.P.	1643	63	26.07	5-41	2	–	–
Wood, M.A.	411	19	21.63	5-78	1	–	–
Wood, S.K.W.	92	3	30.66	3-64	–	–	–
Woolley, R.J.J.	1172	22	53.27	3-54	–	–	–
Wright, B.J.	167	2	83.50	1-14	–	–	–
Wright, C.J.C.	7728	224	34.50	6-22	6	–	1
Wright, L.J.	4397	111	39.61	5-65	3	–	–
Wyatt, A.C.F.	887	29	30.58	3-35	–	–	–
Yardy, M.H.	2078	28	74.21	5-83	1	–	–
Yasir Arafat	18001	749	24.03	9-35	43	5	0+4
Young, E.G.C.	1033	15	68.86	2-23	–	–	–

LEADING CURRENT FIRST-CLASS PLAYERS

These are the leading career batting/bowling averages and wicket-keeping/fielding aggregates among players currently registered for first-class county cricket at the time of going to press. All figures are to the end of the 2012 English season.

BATTING (Qualification: 100 innings)

	Runs	Avge		Runs	Avge
S.Chanderpaul	21332	55.55	D.M.Benkenstein	15690	44.82
R.T.Ponting	22714	55.26	E.C.Joyce	12522	44.56
D.J.Hussey	12339	54.84	N.R.D.Compton	6254	44.35
S.M.Katich	19829	52.04	J.C.Hildreth	9872	44.26
G.C.Smith	11522	50.75	M.A.Carberry	9197	43.17
K.P.Pietersen	14545	49.81	M.E.Trescothick	20221	42.75
T.T.Samaraweera	14156	49.32	M.J.North	12153	42.34
P.A.Jaques	14371	49.04	O.A.Shah	16050	42.23
C.J.L.Rogers	18220	49.01	R.S.Bopara	7895	41.99
A.N.Cook	13194	47.12	R.W.T.Key	16731	41.31
J.W.A.Taylor	5409	47.03	A.C.Voges	7433	41.29
M.W.Goodwin	22113	46.94	C.Kieswetter	4613	41.18
R.N.ten Doeschate	5863	46.90	E.J.M.Cowan	5064	41.17
J.M.Bairstow	3861	46.51	C.L.White	7184	40.58
I.R.Bell	14191	45.48	Z.de Bruyn	13154	40.47
N.D.McKenzie	16647	45.35	G.J.Bailey	5417	40.42
I.J.L.Trott	12343	44.88	M.J.Prior	11502	40.07

BOWLING (Qualification: 100 wickets)

	Wkts	Avge		Wkts	Avge
T.S.Roland-Jones	132	20.78	G.Chapple	883	26.39
M.Davies	289	22.23	G.Onions	359	26.61
A.R.Adams	614	23.15	J.Allenby	166	26.64
T.T.Samaraweera	356	23.50	J.L.Clare	135	26.75
C.R.Woakes	250	25.06	A.C.Thomas	419	26.81
T.E.Linley	133	25.33	J.D.P.Oram	155	26.91
S.J.Magoffin	304	25.39	C.D.Collymore	466	26.92
R.J.Sidebottom	561	25.43	Saeed Ajmal	410	27.13
C.D.Thorp	249	25.69	A.J.Hall	567	27.16
Abdur Rehman	463	25.79	Shahid Afridi	258	27.22
T.A.Copeland	111	25.85	A.Richardson	500	27.27
D.D.Masters	522	25.90	Kabir Ali	483	27.35
Azharullah	182	25.90	J.M.Anderson	524	27.38
J.Lewis	829	26.05	M.J.Hoggard	770	27.52

WICKET-KEEPING (Qualification: 400 dismissals, exc catches taken in the field)

	Total	Ct	St		Total	Ct	St
C.M.W.Read	849	804	45	M.J.Prior	575	536	39
J.S.Foster	626	575	51	M.A.Wallace	545	499	46
G.O.Jones	575	540	35	P.Mustard	501	484	17

FIELDING (Qualification: 200 catches)

M.E.Trescothick	395	N.D.McKenzie	221
V.S.Solanki	317	S.M.Katich	220
D.L.Maddy	289	D.J.Hussey	216
R.T.Ponting	289	D.J.G.Sales	208
P.D.Collingwood	251	A.J.Hall	200
R.Clarke	231		

LIMITED-OVERS CAREER RECORDS

Compiled by Philip Bailey

The following career records, to the end of the 2012 season, include all players currently registered with first-class counties. These records are restricted to performances in limited-overs matches of 'List A' status as defined by the Association of Cricket Statisticians and Historians now incorporated by ICC into their Classification of Cricket. The following matches qualify for List A status and are included in the figures that follow: Limited-Overs Internationals; Other International matches (e.g. Commonwealth Games, 'A' team internationals); Premier domestic limited-overs tournaments in Test status countries; Official tourist matches against the main first-class teams.

The following matches do NOT qualify for inclusion: World Cup warm-up games; Tourist matches against first-class teams outside the major domestic competitions (e.g. Universities, Minor Counties etc.); Festival, pre-season friendly games and Twenty20 Cup matches.

	M	Runs	Avge	HS	100	50	Wkts	Avge	Best	Econ
Abdur Rehman	127	865	13.10	50	–	1	181	26.39	6-16	4.26
Adams, A.R.	165	1504	16.71	90*	–	1	209	28.50	5- 7	4.72
Adams, J.H.K.	70	2201	37.30	131	2	16	1	105.00	1-34	7.97
Agathangelou, A.P.	23	654	32.70	94	–	5	0	–		7.00
Ali, Kabir	164	1150	15.33	92	–	3	237	25.35	5-36	5.20
Ali, M.M.	87	2378	29.72	158	6	10	36	46.16	3-32	5.75
Allenby, J.	75	1488	24.00	91*	–	6	66	28.56	5-43	5.00
Ambrose, T.R.	131	2672	29.36	135	3	11				128/23
Anderson, J.M.	217	297	8.48	20*	–	–	296	28.97	5-23	4.89
Andrew, G.M.	102	973	17.37	104	1	1	99	34.79	5-31	6.24
Ansari, Z.S.	16	236	33.71	60*	–	1	12	31.08	3-28	5.56
Anyon, J.E.	38	34	5.66	12	–	–	41	30.58	3- 6	5.47
Ashraf, M.A.	14	3	–	3*	–	–	15	34.40	2-25	5.55
Azeem Rafiq	17	111	22.20	34*	–	–	13	40.92	3-22	5.26
Azhar Ullah, M.	27	57	9.50	9	–	–	40	27.77	5-56	5.27
Bailey, G.J.	139	3969	34.51	123*	4	24	1	40.00	1-19	4.52
Bairstow, J.M.	49	1046	26.82	114	1	4		–		31/3
Balbirnie, A.	6	30	6.00	17	–	–	0	–		6.75
Balcombe, D.J.	12	10	2.00	6	–	–	16	29.00	4-38	5.76
Ball, A.J.	15	67	16.75	19	–	–	17	25.94	2-31	5.21
Ball, J.T.	15	60	12.00	19*	–	–	11	37.27	3-32	5.56
Ballance, G.S.	39	1570	54.13	135*	4	7		–		
Barker, K.H.D.	43	397	17.26	56	–	1	48	30.58	4-33	5.87
Barrow, A.W.R.	5	108	54.00	72	–	1		–		–
Bates, M.D.	31	73	8.11	24*	–	–		–		20/4
Batty, G.J.	216	2172	16.45	83*	–	5	199	31.85	5-35	4.57
Beer, W.A.T.	23	93	13.28	27*	–	–	17	42.88	3-27	4.89
Bell, I.R.	245	8249	39.09	158	8	59	33	34.48	5-41	5.29
Bell-Drummond, D.J.	5	111	22.20	42	–	–				
Benkenstein, D.M.	297	7275	35.14	107*	1	44	87	30.81	4-16	5.03
Berg, G.K.	49	844	25.57	65	–	4	35	33.22	4-24	5.58
Best, P.M.	13	57	11.40	16*	–	–	11	42.09	3-43	6.27
Billings, S.W.	14	369	36.90	143	1	1		–		6/2
Blackwell, I.D.	254	5765	27.19	134*	3	34	207	34.30	5-26	4.79
Blake, A.J.	33	434	22.84	81*	–	2	3	24.66	2-13	5.28

L-O	M	Runs	Avge	HS	100	50	Wkts	Avge	Best	Econ
Bopara, R.S.	216	6100	37.88	201*	7	36	160	25.65	5-63	5.24
Borrington, P.M.	2	25	25.00	25	–	–	–	–	–	–
Borthwick, S.G.	39	199	11.70	44	–	–	31	38.61	4-51	5.75
Boyce, M.A.G.	51	1116	25.95	80	–	7	–	–	–	–
Bragg, W.D.	14	283	23.58	78	–	1	0	–	–	8.50
Brathwaite, R.M.R.	2	–	–	–	–	–	1	68.00	1-19	7.55
Breese, G.R.	169	1959	20.62	68*	–	3	178	27.80	5-41	4.70
Bresnan, T.T.	203	1905	18.86	80	–	4	226	33.85	5-48	5.13
Briggs, D.R.	42	138	9.85	25	–	–	52	29.50	4-32	4.77
Broad, S.C.J.	110	461	12.13	45*	–	–	173	27.55	5-23	5.18
Brooks, J.A.	23	34	5.66	10	–	–	19	40.00	3-35	4.96
Brown, B.C.	30	351	27.00	60	–	3	–	–	–	30/6
Brown, K.R.	36	1006	37.25	101*	1	5	–	–	–	–
Buck, N.L.	28	71	10.14	21	–	–	32	35.12	4-39	5.81
Burgoyne, P.I.	4	30	30.00	24*	–	–	7	17.85	3-31	5.20
Burns, J.A.	6	205	41.00	82	–	1	–	–	–	–
Burns, R.J.	2	35	17.50	32	–	–	–	–	–	–
Buttler, J.C.	50	1630	60.37	119	2	11	–	–	–	29/4
Carberry, M.A.	134	3528	31.78	148*	4	26	5	42.80	2-11	5.63
Carter, A.	17	35	5.83	12	–	–	24	24.41	4-45	6.13
Chambers, M.A.	6	3	3.00	2	–	–	5	35.80	1-21	5.96
Chanderpaul, S.	385	12293	41.67	150	12	88	56	24.78	4-22	4.95
Chapple, G.	279	2035	17.54	81*	–	9	312	28.76	6-18	4.51
Chopra, V.	60	2255	41.00	115	4	18	0	–	–	6.00
Choudhry, S.H.	22	163	18.11	39	–	–	14	46.14	4-54	6.27
Christian, D.T.	66	1584	33.70	100	1	5	66	31.89	6-48	5.45
Clare, J.L.	39	313	11.59	57	–	1	28	41.32	3-39	5.52
Clark, J.	5	40	20.00	32	–	–	–	–	–	–
Clarke, R.	174	3207	26.28	98*	–	16	96	38.52	4-28	5.63
Claydon, M.E.	62	179	8.13	19	–	–	78	29.83	4-39	5.31
Cobb, J.J.	38	1004	31.37	137	1	6	13	53.15	2-35	6.16
Cockbain, I.A.	24	549	30.50	79	–	5	–	–	–	–
Coetzer, K.J.	87	2505	33.85	127	3	17	2	145.50	1-25	5.93
Coleman, F.R.J.	3	5	2.50	5	–	–	–	–	–	–
Coles, M.T.	24	83	9.22	47	–	–	40	19.35	6-32	6.32
Collingwood, P.D.	382	9950	33.72	120*	8	56	230	35.16	6-31	4.85
Collymore, C.D.	140	155	5.96	13*	–	–	149	31.22	5-27	4.29
Compton, N.R.D.	92	2678	39.97	131	6	16	1	53.00	1- 0	5.21
Cook, A.N.	111	3952	39.52	137	9	23	0	–	–	3.33
Cooke, C.B.	32	790	32.91	137*	2	2	–	–	–	11/2
Copeland, T.A.	12	24	12.00	14*	–	–	12	49.25	5-44	5.25
Cosker, D.A.	222	748	11.33	50*	–	1	225	32.87	5-54	4.77
Coughlin, P.	1	–	–	–	–	–	–	–	–	15.00
Cowan, E.J.M.	58	1749	37.21	131*	3	12	–	–	–	–
Cox, O.B.	13	25	8.33	9*	–	–	–	–	–	9/3
Craddock, T.R.	7	13	–	5*	–	–	5	44.00	2-38	4.68
Croft, S.J.	101	2670	37.08	107	1	20	43	35.55	4-24	5.39
Crook, S.P.	46	369	14.76	72	–	2	41	38.63	4-20	5.89

L-O	M	Runs	Avge	HS	100	50	Wkts	Avge	Best	Econ
Cross, G.D.	66	898	20.88	76	–	3	2	13.00	2-26	44/21
Daggett, L.M.	55	79	15.80	14*	–	–	72	25.36	4-17	4.99
Davey, J.H.	39	783	24.46	91	–	3	36	28.44	5- 9	5.80
Davies, A.L.	1	6	–	6*	–	–	–	–	–	–
Davies, M.	82	169	7.68	31*	–	–	78	30.02	4-13	4.13
Davies, S.M.	134	3880	34.95	119	5	23	–	–	–	118/39
Davis, C.A.L.	3	57	28.50	54	–	1	0	–	–	5.86
Dawson, L.A.	64	1031	25.77	70	–	3	35	41.65	4-45	5.21
de Bruyn, Z.	220	5762	36.23	122*	6	36	148	30.54	5-44	5.55
de Lange, C.D.	127	1451	23.03	66	–	7	130	29.07	4- 8	4.38
Denly, J.L.	91	2686	33.16	115	4	13	5	26.40	3-42	6.18
Dent, C.D.J.	12	125	13.88	36	–	–	7	21.28	4-43	5.13
Dernbach, J.W.	100	179	8.13	31	–	–	159	26.88	5-31	6.06
Dexter, N.J.	73	1570	31.40	135*	2	7	30	49.83	3-17	5.54
Dibble, A.J.	4	–	–	–	–	–	5	34.00	3-52	6.53
Dockrell, G.H.	45	134	11.16	22*	–	–	48	29.06	4-35	4.36
D'Oliveira, B.L.	7	41	41.00	16*	–	–	6	41.83	2-35	5.34
Dunn, M.P.	1	–	–	–	–	–	2	16.00	2-32	5.33
Durham, C.M.	2	–	–	–	–	–	–	–	–	–
Durston, W.J.	92	2121	34.20	120*	2	12	40	35.80	3- 7	5.60
Eckersley, E.J.H.	12	211	26.37	72*	–	1	–	–	–	13/1
Ervine, S.M.	195	4555	31.41	167*	7	19	183	33.86	5-50	5.59
Evans, A.C.	13	4	2.00	2*	–	–	9	55.28	2-34	5.36
Evans, L.	9	19	6.33	18	–	–	7	39.00	2-46	6.82
Evans, L.J.	5	74	18.50	36*	–	–	–	–	–	–
Finn, S.T.	67	132	10.15	35	–	–	95	25.92	5-33	4.89
Fletcher, L.J.	30	99	9.00	40*	–	–	28	38.85	3-27	5.56
Footitt, M.H.A.	11	5	2.50	4	–	–	10	36.30	3-20	6.25
Foster, J.S.	181	2843	28.71	83*	–	15	–	–	–	206/55
Franks, P.J.	183	1964	21.11	84*	–	6	195	28.94	6-27	5.05
Fuller, J.K.	16	224	28.00	43	–	–	31	19.70	6-35	5.54
Gale, A.W.	111	2994	32.19	125*	2	17	–	–	–	–
Gatting, J.S.	39	944	28.60	122	1	4	0	–	–	6.60
Gidman, A.P.R.	178	4200	28.00	116	5	21	68	39.85	5-42	5.12
Gidman, W.R.S.	34	352	20.70	76	–	1	27	32.88	4-36	4.74
Glover, J.C.	5	16	8.00	10	–	–	7	32.85	3-34	6.38
Godleman, B.A.	17	342	21.37	82	–	1	–	–	–	–
Goodwin, M.W.	362	10837	35.76	167	14	67	7	43.71	1- 9	5.23
Gregory, L.	18	115	12.77	39	–	–	23	19.04	4-27	6.11
Griffiths, D.A.	18	15	15.00	7	–	–	22	28.68	4-29	5.84
Groenewald, T.D.	65	360	13.33	36	–	–	65	32.33	4-22	5.38
Gurney, H.F.	26	24	4.80	13*	–	–	22	39.04	5-24	5.29
Hales, A.D.	55	1753	34.37	150*	3	9	0	–	–	15.00
Hall, A.J.	308	5834	29.61	129*	6	32	354	27.46	5-18	4.77
Hamilton-Brown, R.J.	72	1617	26.50	115	2	7	32	36.37	3-28	5.62
Hannon-Dalby, O.J.	5	21	–	21*	–	–	5	40.40	2-22	7.30
Harinath, A.	1	21	–	21*	–	–	–	–	–	–
Harmison, B.W.	54	953	24.43	67	–	3	24	35.62	3-43	5.93

L-O	M	Runs	Avge	HS	100	50	Wkts	Avge	Best	Econ
Harmison, S.J.	143	267	8.09	25*	–	–	184	30.75	5-33	4.96
Harris, J.A.R.	35	179	9.94	29	–	–	44	27.79	4-48	5.48
Harrison, J.	2	7	–	7*	–	–	2	41.50	2-51	6.91
Harrison, N.L.	7	7	–	5*	–	–	8	45.50	2-43	7.13
Hastings, J.W.	36	385	18.33	41*	–	–	53	28.67	4-28	4.91
Henderson, C.W.	257	1203	14.85	45	–	–	319	26.09	6-29	4.38
Higginbottom, M.	1	–	–	–	–	–	0	–	–	8.60
Hildreth, J.C.	149	3702	31.37	151	4	15	6	30.83	2-26	7.40
Hodd, A.J.	42	566	23.58	91	–	1	–	–	–	34/8
Hodgson, D.M.	4	19	9.50	9	–	–	–	–	–	3/1
Hogan, M.G.	21	51	12.75	27	–	–	26	36.38	5-44	4.78
Hogg, K.W.	130	950	16.66	66*	–	1	133	29.59	4-20	4.81
Hoggard, M.J.	150	144	6.00	23	–	–	205	25.72	5-28	4.56
Horton, P.J.	89	2148	30.68	111*	2	12	–	–	–	–
Housego, D.M.	7	269	44.83	132	1	1	–	–	–	–
Howell, B.A.C.	24	643	40.18	122	1	4	6	36.16	2-26	5.16
Hughes, A.L.	7	52	26.00	37*	–	–	3	50.33	1-23	4.57
Hughes, C.F.	52	1090	22.70	81	–	9	22	34.27	5-29	5.15
Hussain, G.M.	8	35	–	18*	–	–	9	33.66	2-17	6.26
Hussey, D.J.	229	7112	38.86	130	8	50	45	40.40	4-21	5.26
Ireland, A.J.	71	116	6.44	22*	–	–	90	30.27	4-16	5.45
James, N.A.	20	212	19.27	43	–	–	15	21.60	3-36	4.90
Jaques, P.A.	159	5968	40.87	171*	14	31	–	–	–	6.33
Javid, A.	3	62	20.66	34	–	–	0	–	–	6.75
Jennings, K.K.	6	286	57.20	71*	–	4	0	–	–	3.66
Jewell, T.M.	2	1	1.00	1	–	–	0	–	–	9.33
Johnson, M.A.	2	16	8.00	14	–	–	–	–	–	–
Johnson, R.M.	16	126	25.20	79	–	1	–	–	–	11/4
Jones, A.J.	5	9	4.50	5	–	–	4	58.25	1-31	7.76
Jones, C.R.	5	126	42.00	45*	–	–	–	–	–	–
Jones, G.O.	181	3013	24.69	86	–	12	–	–	–	197/41
Jones, R.A.	10	23	7.66	11*	–	–	3	126.66	1-25	6.84
Jones, S.P.	54	82	11.71	26	–	–	55	36.00	5-32	5.41
Jordan, C.J.	20	74	6.72	38	–	–	23	32.47	3-28	5.87
Joyce, E.C.	229	7293	37.40	146	11	44	6	51.50	2-10	7.02
Kapil, A.	10	107	21.40	44	–	–	3	74.66	1-18	7.26
Katich, S.M.	240	7235	36.17	136*	7	56	25	34.76	3-21	5.55
Keedy, G.	90	150	9.37	33	–	–	114	25.74	5-30	4.75
Kelsall, S.	1	40	40.00	40	–	–	–	–	–	–
Keogh, R.I.	7	93	18.60	30	–	–	0	–	–	6.05
Kerrigan, S.C.	18	20	5.00	10	–	–	15	39.86	3-21	5.27
Kervezee, A.N.	78	1970	29.84	121*	2	8	0	–	–	9.12
Key, R.W.T.	210	5876	31.42	120*	6	35	–	–	–	–
Khan, A.	74	321	11.46	65*	–	1	76	32.96	4-26	5.15
Kieswetter, C.	122	3887	38.87	143	10	16	1	19.00	1-19	128/25
Kirby, S.P.	92	88	4.19	15	–	–	125	27.73	5-36	5.57
Klinger, M.	96	3502	41.20	133*	9	22	–	–	–	–
Knight, T.C.	4	3	–	2*	–	–	6	27.83	2-27	5.21

L-O	M	Runs	Avge	HS	100	50	Wkts	Avge	Best	Econ
Leach, J.	1	–	–	–	–	–	0	–		11.75
Leach, M.J.	3	2	2.00	2	–	–	1	90.00	1-30	4.73
Leaning, J.A.	1	11	11.00	11	–	–	–	–		–
Lees, A.Z.	2	35	35.00	23	–	–	–	–		–
Levi, R.E.	59	1527	30.54	116	3	5	–	–		–
Lewis, J.	222	918	11.19	54	–	1	289	26.52	5-19	4.58
Liddle, C.J.	39	60	6.00	15	–	–	50	27.36	5-18	5.87
Lilley, A.M.	1	–	–	–	–	–	–	–		–
Linley, T.E.	18	37	37.00	20*	–	–	12	46.16	3-50	5.61
London, A.B.	3	3	3.00	3	–	–	0	–		5.00
Lucas, D.S.	82	229	10.40	32*	–	–	94	31.39	5-48	5.77
Lumb, M.J.	174	4992	31.79	110	3	39	0	–		14.00
Lyth, A.	62	1457	28.01	109*	1	7	0	–		4.66
McCarter, G.J.	2	–	–	–	–	–	6	9.33	3-15	5.89
McKenzie, N.D.	259	7480	37.40	131*	10	52	4	62.00	2-19	5.83
Machan, M.W.	2	227	45.40	126*	1	1	–	–		–
Maddy, D.L.	355	8939	31.03	167*	11	52	215	29.12	4-16	5.18
Madsen, W.L.	47	1291	35.86	75	–	10	5	14.80	2-18	4.35
Magoffin, S.J.	51	225	22.50	24*	–	–	65	30.92	4-58	4.71
Mahmood, S.I.	147	518	9.08	29	–	–	205	27.97	5-16	5.31
Malan, D.J.	65	1718	29.11	134	2	7	15	36.80	2-4	6.14
Marshall, H.J.H.	266	6472	28.26	122	6	43	4	73.75	2-21	6.23
Mascarenhas, A.D.	257	4260	25.05	79	–	27	296	26.42	5-27	4.29
Masters, D.D.	144	503	12.57	39	–	–	139	32.27	5-17	4.51
Maxwell, G.J.	18	353	29.41	61	–	3	9	50.66	2-38	4.92
Meaker, S.C.	38	65	6.50	21*	–	–	37	32.35	4-47	5.71
Meschede, C.A.J.	15	168	18.66	33	–	–	14	25.57	4-27	5.68
Mickleburgh, J.C.	9	163	27.16	56	–	1	–	–		–
Middlebrook, J.D.	177	1563	19.53	57*	–	1	138	35.28	4-27	4.67
Mills, T.S.	12	3	1.50	2*	–	–	9	45.22	2-40	5.58
Mitchell, D.K.H.	79	1539	29.59	92	–	8	41	39.58	4-42	5.72
Moore, S.C.	128	3417	30.78	118	5	22	1	53.00	1- 1	7.75
Morgan, E.J.G.	172	5119	39.37	161	9	30	0	–		7.00
Muchall, G.J.	117	2953	33.55	101*	1	18	1	144.00	1-15	5.14
Muchall, P.B.	2	22	11.00	22	–	–	1	58.00	1-34	9.66
Mullaney, S.J.	42	513	19.00	61	–	2	37	28.37	3-13	5.04
Murphy, D.	19	148	24.66	31*	–	–	–	–		9/4
Murtagh, T.J.	129	629	11.86	35*	–	–	174	28.43	4-14	5.25
Mustard, P.	153	4037	31.05	143	7	24	–	–		153/38
Naik, J.K.H.	28	100	9.09	18	–	–	22	42.77	3-21	5.35
Nannes, D.P.	32	18	3.60	5*	–	–	47	29.70	4-38	4.82
Napier, G.R.	217	2660	18.47	79	–	13	248	26.08	6-9	5.23
Nash, B.P.	71	1121	30.29	71	–	6	15	36.46	4-20	4.20
Nash, C.D.	75	2253	32.65	124*	2	14	34	25.61	4-40	5.30
Newby, O.J.	31	116	16.57	36*	–	–	31	34.87	5-35	6.27
Newton, R.I.	21	484	24.20	66	–	1	–	–		–
North, M.J.	154	4511	35.51	134*	8	31	69	31.94	4-26	5.05
Northeast, S.A.	34	665	26.60	69	–	5	–	–		–

L-O	M	Runs	Avge	HS	100	50	Wkts	Avge	Best	Econ
Norwell, L.C.	3	1	–	1*	–	–	8	16.12	6-52	6.78
O'Brien, K.J.	123	2846	30.27	142	3	11	81	35.67	4-31	5.22
O'Brien, N.J.	144	3081	28.79	121	1	20	–	–	–	120/31
Onions, G.	65	120	6.66	19	–	–	70	33.45	3-39	5.17
Oram, J.D.P.	245	4326	25.75	127	3	23	228	30.05	5-26	4.35
Overton, C.	2	25	12.50	20	–	–	1	72.00	1-35	6.54
Overton, J.	3	19	19.00	10	–	–	6	16.66	4-42	5.88
Owen, W.T.	21	53	8.83	12	–	–	32	19.78	5-49	5.94
Palladino, A.P.	41	162	9.00	31	–	–	39	35.30	4-32	5.42
Panesar, M.S.	84	141	8.81	17*	–	–	81	35.37	5-20	4.64
Pardoe, M.G.	2	27	13.50	16	–	–	–	–	–	–
Parry, S.D.	46	171	11.40	31	–	–	54	30.83	4-21	5.11
Patel, J.S.	130	420	9.54	34	–	–	131	36.11	4-16	4.62
Patel, R.H.	1	–	–	–	–	–	0	–	–	7.60
Patel, S.R.	160	3636	31.89	114	2	19	146	29.65	6-13	5.24
Patterson, S.A.	49	111	27.75	25*	–	–	61	29.18	6-32	5.10
Payne, D.A.	25	30	15.00	13	–	–	45	20.73	7-29	5.80
Peters, S.D.	171	3345	22.60	107	2	20	–	–	–	–
Petersen, A.N.	146	4441	33.90	145*	7	26	7	44.42	2-48	5.39
Pettini, M.L.	137	3251	27.78	144	6	20	–	–	–	–
Phillips, B.J.	137	1042	18.60	51*	–	1	153	30.21	4-25	4.99
Phillips, T.J.	70	403	17.52	58*	–	1	78	24.53	5-28	5.14
Pietersen, K.P.	243	7837	41.46	147	15	44	41	51.75	3-14	5.32
Pinner, N.D.	14	202	15.53	37	–	–	0	–	–	6.75
Piolet, S.A.	25	115	19.16	39	–	–	23	31.91	4-31	5.52
Plunkett, L.E.	118	945	18.52	72	–	2	139	31.84	4-15	5.41
Ponting, R.T.	448	16135	41.90	164	34	98	8	33.62	3-34	4.62
Porterfield, W.T.S.	141	4470	33.35	112*	6	27	–	–	–	–
Powell, M.J.	204	4665	26.96	114*	1	25	1	26.00	1-26	6.50
Poynton, T.	17	124	15.50	40	–	–	–	–	–	11/3
Pringle, R.D.	1	–	–	–	–	–	–	–	–	–
Prior, M.J.	220	5052	27.45	144	4	28	–	–	–	186/31
Procter, L.A.	18	252	28.00	97	–	2	11	38.27	3-29	6.37
Pyrah, R.M.	93	930	18.00	69	–	2	110	25.25	5-50	5.75
Quiney, R.J.	51	1575	36.62	103	1	12	0	–	–	6.73
Rankin, W.B.	73	67	6.09	9*	–	–	86	29.47	4-34	5.02
Rashid, A.U.	74	553	15.36	43	–	–	76	31.75	4-38	5.13
Rayner, O.P.	32	320	26.66	61	–	1	23	42.34	2-20	5.72
Read, C.M.W.	285	4910	28.88	135	2	20	–	–	–	271/64
Redfern, D.J.	40	602	18.81	57*	–	2	5	38.60	2-10	4.99
Reece, L.M.	20	348	24.85	59	–	1	6	69.66	4-35	6.20
Rees, G.P.	44	1317	36.58	123*	3	9	0	–	–	4.00
Riazuddin, H.	23	72	12.00	23*	–	–	16	46.06	3-37	5.11
Richardson, A.	64	105	10.50	21*	–	–	62	35.46	5-35	4.70
Richardson, M.J.	2	45	45.00	45	–	–	–	–	–	–
Riley, A.E.N.	8	3	–	3*	–	–	5	43.20	2-32	5.40
Rippon, M.J.	1	10	10.00	10	–	–	0	–	–	5.50
Roberts, M.D.T.	1	4	4.00	4	–	–	–	–	–	–

L-O	M	Runs	Avge	HS	100	50	Wkts	Avge	Best	Econ
Robson, S.D.	7	168	33.60	65	–	1	–	–	–	–
Roderick, G.H.	4	52	17.33	26	–	–	–	–	–	2/1
Rogers, C.J.L.	147	4777	36.74	140	5	32	2	13.00	2-22	6.50
Roland-Jones, T.S.	18	56	9.33	23*	–	–	30	23.06	3-24	5.55
Root, J.E.	26	748	34.00	110*	1	4	11	32.18	2-10	4.92
Rossington, A.M.	2	22	11.00	17	–	–	–	–	–	1/1
Roy, J.J.	37	819	24.81	131	2	5	0	–		12.00
Rushworth, C.	21	45	6.42	12*	–	–	37	18.43	5-31	5.12
Russell, C.J.	2	–	–	–	–	–	1	68.00	1-23	7.55
Saeed Ajmal	173	408	8.00	33	–	–	262	24.95	5-18	4.38
Sales, D.J.G.	258	7250	34.52	161	4	53	0	–		4.78
Salter, A.G.	2	3	3.00	3	–	–	3	30.00	2-41	5.62
Samaraweera, T.T.	173	2970	32.28	105*	2	16	109	28.63	7-30	4.00
Sandhu, G.S.	1	0	0.00	0	–	–	3	9.33	3-28	4.66
Sarwan, R.R.	251	8142	41.12	118*	10	48	35	28.60	5-10	5.31
Saxelby, I.D.	17	30	6.00	7*	–	–	22	29.59	4-31	6.46
Sayers, J.J.	28	516	19.84	62	–	4	1	79.00	1-31	7.90
Shah, O.A.	355	10374	35.52	134	14	67	27	33.70	4-11	5.90
Shahid Afridi	440	9725	25.06	124	8	52	452	32.93	6-38	4.61
Shahzad, A.	57	356	13.18	59*	–	1	79	29.06	5-51	5.27
Shantry, J.D.	40	71	14.20	18	–	–	57	28.61	4-32	6.00
Shreck, C.E.	52	45	6.42	9*	–	–	63	31.90	5-19	5.22
Sidebottom, R.J.	184	542	11.06	32	–	–	195	30.87	6-40	4.44
Simpson, J.A.	36	418	20.90	82	–	1	–	–		23/4
Smith, G.C.	247	8966	39.67	141	13	65	47	38.21	3-30	5.47
Smith, G.M.	88	1787	22.33	88	–	7	67	34.91	4-53	5.63
Smith, G.P.	21	321	16.89	58	–	1	–	–		–
Smith, T.C.	56	1155	30.39	117	2	7	67	26.83	4-48	5.22
Smith, T.M.J.	33	176	16.00	65	–	1	24	43.00	3-26	5.51
Smith, W.R.	79	1617	24.87	103	1	12	4	24.00	2-22	6.06
Solanki, V.S.	382	10465	32.29	164*	15	60	28	35.25	4-14	5.27
Spriegel, M.N.W.	61	1438	38.86	86	–	10	40	35.77	3-39	5.22
Stevens, D.I.	247	6223	30.50	133	4	41	84	31.65	5-32	4.96
Stirling, P.R.	78	2589	34.98	177	6	11	31	34.32	4-11	4.76
Stokes, B.A.	39	849	26.53	150*	1	3	22	15.04	4-29	5.26
Stone, O.P.	8	10	3.33	7*	–	–	2	92.00	1-12	5.81
Stoneman, M.D.	20	782	46.00	136*	3	3	–	–		–
Styris, S.B.	341	8330	33.32	141	6	·57	300	30.79	6-25	4.59
Suppiah, A.V.	89	1622	27.49	80	–	9	46	32.52	4-39	5.55
Swann, G.P.	260	3118	18.89	83	–	14	298	26.38	5-17	4.41
Sweeney, S.A.	2	–	–	–	–	–	0	–		9.60
Sykes, J.S.	7	15	15.00	12*	–	–	7	27.71	3-39	4.97
Tait, S.W.	98	108	6.75	22*	–	–	178	23.43	8-43	5.10
Taylor, J.M.R.	7	53	26.50	22*	–	–	9	23.00	3-37	4.96
Taylor, J.W.A.	67	2372	46.50	117*	6	13	5	34.00	4-61	7.39
Taylor, R.M.L.	9	106	17.66	29*	–	–	11	26.45	2-26	5.22
ten Doeschate, R.N.	147	3840	45.17	134*	7	22	135	29.39	5-50	5.61
Terry, S.P.	1	–	–	–	–	–	–	–	–	–

L-O	M	Runs	Avge	HS	100	50	Wkts	Avge	Best	Econ
Thakor, S.J.	6	191	38.20	83*	–	2	0	–		8.66
Theron, J.	81	438	17.52	41	–	–	136	21.90	5-44	5.07
Thomas, A.C.	148	573	15.07	28*	–	–	190	27.79	4-18	5.06
Thornely, M.A.	34	926	29.87	105*	1	5	4	57.25	1-20	6.66
Thorp, C.D.	42	323	17.00	52	–	1	53	27.13	6-17	4.54
Tomlinson, J.A.	27	34	3.77	14	–	–	29	31.37	4-47	5.01
Topley, R.J.W.	4	21	10.50	19	–	–	7	22.14	4-46	5.53
Tredwell, J.C.	181	1425	17.59	88	–	4	179	32.17	6-27	4.70
Trego, P.D.	133	2270	24.67	147	2	10	136	31.27	5-40	5.64
Tremlett, C.T.	125	521	10.01	38*	–	–	170	27.75	4-25	4.89
Trescothick, M.E.	351	11592	37.63	184	28	58	57	28.84	4-50	4.90
Trott, I.J.L.	219	7728	46.27	137	14	53	54	27.01	4-55	5.64
Troughton, J.O.	161	3543	27.89	115*	2	21	25	25.76	4-23	5.25
Turner, M.L.	34	60	7.50	15*	–	–	50	26.00	4-36	6.19
Vince, J.M.	47	1622	38.61	131	2	8	–	–		–
Voges, A.C.	138	4375	43.31	104*	3	35	26	51.11	3-25	5.33
Wagg, G.G.	92	1158	17.54	48*	–	–	103	31.78	4-35	5.70
Wainwright, D.J.	60	191	17.36	26	–	–	47	37.87	3-26	4.85
Wakely, A.G.	41	998	29.35	94	–	7	5	21.40	2-14	4.86
Wallace, M.A.	176	2152	19.04	105	1	3	–	–		158/43
Waller, M.T.C.	30	43	10.75	13	–	–	20	40.05	2-24	5.46
Walters, S.J.	67	1485	29.11	91	–	10	3	59.66	1-12	6.50
Wardlaw, I.	8	11	3.66	6*	–	–	8	40.75	3-60	5.96
Waters, H.T.	22	24	4.80	8	–	–	14	60.28	3-47	6.20
Wells, L.W.P.	6	28	9.33	17	–	–	3	20.33	3-19	4.75
Wells, T.J.	1	4	4.00	4	–	–	–	–		–
Wessels, M.H.	110	2577	27.41	100	1	15	1	48.00	1- 0	5.87
Westley, T.	21	506	28.11	82	–	5	4	29.50	1- 9	4.91
Westwood, I.J.	59	929	23.22	65	–	3	3	71.66	1-28	5.11
Wheater, A.J.	36	456	19.82	69	–	2	–	–		11/0
White, C.L.	208	5222	34.13	126*	6	31	96	35.58	4-15	5.36
White, G.G.	35	161	13.41	39*	–	–	36	26.44	5-35	5.36
White, W.A.	55	627	19.00	46*	–	–	46	40.56	6-29	6.41
Whiteley, R.A.	19	197	14.07	40	–	–	3	48.00	1-17	6.00
Willey, D.J.	37	423	17.62	74	–	2	22	39.68	3-49	5.70
Williams, R.E.M.	8	2	–	2*	–	–	2	162.50	2-60	7.76
Wilson, G.C.	97	1801	23.08	113	1	12	–	–		62/18
Woakes, C.R.	69	542	20.07	49*	–	–	72	32.34	6-45	5.39
Wood, C.P.	34	79	6.58	16	–	–	55	22.50	5-22	5.53
Wood, M.A.	5	7	3.50	5	–	–	5	25.00	3-32	4.80
Wood, S.K.W.	4	8	2.66	8	–	–	3	24.00	2-24	6.54
Wright, B.J.	63	1153	23.06	79	–	6	1	126.00	1-19	5.72
Wright, C.J.C.	80	192	10.66	42	–	–	80	34.57	4-20	5.48
Wright, L.J.	155	2723	26.69	125	4	7	104	38.68	4-12	5.28
Wyatt, A.C.F.	12	13	6.50	9*	–	–	10	41.00	2-36	6.47
Yardy, M.H.	195	3391	24.57	98*	–	22	132	38.25	6-27	5.05
Yasir Arafat	230	2533	21.28	110*	1	8	359	25.06	6-24	4.97
Young, E.G.C.	31	230	13.52	50	–	1	27	38.03	3-25	5.01

FIRST-CLASS CRICKET RECORDS

To the end of the 2012 season

TEAM RECORDS

HIGHEST INNINGS TOTALS

1107	Victoria v New South Wales	Melbourne	1926-27
1059	Victoria v Tasmania	Melbourne	1922-23
952-6d	Sri Lanka v India	Colombo	1997-98
951-7d	Sind v Baluchistan	Karachi	1973-74
944-6d	Hyderabad v Andhra	Secunderabad	1993-94
918	New South Wales v South Australia	Sydney	1900-01
912-8d	Holkar v Mysore	Indore	1945-46
910-6d	Railways v Dera Ismail Khan	Lahore	1964-65
903-7d	England v Australia	The Oval	1938
900-6d	Queensland v Victoria	Brisbane	2005-06
887	Yorkshire v Warwickshire	Birmingham	1896
863	Lancashire v Surrey	The Oval	1990
860-6d	Tamil Nadu v Goa	Panjim	1988-89
850-7d	Somerset v Middlesex	Taunton	2007

Excluding penalty runs in India, there have been 34 innings totals of 800 runs or more in first-class cricket. Tamil Nadu's total of 860-6d was boosted to 912 by 52 penalty runs.

HIGHEST SECOND INNINGS TOTAL

770	New South Wales v South Australia	Adelaide	1920-21

HIGHEST FOURTH INNINGS TOTAL

654-5	England (set 696 to win) v South Africa	Durban	1938-39

HIGHEST MATCH AGGREGATE

2376-37	Maharashtra v Bombay	Poona	1948-49

RECORD MARGIN OF VICTORY

Innings and 851 runs: Railways v Dera Ismail Khan	Lahore	1964-65

MOST RUNS IN A DAY

721	Australians v Essex	Southend	1948

MOST HUNDREDS IN AN INNINGS

6	Holkar v Mysore	Indore	1945-46

LOWEST INNINGS TOTALS

12	†Oxford University v MCC and Ground	Oxford	1877
12	Northamptonshire v Gloucestershire	Gloucester	1907
13	Auckland v Canterbury	Auckland	1877-78
13	Nottinghamshire v Yorkshire	Nottingham	1901
14	Surrey v Essex	Chelmsford	1983
15	MCC v Surrey	Lord's	1839
15	†Victoria v MCC	Melbourne	1903-04
15	†Northamptonshire v Yorkshire	Northampton	1908
15	Hampshire v Warwickshire	Birmingham	1922

† *Batted one man short*

There have been 28 instances of a team being dismissed for under 20.

LOWEST MATCH AGGREGATE BY ONE TEAM

34 (16 and 18)	Border v Natal	East London	1959-60

LOWEST COMPLETED MATCH AGGREGATE BY BOTH TEAMS

| 105 | MCC v Australians | Lord's | 1878 |

FEWEST RUNS IN AN UNINTERRUPTED DAY'S PLAY

| 95 | Australia (80) v Pakistan (15-2) | Karachi | 1956-57 |

TIED MATCHES

Before 1949 a match was considered to be tied if the scores were level after the fourth innings, even if the side batting last had wickets in hand when play ended. Law 22 was amended in 1948 and since then a match has been tied only when the scores are level after the fourth innings has been completed. There have been 56 tied first-class matches, five of which would not have qualified under the current law. The most recent are:

Warwickshire (446-7d & forfeit) v Essex (66-0d & 380)	Birmingham	2003
Worcestershire (262 & 247) v Zimbabweans (334 & 175)	Worcester	2003
Habib Bank (245 & 178) v WAPDA (233 & 190)	Lahore	2011-12

BATTING RECORDS
35,000 RUNS IN A CAREER

	Career	I	NO	HS	Runs	Avge	100
J.B.Hobbs	1905-34	1315	106	316*	61237	50.65	197
F.E.Woolley	1906-38	1532	85	305*	58969	40.75	145
E.H.Hendren	1907-38	1300	166	301*	57611	50.80	170
C.P.Mead	1905-36	1340	185	280*	55061	47.67	153
W.G.Grace	1865-1908	1493	105	344	54896	39.55	126
W.R.Hammond	1920-51	1005	104	336*	50551	56.10	167
H.Sutcliffe	1919-45	1088	123	313	50138	51.95	149
G.Boycott	1962-86	1014	162	261*	48426	56.83	151
T.W.Graveney	1948-71/72	1223	159	258	47793	44.91	122
G.A.Gooch	1973-2000	990	75	333	44846	49.01	128
T.W.Hayward	1893-1914	1138	96	315*	43551	41.79	104
D.L.Amiss	1960-87	1139	126	262*	43423	42.86	102
M.C.Cowdrey	1950-76	1130	134	307	42719	42.89	107
A.Sandham	1911-37/38	1000	79	325	41284	44.82	107
G.A.Hick	1983/84-2008	871	84	405*	41112	52.23	136
L.Hutton	1934-60	814	91	364	40140	55.51	129
M.J.K.Smith	1951-75	1091	139	204	39832	41.84	69
W.Rhodes	1898-1930	1528	237	267*	39802	30.83	58
J.H.Edrich	1956-78	979	104	310*	39790	45.47	103
R.E.S.Wyatt	1923-57	1141	157	232	39405	40.04	85
D.C.S.Compton	1936-64	839	88	300*	38942	51.85	123
G.E.Tyldesley	1909-36	961	106	256*	38874	45.46	102
J.T.Tyldesley	1895-1923	994	62	295*	37897	40.60	86
K.W.R.Fletcher	1962-88	1167	170	228*	37665	37.77	63
C.G.Greenidge	1970-92	889	75	273*	37354	45.88	92
J.W.Hearne	1909-36	1025	116	285*	37252	40.98	96
L.E.G.Ames	1926-51	951	95	295	37248	43.51	102
D.Kenyon	1946-67	1159	59	259	37002	33.63	74
W.J.Edrich	1934-58	964	92	267*	36965	42.39	86
J.M.Parks	1949-76	1227	172	205*	36673	34.76	51
M.W.Gatting	1975-98	861	123	258	36549	49.52	94
D.Denton	1894-1920	1163	70	221	36479	33.37	69
G.H.Hirst	1891-1929	1215	151	341	36323	34.13	60
I.V.A.Richards	1971/72-93	796	63	322	36212	49.40	114
A.Jones	1957-83	1168	72	204*	36049	32.89	56
W.G.Quaife	1894-1928	1203	185	255*	36012	35.37	72
R.E.Marshall	1945/46-72	1053	59	228*	35725	35.94	68
M.R.Ramprakash	1987-2012	764	93	301*	35659	53.14	114
G.Gunn	1902-32	1061	82	220	35208	35.96	62

HIGHEST INDIVIDUAL INNINGS

501*	B.C.Lara	Warwickshire v Durham	Birmingham	1994
499	Hanif Mohammed	Karachi v Bahawalpur	Karachi	1958-59
452*	D.G.Bradman	New South Wales v Queensland	Sydney	1929-30
443*	B.B.Nimbalkar	Maharashtra v Kathiawar	Poona	1948-49
437	W.H.Ponsford	Victoria v Queensland	Melbourne	1927-28
429	W.H.Ponsford	Victoria v Tasmania	Melbourne	1922-23
428	Aftab Baloch	Sind v Baluchistan	Karachi	1973-74
424	A.C.MacLaren	Lancashire v Somerset	Taunton	1895
405*	G.A.Hick	Worcestershire v Somerset	Taunton	1988
400*	B.C.Lara	West Indies v England	St John's	2003-04
394	Naved Latif	Sargodha v Gujranwala	Gujranwala	2000-01
390	S.C.Cook	Lions v Warriors	East London	2009-10
385	B.Sutcliffe	Otago v Canterbury	Christchurch	1952-53
383	C.W.Gregory	New South Wales v Queensland	Brisbane	1906-07
380	M.L.Hayden	Australia v Zimbabwe	Perth	2003-04
377	S.V.Manjrekar	Bombay v Hyderabad	Bombay	1990-91
375	B.C.Lara	West Indies v England	St John's	1993-94
374	D.P.M.D.Jayawardena	Sri Lanka v South Africa	Colombo	2006
369	D.G.Bradman	South Australia v Tasmania	Adelaide	1935-36
366	N.H.Fairbrother	Lancashire v Surrey	The Oval	1990
366	M.V.Sridhar	Hyderabad v Andhra	Secunderabad	1993-94
365*	C.Hill	South Australia v NSW	Adelaide	1900-01
365*	G.St A.Sobers	West Indies v Pakistan	Kingston	1957-58
364	L.Hutton	England v Australia	The Oval	1938
359*	V.M.Merchant	Bombay v Maharashtra	Bombay	1943-44
359	R.B.Simpson	New South Wales v Queensland	Brisbane	1963-64
357*	R.Abel	Surrey v Somerset	The Oval	1899
357	D.G.Bradman	South Australia v Victoria	Melbourne	1935-36
356	B.A.Richards	South Australia v W Australia	Perth	1970-71
355*	G.R.Marsh	W Australia v S Australia	Perth	1989-90
355	B.Sutcliffe	Otago v Auckland	Dunedin	1949-50
353	V.V.S.Laxman	Hyderabad v Karnataka	Bangalore	1999-00
352	W.H.Ponsford	Victoria v New South Wales	Melbourne	1926-27
350	Rashid Israr	Habib Bank v National Bank	Lahore	1976-77

There have been 184 triple hundreds in first-class cricket, W.V.Raman (313) and Arjan Kripal Singh (302*) for Tamil Nadu v Goa at Panjim in 1988-89 providing the only instance of two batsmen scoring 300 in the same innings.

MOST HUNDREDS IN SUCCESSIVE INNINGS

6	C.B.Fry	Sussex and Rest of England	1901
6	D.G.Bradman	South Australia and D.G.Bradman's XI	1938-39
6	M.J.Procter	Rhodesia	1970-71

TWO DOUBLE HUNDREDS IN A MATCH

244	202*	A.E.Fagg	Kent v Essex	Colchester	1938

TRIPLE HUNDRED AND HUNDRED IN A MATCH

333	123	G.A.Gooch	England v India	Lord's	1990

DOUBLE HUNDRED AND HUNDRED IN A MATCH MOST TIMES

4	Zaheer Abbas	Gloucestershire	1976-81

TWO HUNDREDS IN A MATCH MOST TIMES

8	Zaheer Abbas	Gloucestershire and PIA	1976-82
8	R.T.Ponting	Tasmania, Australia and Australians	1992-2006
7	W.R.Hammond	Gloucestershire, England and MCC	1927-45
7	M.R.Ramprakash	Middlesex, Surrey	1990-2010

MOST HUNDREDS IN A SEASON

18   D.C.S.Compton   1947   16   J.B.Hobbs   1925

100 HUNDREDS IN A CAREER

	Total		100th Hundred	
	Hundreds	Inns	Season	Inns
J.B.Hobbs	197	1315	1923	821
E.H.Hendren	170	1300	1928-29	740
W.R.Hammond	167	1005	1935	679
C.P.Mead	153	1340	1927	892
G.Boycott	151	1014	1977	645
H.Sutcliffe	149	1088	1932	700
F.E.Woolley	145	1532	1929	1031
G.A.Hick	136	871	1998	574
L.Hutton	129	814	1951	619
G.A.Gooch	128	990	1992-93	820
W.G.Grace	126	1493	1895	1113
D.C.S.Compton	123	839	1952	552
T.W.Graveney	122	1223	1964	940
D.G.Bradman	117	338	1947-48	295
I.V.A.Richards	114	796	1988-89	658
M.R.Ramprakash	114	764	2008	676
Zaheer Abbas	108	768	1982-83	658
A.Sandham	107	1000	1935	871
M.C.Cowdrey	107	1130	1973	1035
T.W.Hayward	104	1138	1913	1076
G.M.Turner	103	792	1982	779
J.H.Edrich	103	979	1977	945
L.E.G.Ames	102	951	1950	915
G.E.Tyldesley	102	961	1934	919
D.L.Amiss	102	1139	1986	1081

MOST 400s: 2 – B.C.Lara, W.H.Ponsford

MOST 300s or more: 6 – D.G.Bradman; 4 – W.R.Hammond, W.H.Ponsford

MOST 200s or more: 37 – D.G.Bradman; 36 – W.R.Hammond; 22 – E.H.Hendren

MOST RUNS IN A MONTH

1294 (avge 92.42)   L.Hutton   Yorkshire   June 1949

MOST RUNS IN A SEASON

Runs			I	NO	HS	Avge	100	Season
3816	D.C.S.Compton	Middlesex	50	8	246	90.85	18	1947
3539	W.J.Edrich	Middlesex	52	8	267*	80.43	12	1947
3518	T.W.Hayward	Surrey	61	8	219	66.37	13	1906

The feat of scoring 3000 runs in a season has been achieved 28 times, the most recent instance being by W.E.Alley (3019) in 1961. The highest aggregate in a season since 1969 is 2755 by S.J.Cook in 1991.

1000 RUNS IN A SEASON MOST TIMES

28   W.G.Grace (Gloucestershire), F.E.Woolley (Kent)

HIGHEST BATTING AVERAGE IN A SEASON

(Qualification: 12 innings)

Avge			I	NO	HS	Runs	100	Season
115.66	D.G.Bradman	Australians	26	5	278	2429	13	1938
104.66	D.R.Martyn	Australians	14	5	176*	942	5	2001
103.54	M.R.Ramprakash	Surrey	24	2	301*	2278	8	2006
102.53	G.Boycott	Yorkshire	20	5	175*	1538	6	1979

Avge			I	NO	HS	Runs	100	Season
102.00	W.A.Johnston	Australians	17	16	28*	102	–	1953
101.70	G.A.Gooch	Essex	30	3	333	2746	12	1990
101.30	M.R.Ramprakash	Surrey	25	5	266*	2026	10	2007
100.12	G.Boycott	Yorkshire	30	5	233	2503	13	1971

FASTEST HUNDRED AGAINST AUTHENTIC BOWLING

35 min	P.G.H.Fender	Surrey v Northamptonshire	Northampton	1920

FASTEST DOUBLE HUNDRED

113 min	R.J.Shastri	Bombay v Baroda	Bombay	1984-85

FASTEST TRIPLE HUNDRED

181 min	D.C.S.Compton	MCC v NE Transvaal	Benoni	1948-49

MOST SIXES IN AN INNINGS

16	A.Symonds	Gloucestershire v Glamorgan	Abergavenny	1995
16	G.R.Napier	Essex v Surrey	Croydon	2011
16	J.D.Ryder	New Zealanders v Australia A	Brisbane	2011-12

MOST SIXES IN A MATCH

20	A.Symonds	Gloucestershire v Glamorgan	Abergavenny	1995

MOST SIXES IN A SEASON

80	I.T.Botham	Somerset and England		1985

MOST FOURS IN AN INNINGS

72	B.C.Lara	Warwickshire v Durham	Birmingham	1994

MOST RUNS OFF ONE OVER

36	G.St A.Sobers	Nottinghamshire v Glamorgan	Swansea	1968
36	R.J.Shastri	Bombay v Baroda	Bombay	1984-85

Both batsmen hit for six all six balls of overs bowled by M.A.Nash and Tilak Raj respectively.

MOST RUNS IN A DAY

390*	B.C.Lara	Warwickshire v Durham	Birmingham	1994

There have been 19 instances of a batsman scoring 300 or more runs in a day.

LONGEST INNINGS

1015 min	R.Nayyar (271)	Himachal Pradesh v Jammu & Kashmir	Chamba	1999-00

HIGHEST PARTNERSHIPS FOR EACH WICKET

First Wicket

561	Waheed Mirza/Mansoor Akhtar	Karachi W v Quetta	Karachi	1976-77
555	P.Holmes/H.Sutcliffe	Yorkshire v Essex	Leyton	1932
554	J.T.Brown/J.Tunnicliffe	Yorkshire v Derbys	Chesterfield	1898

Second Wicket

580	Rafatullah Mohmand/Aamer Sajjad	WAPDA v SSGC	Sheikhupura	2009-10
576	S.T.Jayasuriya/R.S.Mahanama	Sri Lanka v India	Colombo	1997-98
480	E.Elgar/R.R.Rossouw	Eagles v Titans	Centurion	2009-10
475	Zahir Alam/L.S.Rajput	Assam v Tripura	Gauhati	1991-92
465*	J.A.Jameson/R.B.Kanhai	Warwickshire v Glos	Birmingham	1974

Third Wicket

624	K.C.Sangakkara/D.P.M.D.Jayawardena	Sri Lanka v South Africa	Colombo	2006
523	M.A.Carberry/N.D.McKenzie	Hampshire v Yorkshire	Southampton	2011
467	A.H.Jones/M.D.Crowe	N Zealand v Sri Lanka	Wellington	1990-91
459	C.J.L.Rogers/M.J.North	W Australia v Victoria	Perth	2006-07
456	Khalid Irtiza/Aslam Ali	United Bank v Multan	Karachi	1975-76
451	Mudassar Nazar/Javed Miandad	Pakistan v India	Hyderabad	1982-83

Fourth Wicket

577	V.S.Hazare/Gul Mahomed	Baroda v Holkar	Baroda	1946-47
574*	C.L.Walcott/F.M.M.Worrell	Barbados v Trinidad	Port-of-Spain	1945-46
502*	F.M.M.Worrell/J.D.C.Goddard	Barbados v Trinidad	Bridgetown	1943-44
470	A.I.Kallicharran/G.W.Humpage	Warwickshire v Lancs	Southport	1982

Fifth Wicket

520*	C.A.Pujara/R.A.Jadeja	Saurashtra v Orissa	Rajkot	2008-09
464*	M.E.Waugh/S.R.Waugh	NSW v W Australia	Perth	1990-91
420	Mohd. Ashraful/Marshall Ayub	Dhaka v Chittagong	Chittagong	2006-07
410*	A.S.Chopra/S.Badrinath	India A v South Africa A	Delhi	2007-08
405	S.G.Barnes/D.G.Bradman	Australia v England	Sydney	1946-47
401	M.B.Loye/D.Ripley	Northants v Glamorgan	Northampton	1998

Sixth Wicket

487*	G.A.Headley/C.C.Passailaigue	Jamaica v Tennyson's	Kingston	1931-32
428	W.W.Armstrong/M.A.Noble	Australians v Sussex	Hove	1902
411	R.M.Poore/E.G.Wynyard	Hampshire v Somerset	Taunton	1899

Seventh Wicket

460	Bhupinder Singh jr/P.Dharmani	Punjab v Delhi	Delhi	1994-95
347	D.St E.Atkinson/C.C.Depeiza	W Indies v Australia	Bridgetown	1954-55
344	K.S.Ranjitsinhji/W.Newham	Sussex v Essex	Leyton	1902

Eighth Wicket

433	V.T.Trumper/A.Sims	Australians v C'bury	Christchurch	1913-14
332	I.J.L.Trott/S.C.J.Broad	England v Pakistan	Lord's	2010
313	Wasim Akram/Saqlain Mushtaq	Pakistan v Zimbabwe	Sheikhupura	1996-97

Ninth Wicket

283	J.Chapman/A.Warren	Derbys v Warwicks	Blackwell	1910
268	J.B.Commins/N.Boje	SA 'A' v Mashonaland	Harare	1994-95
251	J.W.H.T.Douglas/S.N.Hare	Essex v Derbyshire	Leyton	1921

Tenth Wicket

307	A.F.Kippax/J.E.H.Hooker	NSW v Victoria	Melbourne	1928-29
249	C.T.Sarwate/S.N.Banerjee	Indians v Surrey	The Oval	1946
239	Aqil Arshad/Ali Raza	Lahore Whites v Hyderabad	Lahore	2004-05
235	F.E.Woolley/A.Fielder	Kent v Worcs	Stourbridge	1909

BOWLING RECORDS

2000 WICKETS IN A CAREER

	Career	Runs	Wkts	Avge	100w
W.Rhodes	1898-1930	69993	**4187**	16.71	23
A.P.Freeman	1914-36	69577	**3776**	18.42	17
C.W.L.Parker	1903-35	63817	**3278**	19.46	16
J.T.Hearne	1888-1923	54352	**3061**	17.75	15
T.W.J.Goddard	1922-52	59116	**2979**	19.84	16
W.G.Grace	1865-1908	51545	**2876**	17.92	10
A.S.Kennedy	1907-36	61034	**2874**	21.23	15
D.Shackleton	1948-69	53303	**2857**	18.65	20
G.A.R.Lock	1946-70/71	54709	**2844**	19.23	14
F.J.Titmus	1949-82	63313	**2830**	22.37	16
M.W.Tate	1912-37	50571	**2784**	18.16	13+1
G.H.Hirst	1891-1929	51282	**2739**	18.72	15
C.Blythe	1899-1914	42136	**2506**	16.81	14
D.L.Underwood	1963-87	49993	**2465**	20.28	10
W.E.Astill	1906-39	57783	**2431**	23.76	9
J.C.White	1909-37	43759	**2356**	18.57	14
W.E.Hollies	1932-57	48656	**2323**	20.94	14
F.S.Trueman	1949-69	42154	**2304**	18.29	12

	Career	Runs	Wkts	Avge	100w
J.B.Statham	1950-68	36999	**2260**	16.37	13
R.T.D.Perks	1930-55	53771	**2233**	24.07	16
J.Briggs	1879-1900	35431	**2221**	15.95	12
D.J.Shepherd	1950-72	47302	**2218**	21.32	12
E.G.Dennett	1903-26	42571	**2147**	19.82	12
T.Richardson	1892-1905	38794	**2104**	18.43	10
T.E.Bailey	1945-67	48170	**2082**	23.13	9
R.Illingworth	1951-83	42023	**2072**	20.28	10
F.E.Woolley	1906-38	41066	**2068**	19.85	8
N.Gifford	1960-88	48731	**2068**	23.56	4
G.Geary	1912-38	41339	**2063**	20.03	11
D.V.P.Wright	1932-57	49307	**2056**	23.98	10
J.A.Newman	1906-30	51111	**2032**	25.15	9
A.Shaw	1864-97	24580	**2026**+1	12.12	9
S.Haigh	1895-1913	32091	**2012**	15.94	11

ALL TEN WICKETS IN AN INNINGS

This feat has been achieved 81 times in first-class matches (excluding 12-a-side fixtures).
Three Times: A.P.Freeman (1929, 1930, 1931)
Twice: V.E.Walker (1859, 1865); H.Verity (1931, 1932); J.C.Laker (1956)

Instances since 1945:

W.E.Hollies	Warwickshire v Notts	Birmingham	1946
J.M.Sims	East v West	Kingston on Thames	1948
J.K.R.Graveney	Gloucestershire v Derbyshire	Chesterfield	1949
T.E.Bailey	Essex v Lancashire	Clacton	1949
R.Berry	Lancashire v Worcestershire	Blackpool	1953
S.P.Gupte	President's XI v Combined XI	Bombay	1954-55
J.C.Laker	Surrey v Australians	The Oval	1956
K.Smales	Nottinghamshire v Glos	Stroud	1956
G.A.R.Lock	Surrey v Kent	Blackheath	1956
J.C.Laker	England v Australia	Manchester	1956
P.M.Chatterjee	Bengal v Assam	Jorhat	1956-57
J.D.Bannister	Warwicks v Combined Services	Birmingham (M & B)	1959
A.J.G.Pearson	Cambridge U v Leicestershire	Loughborough	1961
N.I.Thomson	Sussex v Warwickshire	Worthing	1964
P.J.Allan	Queensland v Victoria	Melbourne	1965-66
I.J.Brayshaw	Western Australia v Victoria	Perth	1967-68
Shahid Mahmood	Karachi Whites v Khairpur	Karachi	1969-70
E.E.Hemmings	International XI v W Indians	Kingston	1982-83
P.Sunderam	Rajasthan v Vidarbha	Jodhpur	1985-86
S.T.Jefferies	Western Province v OFS	Cape Town	1987-88
Imran Adil	Bahawalpur v Faisalabad	Faisalabad	1989-90
G.P.Wickremasinghe	Sinhalese v Kalutara	Colombo	1991-92
R.L.Johnson	Middlesex v Derbyshire	Derby	1994
Naeem Akhtar	Rawalpindi B v Peshawar	Peshawar	1995-96
A.Kumble	India v Pakistan	Delhi	1998-99
D.S.Mohanty	East Zone v South Zone	Agartala	2000-01
O.D.Gibson	Durham v Hampshire	Chester-le-Street	2007
M.W.Olivier	Warriors v Eagles	Bloemfontein	2007-08
Zulfiqar Babar	Multan v Islamabad	Multan	2009-10

MOST WICKETS IN A MATCH

19	J.C.Laker	England v Australia	Manchester	1956

MOST WICKETS IN A SEASON

Wkts		Season	Matches	Overs	Mdns	Runs	Avge
304	A.P.Freeman	1928	37	1976.1	423	5489	18.05
298	A.P.Freeman	1933	33	2039	651	4549	15.26

The feat of taking 250 wickets in a season has been achieved on 12 occasions, the last instance being by A.P.Freeman in 1933. 200 or more wickets in a season have been taken on 59 occasions, the last being by G.A.R.Lock (212 wickets, average 12.02) in 1957.

The highest aggregates of wickets taken in a season since the reduction of County Championship matches in 1969 are as follows:

Wkts		Season	Matches	Overs	Mdns	Runs	Avge
134	M.D.Marshall	1982	22	822	225	2108	15.73
131	L.R.Gibbs	1971	23	1024.1	295	2475	18.89
125	F.D.Stephenson	1988	22	819.1	196	2289	18.31
121	R.D.Jackman	1980	23	746.2	220	1864	15.40

Since 1969 there have been 50 instances of bowlers taking 100 wickets in a season.

MOST HAT-TRICKS IN A CAREER

7	D.V.P.Wright
6	T.W.J.Goddard, C.W.L.Parker
5	S.Haigh, V.W.C.Jupp, A.E.G.Rhodes, F.A.Tarrant

ALL-ROUND RECORDS
THE 'DOUBLE'

3000 runs and 100 wickets: J.H.Parks (1937)
2000 runs and 200 wickets: G.H.Hirst (1906)
2000 runs and 100 wickets: F.E.Woolley (4), J.W.Hearne (3), W.G.Grace (2), G.H.Hirst (2), W.Rhodes (2), T.E.Bailey, D.E.Davies, G.L.Jessop, V.W.C.Jupp, J.Langridge, F.A.Tarrant, C.L.Townsend, L.F.Townsend
1000 runs and 200 wickets: M.W.Tate (3), A.E.Trott (2), A.S.Kennedy
Most Doubles: 16 – W.Rhodes; 14 – G.H.Hirst; 10 – V.W.C.Jupp
Double in Debut Season: D.B.Close (1949) – aged 18, the youngest to achieve this feat.

The feat of scoring 1000 runs and taking 100 wickets in a season has been achieved on 305 occasions, R.J.Hadlee (1984) and F.D.Stephenson (1988) being the only players to complete the 'double' since the reduction of County Championship matches in 1969.

WICKET-KEEPING RECORDS
1000 DISMISSALS IN A CAREER

	Career	Dismissals	Ct	St
R.W.Taylor	1960-88	**1649**	1473	176
J.T.Murray	1952-75	**1527**	1270	257
H.Strudwick	1902-27	**1497**	1242	255
A.P.E.Knott	1964-85	**1344**	1211	133
R.C.Russell	1981-2004	**1320**	1192	128
F.H.Huish	1895-1914	**1310**	933	377
B.Taylor	1949-73	**1294**	1083	211
S.J.Rhodes	1981-2004	**1263**	1139	124
D.Hunter	1889-1909	**1253**	906	347
H.R.Butt	1890-1912	**1228**	953	275
J.H.Board	1891-1914/15	**1207**	852	355
H.Elliott	1920-47	**1206**	904	302
J.M.Parks	1949-76	**1181**	1088	93
R.Booth	1951-70	**1126**	948	178
L.E.G.Ames	1926-51	**1121**	703	418
D.L.Bairstow	1970-90	**1099**	961	138
G.Duckworth	1923-47	**1096**	753	343

	Career	Dismissals	Ct	St
H.W.Stephenson	1948-64	1082	748	334
J.G.Binks	1955-75	1071	895	176
T.G.Evans	1939-69	1066	816	250
A.Long	1960-80	1046	922	124
G.O.Dawkes	1937-61	1043	895	148
R.W.Tolchard	1965-83	1037	912	125
W.L.Cornford	1921-47	1017	675	342

MOST DISMISSALS IN AN INNINGS

9	(8ct, 1st)	Tahir Rashid	Habib Bank v PACO	Gujranwala	1992-93
9	(7ct, 2st)	W.R.James	Matabeleland v Mashonaland CD	Bulawayo	1995-96
8	(8ct)	A.T.W.Grout	Queensland v W Australia	Brisbane	1959-60
8	(8ct)	D.E.East	Essex v Somerset	Taunton	1985
8	(8ct)	S.A.Marsh	Kent v Middlesex	Lord's	1991
8	(6ct, 2st)	T.J.Zoehrer	Australians v Surrey	The Oval	1993
8	(7ct, 1st)	D.S.Berry	Victoria v South Australia	Melbourne	1996-97
8	(7ct, 1st)	Y.S.S.Mendis	Bloomfield v Kurunegala Youth	Colombo	2000-01
8	(7ct, 1st)	S.Nath	Assam v Tripura (on debut)	Gauhati	2001-02
8	(8ct)	J.N.Batty	Surrey v Kent	The Oval	2004
8	(8ct)	Golam Mabud	Sylhet v Dhaka	Dhaka	2005-06
8	(8ct)	D.C.de Boorder	Otago v Wellington	Wellington	2009-10
8	(8ct)	R.S.Second	Free State v North West	Bloemfontein	2011-12
8	(8ct)	T.L.Tsolekile	South Africa A v Sri Lanka A	Durban	2012

MOST DISMISSALS IN A MATCH

14	(11ct, 3st)	I.Khaleel	Hyderabad v Assam	Guwahati	2011-12
13	(11ct, 2st)	W.R.James	Matabeleland v Mashonaland CD	Bulawayo	1995-96
12	(8ct, 4st)	E.Pooley	Surrey v Sussex	The Oval	1868
12	(9ct, 3st)	D.Tallon	Queensland v NSW	Sydney	1938-39
12	(9ct, 3st)	H.B.Taber	NSW v South Australia	Adelaide	1968-69
12	(12ct)	P.D.McGlashan	Northern Districts v Central Districts	Whangarei	2009-10
12	(11ct, 1st)	T.L.Tsolekile	Lions v Dolphins	Johannesburg	2010-11
12	(12ct)	Kashif Mahmood	Lahore Shalimar v Abbottabad	Abbottabad	2010-11
12	(12ct)	R.S.Second	Free State v North West	Bloemfontein	2011-12

MOST DISMISSALS IN A SEASON

128 (79ct, 49st) L.E.G.Ames   1929

FIELDING RECORDS
750 CATCHES IN A CAREER

1018	F.E.Woolley	1906-38	784	J.G.Langridge	1928-55
887	W.G.Grace	1865-1908	764	W.Rhodes	1898-1930
830	G.A.R.Lock	1946-70/71	758	C.A.Milton	1948-74
819	W.R.Hammond	1920-51	754	E.H.Hendren	1907-38
813	D.B.Close	1949-86			

MOST CATCHES IN AN INNINGS

7	M.J.Stewart	Surrey v Northamptonshire	Northampton	1957
7	A.S.Brown	Gloucestershire v Nottinghamshire	Nottingham	1966
7	R.Clarke	Warwickshire v Lancashire	Liverpool	2011

MOST CATCHES IN A MATCH

10	W.R.Hammond	Gloucestershire v Surrey	Cheltenham	1928
9	R.Clarke	Warwickshire v Lancashire	Liverpool	2011

MOST CATCHES IN A SEASON

78 W.R.Hammond 1928 77 M.J.Stewart 1957

ENGLAND LIMITED-OVERS INTERNATIONALS 2012

PAKISTAN v ENGLAND

LIMITED-OVERS INTERNATIONALS

Sheikh Zayed Stadium, Abu Dhabi, 13 February. Toss: England. **ENGLAND** won by 130 runs. England 260-7 (50; A.N.Cook 137, R.S.Bopara 50, Saeed Ajmal 5-43). Pakistan 130 (25; S.T.Finn 4-34, S.R.Patel 3-26). Award: A.N.Cook.

Sheikh Zayed Stadium, Abu Dhabi, 15 February. Toss: England. **ENGLAND** won by 20 runs. England 250-4 (50; A.N.Cook 102, R.S.Bopara 58). Pakistan 230 (49; S.T.Finn 4-34). Award: A.N.Cook.

Dubai International Cricket Stadium, 18 February. Toss: Pakistan. **ENGLAND** won by nine wickets. Pakistan 222 (50; Shahid Afridi 51, Umar Akmal 50, S.T.Finn 3-24, S.C.J.Broad 3-42). England 226-1 (37.2; K.P.Pietersen 111*, A.N.Cook 80). Award: K.P.Pietersen.

Dubai International Cricket Stadium, 21 February. Toss: Pakistan. **ENGLAND** won by four wickets. Pakistan 237 (50; Asad Shafiq 65, Azhar Ali 58, J.W.Dernbach 4-45). England 241-6 (49.2; K.P.Pietersen 130, Saeed Ajmal 3-62). Award: K.P.Pietersen. Series award: A.N.Cook. England debuts: D.R.Briggs, J.C.Buttler.

TWENTY20 INTERNATIONALS

Dubai International Cricket Stadium, 23 February. Toss: England. **PAKISTAN** won by 8 runs. Pakistan 144-6 (20; G.P.Swann 3-13). England 136-6 (20; Umar Gul 3-18). Award: Umar Gul.

Dubai International Cricket Stadium, 25 February. Toss: England. **ENGLAND** won by 38 runs. England 150-7 (20; J.M.Bairstow 60*). Pakistan 112 (18.2; S.T.Finn 3-30). Award: J.M.Bairstow.

Sheikh Zayed Stadium, Abu Dhabi, 27 February. Toss: England. **ENGLAND** won by 5 runs. England 129-6 (20; K.P.Pietersen 62*, Saeed Ajmal 4-23). Pakistan 124-6 (20). Award: K.P.Pietersen. Series award: K.P.Pietersen.

ENGLAND v WEST INDIES

NATWEST LIMITED-OVERS INTERNATIONALS

Rose Bowl, Southampton, 16 June. Toss: West Indies. **ENGLAND** won by 114 runs (D/L method). England 288-6 (50; I.R.Bell 126). West Indies 172 (33.4/48; D.R.Smith 56, T.T.Bresnan 4-34). Award: I.R.Bell.

The Oval, London, 19 June. Toss: England. **ENGLAND** won by eight wickets. West Indies 238-9 (50; D.J.Bravo 77, C.H.Gayle 53). England 239-2 (45; A.N.Cook 112, I.R.Bell 53). Award: A.N.Cook.

Headingley, Leeds, 22 June. MATCH ABANDONED. Series award: I.R.Bell.

NATWEST TWENTY20 INTERNATIONAL

Trent Bridge, Nottingham, 24 June. Toss: West Indies. **ENGLAND** won by seven wickets. West Indies 172-4 (20; D.R.Smith 70, D.J.Bravo 54*). England 173-3 (19.4; A.D.Hales 99, R.S.Bopara 59). Award: A.D.Hales.
A.D.Hales made England's highest score in all IT20 games, and the second-wicket partnership of 159 between A.D.Hales and R.S.Bopara was a record for England for all wickets.

ENGLAND v AUSTRALIA

NATWEST LIMITED-OVERS INTERNATIONALS

Lord's, London, 29 June. Toss: Australia. **ENGLAND** won by 15 runs. England 272-5 (50; E.J.G.Morgan 89*, I.J.L.Trott 54). Australia 257-9 (50; M.J.Clarke 61, D.A.Warner 56). Award: E.J.G.Morgan.

Oval, London, 1 July. Toss: Australia. **ENGLAND** won by six wickets. Australia 251-7 (50; S.R.Watson 66, G.J.Bailey 65). England 252-4 (45.4; R.S.Bopara 82, I.R.Bell 75). Award: R.S.Bopara.

Edgbaston, Birmingham, 4 July. MATCH ABANDONED.

Riverside, Chester-le-Street, 7 July. Toss: England. **ENGLAND** won by eight wickets. Australia 200-9 (50; D.J.Hussey 70, S.T.Finn 4-37). England 201-2 (47.5; I.R.Bell 69, I.J.L.Trott 64*). Award: S.T.Finn.

Old Trafford, Manchester, 10 July. Toss: England. **ENGLAND** won by seven wickets (D/L method). Australia 145-7 (32). England 138-3 (27.1/29; A.N.Cook 58, R.S.Bopara 52*). Award: R.S.Bopara. Series award: I.R.Bell.

ENGLAND v SOUTH AFRICA

NATWEST LIMITED-OVERS INTERNATIONALS

Sophia Gardens, Cardiff, 24 August. Toss: South Africa. **NO RESULT**. England 37-0 (5.3/23).

Rose Bowl, Southampton, 28 August. Toss: South Africa. **SOUTH AFRICA** won by 80 runs. South Africa 287-5 (50; H.M.Amla 150, G.C.Smith 52). England 207 (40.4). Award: H.M.Amla.

The Oval, London, 31 August. Toss: South Africa. **ENGLAND** won by four wickets. South Africa 211 (46.4; J.M.Anderson 4-44, J.W.Dernbach 3-44). England 212-6 (48; E.J.G.Morgan 73, I.J.L.Trott 71). Award: E.J.G.Morgan.

Lord's, London, 2 September. Toss: England. **ENGLAND** won by six wickets. South Africa 220-8 (50; J.C.Tredwell 3-35). England 224-4 (46.4; I.R.Bell 88). Award: I.R.Bell.

Trent Bridge, Nottingham, 5 September. Toss: England. **SOUTH AFRICA** won by seven wickets. England 182 (45.2; A.N.Cook 51, R.J.Peterson 3-37). South Africa 186-3 (34.3; H.M.Amla 97*, A.B.de Villiers 75*). Award: H.M.Amla. Series award: H.M.Amla.

NATWEST TWENTY20 INTERNATIONALS

Riverside Ground, Chester-le-Street, 8 September. Toss: South Africa. **SOUTH AFRICA** won by seven wickets. England 118-7 (20). South Africa 119-3 (19). Award: D.W.Steyn (1-13).

Old Trafford, Manchester, 10 September. Toss: England. **NO RESULT**. South Africa 77-5 (9). England 29-2 (4.1).

Edgbaston, Birmingham, 12 September. Toss: South Africa. **ENGLAND** won by 28 runs. England 118-5 (11; C.Kieswetter 50). South Africa 90-5 (11). Award: J.C.Buttler. Series award: C.Kieswetter. England debut: D.R.Briggs.

ICC WORLD TWENTY20 2012

See pages 276-277 for details of these matches.

INDIA v ENGLAND

TWENTY20 INTERNATIONALS

Subrata Roy Sahara Stadium, Pune, 20 December. Toss: India. **INDIA** won by five wickets. England 157-6 (20; A.D.Hales 56, Yuvraj Singh 3-19). India 158-5 (17.5). Award: Yuvraj Singh. England debuts: S.C.Meaker, J.C.Tredwell.

Wankhede Stadium, Mumbai, 22 December. Toss: England. **ENGLAND** won by six wickets. India 177-8 (20). England 181-4 (20; M.J.Lumb 50, Yuvraj Singh 3-17). Award: E.J.G.Morgan (49*). Series award: Yuvraj Singh. England debut: J.E.Root.
This was England's highest successful run chase in IT20s.

ENGLAND'S RESULTS IN 2012

	P	W	L	T	NR	A
Limited Overs	17	12	2	–	1	2
Twenty20	14	7	6	–	1	–
Overall	31	19	8	–	2	2

400 RUNS IN LIMITED-OVERS INTERNATIONALS IN 2012

	M	I	NO	HS	Runs	Avge	100	50	S/Rate
A.N.Cook	15	15	1	137	663	47.35	3	3	79.97
I.R.Bell	11	11	1	126	549	54.90	1	4	82.68
I.J.L.Trott	14	12	2	71	410	41.00	–	3	62.31

15 WICKETS IN LIMITED-OVERS INTERNATIONALS IN 2012

	Pl	O	M	R	W	Avge	Best	4wI	Econ
S.T.Finn	14	119	6	500	25	20.00	4-34	3	4.20
J.M.Anderson	13	101.4	9	479	18	26.61	4-44	1	4.71

ICC LOI Championship

To 10 March 2013

Team	LOIs	Points	Ranking
India	38	4514	119
England	33	3849	117
Australia	37	4285	116
South Africa	22	2514	114
Sri Lanka	39	4291	110
Pakistan	32	3373	105
West Indies	33	2823	86
New Zealand	26	2124	82
Bangladesh	21	1636	78
Zimbabwe	17	804	47

ICC WORLD TWENTY20 2012

The fourth ICC World Twenty20 took place in Sri Lanka between 18 September and 7 October.

GROUP A	P	W	L	T	A	Pts	Net RR
India	2	2	–	–	–	4	+2.82
England	2	1	1	–	–	2	+0.65
Afghanistan	2	–	2	–	–	0	–3.47

R.Premadasa Stadium, Colombo, 21 September. Toss: Afghanistan. **ENGLAND** won by 116 runs. England 196-5 (20; L.J.Wright 99*). Afghanistan 80 (17.2). Award: L.J.Wright.

R.Premadasa Stadium, Colombo, 23 September. Toss: England. **INDIA** won by 90 runs. India 170-4 (20; R.G.Sharma 55*). England 80 (14.4; Harbhajan Singh 4-12). Award: Harbhajan Singh.

GROUP B	P	W	L	T	A	Pts	Net RR
Australia	2	2	–	–	–	4	+2.18
West Indies	2	–	1	–	1	1	–1.85
Ireland	2	–	1	–	1	1	–2.09

GROUP C	P	W	L	T	A	Pts	Net RR
South Africa	2	2	–	–	–	4	+3.59
Sri Lanka	2	1	1	–	–	2	+1.85
Zimbabwe	2	–	2	–	–	0	–3.62

GROUP D	P	W	L	T	A	Pts	Net RR
Pakistan	2	2	–	–	–	4	+0.70
New Zealand	2	1	1	–	–	2	+1.15
Bangladesh	2	–	2	–	–	0	–1.86

SUPER EIGHTS

GROUP 1	P	W	L	T	A	Pts	Net RR
Sri Lanka	3	3	–	–	–	6	+0.99
West Indies	3	2	1	–	–	4	–0.37
England	3	1	2	–	–	2	–0.39
New Zealand	3	–	3	–	–	0	–0.16

Pallekele International Cricket Stadium, 27 September. Toss: New Zealand. **SRI LANKA** won in one-over eliminator. New Zealand 174-7 (20; R.J.Nicol 58). Sri Lanka 174-6 (20; T.M.Dilshan 76). Award: T.M.Dilshan. One over: Sri Lanka 13-1. New Zealand 7-1.

Pallekele International Cricket Stadium, 27 September. Toss: West Indies. **WEST INDIES** won by 15 runs. West Indies 179-5 (20; J.Charles 84, C.H.Gayle 58). England 164-4 (20; E.J.G.Morgan 71*, A.D.Hales 68). Award: J.Charles.

Pallekele International Cricket Stadium, 29 September. Toss: New Zealand. **ENGLAND** won by six wickets. New Zealand 148-6 (20; J.E.C.Franklin 50, S.T.Finn 3-16). England 149-4 (18.5; L.J.Wright 76). Award: L.J.Wright.

Pallekele International Cricket Stadium, 29 September. Toss: West Indies. **SRI LANKA** won by nine wickets. West Indies 129-5 (20; M.N.Samuels 50). Sri Lanka 130-1 (15.2; D.P.M.D.Jayawardena 65*). Award: D.P.M.D.Jayawardena.

Pallekele International Cricket Stadium, 1 October. Toss: New Zealand. **WEST INDIES** won in one-over eliminator. West Indies 139 (19.3; T.G.Southee 3-21, D.A.J.Bracewell 3-31). New Zealand 139-7 (20; L.R.P.L.Taylor 62*, S.P.Narine 3-20). Award: S.P.Narine. One over: New Zealand 17-0. West Indies 19-0.

Pallekele International Cricket Stadium, 1 October. Toss: England. **SRI LANKA** won by 19 runs. Sri Lanka 169-6 (20; S.C.J.Broad 3-32). England 150-9 (20; S.R.Patel 67, S.L.Malinga 5-31). Award: S.L.Malinga.

GROUP 2

	P	W	L	T	A	Pts	Net RR
Australia	3	2	1	–	–	4	+0.46
Pakistan	3	2	1	–	–	4	+0.27
India	3	1	2	–	–	2	–0.27
South Africa	3	–	3	–	–	0	–0.42

R.Premadasa Stadium, Colombo, 28 September. Toss: South Africa. **PAKISTAN** won by two wickets. South Africa 133-6 (20). Pakistan 136-8 (19.4; D.W.Steyn 3-22). Award: Umar Gul (Pakistan, 32).

R.Premadasa Stadium, Colombo, 28 September. Toss: India. **AUSTRALIA** won by nine wickets. India 140-7 (20; S.R.Watson 3-34). Australia 141-1 (14.5; S.R.Watson 72, D.A.Warner 63*). Award: S.R.Watson.

R.Premadasa Stadium, Colombo, 30 September. Toss: Australia. **AUSTRALIA** won by eight wickets. South Africa 146-5 (20; X.J.Doherty 3-20). Australia 147-2 (17.4; S.R.Watson 70). Award: S.R.Watson.

R.Premadasa Stadium, Colombo, 30 September. Toss: Pakistan. **INDIA** won by eight wickets. Pakistan 128 (19.4; L.Balaji 3-22). India 129-2 (17; V.Kohli 78*). Award: V.Kohli.

R.Premadasa Stadium, Colombo, 2 October. Toss: Pakistan. **PAKISTAN** won by 32 runs. Pakistan 149-6 (20; Nasir Jamshed 55, M.A.Starc 3-20). Australia 117-7 (20; M.E.K.Hussey 54*, Saeed Ajmal 3-17). Award: Raza Hasan (Pakistan, 2-14).

R.Premadasa Stadium, Colombo, 2 October. Toss: South Africa. **INDIA** won by 1 run. India 152-6 (20). South Africa 151 (19.5; F.du Plessis 65, Z.Khan 3-22, L.Balaji 3-37). Award: Yuvraj Singh (India, 2-23 and 21).

SEMI-FINALS

R.Premadasa Stadium, Colombo, 4 October. Toss: Sri Lanka. **SRI LANKA** won by 16 runs. Sri Lanka 139-4 (20). Pakistan 123-7 (20; Herath 3-25). Award: D.P.M.D.Jayawardena (Sri Lanka, 42).

R.Premadasa Stadium, Colombo, 5 October. Toss: West Indies. **WEST INDIES** won by 74 runs. West Indies 205-4 (20; C.H.Gayle 75*). Australia 131 (16.4; G.J.Bailey 63, R.Rampaul 3-16). Award: C.H.Gayle.

FINAL

R.Premadasa Stadium, Colombo, 7 October. Toss: West Indies. **WEST INDIES** won by 36 runs. West Indies 137-6 (20; M.N.Samuels 78, B.A.W.Mendis 4-12). Sri Lanka 101 (18.4; S.P.Narine 3-9). Award: M.N.Samuels.

RECORDS
Match

Highest score	205-4		West Indies v Australia	Semi-final	Colombo
Lowest score	93-8	(20)	Zimbabwe v South Africa	Group C	Hambantota
Highest innings	123	B.B.McCullum	New Zealand v Bangladesh	Group D	Pallekele
Fastest fifty	23 balls	G.J.Bailey	Australia v West Indies	Semi-final	Colombo
Highest partnership	133	S.R.Watson/D.A.Warner	Australia v India	Group 2	Colombo
Best analysis	6-8	B.A.W.Mendis	Sri Lanka v Zimbabwe	Group C	Hambantota
Most dismissals	4 (4ct)	A.B.de Villiers	South Africa v Zimbabwe	Group C	Hambantota
	4 (4ct)	M.S.Dhoni	India v Pakistan	Group 2	Colombo

Tournament

Man of the Series	S.R.Watson	Australia (249 runs and 11 wkts @ 16.00)
Most runs	249	S.R.Watson	Australia (ave 49.80, strike rate 150.0)
Highest strike rate	169.2	L.J.Wright	England (193 runs in 114 balls) Qual: 100 runs
Most sixes	16	C.H.Gayle	West Indies (222 runs)
Most wickets	15	B.A.W.Mendis	Sri Lanka (ave 9.80, economy 6.12)
Most economical	4.82	D.W.Steyn	South Africa (82 runs in 17 overs) Qual: 15 overs
Most dismissals	9 (7ct, 2st)	A.B.de Villiers	South Africa
Most catches	6	S.K.Raina	India

DUCKWORTH/LEWIS – A BRIEF EXPLANATION

The Duckworth/Lewis (D/L) method has been around now for 15 years and it is generally accepted as being a very fair method for resetting targets in interrupted one-day matches. However, ask a typical cricket fan as to how the calculations are done and the fallback excuse of not being good at maths at school is frequently trotted out. But if you can work out how much tax you have to pay on your net income then D/L calculations are well within your grasp.

You may well have heard that the D/L method is based on the idea of resources – these are the combination of wickets and overs that a team has for its innings. However, it's not just the numbers of these that matter; it is also their relative value – wickets and overs have different relative importance as an innings progresses. For example, having lots of wickets in hand without overs left in which to use them is of little value, just as if lots of overs remain they have little value if there are no wickets left with which to use them. In conducting their innings, teams need to manage these twin resources in order to maximise the total they set or maximise their chances of winning the match. Through some neat behind-the-scenes mathematics and statistical analysis of hundreds of matches, Duckworth and Lewis have produced a table that represents the average percentages remaining of their twin resources of a 50-over innings. In the extract of the table supplied you will see that teams start with all 50 overs and 10 wickets – and therefore 100% of their resources. As an innings progresses a team receives its overs, loses its wickets and thereby consumes its resources. The table works always in overs left – in that way it can be used for matches that are shorter than 50 overs – and tells us what percentage of their combined resources remains.

Wickets lost:	0	2	4	6	9
Overs remaining:-					
50	100.0	85.1	62.7	34.9	4.7
40	89.3	77.8	59.5	34.6	4.7
30	75.1	67.3	54.1	33.6	4.7
25	66.5	60.5	50.0	32.6	4.7
20	56.6	52.4	44.6	30.8	4.7
10	32.1	30.8	28.3	22.8	4.7
5	17.2	16.8	16.1	14.3	4.6

Suppose that a team has batted for 45 overs and has lost 6 wickets. With 5 overs left, for 6 wickets lost the table shows it has 14.3% of its resources remaining. If its innings is now terminated, these resources are lost and it has had available for its innings 100 – 14.3 = 85.7% resources compared with the 100% for a complete 50-over innings.

These figures came into play in a crucial Group match of the 2003 World Cup in South Africa. Against the host nation, Sri Lanka scored 268 in their 100% resources of 50 overs. Rain began to fall and abandonment looked likely at the end of the 45th over of South Africa's innings. Charts of the D/L method were consulted and the relevant figure was obtained through the comparative resources of the two teams. The calculation was 268 × 85.7/100 = 229.676. This meant that in order to win SA needed to reach 230 by the end of the 45th over if the match were abandoned. A score of 229 would be the score to tie.

How would South Africa know this? You will have seen the D/L par-score displayed on scoreboards. These numbers come from the par-score sheet that is distributed during the interval to team camps, match officials and the media. The par-score is given for the end of every one of the combinations of overs left and wickets lost (and even on a ball-by-ball basis). This sheet is clearly labelled as the score needed to tie. In the World Cup match the SA camp told the batsmen, Boucher and Klusener, that they needed to get to 229 by the end of the over. Thanks to a six from Boucher off the penultimate ball of the over, they achieved this – and to avoid losing his wicket, which would have raised the par-score, Boucher blocked the last ball. Play was duly abandoned at the end of the over but the dismay in the SA camp was palpable when it was finally realised that the 229 the batsmen had been told to score was in fact the score to tie and not to win the match. So a tie it was and the misreading of the clear information available led to the elimination of the host nation from the tournament.

Whenever a stoppage occurs within an innings, the table provides the information by which to calculate the resources lost. Suppose that there are 20 overs left with only 4 wickets down and a stoppage reduces the innings by 10 overs so there are now only 10 overs left on the resumption. You will see from the table that the team went off with 44.6% resources left and came back with 28.3% left. The stoppage would have cost it 44.6 – 28.3 = 16.3% of its resources so that it would have available 100 – 16.3 = 83.7% resources for its innings if there are no more stoppages (but if there are, the resources available are further reduced in the same way) and, in most cases, the target comes from reducing the first innings score in proportion to the resources available as in the World Cup example.

Sometimes teams start with fewer than 50 overs either due to a shorter match competition, such as the Pro40 or Twenty20, or due to a delayed start. For a 25-over innings, for instance, teams start with 66.5% resources compared with a 50-over innings. Although they have half the overs they still have all 10 wickets and therefore more than half their resources – the table says about two-thirds compared with a 50-over innings. Any loss of overs would reduce this further in the same way and using the same figures as in the table.

So you see that it really is simple to calculate targets following interruptions during the second innings. The method is simply to adjust the first innings score in proportion to the resources available to the two teams – rounding up to win and one fewer to tie.

A distinctive feature of the D/L method compared with previous methods of adjusting targets is that it compensates the team batting first for stoppages within its innings – its batting strategy has been based on the full 50 overs and so to have it curtailed is usually a disadvantage. The D/L method usually sets an enhanced target, that is, a target which is quite a few runs more than the team batting first scored. This has the effect of compensating it for the unexpected shortening of the first innings and the advantage that the team batting second has from knowing in advance of its shorter innings.

One of these FAQs concerns the effect that powerplays have on D/L calculations. Data on powerplays are not yet sufficient to do a thorough analysis, but the logic is similar to the old 15-over rule on which there are plenty of data. These show that the greater runs scored in these overs are consistent with what is expected from the D/L method for the overs and the *wickets* used up in those periods of more attacking fields. Consequently it is unlikely that the powerplays have any significant effect on D/L target calculations. But the situation will be kept under review.

Although rain is usually the cause of stoppages and D/L adjusted targets, interruptions have occurred for several other causes including sandstorms, snow, floodlight failures, crowd disturbances and, on a few occasions, due to the sun!

Cases at the higher levels of the game usually run to 80-100 per year and the total usage is approaching 1000 since the method's first use on 1st January 1997 in which England lost to Zimbabwe when they would have won by the old, unfair average run-rate method.

There have been some advances in the methodology since January 1997. With higher totals being more prevalent, and the introduction of Twenty20 matches which fit well into the D/L system, teams need to score a bigger percentage of their runs in the earlier stages of their innings than those suggested by the standard tables. Consequently, higher scores lead to the need for the table to be adjusted and this needs the computer to do the calculations. Whereas what is now known as the Standard Edition, using a single table of resources as described here, is used at lower levels of the game where computers aren't necessary or available, the higher levels of the game now use the more advanced computerised version called the Professional Edition. In this edition, the computer in effect produces a different table of resources for every match, but thereafter the calculations are the same as described here.

LIMITED-OVERS INTERNATIONALS
CAREER RECORDS

These records, complete to 9 March 2013, include all players registered for county cricket for the 2013 season at the time of going to press, plus those who have appeared in LOI matches for ICC full member countries since 11 November 2011.

ENGLAND – BATTING AND FIELDING

	M	I	NO	HS	Runs	Avge	100	50	Ct/St
K.Ali	14	9	3	39*	93	15.50	–	–	1
T.R.Ambrose	5	5	1	6	10	2.50	–	–	3
J.M.Anderson	167	66	35	20*	204	6.58	–	–	43
J.M.Bairstow	7	6	1	41*	119	23.80	–	–	3
G.J.Batty	10	8	2	17	30	5.00	–	–	4
I.R.Bell	127	123	11	126*	4149	37.04	3	25	43
R.S.Bopara	83	77	15	96	1899	30.62	–	10	25
S.G.Borthwick	2	2	–	15	18	9.00	–	–	1
T.T.Bresnan	69	49	13	80	719	19.97	–	1	19
D.R.Briggs	1	–					–	–	–
S.C.J.Broad	96	51	17	45*	416	12.23	–	–	20
J.C.Buttler	6	4	–	21	38	9.50	–	–	7
G.Chapple	1	1	–	14	14	14.00	–	–	–
R.Clarke	20	13	–	39	144	11.07	–	–	11
P.D.Collingwood	197	181	37	120*	5092	35.36	5	26	108
A.N.Cook	64	64	3	137	2456	40.26	5	16	20
S.M.Davies	8	8	–	87	244	30.50	–	1	8
J.L.Denly	9	9	–	67	268	29.77	–	2	5
J.W.Dernbach	22	7	1	5	17	2.83	–	–	5
S.T.Finn	33	12	6	35	80	13.33	–	–	8
J.S.Foster	11	6	3	13	41	13.66	–	–	13/7
P.J.Franks	1	1	–	4	4	4.00	–	–	1
S.J.Harmison	58	25	14	18*	91	8.27	–	–	10
M.J.Hoggard	26	6	2	7	17	4.25	–	–	5
G.O.Jones	49	41	8	80	815	24.69	–	4	68/4
S.P.Jones	8	1	–	1	1	1.00	–	–	–
E.C.Joyce †	17	17	–	107	471	27.70	1	3	6
R.W.T.Key	5	5	–	19	54	10.80	–	–	–
C.Kieswetter	46	40	5	107	1054	30.11	1	5	53/12
D.L.Maddy	8	6	–	53	113	18.83	–	1	1
S.I.Mahmood	26	15	4	22*	85	7.72	–	–	1
A.D.Mascarenhas	20	13	2	52	245	22.27	–	1	4
S.C.Meaker	2	2	–	1	2	1.00	–	–	–
E.J.G.Morgan †	71	65	16	110*	1995	40.71	3	12	25
P.Mustard	10	10	–	83	233	23.30	–	1	9/2
G.Onions	4	1	–	1	1	1.00	–	–	–
M.S.Panesar	26	8	3	13	26	5.20	–	–	3
S.R.Patel	36	22	7	70*	482	32.13	–	1	7
K.P.Pietersen	130	119	16	130	4351	42.24	9	24	38
L.E.Plunkett	29	25	10	56	315	21.00	–	1	7
M.J.Prior	68	62	9	87	1282	24.18	–	3	71/8
A.U.Rashid	5	4	1	31*	60	20.00	–	–	1
C.M.W.Read	36	24	7	30*	300	17.64	–	–	41/2
J.E.Root	8	7	3	79*	326	81.50	–	3	4
O.A.Shah	71	66	6	107*	1834	30.56	1	12	21
A.Shahzad	11	8	2	9	39	6.50	–	–	4
R.J.Sidebottom	25	18	8	24	133	13.30	–	–	6
V.S.Solanki	51	46	5	106	1097	26.75	2	5	16
B.A.Stokes	5	3	–	20	30	10.00	–	–	1
G.P.Swann	76	46	12	34	484	14.23	–	–	28

	M	I	NO	HS	Runs	Avge	100	50	Ct/St
J.W.A.Taylor	1	1	–	1	1	1.00	–	–	–
J.C.Tredwell	14	8	4	16	45	11.25	–	–	5
C.T.Tremlett	15	11	4	19*	50	7.14	–	–	4
M.E.Trescothick	123	122	6	137	4335	37.37	12	21	49
I.J.L.Trott	57	54	7	137	2379	50.61	3	20	12
J.O.Troughton	6	5	1	20	36	9.00	–	–	1
C.R.Woakes	11	8	4	33*	92	23.00	–	–	4
L.J.Wright	46	35	4	52	701	22.61	–	2	17
M.H.Yardy	28	24	8	60*	326	20.37	–	2	10

ENGLAND – BOWLING

	O	M	R	W	Avge	Best	4wI	R/Over
K.Ali	112.1	4	682	20	34.10	4-45	1	6.08
J.M.Anderson	1378.5	110	6885	229	30.06	5-23	12	4.99
G.J.Batty	73.2	1	366	5	73.20	2-40	–	4.99
I.R.Bell	14.4	0	88	6	14.66	3- 9	–	6.00
R.S.Bopara	160.5	8	745	20	37.25	4-38	1	4.63
S.G.Borthwick	9	0	72	0	–	–	–	8.00
T.T.Bresnan	573.1	27	3099	88	35.21	5-48	4	5.40
D.R.Briggs	10	0	39	2	19.50	2-39	–	3.90
S.C.J.Broad	816.1	46	4242	152	27.90	5-23	10	5.19
G.Chapple	4	0	14	0	–	–	–	3.50
R.Clarke	78.1	3	415	11	37.72	2-28	–	5.30
P.D.Collingwood	864.2	14	4294	111	38.68	6-31	4	4.96
J.W.Dernbach	185.4	5	1166	30	38.86	4-45	1	6.28
S.T.Finn	299.5	19	1380	52	26.53	4-34	3	4.60
P.J.Franks	9	0	48	0	–	–	–	5.33
S.J.Harmison	483.1	29	2481	76	32.64	5-33	3	5.13
M.J.Hoggard	217.4	13	1152	32	36.00	5-49	1	5.29
S.P.Jones	58	9	275	7	39.28	2-43	–	4.74
S.I.Mahmood	199.3	7	1169	30	38.96	4-50	1	5.85
A.D.Mascarenhas	137	6	634	13	48.76	3-23	–	4.62
S.C.Meaker	19	1	110	2	55.00	1-45	–	5.78
G.Onions	34	1	185	4	46.25	2-58	–	5.44
M.S.Panesar	218	10	980	24	40.83	3-25	–	4.49
S.R.Patel	197.5	4	1091	24	45.45	5-41	1	5.51
K.P.Pietersen	66.4	0	370	7	52.85	2-22	–	5.55
L.E.Plunkett	227.1	7	1321	39	33.87	3-24	–	5.81
A.U.Rashid	34	0	191	3	63.66	1-16	–	5.61
J.E.Root	21	0	114	0	–	–	–	5.42
O.A.Shah	32.1	1	184	7	26.28	3-15	–	5.72
A.Shahzad	98	5	490	17	28.82	3-41	–	5.00
R.J.Sidebottom	212.5	12	1039	29	35.82	3-19	–	4.88
V.S.Solanki	18.3	0	105	1	105.00	1-17	–	5.67
G.P.Swann	604.5	25	2744	101	27.16	5-28	4	4.53
J.C.Tredwell	115	5	537	22	24.40	4-44	2	4.66
C.T.Tremlett	130.4	2	705	15	47.00	4-32	1	5.39
M.E.Trescothick	38.4	0	219	4	54.75	2- 7	–	5.66
I.J.L.Trott	30.3	0	166	2	83.00	2-31	–	5.44
C.R.Woakes	85.2	2	463	15	30.86	6-45	1	5.42
L.J.Wright	170	2	863	15	57.53	2-34	–	5.07
M.H.Yardy	222	7	1075	21	51.19	3-24	–	4.84

† E.C.Joyce has also made 15 appearances for Ireland and E.J.G.Morgan has also made 23 appearances for Ireland (see below).

AUSTRALIA – BATTING AND FIELDING

	M	I	NO	HS	Runs	Avge	100	50	Ct/St
G.J.Bailey	21	20	3	125*	764	44.94	1	4	15
D.T.Christian	17	17	5	39	250	20.83	–	–	7
M.J.Clarke	227	207	42	130	7375	44.69	7	54	93
P.J.Cummins	5	3	2	11*	21	21.00	–	–	–
B.C.J.Cutting	3	1	–	27	27	27.00	–	–	1
X.J.Doherty	43	18	11	15	84	12.00	–	–	14
J.P.Faulkner	5	3	1	39	72	36.00	–	–	2
A.J.Finch	7	7	–	38	105	15.00	–	–	8
P.J.Forrest	15	14	–	104	368	26.28	1	3	4
B.J.Haddin	96	90	8	110	2614	31.87	2	16	133/9
R.J.Harris	21	13	7	21	48	8.00	–	–	6
M.C.Henriques	5	5	1	12	32	8.00	–	–	1
B.W.Hilfenhaus	25	11	8	16	29	9.66	–	–	10
P.J.Hughes	10	9	1	138*	416	52.00	2	1	2
D.J.Hussey	69	61	6	111	1796	32.65	1	14	29
M.E.K.Hussey	185	157	44	109*	5442	48.15	3	39	105
P.A.Jaques	6	6	–	94	125	20.83	–	1	3
M.G.Johnson	121	68	25	73*	756	17.58	–	2	26
S.M.Katich	45	42	5	107*	1324	35.78	1	9	13
U.T.Khawaja	3	3	1	8*	14	7.00	–	–	–
B.Lee	221	110	44	59	1176	17.81	–	3	54
N.M.Lyon	2	2	1	4*	4	4.00	–	–	1
C.J.McKay	42	21	4	28	105	6.17	–	–	3
S.E.Marsh	37	37	1	112	1314	36.50	2	8	8
G.J.Maxwell	11	11	3	56*	202	25.25	–	2	4
D.P.Nannes	1	1	–	1	1	1.00	–	–	–
M.J.North	2	2	–	5	6	3.00	–	–	1
J.L.Pattinson	11	6	3	13	36	12.00	–	–	2
R.T.Ponting	375	365	39	164	13704	42.03	30	82	160
K.W.Richardson	1	1	–	0	0	0.00	–	–	–
S.P.D.Smith	33	22	4	46*	380	21.11	–	1	14
M.A.Starc	18	6	4	52*	117	58.50	–	1	4
S.W.Tait	35	7	5	11	25	12.50	–	–	8
A.C.Voges	17	16	6	112*	532	53.20	1	2	2
M.S.Wade	32	30	2	75	641	22.89	–	4	37/5
D.A.Warner	38	37	–	163	1124	30.37	2	6	11
S.R.Watson	157	137	24	185*	4761	42.13	7	29	52
C.L.White	87	73	15	105	2037	35.12	2	11	37

AUSTRALIA – BOWLING

	O	M	R	W	Avge	Best	4wI	R/Over
D.T.Christian	109.1	4	528	17	31.05	5-31	1	4.83
M.J.Clarke	417.5	7	2102	56	37.53	5-35	2	5.03
P.J.Cummins	36	1	214	7	30.57	3-28	–	5.94
B.C.J.Cutting	30	1	140	5	28.00	3-45	–	4.66
X.J.Doherty	335.2	11	1573	46	34.19	4-28	3	4.69
J.P.Faulkner	40.1	3	211	8	26.37	4-48	1	5.25
A.J.Finch	1	0	2	0	–	–	–	2.00
R.J.Harris	171.5	13	832	44	18.90	5-19	3	4.84
M.C.Henriques	27	1	123	4	30.75	3-32	–	4.55
B.W.Hilfenhaus	202.4	16	1075	29	37.06	5-33	1	5.30
D.J.Hussey	133.4	1	698	18	38.77	4-21	2	5.22
M.E.K.Hussey	40	1	235	2	117.50	1-22	–	5.87
M.G.Johnson	980.2	56	4732	188	25.17	6-31	9	4.82
B.Lee	1864.1	141	8877	380	23.36	5-22	23	4.76
N.M.Lyon	16	2	77	1	77.00	1-41	–	4.81

AUSTRALIA – BOWLING (continued)

	O	M	R	W	Avge	Best	4wI	R/Over
C.J.McKay	352.5	29	1645	74	22.22	5-28	5	4.66
G.J.Maxwell	58	3	312	6	52.00	4-63	1	5.37
D.P.Nannes	7	1	20	1	20.00	1-20	–	2.85
M.J.North	3	0	16	0	–	–	–	5.33
J.L.Pattinson	92.1	5	468	15	31.20	4-51	1	5.07
R.T.Ponting	25	0	104	3	34.66	1-12	–	4.16
K.W.Richardson	6	3	15	0	–	–	–	2.50
S.P.D.Smith	149.5	0	780	22	35.45	3-33	–	5.20
M.A.Starc	135.4	6	662	36	18.38	5-20	6	4.87
S.W.Tait	281.2	11	1461	62	23.56	4-39	2	5.19
A.C.Voges	25	0	159	1	159.00	1-22	–	6.36
D.A.Warner	1	0	8	0	–	–	–	8.00
S.R.Watson	931	33	4470	155	28.83	4-36	3	4.80
C.L.White	55.1	2	351	12	29.25	3- 5	–	6.36

SOUTH AFRICA – BATTING AND FIELDING

	M	I	NO	HS	Runs	Avge	100	50	Ct/St
H.M.Amla	63	61	6	150	3229	58.70	10	19	23
F.Behardien	2	2	–	31	35	17.50	–	–	–
D.M.Benkenstein	23	20	3	69	305	17.94	–	1	3
J.Botha	78	50	18	46	609	19.03	–	–	36
Q.de Kock	3	3	–	31	74	24.66	–	–	4
M.de Lange	1	–	–	–	–	–	–	–	–
A.B.de Villiers	128	123	22	146	5025	49.75	13	28	104/3
F.du Plessis	29	27	4	72	641	27.86	–	5	15
J.P.Duminy	94	85	20	129	2601	40.01	2	15	39
D.Elgar	5	4	–	42	93	23.25	–	–	3
A.J.Hall	88	56	13	81	905	21.04	–	3	29
C.W.Henderson	4	–	–	–	–	–	–	–	–
C.A.Ingram	18	16	2	124	521	37.21	2	1	6
J.H.Kallis	316	302	53	139	11469	46.06	17	85	125
R.K.Kleinveldt	3	3	–	26	32	10.66	–	–	–
N.D.McKenzie	64	55	10	131*	1688	37.51	2	10	21
R.McLaren	16	12	3	33	98	10.88	–	–	5
D.A.Miller	18	15	4	59	296	26.90	–	2	4
J.A.Morkel	56	41	10	97	760	24.51	–	2	15
M.Morkel	56	20	7	23*	114	8.76	–	–	15
J.L.Ontong	27	15	2	32	184	14.15	–	–	14
W.D.Parnell	27	13	3	49	182	18.20	–	–	2
A.N.Petersen	17	15	1	80	437	31.21	–	4	3
R.J.Peterson	62	29	11	36	312	17.33	–	–	24
A.M.Phangiso	1	1	–	9	9	9.00	–	–	–
V.D.Philander	8	6	3	23	75	25.00	–	–	2
G.C.Smith	188	185	10	141	6887	39.35	10	47	100
D.W.Steyn	66	25	7	35	146	8.11	–	–	17
L.L.Tsotsobe	38	11	7	9	23	5.75	–	–	6

SOUTH AFRICA – BOWLING

	O	M	R	W	Avge	Best	4wI	R/Over
F.Behardien	2	0	9	0	–	–	–	4.50
D.M.Benkenstein	10.5	1	44	4	11.00	3- 5	–	4.06
J.Botha	637.1	13	2916	72	40.50	4-19	1	4.57
M.de Lange	9	1	46	4	11.50	4-46	1	5.11
A.B.de Villiers	2	0	22	0	–	–	–	11.00
F.du Plessis	25	0	142	2	71.00	1- 8	–	5.68

SOUTH AFRICA – BOWLING (continued)

	O	M	R	W	Avge	Best	4wI	R/Over
J.P.Duminy	205.4	3	1032	27	38.22	3-31	–	5.01
D.Elgar	16	1	67	2	33.50	1-11	–	4.18
A.J.Hall	556.5	30	2515	95	26.47	5-18	4	4.51
C.W.Henderson	36.1	2	132	7	18.85	4-17	1	3.64
J.H.Kallis	1754	77	8446	266	31.75	5-30	4	4.81
R.K.Kleinveldt	29	3	126	4	31.50	2-37	–	4.34
N.D.McKenzie	7.4	0	27	0	–	–	–	3.52
R.McLaren	114.4	7	604	17	35.52	4-46	2	5.26
J.A.Morkel	329.3	13	1786	47	38.00	4-29	2	5.42
M.Morkel	454	21	2214	94	23.55	5-38	7	4.87
J.L.Ontong	89.4	3	396	9	44.00	3-30	–	4.41
W.D.Parnell	214.4	11	1196	37	32.32	5-48	3	5.57
A.N.Petersen	1	0	7	0	–	–	–	7.00
R.J.Peterson	424.3	12	1983	56	35.41	4-12	1	4.67
A.M.Phangiso	8	0	43	0	–	–	–	5.37
V.D.Philander	51.5	5	248	7	35.42	4-12	1	4.78
G.C.Smith	171	0	951	18	52.83	3-30	–	5.56
D.W.Steyn	547.2	39	2797	96	29.13	5-50	4	5.01
L.L.Tsotsobe	306.1	27	1427	67	21.29	4-22	5	4.66

WEST INDIES – BATTING AND FIELDING

	M	I	NO	HS	Runs	Avge	100	50	Ct/St
A.B.Barath	14	14	1	113	394	30.30	1	1	3
C.S.Baugh	47	35	11	49	482	20.08	–	–	39/12
T.L.Best	20	13	5	24	68	8.50	–	–	4
D.J.Bravo	137	114	17	112*	2311	23.82	1	8	53
D.M.Bravo	53	50	8	100*	1393	33.16	1	9	13
S.Chanderpaul	268	251	40	150	8778	41.60	11	59	73
J.Charles	11	11	–	130	382	34.72	2	–	3
C.D.Collymore	84	35	17	13*	104	5.77	–	–	12
N.Deonarine	25	23	2	65*	587	29.35	–	4	8
C.H.Gayle	239	234	17	153*	8387	38.64	20	44	104
J.O.Holder	2	2	–	9	16	8.00	–	–	–
D.P.Hyatt	9	9	1	39	112	14.00	–	–	1
A.Martin	9	6	5	4*	10	10.00	–	–	3
J.N.Mohammed	1	1	–	2	2	2.00	–	–	–
S.P.Narine	28	19	3	36	190	11.87	–	–	7
B.P.Nash	9	7	3	39*	104	26.00	–	–	1
V.Permaul	4	2	–	10	11	5.50	–	–	–
K.A.Pollard	75	69	4	119	1752	26.95	3	6	41
K.O.A.Powell	19	19	–	83	486	25.57	–	3	6
D.Ramdin	97	72	17	96	1129	20.52	–	3	125/6
R.Rampaul	73	33	8	86*	339	13.56	–	1	10
K.A.J.Roach	51	32	19	24*	148	11.38	–	–	10
A.D.Russell	34	27	5	92*	660	30.00	–	3	7
D.J.G.Sammy	92	74	20	84	1143	21.16	–	4	49
M.N.Samuels	142	132	20	126	3455	30.84	4	22	39
R.R.Sarwan	179	167	33	120*	5802	43.29	5	38	45
L.M.P.Simmons	42	41	3	122	1152	39.31	1	10	17
D.R.Smith	87	71	5	68	1102	16.69	–	5	27
D.C.Thomas	21	19	2	37	238	14.00	–	–	23/6

WEST INDIES – BOWLING

	O	M	R	W	Avge	Best	4wI	R/Over
T.L.Best	166.4	7	859	26	33.03	4-35	2	5.15
D.J.Bravo	904.1	33	4811	160	30.06	6-43	5	5.32
S.Chanderpaul	123.2	0	636	14	45.42	3-18	–	5.15
C.D.Collymore	679	45	2924	83	35.22	5-51	2	4.30
N.Deonarine	74.3	2	413	6	68.83	2-18	–	5.54
C.H.Gayle	1163.1	38	5487	157	34.94	5-46	4	4.71
J.O.Holder	14.2	1	74	2	37.00	1-18	–	5.16
A.Martin	74	5	296	11	26.90	4-36	1	4.00
S.P.Narine	262.5	19	1019	47	21.68	5-27	3	3.87
B.P.Nash	49	3	224	5	44.80	3-56	–	4.57
V.Permaul	37	0	154	7	22.00	3-40	–	4.16
K.A.Pollard	267.5	4	1460	39	37.43	3-27	–	5.45
R.Rampaul	519.3	28	2633	88	29.92	5-49	8	5.06
K.A.J.Roach	428.1	20	2144	79	27.13	6-27	4	5.00
A.D.Russell	237.5	7	1302	42	31.00	4-35	5	5.47
D.J.G.Sammy	635	32	2929	69	42.44	4-26	1	4.61
M.N.Samuels	680.1	14	3254	74	43.97	3-25	–	4.78
R.R.Sarwan	96.5	3	586	16	36.62	3-31	–	6.05
L.M.P.Simmons	15	0	82	1	82.00	1- 3	–	5.46
D.R.Smith	435.3	18	2149	59	36.42	5-45	4	4.93
D.C.Thomas	1.1	0	11	2	5.50	2-11	–	9.42

NEW ZEALAND – BATTING AND FIELDING

	M	I	NO	HS	Runs	Avge	100	50	Ct/St
A.R.Adams	42	34	10	45	419	17.45	–	–	8
M.D.Bates	2	1	–	13	13	13.00	–	–	1
T.A.Boult	8	4	2	5	8	4.00	–	–	1
D.A.J.Bracewell	6	4	1	8*	14	4.66	–	–	1
D.G.Brownlie	3	3	1	19	22	11.00	–	–	1
C.de Grandhomme	1	1	–	36	36	36.00	–	–	1
G.D.Elliott	43	34	6	115	888	31.71	1	5	8
A.M.Ellis	13	12	1	33	154	14.00	–	–	3
D.R.Flynn	20	17	2	35	228	15.20	–	–	4
J.E.C.Franklin	104	76	26	98*	1235	24.70	–	4	25
M.J.Guptill	69	67	7	122*	2183	36.38	2	17	29
T.W.M.Latham	8	8	1	48	138	19.71	–	–	2
M.J.McClenaghan	4	2	2	2*	2	–	–	–	–
B.B.McCullum	212	183	26	166	4875	31.05	4	25	236/15
N.L.McCullum	46	40	4	65	696	19.33	–	4	17
A.J.McKay	19	10	7	4*	12	4.00	–	–	3
H.J.H.Marshall	66	62	9	101*	1454	27.43	1	12	18
K.D.Mills	147	91	30	54	922	15.11	–	2	36
A.F.Milne	2	1	1	12*	12	–	–	–	1
C.Munro	2	2	–	57	66	33.00	–	1	–
J.D.S.Neesham	3	3	–	13	18	6.00	–	–	–
T.S.Nethula	5	3	1	9*	12	6.00	–	–	2
R.J.Nicol	19	18	1	146	584	34.35	2	2	10
J.D.P.Oram	160	116	15	101*	2434	24.09	1	13	51
J.S.Patel	39	13	7	34	88	14.66	–	–	12
H.D.Rutherford	2	2	–	11	13	6.50	–	–	2
J.D.Ryder	39	33	1	107	1100	34.37	2	6	14
T.G.Southee	66	38	14	32	246	10.25	–	–	12
S.B.Styris	188	161	23	141	4483	32.48	4	28	73
L.R.P.L.Taylor	119	107	14	131*	3558	38.25	7	21	83
B.J.Watling	22	20	2	96*	528	29.33	–	5	16
K.S.Williamson	39	35	5	145*	1092	36.40	3	4	11

LOI　　　　　　　　**NEW ZEALAND – BOWLING**

	O	M	R	W	Avge	Best	4wI	R/Over
A.R.Adams	314.1	15	1643	53	31.00	5-22	3	5.22
M.D.Bates	14	1	52	2	26.00	1-24	–	3.71
T.A.Boult	58.3	3	286	6	47.66	2-45	–	4.88
D.A.J.Bracewell	56	8	281	7	40.14	3-55	–	5.01
C.de Grandhomme	1	0	9	0	–	–	–	9.00
G.D.Elliott	104.3	7	512	19	26.94	4-31	1	4.89
A.M.Ellis	73	3	366	11	33.27	2-22	–	5.01
D.R.Flynn	4	0	25	0	–	–	–	6.25
J.E.C.Franklin	626.2	34	3241	81	40.01	5-42	1	5.17
M.J.Guptill	11.1	0	55	2	27.50	2- 7	–	4.92
M.J.McClenaghan	39.4	2	197	10	19.70	4-20	2	4.96
N.L.McCullum	310.2	4	1510	30	50.33	3-24	–	4.86
A.J.McKay	154.2	7	800	27	29.62	4-53	2	5.18
K.D.Mills	1198	110	5628	214	26.29	5-25	8	4.69
A.F.Milne	9.2	0	38	1	38.00	1-17	–	4.07
J.D.S.Neesham	10.1	0	64	1	64.00	1-20	–	6.29
T.S.Nethula	44	3	249	5	49.80	2-41	–	5.65
R.J.Nicol	50.3	1	286	10	28.60	4-19	1	5.66
J.D.P.Oram	1151.5	93	5047	173	29.17	5-26	5	4.38
J.S.Patel	300.4	9	1513	42	36.02	3-11	–	5.03
J.D.Ryder	63.5	0	399	11	36.27	3-29	–	6.25
T.G.Southee	532.2	30	2768	91	30.41	5-33	4	5.19
S.B.Styris	1019	39	4839	137	35.32	6-25	5	4.74
L.R.P.L.Taylor	7	0	35	0	–	–	–	5.00
K.S.Williamson	70	1	363	12	30.25	4-22	1	5.18

INDIA – BATTING AND FIELDING

	M	I	NO	HS	Runs	Avge	100	50	Ct/St
V.R.Aaron	4	1	1	6*	6	–	–	–	–
R.Ashwin	48	28	10	38	331	18.38	–	–	6
M.S.Dhoni	216	193	55	183*	7085	51.34	7	48	203/65
A.B.Dinda	13	5	–	16	21	4.20	–	–	4
G.Gambhir	147	143	11	150*	5238	39.68	11	34	36
R.A.Jadeja	65	46	12	78	1028	30.23	–	6	24
Z.Khan	194	96	31	34*	753	11.58	–	–	43
V.Kohli	98	95	13	183	4054	49.43	13	22	50
B.Kumar	8	4	1	31	53	17.66	–	–	2
P.Kumar	68	33	12	54*	292	13.90	–	1	11
A.Mithun	5	3	–	24	51	17.00	–	–	1
P.P.Ojha	18	10	8	16*	46	23.00	–	–	7
P.A.Patel	38	34	3	95	736	23.74	–	4	30/9
I.K.Pathan	120	87	21	83	1544	23.39	–	5	21
Y.K.Pathan	57	41	11	123*	810	27.00	2	3	17
A.M.Rahane	16	16	–	91	404	25.25	–	2	6
S.K.Raina	159	138	28	116*	4068	36.98	3	28	64
V.Sehwag	241	235	9	219	7995	35.37	15	37	90
Shami Ahmed	5	2	1	1	1	1.00	–	–	–
I.Sharma	55	20	8	13	61	5.08	–	–	12
R.Sharma	4	1	–	1	1	1.00	–	–	1
R.G.Sharma	88	83	16	114	2065	30.82	2	13	32
S.R.Tendulkar	463	452	41	200*	18426	44.83	49	96	140
M.K.Tiwary	8	8	1	104*	251	35.85	1	1	3
R.Vinay Kumar	22	9	3	18	43	7.16	–	–	3
U.T.Yadav	17	8	8	11*	26	–	–	–	3
Yuvraj Singh	279	257	37	139	8119	36.98	13	50	90

LOI   **INDIA – BOWLING**

	O	M	R	W	Avge	Best	4wI	R/Over
V.R.Aaron	28.1	1	156	6	26.00	3-24	–	5.53
R.Ashwin	433.1	12	2088	66	31.63	3-24	–	4.82
M.S.Dhoni	2	0	14	1	14.00	1-14	–	7.00
A.B.Dinda	99	2	612	12	51.00	2-44	–	6.18
G.Gambhir	1	0	13	0	–	–	–	13.00
R.A.Jadeja	500	22	2392	70	34.17	4-32	2	4.78
Z.Khan	1682.5	117	8301	282	29.43	5-42	8	4.93
V.Kohli	52.3	1	306	2	153.00	1-20	–	5.82
B.Kumar	74	12	315	9	35.00	3-29	–	4.25
P.Kumar	540.2	45	2774	77	36.02	4-31	3	5.13
A.Mithun	30	1	203	3	67.66	2-32	–	6.76
P.P.Ojha	146	5	652	21	31.04	4-38	1	4.46
I.K.Pathan	975.5	53	5142	173	29.72	5-27	7	5.26
Y.K.Pathan	248.2	3	1365	33	41.36	3-49	–	5.49
S.K.Raina	179.2	1	918	19	48.31	2-17	–	5.11
V.Sehwag	715	13	3737	94	39.75	4- 6	1	5.22
Shami Ahmed	38	6	174	4	43.50	1-23	–	4.57
I.Sharma	429.1	20	2393	76	31.48	4-38	3	5.57
R.Sharma	34.2	0	177	6	29.50	3-43	–	5.15
R.G.Sharma	87.5	2	450	8	56.25	2-27	–	5.12
S.R.Tendulkar	1342.2	24	6850	154	44.48	5-32	6	5.10
M.K.Tiwary	21	1	144	1	144.00	1-28	–	6.85
R.Vinay Kumar	164.5	14	925	28	33.03	4-30	1	5.61
U.T.Yadav	134.2	4	841	18	46.72	3-38	–	6.26
Yuvraj Singh	807.2	18	4070	108	37.95	5-31	3	5.04

PAKISTAN – BATTING AND FIELDING

	M	I	NO	HS	Runs	Avge	100	50	Ct/St
Abdul Razzaq	261	225	57	112	5031	29.94	3	23	35
Abdur Rehman	25	18	5	31	104	8.00	–	–	5
Adnan Akmal	5	4	1	27	62	20.66	–	–	3
Aizaz Cheema	14	6	3	9*	26	8.66	–	–	2
Asad Shafiq	35	34	3	78*	930	30.00	–	7	6
Azhar Ali	14	14	3	96	452	41.09	–	4	2
Hammad Azam	8	6	2	36	76	19.00	–	–	3
Imran Farhat	51	51	2	107	1549	31.61	1	12	14
Junaid Khan	16	5	3	1*	2	1.00	–	–	1
Kamran Akmal	143	124	14	124	2930	26.63	5	9	140/29
Misbah-ul-Haq	109	98	24	93*	3052	41.24	–	20	52
Mohammad Hafeez	110	110	4	139*	2892	27.28	4	15	35
Mohammad Irfan	5	3	2	3*	3	3.00	–	–	–
Mohammad Sami	85	46	19	46	314	11.62	–	–	19
Nasir Jamshed	22	22	3	112	955	50.26	3	6	8
Rahat Ali	1	1	1	9*	0	–	–	–	–
Saeed Ajmal	74	44	18	33	219	8.42	–	–	13
Sarfraz Ahmed	23	13	4	46*	172	19.11	–	–	17/8
Shahid Afridi	344	318	20	124	7038	23.61	6	33	112
Shoaib Malik	206	183	22	143	5316	33.01	7	31	70
Sohail Tanvir	50	30	9	59	283	13.47	–	1	11
Umar Akmal	71	62	9	102*	2001	37.75	1	16	31/2
Umar Gul	114	57	16	39	412	10.04	–	–	14
Wahab Riaz	25	16	5	21	88	8.00	–	–	7
Younus Khan	248	238	23	144	6898	32.08	6	48	128
Zulqarnain Haider	4	4	2	19*	48	24.00	–	–	1/1

LOI   PAKISTAN – BOWLING

	O	M	R	W	Avge	Best	4wI	R/Over
Abdul Razzaq	1808.3	107	8452	268	31.53	6-35	11	4.67
Abdur Rehman	224	11	949	21	45.19	2-20	–	4.23
Aizaz Cheema	109.4	3	593	23	25.78	4-43	2	5.40
Azhar Ali	8	0	41	0	–	–	–	5.12
Hammad Azam	25	0	126	2	63.00	1-21	–	5.04
Imran Farhat	19.2	2	110	6	18.33	3-10	–	5.68
Junaid Khan	119.2	7	567	25	22.68	4-12	2	4.75
Misbah-ul-Haq	4	0	30	0	–	–	–	7.50
Mohammad Hafeez	753.5	36	3024	92	32.86	3-17	–	4.01
Mohammad Irfan	38.3	3	209	3	69.66	2-28	–	5.42
Mohammad Sami	698	41	3451	121	28.52	5-10	4	4.94
Rahat Ali	4	0	34	0	–	–	–	8.50
Saeed Ajmal	641	33	2623	117	22.41	5-24	6	4.09
Shahid Afridi	2534.1	66	11667	346	33.71	6-38	12	4.60
Shoaib Malik	1109	35	5031	140	35.93	4-19	1	4.53
Sohail Tanvir	397	22	2041	61	33.45	5-48	4	5.14
Umar Gul	886.1	64	4499	161	27.94	6-42	6	5.07
Wahab Riaz	189.2	9	1030	40	25.75	5-46	1	5.44
Younus Khan	45.2	1	271	3	90.33	1- 3	–	5.97

SRI LANKA – BATTING AND FIELDING

	M	I	NO	HS	Runs	Avge	100	50	Ct/St
L.D.Chandimal	50	48	8	111	1364	34.10	2	9	21/1
T.M.Dilshan	255	230	34	160*	7006	35.74	14	29	97/1
R.M.S.Eranga	5	4	2	2	3	1.50	–	–	2
A.N.P.R.Fernando	2	1	1	0*	0	–	–	–	–
C.R.D.Fernando	146	61	35	20	239	9.19	–	–	27
H.M.R.K.B.Herath	40	15	8	17*	58	8.28	–	–	8
D.P.M.D.Jayawardena	386	360	36	144	10623	32.78	14	66	189
C.K.Kapugedera	92	76	7	95	1521	22.04	–	8	29
C.K.B.Kulasekara	4	3	–	19	38	12.66	–	–	1
K.M.D.N.Kulasekara	131	83	28	73	912	16.58	–	2	32
R.A.S.Lakmal	15	8	5	1*	1	0.33	–	–	5
M.F.Maharoof	104	71	17	69*	1042	19.29	–	2	25
S.L.Malinga	136	65	20	56	374	8.31	–	1	17
A.D.Mathews	90	73	21	80*	1784	34.30	–	13	22
B.A.W.Mendis	61	28	13	15*	109	7.26	–	–	9
B.M.A.J.Mendis	32	24	6	72	412	22.88	–	1	7
M.D.K.J.Perera	4	3	2	22*	50	50.00	–	–	6
M.K.P.A.D.Perera	1	–	–	–	–	–	–	–	–
N.L.T.C.Perera	53	38	7	69*	502	16.19	–	1	22
K.T.G.D.Prasad	12	6	3	31*	63	21.00	–	–	–
S.Prasanna	9	7	2	8*	31	6.20	–	–	1
T.T.Samaraweera	53	42	11	105*	862	27.80	2	–	17
K.C.Sangakkara	330	309	32	138*	10656	38.46	14	70	324/78
S.M.S.M.Senanayake	7	6	3	22*	63	21.00	–	–	2
L.P.C.Silva	75	62	7	107*	1587	28.85	1	13	20
W.U.Tharanga	161	154	8	133	4944	33.86	12	28	31
H.D.R.L.Thirimanne	36	26	2	102*	718	29.91	1	4	16
I.Udana	2	–	–	–	–	–	–	–	–
S.Weerakoon	2	–	–	–	–	–	–	–	–

SRI LANKA – BOWLING

	O	M	R	W	Avge	Best	4wI	R/Over
T.M.Dilshan	677.1	20	3238	68	47.61	4- 4	3	4.78
R.M.S.Eranga	21.4	0	111	5	22.20	2-38	–	5.12
A.N.P.R.Fernando	18	0	115	3	38.33	2-63	–	6.38
C.R.D.Fernando	1074.3	53	5612	183	30.66	6-27	3	5.22
H.M.R.K.B.Herath	303.2	10	1303	30	43.43	3-28	–	4.29
D.P.M.D.Jayawardena	94.4	1	539	7	77.00	2-56	–	5.69
C.K.Kapugedera	44	0	225	2	112.50	1-24	–	5.11
C.K.B.Kulasekara	13	0	80	0	–	–	–	6.15
K.M.D.N.Kulasekara	1030	89	4752	147	32.32	5-22	3	4.61
R.A.S.Lakmal	106	4	670	17	39.41	3-43	–	6.32
M.F.Maharoof	738.2	48	3565	133	26.80	6-14	6	4.82
S.L.Malinga	1110.1	65	5621	213	26.38	6-38	11	5.06
A.D.Mathews	430.4	22	1967	54	36.42	6-20	1	4.56
B.A.W.Mendis	477.1	25	2095	98	21.37	6-13	7	4.39
B.M.A.J.Mendis	150	0	734	22	33.36	3-15	–	4.89
N.L.T.C.Perera	347.5	16	1899	74	25.66	6-44	5	5.45
K.T.G.D.Prasad	90.1	3	497	18	27.61	3-17	–	5.51
S.Prasanna	73.2	5	366	9	40.66	3-32	–	4.99
T.T.Samaraweera	117	2	542	11	49.27	3-34	–	4.63
S.M.S.M.Senanayake	63	1	316	7	45.14	2-38	–	5.01
L.P.C.Silva	7	1	33	1	33.00	1-21	–	4.71
H.D.R.L.Thirimanne	4.1	0	25	1	25.00	1-25	–	6.00
I.Udana	12	0	84	0	–	–	–	7.00
S.Weerakoon	10	0	49	1	49.00	1-49	–	4.90

ZIMBABWE – BATTING AND FIELDING

	M	I	NO	HS	Runs	Avge	100	50	Ct/St
R.W.Chakabva	16	16	1	45	249	16.60	–	–	9
T.L.Chatara	1	–	–	–	–	–	–	–	–
C.J.Chibhabha	63	63	1	73	1312	21.16	–	9	24
E.Chigumbura	139	130	14	79	2786	24.01	–	14	45
C.R.Ervine	25	23	3	85	702	35.10	–	5	3
S.M.Ervine	42	34	7	100	698	25.85	1	2	5
M.W.Goodwin	71	70	3	112*	1818	27.13	2	8	20
A.J.Ireland	26	13	5	8*	30	3.75	–	–	2
K.M.Jarvis	19	13	4	13	38	4.22	–	–	4
H.Masakadza	118	118	4	178*	3076	26.98	3	19	51
S.W.Masakadza	9	6	2	45*	115	28.75	–	–	6
S.Matsikenyeri	112	109	9	90	2205	22.05	–	13	37
T.M.K.Mawoyo	4	4	–	14	42	10.50	–	–	1
K.O.Meth	11	8	–	53	106	13.25	–	1	1
C.B.Mpofu	64	35	19	6	40	2.50	–	–	10
N.Mushangwe	4	4	1	14	22	7.33	–	–	–
T.C.Mutombodzi	1	1	–	13	13	13.00	–	–	2
R.W.Price	102	59	17	46	406	9.66	–	–	17
V.Sibanda	99	98	3	116	2298	23.93	1	18	34
T.Taibu	149	136	21	107*	3383	29.41	2	22	114/33
B.R.M.Taylor	135	134	13	145*	4159	34.37	6	26	67/18
P.Utseya	141	115	44	68*	1222	17.21	–	3	42
B.V.Vitori	6	2	1	3*	3	3.00	–	–	–
M.N.Waller	27	26	2	99*	560	23.33	–	4	8

ZIMBABWE – BOWLING

	O	M	R	W	Avge	Best	4wI	R/Over
T.L.Chatara	8	0	64	0	–	–	–	8.00
C.J.Chibhabha	157	2	1099	20	54.95	2-28	–	7.00
E.Chigumbura	591.2	23	3472	85	40.84	4-28	1	5.87
S.M.Ervine	274.5	10	1561	41	38.07	3-29	–	5.67
T.N.Garwwe	6	0	50	1	50.00	1-50	–	8.33
M.W.Goodwin	41.2	1	210	4	52.50	1-12	–	5.08
A.J.Ireland	221	13	1115	38	29.34	3-41	–	5.04
K.M.Jarvis	156.5	6	978	20	48.90	3-36	–	6.23
H.Masakadza	209.2	4	1134	32	35.43	3-39	–	5.41
S.W.Masakadza	69.1	2	524	16	32.75	4-46	2	7.57
S.Matsikenyeri	153.2	2	778	16	48.62	2-25	–	5.07
K.O.Meth	67.4	2	419	6	69.83	2-52	–	6.19
C.B.Mpofu	511	36	2689	70	38.41	6-52	3	5.26
N.Mushangwe	40	4	184	1	184.00	1-56	–	4.60
T.C.Mutombodzi	10	0	35	2	17.50	2-35	–	3.50
R.W.Price	895.4	75	3575	100	35.75	4-22	1	3.99
V.Sibanda	15.3	0	88	2	44.00	1-12	–	5.67
T.Taibu	14	1	61	2	30.50	2-42	–	4.35
B.R.M.Taylor	66	0	406	9	45.11	3-54	–	6.15
P.Utseya	1213.3	57	5217	111	47.00	4-38	2	4.29
B.V.Vitori	55.3	1	305	13	23.46	5-20	–	5.49
M.N.Waller	32	0	200	2	100.00	1-17	–	6.25

BANGLADESH – BATTING AND FIELDING

	M	I	NO	HS	Runs	Avge	100	50	Ct/St
Abdur Razzak	138	87	32	35	663	12.05	–	–	30
Abul Hasan	2	–	–	–	–	–	–	–	–
Alok Kapali	69	66	3	115	1235	19.60	1	5	29
Anamul Haque	5	5	–	120	195	39.00	1	–	1
Elias Sunny	4	4	2	1	2	1.00	–	–	–
Farhad Reza	34	31	6	50	412	16.48	–	1	13
Imrul Kayes	48	48	1	101	1315	27.97	1	9	14
Jahurul Islam	11	11	1	53	244	24.40	–	1	7
Mahmudullah	85	72	24	68*	1586	33.04	–	8	22
Mashrafe Mortaza	126	95	17	51*	1206	15.46	–	1	38
Monimul Haque	5	4	–	31	69	17.25	–	–	2
Mushfiqur Rahim	113	104	19	101	2251	26.48	1	11	82/33
Naeem Islam	53	45	15	73*	731	24.36	–	3	18
Nasir Hossain	19	17	3	100	498	35.57	1	3	8
Nazimuddin	11	11	–	47	147	13.36	–	–	1
Nazmul Hossain	38	21	13	6*	35	4.37	–	–	6
Rubel Hossain	38	20	12	15*	39	4.87	–	–	7
Shafiul Islam	46	24	7	24*	103	6.05	–	–	8
Shahadat Hossain	50	27	17	16*	79	7.90	–	–	5
Shahriar Nafees	75	75	5	123*	2201	31.44	4	13	13
Shakib Al Hasan	126	121	19	134*	3635	35.63	5	25	35
Sohag Gazi	5	3	–	30	62	20.66	–	–	3
Tamim Iqbal	118	118	1	154	3462	29.58	3	24	33

BANGLADESH – BOWLING

	O	M	R	W	Avge	Best	4wI	R/Over
Abdur Razzak	1204.3	65	5382	195	27.60	5-29	8	4.46
Abul Hasan	9	0	54	0	–	–	–	6.00
Alok Kapali	242	8	1255	24	52.29	3-49	–	5.18
Elias Sunny	34	2	161	5	32.20	2-21	–	4.73
Farhad Reza	189.5	12	1017	22	46.22	5-42	1	5.35
Mahmudullah	437.1	10	2210	52	42.50	3- 4	–	5.05
Mashrafe Mortaza	1068.3	91	4990	162	30.80	6-26	6	4.67
Monimul Haque	5	0	23	2	11.50	2-14	–	4.60
Naeem Islam	289	9	1385	35	39.57	3-32	–	4.79
Nasir Hossain	30.4	0	163	3	54.33	2- 3	–	5.31
Nazmul Hossain	274.5	23	1386	44	31.50	4-40	1	5.04
Rubel Hossain	292.1	10	1615	48	33.64	4-25	4	5.52
Shafiul Islam	321.3	24	1865	54	34.53	4-21	4	5.80
Shahadat Hossain	356.2	18	2072	46	45.04	3-34	–	5.81
Shakib Al Hasan	1075.2	63	4617	160	28.85	4-16	4	4.29
Sohag Gazi	46	8	156	9	17.33	4-29	1	3.39
Tamim Iqbal	1	0	13	0	–	–	–	13.00

ASSOCIATES – BATTING AND FIELDING

	M	I	NO	HS	Runs	Avge	100	50	Ct/St
A.Balbirnie (Ireland)	4	4	–	17	29	7.25	–	–	1
K.J.Coetzer (Scotland)	10	10	1	89*	388	43.11	–	4	6
J.H.Davey (Scotland)	9	9	1	48*	170	21.25	–	–	4
G.H.Dockrell (Ireland)	30	16	8	19	80	10.00	–	–	13
E.C.Joyce (Ireland)	15	15	1	88	464	33.14	–	4	3
A.N.Kervezee (Netherlands)	39	36	3	92	924	28.00	–	4	18
E.J.G.Morgan (Ireland)	23	23	2	115	744	35.42	1	5	9
T.J.Murtagh (Ireland)	2	1	–	15	15	15.00	–	–	–
K.J.O'Brien (Ireland)	68	62	9	142	1749	33.00	2	7	30
N.J.O'Brien (Ireland)	51	51	5	72	1215	26.41	–	8	38/7
W.T.S.Porterfield (Ireland)	60	60	3	112*	1752	30.73	5	8	30
W.B.Rankin (Ireland)	37	16	11	7*	35	7.00	–	–	6
P.R.Stirling (Ireland)	38	38	1	177	1448	39.13	4	6	20
R.N.ten Doeschate (Netherlands)	33	32	9	119	1541	67.00	5	9	13
G.C.Wilson (Ireland)	39	38	4	113	953	28.02	1	6	23/7

ASSOCIATES – BOWLING

	O	M	R	W	Avge	Best	4wI	R/Over
K.J.Coetzer	19	1	125	1	125.00	1-35	–	6.57
J.H.Davey	53.2	6	257	14	18.35	5- 9	1	4.81
G.H.Dockrell	225.3	13	940	37	25.40	4-35	1	4.16
A.N.Kervezee	4	0	34	0	–	–	–	8.50
T.J.Murtagh	8	1	39	0	–	–	–	4.87
K.J.O'Brien	305.4	19	1501	49	30.63	4-71	1	4.91
W.B.Rankin	283.2	19	1391	43	32.34	3-32	–	4.90
P.R.Stirling	156.1	1	692	20	34.60	4-11	1	4.43
R.N.ten Doeschate	263.2	18	1327	55	24.12	4-31	3	5.03

LIMITED-OVERS INTERNATIONALS RESULTS

1970-71 to 9 March 2013

This chart excludes all matches involving multinational teams.

	Opponents	Matches	Won											Tied	NR
			E	A	SA	WI	NZ	I	P	SL	Z	B	Ass		
England	Australia	117	46	67	–	–	–	–	–	–	–	–	–	2	2
	South Africa	50	21	–	25	–	–	–	–	–	–	–	–	1	3
	West Indies	85	40	–	–	41	–	–	–	–	–	–	–	–	4
	New Zealand	73	31	–	–	–	36	–	–	–	–	–	–	2	4
	India	86	35	–	–	–	–	46	–	–	–	–	–	2	3
	Pakistan	72	42	–	–	–	–	–	28	–	–	–	–	–	2
	Sri Lanka	50	26	–	–	–	–	–	–	24	–	–	–	–	–
	Zimbabwe	30	21	–	–	–	–	–	–	–	8	–	–	–	1
	Bangladesh	15	13	–	–	–	–	–	–	–	–	2	–	–	–
	Associates	17	15	–	–	–	–	–	–	–	–	–	1	–	1
Australia	South Africa	80	–	41	36	–	–	–	–	–	–	–	–	3	–
	West Indies	135	–	70	–	59	–	–	–	–	–	–	–	3	3
	New Zealand	124	–	85	–	–	34	–	–	–	–	–	–	–	5
	India	109	–	64	–	–	–	37	–	–	–	–	–	–	8
	Pakistan	89	–	54	–	–	–	–	31	–	–	–	–	1	3
	Sri Lanka	89	–	55	–	–	–	–	–	30	–	–	–	–	4
	Zimbabwe	28	–	26	–	–	–	–	–	–	1	–	–	–	1
	Bangladesh	19	–	18	–	–	–	–	–	–	–	1	–	–	–
	Associates	18	–	17	–	–	–	–	–	–	–	–	0	–	1
S Africa	West Indies	61	–	–	38	12	–	–	–	–	–	–	–	–	1
	New Zealand	58	–	–	34	–	20	–	–	–	–	–	–	–	4
	India	66	–	–	40	–	–	24	–	–	–	–	–	–	2
	Pakistan	57	–	–	38	–	–	–	18	–	–	–	–	–	1
	Sri Lanka	51	–	–	25	–	–	–	–	24	–	–	–	1	1
	Zimbabwe	32	–	–	29	–	–	–	–	–	2	–	–	–	1
	Bangladesh	14	–	–	13	–	–	–	–	–	–	1	–	–	–
	Associates	19	–	–	19	–	–	–	–	–	–	–	0	–	–
W Indies	New Zealand	56	–	–	–	28	21	–	–	–	–	–	–	–	7
	India	106	–	–	–	57	–	46	–	–	–	–	–	1	2
	Pakistan	120	–	–	–	66	–	–	52	–	–	–	–	2	–
	Sri Lanka	49	–	–	–	26	–	–	–	20	–	–	–	–	3
	Zimbabwe	44	–	–	–	34	–	–	–	–	9	–	–	–	1
	Bangladesh	25	–	–	–	16	–	–	–	–	–	7	–	–	2
	Associates	19	–	–	–	17	–	–	–	–	–	–	1	–	1
N Zealand	India	88	–	–	–	–	37	46	–	–	–	–	–	–	5
	Pakistan	89	–	–	–	–	35	–	51	–	–	–	–	1	2
	Sri Lanka	78	–	–	–	–	35	–	–	37	–	–	–	1	5
	Zimbabwe	35	–	–	–	–	25	–	–	–	8	–	–	1	1
	Bangladesh	21	–	–	–	–	16	–	–	–	–	5	–	–	–
	Associates	13	–	–	–	–	13	–	–	–	–	–	0	–	–
India	Pakistan	124	–	–	–	–	–	49	71	–	–	–	–	–	4
	Sri Lanka	139	–	–	–	–	–	75	–	52	–	–	–	1	11
	Zimbabwe	51	–	–	–	–	–	39	–	–	10	–	–	2	–
	Bangladesh	24	–	–	–	–	–	21	–	–	–	3	–	–	–
	Associates	24	–	–	–	–	–	22	–	–	–	–	2	–	–
Pakistan	Sri Lanka	132	–	–	–	–	–	–	77	50	–	–	–	1	4
	Zimbabwe	44	–	–	–	–	–	–	40	–	2	–	–	1	1
	Bangladesh	31	–	–	–	–	–	–	30	–	–	1	–	–	–
	Associates	22	–	–	–	–	–	–	21	–	–	–	1	–	–
Sri Lanka	Zimbabwe	47	–	–	–	–	–	–	–	39	7	–	–	–	1
	Bangladesh	30	–	–	–	–	–	–	–	27	–	3	–	–	–
	Associates	16	–	–	–	–	–	–	–	15	–	–	1	–	–
Zimbabwe	Bangladesh	56	–	–	–	–	–	–	–	–	26	30	–	–	–
	Associates	43	–	–	–	–	–	–	–	–	34	–	6	1	2
Bangladesh	Associates	32	–	–	–	–	–	–	–	–	–	22	10	–	–
Associates	Associates	138	–	–	–	–	–	–	–	–	–	–	133	–	5
		3330	290	497	297	356	272	405	419	318	107	75	155	27	112

MERIT TABLE OF ALL L-O INTERNATIONALS

1970-71 to 9 March 2013

	Matches	Won	Lost	Tied	No Result	% Won (exc NR)
South Africa	478	297	163	5	13	63.87
Australia	808	497	275	9	27	63.63
Pakistan	780	419	338	6	17	54.91
West Indies	690	356	304	6	24	53.45
India	817	405	371	6	35	51.79
England	595	290	278	7	20	50.43
Sri Lanka	681	318	330	4	29	48.77
New Zealand	635	272	325	5	33	45.18
Bangladesh	267	75	190	–	2	28.30
Zimbabwe	410	107	289	5	9	26.68
Associate Members (v Full*)	223	22	195	1	5	10.09

  * Results of games between two Associate Members and those involving multi-national sides are excluded from this list; Associate Members have participated in 361 LOIs, 138 LOIs being between Associate Members.

TEAM RECORDS
HIGHEST TOTALS

443-9	(50 overs)	Sri Lanka v Netherlands	Amstelveen	2006
438-9	(49.5 overs)	South Africa v Australia	Johannesburg	2005-06
434-4	(50 overs)	Australia v South Africa	Johannesburg	2005-06
418-5	(50 overs)	South Africa v Zimbabwe	Potchefstroom	2006-07
418-5	(50 overs)	India v West Indies	Indore	2011-12
414-7	(50 overs)	India v Sri Lanka	Rajkot	2009-10
413-5	(50 overs)	India v Bermuda	Port-of-Spain	2006-07
411-8	(50 overs)	Sri Lanka v India	Rajkot	2009-10
402-2	(50 overs)	New Zealand v Ireland	Aberdeen	2008
401-3	(50 overs)	India v South Africa	Gwalior	2009-10
399-6	(50 overs)	South Africa v Zimbabwe	Benoni	2010-11
398-5	(50 overs)	Sri Lanka v Kenya	Kandy	1995-96
397-5	(44 overs)	New Zealand v Zimbabwe	Bulawayo	2005
392-4	(50 overs)	India v New Zealand	Christchurch	2008-09
392-6	(50 overs)	South Africa v Pakistan	Pretoria	2006-07
391-4	(50 overs)	England v Bangladesh	Nottingham	2005
387-5	(50 overs)	India v England	Rajkot	2008-09
385-7	(50 overs)	Pakistan v Bangladesh	Dambulla	2010
377-6	(50 overs)	Australia v South Africa	Basseterre	2006-07
376-2	(50 overs)	India v New Zealand	Hyderabad, India	1999-00
374-4	(50 overs)	India v Hong Kong	Karachi	2008
373-6	(50 overs)	India v Sri Lanka	Taunton	1999
373-8	(50 overs)	New Zealand v Zimbabwe	Napier	2011-12
372-6	(50 overs)	New Zealand v Zimbabwe	Whangarei	2011-12
371-9	(50 overs)	Pakistan v Sri Lanka	Nairobi	1996-97
370-4	(50 overs)	India v Bangladesh	Dhaka	2010-11
368-5	(50 overs)	Australia v Sri Lanka	Sydney	2005-06
365-2	(50 overs)	South Africa v India	Ahmedabad	2009-10
363-3	(50 overs)	South Africa v Zimbabwe	Bulawayo	2001-02
363-5	(50 overs)	New Zealand v Canada	Gros Islet	2006-07
363-5	(50 overs)	India v Sri Lanka	Colombo (RPS)	2008-09
363-7	(55 overs)	England v Pakistan	Nottingham	1992
361-8	(50 overs)	Australia v Bangladesh	Dhaka	2010-11
360-4	(50 overs)	West Indies v Sri Lanka	Karachi	1987-88
359-2	(50 overs)	Australia v India	Johannesburg	2002-03
359-5	(50 overs)	Australia v India	Sydney	2003-04
358-4	(50 overs)	South Africa v Bangladesh	Benoni	2008-09
358-5	(50 overs)	Australia v Netherlands	Basseterre	2006-07
358-6	(50 overs)	New Zealand v Canada	Mumbai	2010-11

357-9	(50 overs)	Sri Lanka v Bangladesh	Lahore	2008
356-4	(50 overs)	South Africa v West Indies	St George's	2006-07
356-9	(50 overs)	India v Pakistan	Vishakhapatnam	2004-05
354-3	(50 overs)	South Africa v Kenya	Cape Town	2001-02
354-6	(50 overs)	South Africa v England	Cape Town	2009-10
354-7	(50 overs)	India v Australia	Nagpur	2009-10
353-3	(40 overs)	South Africa v Netherlands	Basseterre	2006-07
353-5	(50 overs)	India v New Zealand	Hyderabad, India	2003-04
353-6	(50 overs)	Pakistan v England	Karachi	2005-06
351-3	(50 overs)	India v Kenya	Paarl	2001-02
351-4	(50 overs)	Pakistan v South Africa	Durban	2006-07
351-5	(50 overs)	South Africa v Netherlands	Mohali	2010-11
351-6	(50 overs)	South Africa v Zimbabwe	Bloemfontein	2010-11
351-7	(50 overs)	Zimbabwe v Kenya	Mombasa	2008-09
350-4	(50 overs)	Australia v India	Hyderabad, India	2009-10
350-6	(50 overs)	India v Sri Lanka	Nagpur	2005-06
350-9	(49.3 overs)	New Zealand v Australia	Hamilton	2006-07

The highest for Bangladesh is 320-8 (v Zimbabwe, Bulawayo, 2009).

HIGHEST TOTALS BATTING SECOND

WINNING:	438-9	(49.5 overs)	South Africa v Australia	Johannesburg	2005-06
LOSING:	411-8	(50.0 overs)	Sri Lanka v India	Rajkot	2009-10

HIGHEST MATCH AGGREGATES

872-13	(99.5 overs)	South Africa v Australia	Johannesburg	2005-06
825-15	(100 overs)	India v Sri Lanka	Rajkot	2009-10

LARGEST RUNS MARGINS OF VICTORY

290 runs	New Zealand beat Ireland	Aberdeen	2008
272 runs	South Africa beat Zimbabwe	Benoni	2010-11
258 runs	South Africa beat Sri Lanka	Paarl	2011-12
257 runs	India beat Bermuda	Port-of-Spain	2006-07
256 runs	Australia beat Namibia	Potschefstroom	2002-03
256 runs	India beat Hong Kong	Karachi	2008
245 runs	Sri Lanka beat India	Sharjah	2000-01
243 runs	Sri Lanka beat Bermuda	Port-of-Spain	2006-07
234 runs	Sri Lanka beat Pakistan	Lahore	2008-09
233 runs	Pakistan beat Bangladesh	Dhaka	1999-00
232 runs	Australia beat Sri Lanka	Adelaide	1984-85
231 runs	South Africa beat Netherlands	Mohali	2010-11
229 runs	Australia beat Netherlands	Basseterre	2006-07
224 runs	Australia beat Pakistan	Nairobi	2002
221 runs	South Africa beat Netherlands	Basseterre	2006-07
217 runs	Pakistan beat Sri Lanka	Sharjah	2001-02
215 runs	Australia beat New Zealand	St George's	2006-07
215 runs	West Indies beat Netherlands	Delhhi	2010-11
212 runs	South Africa beat Zimbabwe	Centurion	2009-10
210 runs	New Zealand beat USA	The Oval	2004
210 runs	Sri Lanka beat Canada	Hambantota	2010-11
209 runs	South Africa beat West Indies	Cape Town	2003-04
208 runs	South Africa beat Kenya	Cape Town	2001-02
208 runs	Australia beat India	Sydney	2003-04
208 runs	West Indies beat Canada	Kingston	2009-10
206 runs	New Zealand beat Australia	Adelaide	1985-86
206 runs	Sri Lanka beat Netherlands	Colombo (RPS)	2002-03
206 runs	South Africa beat Bangladesh	Dhaka	2010-11
205 runs	Pakistan beat Kenya	Hambantota	2010-11
203 runs	Australia beat Scotland	Basseterre	2006-07
202 runs	England beat India	Lord's	1975
202 runs	South Africa beat Kenya	Nairobi	1996-97
202 runs	Zimbabwe beat Kenya	Dhaka	1998-99

202 runs		New Zealand beat Zimbabwe	Napier	2011-12
200 runs		India beat Bangladesh	Dhaka	2002-03
200 runs		New Zealand beat India	Dambulla	2010

LOWEST TOTALS (Excluding reduced innings)

35	(18.0 overs)	Zimbabwe v Sri Lanka	Harare	2003-04
36	(18.4 overs)	Canada v Sri Lanka	Paarl	2002-03
38	(15.4 overs)	Zimbabwe v Sri Lanka	Colombo (SSC)	2001-02
43	(19.5 overs)	Pakistan v West Indies	Cape Town	1992-93
43	(20.1 overs)	Sri Lanka v South Africa	Paarl	2011-12
44	(24.5 overs)	Zimbabwe v Bangladesh	Chittagong	2009-10
45	(40.3 overs)	Canada v England	Manchester	1979
45	(14.0 overs)	Namibia v Australia	Potschefstroom	2002-03
54	(26.3 overs)	India v Sri Lanka	Sharjah	2000-01
54	(23.2 overs)	West Indies v South Africa	Cape Town	2003-04
55	(28.3 overs)	Sri Lanka v West Indies	Sharjah	1986-87
58	(18.5 overs)	Bangladesh v West Indies	Dhaka	2010-11
61	(22.0 overs)	West Indies v Bangladesh	Chittagong	2011-12
63	(25.5 overs)	India v Australia	Sydney	1980-81
64	(35.5 overs)	New Zealand v Pakistan	Sharjah	1985-86
65	(24.0 overs)	USA v Australia	Southampton	2004
65	(24.3 overs)	Zimbabwe v India	Harare	2005
67	(31.0 overs)	Zimbabwe v Sri Lanka	Harare	2008-09
68	(31.3 overs)	Scotland v West Indies	Leicester	1999
69	(28.0 overs)	South Africa v Australia	Sydney	1993-94
69	(22.5 overs)	Zimbabwe v Kenya	Harare	2005-06
69	(23.5 overs)	Kenya v New Zealand	Chennai	2010-11
70	(25.2 overs)	Australia v England	Birmingham	1977
70	(26.3 overs)	Australia v New Zealand	Adelaide	1985-86
70	(23.5 overs)	West Indies v Australia	Perth	2012-13

The lowest for England is 86 (v A, Manchester, 2001).

LOWEST MATCH AGGREGATES

73-11	(23.2 overs)	Canada (36) v Sri Lanka (37-1)	Paarl	2002-03
75-11	(27.2 overs)	Zimbabwe (35) v Sri Lanka (40-1)	Harare	2003-04
78-11	(20.0 overs)	Zimbabwe (38) v Sri Lanka (40-1)	Colombo (SSC)	2001-02

BATTING RECORDS
HIGHEST INDIVIDUAL INNINGS

219	V.Sehwag	India v West Indies	Indore	2011-12
200*	S.R.Tendulkar	India v South Africa	Gwalior	2009-10
194*	C.K.Coventry	Zimbabwe v Bangladesh	Bulawayo	2009
194	Saeed Anwar	Pakistan v India	Madras	1996-97
189*	I.V.A.Richards	West Indies v England	Manchester	1984
189	S.T.Jayasuriya	Sri Lanka v India	Sharjah	2000-01
188*	G.Kirsten	South Africa v UAE	Rawalpindi	1995-96
186*	S.R.Tendulkar	India v New Zealand	Hyderabad	1999-00
185*	S.R.Watson	Australia v Bangladesh	Dhaka	2010-11
183*	M.S.Dhoni	India v Sri Lanka	Jaipur	2005-06
183	S.C.Ganguly	India v Sri Lanka	Taunton	1999
183	V.Kohli	India v Pakistan	Dhaka	2011-12
181*	M.L.Hayden	Australia v New Zealand	Hamilton	2006-07
181	I.V.A.Richards	West Indies v Sri Lanka	Karachi	1987-88
178*	H.Masakadza	Zimbabwe v Kenya	Harare	2009-10
177	P.R.Stirling	Ireland v Canada	Toronto	2010
175*	Kapil Dev	India v Zimbabwe	Tunbridge Wells	1983
175	H.H.Gibbs	South Africa v Australia	Johannesburg	2005-06
175	S.R.Tendulkar	India v Australia	Hyderabad, India	2009-10
175	V.Sehwag	India v Bangladesh	Dhaka	2010-11
173	M.E.Waugh	Australia v West Indies	Melbourne	2000-01
172*	C.B.Wishart	Zimbabwe v Namibia	Harare	2002-03

172	A.C.Gilchrist	Australia v Zimbabwe	Hobart	2003-04
172	L.Vincent	New Zealand v Zimbabwe	Bulawayo	2005
171*	G.M.Turner	New Zealand v East Africa	Birmingham	1975
169*	D.J.Callaghan	South Africa v New Zealand	Pretoria	1994-95
169	B.C.Lara	West Indies v Sri Lanka	Sharjah	1995-96
167*	R.A.Smith	England v Australia	Birmingham	1993
166	B.B.McCullum	New Zealand v Ireland	Aberdeen	2008
164	R.T.Ponting	Australia v South Africa	Johannesburg	2005-06
163*	S.R.Tendulkar	India v New Zealand	Christchurch	2008-09
163	D.A.Warner	Australia v Sri Lanka	Brisbane	2011-12
161*	S.R.Watson	Australia v England	Melbourne	2010-11
161	A.C.Hudson	South Africa v Netherlands	Rawalpindi	1995-96
161	J.A.H.Marshall	New Zealand v Ireland	Aberdeen	2008
160*	T.M.Dilshan	Sri Lanka v India	Hobart	2011-12
160	Imran Nazir	Pakistan v Zimbabwe	Kingston	2006-07
160	T.M.Dilshan	Sri Lanka v India	Rajkot	2009-10
159*	D.Mongia	India v Zimbabwe	Gauhati	2001-02
158	D.I.Gower	England v New Zealand	Brisbane	1982-83
158	M.L.Hayden	Australia v West Indies	North Sound	2006-07
158	A.J.Strauss	England v India	Bangalore	2010-11
157*	X.M.Marshall	West Indies v Canada	King City (NW)	2008
157	S.T.Jayasuriya	Sri Lanka v Netherlands	Amstelveen	2006
156	B.C.Lara	West Indies v Pakistan	Adelaide	2004-05
156	A.Symonds	Australia v New Zealand	Wellington	2005-06
156	H.Masakadza	Zimbabwe v Kenya	Harare	2009-10
154	A.C.Gilchrist	Australia v Sri Lanka	Melbourne	1998-99
154	Tamim Iqbal	Bangladesh v Zimbabwe	Bulawayo	2009
154	A.J.Strauss	England v Bangladesh	Birmingham	2010
153*	I.V.A.Richards	West Indies v Australia	Melbourne	1979-80
153*	M.Azharuddin	India v Zimbabwe	Cuttack	1997-98
153*	S.C.Ganguly	India v New Zealand	Gwalior	1999-00
153*	C.H.Gayle	West Indies v Zimbabwe	Bulawayo	2003-04
153	B.C.Lara	West Indies v Pakistan	Sharjah	1993-94
153	R.S.Dravid	India v New Zealand	Hyderabad	1999-00
153	H.H.Gibbs	South Africa v Bangladesh	Potchefstroom	2002-03
152*	D.L.Haynes	West Indies v India	Georgetown	1988-89
152*	C.H.Gayle	West Indies v South Africa	Johannesburg	2003-04
152	C.H.Gayle	West Indies v Kenya	Nairobi	2001-02
152	S.R.Tendulkar	India v Namibia	Pietermaritzburg	2002-03
152	A.J.Strauss	England v Bangladesh	Nottingham	2005
152	S.T.Jayasuriya	Sri Lanka v England	Leeds	2006
151*	S.T.Jayasuriya	Sri Lanka v India	Bombay	1996-97
151	A.Symonds	Australia v Sri Lanka	Sydney	2005-06
150*	G.Gambhir	India v Sri Lanka	Kolkata	2009-10
150	S.Chanderpaul	West Indies v South Africa	East London	1998-99
150	G.Gambhir	India v Sri Lanka	Colombo (RPS)	2008-09
150	H.M.Amla	South Africa v England	Southampton	2012

HUNDRED ON DEBUT

D.L.Amiss	103	England v Australia	Manchester	1972
D.L.Haynes	148	West Indies v Australia	St John's	1977-78
A.Flower	115*	Zimbabwe v Sri Lanka	New Plymouth	1991-92
Salim Elahi	102*	Pakistan v Sri Lanka	Gujranwala	1995-96
M.J.Guptill	122*	New Zealand v West Indies	Auckland	2008-09
C.A.Ingram	124	South Africa v Zimbabwe	Bloemfontein	2010-11
R.J.Nicol	108*	New Zealand v Zimbabwe	Harare	2011-12
P.J.Hughes	112	Australia v Sri Lanka	Melbourne	2012-13

Shahid Afridi scored 102 for P v SL, Nairobi, 1996-97, in his second match having not batted in his first.

| Fastest 100 | 37 balls | Shahid Afridi (102) | P v SL | Nairobi | 1996-97 |
| Fastest 50 | 17 balls | S.T.Jayasuriya (76) | SL v P | Singapore | 1995-96 |

CARRYING BAT THROUGH INNINGS (SIDE ALL OUT)

G.W.Flower	84*	Zimbabwe (205) v England	Sydney	1994-95
Saeed Anwar	103*	Pakistan (219) v Zimbabwe	Harare	1994-95
N.V.Knight	125*	England (246) v Pakistan	Nottingham	1996
R.D.Jacobs	49*	West Indies (110) v Australia	Manchester	1999
D.R.Martyn	116*	Australia (191) v New Zealand	Auckland	1999-00
H.H.Gibbs	59*	South Africa (101†) v Pakistan	Sharjah	1999-00
A.J.Stewart	100*	England (192) v West Indies	Nottingham	2000
Javed Omar	33*	Bangladesh (103) v Zimbabwe	Harare	2000-01
Azhar Ali	81*	Pakistan (199) v Sri Lanka	Colombo (RPS)	2012

† One batsman retired hurt.

5000 RUNS IN A CAREER

		LOI	I	NO	HS	Runs	Avge	100	50
S.R.Tendulkar	I	463	452	41	200*	18426	44.83	49	96
R.T.Ponting	A/ICC	375	365	39	164	13704	42.03	30	82
S.T.Jayasuriya	SL/Asia	445	433	18	189	13430	32.36	28	68
Inzamam-ul-Haq	P/Asia	378	350	53	137*	11739	39.52	10	83
J.H.Kallis	SA/Af/ICC	321	307	53	139	11498	45.26	17	85
S.C.Ganguly	I/Asia	311	300	23	183	11363	41.02	22	72
K.C.Sangakkara	SL/Asia/ICC	337	316	33	138*	10915	38.56	14	73
D.P.M.D.Jayawardena	SL/Asia	391	365	37	144	10892	33.20	15	68
R.S.Dravid	I/Asia/ICC	344	318	40	153	10889	39.16	12	83
B.C.Lara	WI/ICC	299	289	32	169	10405	40.48	19	63
Mohammad Yousuf	P/Asia	288	272	40	141*	9720	41.71	15	64
A.C.Gilchrist	A/ICC	287	279	11	172	9619	35.89	16	55
M.Azharuddin	I	334	308	54	153*	9378	36.92	7	58
P.A.de Silva	SL	308	296	30	145	9284	34.90	11	64
Saeed Anwar	P	247	244	19	194	8824	39.21	20	43
S.Chanderpaul	WI	268	251	40	150	8778	41.60	11	59
D.L.Haynes	WI	238	237	28	152*	8648	41.37	17	57
M.S.Atapattu	SL	268	259	32	132*	8529	37.57	11	59
M.E.Waugh	A	244	236	20	173	8500	39.35	18	50
C.H.Gayle	WI/ICC	242	237	17	153*	8442	38.37	20	45
V.Sehwag	I/Asia/ICC	251	245	9	219	8273	35.05	15	38
Yuvraj Singh	I/Asia	282	260	38	139	8211	36.98	13	50
H.H.Gibbs	SA	248	240	16	175	8094	36.13	21	37
S.P.Fleming	NZ/ICC	280	269	21	134*	8037	32.40	8	49
S.R.Waugh	A	325	288	58	120*	7569	32.90	3	45
A.Ranatunga	SL	269	255	47	131*	7456	35.84	4	49
Javed Miandad	P	233	218	41	119*	7381	41.70	8	50
M.J.Clarke	A	227	207	42	130	7375	44.69	7	54
M.S.Dhoni	I/Asia	219	196	56	183*	7259	51.85	8	48
Salim Malik	P	283	256	38	102	7170	32.88	5	47
N.J.Astle	NZ	223	217	14	145*	7090	34.92	16	41
Shahid Afridi	P/Asia/ICC	349	323	20	124	7075	23.34	6	33
T.M.Dilshan	SL	255	230	34	160*	7006	35.74	14	29
M.G.Bevan	A	232	196	67	108*	6912	53.58	6	46
Younus Khan	P	248	238	23	144	6898	32.08	6	48
G.C.Smith	SA/Afr	189	186	10	141	6887	39.13	10	47
G.Kirsten	SA	185	185	19	188*	6798	40.95	13	45
A.Flower	Z	213	208	16	145	6786	35.34	4	55
I.V.A.Richards	WI	187	167	24	189*	6721	47.00	11	45
G.W.Flower	Z	221	214	18	142*	6571	33.52	6	40
Ijaz Ahmed	P	250	232	29	139*	6564	32.33	10	37
A.R.Border	A	273	252	39	127*	6524	30.62	3	39
R.B.Richardson	WI	224	217	30	122	6248	33.41	5	44
M.L.Hayden	A/ICC	161	155	15	181*	6133	43.80	10	36
D.M.Jones	A	164	161	25	145	6068	44.61	7	46
D.C.Boon	A	181	177	16	122	5964	37.04	5	37
J.N.Rhodes	SA	245	220	51	121	5935	35.11	2	33

		LOI	I	NO	HS	Runs	Avge	100	50
Ramiz Raja	P	198	197	15	119*	**5841**	32.09	9	31
R.R.Sarwan	WI	179	167	33	120*	**5802**	43.29	5	38
C.L.Hooper	WI	227	206	43	113*	**5761**	35.34	7	29
W.J.Cronje	SA	188	175	31	112	**5565**	38.64	2	39
M.E.K.Hussey	A	185	157	44	109*	**5442**	48.15	3	39
A.Jadeja	I	196	179	36	119	**5359**	37.47	6	30
D.R.Martyn	A	208	182	51	144*	**5346**	40.80	5	37
Shoaib Malik	P	206	183	22	143	**5316**	33.01	7	31
G.Gambhir	I	147	143	11	150*	**5238**	39.68	11	34
A.D.R.Campbell	Z	188	184	14	131*	**5185**	30.50	7	30
A.B.de Villiers	SA	133	128	22	146	**5175**	48.82	13	29
R.S.Mahanama	SL	213	198	23	119*	**5162**	29.49	4	35
C.G.Greenidge	WI	128	127	13	133*	**5134**	45.03	11	31
P.D.Collingwood	E	197	181	37	120*	**5092**	35.36	5	26
A.Symonds	A	198	161	33	156	**5088**	39.75	6	30
Abdul Razzaq	P/Asia	265	228	57	112	**5080**	29.70	3	23

The most for Bangladesh 3635 in 121 innings by Shakib Al Hasan.

15 HUNDREDS

		Inns	100	E	A	SA	WI	NZ	I	P	SL	Z	B	Ass
S.R.Tendulkar	I	452	**49**	2	9	5	4	5	–	5	8	5	1	5
R.T.Ponting	A	365	**30***	5	–	2	2	6	6	1	4	1	1	3
S.T.Jayasuriya	SL	433	**28**	4	2	–	1	5	7	3	–	1	4	1
S.C.Ganguly	I	300	**22**	1	1	3	–	3	–	2	4	3	1	4
H.H.Gibbs	SA	240	**21**	2	3	–	5	2	2	2	1	3	–	1
C.H.Gayle	WI	237	**20**	5	2	2	–	2	4	2	–	2	1	3
Saeed Anwar	P	244	**20**	–	1	2	2	–	4	–	7	2	–	–
B.C.Lara	WI	289	**19**	1	3	3	–	2	–	5	2	1	1	1
M.E.Waugh	A	236	**18**	1	–	2	3	3	3	1	1	3	–	1
D.L.Haynes	WI	237	**17**	4	3	2	–	3	2	1	1	–	–	–
J.H.Kallis	SA	307	**17**	1	1	–	4	3	2	1	3	1	1	–
N.J.Astle	NZ	217	**16**	2	1	1	1	–	5	2	–	3	1	–
A.C.Gilchrist	A	279	**16***	2	–	3	2	1	–	1	–	6	1	–
V.Sehwag	I	245	**15**	1	1	–	2	–	–	3	2	1	2	3
Mohammad Yousuf	P	273	**15**	–	1	2	2	4	3	–	2	–	1	–
D.P.M.D.Jayawardena	SL	365	**15***	1	–	1	2	1	2	2	–	1	1	1

* = Includes hundred scored against multi-national side. The most for England is 12 by M.E.Trescothick (in 122 innings), for Zimbabwe 7 by A.D.R.Campbell (184), and for Bangladesh 5 by Shakib Al Hasan (121).

HIGHEST PARTNERSHIP FOR EACH WICKET

1st	286	W.U.Tharanga/S.T.Jayasuriya	Sri Lanka v England	Leeds	2006
2nd	331	S.R.Tendulkar/R.S.Dravid	India v New Zealand	Hyderabad (Ind)	1999-00
3rd	237*	R.S.Dravid/S.R.Tendulkar	India v Kenya	Bristol	1999
4th	275*	M.Azharuddin/A.Jadeja	India v Zimbabwe	Cuttack	1997-98
5th	223	M.Azharuddin/A.Jadeja	India v Sri Lanka	Colombo (RPS)	1997-98
6th	218	D.P.M.D.Jayawardena/M.S.Dhoni	Asia XI v Africa XI	Chennai	2007
7th	130	A.Flower/H.H.Streak	Zimbabwe v England	Harare	2001-02
8th	138*	J.M.Kemp/A.J.Hall	South Africa v India	Cape Town	2006-07
9th	132	A.D.Mathews/S.L.Malinga	Sri Lanka v Australia	Melbourne	2010-11
10th	106*	I.V.A.Richards/M.A.Holding	West Indies v England	Manchester	1984

BOWLING RECORDS
SIX WICKETS IN AN INNINGS

8-19	W.P.J.U.C.Vaas	Sri Lanka v Zimbabwe	Colombo (SSC)	2001-02
7-15	G.D.McGrath	Australia v Namibia	Potchefstroom	2002-03
7-20	A.J.Bichel	Australia v England	Port Elizabeth	2002-03
7-30	M.Muralitharan	Sri Lanka v India	Sharjah	2000-01
7-36	Waqar Younis	Pakistan v England	Leeds	2001
7-37	Aqib Javed	Pakistan v India	Sharjah	1991-92

7-51	W.W.Davis	West Indies v Australia	Leeds	1983
6-12	A.Kumble	India v West Indies	Calcutta	1993-94
6-13	B.A.W.Mendis	Sri Lanka v India	Karachi	2008
6-14	G.J.Gilmour	Australia v England	Leeds	1975
6-14	Imran Khan	Pakistan v India	Sharjah	1984-85
6-14	M.F.Maharoof	Sri Lanka v West Indies	Mumbai	2006-07
6-15	C.E.H.Croft	West Indies v Pakistan	Kingstown	1980-81
6-16	Shoaib Akhtar	Pakistan v New Zealand	Karachi	2001-02
6-18	Azhar Mahmood	Pakistan v West Indies	Sharjah	1999-00
6-19	H.K.Olonga	Zimbabwe v England	Cape Town	1999-00
6-19	S.E.Bond	New Zealand v Zimbabwe	Harare	2005
6-20	B.C.Strang	Zimbabwe v Bangladesh	Nairobi	1997-98
6-20	A.D.Mathews	Sri Lanka v India	Colombo (RPS)	2009-10
6-22	F.H.Edwards	West Indies v Zimbabwe	Harare	2003-04
6-22	M.Ntini	South Africa v Australia	Cape Town	2005-06
6-23	A.A.Donald	South Africa v Kenya	Nairobi	1996-97
6-23	A.Nehra	India v England	Durban	2002-03
6-23	S.E.Bond	New Zealand v Australia	Port Elizabeth	2002-03
6-25	S.B.Styris	New Zealand v West Indies	Port-of-Spain	2002
6-25	W.P.J.U.C.Vaas	Sri Lanka v Bangladesh	Pietermaritzburg	2002-03
6-26	Waqar Younis	Pakistan v Sri Lanka	Sharjah	1989-90
6-26	Mashrafe Mortaza	Bangladesh v Kenya	Nairobi	2006
6-27	Naved-ul-Hasan	Pakistan v India	Jamshedpur	2004-05
6-27	C.R.D.Fernando	Sri Lanka v England	Colombo (RPS)	2007-08
6-27	M.Kartik	India v Australia	Mumbai	2007-08
6-27	K.A.J.Roach	West Indies v Netherlands	Delhi	2010-11
6-28	H.K.Olonga	Zimbabwe v Kenya	Bulawayo	2002-03
6-29	B.P.Patterson	West Indies v India	Nagpur	1987-88
6-29	S.T.Jayasuriya	Sri Lanka v England	Moratuwa	1992-93
6-29	B.A.W.Mendis	Sri Lanka v Zimbabwe	Harare	2008-09
6-30	Waqar Younis	Pakistan v New Zealand	Auckland	1993-94
6-31	P.D.Collingwood	England v Bangladesh	Nottingham	2005
6-31	M.G.Johnson	Australia v Sri Lanka	Pallekele	2011
6-35	S.M.Pollock	South Africa v West Indies	East London	1998-99
6-35	Abdul Razzaq	Pakistan v Bangladesh	Dhaka	2001-02
6-38	Shahid Afridi	Pakistan v Australia	Dubai	2009
6-38	S.L.Malinga	Sri Lanka v Kenya	Colombo (RPS)	2010-11
6-39	K.H.MacLeay	Australia v India	Nottingham	1983
6-41	I.V.A.Richards	West Indies v India	Delhi	1989-90
6-42	A.B.Agarkar	India v Australia	Melbourne	2003-04
6-42	Umar Gul	Pakistan v England	The Oval	2010
6-43	D.J.Bravo	West Indies v Zimbabwe	St George's	2012-13
6-44	Waqar Younis	Pakistan v New Zealand	Sharjah	1996-97
6-44	N.L.T.C.Perera	Sri Lanka v Pakistan	Pallekele	2012
6-45	C.R.Woakes	England v Australia	Brisbane	2010-11
6-46	A.G.Cremer	Zimbabwe v Kenya	Harare	2009-10
6-49	L.Klusener	South Africa v Sri Lanka	Lahore	1997-98
6-50	A.H.Gray	West Indies v Australia	Port-of-Spain	1990-91
6-52	C.B.Mpofu	Zimbabwe v Kenya	Nairobi (Gym)	2008-09
6-55	S.Sreesanth	India v England	Indore	2005-06
6-59	Waqar Younis	Pakistan v Australia	Nottingham	2001
6-59	A.Nehra	India v Sri Lanka	Colombo (RPS)	2005

150 WICKETS IN A CAREER

		LOI	Balls	R	W	Avge	Best	5w	R/Over
M.Muralitharan	SL/Asia/ICC	350	18811	12326	534	23.08	7-30	10	3.93
Wasim Akram	P	356	18186	11812	502	23.52	5-15	6	3.89
Waqar Younis	P	262	12698	9919	416	23.84	7-36	13	4.68
W.P.J.U.C.Vaas	SL/Asia	322	15775	11014	400	27.53	8-19	4	4.18
S.M.Pollock	SA/Afr/ICC	303	15712	9631	393	24.50	6-35	5	3.67
G.D.McGrath	A/ICC	250	12970	8391	381	22.02	7-15	7	3.88
B.Lee	A	221	11185	8877	380	23.36	5-22	9	4.76
Shahid Afridi	P/Asia/ICC	349	15276	11727	348	33.69	6-38	8	4.60
A.Kumble	I/Asia	271	14496	10412	337	30.89	6-12	2	4.30
S.T.Jayasuriya	SL	445	14874	11871	323	36.75	6-29	4	4.78

		LOI	Balls	R	W	Avge	Best	5w	R/Over
J.Srinath	I	229	11935	8847	315	28.08	5-23	3	4.44
S.K.Warne	A/ICC	194	10642	7541	293	25.73	5-33	1	4.25
Saqlain Mushtaq	P	169	8770	6275	288	21.78	5-20	6	4.29
A.B.Agarkar	I	191	9484	8021	288	27.85	6-42	2	5.07
Z.Khan	I/Asia	200	10097	8301	282	29.43	5-42	1	4.93
D.L.Vettori	NZ/ICC	272	12903	8880	282	31.48	5- 7	2	4.12
A.A.Donald	SA	164	8561	5926	272	21.78	6-23	2	4.15
J.H.Kallis	SA/Afr/ICC	321	10636	8558	270	31.69	5-30	2	4.82
Abdul Razzaq	P/Asia	265	10941	8564	269	31.83	6-35	3	4.69
M.Ntini	SA/ICC	173	8687	6559	266	24.65	6-22	4	4.53
Harbhajan Singh	I/Asia	229	12059	8651	259	33.40	5-31	3	4.30
Kapil Dev	I	225	11202	6945	253	27.45	5-43	1	3.72
Shoaib Akhtar	P/Asia/ICC	163	7764	6169	247	24.97	6-16	4	4.76
H.H.Streak	Z/Afr	189	9468	7129	239	29.82	5-32	1	4.51
D.Gough	E/ICC	159	8470	6209	235	26.42	5-44	2	4.39
J.M.Anderson	E	167	8273	6885	229	30.06	5-23	2	4.99
C.A.Walsh	WI	205	10822	6918	227	30.47	5- 1	1	3.83
C.E.L.Ambrose	WI	176	9353	5429	225	24.12	5-17	4	3.48
K.D.Mills	NZ	147	7188	5628	214	26.29	5-25	1	4.69
S.L.Malinga	SL	136	6661	5621	213	26.38	6-38	5	5.06
C.J.McDermott	A	138	7460	5018	203	24.71	5-44	1	4.03
C.Z.Harris	NZ	250	10667	7613	203	37.50	5-42	1	4.28
C.L.Cairns	NZ/ICC	215	8168	6594	201	32.80	5-42	1	4.84
B.K.V.Prasad	I	161	8129	6332	196	32.30	5-27	1	4.67
Abdur Razzak	B	138	7227	5382	195	27.60	5-29	3	4.46
S.R.Waugh	A	325	8883	6761	195	34.67	4-33	–	4.56
C.L.Hooper	WI	227	9573	6958	193	36.05	4-34	–	4.36
L.Klusener	SA	171	7336	5751	192	29.95	6-49	6	4.70
M.G.Johnson	A	121	5882	4732	188	25.17	6-31	3	4.82
C.R.D.Fernando	SL/Asia	147	6507	5648	187	30.20	6-27	1	5.20
Imran Khan	P	175	7461	4844	182	26.61	6-14	1	3.89
Aqib Javed	P	163	8012	5721	182	31.43	7-37	4	4.28
N.W.Bracken	A	116	5759	4240	174	24.36	5-47	2	4.41
J.D.P.Oram	NZ	160	6911	5047	173	29.17	5-26	2	4.38
I.K.Pathan	I	120	5855	5142	173	29.72	5-27	2	5.26
A.Flintoff	E/ICC	141	5624	4121	169	24.38	5-19	2	4.39
Mashrafe Mortaza	B/Asia	128	6411	4990	162	30.80	6-26	1	4.67
Umar Gul	P	114	5317	4499	161	27.94	6-42	2	5.07
Mushtaq Ahmed	P	144	7543	5361	161	33.29	5-36	1	4.26
Shakib Al Hasan	B	126	6452	4617	160	28.85	4-16	–	4.29
D.J.Bravo	WI	137	5425	4811	160	30.06	6-43	1	5.32
R.J.Hadlee	NZ	115	6182	3407	158	21.56	5-25	5	3.31
M.D.Marshall	WI	136	7175	4233	157	26.96	4-18	–	3.54
M.Prabhakar	I	130	6360	4534	157	28.87	5-33	2	4.27
A.Nehra	I/Asia	120	5751	4981	157	31.72	6-23	2	5.19
C.H.Gayle	WI/ICC	242	7026	5545	157	35.31	5-46	1	4.73
G.B.Hogg	A	123	5564	4188	156	26.84	5-32	2	4.51
S.R.Watson	A	157	5586	4470	155	28.83	4-36	–	4.80
S.R.Tendulkar	I	463	8054	6850	154	44.48	5-32	2	5.10
S.C.J.Broad	E	96	4897	4242	152	27.90	5-23	1	5.19
U.D.U.Chandana	SL	147	6142	4818	151	31.90	5-61	1	4.70

HAT-TRICKS

Jalaluddin	Pakistan v Australia	Hyderabad	1982-83
B.A.Reid	Australia v New Zealand	Sydney	1985-86
C.Sharma	India v New Zealand	Nagpur	1987-88
Wasim Akram	Pakistan v West Indies	Sharjah	1989-90
Wasim Akram	Pakistan v Australia	Sharjah	1989-90
Kapil Dev	India v Sri Lanka	Calcutta	1990-91
Aqib Javed	Pakistan v India	Sharjah	1991-92
D.K.Morrison	New Zealand v India	Napier	1993-94
Waqar Younis	Pakistan v New Zealand	East London	1994-95
Saqlain Mushtaq	Pakistan v Zimbabwe	Peshawar	1996-97

E.A.Brandes	Zimbabwe v England	Harare	1996-97
A.M.Stuart	Australia v Pakistan	Melbourne	1996-97
Saqlain Mushtaq	Pakistan v Zimbabwe	The Oval	1999
W.P.J.U.C.Vaas	Sri Lanka v Zimbabwe	Colombo (SSC)	2001-02
Mohammad Sami	Pakistan v West Indies	Sharjah	2001-02
W.P.J.U.C.Vaas[1]	Sri Lanka v Bangladesh	Pietermaritzburg	2002-03
B.Lee	Australia v Kenya	Durban	2002-03
J.M.Anderson	England v Pakistan	The Oval	2003
S.J.Harmison	England v India	Nottingham	2004
C.K.Langeveldt	South Africa v West Indies	Bridgetown	2004-05
Shahadat Hossain	Bangladesh v Zimbabwe	Harare	2006
J.E.Taylor	West Indies v Australia	Mumbai	2006-07
S.E.Bond	New Zealand v Australia	Hobart	2006-07
S.L.Malinga[2]	Sri Lanka v South Africa	Providence	2006-07
A.Flintoff	England v West Indies	St Lucia	2008-09
M.F.Maharoof	Sri Lanka v India	Dambulla	2010
Abdur Razzak	Bangladesh v Zimbabwe	Dhaka	2010-11
K.A.J.Roach	West Indies v Netherlands	Delhi	2010-11
S.L.Malinga	Sri Lanka v Kenya	Colombo (RPS)	2010-11
S.L.Malinga	Sri Lanka v Australia	Colombo (RPS)	2011
D.T.Christian	Australia v Sri Lanka	Melbourne	2011-12
N.L.T.C.Perera	Sri Lanka v Pakistan	Colombo (RPS)	2012

[1] The first three balls of the match. Took four wickets in opening over (W W W 4 wide W 0).
[2] Four wickets in four balls.

WICKET-KEEPING RECORDS
SIX DISMISSALS IN AN INNINGS

6	(6ct)	A.C.Gilchrist	Australia v South Africa	Cape Town	1999-00
6	(6ct)	A.J.Stewart	England v Zimbabwe	Manchester	2000
6	(5ct/1st)	R.D.Jacobs	West Indies v Sri Lanka	Colombo (RPS)	2001-02
6	(5ct/1st)	A.C.Gilchrist	Australia v England	Sydney	2002-03
6	(6ct)	A.C.Gilchrist	Australia v Namibia	Potchefstroom	2002-03
6	(6ct)	A.C.Gilchrist	Australia v Sri Lanka	Colombo (RPS)	2003-04
6	(6ct)	M.V.Boucher	South Africa v Pakistan	Cape Town	2006-07
6	(5ct/1st)	M.S.Dhoni	India v England	Leeds	2007
6	(6ct)	A.C.Gilchrist	Australia v India	Baroda	2007-08
6	(5ct/1st)	A.C.Gilchrist	Australia v India	Sydney	2007-08
6	(6ct)	M.J.Prior	England v South Africa	Nottingham	2008

100 DISMISSALS IN A CAREER

Total			LOI	Ct	St
472‡	A.C.Gilchrist	Australia/ICC	287	417	55
424	M.V.Boucher	South Africa/Africa	295	402	22
392†‡	K.C.Sangakkara	Sri Lanka/Asia/ICC	337	311	81
287‡	Moin Khan	Pakistan	219	214	73
274	M.S.Dhoni	India/Asia	219	206	68
238†‡	B.B.McCullum	New Zealand	212	223	15
233	I.A.Healy	Australia	168	194	39
220‡	Rashid Latif	Pakistan	166	182	38
206‡	R.S.Kaluwitharana	Sri Lanka	187	131	75
204‡	P.J.L.Dujon	West Indies	169	183	21
189	R.D.Jacobs	West Indies	147	160	29
169	Kamran Akmal	Pakistan	143	140	29
165	D.J.Richardson	South Africa	122	148	17
165†‡	A.Flower	Zimbabwe	213	133	32
163†‡	A.J.Stewart	England	170	148	15
154‡	N.R.Mongia	India	140	110	44
145	T.Taibu	Zimbabwe/Africa	150	112	33
142	B.J.Haddin	Australia	96	133	9
136†‡	A.C.Parore	New Zealand	179	111	25
131	D.Ramdin	West Indies	97	125	6

Total			LOI	Ct	St
126	Khaled Masud	Bangladesh	126	91	35
124	R.W.Marsh	Australia	92	120	4
115	Mushfiqur Rahim	Bangladesh	113	82	33
103	Salim Yousuf	Pakistan	86	81	22

† Excluding catches taken in the field. ‡ Excluding matches when not wicket-keeper.

FIELDING RECORDS
FIVE CATCHES IN AN INNINGS

5	J.N.Rhodes	South Africa v West Indies	Bombay (BS)	1993-94

100 CATCHES IN A CAREER

Total			LOI
195	D.P.M.D.Jayawardena	Sri Lanka/Asia	391
160	R.T.Ponting	Australia/ICC	375
156	M.Azharuddin	India	334
140	S.R.Tendulkar	India	463
133	S.P.Fleming	New Zealand/ICC	280
130	M.Muralitharan	Sri Lanka/Asia/ICC	350
127	A.R.Border	Australia	273
125	J.H.Kallis	South Africa/Africa/ICC	321
124	R.S.Dravid	India/Asia/ICC	344
123	Younus Khan	Pakistan	248
123	S.T.Jayasuriya	Sri Lanka/Asia	445
120	C.L.Hooper	West Indies	227
120	B.C.Lara	West Indies/ICC	299
113	Inzamam-ul-Haq	Pakistan/Asia	378
112	Shahid Afridi	Pakistan/Asia/ICC	349
111	S.R.Waugh	Australia	325
109	R.S.Mahanama	Sri Lanka	213
108	P.D.Collingwood	England	197
108	M.E.Waugh	Australia	244
108	H.H.Gibbs	South Africa	248
108	S.M.Pollock	South Africa/Africa/ICC	303
105	M.E.K.Hussey	Australia	185
105	C.H.Gayle	West Indies/ICC	242
105	J.N.Rhodes	South Africa	245
100	I.V.A.Richards	West Indies	187
100	G.C.Smith	South Africa/Africa	189
100	S.C.Ganguly	India/Asia	311

The most for Zimbabwe is 86 by G.W.Flower (221), and for Bangladesh 38 by Mashrafe Mortaza (126).

ALL-ROUND RECORDS
50 RUNS AND 5 WICKETS IN A MATCH

I.V.A.Richards	119	5-41	West Indies v New Zealand	Dunedin	1986-87
K.Srikkanth	70	5-27	India v New Zealand	Vishakhapatnam	1988-89
M.E.Waugh	57	5-24	Australia v West Indies	Melbourne	1992-93
L.Klusener	54	6-49	South Africa v Sri Lanka	Lahore	1997-98
Abdul Razzaq	70*	5-48	Pakistan v India	Hobart	1999-2000
G.A.Hick	80	5-33	England v Zimbabwe	Harare	1999-2000
Shahid Afridi	61	5-40	Pakistan v England	Lahore	2000-01
S.C.Ganguly	71*	5-34	India v Zimbabwe	Kanpur	2000-01
S.B.Styris	63*	6-25	New Zealand v West Indies	Port-of-Spain	2002
R.C.Irani	53	5-26	England v India	The Oval	2002
C.H.Gayle	60	5-46	West Indies v Australia	St George's	2002-03
P.D.Collingwood	112*	6-31	England v Bangladesh	Nottingham	2005
S.Dhaniram	79	5-32	Canada v Bermuda	King City (NW)	2008
Yuvraj Singh	50*	5-31	India v Ireland	Bangalore	2010-11
Shahid Afridi	75	5-35	Pakistan v Sri Lanka	Sharjah	2011-12

APPEARANCE RECORDS
250 MATCHES

463	S.R.Tendulkar	India		288	Mohammad Yousuf	Pakistan/Asia
445	S.T.Jayasuriya	Sri Lanka/Asia		287	A.C.Gilchrist	Australia/ICC
391	D.P.M.D.Jayawardena	Sri Lanka/Asia		283	Salim Malik	Pakistan
378	Inzamam-ul-Haq	Pakistan/Asia		282	Yuvraj Singh	India/Asia
375	R.T.Ponting	Australia/ICC		280	S.P.Fleming	New Zealand/ICC
356	Wasim Akram	Pakistan		273	A.R.Border	Australia
350	M.Muralitharan	Sri Lanka/Asia/ICC		272	D.L.Vettori	New Zealand/ICC
349	Shahid Afridi	Pakistan/Asia/ICC		271	A.Kumble	India/Asia
344	R.S.Dravid	India/Asia/ICC		269	A.Ranatunga	Sri Lanka
337	K.C.Sangakkara	Sri Lanka/Asia/ICC		268	M.S.Atapattu	Sri Lanka
334	M.Azharuddin	India		268	S.Chanderpaul	West Indies
325	S.R.Waugh	Australia		265	Abdul Razzaq	Pakistan/Asia
322	W.P.J.U.C.Vaas	Sri Lanka/Asia		262	Waqar Younis	Pakistan
321	J.H.Kallis	South Africa/Africa/ICC		255	T.M.Dilshan	Sri Lanka
311	S.C.Ganguly	India/Asia		251	V.Sehwag	India/Asia/ICC
308	P.A.de Silva	Sri Lanka		250	C.Z.Harris	New Zealand
303	S.M.Pollock	South Africa/Africa		250	Ijaz Ahmed	Pakistan
299	B.C.Lara	West Indies/ICC		250	G.D.McGrath	Australia/ICC
295	M.V.Boucher	South Africa/Africa				

The most for England is 197 by P.D.Collingwood, for Zimbabwe 221 by G.W.Flower, and for Bangladesh 162 by Mohammad Ashraful.

The most consecutive appearances is 185 by S.R.Tendulkar for India (Apr 1990-Apr 1998).

100 MATCHES AS CAPTAIN

LOI			W	L	T	NR	% Won (exc NR)
230	R.T.Ponting	Australia/ICC	165	51	2	12	75.68
218	S.P.Fleming	New Zealand	98	106	1	13	47.80
193	A.Ranatunga	Sri Lanka	89	95	1	8	48.10
178	A.R.Border	Australia	107	67	1	3	61.14
174	M.Azharuddin	India	90	76	2	6	53.57
150	G.C.Smith	South Africa/Africa	92	51	1	6	63.88
147	S.C.Ganguly	India/Asia	76	66	–	5	53.52
139	Imran Khan	Pakistan	75	59	1	4	55.55
138	W.J.Cronje	South Africa	99	35	1	3	73.33
135	M.S.Dhoni	India	77	47	3	8	60.62
129	D.P.M.D.Jayawardena	Sri Lanka	71	49	1	8	58.67
125	B.C.Lara	West Indies	59	59	–	7	50.42
118	S.T.Jayasuriya	Sri Lanka	66	47	2	3	57.39
109	Wasim Akram	Pakistan	66	41	2	–	60.55
106	S.R.Waugh	Australia	67	35	1	3	63.80
105	I.V.A.Richards	West Indies	67	36	–	2	65.04

The most for England is 62 by A.J.Strauss, for Zimbabwe 86 by A.D.R.Campbell, and for Bangladesh 69 by Habibul Bashar.

100 LOI UMPIRING APPEARANCES

LOI					
209	R.E.Koertzen	South Africa	09.12.1992	to	09.06.2010
181	S.A.Bucknor	West Indies	18.03.1989	to	29.03.2009
176	B.F.Bowden	New Zealand	23.03.1995	to	06.01.2013
174	D.J.Harper	Australia	14.01.1994	to	19.03.2011
174	S.J.A.Taufel	Australia	13.01.1999	to	02.09.2012
172	D.R.Shepherd	England	09.06.1983	to	12.07.2005
152	Alim Dar	Pakistan	16.02.2000	to	22.01.2013
139	D.B.Hair	Australia	14.12.1991	to	24.08.2008
126	R.B.Tiffin	Zimbabwe	25.10.1992	to	20.02.2012
122	E.A.R.de Silva	Sri Lanka	22.08.1999	to	13.06.2012
116	S.J.Davis	Australia	12.12.1992	to	27.01.2013
112	B.R.Doctrove	West Indies	04.04.1998	to	20.01.2012
107	D.L.Orchard	South Africa	02.12.1994	to	07.12.2003
100	R.S.Dunne	New Zealand	06.02.1989	to	26.02.2002

INTERNATIONAL TWENTY20 RECORDS

MATCH RESULTS

2004-05 to 28 February 2013

Opponents		Matches	E	A	SA	WI	NZ	I	P	SL	Z	B	Ass	Tied	NR
England	Australia	7	3	3	–	–	–	–	–	–	–	–	–	–	1
	South Africa	8	3	–	4	–	–	–	–	–	–	–	–	–	1
	West Indies	9	3	–	–	6	–	–	–	–	–	–	–	–	–
	New Zealand	9	7	–	–	–	2	–	–	–	–	–	–	–	–
	India	7	4	–	–	–	–	3	–	–	–	–	–	–	–
	Pakistan	10	7	–	–	–	–	–	3	–	–	–	–	–	–
	Sri Lanka	4	1	–	–	–	–	–	–	3	–	–	–	–	–
	Zimbabwe	1	1	–	–	–	–	–	–	–	0	–	–	–	–
	Bangladesh	0	0	–	–	–	–	–	–	–	–	0	–	–	–
	Associates	3	1	–	–	–	–	–	–	–	–	–	1	–	1
Australia	South Africa	9	–	5	4	–	–	–	–	–	–	–	–	–	–
	West Indies	10	–	5	–	5	–	–	–	–	–	–	–	–	–
	New Zealand	5	–	4	–	–	0	–	–	–	–	–	–	1	–
	India	7	–	4	–	–	–	3	–	–	–	–	–	–	–
	Pakistan	11	–	4	–	–	–	–	6	–	–	–	–	1	–
	Sri Lanka	8	–	2	–	–	–	–	–	6	–	–	–	–	–
	Zimbabwe	1	–	0	–	–	–	–	–	–	1	–	–	–	–
	Bangladesh	2	–	2	–	–	–	–	–	–	–	0	–	–	–
	Associates	1	–	1	–	–	–	–	–	–	–	–	0	–	–
S Africa	West Indies	6	–	–	5	1	–	–	–	–	–	–	–	–	–
	New Zealand	11	–	–	8	–	3	–	–	–	–	–	–	–	–
	India	7	–	–	2	–	–	5	–	–	–	–	–	–	–
	Pakistan	6	–	–	3	–	–	–	3	–	–	–	–	–	–
	Sri Lanka	1	–	–	1	–	–	–	–	0	–	–	–	–	–
	Zimbabwe	3	–	–	3	–	–	–	–	–	0	–	–	–	–
	Bangladesh	2	–	–	2	–	–	–	–	–	–	0	–	–	–
	Associates	2	–	–	2	–	–	–	–	–	–	–	0	–	–
W Indies	New Zealand	6	–	–	–	2	1	–	–	–	–	–	–	3	–
	India	3	–	–	–	2	–	1	–	–	–	–	–	–	–
	Pakistan	1	–	–	–	1	–	–	0	–	–	–	–	–	–
	Sri Lanka	5	–	–	–	1	–	–	–	4	–	–	–	–	–
	Zimbabwe	1	–	–	–	0	–	–	–	–	1	–	–	–	–
	Bangladesh	4	–	–	–	2	–	–	–	–	–	2	–	–	–
	Associates	2	–	–	–	1	–	–	–	–	–	–	0	–	1
N Zealand	India	4	–	–	–	–	4	0	–	–	–	–	–	–	–
	Pakistan	9	–	–	–	–	3	–	6	–	–	–	–	–	–
	Sri Lanka	11	–	–	–	–	5	–	–	4	–	–	–	1	1
	Zimbabwe	5	–	–	–	–	5	–	–	–	0	–	–	–	–
	Bangladesh	2	–	–	–	–	2	–	–	–	–	0	–	–	–
	Associates	3	–	–	–	–	3	–	–	–	–	–	0	–	–
India	Pakistan	5	–	–	–	–	–	3	1	–	–	–	–	1	–
	Sri Lanka	5	–	–	–	–	–	3	–	2	–	–	–	–	–
	Zimbabwe	2	–	–	–	–	–	2	–	–	0	–	–	–	–
	Bangladesh	1	–	–	–	–	–	1	–	–	–	0	–	–	–
	Associates	4	–	–	–	–	–	3	–	–	–	–	0	–	1
Pakistan	Sri Lanka	10	–	–	–	–	–	–	6	4	–	–	–	–	–
	Zimbabwe	3	–	–	–	–	–	–	3	–	0	–	–	–	–
	Bangladesh	6	–	–	–	–	–	–	6	–	–	0	–	–	–
	Associates	5	–	–	–	–	–	–	5	–	–	–	0	–	–
Sri Lanka	Zimbabwe	3	–	–	–	–	–	–	–	3	0	–	–	–	–
	Bangladesh	1	–	–	–	–	–	–	–	1	–	0	–	–	–
	Associates	3	–	–	–	–	–	–	–	3	–	–	0	–	–
Zimbabwe	Bangladesh	1	–	–	–	–	–	–	–	–	0	1	–	–	–
	Associates	2	–	–	–	–	–	–	–	–	1	–	0	1	–
Bangladesh	Associates	8	–	–	–	–	–	–	–	–	–	5	3	–	–
Associates	Associates	39	–	–	–	–	–	–	–	–	–	–	38	–	1
		304	30	30	34	21	28	24	39	30	3	8	42	8	7

MATCH RESULTS SUMMARY

	Matches	Won	Lost	Tied	NR	Win %
South Africa	55	34	20	0	1	62.96
Sri Lanka	51	30	19	1	1	60.00
Netherlands	16	9	6	0	1	60.00
Pakistan	66	39	25	2	0	59.09
Ireland	30	15	12	0	3	55.55
England	58	30	25	0	3	54.54
India	45	24	19	1	1	54.54
Australia	61	30	28	2	1	50.00
Afghanistan	13	6	7	0	0	46.15
West Indies	47	21	22	3	1	45.65
New Zealand	65	28	31	5	1	43.75
Scotland	17	5	11	0	1	31.25
Bangladesh	27	8	19	0	0	29.62
Kenya	17	4	13	0	0	23.52
Canada	15	3	11	1	0	20.00
Zimbabwe	22	3	18	1	0	13.63
Bermuda	3	0	3	0	0	0.00

INTERNATIONAL TWENTY20 RECORDS

(To 28 February 2013)

TEAM RECORDS

HIGHEST INNINGS TOTALS

† Batting Second

260-6	Sri Lanka v Kenya	Johannesburg	2007-08
241-6	South Africa v England	Centurion	2009-10
221-5	Australia v England	Sydney	2006-07
219-4	South Africa v India	Johannesburg	2011-12
218-4	India v England	Durban	2007-08
215-5	Sri Lanka v India	Nagpur	2009-10
214-5	Australia v New Zealand	Auckland	2004-05
214-6	New Zealand v Australia	Christchurch	2009-10
214-4†	Australia v New Zealand	Christchurch	2009-10
214-7	England v New Zealand	Auckland	2012-13
211-5	South Africa v Scotland	The Oval	2009
211-4†	India v Sri Lanka	Mohali	2009-10
209-3	Australia v South Africa	Brisbane	2005-06
209-2	West Indies v New Zealand	Lauderhill	2012
208-8	West Indies v England	The Oval	2007
208-2†	South Africa v West Indies	Johannesburg	2007-08
206-7	Sri Lanka v India	Mohali	2009-10
205-6	West Indies v South Africa	Johannesburg	2007-08
205-4	West Indies v Australia	Colombo (RPS)	2012-13
203-5	Pakistan v Bangladesh	Karachi	2007-08
202-6	England v South Africa	Johannesburg	2009-10
202-5†	New Zealand v Zimbabwe	Hamilton	2011-12
201-4	South Africa v Australia	Johannesburg	2005-06
200-6†	England v India	Durban	2007-08
200-2	Zimbabwe v New Zealand	Hamilton	2011-12

The highest total for Bangladesh is 190-5 (v Ireland, Belfast, 2012).

LOWEST COMPLETED INNINGS TOTALS

† Batting Second

67	(17.2)	Kenya v Ireland	Belfast	2008
68†	(16.4)	Ireland v West Indies	Providence	2009-10
70		Bermuda v Canada	Belfast	2008
71	(19.0)	Kenya v Ireland	Dubai	2011-12
73	(16.5)	Kenya v New Zealand	Durban	2007-08
74	(17.3)	India v Australia	Melbourne	2007-08
74†	(19.1)	Pakistan v Australia	Dubai	2012
75†	(19.2)	Canada v Zimbabwe	King City (NW)	2008-09
78	(17.3)	Bangladesh v New Zealand	Hamilton	2009-10
79†	(14.3)	Australia v England	Southampton	2005
79-7†		West Indies v Zimbabwe	Port-of-Spain	2009-10
80†	(16.0)	Afghanistan v South Africa	Bridgetown	2009-10
80†	(15.5)	New Zealand v Pakistan	Christchurch	2010-11
80†	(17.2)	Afghanistan v England	Colombo (RPS)	2012-13
80†	(14.4)	England v India	Colombo (RPS)	2012-13
81†	(15.4)	Scotland v South Africa	The Oval	2009
81	(17.3)	New Zealand v Sri Lanka	Lauderhill	2010
83†	(15.5)	Bangladesh v Sri Lanka	Johannesburg	2007-08
84	(15.1)	Zimbabwe v New Zealand	Providence	2009-10
85-9†		Bangladesh v Pakistan	Dhaka	2011-12
86†	(15.3)	Netherlands v Ireland	Dubai	2009-10
86	(18.2)	New Zealand v South Africa	Durban	2012-13
87†	(16.2)	Sri Lanka v Australia	Bridgetown	2009-10

The lowest total for South Africa is 114 (v Australia, Brisbane, 2005-06).

BATTING RECORDS
750 RUNS IN A CAREER

Runs			M	I	NO	HS	Avge	50	R/100B
1814	B.B.McCullum	NZ	60	60	8	123	34.88	12	135.2
1293	D.P.M.D.Jayawardena	SL	46	46	7	100	33.15	9	133.2
1206	D.A.Warner	A	44	44	2	90*	28.71	9	139.2
1176	K.P.Pietersen	E	36	36	5	79	37.93	7	141.5
1168	M.J.Guptill	NZ	41	39	6	101*	35.39	6	124.4
1120	T.M.Dilshan	SL	48	47	7	104*	28.00	7	121.3
1080	K.C.Sangakkara	SL	43	41	5	78	30.00	6	120.9
993	C.H.Gayle	WI	32	31	3	117	35.46	11	144.3
982	G.C.Smith	SA	33	33	2	89*	31.67	5	127.5
980	S.R.Watson	A	36	35	3	81	30.62	10	148.4
952	J.P.Duminy	SA	42	39	10	96*	32.82	4	122.3
932	G.Gambhir	I	37	36	2	75	27.41	7	119.0
927	Mohammad Hafeez	P	42	40	–	71	23.17	4	114.1
876	L.R.P.L.Taylor	NZ	50	46	8	63	23.05	4	119.3
873	Shoaib Malik	P	52	48	12	57*	24.25	3	108.7
871	E.J.G.Morgan	E	35	34	10	85*	36.29	4	132.1
863	Umar Akmal	P	42	39	7	64	26.96	4	117.4
848	Kamran Akmal	P	49	44	6	73	22.31	5	123.6
845	Shahid Afridi	P	58	55	5	54*	16.90	4	142.9
840	S.K.Raina	I	36	32	7	101	33.60	4	136.1
791	Yuvraj Singh	I	33	31	5	72	30.42	6	148.6
788	Misbah-ul-Haq	P	39	34	13	87*	37.52	3	110.2
782	A.B.de Villiers	SA	44	42	7	79*	22.34	4	120.6
756	D.J.Hussey	A	39	36	3	88*	22.90	3	121.3

HIGHEST INDIVIDUAL INNINGS

Score	Balls				
123	58	B.B.McCullum	NZ v B	Pallekele	2012-13
117*	51	R.E.Levi	SA v NZ	Hamilton	2011-12
117	57	C.H.Gayle	WI v SA	Johannesburg	2007-08
116*	56	B.B.McCullum	NZ v A	Christchurch	2009-10
104*	57	T.M.Dilshan	SL v A	Pallekele	2011
101*	69	M.J.Guptill	NZ v SA	East London	2012-13
101	60	S.K.Raina	I v SA	Gros Islet	2009-10
100	64	D.P.M.D.Jayawardena	SL v Z	Providence	2009-10
100	58	R.D.Berrington	Sc v B	The Hague	2012
99*	55	L.J.Wright	E v Af	Colombo (RPS)	2012-13
99	68	A.D.Hales	E v WI	Nottingham	2012
98*	55	R.T.Ponting	A v NZ	Auckland	2004-05
98*	56	D.P.M.D.Jayawardena	SL v WI	Bridgetown	2009-10
98	66	C.H.Gayle	WI v I	Bridgetown	2009-10
96*	57	T.M.Dilshan	SL v WI	The Oval	2009
96*	54	J.P.Duminy	SA v Z	Kimberley	2010-11
96	56	D.R.Martyn	A v SA	Brisbane	2005-06
94	45	L.E.Bosman	SA v E	Centurion	2009-10
91*	54	M.J.Guptill	NZ v Z	Auckland	2011-12
91	55	B.B.McCullum	NZ v I	Chennai	2012
90*	55	H.H.Gibbs	SA v WI	Johannesburg	2007-08
90*	62	D.A.Warner	A v SL	Sydney	2012-13
89*	58	G.C.Smith	SA v A	Johannesburg	2005-06
89*	56	J.M.Kemp	SA v NZ	Durban	2007-08
89	43	D.A.Warner	A v SA	Melbourne	2008-09
88*	44	D.J.Hussey	A v SA	Johannesburg	2008-09
88*	61	H.Patel	C v Ire	Colombo (SSC)	2009-10
88*	61	Tamim Iqbal	B v WI	Dhaka	2012-13
88	44	S.T.Jayasuriya	SL v K	Johannesburg	2007-08
88	50	C.H.Gayle	WI v A	The Oval	2009
88	44	G.C.Smith	SA v E	Centurion	2009-10
87*	53	Misbah-ul-Haq	P v B	Karachi	2007-08

The highest score for Zimbabwe is 79 by H.Masakadza (v Can, King City, 2008-09).

HIGHEST PARTNERSHIP FOR EACH WICKET

1st	170	G.C.Smith/L.E.Bosman	SA v E	Centurion	2009-10
2nd	166	D.P.M.D.Jayawardena/K.C.Sangakkara	SL v WI	Bridgetown	2009-10
3rd	137	M.J.Guptill/K.S.Williamson	NZ v Z	Auckland	2011-12
4th	112*	K.P.Pietersen/E.J.G.Morgan	E v P	Dubai	2009-10
5th	119*	Shoaib Malik/Misbah-ul-Haq	P v A	Johannesburg	2007-08
6th	101*	C.L.White/M.E.K.Hussey	A v SL	Bridgetown	2009-10
7th	91	P.D.Collingwood/M.H.Yardy	E v WI	The Oval	2007
8th	64*	W.D.Parnell/J.Theron	SA v A	Johannesburg	2011-12
9th	47*	G.C.Wilson/M.C.Sorensen	Ire v B	Belfast	2012
10th	31*	Wahab Riaz/Shoaib Akhtar	P v NZ	Auckland	2010-11

BOWLING RECORDS
35 WICKETS IN A CAREER

Wkts			Matches	Overs	Mdns	Runs	Avge	Best	R/Over
71	Saeed Ajmal	P	50	186.0	2	1159	16.32	4-19	6.23
69	Umar Gul	P	51	172.4	2	1211	17.55	5- 6	7.01
63	Shahid Afridi	P	58	216.5	3	1371	21.76	4-11	6.32
56	B.A.W.Mendis	SL	29	110.0	5	643	11.48	6- 8	5.84
55	S.C.J.Broad	E	46	163.3	2	1205	21.90	4-24	7.37
51	G.P.Swann	E	39	135.0	4	859	16.84	3-13	6.36
48	S.L.Malinga	SL	42	144.0	–	1070	22.29	5-31	7.43
41	N.L.McCullum	NZ	45	128.2	–	865	21.09	4-16	6.74
39	D.W.Steyn	SA	29	103.0	1	649	16.64	4- 9	6.30
39	M.Morkel	SA	31	111.3	3	762	19.53	4-17	6.83
37	D.L.Vettori	NZ	33	128.1	1	720	19.45	4-20	5.61
37	J.Botha	SA	40	129.0	1	823	22.24	3-16	6.37
36	M.G.Johnson	A	28	101.2	1	724	20.11	3-15	7.14
36	D.J.G.Sammy	WI	38	105.4	–	733	20.36	5-26	6.93
36	T.G.Southee	NZ	31	109.0	2	917	25.47	5-18	8.41
35	Abdul Razzak	P	24	92.0	2	628	17.94	4-16	6.82
35	S.R.Watson	A	36	99.2	1	715	20.42	4-15	7.19
35	K.D.Mills	NZ	35	123.4	1	1029	29.40	3-33	8.32

BEST FIGURES IN AN INNINGS

6- 8	B.A.W.Mendis	SL v Z	Hambantota	2012-13
6-16	B.A.W.Mendis	SL v A	Pallekele	2011
5- 6	Umar Gul	P v NZ	The Oval	2009
5-13	Elias Sunny	B v Ire	Belfast	2012
5-18	T.G.Southee	NZ v P	Auckland	2010-11
5-19	R.McLaren	SA v WI	North Sound	2009-10
5-20	N.Odhiambo	K v Sc	Nairobi (Gym)	2009-10
5-26	D.J.G.Sammy	WI v Z	Port-of-Spain	2009-10
5-31	S.L.Malinga	SL v E	Pallekele	2012-13
4- 6	S.J.Benn	WI v Z	Port-of-Spain	2009-10
4- 7	M.R.Gillespie	NZ v K	Durban	2007-08
4- 8	Umar Gul	P v A	Dubai	2009
4- 9	D.W.Steyn	SA v WI	Port Elizabeth	2007-08
4-10	Mohammad Hafeez	P v Z	Harare	2011
4-10	R.S.Bopara	E v WI	The Oval	2011

HAT-TRICKS

B.Lee	Australia v Bangladesh	Melbourne	2007-08
J.D.P.Oram	New Zealand v Sri Lanka	Colombo (RPS)	2009
T.G.Southee	New Zealand v Pakistan	Auckland	2010-11

WICKET-KEEPING RECORDS
20 DISMISSALS IN A CAREER

Dis			Matches	Ct	St
52	Kamran Akmal	Pakistan	49	22	30
37	K.C.Sangakkara	Sri Lanka	43	20	17
32	D.Ramdin	West Indies	33	25	7
32†	B.B.McCullum	New Zealand	60	24	8
29	M.S.Dhoni	India	42	21	8
26†	A.B.de Villiers	South Africa	44	20	6
26	Mushfiqur Rahim	Bangladesh	26	11	15
20	C.Kieswetter	England	25	17	3

† Excluding catches taken in the field.

MOST DISMISSALS IN AN INNINGS

4 (4 ct)	A.C.Gilchrist	Australia v Zimbabwe	Cape Town	2007-08
4 (4 ct)	M.J.Prior	England v South Africa	Cape Town	2007-08
4 (4 ct)	A.C.Gilchrist	Australia v New Zealand	Perth	2007-08
4 (4 st)	Kamran Akmal	Pakistan v Netherlands	Lord's	2009
4 (3 ct, 1 st)	N.J.O'Brien	Ireland v Sri Lanka	Lord's	2009
4 (4 ct)	M.S.Dhoni	India v Afghanistan	Gros Islet	2009-10
4 (2 ct, 2 st)	A.B.de Villiers	South Africa v West Indies	North Sound	2009-10
4 (3 ct, 1 st)	G.C.Wilson	Ireland v Kenya	Dubai	2011-12
4 (4 ct)	A.B.de Villiers	South Africa v Zimbabwe	Hambantota	2012-13
4 (4 ct)	M.S.Dhoni	India v Pakistan	Colombo (RPS)	2012-13

FIELDING RECORDS

20 CATCHES IN A CAREER

Total			Matches	Total			Matches
33	L.R.P.L.Taylor	New Zealand	50	22	Umar Akmal	Pakistan	42
25	D.A.Warner	Australia	44	21	C.L.White	Australia	38
24	D.J.Hussey	Australia	39	20	J.M.Bairstow	England	18
24	Shoaib Malik	Pakistan	52	20	M.E.K.Hussey	Australia	38
22	A.B.de Villiers	South Africa	44	20	S.C.J.Broad	England	46

MOST CATCHES IN AN INNINGS

4	D.J.G.Sammy	West Indies v Ireland	Providence	2009-10
4	P.W.Borren	Netherlands v Bangladesh	The Hague	2012
4	C.J.Anderson	New Zealand v South Africa	Port Elizabeth	2012-13

APPEARANCE RECORDS

40 APPEARANCES

60	B.B.McCullum	New Zealand		44	D.A.Warner	Australia
58	Shahid Afridi	Pakistan		43	K.C.Sangakkara	Sri Lanka
52	Shoaib Malik	Pakistan		42	M.S.Dhoni	India
51	Umar Gul	Pakistan		42	J.P.Duminy	South Africa
50	Saeed Ajmal	Pakistan		42	S.L.Malinga	Sri Lanka
50	L.R.P.L.Taylor	New Zealand		42	Mohammad Hafeez	Pakistan
49	Kamran Akmal	Pakistan		42	J.A.Morkel	South Africa
48	T.M.Dilshan	Sri Lanka		42	Umar Akmal	Pakistan
46	S.C.J.Broad	England		42	L.J.Wright	England
46	D.P.M.D.Jayawardena	Sri Lanka		41	M.J.Guptill	New Zealand
45	N.L.McCullum	New Zealand		40	J.Botha	South Africa
44	A.B.de Villiers	South Africa				

20 MATCHES AS CAPTAIN

			W	L	T	NR	%age wins
41	M.S.Dhoni	India	20	19	1	1	50.00
30	P.D.Collingwood	England	17	11	–	2	60.71
30	W.T.S.Porterfield	Ireland	15	12	–	3	55.55
28	D.L.Vettori	New Zealand	13	13	2	–	46.42
27	G.C.Smith	South Africa	18	9	–	–	66.66
22	K.S.Sangakkara	Sri Lanka	13	9	–	–	59.09

UNIVERSITY MATCH RESULTS

Played: 167. Wins: Cambridge 58; Oxford 54. Drawn: 55. Abandoned: 1

In 2001, for the very first time, Cambridge hosted the University Match, cricket's oldest surviving first-class fixture, after the ECB's re-organisation of university cricket around six centres of excellence had removed it from Lord's. Dating from 1827 it has, wartime interruptions apart, been played annually since 1838. With the exception of five matches played in the area of Oxford (1829, 1843, 1846, 1848 and 1850), all the previous fixtures had been staged at Lord's. Since 2001 it has been played over four days rather than three.

In 2003, Oxford (with Brookes), Cambridge (with Anglia) and Durham were joined by Loughborough in playing three first-class matches against counties. In 2012, two other centres – Cardiff (with UWIC and Glamorgan), and Leeds (with Bradford and Leeds Metropolitan) – were also granted first-class status. All six university sides now play two games each against the counties.

1827	Drawn	1877	Oxford	1923	Oxford	1971	Drawn
1829	Oxford	1878	Cambridge	1924	Cambridge	1972	Cambridge
1836	Oxford	1879	Cambridge	1925	Drawn	1973	Drawn
1838	Oxford	1880	Cambridge	1926	Cambridge	1974	Drawn
1839	Cambridge	1881	Oxford	1927	Cambridge	1975	Drawn
1840	Cambridge	1882	Cambridge	1928	Drawn	1976	Oxford
1841	Cambridge	1883	Cambridge	1929	Drawn	1977	Drawn
1842	Cambridge	1884	Oxford	1930	Cambridge	1978	Drawn
1843	Cambridge	1885	Cambridge	1931	Oxford	1979	Cambridge
1844	Drawn	1886	Oxford	1932	Drawn	1980	Drawn
1845	Cambridge	1887	Oxford	1933	Drawn	1981	Drawn
1846	Oxford	1888	Drawn	1934	Drawn	1982	Cambridge
1847	Cambridge	1889	Cambridge	1935	Cambridge	1983	Drawn
1848	Oxford	1890	Cambridge	1936	Cambridge	1984	Oxford
1849	Cambridge	1891	Oxford	1937	Oxford	1985	Drawn
1850	Oxford	1892	Oxford	1938	Drawn	1986	Cambridge
1851	Cambridge	1893	Cambridge	1939	Oxford	1987	Drawn
1852	Oxford	1894	Oxford	1946	Oxford	1988	Abandoned
1853	Oxford	1895	Cambridge	1947	Drawn	1989	Drawn
1854	Oxford	1896	Oxford	1948	Oxford	1990	Drawn
1855	Oxford	1897	Cambridge	1949	Cambridge	1991	Drawn
1856	Cambridge	1898	Oxford	1950	Drawn	1992	Cambridge
1857	Oxford	1899	Drawn	1951	Oxford	1993	Oxford
1858	Oxford	1900	Drawn	1952	Drawn	1994	Drawn
1859	Cambridge	1901	Drawn	1953	Cambridge	1995	Oxford
1860	Cambridge	1902	Cambridge	1954	Drawn	1996	Drawn
1861	Cambridge	1903	Oxford	1955	Drawn	1997	Drawn
1862	Cambridge	1904	Drawn	1956	Drawn	1998	Cambridge
1863	Oxford	1905	Cambridge	1957	Cambridge	1999	Drawn
1864	Oxford	1906	Cambridge	1958	Cambridge	2000	Drawn
1865	Oxford	1907	Cambridge	1959	Oxford	2001	Oxford
1866	Oxford	1908	Oxford	1960	Drawn	2002	Drawn
1867	Cambridge	1909	Drawn	1961	Drawn	2003	Oxford
1868	Cambridge	1910	Oxford	1962	Drawn	2004	Oxford
1869	Cambridge	1911	Oxford	1963	Drawn	2005	Oxford
1870	Cambridge	1912	Cambridge	1964	Drawn	2006	Oxford
1871	Oxford	1913	Cambridge	1965	Drawn	2007	Drawn
1872	Cambridge	1914	Oxford	1966	Oxford	2008	Drawn
1873	Oxford	1919	Oxford	1967	Drawn	2009	Cambridge
1874	Oxford	1920	Drawn	1968	Drawn	2010	Oxford
1875	Oxford	1921	Cambridge	1969	Drawn	2011	Cambridge
1876	Cambridge	1922	Cambridge	1970	Drawn	2012	Drawn

CAMBRIDGE UNIVERSITY RECORDS

ALL FIRST-CLASS MATCHES

Highest Total	For 703-9d		v	Sussex	Hove	1890
	V 730-3		by	W Indians	Cambridge	1950
Lowest Total	For 30		v	Yorkshire	Cambridge	1928
	V 32		by	Oxford U	Lord's	1878
Highest Innings	For 254*	K.S.Duleepsinhji	v	Middlesex	Cambridge	1927
	V 304*	E.de C.Weekes	for	W Indians	Cambridge	1950
Highest Partnership						
(2nd wicket)	429*	J.G.Dewes/G.H.G.Doggart	v	Essex	Cambridge	1949
Best Innings Bowling	10-69	S.M.J.Woods	v	Thornton's XI	Cambridge	1890
Best Match Bowling	15-88	S.M.J.Woods	v	Thornton's XI	Cambridge	1890
Most Runs – Season	1581	D.S.Sheppard	(av 79.05)			1952
Most Runs – Career	4310	J.M.Brearley	(av 38.48)			1961-68
Most 100s – Season	7	D.S.Sheppard				1952
Most 100s – Career	14	D.S.Sheppard				1950-52
Most Wkts – Season	80	O.S.Wheatley	(av 17.63)			1958
Most Wkts – Career	208	G.Goonesena	(av 21.82)			1954-57

UNIVERSITY MATCH RECORDS

Highest Total	604		Oxford	2002
Lowest Total	39		Lord's	1858
Highest Innings	211	G.Goonesena	Lord's	1957
Best Innings Bowling	8-44	G.E.Jeffery	Lord's	1873
Best Match Bowling	13-73	A.G.Steel	Lord's	1878

Hat-Tricks: F.C.Cobden (1870), A.G.Steel (1879), P.H.Morton (1880), J.F.Ireland (1911), R.G.H.Lowe (1926)

OXFORD UNIVERSITY RECORDS

ALL FIRST-CLASS MATCHES

Highest Total	For 651		v	Sussex	Hove	1895
	V 679-7d		by	Australians	Oxford	1938
Lowest Total	For 12		v	MCC	Oxford	1877
	V 24		by	MCC	Oxford	1846
Highest Innings	For 281	K.J.Key	v	Middlesex	Chiswick Park	1887
	V 338	W.W.Read	for	Surrey	The Oval	1888
Highest Partnership						
(3rd wicket)	408	S.Oberoi/D.R.Fox	v	Cambridge U	Cambridge	2005
Best Innings Bowling	10-38	S.E.Butler	v	Cambridge U	Lord's	1871
Best Match Bowling	15-65	B.J.T.Bosanquet	v	Sussex	Oxford	1900
Most Runs – Season	1307	Nawab of Pataudi sr	(av 93.35)			1931
Most Runs – Career	3319	N.S.Mitchell-Innes	(av 47.41)			1934-37
Most 100s – Season	6	Nawab of Pataudi sr				1931
	6	M.P.Donnelly				1946
Most 100s – Career	9	A.M.Crawley				1927-30
	9	Nawab of Pataudi sr				1928-31
	9	N.S.Mitchell-Innes				1934-37
	9	M.P.Donnelly				1946-47
Most Wkts – Season	70	I.A.R.Peebles	(av 18.15)			1930
Most Wkts – Career	182	R.H.B.Bettington	(av 19.38)			1920-23

UNIVERSITY MATCH RECORDS

Highest Total	611-5d		Oxford	2010
Lowest Total	32		Lord's	1878
Highest Innings	247	S.Oberoi	Cambridge	2005
Best Innings Bowling	10-38	S.E.Butler	Lord's	1871
Best Match Bowling	15-95	S.E.Butler	Lord's	1871

Match Doubles: P.R.le Couteur (160 and 11-66 in 1910); G.J.Toogood (149 and 10-93 in 1985)

INDIAN PREMIER LEAGUE 2012

The fifth IPL tournament was held in India between 4 April and 27 May.

Team	P	W	L	T	NR	Pts	Net RR
1 Delhi Daredevils (10)	16	11	5	–	–	22	+0.61
2 Kolkata Knight Riders (4)	16	10	5	–	1	21	+0.56
3 Mumbai Indians (3)	16	10	6	–	–	20	–0.10
4 Chennai Super Kings (2)	16	8	7	–	1	17	+0.10
5 Royal Challengers Bangalore (1)	16	8	7	–	1	17	–0.02
6 Kings XI Punjab (5)	16	8	8	–	–	16	–0.21
7 Rajasthan Royals (6)	16	7	9	–	–	14	+0.20
8 Deccan Chargers (7)	16	4	11	–	1	9	–0.50
9 Pune Warriors (9)	16	4	12	–	–	8	–0.55

1st Qualifying Match: At Subrata Roy Sahara Stadium, Pune, 22 May (floodlit). Toss: Kolkata Knight Riders. **KOLKATA KNIGHT RIDERS** won by 18 runs. Kolkata Knight Riders 162-4 (20). Delhi Daredevils 144-8 (20). Award: Y.K.Pathan (40*) KKR.

Elimination Final: At M.Chinnaswamy Stadium, Bangalore, 23 May (floodlit). Toss: Mumbai Indians. **CHENNAI SUPER KINGS** won by 38 runs. Chennai Super Kings 187-5 (20; M.S.Dhoni 51*, D.S.Kulkarni 3-46). Mumbai Indians 149-9 (20). Award: M.S.Dhoni.

2nd Qualifying Match: At M.A.Chidambaram Stadium, Chennai, 25 May (floodlit). Toss: Delhi Daredevils. **CHENNAI SUPER KINGS** won by 86 runs. Chennai Super Kings 222-5 (20; M.Vijay 113). Delhi Daredevils 136 (16.5; D.P.M.D.Jayawardena 55, R.Ashwin 3-23). Award: M.Vijay.

FINAL: At M.A.Chidambaram Stadium, Chennai, 27 May (floodlit). Toss: Chennai Super Kings. **KOLKATA KNIGHT RIDERS** won by five wickets. Chennai Super Kings 190-3 (20; S.K.Raina 73, M.E.K.Hussey 54). Kolkata Knight Riders 192-5 (19.4; M.S.Bisla 89, J.H.Kallis 69). Award: M.S.Bisla. Series award: S.P.Narine (Kolkata Knight Riders).

IPL winners:	2008	Rajasthan Royals	2009	Deccan Chargers
	2010	Chennai Super Kings	2011	Chennai Super Kings

TEAM RECORDS
HIGHEST TOTALS

246-5 (20)	Chennai v Rajasthan	Chennai	2010
240-5 (20)	Chennai v Punjab	Mohali	2008

LOWEST TOTALS

58 (15.1)	Rajasthan v Bangalore	Cape Town	2009
67 (15.2)	Kolkata v Mumbai	Mumbai	2008

LARGEST MARGINS OF VICTORY

140 runs	Kolkata (222-3) v Bangalore (82)	Bangalore	2008
10 wickets	Mumbai (154-0) v Deccan (155-0)	Mumbai	2008
10 wickets	Rajasthan (92) v Bangalore (93-0)	Bangalore	2010
10 wickets	Mumbai (133-5) v Rajasthan (134-0)	Mumbai	2011
10 wickets	Rajasthan (162-6) v Mumbai (163-0)	Jaipur	2012

Delhi beat Punjab by ten wickets in a reduced game in 2009.

BATTING RECORDS
600 RUNS IN A SEASON

Runs			Year	M	I	NO	HS	Ave	100	50	6s	4s	R/100B
733	C.H.Gayle	Bangalore	2012	15	14	2	128*	61.08	1	7	59	46	160.7
618	S.R.Tendulkar	Mumbai	2010	15	15	2	89*	47.53	–	5	3	86	132.6
616	S.E.Marsh	Punjab	2008	11	11	2	115	68.44	1	5	26	59	139.7
608	C.H.Gayle	Bangalore	2011	12	12	3	107	67.55	2	3	44	56	183.1

HIGHEST SCORES

Score	Balls				
158*	73	B.B.McCullum	Kolkata v Bangalore	Bangalore	2008
128*	62	C.H.Gayle	Bangalore v Delhi	Delhi	2012
127	56	M.Vijay	Chennai v Rajasthan	Chennai	2010
120*	63	P.C.Valthaty	Punjab v Chennai	Mohali	2011

FASTEST HUNDRED

37 balls	Y.K.Pathan (100)	Rajasthan v Mumbai	Mumbai (BS)	2010

MOST SIXES IN AN INNINGS

13	B.B.McCullum	Kolkata v Bangalore	Bangalore	2008
13	C.H.Gayle	Bangalore v Delhi	Delhi	2012

HIGHEST STRIKE RATE IN A SEASON (Qualification: 100 runs or more)

R/100B	Score	Balls			
204.34	188	92	B.B.McCullum	Kolkata	2008

HIGHEST STRIKE RATE IN AN INNINGS (Qualification: 25 runs, 300+ strike rate)

R/100B	Score	Balls				
400.0	28	7	J.A.Morkel	Chennai v Bangalore	Chennai	2012
385.7	27*	7	B.Akhil	Bangalore v Deccan	Hyderabad	2008
346.1	45*	13	K.A.Pollard	Mumbai v Delhi	Mumbai (BS)	2010
316.6	38	12	C.H.Gayle	Bangalore v Kolkata	Bangalore	2011
306.2	49	16	Yuvraj Singh	Punjab v Rajasthan	Mohali	2008

BOWLING RECORDS
MOST WICKETS IN A SEASON

Wkts			Year	P	O	M	Runs	Avge	Best	4w	R/Over
28	S.L.Malinga	Mumbai	2011	16	63.0	2	375	13.39	5-13	1	5.95
25	M.Morkel	Delhi	2012	16	63.0	1	453	18.12	4-20	1	7.19
24	S.P.Narine	Kolkata	2012	15	59.1	1	324	13.50	5-19	2	5.47
23	R.P.Singh	Deccan	2009	16	59.4	1	417	18.13	4-22	1	6.98

BEST BOWLING FIGURES IN AN INNINGS

6-14	Sohail Tanvir	Rajasthan v Chennai	Jaipur	2008
5- 5	A.Kumble	Bangalore v Rajasthan	Cape Town	2009
5-12	I.Sharma	Deccan v Kochi	Kochi	2011
5-13	S.L.Malinga	Mumbai v Delhi	Delhi	2011

MOST ECONOMICAL BOWLING ANALYSIS

O	M	R	W				
4	1	6	0	F.H.Edwards	Deccan v Kolkata	Cape Town	2009
4	1	6	1	A.Nehra	Delhi v Punjab	Bloemfontein	2009

MOST EXPENSIVE BOWLING ANALYSIS

O	M	R	W				
4	0	63	2	V.R.Aaron	Delhi v Chennai	Chennai	2012
4	0	59	1	R.P.Singh	Deccan v Kolkata	Hyderabad	2008
4	0	59	0	S.K.Trivedi	Rajasthan v Punjab	Mohali	2011

CHAMPIONS LEAGUE TWENTY20 2012

The fourth Champions League Twenty20 tournament took place in South Africa between 9 and 28 October. Fourteen teams took part, having qualified from their domestic Twenty20 competitions: four from India's IPL, two each from Australia, England and South Africa, and one each from New Zealand, Pakistan, Sri Lanka and West Indies. Hampshire, Sialkot Stallions, Trinidad & Tobago and Uva Next were eliminated in a qualifying round.

GROUP A

Team	P	W	L	T	NR	Pts	Net RR
1 Delhi Daredevils	4	2	–	–	2	12	+1.44
2 Titans	4	2	1	–	1	10	–0.01
3 Kolkata Knight Riders	4	1	2	–	1	6	+0.48
4 Perth Scorchers	4	1	2	–	1	6	–0.47
5 Auckland	4	1	2	–	1	6	–0.96

GROUP B

Team	P	W	L	T	NR	Pts	Net RR
1 Sydney Sixers	4	4	–	–	–	16	+1.65
2 Lions	4	3	1	–	–	12	+0.14
3 Chennai Super Kings	4	2	2	–	–	8	–0.04
4 Mumbai Indians	4	–	3	–	1	2	–0.47
5 Yorkshire	4	–	3	–	1	2	–1.79

1st Semi-Final: At Kingsmead, Durban, 25 October (floodlit). Toss: Delhi Daredevils. **LIONS** won by 22 runs. Lions 139-5 (20; G.H.Bodi 50). Delhi Daredevils 117-9 (20; K.P.Pietersen 50). Award: N.D.McKenzie (Lions, 46*).
2nd Semi-Final: At SuperSport Park, Centurion, 26 October (floodlit). Toss: Titans. **SYDNEY SIXERS** won by two wickets. Titans 163-5 (20; D.Wiese 61*, H.Davids 59*). Sydney Sixers 164-8 (20). Award: S.N.J.O'Keefe (Sydney Sixers, 32 and 0-19).
FINAL: At New Wanderers Stadium, Johannesburg, 28 October (floodlit). Toss: Sydney Sixers. **SYDNEY SIXERS** won by ten wickets. Lions 121 (20; J.Symes 51, J.R.Hazlewood 3-22, N.L.McCullum 3-24). Sydney Sixers 124-0 (12.3; M.J.Lumb 82*). Award: M.J.Lumb. Series award: M.A.Starc.

Champions League winners:	2009	New South Wales	2010	Chennai Super Kings
	2011	Mumbai Indians		

TOURNAMENT RECORDS 2009-12

Highest total	215-8		RC Bangalore v S Australia	Bangalore	2011
Lowest total	70		Central Districts v Wayamba	Port Elizabeth	2010
Largest victory	99 runs		KKR (188-5) v Titans (89)	Cape Town	2012
	10 wkts		Sydney (124-0) v Lions (121)	Johannesburg	2012
Highest score	135*	D.A.Warner	New South Wales v Chennai	Chennai	2011
Most runs overall	556	D.A.Warner (ave 55.60)	New South Wales	Delhi	2009-12
Most runs in season	328	D.A.Warner (ave 109.33)	New South Wales		2011
Highest partnership	147	D.J.Jacobs/A.G.Prince	Warriors v CD	Port Elizabeth	2010
Best bowling	5-24	Azhar Mahmood	Auckland v Hampshire	Centurion	2012
Most wickets overall	24	S.L.Malinga (ave 13.37)	Mumbai Indians		2010-12
Most wickets in season	14	M.A.Starc (ave 12.35)	Sydney Sixers		2012
Most economical	4-1-6-2	K.D.Mills	Auckland v Sialkot	Johannesburg	2012
Most expensive	4-0-69-0	S.Aravind	Bangalore v S. Australia	Bangalore	2011
Most catches in field	4	O.A.Shah	Cape Cobras v Mumbai	Bangalore	2011

WOMEN'S LIMITED-OVERS RECORDS

1973 to 1 April 2013

RESULTS SUMMARY

	Matches	Won	Lost	Tied	NR	% Won (exc NR)
Australia	265	205	53	1	6	79.15
England	276	156	109	2	9	58.42
India	203	103	95	1	4	51.75
West Indies	113	56	53	1	3	50.90
New Zealand	268	132	128	2	6	50.38
Sri Lanka	104	49	52	–	3	48.51
South Africa	105	46	53	1	5	46.00
Trinidad & Tobago	6	2	4	–	–	33.33
Ireland	124	38	81	–	5	31.93
Bangladesh	8	2	5	–	1	28.57
Pakistan	96	25	69	–	2	26.59
Jamaica	5	1	4	–	–	20.00
Netherlands	101	19	81	–	1	19.00
Denmark	33	6	27	–	–	18.18
International XI	18	3	14	–	1	17.64
Young England	6	1	5	–	–	16.66
Scotland	8	1	7	–	–	12.50
Japan	5	–	5	–	–	0.00

TEAM RECORDS

HIGHEST INNINGS TOTALS

455-5 (50 overs)	New Zealand v Pakistan	Christchurch	1996-97
412-3 (50 overs)	Australia v Denmark	Mumbai	1997-98
397-4 (50 overs)	Australia v Pakistan	Melbourne	1996-97
376-2 (50 overs)	England v Pakistan	Vijayawada	1997-98

HIGHEST MATCH AGGREGATES

577-12 (96.4 overs)	Australia v New Zealand	Sydney	2012-13
570-14 (98 overs)	New Zealand v Australia	Hamilton	2008-09
563-16 (98.2 overs)	England v New Zealand	Chennai	2006-07

LARGEST RUNS MARGIN OF VICTORY

408 runs	New Zealand beat Pakistan	Christchurch	1996-97
374 runs	Australia beat Pakistan	Melbourne	1996-97

LOWEST INNINGS TOTALS

22 (23.4 overs)	Netherlands v West Indies	Deventer	2008
23 (24.1 overs)	Pakistan v Australia	Melbourne	1996-97
24 (21.3 overs)	Scotland v England	Reading	2001

BATTING RECORDS

HIGHEST INDIVIDUAL INNINGS

229*	B.J.Clark	Australia v Denmark	Mumbai	1997-98
173*	C.M.Edwards	England v Ireland	Pune	1997-98
171	S.R.Taylor	West Indies v Sri Lanka	Mumbai	2012-13
168	S.W.Bates	New Zealand v Pakistan	Sydney	2008-09
156*	L.M.Keightley	Australia v Pakistan	Melbourne	1996-97

156*	S.C.Taylor	England v India	Lord's	2006
154*	K.L.Rolton	Australia v Sri Lanka	Christchurch	2000-01
153*	J.Logtenberg	South Africa v Netherlands	Deventer	2007
151	K.L.Rolton	Australia v Ireland	Dublin	2005

2000 RUNS IN A CAREER

Runs		Career	M	I	NO	HS	Avge	100	50
5075	C.M.Edwards (E)	1997-2013	167	156	20	173*	37.31	8	38
4844	B.J.Clark (A)	1991-2005	118	114	12	229*	47.49	5	30
4814	K.L.Rolton (A)	1995-2009	141	132	32	154*	48.14	8	33
4622	M.Raj (I)	1999-2013	145	132	32	114*	48.65	4	36
4101	S.C.Taylor (E)	1998-2011	126	120	18	156*	40.20	8	23
4064	D.A.Hockley (NZ)	1982-2000	118	115	18	117	41.89	4	34
2919	H.M.Tiffen (NZ)	1999-2009	117	111	16	100	30.72	1	18
2856	A.Chopra (I)	1995-2012	127	112	21	100	31.38	1	18
2844	E.C.Drumm (NZ)	1992-2006	101	94	13	116	35.11	2	19
2728	L.C.Sthalekar (A)	2001-2013	125	111	22	104*	30.65	2	16
2630	L.M.Keightley (A)	1995-2005	82	78	12	156*	39.84	4	21
2444	S.R.Taylor (WI)	2008-2013	64	64	8	171	43.64	4	16
2398	S.J.Taylor (E)	2006-2013	77	71	8	129	38.06	4	10
2235	A.J.Blackwell (A)	2003-2013	100	88	17	106*	31.47	2	15
2201	R.J.Rolls (NZ)	1997-2007	104	91	3	114	25.01	2	12
2125	L.S.Greenway (E)	2003-2013	104	92	23	125*	30.79	1	10
2121	J.A.Brittin (E)	1979-1998	63	59	9	138*	42.42	5	8
2093	S.J.McGlashan (NZ)	2002-2013	115	109	15	97*	22.26	–	9
2091	J.Sharma (I)	2002-2008	77	75	7	138*	30.75	2	14
2047	S.Nitschke (A)	2004-2011	80	69	9	113*	34.11	1	14

HIGHEST PARTNERSHIP FOR EACH WICKET

1st	268	S.J.Taylor/C.M.G.Atkins	England v South Africa	Lord's	2008
2nd	262	H.M.Tiffen/S.W.Bates	New Zealand v England	Sydney	2008-09
3rd	244	K.L.Rolton/L.C.Sthalekar	Australia v Ireland	Dublin	2005
4th	224*	J.Logtenberg//M.du Preez	South Africa v Netherlands	Deventer	2007
5th	188*	S.C.Taylor/J.Cassar	England v Sri Lanka	Lincoln	2000-01
6th	139*	S.J.McGlashan/N.J.Browne	New Zealand v South Africa	Bowral	2008-09
7th	104*	S.J.Tsukigawa/N.J.Browne	New Zealand v England	Chennai	2006-07
8th	85*	S.L.Clarke/N.J.Shaw	England v Scotland	Reading	2001
9th	73	L.R.F.Askew/I.T.Guha	England v New Zealand	Chennai	2006-07
10th	58	A.Sharma/G.Sultana	India v England	Taunton	2012

BOWLING RECORDS

SIX WICKETS IN AN INNINGS

7- 4	Sajjida Shah	Pakistan v Japan	Amsterdam	2003
7- 8	J.M.Chamberlain	England v Denmark	Haarlem	1991
7-14	A.Mohammed	West Indies v Pakistan	Dhaka	2011-12
7-24	S.Nitschke	Australia v England	Kidderminster	2005
6-10	J.Lord	New Zealand v India	Auckland	1981-82
6-10	M.Maben	India v Sri Lanka	Kandy	2003-04
6-10	S.Ismail	South Africa v Netherlands	Savar	2011-12
6-20	G.L.Page	New Zealand v Trinidad & T	St Albans	1973
6-31	J.Goswami	India v New Zealand	Southgate	2011
6-32	B.H.McNeill	New Zealand v England	Lincoln, NZ	2007-08

100 WICKETS IN A CAREER

		LOI	Balls	R	W	Avge	Best	4w	R/Over
C.L.Fitzpatrick (A)	1993-2007	109	6017	3023	**180**	16.79	5-14	11	3.01
J.Goswami (I)	2002-2013	130	6198	3315	**154**	21.52	6-31	6	3.20
L.C.Sthalekar (A)	2001-2013	125	5964	3646	**146**	24.97	5-35	2	3.66
N.David (I)	1995-2008	97	4892	2305	**141**	16.34	5-20	6	2.82
C.E.Taylor (E)	1988-2005	105	5140	2443	**102**	23.95	4-13	2	2.85
I.T.Guha (E)	2001-2011	83	3767	2345	**101**	23.21	5-14	4	3.73
N.Al Khadeer (I)	2002-2012	78	4036	2402	**100**	24.02	5-14	5	3.57

WICKET-KEEPING AND FIELDING RECORDS
SIX DISMISSALS IN AN INNINGS

6 (4ct, 2st)	S.L.Illingworth	New Zealand v Australia	Beckenham	1993
6 (1ct, 5st)	V.Kalpana	India v Denmark	Slough	1995
6 (2ct, 4st)	Batool Fatima	Pakistan v West Indies	Karachi	2003-04
6 (4ct, 2st)	Batool Fatima	Pakistan v Sri Lanka	Colombo (PSS)	2011

80 DISMISSALS IN A CAREER

Total			LOI	Ct	St
133	R.J.Rolls	New Zealand	104	89	44
114	J.Smit	England	109	69	45
99	J.C.Price	Australia	84	69	30
89	S.J.Taylor	England	77	59	30
81	A.Jain	India	65	30	51

FOUR CATCHES IN AN INNINGS IN THE FIELD

4	Z.J.Goss	Australia v New Zealand	Adelaide	1995-96

40 CATCHES IN THE FIELD IN A CAREER

Total			LOI	Career
49	L.C.Sthalekar	Australia	125	2001-2013
48	J.Goswani	India	130	2002-2013
46	L.S.Greenway	England	104	2003-2013
45	B.J.Clark	Australia	118	1991-2005
41	D.A.Hockley	New Zealand	118	1982-2000
41	C.M.Edwards	England	167	1997-2013

APPEARANCE RECORDS
120 APPEARANCES

167	C.M.Edwards	England	1997-2013
145	M.Raj	India	1999-2013
141	K.L.Rolton	Australia	1995-2009
130	J.Goswami	India	2002-2013
127	A.Chopra	India	1995-2012
126	S.C.Taylor	England	1998-2011
125	L.C.Sthalekar	Australia	2001-2013

MOST CONSECUTIVE APPEARANCES

109	M.Raj	India	17.04.2004 to 07.02.2013

75 MATCHES AS CAPTAIN

			Won	Lost	No Result	
101	B.J.Clark	Australia	83	17	1	1994-2005
93	C.M.Edwards	England	57	30	6	2005-2013

WOMEN'S INTERNATIONAL TWENTY20 RECORDS

2004 to 28 February 2013

MATCH RESULTS SUMMARY

	Matches	Won	Lost	Tied	NR	Win %
England	63	46	15	1	1	74.19
West Indies	51	32	17	1	1	64.00
Australia	56	32	22	2	–	57.14
New Zealand	54	28	25	1	–	51.85
Bangladesh	7	3	4	–	–	42.85
India	38	15	23	–	–	39.47
Ireland	16	6	10	–	–	37.50
Pakistan	30	10	19	1	–	33.33
Sri Lanka	26	6	18	–	2	25.00
South Africa	30	7	22	–	1	24.13
Netherlands	11	–	10	–	1	0.00

WOMEN'S INTERNATIONAL TWENTY20 RECORDS
(To 28 February 2013)

TEAM RECORDS
HIGHEST INNINGS TOTALS

205-1	South Africa v Netherlands	Potchefstroom	2010-11
191-4	West Indies v Netherlands	Potchefstroom	2010-11
186-7	New Zealand v South Africa	Taunton	2007
184-4	West Indies v Ireland	Dublin	2008
180-5	England v South Africa	Taunton	2007
180-5	New Zealand v West Indies	Gros Islet	2010

HIGHEST INNINGS TOTAL BATTING SECOND

165-2	England v Australia	The Oval	2009

LOWEST COMPLETED INNINGS TOTALS
† Batting Second

57† (19.4)	Sri Lanka v Bangladesh	Guangzhou	2012-13
60† (16.5)	Pakistan v England	Taunton	2009
62 (18.2)	India v Australia	Billericay	2011
62 (18.0)	Bangladesh v Sri Lanka	Guangzhou	2012-13
63† (19.1)	Pakistan v India	Guangzhou	2012-13
65-9	Pakistan v New Zealand	Basseterre	2010
65 (18.5)	Pakistan v West Indies	St Andrew's	2011

The lowest total for England is 96 (v India, Mumbai, 2009-10).

BATTING RECORDS
800 RUNS IN A CAREER

Runs			M	I	NO	HS	Avge	50	R/100B
1599	C.M.Edwards	E	61	59	9	76*	31.98	6	108.5
1219	S.J.Taylor	E	46	44	7	73	32.94	8	112.2
1090	S.W.Bates	NZ	50	50	2	68	22.70	5	104.3
1021	S.R.Taylor	WI	41	40	8	90	31.90	9	99.4†
885	M.Raj	I	37	37	10	52*	32.77	3	90.9†
879	D.J.S.Dottin	WI	51	50	12	112*	23.13	6	137.0†
837	L.S.Greenway	E	54	49	15	61*	24.61	1	97.2
827	A.J.Blackwell	A	53	47	6	61	20.17	1	94.0

† No information on balls-faced for games at Roseau on 22 and 23 February 2012.

318

HIGHEST INDIVIDUAL INNINGS

Score	Balls					
116*	71	S.A.Fritz	SA v Neth	Potchefstroom	2010-11
112*	45	D.J.S.Dottin	WI v SA	Basseterre	2010
96*	53	K.L.Rolton	A v E	Taunton	2005
90	49	S.R.Taylor	WI v Ire	Dublin	2008
90	61	A.J.Healy	A v I	Visakhapatnam	2011-12

The highest score for England is 76* by C.M.Edwards (v SA, Northampton, 2008) and by S.C.Taylor (v A, The Oval, 2009).

HIGHEST PARTNERSHIP FOR EACH WICKET

1st	170	S.A.Fritz/T.Chetty	SA v Neth	Potchefstroom	2010-11
2nd	118*	S.W.Bates/A.L.Watkins	NZ v A	Taunton	2009
3rd	124	T.D.Smartt/S.A.C.A.King	WI v Neth	Potchefstroom	2010-11
4th	147*	K.L.Rolton/K.A.Blackwell	A v E	Taunton	2005
5th	118	S.F.Daley/D.J.S.Dottin	WI v SA	Basseterre	2010
6th	68	K.L.Rolton/A.J.Blackwell	A v SA	Taunton	2009
7th	51	S.R.Taylor/M.R.Aguilleira	WI v SL	Cayon	2010
8th	32*	M.A.D.D.Surangika/S.S.Weerakkody	SL v WI	Port of Spain	2012
9th	32*	K.J.Martin/M.J.G.Nielsen	NZ v A	Sydney	2011-12
10th	22	H.Kaur/E.Bisht	I v A	Billericay	2011

BOWLING RECORDS

40 WICKETS IN A CAREER

Wkts			Matches	Overs	Mdns	Runs	Avge	Best	R/Over
64	A.Mohammed	WI	49	164.4	3	853	13.32	5-10	5.18
60	L.C.Sthalekar	A	54	199.2	1	1161	19.35	4-18	5.82
59	H.L.Colvin	E	43	161.5	4	823	13.94	4- 9	5.08
51	L.A.Marsh	E	55	205.1	4	1073	21.03	3-17	5.22
48	S.F.Daley	WI	45	146.5	4	699	14.56	3- 9	4.76
47	E.A.Perry	A	44	153.1	3	908	19.31	4-20	5.92
44	S.R.Taylor	WI	41	127.1	3	691	15.70	3-10	5.43
43	S.Nitschke	A	36	128.0	4	705	16.39	4-21	5.50
43	D.Hazell	E	35	133.5	1	721	16.76	4-12	5.38

BEST FIGURES IN AN INNINGS

6-17	A.E.Satterthwaite	NZ v E	Taunton	2007
5-10	A.Mohammed	WI v SA	Cape Town	2009-10
5-11	A.Shrubsole	E v NZ	Wellington	2011-12
5-11	J.Goswami	I v A	Visakhapatnam	2011-12
5-16	P.Roy	I v P	Taunton	2009
5-22	J.L.Hunter	A v WI	Colombo (RPS)	2012-13
4- 5	S.J.Coyte	A v I	Billericay	2011
4- 6	Salma Khatun	B v WI	Guangzhou	2012-13
4- 9	J.L.Gunn	E v SA	Taunton	2007
4- 9	A.Mohammed	WI v SL	Cayon	2010
4- 9	A.Mohammed	WI v P	St Andrew's	2011
4- 9	H.L.Colvin	E v P	Galle	2012-13

HAT-TRICKS

Asmavia Iqbal	Pakistan v England	Loughborough	2012
Ekta Bisht	Sri Lanka v India	Colombo (NCC)	2012-13

WICKET-KEEPING RECORDS
20 DISMISSALS IN A CAREER

Dis			Matches	Ct	St
42	S.J.Taylor	England	46	14	28
39	J.M.Fields	Australia	34	24	15
31	S.Naik	India	31	10	21
30	R.H.Priest	New Zealand	31	14	16
28	M.R.Aguilleira	West Indies	44	11	17
21	Batool Fatima	Pakistan	25	3	18

MOST DISMISSALS IN AN INNINGS

4 (3 ct, 1 st)	J.M.Fields	Australia v New Zealand	Brisbane	2009
4 (1 ct, 3 st)	S.Naik	India v England	Mumbai	2009-10
4 (4 st)	S.A.Campbell	West Indies v Sri Lanka	Cayon	2010
4 (2 ct, 2 st)	S.Naik	India v Pakistan	Guangzhou	2012-13

FIELDING RECORDS
18 CATCHES IN A CAREER

Total			Matches	Total			Matches
42	J.L.Gunn	England	61	21	A.J.Blackwell	Australia	53
29	L.S.Greenway	England	54	18	N.J.Browne	New Zealand	41
24	J.E.Cameron	Australia	44	18	H.L.Colvin	England	43
24	S.J.McGlashan	New Zealand	51	18	S.A.C.A.King	West Indies	47

MOST CATCHES IN AN INNINGS

4	L.S.Greenway	England v New Zealand	Chelmsford	2010

APPEARANCE RECORDS
45 APPEARANCES

61	C.M.Edwards	England	51	S.J.McGlashan	New Zealand
61	J.L.Gunn	England	50	S.W.Bates	New Zealand
55	L.A.Marsh	England	49	A.Mohammed	West Indies
54	L.S.Greenway	England	48	A.E.Satterthwaite	New Zealand
54	L.C.Sthalekar	Australia	47	S.A.C.A.King	West Indies
53	A.J.Blackwell	Australia	46	S.J.Taylor	England
51	D.J.S.Dottin	West Indies	45	S.F.Daley	West Indies

20 MATCHES AS CAPTAIN

			W	L	T	NR	%age wins
59	C.M.Edwards	England	45	12	1	1	77.58
43	M.R.Aguilleira	West Indies	25	16	1	1	59.52
29	A.L.Watkins	New Zealand	19	10	–	–	65.51
28	Sana Mir	Pakistan	9	18	1	–	32.14
23	J.M.Fields	Australia	16	7	–	–	69.56

MCCA FIXTURES 2013

Sun 21 April

Venue	Fixture
Bovey Tracey	**KNOCK-OUT TROPHY**
Shifnal	Devon v Oxfordshire (1)
Devizes	Shropshire v Lincolnshire (2)
March	Wiltshire v Norfolk (2)
Brockhampton	Cambridgeshire v Cumberland (3)
Dean Park	Herefordshire v Cheshire (3)
Stone	Dorset v Wales MC (4)
	Staffordshire v Buckinghamshire (4)

Sun 5 May

Venue	Fixture
Werrington	**KNOCK-OUT TROPHY**
Bicester & N Oxford	Cornwall v Hertfordshire (1)
Woodhall Spa	Oxfordshire v Bedfordshire (1)
Ipswich S	Lincolnshire v Wiltshire (2)
Tattenhall	Suffolk v Shropshire (2)
Jesmond	Cheshire v Cambridgeshire (3)
Burnham	Northumberland v Herefordshire (3)
Cresselly	Berkshire v Dorset (4)
	Wales MC v Staffordshire (4)

Mon 6 May

Venue	Fixture
North Devon	**KNOCK-OUT TROPHY**
Manor Park	Devon v Hertfordshire (1)
	Norfolk v Shropshire (2)

Sun 19 May

Venue	Fixture
Redruth	**KNOCK-OUT TROPHY**
Radlett	Cornwall v Devon (1)
Manor Park	Hertfordshire v Oxfordshire (1)
Devizes	Norfolk v Lincolnshire (2)
Leys S	Wiltshire v Suffolk (2)
Kendal	Cambridgeshire v Northumberland (3)
Dinton	Cumberland v Cheshire (3)
West Brom Dart	Buckinghamshire v Wales MC (4)
	Staffordshire v Berkshire (4)

Sun 26 May

Venue	Fixture
Harpenden	**KNOCK-OUT TROPHY**
Challow & C	Hertfordshire v Bedfordshire (1)
Oswestry	Oxfordshire v Cornwall (1)
Bury St Edmunds	Shropshire v Wiltshire (2)
Colwall	Suffolk v Norfolk (2)
Jesmond	Herefordshire v Cambridgeshire (3)
Kidmore End	Northumberland v Cumberland (3)
Dean Park	Berkshire v Buckinghamshire (4)
	Dorset v Staffordshire (4)

Mon 27 May

Venue	Fixture
Cople	**KNOCK-OUT TROPHY**
	Bedfordshire v Cornwall (1)

Thu 30 May

Venue	Fixture
Sidmouth	MCCA v MCC

Sun 2 June

Venue	Fixture
Dunstable	**KNOCK-OUT TROPHY**
	Bedfordshire v Devon (1)

Bracebridge Heath	Lincolnshire v Suffolk (2)
Hyde	Cheshire v Northumberland (3)
Penrith	Cumberland v Herefordshire (3)
Tring Park	Buckinghamshire v Dorset (4)
Mumbles	Wales MC v Berkshire (4)

Sun 9 – Tue 11 June	**MCCA CHAMPIONSHIP**
Ampthill	Bedfordshire v Buckinghamshire
Henley	Berkshire v Dorset
Wisbech	Cambridgeshire v Norfolk
Exeter	Devon v Cornwall
Sleaford	Lincolnshire v Suffolk
Jesmond	Northumberland v Hertfordshire
Gt & Little Tew	Oxfordshire v Cheshire
Hem Heath	Staffordshire v Cumberland
Pontarddulais	Wales MC v Herefordshire
South Wilts	Wiltshire v Shropshire

Sun 16 June	**KNOCK-OUT TROPHY Quarter-finals**
Match 1	Winner Gp 4 v Runner-up Gp 1
Match 2	Winner Gp 2 v Runner-up Gp 4
Match 3	Winner Gp 1 v Runner-up Gp 3
Match 4	Winner Gp 3 v Runner-up Gp 2

Sun 23 – Tue 25 June	**MCCA CHAMPIONSHIP**
Luton	Bedfordshire v Staffordshire
High Wycombe	Buckinghamshire v Northumberland
Chester BH	Cheshire v Wiltshire
Truro	Cornwall v Oxfordshire
Furness	Cumberland v Norfolk
Eastnor	Herefordshire v Berkshire
Hertford	Hertfordshire v Lincolnshire
Bridgnorth	Shropshire v Dorset
Bury St Edmunds	Suffolk v Cambridgeshire
Usk	Wales MC v Devon

Sun 7 – Tue 9 July	**MCCA CHAMPIONSHIP**
Falkland	Berkshire v Wales MC
Saffron Walden	Cambridgeshire v Hertfordshire
Dean Park	Dorset v Cheshire
Colwall	Herefordshire v Devon
Cleethorpes	Lincolnshire v Cumberland
Jesmond	Northumberland v Bedfordshire
Banbury	Oxfordshire v Shropshire
Ipswich S	Suffolk v Staffordshire
Corsham	Wiltshire v Cornwall

Sun 14 July	**KNOCK-OUT TROPHY Semi-finals**
tbc	Winner 3 v Winner 2
tbc	Winner 1 v Winner 4
Reserve day Mon 15 July	

Sun 21 – Tue 23 July	**MCCA CHAMPIONSHIP**
Bedford S	Bedfordshire v Hertfordshire
Finchampstead	Berkshire v Cheshire
Gerrards Cross	Buckinghamshire v Suffolk

Barrow	Cumberland v Cambridgeshire
Exmouth	Devon v Wiltshire
Dean Park	Dorset v Herefordshire
Manor Park	Norfolk v Northumberland
Shrewsbury	Shropshire v Cornwall
Longton	Staffordshire v Lincolnshire
Abergavenny	Wales MC v Oxfordshire

Sun 28 – Tue 30 July   **MCCA CHAMPIONSHIP**
Manor Park   Norfolk v Buckinghamshire

Sun 4 – Tue 6 August   **MCCA CHAMPIONSHIP**

Marlow	Buckinghamshire v Cumberland
March	Cambridgeshire v Bedfordshire
Bowdon	Cheshire v Devon
Truro	Cornwall v Dorset
Harpenden	Hertfordshire v Staffordshire
Manor Park	Norfolk v Lincolnshire
Aston Rowant	Oxfordshire v Herefordshire
Whitchurch	Shropshire v Berkshire
Copdock	Suffolk v Northumberland
Trowbridge	Wiltshire v Wales MC

Sun 18 – Tue 20 August   **MCCA CHAMPIONSHIP**

Nantwich	Cheshire v Shropshire
St Austell	Cornwall v Berkshire
Sedbergh S	Cumberland v Suffolk
Sidmouth	Devon v Oxfordshire
Dean Park	Dorset v Wales MC
Brockhampton	Herefordshire v Wiltshire
Long Marston	Hertfordshire v Buckinghamshire
Grantham	Lincolnshire v Bedfordshire
Jesmond	Northumberland v Cambridgeshire
Old Hill	Staffordshire v Norfolk

Wed 28 August   **KNOCK-OUT TROPHY Final**
Wormsley   (Reserve day, Thu 29 August)

Sun 8 – Wed 11 September   **MCCA CHAMPIONSHIP**
Winners of East   Championship Final

MCCA KNOCK-OUT TROPHY GROUPS

Group 1	*Group 2*	*Group 3*	*Group 4*
Bedfordshire	Lincolnshire	Cambridgeshire	Berkshire
Cornwall	Norfolk	Cheshire	Buckinghamshire
Devon	Shropshire	Cumberland	Dorset
Hertfordshire	Suffolk	Herefordshire	Staffordshire
Oxfordshire	Wiltshire	Northumberland	Wales MC

SECOND XI CHAMPIONSHIP FIXTURES 2013

THREE-DAY MATCHES

APRIL

Mon 8	The Oval	Surrey v Glos
Wed 10	Radlett	Middx v Northants
Tue 23	Radlett	MCC YC v Notts
Tue 30	Southampton	Hants v Northants

MAY

Wed 1	Cardiff CC	Glamorgan v Worcs
Tue 7	Radlett	Middx v Sussex
	Notts SC	Notts v Durham
Wed 8	tbc	Derbys v Lancs
	H Wycombe	MCC YC v Worcs
Tue 14	Southampton	Hants v Kent
	Taunton Vale	Somerset v Northants
	Kidderminster	Worcs v Derbys
Wed 15	Southend GP	Essex v Glos
	Hinckley Town	Leics v Glamorgan
	Welbeck Coll	Notts v Warwicks
Wed 22	Manchester	Lancs v Durham
	Taunton Vale	Somerset v Sussex
Tue 28	tbc	Glamorgan v Durham
Wed 29	Clifton Coll	Glos v Somerset
	Stowe S	Northants v Essex
	Harrogate	Yorks v Derbys

JUNE

Tue 4	Middlesbro	Durham v MCC YC
	Milton Keynes	Northants v Surrey
Wed 5	Mkt Harboro	Leics v Yorks
Tue 11	tbc	Derbys v Notts
	Bristol CC	Glos v Kent
Wed 12	West Brom	Warwicks v Lancs
Tue 18	Radlett	Middx v Somerset
Tue 25	Bish Stortford	Essex v Surrey
	Notts SC	Notts v Leics
Wed 26	Horsham	Sussex v MCC Univs

JULY

Tue 2	Southampton	Hants v Susssex
	Beckenham	Kent v Somerset
	Newclose IoW	MCC YC v Glamorgan
Wed 3	Ashby Hastings	Leics v Derbys
	Bish Stortford	MCC Univs v Essex
	Guildford	Surrey v Middx
Tue 9	Southampton	Hants v Somerset
	Cheltenham CC	MCC Univs v Glos
	Ombersley	Worcs v Warwicks
	Stamford Brg	Yorks v MCC YC
Tue 16	Coggleshall	Essex v Middx
	Southampton	MCC Univs v Hants
	Leeds	Yorks v Glamorgan
Wed 17	Chester-le-St	Durham v Warwicks
	Frocester	Glos v Sussex
	Leicester	Leics v Lancs
	Welbeck Coll	Notts v Worcs
	tbc	Surrey v Kent
Tue 23	Darlington	Durham v Leics
	Thornbury	Glos v Middx
	Maidstone	Kent v Essex
	Taunton	Somerset v Surrey
Wed 24	Cardiff CC	Glamorgan v Notts
	Liverpool	Lancs v Worcs
	Knowle & Dor	Warwicks v Derbys
Tue 30	Repton S	Derbys v Glamorgan
	Beckenham	Kent v Sussex
	Leicester Ivan	Leics v MCC YC
	Milton Keynes	Northants v Glos
	Kidderminster	Worcs v Durham
Wed 31	Taunton Vale	Somerset v MCC Univs
	Coventry NWk	Warwicks v Yorks

AUGUST

Tue 6	Lansdown	Glos v Hants
	Arundel	Sussex v Surrey
	Barnt Green	Worcs v Yorks
Wed 7	tbc	Derbys v MCC YC
	Cardiff CC	Glamorgan v Warwicks
	Crosby	Lancs v Notts
	Radlett	Middx v MCC Univs
Tue 13	South North	Durham v Yorks
	Halstead	Essex v Hants
	Beckenham	Kent v Northants
	Kidderminster	Worcs v Leics
Wed 14	Blackpool	Lancs v Glamorgan
	Cambridge	MCC Univs v Surrey
	Walmley	Warwicks v MCC YC
Tue 20	Southampton	Hants v Middx
	Horsham	Sussex v Northants
Wed 21	Stockton	Durham v Derbys
	Canterbury PF	Kent v MCC Univs
	Taunton Vale	Somerset v Essex
	Kenilworth	Warwicks v Leics
	Todmorden	Yorks v Lancs
Wed 28	Desborough	Northants v MCC Univs
	Wimbledon	Surrey v Hants
	Hove	Sussex v Essex
	York	Yorks v Notts

SEPTEMBER

Tue 3	Shenley	MCC YC v Lancs
	Radlett	Middx v Kent
Mon 16	tbc	FINAL (four days)

SECOND XI TROPHY FIXTURES 2013

ONE DAY

APRIL

Tue 9	Radlett	Middx v Northants		Leeds, Weet	Yorks v MCC YC
Thu 11	The Oval	Surrey v Glos	Wed 10	Kings S, Cant	Kent v Unicorns A
Mon 22	Radlett	MCC YC v Notts	Mon 15	Radlett	MCC YC v Lancs
Mon 29	Southampton	Hants v-Northants	Tue 16	Chester-le-St	Durham v Warwicks
	Taunton Vale	Somerset v Unicorns A		Frocester	Glos v Sussex
Tue 30	Cardiff CC	Glamorgan v Worcs		Lutterworth	Leics v Lancs
MAY				Welbeck Coll	Notts v Worcs
Mon 6	Radlett	Middx v Sussex		tbc	Surrey v Kent
	Notts SC	Notts v Durham	Fri 19	Coggleshall	Essex v Middx
Tue 7	H Wycombe	MCC YC v Worcs		Pudsey Congs	Yorks v Glamorgan
Mon 13	Southampton	Hants v Kent	Mon 22	Darlington	Durham v Leics
	Taunton Vale	Somerset v Northants		Thornbury	Glos v Middx
	Kidderminster	Worcs v Derbys		Maidstone	Kent v Essex
Tue 14	Southend GP	Essex v Glos		Taunton Vale	Somerset v Surrey
	Leicester	Leics v Glamorgan	Tue 23	Cardiff CC	Glamorgan v Notts
	Welbeck Coll	Notts v Warwicks		Middlewich	Lancs v Worcs
Tue 21	Westhoughton	Lancs v Durham		Knowle & Dor	Warwicks v Derbys
	Taunton Vale	Somerset v Sussex	Mon 29	Derby	Derbys v Glamorgan
Mon 27	tbc	Glamorgan v Durham		Leicester	Leics v MCC YC
Tue 28	Clifton Coll	Glos v Somerset		Dunstable	Northants v Glos
	Stowe S	Northants v Essex		Sunbury	Surrey v Hants
	Harrogate	Yorks v Derbys		Kidderminster	Worcs v Durham
Wed 29	Eastbourne	Sussex v Unicorns A	Tue 30	Rugby S	Warwicks v Yorks
Fri 31	Sidmouth	Unicorns A v Hants	Wed 31	Luton WP	Unicorns A v Surrey
JUNE			**AUGUST**		
Mon 3	tbc	Derbys v Lancs	Fri 2	Beckenham	Kent v Surrey
	Middlesbro	Durham v MCC YC	Mon 5	Lansdown	Glos v Hampshire
	Milton Keynes	Northants v Surrey		Arundel	Sussex v Surrey
Tue 4	Leicester	Leics v Yorks		Barnt Green	Worcs v Yorks
Wed 5	Radlett	Middx v Kent	Tue 6	tbc	Derbys v MCC YC
	Long Marston	Unicorns A v Essex		Cardiff CC	Glamorgan v Warwicks
Thu 6	Radlett	Middx v Unicorns A		Crosby	Lancs v Notts
Mon 10	tbc	Derbys v Notts	Mon 12	South North	Durham v Yorks
	Bristol CC	Glos v Kent		Halstead	Essex v Hants
Tue 11	Coventry/N Wk	Warwicks v Lancs		Beckenham	Kent v Northants
Fri 14	Preston Nom	Sussex v Essex		Kidderminster	Worcs v Leics
Mon 17	Radlett	Middx v Somerset	Tue 13	Middleton	Lancs v Glamorgan
	Bradfield C	Unicorns A v Glos		Olton & WWk	Warwicks v MCC YC
Mon 24	Bish Stortford	Essex v Surrey	Mon 19	Southampton	Hants v Middx
	Notts SC	Notts v Leics		Horsham	Sussex v Northants
Thu 27	Oundle S	Northants v Unicorns A		Barnsley	Yorks v Notts
JULY			Tue 20	Stockton	Durham v Derbys
Mon 1	Southampton	Hants v Sussex		Taunton Vale	Somerset v Essex
	Beckenham	Kent v Somerset		Coventry NWk	Warwicks v Leics
	Newclose IoW	MCC YC v Glamorgan		Todmorden	Yorks v Lancs
Tue 2	Leicester	Leics v Derbys	Tue 27	tbc	Semi-finals
	Sunbury	Surrey v Middx	**SEPTEMBER**		
Mon 8	Southampton	Hants v Somerset	Wed 11	tbc	FINAL
	Ombersley	Worcs v Warwicks			

SECOND XI TWENTY20 CUP FIXTURES 2013

JUNE

Mon 10	Southampton	Hants v Sussex
	Hinckley Town	Leics v Essex
	Walmley	Warwicks v Somerset
Tue 11	Southend GP	Essex v Middx
	Taunton	Somerset v Glamorgan
	Preston Nom	Sussex v Surrey
Wed 12	Uxbridge	Middx v Unicorns A
Thu 13	Newport	Glamorgan v Worcs
Fri 14	Uxbridge	Middx v Leics
	Leeds	Yorks v Notts
Mon 17	Ormskirk	Lancs v Derbys
	Hinckley Town	Leics v Northants
	Trent Coll	Notts v Durham
	Purley	Surrey v MCC YC
	Kidderminster	Worcs v Warwicks
Tue 18	Neston	Lancs v Durham
	Shenley	MCC YC v Sussex
	Ombersley	Worcs v Glos
Wed 19	tbc	Derbys v EDP U19s
	Chelmsford	Essex v Northants
	Panteg	Glamorgan v Warwicks
	Purley	Surrey v Hants

	Bish Stortford	Unicorns A v Leics
Thu 20	Loughboro U	EDP U19s v Notts
	Chichester	Sussex v Kent
	Bish Stortford	Unicorns A v Essex
	Marske	Yorks v Lancs
Fri 21	Loughboro U	EDP U19s v Yorks
	Canterbury PF	Kent v Surrey
	Bedford S	Northants v Middx
	Worksop Coll	Notts v Lancs
Mon 24	tbc	Derbys v Yorks
	Brandon	Durham v EDP U19s
	Bristol	Glos v Somerset
Tue 25	Bristol	Glos v Glamorgan
	Southampton	Hants v MCC YC
	Taunton Vale	Somerset v Worcs
Wed 26	Brandon	Durham v Derbys
	Radlett	MCC YC v Kent
	Northampton	Northants v Unicorns A
	Olton/W Wk	Warwicks v Glos
Thu 27	Folkestone	Kent v Hants
JULY		
Fri 12	Arundel	Semi-finals and FINAL

326

WOMEN'S INTERNATIONAL FIXTURES 2013

Sun 11 – Wed 14 August
TM   Wormsley   England v Australia

Tue 20 August
LOI   Lord's   England v Australia

Fri 23 August
LOI   Hove   England v Australia

Sun 25 August
LOI   Hove   England v Australia

Tue 27 August
IT20 F   Chelmsford   England v Australia

Thu 29 August
IT20   Southampton   England v Australia

Sat 31 August
IT20   Chester-le-St   England v Australia

INTERNATIONAL UNDER-19 CRICKET TRIANGULAR SERIES

Mon 5 August
LOI   Loughborough   Pakistan v Bangladesh

Tue 6 August
LOI   tbc   England v Pakistan

Wed 7 August
LOI   tbc   England v Bangladesh

Fri 9 August
LOI   tbc   Pakistan v Bangladesh

Sat 10 August
LOI   tbc   England v Bangladesh

Mon 12 August
LOI   Leicester   England v Pakistan

Tue 13 August
LOI   Leicester   Pakistan v Bangladesh

Thu 15 August
LOI   Worcester   England v Bangladesh

Fri 16 August
LOI F   Derby   England v Pakistan

Mon 19 August
LOI   Nottingham   FINAL

MCC UNIVERSITIES CHALLENGE

Thu 11 – Fri 12 April
Cambridge   Cambridge v Oxford
Leeds, Weetwood   Leeds/Bradford v Loughborough

Thu 18 – Fri 19 April
Usk   Cardiff v Oxford
Leeds, Weetwood   Leeds/Bradford v Cambridge

Thu 25 – Fri 26 April
Loughborough   Loughborough v Cardiff
Oxford   Oxford v Durham

Thu 2 – Fri 3 May
Durham   Durham v Leeds/Bradford
Loughborough   Loughborough v Cambridge

Thu 9 – Fri 10 May
Cambridge   Cambridge v Cardiff
Durham   Durham v Loughborough

Thu 30 – Fri 31 May
Durham   Durham v Cardiff
Leeds, Weetwood   Leeds/Bradford v Oxford

Mon 10 – Tue 11 June
Cambridge   Cambridge v Durham

Tue 11 – Wed 12 June
Usk   Cardiff v Leeds/Bradford
Oxford   Oxford v Loughborough

Fri 21 June
Lord's   MCCU Challenge Final

PRINCIPAL FIXTURES 2013

CC1   LV= County Championship (1st Div)
CC2   LV= County Championship (2nd Div)
F   Floodlit
FCF   First-Class Friendly
LOI   NatWest Limited-Overs International
40L   Yorkshire Bank 40

T20   Friends Provident t20
IT20 Twenty20 International
[T20] Other Twenty20 Match
TM   npower Test Match
MCCU MCC University

Sun 24 – Wed 27 March
FCF F	Abu Dhabi	MCC v Warwicks

Fri 5 – Sun 7 April
FCF	Cambridge	Cambridge MCCU v Essex
FCF	Chester-le-St	Durham v Durham MCCU
FCF	Cardiff	Glamorgan v Cardiff MCCU
FCF	Oxford	Oxford MCCU v Warwicks
FCF	Hove	Sussex v Loughborough MCCU
FCF	Leeds	Yorkshire v Leeds/Bradford MCCU

Wed 10 – Sat 13 April
CC1	Chester-le-St	Durham v Somerset
CC1	Nottingham	Notts v Middlesex
CC1	Birmingham	Warwicks v Derbyshire
CC1	Leeds	Yorkshire v Sussex
CC2	Chelmsford	Essex v Glos
CC2	Cardiff	Glamorgan v Northants
CC2	Southampton	Hampshire v Leics
CC2	Manchester	Lancashire v Worcs

Wed 10 – Fri 12 April
FCF	Canterbury	Kent v Cardiff MCCU

Wed 17 – Sat 20 April
CC1	Lord's	Middlesex v Derbyshire
CC1	The Oval	Surrey v Somerset
CC1	Birmingham	Warwicks v Durham
CC2	Cardiff	Glamorgan v Worcs
CC2	Leicester	Leics v Kent
CC2	Northampton	Northants v Essex

Wed 17 – Fri 19 April
FCF	Durham	Durham MCCU v Notts
FCF	Southampton	Hampshire v Loughborough MCCU

Wed 24 – Sat 27 April
CC1	Derby	Derbyshire v Notts
CC1	Chester-le-St	Durham v Yorkshire
CC1	The Oval	Surrey v Sussex
CC2	Bristol	Glos v Northants
CC2	Southampton	Hampshire v Worcs
CC2	Manchester	Lancashire v Kent

Wed 24 – Fri 26 April
FCF	Cambridge	Cambridge MCCU v Middlesex
FCF	Leicester	Leics v Leeds/Bradford MCCU

Thu 25 – Sun 28 April
CC1	Taunton	Somerset v Warwicks

Mon 29 Apr – Thu 2 May
CC1	Nottingham	Notts v Durham
CC1	Leeds	Yorkshire v Derbyshire

CC2	Chelmsford	Essex v Hampshire

Tue 30 – Fri 3 May
CC2	Leicester	Leics v Glos

Wed 1 – Sat 4 May
CC1	Hove	Sussex v Warwicks
CC2	Colwyn Bay	Glamorgan v Lancashire
CC2	Canterbury	Kent v Northants

Wed 1 – Fri 3 May
FCF	Oxford	Oxford MCCU v Worcs
FCF	Taunton Vale	Somerset v Cardiff MCCU

Thu 2 – Sun 5 May
CC1	Lord's	Middlesex v Surrey

Fri 3 May
40L F	Chelmsford	Essex v Hampshire

Sat 4 – Mon 6 May
FCF	Derby	Derbyshire v New Zealanders

Sat 4 May
40L	Leicester	Leics v Glos

Sun 5 May
40L	Chester-le-St	Durham v Essex
40L	Colwyn Bay	Glamorgan v Yorkshire
40L	Southampton	Hampshire v Scotland
40L	Northampton	Northants v Notts
40L	Taunton	Somerset v Unicorns
40L	Hove	Sussex v Worcs

Mon 6 May
40L	Manchester	Lancashire v Durham
40L	Lord's	Middlesex v Glamorgan
40L	The Oval	Surrey v Hampshire
40L	Wormsley	Unicorns v Glos
40L	Birmingham	Warwicks v Kent

Tue 7 – Fri 10 May
CC1	Leeds	Yorkshire v Somerset
CC2	Manchester	Lancashire v Essex

Wed 8 – Sat 11 May
CC1	Birmingham	Warwicks v Middlesex
CC2	Bristol	Glos v Hampshire
CC2	Worcester	Worcs v Leics

Wed 8 May
40L F	Nottingham	Notts v Kent

Thu 9 – Sun 12 May
FCF	Leicester	England Lions v New Zealanders

Thu 9 May
40L F	The Oval	Surrey v Durham

Fri 10 – Mon 13 May
CC1   The Oval   Surrey v Durham

Fri 10 May
40L   Deventer   Netherlands v Kent
40L [F] Northampton   Northants v Sussex

Sat 11 May
40L   Leeds   Yorkshire v Somerset

Sun 12 May
40L   Derby   Derbyshire v Lancashire
40L   Cardiff   Glamorgan v Unicorns
40L   Bristol   Glos v Middlesex
40L   Edinburgh   Scotland v Essex
40L   Birmingham   Warwicks v Sussex
40L   Worcester   Worcs v Notts

Wed 15 – Sat 18 May
CC1   Derby   Derbyshire v Sussex
CC1   Nottingham   Notts v Surrey
CC1   Taunton   Somerset v Middlesex
CC1   Birmingham   Warwicks v Yorkshire
CC2   Cardiff   Glamorgan v Essex
CC2   Northampton   Northants v Leics

Wed 15 – Fri 17 May
FCF   Cambridge   Cambridge MCCU v Glos

Wed 15 May
40L [F] Canterbury   Kent v Worcs

Thu 16 – Mon 20 May
TM1   Lord's   ENGLAND v NEW ZEALAND

Fri 17 – Mon 20 May
CC1   Canterbury   Kent v Worcs

Sun 19 May
40L   Cardiff   Glamorgan v Glos
40L   Southampton   Hampshire v Durham
40L   Manchester   Lancashire v Surrey
40L   Taunton   Somerset v Middlesex
40L   Chesterfield Unicorns v Yorkshire

Mon 20 May
40L   Rotterdam   Netherlands v Sussex

Tue 21 – Fri 24 May
CC2   Leicester   Leics v Glamorgan

Tue 21 May
40L   Rotterdam   Netherlands v Northants

Wed 22 – Sat 25 May
CC1   Chester-le-St Durham v Middlesex
CC1   Horsham   Sussex v Somerset
CC2   Chelmsford   Essex v Kent
CC2   Worcester   Worcs v Glos

Wed 22 – Fri 24 May
FCF   Oxford   Oxford MCCU v Surrey

Wed 22 May
40L [F] Southampton   Hampshire v Lancashire

Thu 23 – Sun 26 May
CC2   Southampton   Hampshire v Lancashire

Thu 23 – Sat 25 May
FCF   Loughborough Loughborough MCCU v Northants

Thu 23 May
40L   Birmingham   Warwicks v Notts

Fri 24 –Tue 28 May
TM2   Leeds   ENGLAND v NEW ZEALAND

Sun 26 May
40L   Bristol   Glos v Unicorns
40L   Leicester   Leics v Somerset
40L   Nottingham   Notts v Netherlands
40L   Edinburgh   Scotland v Derbyshire
40L   Horsham   Sussex v Kent
40L   Worcester   Worcs v Northants

Mon 27 May
40L   Chester-le-St Durham v Derbyshire
40L   Tunbridge W   Kent v Netherlands
40L   Radlett   Middlesex v Yorkshire
40L   Northampton   Northants v Warwicks
40L   Edinburgh   Scotland v Surrey
40L   Wormsley   Unicorns v Leics

Tue 28 – Fri 31 May
CC1   Taunton   Somerset v Yorkshire
CC2   Worcester   Worcs v Essex

Wed 29 May – Sat 1 June
CC2   Tunbridge W   Kent v Leics
CC2   Liverpool   Lancashire v Glos
CC2   Northampton   Northants v Hampshire

Wed 29 May
40L [F] Derby   Derbyshire v Surrey

Thu 30 May – Sun 2 June
CC1   Derby   Derbyshire v Surrey

Thu 30 May
40L [F] Hove   Sussex v Warwicks

Fri 31 May – Mon 3 June
CC1   Hove   Sussex v Notts

Fri 31 May
LOI   Lord's   England v New Zealand

Sat 1 June
40L   Worcester   Worcs v Warwicks

Sun 2 June
LOI   Southampton   England v New Zealand
40L   Chester-le-St Durham v Lancashire
40L   Chelmsford   Essex v Scotland
40L   Tunbridge W   Kent v Northants
40L   Leicester   Leics v Middlesex
40L   Taunton   Somerset v Glamorgan
40L   Leeds   Yorkshire v Glos

Mon 3 June
40L [F] Chelmsford   Essex v Surrey
40L   Rotterdam   Netherlands v Worcs

Tue 4 June
40L [F] Lord's   Middlesex v Somerset

Wed 5 – Sat 8 June		
CC1	Lord's	Middlesex v Sussex
CC1	Guildford	Surrey v Warwicks
CC1	Scarborough	Yorkshire v Notts
CC2	Bristol	Glos v Glamorgan
CC2	Southampton	Hampshire v Kent
CC2	Northampton	Northants v Worcs
Wed 5 – Fri 7 June		
FCF	Derby	Derbyshire v Durham MCCU
FCF	Leeds, W'wd	Leeds/Bradford MCCU v Lancashire
Wed 5 June		
LOI	Nottingham	**England v New Zealand**
Thu 6 – Sun 9 June		
CC1	Taunton	Somerset v Durham
Sun 9 June		
40L	Leek	Derbyshire v Essex
40L	Guildford	Surrey v Lancashire
40L	Southend	Unicorns v Glamorgan
40L	Scarborough	Yorkshire v Leics
Tue 11 – Fri 14 June		
CC1	Lord's	Middlesex v Yorkshire
CC2	Leicester	Leics v Northants
Wed 12 – Sat 15 June		
CC1	Chester-le-St	Durham v Warwicks
CC1	Nottingham	Notts v Derbyshire
CC1	Arundel	Sussex v Surrey
CC2	Chelmsford	Essex v Lancashire
CC2	Southampton	Hampshire v Glos
CC2	Canterbury	Kent v Glamorgan
Fri 14 June		
40L	Truro	Unicorns v Somerset
Sat 15 June		
	Lord's	Cambridge U v Oxford U
Sun 16 June		
40L	Chester-le-St	Durham v Scotland
40L	Chelmsford	Essex v Lancashire
40L	Bristol	Glos v Yorkshire
40L	Nottingham	Notts v Warwicks
40L	Taunton	Somerset v Leics
40L	Arundel	Sussex v Northants
40L	Worcester	Worcs v Netherlands
Tue 18 June		
40L F	Southampton	Hampshire v Derbyshire
40L F	Manchester	Lancashire v Scotland
Wed 19 June		
40L F	Canterbury	Kent v Sussex
40L	Leicester	Leics v Glamorgan
40L	Truro	Netherlands v Notts
Thu 20 – Sun 23 June		
CC2	Manchester	Lancashire v Northants
CC2	Worcester	Worcs v Glamorgan
Thu 20 June		
40L F	Derby	Derbyshire v Scotland
40L	Leeds	Yorkshire v Middlesex

Fri 21 – Mon 24 June		
CC1	Derby	Derbyshire v Somerset
CC1	Leeds	Yorkshire v Surrey
CC2	Leicester	Leics v Essex
Fri 21 – Sun 23 Jun		
FCF	Bristol	Glos v Australia A
Fri 21 June		
40L	Amsterdam	Netherlands v Warwicks
40L F	Nottingham	Notts v Sussex
Sat 22 – Tue 25 June		
CC1	Nottingham	Notts v Sussex
Sat 22 June		
40L	Chester-le-St	Durham v Hampshire
[T20] F	Canterbury	Kent v New Zealanders†
† Cancelled if NZ in final of ICC Champions Trophy		
Sun 23 June		
40L	Southend	Unicorns v Middlesex
Mon 24 June		
40L F	Northampton	Northants v Worcs
Tue 25 June		
IT20	The Oval	**England v New Zealand**
Wed 26 – Sat 29 June		
FCF	Taunton	Somerset v Australians
Wed 26 June		
T20 F	Southampton	Hampshire v Surrey
Thu 27 June		
IT20	The Oval	**England v New Zealand**
Fri 28 June		
T20	Chester-le-St	Durham v Lancashire
T20 F	Chelmsford	Essex v Hampshire
T20 F	Canterbury	Kent v Middlesex
T20 F	Northampton	Northants v Glos
T20	Nottingham	Notts v Leics
T20 F	Hove	Sussex v Surrey
T20	Worcester	Worcs v Glamorgan
T20	Leeds	Yorkshire v Derbyshire
Sat 29 June		
T20	Leicester	Leics v Derbyshire
Sun 30 June – Wed 3 July		
FCF	Chelmsford	Essex v England
Sun 30 June		
T20	Bristol	Glos v Worcs
T20	tbc	Kent v Surrey
T20	Lord's	Middlesex v Sussex
T20	Scarborough	Yorkshire v Durham
Mon 1 July		
T20 F	Manchester	Lancashire v Notts
Tue 2 – Fri 5 July		
FCF	Worcester	Worcs v Australians
FCF	Cambridge	Cambridge U v Oxford U
Tue 2 July		
T20 F	Derby	Derbyshire v Lancashire

Wed 3 July
T20 [F]	Cardiff	Glamorgan v Warwicks
T20 [F]	The Oval	Surrey v Sussex

Thu 4 July
T20 [F]	Lord's	Middlesex v Essex

Fri 5 July
T20 [F]	Derby	Derbyshire v Notts
T20 [F]	Canterbury	Kent v Essex
T20	Leicester	Leics v Durham
T20 [F]	Northampton	Northants v Warwicks
T20	Taunton	Somerset v Glos
T20 [F]	The Oval	Surrey v Middlesex
T20	Hove	Sussex v Hampshire
T20	Leeds	Yorkshire v Lancashire

Sat 6 July
T20	Chester-le-St	Durham v Notts
T20	Rugby S	Warwicks v Glamorgan

Sun 7 July
T20	Manchester	Lancashire v Leics
T20	Uxbridge	Middlesex v Kent
T20	Taunton	Somerset v Northants
T20	Worcester	Worcs v Glos

Mon 8 – Thu 11 July
CC1	Chester-le-St	Durham v Derbyshire
CC1	Uxbridge	Middlesex v Warwicks
CC1	Taunton	Somerset v Sussex
CC1	The Oval	Surrey v Notts
CC2	Cardiff	Glamorgan v Hampshire
CC2	Northampton	Northants v Lancashire

Mon 8 July
T20 [F]	Chelmsford	Essex v Kent

Tue 9 July
T20	Leeds	Yorkshire v Leics

Wed 10 – Sun 14 July
TM1	Nottingham	ENGLAND v AUSTRALIA

Wed 10 – Sat 13 July
CC2	Cheltenham	Glos v Kent

Fri 12 July
T20	Chester-le-St	Durham v Yorkshire
T20 [F]	Chelmsford	Essex v Middlesex
T20 [F]	Cardiff	Glamorgan v Somerset
T20 [F]	Southampton	Hampshire v Sussex
T20 [F]	Manchester	Lancashire v Derbyshire
T20	Leicester	Leics v Notts
T20	Worcester	Worcs v Warwicks

Sun 14 July
T20	Chesterfield	Derbyshire v Yorkshire
T20	Chelmsford	Essex v Sussex
T20	Cheltenham	Glos v Warwicks
T20	Manchester	Lancashire v Durham
T20	Richmond	Middlesex v Hampshire
T20	Northampton	Northants v Glamorgan
T20	Taunton	Somerset v Worcs

Mon 15 – Thu 18 July
CC1	Birmingham	Warwicks v Notts
CC2	Canterbury	Kent v Hampshire
CC2	Manchester	Lancashire v Glamorgan

Mon 15 July
T20 [F]	The Oval	Surrey v Essex

Tue 16 July
T20 [F]	Cheltenham	Glos v Northants
T20 [F]	Hove	Sussex v Middlesex

Wed 17 – Sat 20 July
CC1	Chesterfield	Derbyshire v Yorkshire
CC1	Hove	Sussex v Middlesex
CC2	Chelmsford	Essex v Leics
CC2	Cheltenham	Glos v Worcs

Wed 17 July
T20 [F]	Northampton	Northants v Somerset

Thu 18 – Mon 22 July
TM2	Lord's	ENGLAND v AUSTRALIA

Fri 19 July
T20	Nottingham	Notts v Durham
T20	Taunton	Somerset v Glamorgan
T20 [F]	The Oval	Surrey v Hampshire

Sat 20 July
T20	Birmingham	Warwicks v Northants

Sun 21 July
T20	Chesterfield	Derbyshire v Durham
T20	Cheltenham	Glos v Glamorgan
T20	Southampton	Hampshire v Kent
T20	Taunton	Somerset v Warwicks
T20	Hove	Sussex v Essex
T20	Worcester	Worcs v Northants
T20	Leeds	Yorkshire v Notts

Tue 23 July
T20 [F]	Cardiff	Glamorgan v Worcs
T20	Leicester	Leics v Lancashire
T20	Nottingham	Notts v Derbyshire

Wed 24 July
T20 [F]	Canterbury	Kent v Sussex
T20 [F]	Manchester	Lancashire v Yorkshire
T20 [F]	Birmingham	Warwicks v Glos

Thu 25 July
T20	Chester-le-St	Durham v Leics
T20 [F]	Lord's	Middlesex v Surrey

Fri 26 – Sun 28 July
FCF	Hove	Sussex v Australians

Fri 26 July
T20	Derby	Derbyshire v Leics
T20 [F]	Cardiff	Glamorgan v Northants
T20 [F]	Bristol	Glos v Somerset
T20 [F]	Southampton	Hampshire v Essex
T20 [F]	Nottingham	Notts v Yorkshire
T20 [F]	The Oval	Surrey v Kent
T20 [F]	Birmingham	Warwicks v Worcs

Sat 27 July

T20	Worcester	Worcs v Somerset

Sun 28 July

T20	Chester-le-St	Durham v Derbyshire
T20	Leicester	Leics v Yorkshire
T20	Nottingham	Notts v Lancashire

Mon 29 July

T20 F	Canterbury	Kent v Hampshire

Tue 30 July

T20 F	Cardiff	Glamorgan v Glos
T20 F	Northampton	Northants v Worcs
T20 F	Birmingham	Warwicks v Somerset

Wed 31 July

T20 F	Chelmsford	Essex v Surrey
T20 F	Southampton	Hampshire v Middlesex
T20 F	Hove	Sussex v Kent

Thu 1 – Mon 5 August

TM3	Manchester	ENGLAND v AUSTRALIA

Fri 2 – Mon 5 August

CC1	Lord's	Middlesex v Durham
CC1	Taunton	Somerset v Notts
CC1	Hove	Sussex v Derbyshire
CC1	Leeds	Yorkshire v Warwicks
CC2	Southampton	Hampshire v Glamorgan
CC2	Leicester	Leics v Lancashire
CC2	Northampton	Northants v Glos
CC2	Worcester	Worcs v Kent

Fri 2 August

40L F	The Oval	Surrey v Essex

Sun 4 August

40L	The Oval	Surrey v Scotland

Tue 6 August

T20 F	tbc	Quarter-finals 1 & 2
	Southampton	Hampshire v Bangladesh A

Wed 7 August

T20	tbc	Quarter-final 3

Thu 8 August

T20	tbc	Quarter-final 4

Fri 9 – Tue 13 August

TM4	Chester-le-St	ENGLAND v AUSTRALIA

Fri 9 August

	Leeds	Yorkshire v Bangladesh A

Sun 11 August

40L	Southampton	Hampshire v Essex
40L	Leicester	Leics v Yorkshire
40L	Lord's	Middlesex v Unicorns
40L	Nottingham	Notts v Northants
40L	Glasgow	Scotland v Durham
40L	Taunton	Somerset v Glos
40L	The Oval	Surrey v Derbyshire
40L	Birmingham	Warwicks v Netherlands
40L	Worcester	Worcs v Kent
	Manchester	Lancashire v Bangladesh A

Mon 12 August

40L F	Cardiff	Glamorgan v Somerset

Tue 13 August

40L	Chelmsford	Essex v Durham
40L	Bristol	Glos v Leics
40L F	Manchester	Lancashire v Derbyshire
40L F	Northampton	Northants v Kent
40L F	Nottingham	Notts v Worcs
40L F	Glasgow	Scotland v Hampshire
40L F	Hove	Sussex v Netherlands
40L	Leeds	Yorkshire v Unicorns

Wed 14 August

40L F	Cardiff	Glamorgan v Middlesex
	Nottingham	Notts v Bangladesh A

Thu 15 August

40L F	Derby	Derbyshire v Durham
40L F	Southampton	Hampshire v Surrey
40L F	Canterbury	Kent v Warwicks
40L	Leicester	Leics v Unicorns
40L F	Lord's	Middlesex v Glos
40L F	Northampton	Northants v Netherlands
40L	Glasgow	Scotland v Lancashire
40L	Bath	Somerset v Yorkshire
40L F	Hove	Sussex v Notts

Fri 16 – Sat 17 August

	Northampton	Northants v Australians

Fri 16 August

	Worcester	Worcs v Bangladesh A

Sat 17 August

T20 F	Birmingham	Semi-finals and FINAL

Sun 18 August

40L	Bristol	Glos v Glamorgan

Mon 19 August

40L F	Birmingham	Warwicks v Worcs

Tue 20 – Fri 23 August

CC1	Derby	Derbyshire v Middlesex
CC1	Birmingham	Warwicks v Somerset
CC2	Colchester	Essex v Northants

Tue 20 August

40L F	Manchester	Lancashire v Hampshire
	Bristol	England Lions v Bangladesh A

Wed 21 – Sun 25 August

TM5	The Oval	ENGLAND v AUSTRALIA

Wed 21 – Sat 24 August

CC1	Nottingham	Notts v Yorkshire
CC2	Swansea	Glamorgan v Leics
CC2	Canterbury	Kent v Glos

Thu 22 – Sun 25 August

CC1	Chester-le-St	Durham v Surrey
CC2	Worcester	Worcs v Lancashire

Thu 22 August

	Taunton	England Lions v Bangladesh A

Sat 24 August

	Taunton	England Lions v Bangladesh A

Sun 25 August

40L	Colchester	Essex v Derbyshire
40L	Swansea	Glamorgan v Leics

Mon 26 August

40L	Derby	Derbyshire v Hampshire
40L	Chester-le-St	Durham v Surrey
40L	Bristol	Glos v Somerset
40L	Canterbury	Kent v Notts
40L	Manchester	Lancashire v Essex
40L	Lord's	Middlesex v Leics
40L	Birmingham	Warwicks v Northants
40L	Worcester	Worcs v Sussex
40L	Leeds	Yorkshire v Glamorgan

Wed 28 – Sat 31 August

CC1	Lord's	Middlesex v Somerset
CC1	Birmingham	Warwicks v Sussex
CC1	Scarborough	Yorkshire v Durham
CC2	Bristol	Glos v Essex
CC2	Southport	Lancashire v Hampshire
CC2	Leicester	Leics v Worcs
CC2	Northampton	Northants v Glamorgan

Thu 29 August – Sun 1 September

CC1	The Oval	Surrey v Derbyshire

Thu 29 August

IT20 F	Southampton	England v Australia

Sat 31 August

IT20	Chester-le-St	England v Australia

Tue 3 – Fri 6 September

CC1	Chester-le-St	Durham v Sussex
CC1	Nottingham	Notts v Warwicks
CC1	Taunton	Somerset v Derbyshire
CC1	The Oval	Surrey v Middlesex
CC2	Chelmsford	Essex v Worcs
CC2	Cardiff	Glamorgan v Kent
CC2	Bristol	Glos v Leics
CC2	Southampton	Hampshire v Northants

Tue 3 September

LOI	Dublin	Ireland v England
	Edinburgh	Scotland v Australia

Fri 6 September

LOI	Leeds	England v Australia

Sat 7 September

40L	tbc	Semi-final

Sun 8 September

LOI	Manchester	England v Australia

Mon 9 September

40L	tbc	Semi-final

Wed 11 – Sat 14 September

CC1	Derby	Derbyshire v Durham
CC1	Lord's	Middlesex v Notts
CC1	Taunton	Somerset v Surrey
CC1	Hove	Sussex v Yorkshire
CC2	Canterbury	Kent v Essex
CC2	Manchester	Lancashire v Leics
CC2	Worcester	Worcs v Hampshire

Wed 11 September

LOI F	Birmingham	England v Australia

Sat 14 September

LOI	Cardiff	England v Australia

Mon 16 September

LOI F	Southampton	England v Australia

Tue 17 – Fri 20 September

CC1	Chester-le-St	Durham v Notts
CC1	Birmingham	Warwicks v Surrey
CC1	Leeds	Yorkshire v Middlesex
CC2	Chelmsford	Essex v Glamorgan
CC2	Bristol	Glos v Lancashire
CC2	Leicester	Leics v Hampshire
CC2	Northampton	Northants v Kent

Sat 21 September

40L	Lord's	FINAL

Tue 24 – Fri 27 September

CC1	Derby	Derbyshire v Warwicks
CC1	Nottingham	Notts v Somerset
CC1	The Oval	Surrey v Yorkshire
CC1	Hove	Sussex v Durham
CC2	Cardiff	Glamorgan v Glos
CC2	Southampton	Hampshire v Essex
CC2	Canterbury	Kent v Lancashire
CC2	Worcester	Worcs v Northants

TEST MATCH CHAMPIONSHIP SCHEDULE

Months indicate the start of a series. Number of Tests in brackets. All series, especially those involving Pakistan and Zimbabwe, are subject to confirmation.

2013	Apr	West Indies hosts Sri Lanka (2)		Oct	Pakistan hosts Australia (3)
	May	**England hosts New Zealand (2)**			Bangladesh hosts Zimbabwe (2)
	June	**England hosts Australia (5)**			West Indies hosts India (3)
		West Indies hosts Pakistan (2)		Nov	Pakistan hosts New Zealand (3)
	July	Sri Lanka hosts South Africa (3)		Dec	Australia hosts India (4)
	Oct	Pakistan hosts South Africa (2)			Pakistan hosts Zimbabwe (2)
		Zimbabwe hosts Sri Lanka (2)			South Africa hosts West Indies (3)
		Bangladesh hosts New Zealand (2)			New Zealand hosts Sri Lanka (2)
	Nov	**Australia hosts England (5)**	2015	Jan	Bangladesh hosts Pakistan (2)
		South Africa hosts India (3)		Apr	**West Indies hosts England (3)**
	Dec	New Zealand hosts West Indies (3)		May	**England hosts New Zealand (2)**
		Pakistan hosts Sri Lanka (3)			Sri Lanka hosts South Africa (3)
2014	Feb	New Zealand hosts India (3)			West Indies hosts Australia (3)
		South Africa hosts Australia (3)		June	Zimbabwe hosts Pakistan (2)
		Bangladesh hosts Sri Lanka (2)			Bangladesh hosts India (2)
	May	**England hosts Sri Lanka (2)**			**England hosts Australia (5)**
		West Indies hosts New Zealand (3)		July	Bangladesh hosts South Africa (2)
	June	**England hosts India (5)**			Zimbabwe hosts West Indies (2)
	July	West Indies hosts Bangladesh (2)			Sri Lanka hosts New Zealand (2)
		Zimbabwe hosts South Africa (2)			

CHAMPIONS TROPHY 2013

Thu 6 June			**Sat 15 June**		
Gp B	Cardiff	India v South Africa	Gp B	Birmingham	India v Pakistan
Fri 7 June			**Sun 16 June**		
Gp B	The Oval	Pakistan v West Indies	Gp A	Cardiff	**England v New Zealand**
Sat 8 June			**Mon 17 June**		
Gp A	Birmingham	**England v Australia**	Gp A [F]	The Oval	Australia v Sri Lanka
Sun 9 June			**Wed 19 June**		
Gp A	Cardiff	New Zealand v Sri Lanka		The Oval	Semi-final 1
Mon 10 June					
Gp B	Birmingham	Pakistan v South Africa	**Thu 20 June**		
Tue 11 June				Cardiff	Semi-final 2
Gp B	The Oval	India v West Indies			
Wed 12 June			**Sun 23 June**		
Gp A [F]	Birmingham	Australia v New Zealand		Birmingham	FINAL
Thu 13 June				*Group A*	Group B
Gp A [F]	The Oval	**England v Sri Lanka**		Australia	India
Fri 14 June				England	Pakistan
Gp B	Cardiff	South Africa v West Indies		New Zealand	South Africa
				Sri Lanka	West Indies

FIELDING CHART

(For a right-handed batsman)

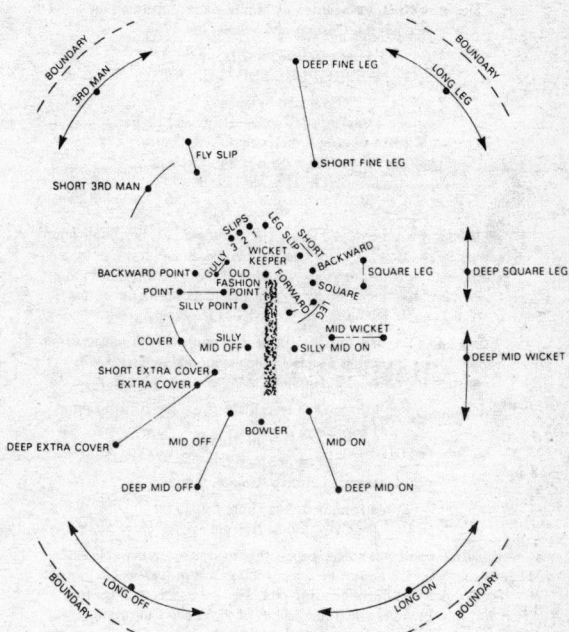

First published in 2013 by
HEADLINE PUBLISHING GROUP

Cover photographs:
(*Front and spine*) Alastair Cook, Essex and England
© Mike Egerton/Empics Sport /PA Photos
(*Back*) Matt Prior, Sussex and England
© Action Images/Jed Leicester

1

Cataloguing in Publication Data is available from the British Library

ISBN 978 0 7553 8752 6

Typeset in Times by
Letterpart Limited, Reigate, Surrey

Printed and bound in Great Britain by
Clays Ltd St Ives plc

Headline's policy is to use papers that are natural, renewable and
recyclable products and made from wood grown in sustainable forests.
The logging and manufacturing processes are expected to conform
to the environmental regulations of the country of origin.

HEADLINE PUBLISHING GROUP
An Hachette UK Company
338 Euston Road
London NW1 3BH

www.headline.co.uk
www.hachette.co.uk